To Koei-Liang Liauw, the former graduate student who did excellent research in invading a rather new field of study, with compliments from the author

Jim Casn

THINGS REMEMBERED

James Cason, M.S., Ph.D.

THINGS REMEMBERED

James Cason, M.S., Ph.D.

Rutledge Books, Inc.   Danbury, CT

Rutledge Books, Inc.
107 Mill Plain Road, Danbury, CT 06811
1-800-278-8533
www.rutledgebooks.com

Manufactured in the United States of America

Cataloging in Publication Data
Cason, James
   Things Remembered

ISBN: 1-58244-070-0

   1. Cason, James. 2. Memoirs. 3. Chemists -- United States --
Biography.

Library of Congress Catalog Card Number: 00-100849

CONTENTS   PAGE

Preface

Several years ago, as arthritis began to limit my mobility enough to inter-fere with my doing most of the things which I enjoyed most, such as felling trees at our timber property, which we call Camelot, and cutting them into firewood, I began to think of writing something. During my professional-ly active years I had always enjoyed writing research papers, textbooks, and letters. I even enjoyed—most of the time—serving a stint on the edi-torial board of two publications. So perhaps it was natural for me to think of writing something. These thoughts gradually simmered down to writ-ing a chronicle, which would probably be called an autobiography; how-ever, it would be a rather unusual autobiography. Eventually, my ideas crystallized into something definite. This is a chronicle of people, places, and events which touched my life. Many of these "touches" would be light; some would develop into an impact of significance, sometimes of enduring significance; some would become a powerful, persistent force destined to shape my life. In some situations the author would be the cen-tral character; however, in many developments the author would become the raconteur, reporting on events and people who generate events. In such situations as these, the raconteur will feel free to express opinions and/or recommendations, frequently highly controversial.

After having developed these plans over a period of a few years, dur-ing spasmodic periods of attention, I realized that time was running out; I must do something or else get off the pot. Furthermore, I have no ambition to become classified as one of those who makes vast plans, followed by half-vast execution. The first and principal problem which must be solved results from the fact that my typing has degenerated badly from the days when I typed the final copy of my Ph.D. thesis. My wife kept our typewriter going during most of our waking hours, in order to pay for the type-writer, by typing the thesis of my good friend George Waters. This knotty problem was resolved by what is sometimes called "a bolt from the blue." One day in the spring of 1997, Randall (Randy) Marsden, nephew of my wife, Rebecca, telephoned us that he and his wife were taking a weekend in San Francisco and would like to visit us for a couple of hours. Rebecca naturally invited them for lunch. Randy owned his own business, which was devoted to making computer graphics for use on the Internet, and he had brought his computer along to show us some of his work. One thing led to another, until Randy asked if I would like his advice on what computer to buy for use as a word processor for writing my proposed book. When I answered enthusiastically in the affirmative, one thing continued to lead to another until we reached the conclusion that Randy would buy the computer for me, get it set up with the operating system ready for me to start using it, get it adjusted to drive the printer which he would select for me, and finally deliver the whole thing to me, along with accessories such as a modem, and give me a few hours of instruction in order to get me started, since I had never before touched a computer. All of this would be done as rapidly as he could fit it in with running his business. Not only that, but Randy delivered the goods within a very few weeks. If I can be pardoned for making an understatement, I will comment that Randy Marsden made it possible for me to write this book, and I appreciate it.

Of course, I had a rough time at the start, made a few telephone calls to Randy, and made continual reference to the book Macs for Dummies, which granddaughter Kristen had given me. Nevertheless, by September I had reached the point where I could solve my problems as they arose by referring to the user's manual. By year-end, I was moving at a rate suffi-cient to allow me to complete my chronicle by October 1998. Of course, I was attending to the other things demanding my attention, and these all went much faster with my increased speed at letter writing. Regarding these other things, I also had to learn how to organize my files so that I could find things I had written.

So much for my adventures with my computer.

As for other people who helped me in many ways, of course my beau-tiful wife of sixty-four years' tenure with me stands at the top of the list. Whenever I use that adjective in referring to Rebecca, I am thinking of the picture that hangs on the wall in front of my desk, which I took of her at Bryce Canyon about 1950. She cheered me up when I became discouraged about learning to handle the word processor, and also did a great service for me in proofreading the entire chronicle. After I had finished each chapter and proofread it on the screen, I used the spelling checker, and finally printed a copy which Rebecca read. In addition to picking up things which the computer could not detect—such as a typo error which was also a good word—she also detected sentences or parts of sentences which did not make sense to anybody except the author of that sentence. Whatever may be the merits or demerits of the subject matter of my writing, I think that we have produced good copy.

Several people have helped me by reading and criticizing certain chapters in which they had expertise and/or information. Among these are Charlie Koch and Henry Rapoport, who are retirees of the faculty of the College of Chemistry at Berkeley, and Clayton Heathcock, who is continuing as a professor at this same institution. Christopher Jolles, M.D., of Salt Lake City, was also very helpful in reading and criticizing one important chapter. My friend Noel Vietmeyer provided me with a highly professional critique of Chapter 20, for which I am grateful. There was only one person who was living and also available to me for reading and criticizing Chapter 1. This was Alvin Moore, a prominent attorney in Chattanooga, Tennessee, who was mentioned in both Chapter 1 and Chapter 3. I had learned in Alvin's 1996 Christmas card that he was suffering from infirmities characteristic of his age. Thus, I sent a copy of Chapter 1 to Alvin at the time we sent his 1997 Christmas card. Alas, Alvin died early in January, after receiving a concussion from a fall, and so I did not receive his commentary on Chapter 1. However, I did receive a letter from his wife, Annie Kate, in which I learned of his death. She reported that Alvin had read my chapter more than once, and that he did a lot of chuckling while reading it. I judge from this that he had no major adverse comment to deliver.

As I proceeded through the writing of this autobiography, I began to real-ize that although I am constructing a report concerning many people, many places, and many topics extending over a period of about seven decades, there are a few basic themes which extend through many chapters. Of course, some of these themes extend through more chapters than do others. Naturally enough, the first theme to be presented appears in Chapter 1. This involves the great respect and affection existing between the writer and his family, which consists of his mother and father and his brother. His mother was confronted in her teen years with such a heavy burden in being required to raise her younger brother and younger sister that she sought assistance and love by marrying at age nineteen a young dandy of age thirty-five who had come to town to go into business with his brother-in-law. This marriage lasted until death did them part, in spite of the major problems encountered in raising their two sons, each with his own "pecu-liar" characteristics.

My mother appears in many chapters, for Rebecca and I spent many summers with my parents while I was at graduate school at Yale or work-ing at Harvard. I learned that Memur (as John and I called our mother) had some steel in her soul when she drove with me from Tennessee to California in December to be able to attend my wedding to Rebecca. Even when I skid-ded a little on the frozen bridges which we crossed in the Arkansas swamp, she never complained or told me to slow down. She knew that I was anx-ious to get there, and would surely do my best to succeed. She later came to Boston to help Rebecca when our first son was born.

My father made an impression early in my life when he explained a few things to me about judging a person by how good and kind and honest he was, not by what color he might be, or who his father or grand-mother was. In a later year, as I was leaving to drive to Berkeley, Dad had quite a discussion with me as I set out into the world at a distance too great to drive home for help or advice. Three sentences which were included in his comments became firmly fixed in my mind, and frequently comforted or guided me throughout my life. "Now, James, you know what is right and what is wrong, so I don't need to discuss that sort of thing with you. I hope you will always do what is right. Whatever you do, please remember that I stand ready to assist you if you need help, to the best of my ability."

Five years after I had left home, in the first term that I was in graduate school at Yale, I decided that I wanted Rebecca now, not next summer when we were scheduled to be married. After I had received an enthusiastic endorsement of this idea from Rebecca, I wrote Dad to ask him if he would be able to supply the money for me to drive to California to get married during the Christmas holidays. Among other things in the letter in which he responded was the statement: "I will find the money if I have to steal it." How could I ever do anything that would disappoint such a man?

Throughout the first ten years that Rebecca and I were married, we were nomads. We lived in nine different cities in five different states as I was fighting for a place in the sun. Our two sons were born during that period. On several occasions, especially during the war, when our second son was born in Nashville while I was in Pittsburgh, Pennsylvania, work-ing for The National Defense Research Committee, I needed to bolster my flagging morale by remembering the words spoken by my dad in 1934.

My relationship with my brother, John, during the early years of my life is retained in my memory as a few scenes connected by no narrative. The earliest scene that I recall involved his reading to me from the series of books about different animals, written by Thornton W. Burgess. Each book was devoted to the adventures of a certain animal, such as Reddy Fox or Paddy the Beaver. This reading to me of these very interesting stories occurred at about the time of my starting to attend Miss Eliza Ransom's school. This no doubt encouraged me to learn to read early in life so that I could enjoy this very interesting activity. This in turn led to my associating with a group of boys who spent much time reading at an early age.

John also included me, whenever it was appropriate, in many of his activities with his friends, and this became especially interesting to me when

Dad bought a big tent which was used for camping for a period each summer. John always took me along, and this eventually led to my best friend, Kit Haynes, John, and me building the cabin on Rocky River, with some help from Dad. We enjoyed many years staying in this cabin in the summer, and this led to a valuable association between my dad, John, Kit and me.

John was of greatest value to me during my teen years. His experiences in life were so close to the time in which I was living that he was even more valuable than my dad during that period. The situation in which John's advice was so important in affecting my entire life developed during my junior year at Vanderbilt, at which time John was in his Junior year in medical school on the same campus. After I had spent much time and thought in the process of finally arriving at the conclusion that I was not adapted to becoming a lawyer, I began to think of following in my brother's footsteps to medical school. Naturally enough, I sought John's advice, knowing that he probably knew me better than I knew myself, after those years of camping together. After some conversation, John warned me that I should realize that, sooner or later, one of my patients would die while I was attending him or her. As I was emitting groans of anguish following this message, he added, "And there might come a time when you would think that the patient died because of a mistake you had made!" I got the message loud and clear. I decided that I would go to graduate school in chemistry or biochemistry. Subsequent events have demonstrated that this decision, which John made stand out so clearly, was the second most important decision of my life. The most important decision I made was to marry Rebecca.

The second theme in this autobiography develops when the blonde from Southern California comes on the scene in Chapter 4. My love affair with Rebecca, which has lasted sixty four years as of this writing, could hardly have been predicted on the basis of the circumstances in which we met. I was sitting on the wood box beside the big fireplace in The Great Hall of the International House in Berkeley, chatting with a group of men and women from several lands, when another group came up, and there were introductions all around. When my turn to be introduced came up, this blonde named Rebecca said, "I know who you are; there are only two people who eat breakfast in this International House who want tea for breakfast. One is a handsome black man from The Gold Coast in Africa, and the other is you," said she while wagging a finger at me. It turned out that she could push out coffee at six A.M. without really waking up, but gathering up a tea pot with hot water, a tea bag, and a cup was quite a nuisance. I countered with approximately, "Oh, so you are that sleepy blonde with uncombed hair who dishes out coffee and tea to early risers. I didn't recognize you; with your face on, you are a nice looking gal."

About fourteen months after that improbable beginning, we were married during another rather improbable sequence of events. My drive, starting in a snowstorm in New Haven, Connecticut, to Murfreesbooro, Tennessee, to pick up my mother who wanted to attend my wedding; then to Fullerton, California, where I was married; then back to New Haven with Rebecca, has been mentioned briefly in connection with the first theme in this prologue. As already mentioned, our first ten years of marriage were spent as nomads. Our migrations ended in 1945, immediately after the war, and after we had driven with our two sons from Tennessee to California at a maximum pace of 45 miles per hour in our 1938 Chevrolet whose tires had been recapped three times. After we had gotten settled down in our house at 486 Michigan Ave., I commented to Rebecca, "I don't plan to move from here soon." She indicated her agreement with that sentiment. We are still at that address. Recently, as Rebecca was looking out of our sunroom window at our lovely garden, with the Golden Gate visible in the distance, she commented, "I want to live in this home until my remains are carried out in a box." Our world traveling has been confined to a glorious four weeks in New Zealand, driving our rented cars about 6,000 kilometers on the left side of the road. As always, I enjoyed learning something new—such as driving on the left side of the road and learning to understand the delightful New Zealand brand of the English language. When we turned in our last car, the woman at the desk was surprised that there was not a scratch on the car. We went to New Zealand because of our interest in their unique horticulture, but wound up enjoying the people even more than their beautiful land.

Our family life is intertwined with the action throughout this autobiography, with the story of our New Zealand trip being a nice ending for the book. However, the third theme becomes dominant after our arrival in Berkeley.

The third theme, which became apparent in Chapter 3, refers to my powerful drive to be an iconoclast, to strive mightily to do things differently—and better than the ways in vogue. An iconoclast can strive to do things differently, even if the difference leads to a worse system. Such types frequently attract much attention from the news media, and this is likely to result in iconoclasts getting bad press as regards public opinion. For this reason, an iconoclast who is interested in improving things is likely to be rather violently opposed to those who seek to damage society—frequently for their personal gain. During the "Free Speech Movement" on the Berkeley campus of the University of California, I was adamantly against the whole idea, and prone to ask, "Free speech for whom?"

During my early years, my iconoclastic instincts became evident in relatively minor things. During my tenure at the McCallie School, which at that time was a strict military school, my roommate, Bill Massie, and I were able to generate rather significant changes in the system of hazing which was prevalent. We also did some experiments with hypnotizing fellow students. The results of this caused us to adopt a firm policy to never again have any involvement with hypnotism, and we never departed from that resolve throughout our lives.

At Vanderbilt, my instincts became more significant, in that I came into conflict with tradition or university officials. Fortunately, my instinct for fair play and respect for authority saved me from suffering serious consequences. Upon entering Vanderbilt, I had my curriculum all made out to fit my long range plans for being a lawyer. The only problem was that my schedule did not allow my taking a course in either biology or chemistry in my freshman year. After I had argued with all the officials who would listen to me, I realized that I must take the required course. Thus, I naturally asked my brother, who was in medical school on the same campus, which course I should take. He advised me that the biology course designed for people who had not had any chemistry was not very useful, and so I should take the chemistry course which Breckenridge gave for those who were required to take a chemistry course. Ergo, I took that chemistry course—and liked it better than any course I had ever taken. Perhaps, the instinct for seeking change causes an iconoclast to be prone to accept and support change, even when forced to face it. In any case, however a psychiatrist would psychoanalyze me, I graduated with a double major in chemistry and physics, with the highest scholastic record ever recorded at Vanderbilt at that time. I enjoyed winning the Founders Medal because it made my mother quite happy.

James Cason / xv

Throughout my years at Vanderbilt, I never went to the chapel services, which consisted to a major extent of announcements about social events on the campus. I felt that my time was spent more productively in studying or working out in the gym doing gymnastics. At that time, Vanderbilt had a rule which operated more in theory than in practice, that attendance in class was mandatory, with only a few "cuts" per term allowed. Since I never cut a class, I assumed that if attendance at chapel should be required, I had more than enough cuts to my credit to take care of the situation. For reasons never revealed to me, during my senior year the dean of men called me into his office and advised me that I must go to chapel because no cutting of chapel was allowed. When I asked for the university regulation which specified this, he lost his temper and threatened to expel me from college unless I started going to chapel. And so I started going to chapel. Nevertheless, the dean went to the committee in charge of deciding who was awarded the Founders Medal, and demanded that I not receive such an honor because of a faulty character. Fortunately for my mother, every member of the faculty who had any contact with me combined to cut down this dean. Professor E. E. Reinke, who had contact with me only in a large lecture course in biology, told me this story. Judging from his mien while relating the story, I concluded that he approved of my behavior.

Fortunately, my iconoclastic instincts were directed toward useful endeavors in later life. Perhaps I finally learned something. After marriage to Rebecca, my life became much happier. After finishing my Ph.D. degree at Yale, I worked for two years with Professor Louis Fieser at Harvard. I was a part of the group that did synthetic work that established the basis for chemical carcinogenesis. My account includes a very intimate and personal history of Professor Louis Fieser during that critical period in his life. In view of his voluminous writing, splendid and enthusiastic teaching, and top-notch research, I regard Louis Fieser as probably the best organic chemist that this country has produced. I am aware that many—perhaps most—organic chemists will disagree with this assessment. Perhaps they are unaware of all the facts in the case, some of which are reported in this autobiography.

After a year of teaching at DePauw University and a summer of work for the Union Oil Co. in San Pedro, California, I arrived at Vanderbilt University as a faculty member. Soon after my arrival at Vanderbilt, the

Japanese made their sneak attack on Pearl Harbor, and we were into World War II. About a year later, I spent a few months working for the National Defense Research Committee (NDRC) at the Explosives Research Laboratory near Pittsburgh, Pennsylvania, then returned to Vanderbilt as Principal Investigator on a project directed toward the high explosive called RDX. Chapter 9 recounts many interesting things that occurred during the war. Perhaps most notable is the account of how American chemists defeated the German chemists in learning to produce RDX in quantity without blowing up any plants. This success was based centrally on the behavior of a graduate student at Cornell who was a determined iconoclast.. He refused to follow traditional methods used to identify chemical compounds. He insisted on using a polarizing microscope to accomplish this job, in spite of the fact that his Ph.D. dissertation was delayed. As a result, he learned that the compound RDX existed in three different crystal forms, which differed from each other in sensitivity to detonation by shock. The German chemists had no chance of learning these things, since an iconoclast would never have been tolerated in Germany, even if such a person had been present. And so they blew up several plants while trying to manufacture RDX, whose explosive properties were first learned by German chemists.

As the war was grinding to a close, I received a letter from Professor Wendell Latimer, dean of the College of Chemistry at Berkeley, inquiring if I would be interested in a faculty position there. After some exchange of letters, Dean Latimer offered me a job on the Berkeley faculty as an assistant professor. This was very good news for Rebecca and me, for both of us were very anxious to return to the favored place on earth that lies just opposite the Golden Gate. However, there was a problem. I was familiar with the Berkeley chemistry department, and knew that there was no organic chemistry there; no faculty member that understood modern organic chemistry. That is why I had left there after one year as a postgraduate, in spite of Rebecca being there, and gone to Yale for my Ph.D. work. Rebecca was very helpful to me during those days of soul searching. Finally, I decided to seek advice from Professor Homer Adkins at the University of Wisconsin. He was the director of the NDRC division in which I worked, and I had become friendly with him, partly because of the dangerous work we were doing.

At Madison, I explained my problem to Homer, who listened intently, making no movements except to cross his legs frequently, a maneuver for which he was famous. After I finished, he stated approximately, "I would not advise most people to dive into that den of narrow-minded physical chemists, but you are such a stubborn son-of-a-bitch that I advise you to take the job. They will never be able to budge you." I was so happy to receive this advice that I accepted the job, without even trying to decide whether the comment was complimentary or derogative.

Chapters 10, 11, and 12 give a detailed report of the history of organic chemistry at Berkeley, rising from nothing to becoming a highly respected center of organic chemistry. I was at Berkeley for more than a year before I discovered that the Powers That Be in organic chemistry at that time had decided that something had to be done about the absence of organic chemistry at such a prestigious university as Berkeley. I was "chosen," and Homer Adkins was appointed to see to it that I accepted the job. Dean Wendell Latimer was clearly the kingpin in this operation. The rest of us worked very hard to justify his faith in us, but it was that faith and the many things that he did for us that made success possible. Most chemists in the U.S. at that time were astonished that such a revolution could be accomplished.

Chapters 11 and 12 also contain much history of the Berkeley campus at that time, which was very critical to the shape of the Berkeley campus in the future. Of particular interest is the account of the development of the chancellor's office at Berkeley during the first years of Clark Kerr's tenure there. This report is intimate and real, for this writer was there. Clark Kerr had some mountains to move, and he moved them—even to becoming president of the Statewide University of California.

Chapter 14 is devoted in large measure to my personal experiences with use of vitamin C as a potent agent for counteracting many of the ills of the human race. My first experience with vitamin C occurred soon after 1950, several years before Linus Pauling came on the scene. My information came indirectly from Irwin Stone, who began writing about the virtues of vitamin C sometime around 1940. Pauling's information came directly from Stone, after he had retired to California. A few people listened to Stone prior to his contact with Pauling, but when the famous and eloquent Linus Pauling came on board, things were different. However, in spite of so much endorsement by competent and prominent people, the medical profession has been reluctant to admit the full virtues of this natural product.

My first encounter with vitamin C occurred sometime around 1952 when a chemist named Kvalnes who worked for DuPont, stopped by my office to visit me since I had used some of the data from his Ph.D. thesis work in my research. I learned that he was so badly afflicted with asthma that he periodically took leave without pay from his job to learn if he could find a climate more kind to his allergies. San Francisco proved to be no improvement. When I met Kvalnes at an American Society meeting , I asked how his asthma was, and he replied that he had none. As a result of this startling news, I stuck to eating one or two grams of vitamin C per day, and eventually, I got completely rid of asthma, and have remained so until the present time.

Many details of the dramatic effects of vitamin C are described in detail in Chapter 14, including its effect in causing rapid healing of wounds. But the medical profession as a whole refuses to admit the facts which are so widely reported. Perhaps this is not surprising. Think of the impact on medical practice if viral infections should be reduced by 50 percent or more, wounds heal very rapidly, and asthmatics frequently recover without assistance of drugs.

Chapter 16 is basically a history of my thirty-year struggle to reduce the painful effects of arthritis. I encountered many roadblocks presented partly by agencies of the government and partly by business enterprises. I have experienced some successes in that I am still walking around with a cane, and have not had any of my joints replaced with plastic and metal. The natural product, glucosamine, introduced in the early 1990s, appears to offer much hope for improving the lot of arthritics. This development and its impact on me is discussed in a tentative fashion in an epilogue to Chapter 16. In that chapter is also discussed the hazards and traps that are encountered when one is without a reliable source of the facts in the case.

Chapter 15, "The Cancer Controversy," is probably the most important part of this autobiography, because of its importance to so many people, and the widespread misunderstanding of the causes and therapy of this affliction by both the public and the medical profession. In contrast with other medical problems discussed in this book, I am not personally involved with cancer in that I have not had the misfortune of being a cancer victim. On the other hand, circumstances have caused me to become deeply involved with the efforts of a group of brave and dedicated people who have spent a significant part of their adult lives, and a part of their personal assets, in a determined effort to prevent a combination of the Food and Drug Administration (FDA), other government agencies, a segment of the medical profession, and, foremost of the group, the American Cancer Society, from contributing to the death of some two to three hundred thousand people per year in the U.S. alone. This group of people and organizations became known to their opponents as the "Cancer Establishment." The worst part of this ghastly situation is that there is abundant evidence, available to anyone who can read and hear, which clearly supports the contention that it is unnecessary for many—perhaps most—of these people to die.

I became involved in the struggle against the cancer establishment in an unexpected manner. I received a telephone call, as I was working at my desk in Latimer Hall, from my prep school roommate, Bill Massie, who had become a prominent orthopedic surgeon. After some chitchat about our families, Bill asked what I knew about Laetrile. I responded by saying that the name sounded familiar, but I did not know anything about it. After asking if I had been living in a cave, he informed me that I was living in the middle of a frantic controversy about the merits of using the substance Laetrile, which had reportedly cured many people, as a cancer treatment. He asked me if I would find out everything that I possibly could about Laetrile, and pass the information along to him. I knew that Bill was a cancer victim, and with the exception of my brother, he was my oldest and best friend. I could not refuse his request. Even if I had known what a hornet's nest I was walking into, I still could not have refused.

As I set out to investigate Laetrile, my friend Charlie Koch, who was on the faculty of the College of Chemistry at the time, told me that he had a friend, Mike Culbert, who was involved with the Laetrile affair. Mike was editor of the Berkeley Gazette, a good, very conservative newspaper. Charlie offered to invite Rebecca and me to dinner with him and his family, and also invite Mike Culbert. This proved to be the lunging start that propelled me into the cancer controversy.

Mike related some events that occurred in the trial of John Richardson, M.D. I remember vividly the incident where Richardson's attorney was questioning a typical "little old lady." The attorney said approximately the following to the lady: "Dr. Richardson is being tried as a criminal and will probably go to jail if convicted. Do you think that Dr. Richardson is a criminal?" At this point the lady exploded like a volcano: "Oh no, I think he is an angel." When asked for the basis of her opinion, she related how she had been diagnosed as a terminal cancer victim, and in despair, had decided to visit Dr. Richardson, who had been recommend to her by a friend. Her life had changed from that day until the present, when she had been diagnosed as entirely free of cancer. The jury acquitted Dr. Richardson, and the same sort of thing happened when the cancer establishment charged Richardson for the second time with violation of the California "Anti-Quackery Law." In a third attempt, the judge threw the case out of court as harassment.

Mike Culbert was fired by the Berkeley Gazette for persisting in writing editorials condemning the persecution of Dr.Richardson. He had already joined the group headed by Bob Bradford, the Committee for Freedom of Choice in Cancer Therapy. I later told Bill Massie that I really had been living in a cave in certain respects.

It was a few years later, when the book by John Richardson, M.D. and Patricia Griffin, R.N., was published that I learned about this respected medical doctor being arrested—the arrival of police cars with sirens screaming; police tramping through his clinic searching for Laetrile; finally the doctor being led away in handcuffs as the T.V. cameras rolled.

This is just one illustration of the tactics used by the cancer establishment in their multi-million dollar effort to discredit metabolic therapy of cancer. In view of the unlimited dollar resources and legal authority possessed by the cancer establishment, there is small wonder that they won. They even set up an official test which was alleged to settle the Laetrile farce forever. This "test" used only cancer victims whose immune systems had been beaten up by chemotherapy, acting against the advice of Nobel Laureate Linus Pauling, and also used their own Laetrile, which could not have contained more than 15 percent Laetrile. The infrared spectrum supplied by the FDA, under the Freedom of Information Act, did not show the strong line in the infrared, which Laetrile does show. I personally inspected the printout of this spectrum. Of course, the cancer establishment reported in the news media the failure of this test to find any support for the use of Laetrile in cancer therapy.

In Chapter 15, there is much, much more evidence of the frantic determination of the cancer establishment to stop demonstration of the fact that metabolic therapy is much more effective than anything else presently known. According to the last reports that I have received, the method developed by biochemist Vladislaw Burzynski, M. D. and Ph. D. in biochemistry, has not been successfully blocked by the cancer establishment, and it appears very promising indeed.

Why would the cancer establishment be so determined to block recognition of successful methods for curing cancer? I leave the answer to that question up to the reader.

Three of my oldest and best friends, now deceased, one of them my brother, were medical doctors, and they were among the most dedicated and successful people that I have known. My present family doctor is capable and has the highest ideals. The surgeons that he has recommended to me have the same characteristics.

Any reader who thinks that my writing of Chapter 15 was difficult is dead right.

I will close this prologue with a bit of philosophy. As everybody must be aware, the medical profession is the most important of all professions, and has traditionally been the most honorable and the most honored. What an inviting target for scoundrels to move in and take over! The more brilliant and capable the scoundrel, the more able he is to seize control. The conscientious medical doctors are busy taking care of their patients. The advent of the Health Maintenance Organization (HMO) has greatly facilitated seizure of control by scoundrels. Abuses by the HMOs have caused politicians to step in and try to mitigate the damage. But politicians do not have the honorable traditions that medical doctors have.

CHAPTER 1

A PECULIAR CHILD

One of my earliest memories from childhood involves a scene in the front hall of my parents home at 515 N. Maple Street, Murfreesboro, Tennessee. This large brick house was heated only by coal-burning fireplaces, except for the front hall, which was heated by an ornate coal-burning stove that had a pipe rising straight up from it to a hot air register in the room directly above. This made the upstairs room the warmest room in the house, except for the front hall where the stove was located.

It was this warm front hall where a few local relatives would frequently gather on a cold winter afternoon, after eating a good "Sunday dinner" which had been prepared by my mother's cook while those attending the dinner were at church. The events being described here occurred some time when I was less than six years old, for I was not at that time in first grade at Miss Eliza Ransom's School. All my recollections of such early dates consist of scenes, not narratives. On such a cold winter afternoon as this, my brother, John, who was about seven years older than me, would chat with the relatives for a few minutes, then excuse himself and go out to visit with friends his own age. I would remain playing games by myself on the floor. A game I remember best was called "Keep Off the Rug." This involved certain maneuvers on the carpets between the rugs with a marble used as a taw. Each player had a taw. In playing by myself, of course I shot the taw for each side.

As I played my game on the floor and the relatives chatted (gossiped), I don't recall any exchanges between me and the adults. I seemed to function as part of the furniture; however, I had ears which the furniture did not have, and I did a certain amount of thinking about what I heard. It was not uncommon for the conversation to refer to "James, who was playing on the floor," especially with reference to what kind of man James would grow up to be. There were two topics on which the adults usually agreed. One such topic was that James would be a small man. The other was that James was a peculiar child. They were dead right on one count. During the period when I was in college, and for several years after that, my weight held between 180 and 185 pounds, with my height being about 5 ft., 11 in.

Another scene that is fresh in my memory is of great importance concerning problems encountered throughout my life. I was lying in bed during the wee hours of the night, propped up with pillows, gasping desperately in the effort to pull a little more air into my lungs. My mother was rubbing camphorated oil on my chest and encouraging me to "pull hard." She would then put a flannel cloth over my chest and put a wool blanket on top of that. My memory carries nothing more beyond this point, but it is clear that I survived.

In terms of what was known about the treatment or alleviation of asthma during the period before 1920, my mother was doing all that she could for me. In retrospect, this scene, repeated often in the hay fever allergy season occurring each year during August and September, must have been very distressing to my mother. Especially so since the problems with her younger child were trivial compared to the problems with my older brother, John. He came very close to dying twice during the same year, with his mother staying at his bedside all night for many consecutive nights. He was hit first with typhoid fever, then with pneumonia. John was a member of the last generation for whom typhoid fever was a major cause of death in the limestone regions of the country. Tennessee and Kentucky occupied one of the largest limestone regions in this country. The caves of Kentucky which are, of course, famous throughout the world, result from erosion of the limestone strata by underground streams. Surface run-off becomes commingled with the underground water, with the result that any bacterial infection from human feces becomes very widespread and is likely to be present in any spring or river. Thus arose the necessity for chlorination of the public water supply. This did not eliminate typhoid fever, however, because of the amount of water drunk from springs. I was saved by the introduction of the vaccine against typhoid. Good luck by being born at just the right time; considering my struggles with asthma, surviving an attack by the typhoid bacillus would have been doubtful.

My mother's burden in nursing her two sons followed a longer-lasting burden of nursing her mother. In my adult years, I made a particular point of never asking any questions about this traumatic period in my mother's life; however, my wife Rebecca gave me some information concerning that period. Rebecca and my mother were so close that discussion of such things was appropriate. According to this information, my mother's father died of pneumonia when my mother was in her mid-teens. After that, her mother went to bed and stayed there until her death, leaving her oldest child, Madeliene, my mother, to manage the family. Madeliene had two siblings, a brother named Ridgeley (family name) and a sister named Sara. The perennial disagreements between her siblings increased my mother's burden

One could speculate at great length as to why Madeliene Park, a beautiful young woman of nineteen, who had many beaux, would decide to marry a thirty-five-year-old young dandy who had recently come to town in order to go into business with his brother-in-law, Gentry Smith, who had married his sister, Indiana. I have thought a great deal about this unusual situation, and feel that the following scenario carries a high probability of bearing a considerable resemblance to the actual events. Judging from his pictures, my dad, Jim Cason, was a handsome man who had lived in several cities before coming to Murfreesboro. He had decided that he wanted to get married and settle down, and so this beautiful young woman whose family were land-owners was very attractive to him, so attractive that he decided he would marry her even though it involved living with her in the room next to the invalid mother for whom she was caring. On the other side, teen-age Madeliene had become so distraught over her situation that she felt that she must have someone to help her with this heavy burden. And so, when Jim agreed to live with her and share this burden, she accepted his proposal. However much this scenario may or may not fit the facts in the case, one thing is clear; both parties showed great intelligence and confidence in their judgment. The marriage lasted until "death did them part "after fifty-six years. One can imagine the gossip that flew around town when that marriage was announced.

The predicted peculiarities of James began to show up at about the time that he began to attend, at the normal age of six, Miss Eliza Ransom's School. This was a very small school, with a total of fifteen to twenty students, divided into three or four grades. When I entered there were five other boys in the first grade with me. All teaching in the school was done by two old maids, Miss Eliza and Miss Belle. Miss Eliza presided over the main room, which contained all the students all the time except for those in the reading class, taught by Miss Belle, which also included spelling and pronunciation (diacritical marks). As soon as practical, use of a dictionary was introduced. A small dictionary was one of the books each student was required to buy. I do not remember the chronology of introduction into study of the dictionary, but for a period of many months the dictionary was the focus of Miss Belle's teaching. A frequent exercise was for Miss Belle to hold up a card with a word printed on it. The students then scrambled to find that word in their personal dictionary. The first to find it held up his hand. Miss Belle then asked him to read what the dictionary had to say about that word. Miss Belle would correct any errors in pronunciation. She would then ask another student to say something which included the proper use of that word. My recollection of events in these days of long ago do not include many other events, such as spelling contests. Although Miss Belle taught only one class it is apparent that she had a profound impact on what was taught in that school and how it was taught. Miss Eliza taught everything else and managed discipline in that room, which contained not only the class she was teaching but also the rest of the students who were not in Miss Belle's class at a given time. This daunting task proved possible with only fifteen to twenty students and with the exercise of no-nonsense discipline.

Some of the peculiarities predicted for James became evident during his tenure at Miss Eliza's school, more specifically in his relations with Miss Eliza. During his preteen years, there was no reasonable doubt that James was shy, painfully shy. Some people, especially professionals in the field of judging character and personality, would be likely to use the adjective timid; however, from my perspective of old age, I judge this to be the wrong word. I was so reluctant to meet people whom I did not know that I would hide whenever overnight guests came into the house. My ever-patient mother would track me down and persuade me to meet the new people. After that I was okay; on one occasion I had fun "passing" a baseball back and forth with one of the younger visitors. I still remember his name; it was Procter Bell, a member of the Procter and Gamble dynasty.

When I was faced with a new situation, problem, or opportunity, my reaction was radically different. I would be eager to plunge into the new territory, solve a new puzzle, or gain knowledge I never had before. In my preteen years, the basis of the present discussion, I was the kid who organized a vacant-lot baseball team—possibly because my dad bought me a catcher's mitt and mask. At Miss Eliza's school I frequently devised a new game to play; however, I was most conspicuous in the classroom where Miss Eliza was in charge. A common practice in a class was to have a contest among the students (six students in my class). The students were seated on a long bench at the front of the room, with the student at the right end (with the students facing forward) being described as at the head of the class. Of course, the student at the other end of the bench was at the foot of the class. On a designated Monday morning, positions in the row on the bench were assigned by drawing straws. The student drawing the longest straw was assigned the position at the head of the bench.

Each day the class would begin by Miss Eliza directing a question to the student at the head of the class. These questions were not limited to any specific field. Arithmetic, spelling, grammar, history, and geography were included. And, of course, the nature of the questions changed as the pupils progressed through the first grade, on to the second grade, and so forth. The "trapping class" was held each day for a week, and applied to what was studied during the preceding week in any field. In retrospect, I realize that holding a class of this sort amounted to a weekly exam, with very powerful social pressure to succeed. One's performance was reviewed at close range by the rest of the class, with no possibility for claims that one person was graded more harshly than another. I also remember that if a student held the position at the head of the class for a week, according to the procedure to be described, he was given a little gold star to be pasted in the front of one of his books. Thus, the element of competition, so fundamental to the spectacular success of our nation, was introduced to the classroom. A student's performance was publicly viewed, just as it was when he was at bat in a baseball game. This situation carries a lot of serendipity. When a person is young and able to learn fast, what an appropriate time to introduce competition into the classroom. Nothing like injecting a dose of adrenaline into the system to generate a top performance. Every athlete knows that. Every athlete also knows that delivery of a top performance requires the ability to do well while under pressure—to take the heat. As then-President Harry Truman said long ago, in response to a rather impertinent question from a reporter, "Those who cannot take the heat should stay out of the kitchen."

Now let us describe the atmosphere that developed during a session of the "trapping class." As noted previously, the class was opened each day by Miss Eliza asking a question of the student at the head of the class. If he answered it correctly, then she asked another question of the next student below the head. If the student at the head missed the question, this same question was passed to the next student. If this student answered the question correctly, then he trapped the head student and took his position at the head of the class. If a student who had been at the head for a few days hesitated for a brief period, someone in the class or at a desk behind the class where the rest of the students were supposed to be studying, might be unable to restrain himself and yell, "TRAP HIM." Quite a strain on the composure of the head! As a matter of fact, Miss Eliza rated this as overdoing the competitive atmosphere. She would not say anything, but would get up from her seat, quietly go to the blackboard and write the student's name at a corner reserved for such events, and place a 10 after his name. This meant that the offender must stay after school was dismissed, and stay there until he had memorized and recited to Miss Eliza whatever ten lines of poetry she had assigned to him. Ten lines was the most that she would assign for a single offense; but she could also vary the severity of the penalty up or down by the particular poem she chose . For a severe infraction, Robert Browning was always available. If the victim of a severe penalty was still unable to recite his poetry by 5:00 P.M., Miss Eliza would call his mother and ask if she wanted to pick him up since it was after dark (at certain seasons).

To return to the classroom scene, if the student next below the head was able to answer the question, then he "trapped" the head, and walked over to occupy the head seat. The person who was next in line was the recipient of the next question, and things then proceeded as described before. As mentioned earlier, positions on the bench were assigned by drawing straws at a beginning Monday. I do not remember whether this initial assignment by lot occurred each month or each semester, or for some other period, but it was for a long period. My recollections apply to long equilibrium periods, where positions changed only because of trapping. Perhaps a new start was declared by Miss Eliza whenever the distribution had become too stable, to stir up the desired competitive spirit.

The preceding discussion has been devoted largely to describing the technique developed by Miss Eliza for the purpose of developing a competitive spirit in young people. The utility of this technique, and others, is obviously a subject likely to be debated. As a matter of fact, it has been debated vigorously for many decades. The effects of Miss Eliza's teaching on James, the peculiar child, can also be debated; however, in this instance we do know how Miss Eliza's school was run and we can evaluate the behavior of the peculiar child in later life in terms of the possible impact of Miss Eliza's teaching. Thus, a description of certain events impacting the peculiar child are in order.

As has been described, my shyness about meeting new people did not apply at all in meeting new challenges. Indeed, the opposite would apply; I was eager to search for the solution to a new problem, acquire information which I had never had before.

Miss Eliza's iron discipline in maintaining quietness and order in a room where some students were reciting and some were studying has been described. This was especially important since there was no homework at Miss Eliza's school. Anyone who had not finished his written assignments would be required to stay after school until they were finished—joining those who had poetry to memorize. I was never one of those who had not completed his written work, but was frequently one of those who was memorizing poetry. And so there was inevitably another competition about who would finish his task and get out to play in the vacant lot in our neighborhood before the kids arrived from the grammar school nearby. For those at Miss Eliza's school who did not have to "stay after school," school was "let out" one hour earlier than was the case at the grammar school. Even with my poetry to memorize, I usually arrived at the playground before the other kids. And so a hierarchy developed.

Memorizing poetry for Miss Eliza probably had a greater impact on my academic success than any other factor in her game plan. By the time I arrived in college, I was regarded by my friends and acquaintances as some kind of a freak who could memorize things in "nothing flat" and remember it for an exam weeks later. Even as a professor at the University of California, where I frequently taught classes of several hundred, students would frequently express amazement when I greeted them by name when they walked into my office. An event which I remember with particular satisfaction occurred during my freshman year at Vanderbilt University. At that time at Vanderbilt, every entering freshman was required to take the three-unit course in English which consisted of two units of composition taught by various people and one unit of literature, which was taught by Eddie Mims, who was famous as the leader of the group of writers known as the Agrarians. Eddie Mims was also notorious for the way he taught the English class, particularly for the kind of exams he gave. Locksley Hall, by Tennyson, was a favorite of his, and one could anticipate a question about Locksley Hall on the final exam. I had memorized a lot of Locksley Hall for Miss Eliza, so I memorized the rest of it for Eddie Mims. Sure enough, the question came: "Give the content of the one hundred lines between the following two lines." I wrote out all of it verbatim. My grade for the exam and for the course was "A". My grades for the rest of the courses I took at Vanderbilt were also "A"—a feat accomplished previously by only three Vanderbilt students. I also won the Founders Medal for Scholarship.

In spite of my failure to keep my big mouth shut on some inappropriate occasions, Miss Eliza never lost patience with me, although she occasionally warned me that if I did not get better control there would be longer and more difficult lines of poetry to memorize. On my side of the relationship, I never rebelled at what Miss Eliza assigned me to memorize. In retrospect, I suppose one might be prone to rationalize that the genes I carried were not the sort to cause a rebellious individual; however, this idea is contradicted by the simple fact that in later years I became a definitely rebellious individual. This characteristic caused me to have serious problems sometimes, at other times caused me to rebel at the status quo and seek new ways of doing things. In the case of my early childhood, I now believe that my docile cooperation resulted from my belief that the rules and regulations were made because they were desirable and necessary, and to everybody's benefit, including mine. After all, my dealings with rule makers were restricted largely to my mother and Miss Eliza, and so such an attitude was well justified. One experience with Miss Eliza caused that idea to be embedded in concrete. It was rather remarkable that I was later to take a more tolerant view of the subject.

Miss Eliza had only a few rules regarding what we did during our one recess; however, she maintained a surveillance of the playground in order to know if any of those rules were broken. I learned this the hard way! On one particular occasion, I decided to climb up into the apple tree to pick one of the nice red apples. I have no recollection of why I reached such a decision. A good guess would be that another kid dared me to do it, or bet me a few marbles that I could not do it. All of us knew that climbing in the apple tree was forbidden. In any case, as I crept out on the limb to reach the apple, the limb split off at the trunk, as limbs do, and the limb and I crashed to the ground. I got to my feet and ran to the house, crying hysterically. What my thoughts were, I do not remember. Miss Eliza met me at the door and said, "Sit down on the front bench." She then sat down beside me, put an arm around me and said, "Stop crying, James." She then quietly explained to me that she made rules concerning our playing for good reasons.The rule about climbing in the apple tree was made because she was concerned that one of the kids might fall out of the tree and get hurt. Finally, she said, "Go back out and play. I will be very disappointed if, ever again, you intentionally break one of my rules." At the end of recess, I came back into the room, trembling with apprehension. My name was not on the board, with a number after it. After that sequence of events, in my mind, Miss Eliza could do no wrong!

Before leaving the subject of Miss Eliza's school, perhaps it is in order to consider whether significant credibility should be credited to these accounts involving only a peculiar child. I can report on only two other men who were graduates of Miss Eliza's school, and whom I have been associated with over a long enough period of time to allow a significant report on their subsequent behavior in life. After all, there were only six students in my class at Miss Eliza's, and a lot of water has gone over the dam since we graduated.

One of these former students, whose name is Alvin Moore, has remained in contact with me to the day of this writing (September 21, 1997). We were in frequent close contact during the years that we were undergraduates together at Vanderbilt University. This resulted not only because we were from the same home town, but because each of us had started out to be a lawyer and had taken high school courses in preparation for that career. By the middle of our freshman year, I had begun to have serious doubts about continuing with that career in mind. I do not remember whether Alvin was unduly influenced by my uncertainty, or if he had reasons of his own for doubting his intention of becoming a lawyer. What I do remember is the warm afternoons that we spent lying on the grass in Centennial Park, watching the swans and squirrels, as we debated with ourselves and sought the counsel of each other in the effort to reach intelligent decisions. We finally decided that Alvin would continue the pursuit of law and I would shift into a scientific career. Subsequent events proved that both of us were right. Alvin had a very successful career in the practice of law in Chattanooga, and wound up as the head of his law firm. In his Christmas card for 1996, he reported that he was enjoying his semi-retirement, keeping in touch with the office, doing whatever he wanted to do. Whatever effect Miss Eliza had on Alvin, it must have been good. As to the effect of Miss Eliza on the peculiar child, that will be discussed in future chapters.

The other former student that I kept in close touch with was my brother, John, with whom I kept in very close touch until his death a few years ago. Of course, my information regarding John's early years was passed to me by relatives or friends of my mother. John was seven years older than me, and as will be reported subsequently, this proved to be a great advantage to me. According to information which I received about John's early years, he was a normal child during the first few years of his life, except for a pronounced difficulty in handling the English language. This difficulty consisted of learning to associate an object with a word, then learning to pronounce the word. For example, mother finally turned out to be Memur, and so she was always addressed in that way by John and me, as well as John's children. There were similar problems with my father's sister, whose name was Indiana. After a struggle, John began to address her as Nin, and so both John and I called her Nin until her death. At the time of Nin's death, John was serving as her attending medical doctor. In view of this circumstance, it is clear that this rather formidable early handicap did not blight John's career. He graduated from college as a member of Phi

Beta Kappa, turned in a distinguished performance in medical school, and was a highly respected doctor in his home town, where he spent most of his career. And so, again, who can say how much Miss Eliza helped this man? It is known, however, that my mother persuaded my father to somehow scrape up enough money to send their troubled son to Miss Eliza Ransom's School.

In September, following completion of my fourth year at Miss Eliza's School, I was enrolled in the seventh grade at the public Crichlow Grammar School, which was only one block up Maple Street from my home. Before enrollment, I was told that I would enter the seventh grade because of previous experiences with Miss Eliza's students. I do not recall any great apprehensions about this circumstance, and I do not recall any timidity about facing the horde of new faces with which I was surrounded. Perhaps I was too excited about the prospect of exploring new territory. And there was plenty to be explored. Whereas I had played when out of school, for the most part, with a group of kids who played everything from baseball to various marble games in a large vacant lot near my home, at the public school I was literally surrounded by a horde of kids of all ages. It did not make much difference that I was the youngest member in my class. All, or perhaps most, of the grades had recess at the same time.

There was one very large difference, however, in the public school, where I was associated for the first time with large numbers of girls. This applied in the classroom, of course, but did not apply in the play-yard, where the boys and girls played entirely different games and had different playgrounds. Since my new friendships developed on the playground, I was shielded to a significant extent from the adjustments I had to contend with when I reached high school. Of course, this adjustment in sexual relations would become necessary in high school because of my being two or three years younger than the rest of the students in my class. I continued playing games with the boys at recess and naturally adjusted to playing with those of compatible physical capability.

In the classroom, however, there developed a conspicuous difference between me and the rest of the people, whether boys or girls. This difference resulted not because I was younger than the rest of the people, but because I was ahead of them academically. It seems rather improbable that I would just happen to have inherited such a superb set of genes that I would be three or four grades in school ahead of all members of a group of a few hundred young people, picked at random among the children in a middle Tennessee town of about eight thousand population. Indeed, if one would like to explain such a phenomenon by relating academic accomplishment to social and/or economic position, I have some news for such people. My dad had a hard time raising the money to pay the few dollars a month which Miss Eliza charged. He did it because my mother insisted that it was very important and she helped by scrimping on house-hold expenses. My home was not on East Main Street, where lived the members of the only country club in town. My home was a few blocks from The Square in a neighborhood that was somewhat upscale in the 1890s, when this house was built. My mother's father did not trust this remarkable new idea of getting lights over a little wire. Each chandelier in the house had alternate gas lights and electric lights. But by the time I was born, the neighborhood had deteriorated considerably. The large old house directly across the street from us had become a boarding house, with no interior plumbing. Another neighborhood from which students attend-ed the Crichlow Grammar School was across the railroad tracks where the pencil factory and the whorehouses were located. The children who lived on East Main Street went to another grammar school. I did not realize what the rest of the world was like until I met these students in high school.

So much for the idea that Miss Eliza really had a major impact on my academic success in life. Since Miss Eliza did not believe in wasting time with exams, I had never taken an exam at the time I entered grammar school. As interested as I was in exploring new things, I was rather appre-hensive about this Great Unknown, an Exam. For the first time in my life, I took books home with me to study for the exam, and got up at four A.M. to do some extra study. The teacher commented to the class on my scoring 100% on the exam. This rather embarrassed me, because I was not accus-tomed to being conspicuous in society. Of course, I did not realize that this same instinct would become a very important guiding factor in my later life. This announcement also had some effect on my playmates during recess. There appeared to be a significant number of kids in this very het-erogeneous group who regarded me as some kind of a nut. This proved to be another thing that I encountered on a few occasions in later life.

At grammar school I continued the practice, as far as possible, of doing all my "homework" at school. As I walked the few blocks to my home after school with a few other kids who lived further away, I would be conspicuous by having only one or two books in my bookstrap, frequently only one. I was quite interested in arithmetic, especially after I reached the eighth grade, because of the variety of problems that were presented. This interest was shared by another student named Horace Reed, whom I encountered for the first time in the eighth grade. (More below about my being in the eighth grade.) This interest became so intense that we would sometimes skip recess and meet at adjacent desks in the classroom in order to help each other work out problems that seemed difficult. At graduation from grammar school, I received a little gold medal for scoring the highest grade in arithmetic. Horace and I did not do all of our arithmetic together. We also did not engage in competition with each other in solving the tough problems. This proved to be another practice in which I engaged in later life, in college years when studying with other students.

By the end of the seventh grade, I began to feel more and more aware of the effects of the differences between me and the rest of the students in my class. There were still no opportunities for social life between the boys and girls, but there were other differences, such as the kinds of books that I enjoyed reading. These things were noticed by my astute parents, especially the way that I showed no interest in girls, in marked contrast to the way my older brother showed a very great interest in girls by the time he entered high school. This difference was exaggerated by the fact that John was at least a year behind his age group because of illness. This same difference between the two of us persisted through our respective college years.

In view of the changing relationship between me and my environment as time marched on, both of my parents and I agreed that it would be a good idea for me to not go to summer school in order to "skip" the eighth grade. At that time in Murfreesboro, it was common practice for all the "better" students to skip the eighth grade. Of course this brought me one year closer to the average age of students in my class. In addition, this freed me to enjoy camping with my brother and his friends. John had already been camping on Stones River with friends for several weeks each summer. Our Dad had supplied us with a large tent, a smaller tent, cook stove, cots, and the other paraphernalia necessary for a group of people to go camping. I had been along for short periods at the camp in earlier years, but it was just a matter of my tagging along, due to the consideration my older brother accorded me on so many occasions. But the summer before I entered high school was a very special one. John invited my best friend, Kit Hill Hayes, to go camping with us. It was the beginning of a period of several years when John, Kit and I were the central core of the camp. Many others came and went, but we three carried on. I remember this period as a critical time when the advice and friendship of John was so important to me.

CHAPTER 2

PECULIAR CHILD GROWS UP—SLOWLY

When I passed from grammar school to high school I expected to find a difference in my relations with the other students; however in my high school this did not occur with the girls. I continued to have no opportunity to associate with them during school hours, unless accidentally because of proximity of seating in the various classrooms. As for my relations with other boys, these tended to decrease significantly because there was no playground. Only students involved with interscholastic athletics engaged in any sort of physical activity associated with being enrolled in the school. There were groups of students talking to each other during recess while standing around in the halls, on the campus, or walking on the sidewalks. Going off the campus during school hours was not allowed, but walking on the public sidewalk in front of the school grounds was allowed. Since my home was only one house removed from the school, I frequently walked home on the sidewalk by simply continuing from a group I was with. I assumed that nobody would notice my defection, which always proved to be the case. Sometimes I would invite a friend to have lunch with me when it was convenient for my mother. However, these friends were always boys. I continued to be completely unsophisticated in my relations with girls. Occasionally, in a large group of boys, I would hear some older boy broadcasting his wisdom about how to get a girl "hot enough to go all the way"; however, none of the boys with whom I normally associated engaged in such conversations, and most of us would drift away from such groups. I think that most of my group was as embarrassed as I was by such conversations. In retrospect, and in consideration of other events in my later life, I believe that a major factor with me was my apprehension at getting into a situation that might get out of my control and get me into serious difficulties. Indeed, I am cognizant of several situations in my later life where this same instinct kept me out of serious difficulties. I suspect that a combination of timidity and caution frequently served me well during this period in my life, as well as later.

Due to such things as just described, my two years at Central High School tend to be a gap in my memories, except for two things that I do recall with pleasure. One of these was the opportunity to get acquainted with boys whom I had never met before because they did not go to Crichlow Grammar School, but to a grammar school in the east side of town. Most of these acquaintances arose, not because of contacts with groups that were "shooting the breeze" in the halls at the high school, but by chain reactions resulting from some of this group who were quite interested in reading, getting together with others with the same interests. We loaned books to each other, and told each other of interesting books to investigate. I remember that one of our favorites, sometimes read more than once, was Jules Verne's Twenty Thousand Leagues Under the Sea. One of this group, with whom I maintained contact for the rest of our lives, was Charles Travis. He attended the Naval Academy at Annapolis and subsequently served with distinction as a naval officer. Indeed, he was the captain in command of one of the battleships which laid down a barrage of heavy artillery shells protecting landing forces at the beach in Normandy in World War II. We have maintained contact through the years primarily via exchange of Christmas cards; however there is one other occasion that remains vividly in my memory. Charles and his wife Esther were the only people other than my mother who were sitting on the side of the church aisle devoted to the family and friends of the groom when I was married to Rebecca Marsden on December 28, 1935. His ship just happened to have docked in Long Beach in time for him to be able to attend this occasion. (A full account of said occasion will occur in a later chapter.)

Another series of events occurring in this interlude of my two years in high school, which occupy much space in my memories , were the summers in which John, Kit Haynes and I spent most of those summers camping. The summer in which I did not go to summer school was what might be called an epoch-making summer. We were able to develop our camping into a much larger and more enjoyable operation because the bus line which my dad had started soon after World War II had prospered to the extent that he could afford to spend enough money to buy more expensive equipment for us. Indeed, my pleasures and opportunities in life, beginning at this time, were intimately associated with the success of Dad's bus line.

To consider the genesis of this important development in my life, I must go back to the period just before my birth when my dad bought the second automobile to be bought in Rutherford County, Tennessee. Dad was always a forward-thinking sort, always one step ahead of current thinking. And my mother obviously enjoyed being married to this young dandy. Her reputation as an adventuress was amplified by an event which developed as a result of Dad going into business with his brother, John, to raise racehorses on the family farm, which John inherited. My mother began using one of the racehorses, named Lady Cason, to pull her buggy. And so the day came when Lady was frightened by something and "ran away." The 115-pound driver hung in there, and eventually pulled Lady in, after she had torn up several lawns. The stories that I heard about this event were inconsistent as to whether Madeliene was "heavy with child" at the time of the run-away. And so there appeared to be no great surprise among the townspeople when Jim bought the Buick. Again according to the stories, however, there was great surprise when Jim dropped out of the business venture with his brother-in-law, Gentry Smith. Regarding this situation I have the report from Dad. The Smith and Cason dry goods business (selling cloth for home sewing) had become so prosperous that Cason wanted to borrow money against their good credit and open a store in nearby Lebanon. Cason had been reading stories in the newspapers about a company called F. W. Woolworth that was expanding at a simply terrifying rate. But Mr. Smith considered gambling with hard earned money by borrowing more money lunacy, so Jim went into the garage business with his brother John. This eventually led to the decision to apply to the Postal Service to deliver the U. S. mail to Woodbury, a very small town some twenty miles from Murfreesboro and not on the railroad. Since the mail was being delivered in a wagon, Dad got the contract to deliver the mail in a motor vehicle. I remember the vehicle, made by the Reo company. It was something like a modern day pickup truck with a canopy cover. The road to Woodbury was not paved, but the worst part was that there was no bridge across a creek which was dry in summer but ran with a lot of water after a winter storm. Communication by telephone was unreliable or non-existent, so Dad had a contract with a farmer living near the creek to bring his mule down to the ford after every heavy rain to pull the Reo across. The mail must go through!

Soon after Dad got the contract to deliver the mail to Woodbury, the paving of the road from Murfreesboro to Nashville was completed, and Dad was ready with the necessary vehicles to launch the Red Bus Line to Nashville. Of course his acquisition of vehicles of suitable design was greatly facilitated by his being an automobile dealer. The garage also had a large repair shop, needed to keep the buses running in those days. Dad kept up a steady supply of mechanics and bus drivers by attracting young men and boys from the surrounding farms. Before I entered college he had taken in two partners, the main office was in Nashville, and they were operating buses to Knoxville, Atlanta, Birmingham, and Chattanooga. I do not remember whether they also went to Memphis. But very black clouds were piling up on the horizon!

At this time, Tennessee politics were controlled by political machines in the cities. Ed Crump virtually owned and operated Memphis, the largest city in the state, and the satanic combination of Rogers Caldwell and Luke Lea occupied a similar position in Nashville. Between the two of them, Tennessee was pretty much in bondage. Word came through to Dad that Lea and Caldwell had fully developed plans to take over the booming bus business as well as the trucking industry. The plan was very simple. The legislature would pass a law that all bus and truck lines must have a franchise from the state. And L. and C. would naturally control who got the franchises. A man in Murfreesbooro named Eph Hoover was a leading truck operator. Eph and Dad began circling the wagons by forming an alliance not to compete with each other and thus be more able to fight the political bosses. Eph's son-in-law, Ed Miller, became a partner in Dad's bus line. Eph and Dad went to work at the local level in many political districts raising money and generating allies. Since I was in prep school at Chattanooga during these critical times, I never knew whether the political actions of Eph and Dad saved them or they were saved by the unbridled greed of L. and C. In any case, L. and C. apparently became so mesmerized by their success in taking over control of Tennessee that they branched out into new territory in North Carolina. This attracted the attention of the federal government, and the upshot of that was that both of them wound up in a federal penitentiary. Eph's trucking business prospered, and Ed and Jim's bus business prospered. At some stage along the way, a third partner was taken into the bus business, Ray Quarles, and he seemed to fit in excellently with Ed and Jim. Ed Miller was much younger than Dad, but his family became quite friendly with the Casons. Ed took John and me fishing on certain occasions before we had an outboard motor. Later, he visited us in our new cabin on Rocky River. It is appropriate at this point to shift our attention to the site of our cabin on Rocky River.

Caney Fork River is the largest stream arising in the Cumberland Plateau and then flowing west and south across the Highland Rim towards the Cumberland River. The Highland Rim is on the east and west of the central lowland in middle Tennessee. Murfreesboro and Nashville are near the center of this central lowland. In the years before I became acquainted with this area of east central Tennessee, the Tennessee Electric Power Co. had built a large high dam at a strategic location just barely down-stream from where the Collins River flows into the Caney Fork from the west. At a point some two or three miles upstream from the dam, the Rocky River flows into the Caney Fork from the west. This confluence of the three rivers resulted in a rather wide valley which in turn led to a large and deep lake. Just below where Rocky River flowed into this lake there was an island projecting above the water even when the dam was filled to overflowing. This little parcel of rocky land was known as Rock Island, and the accumulation of summer homes with their boat landings on the shores of the lake was also known as Rock Island. This area was populated by wealthy people who were interested in water sports, in less abbreviated bathing suits than were to become popular in later days, and in driving around in power boats, frequently pulling water skiers.

Our cabin on Rocky River was about ten miles upstream from Rock Island, and in an entirely different environment. This location was only about two miles from the head of the backwater from the dam, and at that point was located the remains of an old wooden dam. Above that point, Rocky River was a beautiful mountain stream extending into the Cumberland Plateau. After the Rocky River reached the point where the land began rising rather steeply up to the Cumberland Plateau the stream became too small and swift for fishing. Between that point and the head of the backwater the river was a beautiful mountain stream ideally adapted to fly fishing. Since the three of us, John, Kit and I, were all fly fishing enthusiasts, we spent a lot of time in this part of Rocky River. We would paddle up there in a canoe to where the old wooden dam was, crawl through the remains of the dam, and continue wading up the river with our fly rods in action. Since there were usually two of us involved in such expeditions, we would take turns, with one of us simply hiking up the river without fishing until reaching the headwaters, then turning around and assembling the fly rod to start downstream fishing. When the two of us met, we usually sat down on a rock with our feet in the water and rested for a while, fishing and talking about anything that interested us, or things we planned to do after getting back to our cabin. I still remember rather vividly an item that Kit reported during one of these rest and relax periods. He was the upstream man on this occasion. He reported that he had noticed for the first time what appeared to be slabs of stone standing upright high up on the bank. We decided to investigate, went back upstream to the point Kit remembered, and found what appeared to be a very old, small graveyard. The gravestones had been engraved; however, they had been weathered for so long that it was difficult to make out the writing. On one of them we were able to make out the following:

> As you are now so once was I.
>
> As I am now so you must be.
>
> Prepare for death and follow me.

Before proceeding with further description of the location of our cabin and the characteristics of that location, it is no doubt in order to recall some of our adventures in building this cabin.

None of the three of us knew much about carpentry, although I knew a little, having worked with my dad building a small flat-bottom boat. Also, Dad had not become sufficiently prosperous at that time to offer much money. Nevertheless, we proceeded to the task by first taking the big

---

tent we had used on Stones River and setting it up on the bank above the place we planned to put the cabin, which was about thirty feet from the water's edge when the dam on Caney Fork was filled to the brim. This location had been picked by John through his acquaintance with an old medical doctor who had a cabin about a quarter mile downstream from our location. The land was owned by an old farmer named Witt, always known to us as Mr. Witt. His forty-five year old son was known to us as Mr. Norman (his first name). For rental of the place to build the cabin and use of his dirt road to get to the site-well, close to the site—we paid $35 per year. During the first night after we set up the tent, we learned some things about maintaining a tent in a cow pasture. During that moonlit night, the cows gathered around this new object and, of course, stumbled over the guy ropes extending from the tops of the side poles supporting our tent to large stobs in the ground. By the time we woke up, a couple of side poles were down. Also, we had brought up a couple of baseball gloves and a ball, which we had used to "pass" the ball for relaxation on some occasions when camping on Stones River. The cows had chewed on the gloves until they bore only a casual resemblance to a baseball glove, and the ball was nowhere to be found. We never knew whether the ball had rolled off towards the river or a cow had eaten it. In any case, we were happy not to receive any report that one of Mr. Witt's cows had developed a strange illness. We later learned to prevent this sort of occurrence by tying white cloths on the guy ropes. We also learned that we had no use for the gloves and ball. Since we were working eight or more hours per day to increase our chances of getting a roof on the cabin before the winter rains set in and turned the dirt roads into a quagmire, we had no inclination to pass a baseball for relaxation.

Our next move, after getting our temporary living quarters established, was to buy lumber from an old sawmill located up the road, which had gone out of business and was selling seasoned oak lumber cheap. We bought most of what we needed for the cabin for about $80. We next bought nine cedar trees from Mr. Witt for $1 each to be used as posts under the house. Tennessee red cedar (juniperus virginiana) is quite resistant to rotting even when underground. We felled the trees using an ax, then we cut the trunks into suitable lengths using a carpenter's saw. (This was before the invention of the chain saw.) After that it was many days spent

in putting the sills on the posts, then the sleepers for the flooring, and finally putting up the studs, vertically, of course. Putting the two-by-four's
across the tops of the studs, and nailing them to the studs as the studs were
held in a vertical position, parallel to each other, was difficult. We were
able to accomplish this after much tedious work. However, putting up the
rafters for the roof simply stymied us. We had never heard of a framing
square. So we decided that this would be an excellent time to go to
Murfreesboro—we had to ask Dad to buy us some roofing, anyhow. As
usual, Dad came through cheerfully and with encouragement. He found
an old carpenter who had worked for him on previous occasions, and took
him up to our building site as the three of us drove along in our beat-up
old Studebaker touring car with no top. Of course my brother was always
the driver of this old car which came to us from Dad's garage. Happily
enough, we had no rain for a couple of days , which was all the time it took
for the carpenter to put up the rafters and nail the sheeting to them. The
carpenter was really impressed by how hard the seasoned oak was. Of
course, we had learned about this from the very beginning. It was difficult,
if not impossible, to drive nails into it unless the nails were first rubbed on
a cake of soap. I remember the old carpenter's comment soon after he started to work: "This lumber is as hard as elkhorn, lucky that I just had my
saw sharpened!" And so it became Elkhorn Cabin. Even before we finished, we put a large sign on the front of the cabin facing the stream, which
proudly displayed its name. And so the cabin was finished, and we lived
in it for a few days before the inevitable return to school. John, Kit and I
were living alternately in two different worlds. All three of us enjoyed both
worlds, and each world made the other happier for us.

For the next two years after we built the cabin, which had a large
sleeping room, a kitchen half the size of the sleeping room, and a porch of
the same size as the kitchen, the three of us enjoyed the good life at
Elkhorn Cabin. Dad bought us a canoe and a new boat which was built like
a canoe, with a canvas cover over a light wood supporting framework, but
with a square two-inch thick solid wood back for supporting an outboard
motor. Except for the motorboat, all our facilities were primitive. Our
latrine was a board supported between two trees, located in a grove of little trees about two hundred feet from the cabin.

Our windows were wooden flaps which swung shut on hinges, with latch bolts for locking them while we were away. The doors to the porch from the kitchen and sleeping room had similar bolts on them, but the door to the outside from the sleeping room had a conventional hasp with a padlock. There were no screens, hence lots of flies. Our only defense against the flies was swatting them. Fortunately, we did not have mosquitos to harass us at night. Our lights were kerosene lanterns, so we did not do much reading at night. Of course, we have all heard the stories about Abe Lincoln doing his schoolwork in front of the fire at night. Regardless of whether this was factual or fictional it does not apply to our cabin. Our only fire was in the wood-fired cookstove. Our primitive facilities were a bother only to the occasional visitors who would spend a day or three with us. Our facilities were probably a major reason that the principal occupants of our camp were John, Kit and me. Which obviously suited us just fine.

During this pleasant hiatus, the three of us spent time as we desired, doing things on the enormous lake generated by the dam on the Caney Fork River. The backwater extended about twelve miles up the Rocky River, and probably extended as much as twenty-five miles up the Caney Fork. A really big lake. We never drove our motorboat up the Collins River because of the urban population extending several miles from its junction with the Caney Fork. On only one occasion did we explore the Caney Fork above its junction with Rocky River. That was an expedition, started early one morning, by me and our favorite uncle, my mother's brother and an avid fisherman. He spent many days with us at Elkhorn Cabin. He was known to the family, except for my mother, as "Chicken," or Chick. In those days this nickname carried none of the insulting inferences that became standard in much later days. Indeed, this nickname had a completely different origin than would ever be guessed by anyone. His name was Ridgeley Park. While he was in college he came down with chicken pox, which attracted a lot of attention because of the much more usual occurrence of this malady in younger people. By a not uncommon stretch of the imagination in designation of nicknames, the resemblance of Pox and Park resulted in Chicken Park. Well, anyway, that is the way that I heard it from older members of the family.

Whatever the origin of the nickname, Chicken and I started out in the early morning for a trip up the Caney Fork. A fishing buddy had told him that the Calfkiller River, which flowed into the Caney Fork, was a marvelous fishing stream. Judging from a map, the Calfkiller seemed to join the Caney Fork some twenty miles above Rock Island, but we were undaunted. We did take the precaution of taking a five-gallon can of gasoline with us. I do not remember how fast our little outboard motor drove our boat, but I daresay that it was less than ten mph. I remember that it took us more than an hour to get down to Rock Island, which was about ten miles from Elkhorn Cabin. All went well as we drove down Rocky River, turned right up the Caney Fork after more than an hour, and continued upstream into territory which I had not previously seen. After about an hour traveling up the Caney Fork, the motor stopped, and we were not out of gas! Chicken looked very worried, and said, "That certainly is a long ways to paddle." After addressing the motor with a few expletives, I said, "Don't start rowing yet." I would have been more worried than I was if the motor had not behaved in a similar fashion previously. And I thought that I remembered what John and I had worked out at that time. We pulled the boat up on a sloping shore to eliminate the hazard of dropping tools into the water. (We never traveled even for short distances without our tool box.) I took the carburetor apart, blew out the jet, made sure that the float was not sticking, and put it back together again. The motor started on about the third crank! After another hour of traveling upstream we got into an area where we began to encounter a lot of dead trees. The appearance was similar to that at Elkhorn Cabin, which we knew to be only a couple of miles from the head of the backwater from the dam on Caney Fork. We began to be concerned that we had missed the place where the Calfkiller came in, because of the rather wide channel full of dead trees. As we were pondering what to do, a fisherman came along paddling a boat which was obviously a homemade job. Chicken hailed him and asked if he knew where Calfkiller River flowed into the Caney Fork. He responded, "Mister, I ain't never been here before, and I don't know where I am now." At that point we decided to head for home before we got into that same condition. Our Evinrude purred along like a champ. When we turned into Rocky River, Chicken turned around with a big grin on his face and yelled, "We could row home from here." About a half hour later we passed a landmark that he recognized, and this time he yelled, "Hell,

I can swim home from here."When we were getting into our sleeping clothes that night, Chicken looked at a certain place on me, turned to John and said, "James is slung like a stallion." This embarrassed me considerably more than somewhat. I was simply not accustomed to such comments. After I had gathered my wits together a little, I wondered if Chicken was complimenting me for action more worthy of a man rather than a kid when I was able to get the motor running.

This was only one of the many excursions that John and I enjoyed with Uncle Chicken. Over many years, we also enjoyed frequent reminiscing about Uncle Chicken.

For four summers after the completion of Elkhorn Cabin, John, Kit and I enjoyed the boating and fishing on the lake behind the dam, and fishing in the flowing stream above the backwater. After this, the pleasure of The Trio spending rather idyllic summers at Elkhorn Cabin had to yield to the march of time. John was in medical school, and this placed heavy demands on his time during the summer. I was at McCallie School in Chattanooga, hence not in Murfreesboro except in summer, and this tended to build up things requiring attention there. Kit had reached an age where he felt obligated to contribute as much as possible to his living expenses. He had been orphaned at an early age, before I had become acquainted with him, when his father was killed by a bull. In spite of these contingencies, Kit and I were able to spend two or three weeks at Elkhorn Cabin during that summer. But an event occurred that certainly cast a pall over Elkhorn Cabin as we had known it. There was a severe drought affecting the headwaters of the Caney Fork River, as well as a very large surrounding area. Tennessee Electric Power Co. had to pull down the water level in their reservoir until the head of the backwater was two miles or more below the location of Elkhorn Cabin. Between our cabin and what the drought had left of Rocky River was a mud flat. Small wonder that Kit and I decided to give up after about two weeks of trying to find something to do of interest. Finally, we pulled the boats out of the water and stored them under the house. We took the Evinrude, two guns we had previously left at the cabin, and all the fishing tackle home. Everything else we left in the cabin because we knew that we would not have further use for those things unless some happy event allowed one of the trio to return to Elkhorn Cabin. As we left without even taking a last look around, we felt no regrets. Elkhorn Cabin had rewarded us magnificently. It didn't owe us anything more.

Writing these preceding paragraphs was a severe emotional strain on me. I would frequently stop to think of the way that John, or Kit, or Chicken looked on various occasions. Or I would smile or laugh out loud at something that was said—such as Chicken's comments about the "footballs," rocks that lined the bed of Rocky River where we waded when fishing above the backwater. We wore heavy hobnail boots which would cut into the sandstone boulders sufficiently to prevent our feet from sliding between the rounded boulders. Before we wised up to the hobnailed boots, we frequently fell into the water and got bruised feet. Chicken's comments on "footballs" came before he was equipped with the hobnails. And there was the episode that occurred one morning as John, Kit and I were getting dressed after waking up. Kit made the announcement: "I am accustomed to hearing both of you talking in your sleep, and seeing James walking around in his sleep, sometimes outside the cabin, but last night was the first time that I saw and heard the two of you carrying on a long conversation while both of you were sound asleep." Neither John nor I could think of any reason to doubt this allegation, and we could remember nothing about the conversation which Kit reported. He said that it was something about which fly to use when fishing at a certain spot in the stream above the backwater, so we had to accept his report in good faith. Reams of this sort of thing have persisted in intruding into my mental cyberspace. I have enjoyed it, but feel a little wrung out. Time to get on into another world—to McCallie School.

As in the case of Miss Eliza Ransom's school, my brother John was my fore-runner at McCallie School. John's experiences at McCallie and his intimate knowledge of my unusual personality made him very helpful to me when my time to go to McCallie came. In light of this background I will report, according to what I heard, on the reasons that John, and therefore I, went to the McCallie School. As the beginning of this story, my mother, Memur, became quite perturbed about John's associations with the boys and girls in Murfreesboro. John was not afflicted with my timidity about approaching girls. Memur's sister, my Aunt Sara, had lived in Chattanooga for many years after marrying Charles Twinam of that city. There were two prep schools with excellent reputations in Chattanooga, the Baylor School and the McCallie School, and so this was a logical place to select a school for John. On a nice spring day, a Sunday, Aunt Sara took Memur to visit the two schools. Both seemed very nice, but there was one significant difference. At Baylor, the boys were having a baseball game on one of the athletic fields. At McCallie, there was no activity on the playing fields. That did it! My religious mother, who virtually owned and operated the First Presbyterian Church in Murfreesboro, regarded such a boisterous game as baseball entirely inappropriate for the sabbath. Memur softened up some as her sons got older and acquiesced to Dad taking his sons to baseball games in Nashville on Sunday, to see the Nashville Vols play. At the time of choosing between the two schools, however, playing baseball on Sunday was the deciding factor. The irony of this story is that Memur picked the right school for the wrong reason.

Since McCallie was owned and operated by two brothers who were sons of a Presbyterian missionary, it would seem impossible that the influence of religion at Baylor could be even stronger than it was at McCallie. Ergo, Memur picked the right school. However, after I arrived at McCallie, I discovered that the McCallie brothers were very enthusiastic about athletics. Indeed, they seemed to be ahead of their time in regarding athletics as a topnotch device for giving youth something to do that would be so interesting as to prevent them from doing something else that might be undesirable. The school had splendid facilities for athletics including an outdoor gym equipped with swinging rings, horizontal bars, parallel bars, etc.; several athletic fields with a track around one of them; a well equipped gym with lockers and a basketball floor; and last but not least, a lake for swimming which was about an acre in size and equipped with a toboggan slide, springboards and a dressing room for girls. The lake was rented to outside interests for public use in the summer. My interest in athletics escalated rapidly after my arrival at McCallie, and so this choice of schools was also very good for me. Furthermore, I also learned that the McCallie brothers felt that playing athletic games on Sunday afternoon was a very desirable Christian activity.

As for Memur's primary objective in choosing McCallie School, this also was attained magnanimously. As might be expected, the McCallie brothers were very big on religion. Every boarding student was required to attend church on Sunday—any Christian or Jewish church would satisfy the requirement. Most of the boarding students attended the Presbyterian church which was about a half mile towards town from McCallie School. The minister of that church was a third McCallie brother. Not only that, but every student, whether day or boarding, was required to take a one-year course studying the Bible. Either the Old Testament or the New Testament could be chosen. This follows logically from the fact that many of the wealthy Jewish business men in Chattanooga sent their sons to McCallie because of its well-deserved reputation for high scholastic standards. (Parenthetically, as will be noted later, I learned a lot about those high scholastic standards as soon as I started attending classes.) In any case, I figured that I had learned enough about the New Testament from attending Sunday school for many years in my mother's class. This was not Memur's idea but mine. At the age I started Sunday School, I was mired deeply in timidity. And so I elected to take the Old Testament as my Bible course at McCallie. This proved to be a happy choice. I found the Old Testament to be much more interesting than the New Testament in many ways. It is largely a combination of Jewish civil law, including the Ten Commandments, with history slanted to make the Jewish people seem better than reality. Among the interesting things I still remember was the scenario about the king (it may have been David) who was wounded in one of the numerous battles described in the Old Testament. Anxious to show that he was still a virile and able king, he directed that a platform be built and the people gathered to observe as he "went in unto his wives." The elderly gentleman who taught the course was rather embarrassed by a question asked by one of the students. He responded by saying, "Of course he had a tent erected on the platform." After the Children of Israel escaped from bondage in Egypt and fled to the Promised Land, which was represented as "flowing with milk and honey," there was a period of fighting with the former occupants. There appeared to be a considerable resemblance to more recent colonization of "primitive" countries by powerful European nations. Some of the accounts of this period were rather bloody. After storming and conquering one walled city, there was left alive no person that "pisseth against the wall." Since I was becoming quite interested in history at the time that I entered McCallie, perhaps that was the reason that I did quite well in that class in the Old Testament. I have a small gold medal which I was awarded for scoring the highest grade in the class.

Upon my arrival on the campus at McCallie, I was directed to the teacher assigned to go over my entrance credentials and advise me on what courses I should take. His first action was to inform me that I just thought that I had taken two years of algebra at Central High School in Murfreesboro. I had covered only one year of algebra; and hence would be required to take the second year of algebra rather than plane geometry, which was normally scheduled for the junior year. Since I had never made any grade except A since I had left Miss Eliza's school, this was quite a jolt to me. I realized that unless something was done about this situation, I would be behind my classmates. Unbelievable! I asked if taking plane geometry and the second year of algebra at the same time would generate any serious problems. After some thought my adviser said that this would work out okay except that if I took the other normal junior courses it would be a very heavy load for the first year in a new school. Thinking of the way I had breezed through every course I had ever taken, I responded without hesitation that I wanted to try it because I was sure that I could at least pass, and a low grade would not be as bad as falling behind. He responded approximately,"I will approve it if you insist, but you are in for a big surprise." Truer words were never spoken! In retrospect, I now realize that this scenario illustrates a characteristic which I had as early as when I attended Miss Eliza's school. There was nothing I enjoyed as much as attacking new problems. Although I was painfully timid about meeting people, especially new people, I seemed to have no fear about tackling new intellectual challenges without even considering the consequences. This instinct no doubt had a major impact on what I could accomplish in later life. Fortunately, when a wife and children would be affected by my actions, I began to do a little thinking before charging. One of my sons who inherited these characteristics has been phenomenally successful in business, but has taken some hard falls on account of insufficient thinking before charging. He was never able to profit from my advice.

Before the end of two weeks I began learning what that advisor was thinking about when he commented about a big surprise. I had decided to try out for football because of my interest in athletics and football being the sport that was in season. In retrospect, I obviously should have dropped football at once since there was no hope of my earning a letter that year. However, I was constrained by the idea of being a quitter, and so stuck it out, although it soon became apparent that there were not enough hours in the day for me to meet my commitments. McCallie was not only a religion-dominated school; it was also a strict military prep school, with an ROTC unit to which all male students must belong unless excused for medical reasons. Our lives were highly regimented: dressed properly and standing at the foot of our bed at attention for inspection at 7 A.M.; in the dining hall for breakfast at 7:30; classes started at 8 A.M. and ended at 3 P.M During the day, there was one period for chapel, except for military drill on Friday at that period. Of course there was a dinner period. When classes were over at 3 P.M., an hour of physical activity was required, again unless a medical excuse was provided. And those out for athletic teams spent more than an hour. The football team practiced until dark and were excused if they were late for the six o'clock dinner. Study hall was 7:30 to 9:30, and lights out was at 10:00. There is a limit to how much study time can be crammed into that kind of a schedule, and I was not in the mood to give up Saturday, which was allowed off campus, especially since I could occasionally get a waiver of church in order to stay overnight with my Aunt Sara who lived on Signal Mountain. The obvious answer was to get up at five o'clock in the morning. There developed a problem with my getting up at five o'clock.

The rooms in South Hall where most new students lived were small and had double decker beds in them. The roommate who had been assigned to me was a small, quiet chap named Chauncey Gilchrist who took a dim view of my getting up at five A.M. About the only solution was for him to sleep in the upper bunk, and for me to be as quiet as possible. This worked out fairly well until Chauncey discovered that I was using a pony (a translation of Cicero from Latin to English) in order to save at least half the time consumed in translating the daily assignment in Latin class. I had started this practice because of the significant time saving, and because I was unable to discover any way in which it would damage me in regard to the final exam or in any other way. But Chauncey regarded this as cheating, and reported my use of the pony to whoever was appointed to receive such complaints. A few days later, Mr. McElwaine, the Latin teacher whom I liked, asked for all students who were using a pony to hold up their hands. I responded immediately. After a few seconds, about half the class had their hands up. Mr. McElwaine looked around the class for a few moments, then said, approximately, "It has been traditional to frown on the use of a pony; however, when I note that many of the best students in this class have declared that they use a pony, I find it difficult to justify that position." I heard nothing more about this matter, and Chauncey was relieved of rooming with me at the end of the quarter. I was moved across the hall to room with a chap named Bill Hill, from Knoxville. We got along quite well with each other, but I felt sorry for him because he was quite homesick, possibly because of a girl back home. For better or worse, I was never bothered with that particular problem. By an ironic twist of fate, I was able to overcome the need to get up at 5 A.M in order to have enough study time. McCallie had a system of displaying each student's scholastic standing for all to see by posting colored cards in the main assembly room in a card rack extending along the walls of the room. The top group had a white card posted, the next group a blue card, and so on down to the black card. For boarding students, a black card student was campused (no off-campus privilege on week ends) and a white card student was excused from study hall at night. After a few weeks, a white card showed up in my box. This allowed me more than a half hour of extra study time per day by eliminating the necessity for walking back and forth to study hall—and, of course, visiting with friends along the way. Ergo, no more early arising.

As implied in a statement above, I was able to handle the matter of carrying an extra course. I also had no further problems from forced association with a student with whom I was not compatible. There was also no problem with the one thing that bothered me considerably about going to McCallie, a semi-military school. At such schools, hazing was frequently practiced in those days. As I have mentioned previously, from an early age I was apprehensive about getting into situations where things could get out of my control. I had talked to my older brother about hazing at McCallie, and he had suggested that I might profit by looking up Delbert Martin, younger brother of Frank Martin, who was his best friend at McCallie. I followed John's advice. As soon as I had gotten settled into my new surroundings, I looked up Delbert, and after some chit-chat got down to telling him that my brother John had told me that I might profit by asking his advice on how I could best deal with hazing. John's advice proved to be excellent. Delbert told me that obnoxious hazing such as paddling is nearly always carried out by cowards, and cowards do not pick on anyone that they fear might retaliate in some way. We don't have many of that type at McCallie, he said, and I think that they are unlikely to pick on anybody as big as you are, and who is out for football. Delbert was right. I had no problem at all. As a matter of fact, I and my future roommate made an attack on hazing during the next two years.

After the end of the football season there were no interscholastic athletics in which I had either interest or experience. I think that I had never touched a basketball. So after the Christmas vacation I went down to the gym, where I was able to retain my football locker, and signed up for gymnastics as my athletic activity. There were only eight or ten people in the class, and we had no instructor, only a person who came around now and then to see if all of us were there. An ideal situation for what I wanted to do. This group was not interested in complicated gymnastics, but rather in learning to do things that were fun, without months or years of training. This type of thing was normally referred to as tumbling. We worked on learning to do such things as forward and backward handsprings; back flips and forward flips; cartwheels and roundoffs; and a few other simple maneuvers. We also worked in pairs for various kinds of lifts. One of the group, Bill Massie from Lexington, Kentucky, quickly became a good friend of mine. Our ability at tumbling was similar, and our respective sizes were ideal for working as a pair. After a few months of living in an orderly fashion at a military school, I gained about twenty-five pounds, which brought me to the 180-185 pound range. Bill was at 155-160 pounds. Thus, when we worked as a pair, I was always the floor man. Bill and I worked hard at learning tumbling, usually staying after the required time for physical activity, often staying as late as we could and still get a shower before rushing up the hill to get to dinner on time. Naturally enough, I have no recollection of anything about the other members of this group, whereas Bill and I became roommates at the beginning of my second year at McCallie. After graduation from McCallie, we followed very different paths, but always kept in touch, and frequently visited each other, until Bill died a few years ago.

All of my first year at McCallie was dominated by the need to devote as much time as possible to studying, in order to keep my grades as high as I had become accustomed to having them. I do not remember whether

I planned to go out for baseball in the spring, because I had no opportunity to do so. An epidemic of scarlet fever swept through the McCallie dormitories. After the wave of infection had died down, I noticed a rash in my armpits which looked like the description I had heard of one of the symptoms of scarlet fever, so I went to the infirmary. The nurse said it looked like scarlet fever, but she wanted to get the doctor's opinion because my temperature was normal. The doctor decided that I should be put into quarantine as a precaution against my causing a flare-up of the infection just when it seemed to be abating. I was put into a room with two others who were recovering and were symptom-free and feeling fine. At that time, a four-week quarantine period was required, and I was required to remain quarantined for that period even though I never ran any temperature. Since the number of scarlet fever patients had swamped the infirmary, some rooms normally occupied by teachers were pressed into service. The room I was in was that of Mr. McElwaine, my Latin teacher. There was a poem on the wall in a frame, which seemed to me to be a nice little satire on the kind of language used by too many people. I memorized the poem, but can now recall only the title and first
four lines:

> HELL
> Hell yes, hell no, and oh hell too;
> The hell you don't, and the hell you do;
> Now who the hell, and oh hell where;
> And what the hell do you think I care.

There were eight or ten more lines, but I do not remember them, probably because they added nothing to the concept and objective of the poem.

During the last ten days of my quarantine I was alone in the room because my roommates had served their time. I was not lonesome, however, because there was a lot of yelling back and forth between my third-story window and people passing below between classes or for other reasons. There was another reason that I was rather busy during these days. I missed a month of classes. My books were sent up to me, even the Cicero pony, and I had to study because of final exams coming up in a few weeks. I had a stack of "homework" to do, especially in the two math classes. I wrote out all the assignments, then took the papers out to nearby tennis courts where there were several long benches, and spread each one out in the sun for about an hour. Somebody else was sent to gather up the papers and take them to the teachers. There were some pretty weird ideas about contagion in those days, compared to what is known today. I had no trouble at all on the final exams. My white card was not endangered.

When Bill Massie and I returned as roommates in the fall of my second year at McCallie, both of us began to enjoy life at McCallie a great deal more, especially me. For one thing, I was relieved of the double load in math; hence had more time to engage in things of my choice. Also, regarding hazing, I was no longer a "rat," but an "old man." Rather early in the year, Bill and I began to have discussions with Dr. McCallie about hazing. Dr. J.P. McCallie was the older of the brothers and was clearly in charge. His title was justified, for he had a Ph. D. degree in astronomy. He sometimes gave a rather interesting talk on astronomy in chapel. The younger brother did not have a doctorate degree of any kind, and he was known as Professor McCallie. He appeared to be in charge of the business side of the school. Dr. McCallie appeared receptive to the idea of reducing hazing to a rather friendly relationship. As well as I can remember, the plan was developed largely by Dr. McCallie, with consultation with Bill and me, as well as other students. I think that the crux of the plan was to have each "rat" (new student) assigned to an "old man" who would act as his advisor and manager. Something of a father-son relationship. The old man was responsible for the behavior of his rat, but the rat was supposed to do what the old man told him to do, in order to keep his nose clean. I have no recollection of what recourse, if any, was provided to either party, but I presume that Dr. McCallie took care of that sort of thing. At sometime in the spring, the rat was to repay the old man for taking care of him by acting as his servant for a week. This was called "Rat Week." I do not recall any problem with an old man requiring abusive or embarrassing service from his rat, but I presume it sometimes occurred. In any case, it was a big improvement over the system in effect when I arrived at McCallie, and so Bill and I felt rather elated over the evolution.

Both Bill and I went out for football in the fall, but neither of us earned a letter. We continued to spend a lot of time doing gymnastics, and were guilty of "showing off" sometimes; doing things such as walking down stairs on our hands. (The last time I walked down stairs on my hands was in about 1948 when Bill, his wife and two of his children visited us in Berkeley. Bill and I walked down a few of the stairs in our living room in order to impress our children that we were not yet over the hill.) I recall an incident that involved hand walking which occurred at McCallie in the fall of the year that Bill and I did not earn letters in football. In the dining room at McCallie, students were assigned seats at large round tables seating about ten. Each table had a teacher assigned to it. On one evening at dinner, the teacher assigned to my table said, "Cason, I have never seen a good student eat as much as you do." I could not think of anything appropriate to say, but another student said, "Have you ever known another good student who raced his roommate across the football field after practice, wearing his football clothes, and walking on his hands?". The teacher looked rather startled and asked me if that were true. I told him that it was true but that it was a rather unusual kind of race in that the winner was not the one who went the fastest, but the one who was able to go the farthest without getting down on his feet.

At sometime during the winter quarter, I began to think about returning to McCallie for a third year. Of course this clearly indicated that I was enjoying myself and felt that McCallie was doing a lot for me. Many factors were involved, such as my enjoyment of the athletic facilities; however, a major consideration was delaying for a year my entrance into college. This would bring me into step with the majority of my classmates, and I realized that this would become more important in college. I assumed that I would follow my brother to Vanderbilt University, which was coeducational. This assumption proved correct. At the college level, my brother's advice proved to be very important indeed, in many respects. And so I wrote my father to ask if he could afford to send me to McCallie for a third year. He immediately responded in the affirmative; the bus business had prospered to the extent that this was possible. In those days, even important decisions such as this were unlikely to inspire a telephone call. As a matter of fact, I cannot remember having ever made a long distance telephone call at that time. McCallie School required that each student write a letter home every Sunday night, and the letters were collected and mailed for the students. That weekly letter was always addressed to my mother, a letter to my dad was an extra. During my first year, when I was hard-pressed for time, I occasionally mailed my mother a blank piece of paper.

I heard from one of my mother's friends that she told people: "That blank piece of paper does not bother me in the least. I know that he is very busy making good grades with a heavy course load."

I do not remember whether Bill Massie was influenced by my decision, but he also decided on an extra year at McCallie. I daresay that I would not have returned if Bill's decision had been negative. As things developed, there was plenty of serendipity to go around. My mother was very happy to learn that I graduated as valedictorian of my class and this made me happy. This could not have happened if I had not returned for the extra year. It was rare, if not unprecedented, for a three-year man to be valedictorian. I doubt if a two-year man would have been considered under any circumstances.

I won a letter in baseball in my second year at McCallie, and enjoyed that season very much. This proved to be my only season in baseball, for there was no baseball team during my third year. There were so few people who turned out for baseball that the brothers decided it was not desirable to field a team. They gave each man who had turned out for baseball a letter, and encouraged them to go out for track, in which McCallie excelled. I was not pleased about this decision and did not regard it as entirely fair and square. I did not complain, however, but went out for pole vaulting, since there were few candidates for that activity and I had previously done some practicing at it. Since I was in a hurry to build up my pole vaulting ability, I practiced on a wet day, slipped off the pole and landed on my hands in the sawdust pit, which broke one bone in my right forearm. In those days, there was hardly anything known about setting bones, and the muscles in my forearm pulled against the two pieces of bone so that they could not be fit together properly except in an open operation. My brother, who was in medical school at the time, advised strongly against such an operation. This was long before the day of antibiotics, and an open operation involving a bone presented a serious risk of a bone infection, which would result in death unless the arm, or at least the forearm, were amputated. The arm was set with only about 50 percent contact between the pieces. This was judged to require keeping the forearm in a sling and a cast for two months or longer, which extended well into the summer. At graduation time, the surgeon put on a lighter cast so that I could wear my dress uniform with my lieutenant's chevrons. This pleased my mother very much. Naturally enough, she attended graduation exercises, and a little serendipity became involved. Several people spoke to her of what they called my courageous behavior when I broke my arm.

Of course this affair of the broken arm consumed most of my time during my last quarter at McCallie, but that was not the half of it. When the cast finally came off I was able to straighten the arm only part way. The best I could do left a dihedral angle of about 25 degrees. The doctors said that I would never be able to straighten out the arm completely. Well, I showed them a thing or two. I began thinking about the orthodontistry which was done on my teeth at an earlier date. If an orthodontist could move teeth around in my jawbone why couldn't pressure against the cartilage which had formed on the ends of those bones cause it to wear enough so that I could again straighten out the arm? I spent most of my time that summer working on that arm, first soaking in hot water, then carrying around a bucket of sand. And so on, ad infinitum. Not really ad infinitum, but it seemed that way before I was able to straighten out the arm just before entering Vanderbilt in the fall. It did not interfere with walking on my hands or in other ways in tumbling, although I was very cautious about jolting my arms for several months. I did experience a significant handicap in using my right arm because of an inability to rotate that forearm. The healing of the poorly mended bone, which was broken just below the elbow, caused development of such a lump that the bones could not slide over each over as required for rotation of the forearm. I cannot receive in my right hand a group of small objects, such as change after making a purchase. Anyone handing me such things will extend it toward my right hand. This is actually a minor nuisance compared to interference with typing; however, this, also, has been eliminated since I bought a computer and type on a word processor. I can type faster than I ever could on an electronic typewriter.

I will report on one other sequence of events before passing on to my entrance into Vanderbilt University. I have chosen, from a large number of events happening at McCallie school, those which I judge as likely to have had some impact, in one way or another, on my life in the future.

On one occasion during my last year at McCallie, a man gave a talk on hypnotism at the chapel assembly. He spoke on the realism of hypnotism, methods of inducing it, and methods of bringing a person out of a hypnotic state. At the end of his talk, he said that he would give a demonstration of hypnotism if he could get a volunteer from the audience to be the subject. He allowed himself an escape route in case his demonstration failed. He said that some people were harder to hypnotize than others. After a pause, one of the younger teachers volunteered. He happened to be the teacher in charge of my table in the dining room. The speaker got the subject seated comfortably, and then began talking to him after he had instructed him to look at a light which the speaker held to one side, without turning his head away from pointing straight forward. After what I remember as a short interval, the speaker said to the subject, "There has been an elephant walking around on this campus recently, and you are worried about it. I want you to make inquiry as to who else has seen this elephant." Soon after that, the session ended, and the students went out to lunch while laughing and talking about the interesting chapel talk. The subject of hypnotism came in to lunch a little late, and seemed rather distracted. After a while, he said, "I know that this sounds rather crazy, but have any of you seen the elephant that has been walking around on campus?" This was followed by a roar of laughter, with such comments as, "I still don't believe it; it must be a frame-up!" I have no recollection of having looked at the hypnotism victim, or hearing him say anything.

Bill Massie and I were very skeptical, but very interested. Acting in a manner characteristic of the two of us, we decided to investigate, rather than joining in on the blue sky speculation. On the following Saturday we went down to the Chattanooga library, and came home with a few books which we found on hypnotism. After studying these books during all the time we had available during the weekend, we concluded that the time had come to try an experiment. We would try to hypnotize someone if we could find a volunteer. Someone volunteered, and we hypnotized him! We then brought him out of it, according to instructions in the book. We purposely avoided any publicity about this feat because we were rather scared. We wanted to study the books some more. On the next weekend, we hypnotized another volunteer. After a few more successes, with much exchange of sensations among those hypnotized, disaster struck! We hypnotized a boy and were unable to bring him out of it. To put it mildly, we were terrified! Our first instinct was to forget about the dire consequences of reporting what we had been doing, and seek help. But before doing such a thing, we realized that we had no idea who would be a professional competent to help. So we agreed to disperse the crowd, then Bill would stay with the hypnotized victim to make sure that nothing unfortunate happened to him and continue to try and snap him out of it while I studied the books. I worked intently, and after a period, whose length I do not remember, I came up with something new to try. It worked! It is probable that I have never since experienced such relief over anything. After getting our wits together and taking those books back to the library, Bill and I reached two conclusions which we regarded as engraved in stone, and I have never changed my mind on the subject. I was really frightened! These conclusions were:

1. We would never have anything more to do with hypnotism. It is dangerous stuff.

2. Hypnotism is very real. Anyone who fails to realize that may suffer serious consequences.

Regarding the second item above, history is full of incidents where failure to recognize this principle had serious consequences, Recent large scale incidents include Jones Temple, Heaven's Gate, the people in a sect in Texas who were slaughtered, and numerous smaller groups. Hypnotism between married couples seems quite widespread. One often hears such an expression as, "How could two people like that be married?" Be that as it may, there is little likelihood that anything will be accomplished in understanding and defending against hypnotism. Not only is the subject very complicated, but subject to abuse by politicians and numerous self-interest groups. However these things may turn out, I am sticking to the two Cason & Massie Principles.

And so this report on a few highlights of the experiences of Cason and Massie at the McCallie School must come to an end, but the friendship and association between them continued until death did us part. Bill graduated from the University of Kentucky, then from Harvard Medical School, served in England during World War II, and finally became a prominent orthopedist. I graduated from Vanderbilt University, obtained an M.S. in organic chemistry from the University of California in Berkeley, then a Ph.D. in organic chemistry from Yale. After serving as a Postdoctoral Research Fellow with Louis Fieser at Harvard and working for the National Defense Research Committee during WW II, I started teaching at

DePauw University, after a year shifted to Vanderbilt, and after WW II wound up going full circle as a Professor of Organic Chemistry at Berkeley. During all these peregrinations, we remained in contact. I saw Bill just days before he died a few years ago.

CHAPTER 3

VANDERBILT DAYS

During the summer before I entered Vanderbilt, my dad offered to buy me one of the new portable typewriters if I would learn to type rapidly—hopefully forty words per minute—during the summer. Never one to refuse a challenge, I set to work immediately typing on the mammoth office machine, a reject from my dad's office. I also bought a book on the subject which was considerably more simple than the books I used learning to type on a word processor. I spent many days typing sentences which contained all the letters in the alphabet, such as: Whenever the black fox jumped, the squirrel gazed suspiciously. Check them out; they are all there. And there were many more sentences with most of the letters present, such as: Now is the time for all good men to come to the aid of their country. Before the end of the summer, I reached my goal and became the proud owner of a new portable typewriter. I treasured that machine, and was still typing on it when I entered graduate school at Yale. I realized immediately that this simple little machine would add a great many weeks, or even months, to what I could accomplish if I should become engaged in any kind of scholarly work. Having no powers of prophecy, I certainly was not thinking of typing all of the first draft copy for more than a hundred research papers and three college textbooks. However, I did know that I had every intention of becoming a lawyer, and had shaped all my reading and course work in that direction. During that extra year at McCallie I had taken a third year of French, a second year of classical Greek, a fifth year of Latin, and a fifth year of English. Rather discouraging to think of how profitable it would have been to put in those seven course years studying modern languages rather than dead languages. But there is no point in contemplating that sort of thing. In those days, there seemed to be a general consensus among scholars that studying Latin makes the brain strong; therefore, good students should study Latin. The one saving grace among the courses I took in my extra year at McCallie was the English course, which was called English IV. It was taught by a young man named Varner, who was working for a graduate degree in English. There were only four or five students enrolled in the course, and the subject matter consisted of whatever Mr. Varner chose. He chose to have us read books of his choice; sometimes different books were read by different students. I remember one occasion on which Mr. Varner stopped me as I was going into the dining room at lunch, and said: "I want you to read at least one book by an author who should be getting more recognition than he is getting. His name is James Conrad and he is a native of Poland, but he writes his books in English. He says that English is such a beautiful language because he can express his thoughts more accurately and attractively than is possible in Polish." This commentary certainly stirred up my imagination and ambitions, and may have occurred because I had told Mr. Varner that I was planning to become a lawyer.

Although much of my time during the summer before I entered Vanderbilt was spent learning to type, some other things demanded my attention. Two things in particular had developed as a result of my prep school record. One problem was being offered a scholarship if I would attend a small college in South Carolina named Presbyterian College. Because of having been exposed to such an abundance of religion during previous years, I was rather unimpressed by the name of this college. Moreover, I was geared to follow in my brother's footsteps at Vanderbilt , so I gave the solicitors from Presbyterian College no encouragement. Nevertheless, these people mounted a powerful sales pitch based on their knowledge of my mother's strong religious convictions. I regarded this behavior as highly reprehensible and unfair—what I called, in the language of a college student of those times, "dirty pool." This hardened my determination not to go to Presbyterian College. Fortunately, my dad behaved in characteristic fashion. He said that he could afford to pay my way at Vanderbilt, and did not need to seek charity from some other college. Ergo, I went to Vanderbilt.

Another thing which required some attention during that summer before entering Vanderbilt was the ambition of the fraternities at Vanderbilt to snag a freshman who had high grades and two varsity athletic letters. No matter that there was no possibility of my winning an athletic letter at the college level; having a "straight A" student in the chapter would give them "standing" with the Dean. To complicate the matter, there were a lot of Murfreesboro boys, including my brother, who were members or alumni of the Kappa Alpha fraternity. As I noted on some occasions in Chapter 2, I had been wary at an early age of getting into situations where things might get out of my control. This attitude had become hardened concerning a college fraternity. The news was replete with reports of brutal and nonsensical treatment of new fraternity members under the guise of initiation—or for no reason at all in some flagrant instances. On the other side of the coin, some 95 percent of the male students at Vanderbilt were fraternity members. Naturally enough, I guess, I consulted John on the subject. We had a long discussion, during which John said that he felt uncertain on how to advise me, due to the dichotomy which I have just mentioned. He knew me well enough to know exactly what was bothering me. Finally, after much discussion, he stated: "There is one item of advice on which I will speak with complete confidence; for God's sake, do not join the same fraternity that I did." My response: "I get the message." So I told the fraternity boys to go to hell, and thus cut off nearly all my opportunities for association with girls. This decision turned out surprisingly well.

As things developed, I had the opportunity to make many friends among the male students, whom I met in various normal activities such as contacts in the dormitory, in the laboratories which I took in later years, or in the cafeteria where I ate most of my meals during all my four years at Vanderbilt. Of particular importance were contacts made in the physical education class which was required once a week for the first two years. In retrospect, I am prone to wonder if there are not great advantages during college years for a boy who has numerous interests not involving girls, to be rid of the problems associated with girls at this stage in life. If a major objective of associating with girls in college is finding a girl who will make a suitable mate for life, there is no reasonable doubt that a boy is better off not to be involved with the problems arising from association with girls during college. However, there is an obvious flaw in this rather simplistic reasoning. For well-known biological reasons, involving the necessity for propagation of the species, the teenage boy is likely to be more interested in copulation with the girl than in marrying her at a later date. So it may make things easier for the boy if he is able to avoid an undue strain on his ability to refrain from acting according to his biological instincts. In such a quandary, it might reasonably be concluded that the boy, as well as the girl, is not helped any by receiving official instruction, even in high school, on how to enjoy copulation without pregnancy. This sort of reasoning is not likely to have a significant impact on most members of society; however, it may help some members of society feel a little better about what they are doing. In my case, in deja vu, I have no regrets whatsoever that I made the decision not to join a fraternity. My brother did a masterful job of guiding me to the correct decision.

As soon as I had completed enrollment at Vanderbilt, I consulted the person who was assigned to advise me about my schedule of classes. I did not make a big hit with this adviser when I showed him the paper on which I had made out my schedule of classes for my entire four years at Vanderbilt. He objected especially strenuously to my idea of postponing to a later year the course in biology or chemistry that was required of all entering freshmen. He told me: "This regulation has been adopted to prevent a person like you, who has not even entered college, from going into a program unsuitable to him without even considering a different field. Since most students entering college these days know little, if anything, about physical and biological sciences, this regulation has been adopted." Truer words were never spoken! I explained to him that I had very good reasons for planning to become a lawyer. My dad had a law degree, which was not common in the preceding century among people raised in the backwoods of Tennessee. After he had practiced for only a few years, his hearing went bad which forced him to give up the practice of law. Since he had two sons and my older brother was in medical school, it was natural for him to hope that I would become a lawyer, and he had treated me so well for all of my life that I could not bear to disappoint him. The adviser noted that I did not have to give up being a lawyer because of not taking one course in my freshman year, and that he did not want to hear any more argument. I was so anxious to defer that course (self hypnotism?) that I decided to appeal to the dean of the College of Letters and Science. The dean was not as patient with me as was my adviser. After hearing my story, he responded without hesitation: "Young man, the function of my office in this university is to see to it that the rules and regulations are followed, not to make exceptions to them. Have I made myself clear?" My response: "Yes sir, Dean, you have made yourself disgustingly clear."

Naturally enough, my next move was to hunt up my brother who was in medical school on the same campus. He laughed out loud at my story about the dean, and said that I deserved rough treatment for taking up several professors' time over such a trivial matter. He followed up by saying, "You have no recourse except to take that lousy freshman chemistry course that is taught by old Breckenridge for the poor souls like you who are required to take it. There is a problem about the beginning biology course. Studying biology before studying chemistry is a complete waste of time."

Since John had majored in chemistry before entering medical school, I realized that if anybody in the world was qualified to make such a statement, it was John Cason. So I enrolled in that lousy chemistry course. Let us jump forward in time to about the middle of the winter quarter. I was walking across campus with a group who had lunch together to the one laboratory which this freshman chemistry course had. Along the way I commented, "I really like this course, especially the laboratory." The entire group stopped walking and stared at me as if I had two heads. Somebody observed, "I didn't notice you drinking anything unusual at lunch."

The long continuation of this story must come later.

Each entering freshman at Vanderbilt was required to enroll in five courses, of which three or four were required. Among the required courses was Freshman English. This was my favorite course in my first year at Vanderbilt and fit perfectly with my intention of becoming a lawyer. At that time the course consisted of one unit taught by the well-known Eddie Mims, lecturing to the whole class in a large lecture room, and two units where the class was broken up into sections of twenty to twenty-five students. Each section was taught by a different person, and in those days I think faculty members taught all sections. I had the incredible good luck to draw as my teacher John Crowe Ransom, a prominent man of letters who later left Vanderbilt to go to Kenyon College to become editor of the Kenyon Quarterly Review. At my time at Vanderbilt, he was prominent in a group of writers known as "The Agrarians." Eddie Mims seemed to be the head honcho in "The Agrarians." I never knew whether he was the founder. My chief attraction to the course was Professor Ransom. According to my preferences, he certainly knew how to teach a course about the writing of the English language. He gave a writing assignment for each of the periods into which he divided a quarter. (I do not remember how long a period was, or if it was variable.) He was very strict about assignments being late, except that once, possibly twice, per quarter he would excuse lateness on such grounds as "genius simply was not working." He spent class periods reading to us from various authors and made commentary on the significance and meaning of style, good syntax, and balanced clauses and phrases. Sometimes he read things that those in the class had written, and commented mostly on good features, only occasionally on bad ones. Near the end of the spring quarter he returned a paper I had written with an A+ on it. I have treasured that paper, not because of the A+ but because John Crowe Ransom had written on it. Quite a few years after I had become a professor of chemistry at the University of California, I noticed a short article in the news that Professor Ransom had retired from teaching at Kenyon and as editor of the Kenyon Quarterly Review. If my memory is correct, the Kenyon Quarterly Review was closed down after Ransom's retirement; in fact, I think that was what the news article was about. In any case, I sent him a copy of a textbook I had written recently, and I wrote on the fly leaf the following: "Any good features that appear in the writing of this book are due to what I learned in 1935 during my freshman year at Vanderbilt in the class taught by Professor John Crowe Ransom. Any poor writing in this book is due to my failure to learn as much as I should have learned from Professor Ransom." I did not receive a response from him and I wondered if he might be too far along in age to take care of such things. On one occasion, when I was teaching a class in organic chemistry and using the text I wrote for such a course, a student enrolled in the class who was an English major complimented me on the quality of my writing, which he said he hardly ever found in science texts. I gave him the same story that I had written to Professor Ransom.

The other courses I took in my freshman year were rather dull. The mathematics course was downright boring, because the senior math course I took at McCallie covered essentially everything that was in the so-called college algebra course. I doubt if I ever earned a cheaper A grade. As for the Latin and Greek courses, dullsville is the only proper description. In retrospect, I have no idea how I could have taken so much of that stuff; probably a combination of following tradition as defined for "good" students, and being ignorant of what a good course is like. The chemistry course was certainly very different, even more interesting than Professor Ransom's English course. I became increasingly fascinated by all these things I had not even known existed. By the middle of the third quarter, the instructor in charge of the labs was giving me some extra experiments to do. Wow! Real fun! By the end of the quarter, I had definitely decided to take the first courses in geology and physics, along with calculus and the second year of chemistry, if they would let me do so after having taken this lousy course given by Breckinridge for those who were forced to take it. This second year of chemistry, which was entirely quantitative analysis in those days, was taught by a professor named Fritz Conover, who had a well-earned reputation for being an oddball. For example, he would walk into a drugstore and soda fountain across the street from the campus, and as he came in the door he would start yelling, "One Coca Cola, no ice!" He expected the drink to be ready by the time he reached the soda fountain in the back of the store. He proved to be very understanding of my wanting to take the course he taught in spite of having taken the freshman course, which was not intended for those who wanted to take advanced chemistry courses. After hearing that I had made A grades in the first two quarters of Breck's course, and was doing extra work in the lab during the third quarter, he said, "If you are willing to work your ass off, you should have no trouble with my course." I assured him that I was willing, and signed up for the course in the fall.

In the following fall semester, when I was taking elementary geology and physics, along with chemistry and calculus, I was like a kid in a toy shop, encountering this array of new things that I had never known before. In retrospect, at the time that I am writing this, a few lines from the poem Ulysses seem appropriate:

"Come, my friends, "tis not too late to seek a newer world,
Push off, and sitting well in order, smite the sounding furrows.

My purpose holds to sail beyond the sunset and the baths of all the western stars;
To follow knowledge like a sinking star, beyond the utmost bounds of human thought".

Since I had not studied calculus prior to the beginning of the semester, I signed up for the "non-engineering" physics, which did not require the use of calculus. I was taking physics in an exploratory sense, as was the case with geology. I judged that if I should find physics sufficiently interesting to justify advanced courses, I could manage that as I had in chemistry. There were no requirements for advanced geology courses which I did not have. As things worked out, I did take advanced courses in both physics and geology in my junior year, along with the first year of biology. In that year, I began to have trouble with having more laboratories than I could fit into the usual schedule at Vanderbilt, which was a three-hour lab each afternoon on each weekday. I had six labs, but was able to solve the problem by the fact that the Biology 1 course had one of its two scheduled labs on Saturday. During all my days at Vanderbilt I went home each weekend, but ordinarily left Nashville late Saturday afternoon, and returned from Murfreesboro on Sunday night.

At this stage of my tenure at Vanderbilt, the pattern of my academic activities had become rather firmly fixed, so it is no doubt in order to return to square one and consider other activities in which I was engaged and the people with whom I became associated. I started my life at Vanderbilt as a resident of Kissam Hall, named after its donor, Maria Louisa Kissam Vanderbilt. This was a large four-story brick building, with a basement which was partly above ground level. It was in the shape of a U, with about a hundred feet between the parallel wings. There was a paved U-shaped driveway next to the building, with a planted area in the center of the U. As one can well imagine, this geometry was conducive to considerable commotion in the U, with a large captive audience of the occupants of the rooms facing toward the U. My room was at the end of the U, first floor, facing into the U. I have no recollection of the commotion in the U generating any problems for me—possibly because Kissam Hall was inhabited mostly by non-fraternity undergraduates, graduate students, and students in the Vanderbilt Divinity School. Vanderbilt, like many other universities, was founded near the middle of the nineteenth century by the Methodist Church. It expanded greatly and changed its name after generous gifts from the Vanderbilt family. By the time of my arrival there was no visible influence by the Methodist Church—a situation very different than that at DePauw University where I taught for one year just before World War II.

In many ways, Kissam Hall was a rather archaic structure, especially the toilet facilities, but this did not bother me as much as it did many of the other students, possibly because it was reminiscent of the house in which I grew up in Murfreesboro. That house had a large kitchen with a coal-burning stove; a very large dining room; a smaller eating room in which the family ate breakfast and lunch; a large parlor, used on only rare occasions, such as a meeting of the "sewing circle" of the Presbyterian Church; a large front hall where guests were entertained; a large library with bookcases full of books, where I spent a great deal of my time during my teen years; four bedrooms and one bathroom upstairs. Kissam Hall was not dissimilar. The only toilets on each floor were in a little room at the end of each wing. Each of these end rooms had one toilet and one wash basin, no shower. In the basement of the wing opposite my wing was one large room with a row of toilets and another large room with a row of showers. I always showered after spending an hour in the gym each day, and in the morning I got up before anyone else in my wing to get breakfast in the cafeteria and get to an eight o'clock class on time. The facilities were about as good as I was accustomed to; a little better, on average, than most of my rooms at McCallie.

The little toilets at the ends of the halls in Kissam were the width of the hall, thus the door to this little room was at the end of the hall. The door to my room opened into the hall immediately adjacent to the door to the toilet and was directly across the hall from the door to the other single occupant room at this end of the wing. As I was getting my clothes unpacked on my day of arrival I had left my door open, following the custom of my prep school days. The man in the room directly across from me walked into my room and introduced himself as Henry Harrell, from Murfreesboro. I was unaware of the existence of anybody named Henry Harrell in Murfreesboro. There proved to be a very good reason for this. I was unaware of Henry's existence, not because he lived on east Main

Street where the country club types lived, but because he lived on a farm about four miles from the city limits at the end of Main Street . His father was a retired minister in the Methodist Church and was operating this farm to supplement any meager savings he may have accumulated as a minister in those days. The fact that Henry and I were occupying the very scarce single occupant rooms in Kissam Hall may offer a rational explanation why we rapidly became good friends, and the relationship lasted until death did us part. An obvious and important characteristic common to the two of us was that both of us were obviously social introverts. Neither of us had dates with girls during the time we were together at Vanderbilt, which was quite satisfactory for both of us. As will be encountered later, we began rooming together at the beginning of our junior year. He was an engineering student—civil engineering, which became very useful to him in later life.

Since I had only one laboratory, in the chemistry course, during my freshman year, I had more "free" time available than was the case during the later three years, when most of my courses had one or more labs per week. The situation was diametrically opposite to that during my first year at McCallie. I spent much of this potentially free time in "hitting the books." I suppose that a psychologist might choose to label my motivation in several ways: I was in the habit of making top-notch grades; I was motivated by a powerful "will to win," to stand at the top of the heap; I wanted to stand out in the crowd, to be a person whom people would recognize on seeing me in a crowd; I wanted to prepare myself for being able to earn a good living in later life, and thus be able to lead a healthy and happy life. There has been a considerable expenditure of printer's ink setting forth the idea that self-psychoanalysis is futile, and there is nothing in my background that would seem to qualify me to comment on that subject. Nevertheless, I will point out that subsequent events in my life, when considered together, indicate clearly that the second of the above-cited options is correct.

Although I did spend much time in hitting the books, I also had considerable time to enjoy myself while getting acquainted with my new environment. Naturally enough, I guess, one of my first moves was spending an hour every day at the end of the afternoon in the gym. I met several interesting people in a room that was equipped for tumbling (amateur gymnastics); however, I formed a lasting friendship with only one of them, a man named Tom Weaver. Tom was a member of a prominent, wealthy family, a handsome chap who was active as a fraternity man during his undergraduate days at Vanderbilt. After graduation, he went to medical school, beginning the fulfillment of a long-held ambition to become a medical doctor. As an undergraduate, he had become so interested in tumbling that, as one of his first moves after enrolling in medical school, he decided to investigate what was going on in the tumbling room at the undergraduate gym. This was facilitated by the fact that the medical school was on the same campus with the undergraduate school. As soon as Tom and I met, it became apparent that we were ideally adapted to becoming companions in tumbling. At about 160 pounds, he was twenty pounds lighter than me, thus ideal as the top man in a two-man stunt with me. For much of the time during my undergraduate years and Tom's four years at medical school, we enjoyed working out at the gym four or five days a week. We really got acquainted with each other during the summer between our junior and senior years. We took a six or seven day canoe trip down the Caney Fork River, starting at an accessible place about a mile below the dam at Rock Island, and were picked up by my dad and Kit Haynes at Carthage, which is on the Cumberland River at the location of a dam a few miles below the junction of the Cumberland River and the Caney Fork. They had responded to the telephone call we had made early that morning from a house we had spotted on the quadrangle map we were carrying with us. The house was on a country road near the river, and we had to climb up the steep bank for several hundred feet to get to it. During our entire route, the Caney Fork flowed through a small canyon with only occasional houses shown near the river on the quadrangle map. The telephone we used was the kind, which I haven't seen since, where one turned a little crank to ring up the operator, then gave the number desired and the town. After a while, she got the number for us. After I talked, following the instructions of our kind host, I rang up the operator again to find out what we owed for making the call. I cannot recall why Tom and I made this trip, perhaps a survival of the old pioneer spirit, or maybe it was the response to a challenge. The entire route we traveled was through a deep uncharted canyon. Except for a pup tent we had bought for the trip, most of the equipment was inherited from Elkhorn Cabin. Whatever our reasons for making the trip, our friendship survived, even when Tom developed diarrhea and decided that what he needed was some eggs. He had always had eggs for breakfast. Fortunately, the quad map showed a house only a mile or two downstream, so we climbed out and bought some eggs from the farmer. I remember nothing more about the incident, so the eggs—or something else—must have done the job.

My friendship with Tom Weaver not only survived the canoe trip, but became entrenched, and lasted until death did us part. Indeed, by a curious twist of fate, our friendship expanded to include my brother. After Tom had finished medical school and the required years of internship and residency, he went into practice in Nashville and became a pediatrician. By this time my brother had developed a flourishing practice in Murfreesboro as an obstetrician and pediatrician. Such a combination was not uncommon in relatively small cities such as Murfreesboro. Since John had met Tom on several occasions while he was associated with me at Vanderbilt, it was natural, indeed inevitable, that the two of them should see each other frequently, especially because of the small city, larger city relationship. Eventually Tom began serving as pediatrician for John's grandchildren, who were living in Nashville. The last time that I saw Tom was when he attended my mother's funeral, which was on a day when rain was falling in the cemetery. Tom arrived late, not because of the rain, but because he had received an emergency call to attend one of the children of John's daughter Sally.

Tom Weaver was one of a few lifelong friends whom I met at Vanderbilt. This, of course, is reminiscent of my similar experience at McCallie, where I first met my lifelong friend Bill Massie. I believe that this sort of thing is regarded by psychologists as characteristic of social introverts. If so, I was continuing to run true to form. This does not mean that I did not have other friends at McCallie, and I had still more friends at Vanderbilt, resulting no doubt from the much greater opportunities for meeting people and eventually becoming rather closely associated with them. One such opportunity derived from my outstanding scholastic ability. As time marched on through my freshman year, I was asked by students living in Kissam Hall to assist them with their classwork. This was especially common in Latin and mathematics where I knew, from courses taken at McCallie, most of what was being taught. I was always glad to help people who needed it, probably because of genes inherited honestly from my mother. I remember especially well a group of Kissam residents whom I helped frequently during my freshman year. I was first approached by two men from McMinville who were roommates. One was named Ivan Gestner and I forget the name of the other—possibly Jack Smith. The two-man rooms in Kissam were quite large and rather adequate except for the galvanized sheet metal which was put on the walls during World War I when Kissam was used as an army barracks. There was a large living room with tables and chairs, and a bedroom off each side of the living room. The bedrooms were large enough to accommodate a bed, chest of drawers, closet, and table with bookshelves and chair. Most of the belongings of each student were kept in the bedroom, and the bedroom doors could be shut for studying while a party or something else noisy was going on in the living room. Thus, the living room of Gestner and his roommate was ideal for such things as a session of studying Latin.

Another kind of help that was sometimes requested of me resulted from the so-called Honor System that was followed at Vanderbilt at that time. There was a prevalent saying: "The teachers have the honor and the students have the system". A simply disgraceful system! There was no proctoring of exams, and there was much talking during exams in some courses. Thus, it was inevitable that I would receive requests to copy my math problems. My refusal was usually greeted with insults, and this did not bother me at all. I knew that I was right! In only one instance did things get sticky. Naturally enough, this involved a football player. When his plea that I would be helping the football team was ignored, he then offered to "beat me up." He was bigger than me, but I was not frightened because I knew that I was fast and strong. In any case, he backed off while uttering a stream of profanity. It could have been that he had heard of my gymnastic activities, but I think it is more probable that he was like nearly all people who behave as he did. He was a coward. Happily enough, the cheating was far less flagrant after my first year.

By the end of my sophomore year, I had accumulated some items of reputation which were variously described as: "just what you can expect from that guy Cason"; "how the hell does he get away with it?"; "nutty as a fruitcake" and a few others I don't care to repeat. A minor idiosyncrasy that attracted attention was my practice of always going to a movie the night before an exam. I had not wised up to this sort of thing prior to entering Vanderbilt, where everybody was entirely free to study when, as, and if they so chose. I soon learned by some simple experiments and reading an article in a magazine that the way to get things embedded in permanent memory is to go over the item with understanding, review it a little later, and then review it again the next day. My version of this was to study everything on the day the class met (in lecture courses, I typed an expanded version of my rough and ready lecture notes as soon as possible after class). The next step was to review these notes before class the next time that it met. If there was a midterm exam, everything was reviewed after the last class before the midterm. Before a final exam, everything was reviewed lightly during one or three days before the exam. With this system, two exams in one day was no problem. The idea of a movie on the night before the exam was to get the whole thing out of mind so that the last thing studied was not uppermost in mind. The system did not require a great deal of time, but it did require a lot of organization. I was able to sell this system to a couple of friends who went to the movies with me. It worked fine for them.

After my freshman year I usually had a laboratory every afternoon during week-days, so there developed considerable pressure on my time. I reluctantly decided to get away from the idea of spending an hour every day in gymnastics, especially in the spring when the weather was good, in order to develop some type of physical activity outdoors. Tennis seemed attractive, although I had never swung a tennis racquet before. A friend who lived in Kissam named Bob Smith volunteered to advise me on buying a racquet, and to play with me so I could learn something about the game. This worked out very well. I soon learned to play well enough to give Bob a good game, although it was uncommon for me to win. We worked out a system where the difference in our abilities did not spoil the competitiveness. In my junior year my dad gave me an old car, which was very helpful to our tennis playing. Vanderbilt had a rather limited supply of tennis courts; however, there were quite a few tennis courts in Centennial Park, not far from the campus. On some days we played tennis during the lunch hour instead of eating, then went downtown for a big meal at a very good cafeteria in Nashville. Bob and I played tennis frequently during my last two years at Vanderbilt. When I was driving to

Berkeley to enroll in the university, my first stop on the route was to spend a day and night with Bob Smith in Owensboro, Kentucky. We played tennis on his family's tennis court.

During my freshman year, when I had some time available for relaxing, I developed a practice of going to the student union after supper and shooting pool for about an hour. "Pool" was the name commonly used in reference to pocket billiards, and the pool parlor in a small town such as Murfreesboro was not regarded as a proper place for solid citizens to hang around. The pool parlor was likely to be a good place to buy condoms. Later on in my sojourn at Vanderbilt there developed some discussion about a guy like Cason shooting pool—and being a "shark," no less. And it was true that the people I shot pool with were a different type than I otherwise associated with. I never told anybody why I happened to be a pool shark—probably because I enjoyed letting people know that not all people who make good grades are oddballs. The facts in the case are so simple that it would have either spoiled the story or else gotten me classified as a liar if I had spoken up. At about the time that I entered high school in Murfreesboro, I engaged in a three-way trade with a friend named Vincent DeGeorge and the fire house. I don't remember who engineered the trade, but I traded a camera to Vincent, who traded a radio to the fire house, which traded me the pool table. The pool table was in a really run-down condition, needing new cushions, new cover, new pockets, new cues and a few other things. What with the massive oak legs and frame required to support the stone slabs that served as the top on which the cover was placed, the total weight of this thing must have been close to a ton. The father of a friend named Bob Overall, who lived a couple houses down the street from me, owned a coal yard and had a truck and a couple of husky colored men working for him. (People that I associated with never used the term "blacks"; that term was insulting, because it was used in the slave days. That term "blacks" still sticks in my throat, but I try to become accustomed to it.) Mr. Overall told me that he would supply us with the truck and the two workers if I would give them a good tip. The truck showed up with the pieces of the pool table, and the workers carried the pieces up the three flights of stairs to our big attic. I tipped the workers $10 each, and they acted very pleased. Kit Haynes and I cleaned up the attic, which was used mostly for storing useless things and had no heat, but it had electricity, so we hung a light over the table just like in the pool hall. We worked a long time getting the stone tops to the table perfectly smooth and level, but we were all ready when the cloth and new cushions came. My friends and I shot a lot of pool on cold winter days in that cold attic. Since I practiced a lot while others were not there, I naturally became the shark. But I never could beat Uncle Chicken. I never inquired as to how he got to be such a pool shark, but this discussion reminds me of an incident that happened in my junior year while I was taking second year German from Professor Mayfield, a popular teacher who was known as "Birdie" because of his great interest in birds and bird-watching. He was responsible for the Tennessee legislature adopting the robin as the state bird. To return to the incident: I was shooting pool in a game of "call shot" pool. In this game, the shooter did not get credit for anything that happened to fall in a pocket unless he sank the ball that he called. I had a difficult lay, and the only way I could get the 9 ball which was next up, was in a bank shot. After some sighting down different angles, I called, "9 ball in the side pocket next to me." I sank it without touching the sides of the pocket. At that point, a voice boomed out behind me, "Cason, I believe that it was Samuel Johnson, a British man of letters who stated, after losing a game of billiards, 'Proficiency in sports is commendable; however, such expertise at billiards as just shown by you is a sign of a wasted youth." When I whirled around to see who was delivering such an oration, I found Birdie Mayfield standing in the door laughing, as were the others who happened to be there. I could not think of anything else to do except join in the laughter.

At the end of my second quarter at Vanderbilt, I moved out of Kissam Hall into a room in one of the small brick buildings known as Westside Row. Each of these buildings had two stories, and each level had four rooms and a bathroom. These rooms were the best on campus for men, and hence sought after. I got the opportunity to move into one of these rooms because it was vacated by my brother when he got married. He and his best friend at medical school, Tom Huey, occupied two of these rooms on the second floor. They used one room as a bedroom and the other as a living room. The two occupants of the two rooms on the other side of the building, which was also on the other side of the bathroom, were law students. Thus, I moved into the bedroom with Tom Huey. Tom proved to be quite a character, very funny sometimes, and I enjoyed living with him. There was never any conflict for use of the living room as a study room because of the demands on Tom from the medical school.

Some of the hilarious things that Tom did remain vividly in my memory although it is now ten or fifteen years since Tom passed away from this world. He had big feet; according to his story, he wore size 12 shoes, but size 13 felt so good that he had size 14 specially made. Some mornings, when he had come to bed late the night before, he would sit on the side of the bed and put on his shoes first thing, then moan, "Aaah, practically dressed." He would sometimes thank someone by saying, "mercy buckets," a Hueyism for the French, "merci beaucoup." This sort of thing was regularly laced into his conversation—and sometimes appeared in his writings. In one course he was taking, it was a uniform practice for the students to take notes in a large book bound like a ledger. One day, I was looking through his notebook, sometimes laughing out loud at his notations in the margins. The one I remember most vividly was a cartoon of a man labeled, "Man with boil on neck and ass in sling." What a pitiful condition that man was in. One night just after I had come in from eating supper, Tom rushed through the room, saying, "I have to really hurry if I'm going to get a shoe shine, shit, shower, shampoo, and make it to the party on time." Speaking of parties, I heard a lot of conversation about the "interesting" parties the medical students threw, but this had no impact on me, or the interesting world in which I lived with Tom Huey. An interesting expression that I have never heard except from the group of medical students which included Huey, my brother, and their associates, involved the word "pupats." There appeared no reason for using the word except for its unusual sound. Actually, if my memory serves me correctly, it is the name of a small muscle in the leg, whose function I never knew. It was used in such expressions as "my pupats is sagging" to indicate weariness. The comparative was "my pupats is dragging," or the superlative, "my pupats is dipping sand." Such a vivid and useful expression, suggesting a sort of fraternal relationship between those using it. Kit Haynes and I and some of our associates used it; and my wife, Rebecca, and I still use it at this late date.

Tom had a Ford Model A convertible coupe, in which we did a lot of riding around. I did not have an old car until my junior year. Oddly enough, Tom did not give a name to this car, but it had enough idiosyncrasies to deserve a name. It had a little metal ball, possibly a lump of solder, which rolled around in the gas tank and occasionally got lodged in the gas outlet. In such an emergency, Tom and I, or whoever might be with him, gave the car a good shaking, jumped back in and went on our way. One night, this happened to us when the car stopped at a traffic light in downtown Nashville. We hopped out, gave it the usual treatment, then jumped in to go on our way. Before we could get started and get away, some guy on the sidewalk yelled, "Hey bud, have you tried kicking it?"

Among the experiences we had in the convertible was an event that happened as we were driving along at the usual speed on our way to Murfreesboro. At one point there was an embankment some eight to ten feet high beside the road as it turned to the right. This put us close to the embankment. Just as we got there, a big rooster took off from the bank and timed his flight just right to collide with the middle of our windshield. We saw it coming for a second or two before impact, so we crouched down against the windshield. The windshield did not break, probably because windshields were not as large in those days and were very thick to resist the flying rocks from gravel roads. We were able to get low behind the windshield so that not much of the viscera of that big bird hit us, but Tom's Ford was a mess.

Probably the most unconventional escapade in which Tom and I engaged was buying a blue racer snake about five feet long. I have no recollection of why we bought that snake, which came from some company in Texas. In rolling back my memory from this great distance, I am able to think of only one theoretically possible explanation. Tom and my brother John appear to have been engaged in a periodic, unadvertised contest to outdo each other by engaging in some sort of eccentric activity which was not particularly damaging to anybody, including them. At some time before John and Tom began rooming together, John bought a monkey. Again, I can think of no rational explanation for this action except that just stated. Whatever may have been the reason, John's monkey turned out to be a first class disaster. He kept the monkey in his room while he was gone all day at medical school . As I recall the events, there was no problem about getting the monkey housebroken, but there was a big problem about getting everything in the room protected from the monkey's inquisitiveness. The final blow occurred on one night when John returned to his room to find the monkey squatting on a table with a copy of Gray's Anatomy in front of him. Gray's Anatomy was a huge book required of every freshman medical student, since he spent about half of that year dissecting a "stiff" (preserved human body). The book was open, of course, and on one side of the monkey was a neat pile of pages torn from the book., As John entered, the monkey ripped out another page, held it in front of his face and saw a picture on it , then yelled "OUK." This is my recollection of John's story of the event. Needless to say, that was the end of the monkey in John's room.

The experience of Tom and me with our snake was considerably different from John's monkey episode. We had problems, especially with doing anything entertaining with the snake. People just weren't ready for viewing snakes with equanimity. We named our snake "Damit," a German word meaning approximately in English, "following upon that." It is a word used frequently in scientific writings in describing procedures. The name was chosen principally because its pronunciation according to normal English usage caused it to come out as a mild expression of profanity. My mother seemed to enjoy referring to the snake as "Dammit." I think that, since this was the name of the snake, she felt released from her normal inhibitions against the use of such language.

Before the snake arrived, we had prepared a large box for it made from a sturdy cardboard packing box. The top of the box was carefully cut off to keep it intact, and one end was attached with a band of adhesive tape, which acted as a hinge. (Medical doctors tend to use adhesive tape for any kind of repair job, whether applied to an animate or inanimate object.) We cut a rectangular hole in the top and put a piece of glass over it, holding the glass in place with adhesive tape, of course. We put a plank across the end that opened and put a couple of weighty books on the plank to make sure the snake could not push it open. It was surprising how strong that snake was. When the snake arrived in a box labeled "live animal" I was present, but the janitor who cleaned up our room was also present. When told that the "animal" was a snake, he went into orbit: "Let me tell you that your room is never going to get cleaned up as long as that snake is there." A couple of days later, when he was cleaning up the rooms on the other side of our floor, Tom gave him a big pitch (he and Tom were good friends) about how the snake was harmless and how we had fixed the box so that the snake could not get out. Finally the janitor agreed to look at the box, and then agreed to give our rooms a real fast cleaning. At that time I did not know much about snakes, that they are cold-bloodied animals, and hence do not need to use a lot of food keeping warm. So Tom got a mouse from the medical school and put it into Damit's box, expecting him (?) to gulp it down in one gulp. Instead of that, the darn snake ignored the mouse. Later, we found that the mouse was eating part of the snake, without Damit objecting. And so out with the mouse. When we put a little flat plate containing some milk into the box, we found later that Damit had consumed some of the milk, so that solved the feeding problem.

We found that there really was not much we could do with Damit outside of his box. We could not carry him around campus, unless in a box, for he was so strong and slippery that he would surely get away from us. We carried him to Tom's car in a box, then let him out, whereupon he climbed up above the dashboard to the windshield, presumably because it was warm there. This also proved to be a no-no. People in nearby cars would see the snake, scream or engage in other antics such that we were afraid of creating traffic accidents. Back to his box with Damit.

After a few weeks, during which our enthusiasm for the snake waned, I came back to the room after supper and found no snake in the box. The box seemed in good shape. I suspected the new tenants in the rooms on the other side of our floor, but there obviously was nothing I could do about that. I also realized that Damit might have really muscled up and pushed up the top enough to squeeze his slippery carcass out. In any case, I was frantically looking in the corners and moving furniture around when Tom came in. Since snakes are cold-blooded animals, Tom suggested that if Damit is in the room he should be in our clothes. Sure enough, there he was snuggled up under some shirts and socks in a drawer. By this time it was near the end of the spring quarter, and so something had to be done about Damit's future. My mother made it quite clear that no snake was coming into her house, and I was not at all keen about that solution anyhow. Tom began inquiring around among his acquaintances, and finally found a barber shop which would like to have Damit to display in a box with glass sides in a window. And so that was the end of our most futile undertaking. It was also the end of our rooming together, for Tom, as well as my brother, was graduating from medical school.

If I were going to retain this desirable room, I would have to find a

---

roommate. Since the location was about the best on campus, this proved to be no problem. A physics major with whom I had become acquainted named Jimmy Peoples, who lived in a fraternity, had decided that he could handle a tough major such as physics better if he got out of the fraternity house. Thus, he was pleased to come in with me in West Side Row. In order to make sure of not losing these very desirable rooms, I paid the rent for the fall quarter for both rooms and made sure that I got a receipt ,which I carefully preserved. This was to prove to be a very smart move.

During my four years at Vanderbilt I liked and respected every professor who ever taught me. Several of them were simply outstanding, such as Arthur W. Ingersoll, who taught organic chemistry, Willard Jewel, who taught geology, John Hyden, who taught calculus, Francis Slack, who taught physics, Warren Deacon, who taught bacteriology, and last but not least , John Crowe Ransom, who taught English. My relationships with the business and administrative side of the University were less fortunate, especially in relation to two incidents.

When I returned in the fall of my junior year, thinking happy thoughts about my living quarters, I received quite a shock. When I went over to our rooms, they were already occupied by other students! After recovering from the shock, I went over to the business office to discuss the matter with Gerald Henderson, the business manager. He commented that he had no way of knowing that I wanted the rooms. When I produced my receipt, he tried to ignore it, and we had a heated discussion which finally came down to my threatening to go to the chancellor with my receipt. He eventually offered a compromise, giving me a double room in Kissam Hall for the full year without charging me anything more than the money already paid for the West Side Row rooms for the fall quarter. In spite of being completely crushed, and knowing that I was being cheated, I managed to restrain myself and accept the compromise. I knew that I had no alternative, and I knew that Jimmy Peoples would not be interested in living in Kissam Hall. Another thing that made my restraint difficult was the knowledge that Kissam Hall had many vacant rooms, so that he was giving me nothing and getting paid for rental of a double room in Kissam for a quarter. Fortunately for my equilibrium, it was several months later that I learned that one of the boys in the room I had paid for was a fraternity brother of the business manager, Henderson. I also did not know until some twelve years later just what sort of scoundrel Henderson was. After I had returned to Vanderbilt as a professor in 1942, and volunteered to help with the war effort by accepting a research contract to work on high explosives, this same Henderson, still business manager, gave me a very bad time about approving the contract with the National Defense Research Committee.

The other sad experience which I had with an administrator at Vanderbilt occurred during the winter quarter of my senior year. This experience involved a faculty member named Madison Sarratt, who was also the Dean of Men. Since my freshman year, I had rarely gone to the weekly "chapel" meeting. Since the courses I was taking involved a total of five or six labs per week, there developed enough pressure on my time that I had to cut out something or other, and I had no tendency to want to eliminate anything such as my hour per day of enjoyable physical activity or an occasional hour of shooting pool, especially since chapel tended to be involved heavily with announcements about current activities on the campus, particularly those involving fraternities and sororities. Unbelievable though it seems, Vanderbilt had a rule requiring mandatory attendance at classes. A certain number of "cuts" per quarter were allowed, probably in the range of ten to fifteen, but I have no recollection of that number. I had never cut a class since entering Vanderbilt, although I had attended on a few occasions when I was sick from a virus infection. As a matter of fact, I was not aware of a roll being taken in any class that I attended, and it was apparent that nobody, faculty or students, paid any attention to the rule about compulsory class attendance. I suspect that there was no definition of what penalty might ensue.

When I received a written notice to appear at the office of the Dean of Men at a specified date and time, I was puzzled since I was unaware of having been involved in any infraction of the rules and regulations, and had never spoken to the Dean of Men since my arrival at Vanderbilt. When I arrived in the presence of the dean, without any introductory formalities, he announced that it had come to his attention that I had not attended chapel during the entire school year. I agreed to that, and in answer to a question explained that chapel was usually uninteresting to me and that a lot of things made demands on my time, and that I had judged chapel to be less important than these other things. When he reminded me of the rule about mandatory attendance at classes, I said that I had never cut a class since attending Vanderbilt, so I had plenty of cuts that could be applied to chapel. After some hesitation, he responded that cuts allowed in classes did not apply to chapel. When I asked why he had brought up the matter of mandatory attendance at classes, he blew his stack, and delivered in a loud stern tone the following: "Young man, if you persist in not going to chapel, then pack up your clothes and get out of this university." I realized that he was furious at having no case against me for not going to chapel, and that he would become ever more furious if I should question his authority to enforce his threat against me. Ergo I responded, after only a minor delay: "You must be aware, Dean, that I have never made any grade except 'A' since I entered this university, and that it would be likely to seriously interfere with my opportunities in life if I should be thrown out of the university at a time so close to my graduation. Since I am not as stupid as you are, I shall attend chapel regularly, even if I should become so sick as to need to be carried in." Without delay, I turned and walked out of the office.

It has been my experience that the gods and the fates have a way of generating sequels to such events as just described. I do not ascribe this to the influence of some supernatural All Powerful Being. It seems more rational to believe that everything that happens on this orb called Earth is the result of interactions between parts of this Earth, both animate and inanimate, both large and small. In any case, there developed two sequels to the above-described event. One of them was reported to me by Professor E. E. Reinke, chairman of the biology department. This report was about the meeting of the Committee to determine who should receive the Founders Medal in Scholarship, which had been awarded annually for many years to the student with the highest scholastic average. Since I was the only graduating student with all grades "A," the chairman of the committee opened the meeting by announcing that, as the members knew, the decision was quite easy this year. This was followed by a tirade from Dean Sarratt to the effect that such an honor should not go to a person who was so obnoxious about following the rules of the university. Fortunately for me, several professors who had had me in class were on the committee. One of them had come prepared, and obviated any discussion by pointing out the terms of the bequest which had established the Founders Medal in Scholarship. Apparently, Professor Reinke approved of my actions, for he was laughing during most of the time that he was making his report.

As for sequels to this affair, one occurred after I had returned to Vanderbilt in 1942, as the first new instructor hired by the chemistry department in many years. (There is a long story concerning the devious and partly accidental route followed by me in arriving at Vanderbilt as a faculty member.) My job was teaching an upper division course in organic chemistry, and running the laboratory in the first course in organic chemistry, which was taught by Professor A. W. Ingersoll. During my second year running this laboratory, a student enrolled in the course was the son of Dean Madison Sarratt. He was a premedical student, and for entrance into Vanderbilt Medical School an "A" in Ingersoll's organic chemistry was widely regarded as a must. Sarratt's son was almost certainly unaware of the damage that his father attempted to inflict on me, but I wondered what were the sentiments of his father when his son told him how helpful and friendly I was.

The second sequel was short and nasty. It occurred after I had been teaching at Berkeley for a few years. One day, as I was eating lunch at home, the telephone rang and the caller identified himself as the chairman of the Vanderbilt Club of San Francisco. He said that he wanted to invite me to a luncheon which they were giving in honor of Dean Madison Sarratt, who was visiting in San Francisco. With no significant delay, I responded, "Madison Sarratt is a stupid dope. If he were a cow on a concrete pasture I would not give him hay." After an interval of sputtering, the caller finally articulated, "Why in the world would you make a statement like that about Dean Sarratt ?" My response: "If you so desire, I will give you the full story as to why I would make such a statement. Do you want to hear it?" He hung up.

If these lines should be read by people who tend to be critical of my carrying a grudge to this extent, I have a message for them: Even at this late date in my life, I shudder to think of the impact it would have made on my sainted mother if Dean Sarratt had succeeded in his determined effort to destroy my good reputation. I have not the slightest idea why Sarratt was so determined to force me to attend chapel, but it is inconceivable that his motivation was more than trivial compared to the damage that he would have done if he had succeeded in his efforts. As a matter of fact, is it not true that the majority of the mass slaughtering and humiliation which is occurring in the world today, such as that in Bosnia, is happening due to similarly trivial matters?

Before leaving the subject of the Founders Medal, it may be of interest for me to relate another incident involving this matter. As I have not specifically noted, my major was chemistry. I also had enough physics courses to declare a major in that subject; however, I declared chemistry as my major, with physics as my minor, since I had decided to go to graduate school in chemistry. In the year immediately following my award of the Founders Medal, it was won by a man named Stanford Moore, who was also a chemistry major. So far as anything I have heard, we were the only chemistry majors who had ever won the Founders Medal. Another amazing coincidence. While I was teaching at Vanderbilt during World War II, my wife Rebecca met Stan Moore's mother at some organization of faculty wives. Stan's father was a professor at Vanderbilt. I am unsure of it, but I think that Professor Moore was a professor of Greek. After taking a year of Greek in my freshman year, I continued to take some notice of events in the classics department on account of my good friend Tommy Lynn, who majored in classics. Tommy took the same amount of physics that I did, and eventually got a Ph.D. degree in physics. He must have been one of a kind. In any case, Rebecca and Mrs. Moore had fun swapping stories about the son of one of them and the husband of the other. Quite a generation gap. Rebecca was about thirty years old at the time.

Stan Moore and I shared certain characteristics, those required to win a Founders Medal at Vanderbilt University; however, it is equally obvious that a great many of our characteristics were not common to the two of us. Stan also became a university professor, at Rockefeller University in New York City; however, after that point our careers diverged sharply. Stan was not reclusive, but was a rather private sort of person. He appeared to have a one-track non-skid sort of mind which can produce a Nobel Laureate. He won the Nobel Prize in biochemistry for developing very effective methods for synthesis of high molecular weight polypeptides.

Even the most casual examination of the document that I am writing at present will reveal that I could never become a Nobel Laureate. This concept has been experimentally verified. Indeed, it may develop that I am one of a very small group of people who have defeated the Peter Principle.

As my junior year at Vanderbilt University drew to a close, it became increasingly apparent to me that I must not delay any further about advising my dad that I did not want to become a lawyer. He knew what courses I was taking, and I knew that he must be aware of my intentions; however, I had cringed for too long from the idea of telling him. I decided to consult my mother about the problem, on the grounds that she would understand my Dad better than anyone else in the world. She advised me that she had found my Dad to be a wise man and that I should expect a very reasonable response to my explanation of my decision to switch from law to chemistry. Following her advice, I spent some time preparing my presentation to Dad, then interrupted his working on a crossword puzzle, and asked if this would be a convenient time for some conversation. Of course I knew that Dad was hard of hearing and I also knew that he did a lot of lip-reading, so I sat fairly close directly in front of him and spoke slowly, not too loudly. He looked at me intently as I spoke, which I had expected. When I had finished he spoke without significant delay: "I don't know anything about this science stuff, but I hear that it is the coming thing." What a man! What a relief! This was one of many times that Dad came through like a champ, just when I needed him.

The initiation ceremony for Phi Beta Kappa came late in my senior year, and generated a collision with my instinct for resentment against ceremonies which serve no useful purpose, and cost time and money—probably a factor in my collision with Dean Sarratt. The invitation to the ceremony called for formal dress, but I figured that there would surely be others besides me who did not own a tuxedo. The idea of renting a tuxedo did not occur to me, since I had never been exposed to such things. Furthermore, I had a new tailored suit, my first, which Dad had made for me a short time before. To put it mildly, I underestimated how much people in those parts cherished formality and protocol. The report in the Nashville Banner, to which many people in Murfreesboro subscribed, was occupied largely with the two iconoclasts who did not have formal wear. Seemed to be something inconceivable, almost as bad as endorsing the theory of evolution. Remember the famous "monkey trials" which occurred in Tennessee soon after the turn of the century? At the time of which we are speaking it was against the law to teach evolution in the public schools, including the University of Tennessee. I was blindsided by the whole affair; at least that was my story. Dad insisted that, on my first visit to

Murfreesboro, he would take me down to Goldstein's to be measured for a tuxedo. It would never do for me to set out for California without a tuxedo. I did wear it on one memorable occasion in California; however, the most important occasion on which I wore it was when I was initiated into Sigma Xi, the honorary scientific society, at Yale. On that occasion, the person sitting next to me wore tails. I watched as he flipped the tails when he sat down to avoid crumpling them.

During my senior year, I began to feel more strongly the urges that most people would say were long overdue; however, I had formal dates with only one girl, a beautiful brunette named Gladys Hanover. When I went home for the Christmas holidays, which lasted for one month at that time, during my year at the University of California graduate school, I visited my friend Bob Smith who was still on the Vanderbilt campus in his senior year. According to the gossip that Bob supplied to me, there had been quite a bit of interest in Gladys Hanover "going after" the iconoclast, Jim Cason. According to this story, Gladys noticed on the bulletin board at the gym that Cason had tied for first place in the physical fitness contest. Since Gladys had placed No. 1 on the women's side, she decided that we would make a great pair. Since I was not in the fraternity-sorority whirl, I was completely unaware of any such story going around; however, I would have agreed that Gladys might deserve to win a physical fitness contest. On one occasion when I called Gladys at her sorority, the person who answered the phone yelled, "Glad Ass, it's for you"; however, I observed no behavior on her part that would suggest any significance to that nickname.

I first became acquainted with Gladys because she was enrolled in the bacteriology course taught by Professor Deacon, which I took in my senior year. In this course there was a lot of milling around, going to the autoclaves, incubation ovens, etc., and so the people in the class got acquainted with each other. One day Gladys asked me if I would be one of the guinea pigs in an experiment she was doing in a psychology course. In answer to my inquiry, she said that it was an experiment to learn what correlation there might be between judging weights and general intelligence. That sounded harmless, so I agreed to meet her in a room in the psychology department. She had a group of some fifteen small opaque glass vials, which consisted of a round bulb with a flat bottom and a narrow stem on top. My job was to arrange the vials in a row according to their weight. I assumed that they had small lead shot in them. Following my instinct to do the best job that I could, I spent quite a lot of time picking up a vial, then another, arranging them in a line, finally checking the weight of each vial against the one on each side of it. Gladys did not make a sound, and I was concentrating so heavily that I was unaware of whether she was there or had gone out of the room. Finally, I looked up and said, "That's it." Whereupon, she let out a yelp and said, "You are the first person who has been tested who got every one of them right." After that, we had several dates such as going to a movie, or to dinner, and engaging in what was known as "light necking," as we parked my car in the driveway to the enormous house on Belle Meade Avenue where her aunt lived with her big white Cadillac. Her aunt was one of the German Jews who virtually owned and operated most of the businesses in Nashville. By the time the school year was over, I began to suspect that her parents were not overly enthusiastic about her dating a non-Jew. We corresponded during the summer, and in one letter I asked her what her parents and relatives thought of her dating a non-Jew. She said that they did not like it but had not really objected. Both of us began to think of the problems that would ensue if we should get married, and so our relationship tapered off amicably.

Prior to my going to the University of California, I had relations that could have become permanent with only one other girl. This was Margaret Massie, sister of my McCallie roommate Bill Massie. Bill and I had maintained close relations, and during our senior years in college had made plans to spend about a week at the Chicago World Fair during the upcoming summer. Margaret's Agnes Scott roommate, Laura Spivey, was living in Chicago. Bill had already developed a very serious interest in Laura, and so our plan was for Bill, Margaret and I to go to Chicago after I had spent several days with the Massies, who lived in Lexington. Mrs. Massie's mother lived on the old family estate in the blue grass region of Kentucky. When I spent a day visiting there, with the objective of playing tennis on the tennis court near the house, which was surrounded by a large lawn, I learned a few things about the family. The grandmother was confined to a large easy chair, and was cared for by the two unmarried sisters of Bill's mother, i.e., his aunts. It was apparent to me that Grandma was the ruler of the family. When Bill, Margaret and I had an audience with Grandma, I noticed that she gave each of them money. There were some interesting rules about the tennis court. For example, nobody was allowed to play on the court unless they wore white clothes. I had been warned about this.

When I accepted the invitation to visit the Massies, I was well aware that there were probably some plans afoot to show how nice it would be for me to marry Margaret, since Bill was planning to marry Spivey. (At Agnes Scott School, the girls were always addressed by their last name.) The above-described situation had impressed me sufficiently that I had no tendency to do more than put my arm around Margaret as we sat on the porch in the moonlight. However, a development occurring when I arrived at the Lexington home gave me an equally clear message. Immediately after my arrival, before I had brought in my bag, Bill's father, a pompous overweight sort, summoned Margaret to play the piano for me. When I said that I would enjoy it more after dinner, the father insisted. And so Margaret played.

I decided that I would be better off marrying a beautiful rich Jewess.

CHAPTER 4

GO WEST YOUNG MAN AND GROW UP WITH THE COUNTRY

After I had visited Bill Massie and his family in Lexington, and taken a trip with Bill and Margaret to visit the Chicago World Fair, I returned to Murfreesboro to pack my belongings into the new Chevrolet coupe with rumble seat that Dad had recently bought for me. Among the things packed was my equipment for developing, enlarging, and printing pictures taken with my new Zeiss Contax 35mm camera, which I had bought during my junior year at Vanderbilt. I was very much into picture taking at that time, and had saved money for a couple of years to buy this camera. It was one of the two upscale 35mm cameras that first came on the market at that time; the other was the Leica. I also bought an enlarger which used a detachable lens also used on the camera. Packing this equipment into the coupe was not easy, but possible. I remember vividly some of the things Dad told me as I was setting out on this long trip to go far from the control or assistance of my parents. In particular, I have never forgotten one comment Dad made: "Now, James, you know what is right and what is wrong, so I don't need to discuss that sort of thing with you. I hope that you will always do what is right. Whatever you do, please remember that I stand ready to assist you if you need help, to the best of my ability." I knew that my voice would break if I tried to say something, so I shook his hand in silence. I have never forgotten those simple words, and have done my best to never do anything that would not make Dad proud of me.

I knew that my mother would endorse the same sentiment; however, it was a little different with Memur. She was an unshakable believer in the doctrine of predestination, which was a part of the code of the Presbyterian Church, and I certainly respected her for the firmness of her faith. However, I had more faith in getting help from Dad than from the Lord. In spite of my confidence that I could take care of myself, as I set out across the continent for the first time that I had been further from home than Chicago, I felt quite comforted by knowing that Dad would always be there if I needed help.

When I set out for the West in my loaded Chevrolet, I made a minor detour from my direct route. I went to Owensboro, Kentucky, to spend a day with my Vanderbilt friend, Bob Smith. We played tennis on his privately owned tennis court, and he took me on a tour of a big whiskey distillery in Owensboro. At the point where the distillate was pouring out of the still, the person guiding our tour dipped out a little and asked me if I wanted to sample it. Being a blossoming chemist, I did not bite on that one, and so the big joke fell flat.

After leaving Owensboro I have no recollections of my trip of the sort that could be pieced together into a narrative. There is not much to narrate about driving alone for eight or ten hours a day across Missouri and Kansas. I remember separate incidents, such as an event that happened in the tourist parking lot at Crater Lake. As I was getting out of my car, a stranger got out of a nearby car with several people in it , walked up to me and handed me a $5 bill. Assuming this to be some kind of con game, I said, "What's going on here?" whereupon he explained that the group in his car had been spending much of the summer traveling around the USA, and he had made a fifty-dollar bet with another person in the car that they would see a license plate from every state in the Union. (This was before Alaska and Hawaii came aboard.) He ended by saying, "Tennessee is state number 48 whose license plate we have seen, so I figure it is only fair to share my winnings with you." And so I took the five bucks and commented that he had made this a lucky day for me. In those days five bucks would pay for a night's lodging. Except for an occasional event of this sort which one is likely to remember, most of my other recollections were directed to scenes where I took pictures, whether or not there was another incident such as at Crater Lake.

After I left Owensboro and headed west, most of the driving was across the monotonous Great Plains. I do not remember whether I spent two or three days at this dreary task; indeed, I have hardly any recollection of how much time I spent at any place. This seems hardly surprising since I had a lot of other things to think about, such as where I would stay on the next day, where I wanted to visit, keeping the car serviced, and last, but not least, paying great attention to my driving—I wanted to get there. Since I had never seen anything like the Rocky Mountains before, it was very exciting when they began coming into view after that seemingly endless expanse of nothing worth looking at. Of course, I had spent many hours poring over road maps before starting on such a trip. The oil companies were so anxious to sell gasoline that they offered all kinds of freebies, such as maps with a full outline of any trip, the longer the better. After studying advertisements from several oil companies, I had decided that the offer from Conoco was the best. I took pleasure in using a brand of gasoline which I had never heard of previously. Following the route which Conoco had outlined to visit the places I had specified, I turned off of US 70 somewhere near the Colorado state line to spend the night in Pueblo.

In those days Pueblo was a rather small city where much mining and manufacturing was located. I had decided to stop there because it was the first city of any size after the drive across the plains, and it fit in with my plan to proceed north through Colorado Springs and Denver, then north into Wyoming. The reason for going up into southern Wyoming was because the roads over the Rockies from Denver to Salt Lake City had not been developed to the point that anyone wanting to get to Salt Lake City would choose that route, which Conoco had warned me about. As a matter of fact, I saw very few roads in the state of Colorado that were pleasant to drive on. Even main routes sometimes had sections of cobblestone roads. Of course, the word "freeway" was not a part of the English language in those days.

I spent several days in that part of Colorado, staying overnight in Pueblo, Colorado Springs, and Denver as I worked north. In addition to the usual tourist attractions, I was especially interested in the region from having studied enough geology at Vanderbilt to have a minor in it, if I had so desired. The Royal Gorge was especially fascinating to me because of the exposure of so many layers of rock that were near enough to be seen with binoculars. In later years, when Rebecca and I visited the Grand Canyon, I found it rather dull as a geological exhibit because one could not really see anything without walking or riding a burro down into the canyon. Even in my youth (less than sixty years of age) I never had much interest in such masochistic undertakings. Of course, the Rocky Mountains also interested me greatly, because of the great contrast with the mountains of Tennessee where I had spent so much time. There was a road leading almost to the top of one of the higher mountains near Colorado Springs, and I decided to drive to the top of it. I learned a lot about driving up steep grades at high altitudes. Somewhere above 10,000 feet my engine started boiling. There was a little stream below the road at that point, but I had no container of any size. After the car cooled down enough to make it safe to take the cap off the radiator, I emptied my thermos bottle into it, then climbed down to the creek for a refill. During this time not a single car had come by me, so I got the message that I would be a damn fool to go any further up this mountain. The absence of traffic made it simple to back up downhill until I arrived at a place where a small area had been constructed so that sightseers could pull off the road—if their engine began to overheat.

On the day after my abortive attempt to climb up to the top of the high mountain, I bought a ticket to ride up to the top of Pike's Peak in one of the big cars used to take tourists up there. This trip proved much more enjoyable than when I was driving my car the previous day. At a halfway station our driver pulled off the road and waited a few minutes. Soon a big car that looked like a racing car came roaring by at very high speed. I asked our driver, "What is that idiot trying to do?" His response, "He's no idiot; he's one of the drivers who is practicing for the upcoming Pike's Peak race." He then explained that the road is sometimes cleared so that these drivers can practice without killing anybody except themselves. At the top of Pike's Peak there was a large area fitted out to cater to tourists. The view was magnificent, either toward the mountains all around the peak or across the plains to the east.

After a few days in the south central area of Colorado, I headed north to Cheyenne in order to drive across southern Wyoming and turn south to Salt Lake City. About the most that I can say for Wyoming is that it is better than west Texas. I found it very refreshing to pull into Salt Lake City and stay there for a day or two; but I was not there long enough to learn how to locate anything by its street address. What a queer system of naming streets! Instead of driving around the south end of Salt Lake and across the desert to California, I took the Conoco's advice and headed north to Idaho. This was a very interesting drive, especially when I began to go along the Snake River. In prehistoric times, when Salt Lake was a fresh water lake called Lake Bonneville, the Snake River was its drainage, and eventually went to the sea after joining the Columbia River. In southern Idaho and to the west after the river turns north, there are numerous hydroelectric dams on the Snake, and there is much irrigation all over southern Idaho. Long before my drive through this area there was irrigation there. I had heard about irrigation being done in California, but had never seen any. On the first occasion that I drove out of the desert to encounter the panorama of lush green fields stretching out to the edge of my view, I was simply enchanted! No exaggeration! I pulled off the road and just sat in the car and gazed around for quite a time. I kept thinking of the poor farmers in Tennessee, where summer droughts were frequent. The only recourse they had was to pray for rain, which is notably unreliable in producing it. All along the course of the Snake River up to the state of Washington there are beautiful gorges. On two occasions a farmer had a sign on the road to the effect that I could pay a buck and drive across his land to the river. I assumed rightfully that the sign would be out only if the location was worthy of picture taking. That proved to be correct. I finally tore myself away from the beautiful Snake River, and proceeded to Walla Walla, Washington, where I spent the night.

Walla Walla is near the junction of the Columbia and Snake Rivers. In proceeding west from Walla Walla, I soon returned to the state of Oregon, and drove south of the Columbia River to Portland. The scenery along the Columbia is picturesque, but in no way comparable to the scenery along the Snake River. I spent a day in Portland to get the engine of my car tuned up. Somehow or other I had not previously realized that Portland is a considerable distance from the mouth of the Columbia River.

I left Portland very early in the morning because my plan was to drive to Berkeley in one day. Thus, I drove south on US 5, which is a direct route to California; however, I did detour temporarily from US 5 to visit Crater Lake. Even though I was getting anxious to get to Berkeley, I had placed

Crater Lake as a "must stop" on my route plan. This proved to be wise. Crater Lake is a unique phenomenon, very interesting to anyone, especially a person with some knowledge of geology. As far as any activity is concerned, however, there is not much to do other than take pictures. I took several interesting pictures, pocketed five dollars proffered by a stranger, and set out for Berkeley. I was quite surprised by the size and prominence of Mt. Shasta, but I was destined to encounter several surprises as I proceeded into the Golden State. Soon after entering the state, I was stopped at an inspection station where all foreign cars were required to stop. In all the states I had driven through I had never encountered anything like that. The guard wanted to see all kinds of things: first my driver's license, which I did not have since Tennessee did not require such a thing. That really stirred him up. He wanted to see my certificate of ownership for the car, which I had on account of my dad's foresight. It was made out to James Cason, since he had bought the car. But the registration of the car was to James Cason, Jr., and that stirred up the guard again. (This was the last straw in my lifelong struggles with the Jr. thing. My resistance to Jr. became embedded so firmly in stone that I even resisted my sainted mother's ambition to have her first-born grandson named Jr.; I never did discuss the fact that it would have been III.) I got pretty frustrated during my discussion with that guard, but he finally agreed to let me go ahead after giving me a stern lecture about the consequences if I failed to get a driver's license within thirty days. And so I drove down the Central Valley, wondering why nobody had ever told me about California being as hot as the hinges of hell.

I had an add-on radio in the car which I usually listened to as I drove. As I was coming down the valley, the dedication of the new bridge across the Carquinez Straits was being broadcast, with none other than Franklin D. Roosevelt giving the address. At one point, FDR referred to, "this beautiful bridge across the Carquinez Straits at Valley Joe." At this point, a burst of raucous laughter interrupted the proceedings. Since I grew up in Tennessee where high school students studied French rather than Spanish, I was at a loss to figure out what the hilarity was about. After being in California for a period of time, I learned what it was about. Accenting the last syllable of Carquinez and pronouncing it as "nay" was enough to cause people to look at each other with a knowing expression, but that pronunciation of Vallejo was just too much—there appeared to be more than a little laughter.

When I arrived in Berkeley I went to the Whitecotton Hotel to stay overnight, since it was just off of Shattuck Avenue and close to the university campus. By the date of this writing, this hotel has had at least two name changes, and I think that it is now a residence hotel frequented by elderly people who like to be downtown. When the bellhop took me to my room, he went over to a corner and began turning a valve on something that looked like a radiator. Since I had been sweating all day coming down the central valley, I asked what he was doing. I received another surprise when he responded, "I'm turning on your heat, it gets pretty cold at night in August." Between me and Berkeley, it was love at first contact—and it has never waned! Surprises continued. When I got change paying for my breakfast, I received several silver dollars. I could not recall having seen one before. As I stood staring at them, the cashier asked what was wrong. When I told him I was accustomed to paper dollars, he replied that he did not ordinarily keep them on hand, but I could get them at the bank. Spirit of the old west! When Rebecca and I came back to Berkeley in 1945, only old-timers remembered the prewar days in Berkeley when the only way to get to San Francisco was on the Oakland passenger ferry or the Berkeley auto ferry. My final surprise on my first day was when I started across Shattuck Avenue and before I stepped off the curb onto the street a car about 100 feet away stopped. As I stared open-mouthed at him, he finally motioned me to go across the street. As I was ready for just about anything by that time, I proceeded across the street, and a couple of cars going in the other direction also stopped for me. As I proceeded, I kept thinking to myself, "Am I underground with Alice? I'm going to like it around here better than I expected."

I had a map of the campus which I had received when I was admitted for graduate work, while holding an appointment as a teaching assistant. When I went to the administrative office of the College of Chemistry, I met Miss Kittredge, secretary to the dean of the college. Of course then I did not realize what an important person this attractive young woman was. She escorted me in to meet the Chief, Gilbert N. Lewis. To put it mildly, I was awe-stricken. A major reason for my choosing Berkeley for graduate work was my great interest in thermodynamics. The Bible on the subject was the textbook written by Lewis and Randall. My interest in thermodynamics was equaled by my conviction that theories concerning reaction mechanisms of organic molecules were a total mess. I was looking forward to studying applications of thermodynamics to organic reaction mechanisms. Subsequent history has proven that I had a very good idea; however, much history has demonstrated that Robert Burns was dead right when he said, "The best-laid schemes o' mice and men gang aft agley."

The Chief was smoking a big, black, evil-smelling cigar. I later learned that those cigars were rather famous—or infamous. They were imported from the Philippines, where he had worked at one time, and he had become the only customer in this country. He gave me a big, attractive smile, for which he was also famous, and after some casual chit-chat, asked me, "In what field do you plan to work?" I replied, "Organic chemistry." His only immediate response was to puff on the cigar and blow smoke around. After what seemed an eternity to this green graduate student, he finally responded, "You'll change." As usual, the Chief was right. I did change—to another university for my graduate work. He concluded the interview by telling me that Miss Kittredge would give me the names of the three professors who were in organic, and would give me the location of their offices. Miss Kittredge also gave me the name and office location of Professor Ernest Gibson, who would advise me on what courses to take and sign my study list. Since I was supposed to report for duty as a teaching assistant the next day and complete registration during this same week, I decided to look up Professor Gibson and get my study list filled out. Miss Kittredge had told me his office was on the next floor up in Gilman Hall.

When I reached Professor Gibson's office, the door was open and there was a young man, presumably a graduate student, working at a large rack filled with glass tubing, with a noisy vacuum pump going. I told him that I was looking for Professor Gibson's office, and he told me that this was it. When I asked him why he was working in this room, he said, "I'm doing my graduate work under his direction, and he is not in his office very much, so I am using it as my laboratory." I told him that I was a new graduate student from Vanderbilt University, and had been told that I should consult Gibson about making out my study list. He responded by telling me that he was a Vanderbilt graduate, Merlin D. Peterson, and this was his third year at Berkeley, so he expected to get his Ph.D. after this year. This chance meeting was very useful and helpful to me. He was the only person during my first week at Berkeley who gave me information that got me moving on my way. He told me how to fill out my study list: Put down Chemistry 14, the thermodynamics course, any courses I wanted to take in another department; and no other courses in chemistry except the research course. I was supposed to take the inorganic chemistry course taught by Professor Bray, but the graduate students do not take the lab, so it did not appear on my course card. He also told me that I did not have to file my study list until several days later, so I should make it out and leave it with him for Gibson to sign. I kept wondering what would happen to new students who did not have the good fortune to happen upon Merlin D. Peterson. Merlin also told me that any time I wanted to know something, ask Mabel Kittredge. Of all the useful things that Merlin told me on that day, the most important of all proved to be, "Ask Mabel." As a matter of fact, that still proved to be the best of advice when I returned to Berkeley as a faculty member in 1945.

Following instructions to teaching assistants (TAs) posted on the bulletin board outside the dean's office, I reported the next day to help with assignment of lockers to students taking the first chemistry course, Chem 1A. I sat at a long table in a line of teaching assistants as the students passed through on the other side of the table. I knew nothing, of course, about the system being used for locker assignments, but I was instructed by the faculty member in charge of the course on what my duty was. The man sitting on one side of me was a long lanky chap with jet black hair whose name was Glenn Seaborg. He was from southern California and already had an M.S. degree in chemistry from UCLA. At that time, UCLA did not offer a Ph.D. program. Since neither of us knew anybody else, we chatted and got acquainted with each other during our work day, and decided to go to a movie together that night. Glenn had gotten in early and had already been able to rent a room; however, I stayed at the hotel that night. The next day, I followed Merlin Peterson's advice and asked Miss Kittredge how I could best find a place to live. She telephoned one of the graduate students named Alan Nixon and asked if he had time to help me find a place to live. He cheerfully responded in the affirmative, and we began going around in my car looking at boarding houses. Even compared to Kissam Hall, these places looked pretty dismal to me, and so I asked Alan if the university had any housing for graduate students. He answered that they did not, but that the place called International House was near the campus and near the chemistry buildings. He said that the only problem was its expense, which was about $35 per month for room and board. I knew that TAs were paid $50 per month for 10 months, but I was receiving $75 per month from my dad. This was the rent of two nice little houses he had given to me, and he had also given two similar houses to my brother. Dad was also paying my out-of-state tuition. I realized at once that I was wealthy—never had that sensation before. I told Alan that I thought I could handle the fees at the I House, thanked him profusely, and took him back to campus before going to the I House to investigate. After the boarding houses I had seen, I had no doubts about living at the International House. I found that if I paid about $10 more for my room I could get a room on the seventh floor which faced towards the west. The front part of the I House was lower than the back part where the upper floors were, so that my window provided a view across San Francisco Bay to the Golden Gate. I was very fortunate to find such a wonderful place to live, and I have many beautiful pictures, including spectacular sunsets, taken from that window.

During my first weeks, I was quite busy with my school work and learning how to be a TA. I was given one lab section in organic chemistry and one in quantitative analysis, which was normally the second year of chemistry required of chemistry majors as well as premedical students in any major. I received no instructions whatever in how to run the lab. The only direction I received was the assignment which the students were supposed to follow. I was assigned to the quant lab because one of the biochemistry courses which I was taking had two afternoon labs and this interfered with my assisting in the organic labs. The quant course had one morning lab, so I was the fall guy for that. By incredible good luck, my quant lab section was in the same room with Glenn Seaborg's lab section. Glenn had signed up to do his graduate work in nuclear chemistry with an instructor named Bob Fowler. It was unprecedented to have a Ph.D. student do graduate work with an instructor rather than with some rank of professor; however, this field was so new that there was nobody else qualified to direct Glenn's research. Since Glenn was sort of a maverick, similar to me taking biochemistry, it was natural for us to fall into assisting in the morning quant lab. Incredible good luck for me; whenever a student asked me a question I could not answer, I admitted ignorance in this field and suggested that he ask the tall guy assisting in the next section. Glenn did not complain. I lucked out; he was a nice guy. We began studying thermodynamics together quite frequently, another time that I lucked out. I was so busy in my undergraduate days taking courses in every field of science that I did not take a course in differential equations, and occasionally a problem came up that required them. Since Glenn was taking a graduate course in mathematics, differential equations were simple stuff for him. This thermodynamics course was taught by a professor named Axel Olson, who used some rather unusual tactics in his teaching. At the first midterm exam, he gave two questions. Each counted 50 percent of the grade, and each was scored as fifty points. This made grading easy for the TA. Glenn got both problems right, and therefore scored 100%; I missed one problem and therefore got 50%. I had never been so shocked in my life. Glenn consoled me by pointing out that Olsen had a reputation for using a lousy grading system on peculiar exams. Of course, neither Glenn nor I had powers of prophecy; hence, no way of knowing that the man who made a higher grade than me would be awarded a Nobel Prize at about the same time that I was returning to Berkeley as a professor. During my years as a professor, I cheered up several students by telling them this true story. To conclude this paragraph on a happy note, I will report that by persistence, a little bit of luck, and coaching by Glenn, I made an "A" in the course.

During the first week of classes, I took time to go down to the gym, check out a locker, and visit the gymnastics room. The men in there were doing things which I had never heard of. I was astonished to see one of them start around on a giant swing, come to a stop at the top, turn around and come back down going in the opposite direction. I turned to a man standing near me and said, "That man is good!"; his reply: "He certainly is, he is a member of the U. S. Olympic team." I walked out of that room, went out into the hall and signed up for the 4-wall handball ladder which was marked: "Those with little or no prior experience." I had played a little 4-wall handball at Vanderbilt, but there was only one court, so it was hard to get on. I figured that if handball players differed from those I had known at Vanderbilt as much as was the case for gymnastics, I should be cautious. It was fortunate that I did so. When I was looking at the names on the tyro ladder, I noticed the name of Mike Kraus, a new graduate student in chemistry. I contacted him and we began to play two or three times per week together, in addition to the weekly scheduled ladder game. I found that I enjoyed 4-wall handball at least as much as tennis. It is much more vigorous exercise than tennis because it involves essentially non-stop running. Also, a pair of handball gloves is much cheaper than a tennis racquet, requires no upkeep, and can be carried around in a coat pocket.

During the first week and extending into the second week, I interviewed the three professors whom Dean Lewis had told me were the organic chemists on the faculty. This was a rather sobering experience. Two of these professors were not really organic chemists in the terminology that was in use in those days. Ten years later they would become classified as physical organic chemists, and one of them, Gerald K. Branch, became a leader in that field. A principal reason for my coming to Berkeley was the idea that application of thermodynamics to organic chemistry would be very interesting indeed; however, that idea could not be pursued by a green graduate student except by finding a professor to work with who was studying this field. Gerald Branch and Dale Stewart, the other "physical organic chemist" whom I interviewed, were not discussing thermodynamics in connection with what they were doing. The Gilbert Lewis school of thermodynamics regarded organic chemistry as a wishy-washy sort of thing, a back alley of chemistry. No decent thermodynamicist would be caught studying something where it was not possible to know where all the electrons were. I began to understand what Dean Lewis was thinking about as he puffed on his cigar, blew smoke around the room, and eventually said, "You'll change." Even at this early date after my arrival in Berkeley, I began feeling that I had been wise in not becoming so preoccupied with thinking about thermodynamics that I failed to include in my plans provision for my second strong interest, biochemistry. Fortunately, this also led me to Berkeley. In those days it was very difficult to find a university whose biochemistry department was not in the medical school. In Berkeley at that time, the biochemistry Department was in the medical school, but it was physically located in Berkeley, not on the San Francisco campus where the major functions of the medical school were located. The graduate division of the biochemistry department was in Berkeley, as were several courses for graduate and undergraduate students. Two of these courses were those which I had put on my study list, and which Professor Gibson had approved—probably without reading it.

The third professor whom I interviewed was Walter Porter. I took an instinctive liking to him, and his research was in the field which was commonly regarded in those days as organic chemistry. Specifically, it was synthetic chemistry, the making of chemical compounds, the backbone of the chemical industry. The problem which he suggested to me was very interesting. In spite of my being a tyro in the science of organic chemistry, I realized that this problem was quite important in developing basic structural theory in organic chemistry. It had been well established by the end of the nineteenth century that if a carbon atom has four different groups attached to it, the carbon becomes asymmetric. With the discovery of "heavy" hydrogen, there developed great interest in the question of whether a carbon atom would become asymmetric if two of the groups attached to it were "ordinary" hydrogen and "heavy" hydrogen, with the other two groups different from each other and hydrogen. In other words, in the sense of development of asymmetry, do "ordinary" hydrogen and "heavy" hydrogen qualify as different groups? Thus, I signed on with Professor Porter and was assigned a tiny laboratory with another new graduate student named Tom Schultz. I never did become well acquainted with Tom because he spent so little time in the laboratory. It developed that first year students frequently spent a minor amount of time on research, and the professors did not usually expect much. Tom's infrequent appearance in the lab worked out excellently for me. For most purposes I had a private lab, very fortunate on account of the size of the room.

To my surprise, the stockrooms were open to the graduate students at any time of the day or night. Dean Lewis felt that it would interfere with the progress of research if a student should have to wait until "business hours" in order to get materials which proved to be needed for his research in the middle of the night. It is a great system if one can afford it, and Lewis had enough influence on the campus to allow him to "get away" with just about anything. Under this system, I was able to rummage around in the stockrooms and find everything I needed for my research. I started right in, spending about half my available time on experimental work, and the other half in the library. Professor Porter had outlined for me the reactions he proposed to use for synthesis of the type of compound desired for testing out the objective of the research, and so I began the necessary experimental work. In the library, I searched for everything known about these reactions, and evaluated their appropriateness for the desired result. In this pattern, I continued until the end of the semester.

After three or four weeks I had gotten my school work and teaching assisting sufficiently under control so that I began to have time to enjoy the social life at the I House. It was my understanding that the managers of the I House tried to keep the ratio of foreign students to American students at about 2:1. This made it possible for the American students to become acquainted with men and women from many lands. I found this a very enjoyable experience since I had previously known only a few people from states other than Tennessee. Also, the physical setup at the I House was purposely adapted to encouraging association in groups and discouraging the development of cliques. The dining hall had long tables with people seated on each side, so that any person was within view and earshot of several people. Periodically, the dinner would be that eaten in a foreign land, with chopsticks required at the Japanese and Chinese dinners. In the Great Hall there were many chairs, couches, sofas, etc. which were well occupied at certain periods, such as after dinner. Next to the fireplace was a big box for firewood with a curved, hinged top on it. On one evening, after dinner, I was sitting on top of the firewood box with a man from South Africa beside me. Several people were standing in a rather loose group in front of us, and conversation was flowing about as another group of three or four people came up. The object of the encounter was to introduce the new group to those in my group. When a nice looking blonde was introduced to me, she did not respond with any of the usual expressions, but said, "I know who you are." After I disclaimed having ever met her before, she offered an explanation: "I work the early breakfast shift pushing out coffee. I can pull the handle and pass out a cup of coffee without waking up enough to see who is getting it. Periodically, some character comes along and wants hot tea. So I have to wake up enough to get out a pot of hot water, a pot in which to brew the tea, a tea cup and tea bag, then pass it all out to this individual. There are only two people who eat early breakfast at the I House who ask for hot tea in the morning. One of them is a jet black man from the Gold Coast, and the other one is you." After the laughter had subsided, I responded, "So you are that sleepy blond with uncombed hair who feeds me hot tea in the morning. With combed hair and your face put on, I didn't recognize you. You are a nice looking gal." Except for more laughter, I don't remember anything else that happened on that particular night. I had no way of knowing that this was anything other than some of the repartee that is commonly heard at the I House.

I have no recollections of a serial nature regarding what followed immediately after my first encounter with the blonde; however, I do remember several events. On the next occasion that I had early breakfast when the blonde was at the coffee station, I asked for coffee. Before handing it to me, she looked up, probably alerted by my southern accent, and said, "Thank you." As the line accumulated at the cash register, the man behind me said, "What the hell is going on here; why would that coffee gal thank you for taking a cup of coffee from her; she didn't even look up as I took my coffee, just as she always does." Not being well acquainted with people and places, I decided that I should play it carefully. I did not know the man who asked the question, so I said, "It is a long story, sort of a joke between us." On the next occasion that the blonde and I were in the same group that was chatting in the Great Hall, I told her that I had failed to get her name, and she said that her name was Rebecca Marsden and that she was from Fullerton, in Southern California. She also said that she already knew my name when we were introduced because everybody knows the name of the guy with the southern accent. This was neither the first time nor the last time I was reminded that as soon as I spoke three words or less I generated a conspicuous identifying label across my forehead. This was a big nuisance, to put it mildly, especially in connection with my teaching assisting. On some occasions, the student could not understand me well enough to get the answer to his question, and on a few occasions the student became irritated. On more frequent occasions, however, I began to grow suspicious that the student was feigning lack of understanding to hear me talk some more. The only adverse effect that became apparent was when I was shifted out of TAing the organic lab and set to grading papers. This made my work easier and less time consuming, but I was upset by it. I began to try and learn the words and expressions that were giving me trouble, but with little success until later on in the second semester when I began to get help from Rebecca. Having no powers of prophecy, I was unaware that my experience in these labs would be of use to me when, as a professor working in these same labs, I was able to be helpful to TAs from foreign lands who were having more trouble than I was having now.

On one afternoon, as I was going through the Great Hall on my way to dinner, I met Rebecca and we decided to sit together at dinner. We talked mostly about our respective families and friends in our home towns. This proved quite interesting to both of us because of the vast differences in our backgrounds in some respects, and the surprising similarities in others. As we talked, I began to realize that we had a lot going for us as far as enjoying each other's company. The contrast was especially great when compared to the other two women with whom I had become sufficiently acquainted to allow consideration of such matters. My mother was the backbone of the First Presbyterian Church in Murfreesboro; Rebecca's mother was only slightly less active in the Methodist Church in Fullerton. Rebecca commented that I seemed to love my parents, who were nice people, and I enjoyed hearing from her about the things that she had done with her parents and her siblings. I kept making comparisons with Margaret Massie's odd family and Gladys Hanover's very rich Jewish family. The obvious outcome of all this was that I asked Rebecca what movie she would like to see tonight. I have no recollection what movie she picked, but we walked down the hill for a couple of blocks to where I stored my car for the night in the garage at a fraternity house. In those days, it was illegal in Berkeley to park a car overnight on the street, so it was common for people with garages, especially fraternity houses, to make money by renting them. We drove down to Oakland and enjoyed a good movie—good movies were common in those days. After the movie, we came back to Berkeley and followed another UC tradition which we had heard discussed. We went to Edy's for an ice cream sundae or something similar. After that I took Rebecca back to the I House, and we parted with both of us expressing pleasure at such an enjoyable evening. No embrace; no comment even suggesting "necking." After returning to my room, I sat for quite a while looking out my window across San Francisco Bay to the Golden Gate, and thinking how much the evening had brightened my life. Naturally enough, I planned encores.

In the days of which I am writing, the University of California had a simply wonderful schedule of operation. For the fall semester, classes started in about the middle of August. That is why I arrived in August and was surprised to find the weather rather cool. That cool August weather made it not only practical but highly desirable to start the fall semester at that time. This made it possible to end a semester of normal length early in December. Next joyful item: the spring semester started about a week after New Year's Day and ended about the middle of May. All kinds of serendipity ensued. People such as me, who wanted to drive back to Tennessee to visit his home during the holidays had more than two weeks to be there. Everybody, students and teachers alike, could enjoy the year-end holidays much more if they had a week before returning to the old grind. Last and definitely not least, UC students had an inside track at landing the most desirable summer jobs, those at the several National Parks and other recreation areas. The recreational areas were desperately in need of manpower, beginning at about the middle of May, to prepare for the onslaught when the rest of the schools and colleges let out. Only at Berkeley, and no place else in the US, is it practical to start school in mid-August. Such an ideal system! What a pity that when the University of California became the University of California at Berkeley, Berkeley was forced to knuckle under to the concept that it was impractical to have the new campuses on a different schedule from the Father of Them All. Old Blues know better! It was raw jealously, backed by the authority that goes with the majority. As an Old Blue, famed newspaper columnist Herb Caen, put it at the time of the change: "The University of California has been at Berkeley for almost one hundred years, and it will always be at Berkeley, just as intended by Benjamin Ide Wheeler, Robert Gordon Sproul and God."

After that wonderful night of realization, Rebecca and I saw a lot of each other, doing the usual sorts of things, such as movies, dinner together, sometimes at restaurants, walking through the fields of poppies on the hills above the I House, exploratory "light necking" while in my car parked in a viewing area on Grizzly Peak Boulevard, looking at the million lights around San Francisco Bay. It was safe for lovers to park in that fabulous spot in those days, even for a while after I returned to Berkeley as a professor. Not any more! It is natural enough, I guess, for hoodlums to invade any spot that resembles the Garden of Eden, kick out those who planted the garden, and eat the apples. I blame television as the prime culprit. Rebecca and I knew Berkeley, lived in Berkeley in the glory days of old. By the time the semester ended and I had told Rebecca of my plans to drive to Tennessee for the holidays, relations between us had reached the point where she invited me to come to her home on my way back to Berkeley, spend the night with her family and bring her back to Berkeley. I had already agreed with Glenn Seaborg to bring him back to Berkeley. Since Glenn lived in Southgate, it was simple to pick him up on the way from Fullerton. I knew where Glenn lived with his parents for I had spent the night with them when Glenn invited me to drive down with him to attend the UCLA-UC football game and spend two nights with him. Glenn's research director, Bob Fowler, rode down with us but did not spend the night with Glenn or come back with us. On the first night I spent with Glenn, I went to the bathroom last and noticed that the back door, adjacent to the bathroom door, was not quite shut. I could not get it shut, so I told Glenn that I could not get the back door shut. His reply: "We never have been able to get that door shut since the Long Beach earthquake. It is okay." In today's Los Angeles, can you imagine not bothering to get a back door fixed so that it could be locked? Incidentally, Southgate is completely surrounded by Los Angeles. So my plans were made to bring Rebecca and Glenn back with me after the holidays; however, I did not take either of them down to southern California when I went east. Rebecca decided to go home on one of the party boats which were popular for the trip home for the Christmas holidays. Unfortunately, she got seasick. What a party! I took a man from Texas named Jack Warren, a graduate student in petroleum engineering, as far as Dallas. I was alone for the last half of the trip to Murfreesboro.

Tennessee, here I come, after the longest absence of my life!

CHAPTER 5

WE LAUNCH THE GOOD SHIP MARRIAGE

— destined to stay afloat for more than sixty-four years

During my two-week vacation in Murfreesboro, I enjoyed visiting a few friends who were still there, but particularly enjoyed visiting with my parents. They were especially interested in the unexpected things I had encountered in Berkeley: automobile drivers waiting for pedestrians to cross the street in front of them; silver dollars in circulation; cold weather in August; and white buildings in San Francisco, as viewed from my window. I had already sent them pictures from my window. Memur was especially interested, of course, in the blonde whom I said was far, far ahead of any other woman that I had become familiar with. I told her as much as I knew about her family, and she was most interested in the affiliation with the Methodist church. I think there was nothing about my trip to the far west which displeased them. Memur was almost to the point of understanding why the Lord had sent me so far from home.

I left 515 N. Maple Street early in the morning and followed the southern route back to California, reversing the route used for my trip east. The weather was good for that time of year, and on the fifth day, before dark, I pulled into 615 S. Highland Avenue, Fullerton California. I had written to give the day that I expected to arrive, and came in right on schedule. I got the impression that this made a good impression on Rebecca's parents. I slept on a sleeping porch with Rebecca's brother Ralph, and I just about froze to death. The top half of the walls on each side of the long narrow room were screened, with no provision for closing them. I asked Ralph if there were any extra blankets around, and he brought me some kind of heavy comforter, which saved me from frostbite. Mrs. Marsden got up early to fix us a good breakfast so that Rebecca and I could get off to an early start. We found the Seaborg's address in Southgate with no difficulty; Glenn was all ready to go, and so we took off up the valley. With Rebecca between us in my coupe, we had a good chance to get acquainted with each other during the long drive to Berkeley. Rebecca had warned us that there might be heavy fog in the valley at this time of year, but we lucked out. It was a nice sunny day. Even with the kind of roads in the valley in those days, we got in before dark, deposited Glenn at his place, then Rebecca and I went to the garage where I kept my car. After loving each other more than a little, and expressing our pleasure to be back together again with no mishaps along the way, we went to the I House and then to our rooms. I still remember how tired I was—and how happy.

Rebecca and I continued to enjoy doing many things together. In particular, she taught me how to dance, "working" at it during the noon hour for several days. She concentrated her instruction on the fox trot and the waltz, both of which were popular in those days. There was also something known as jazz, which Rebecca did not know, fortunately. There were three or four places in Oakland where there were public dance halls, which were nice places and frequented by Cal students. The ones at the hotels had dinner with dancing, and hence were more expensive. We went more often to the dance hall operated by the Athens Club. I do not remember just what the charge was, but I think it was not more than $1.50, which was quite a bit more than the movies cost. I also do not remember how often we went dancing, but I think it was about once every two weeks. Occasionally, we had a big date such as going to San Francisco to have dinner at a restaurant called Lucca's. The first things brought to the table were appetizers, consisting of ravioli and other items in quantity sufficient for a meal. Next the dinner menu was presented, with a notice at the top which read: "You may select any one or all of the following if you so desire." Of course college students would probably go without lunch before going to Lucca's, then lay off the appetizers so that two main menu items could be accommodated. However, there was another item to be considered: a big dessert consisting of the Italian ice cream called spumoni. Being a dessert fan, I always held off of the previous items in order to be able to handle the serving of spumoni, which was shaped like a big cantaloupe. Unfortunately, Lucca's was out of business by the time we returned to Berkeley in 1945. A great many other things had changed by the time we returned—rarely for the better.

We spent many evenings loving each other in my car while parked in one of the viewing areas along Grizzly Peak Drive near the top of the Berkeley Hills. On a clear night, of which there were many in those days, the sweep of the view to the many cities around San Francisco Bay was simply magnificent. During this period the "loving" never went beyond "heavy necking." We never had any discussion of having sexual inter-course. I think there were two principal reasons for this. Dating back to my preteen years, I have always had a strong instinct for fair play, and I still have it at the time of this writing. During those times, a girl who became pregnant out of wedlock was faced with the prospect of having her life ruined, or at least denigrated seriously. Her only hope of escaping delivery of a baby was to find a sympathetic physician or go to a person with no medical training who specialized in helping such unfortunate girls. On some more fortunate occasions, where both families were helpful, the boy and girl would get married, and this sometimes worked out well. On the other hand, the boy took no risk at all, at least none for which he was like-ly to be held liable. And in those days condoms were much less reliable than is the case today. Another factor involved in our abstinence was that we were thinking a great deal about living together for a long time and enjoying indefinitely the fun and satisfaction which we were experiencing as we gazed around San Francisco Bay. After we pledged to each other that we were engaged to be married, we talked a great deal about what we would do with our lives. About the only thing we did not discuss was sex-ual intercourse, although we certainly felt powerful biological urges and looked forward to gratifying those urges. Of course we had no inkling of what an ecstatic experience that act could become if worked out over a period of years by an understanding couple.

I think that neither of us remembers the date at which we formally declared our commitment to be married, but I well remember that it was on a beautiful clear night as we gazed in ecstasy around the Bay. I also remember that it occurred shortly before I fully realized that I would not be coming back to graduate school at Berkeley for the next year. It is possible that I had a foreboding that it was really inevitable that I would have to reach that decision, and hence wanted to develop a formal and lasting attachment to Rebecca. I did not want to lose her. To celebrate our engagement, we decided to go to the Lake Merrit Hotel for dinner and dancing, dressed in formal attire. Rebecca had brought a long dress with her to Berkeley, and I had the tuxedo which my Dad had bought for me after the Phi Beta Kappa affair. I had never worn it before, but Dad had provided me with the necessary accessories, such as dress shirt, cuff links and bow tie. After that night, I did not wear it again except for initiation into Sigma Xi at Yale. On that occasion, a friend sitting next to me wore tails. I learned how to flip tails to avoid sitting down on them; however, I have not had any use for that knowledge. I think that we did not decide, on the night that we pledged our faith to each other, just when we would plan for our wedding. Our minds were too fully occupied with other things. It was not much later, however, that we decided the marriage should wait until Rebecca finished her senior year at Cal and got her degree. This put it in the summer of 1936. I have no recollection of whether Rebecca's parents had any influence on that decision, but I do remember that I became quite worried about it when I became aware that I would have to go to another university to finish my graduate work.

Near the middle of the spring semester, Professor Porter advised me that experiments he had run revealed that the synthetic route which he had recommended to me had failed. A key step in the synthesis had resulted in what is known as racemization, and the objective of the synthesis required avoidance of racemization. The long hours I had spent in the library searching for everything that was known about that synthesis had made me apprehensive that racemization would occur. (As an astonishing revelation of the lightning speed with which information retrieval can be accomplished today, I will comment that the literature search I did could be done in a few minutes—or a few hours at the most—by use of the Internet.) Thus, I was not surprised by Professor Porter's revelation. He said that he was very sorry about having recommended to me a project that had failed so soon, but that it would be necessary for me to shift to another project. Since I was apprehensive about this development, I had been searching the catalog to learn exactly what the requirements were for earning a Master of Science (M.S.) degree. I had learned that if I could produce a satisfactory thesis I had enough hours of course credits to qualify for the M.S. degree after completion of my second semester. This was due partly to the two biochemistry courses which I had taken, and partly to the fact that the chemistry department always assigned a large number of hours to the research course. This was done to emphasize to graduate students that the principal objective of their graduate work is experimental research. I was—and still am—very much in favor of such a requirement. In my case, it made it possible for me to earn an M.S. degree in a single year. In view of this, I told Professor Porter that I had already decided that I would go to another university the next year in order to pursue a biochemical problem in the department of chemistry. I then asked him if he considered my work so far qualified for a thesis for an M.S. degree—and held my breath in anxiety. He responded promptly that he was confident that my work would qualify for the thesis, especially since I had accumulated so much information from my library searching that would be quite appropriate in the thesis. I worked very hard to promptly gather up loose ends in my experimental work, and get my library work organized for use in the thesis. Professor Porter was very helpful to me; he even arranged for one of the department's WPA workers to type my thesis. I was quite grateful. I assume that he was happy to have a potentially messy situation work out to everybody's advantage.

As soon as it became clear that I would be able to finish up everything necessary for getting the M.S. degree, I wrote my mother the news. She responded at once to report that she wanted to attend my graduation exercises. "Advise me as soon as possible when the event is scheduled," she wrote. Both Rebecca and I felt that a major reason she wanted to attend the graduation was to get acquainted with the girl I planned to marry. I assume that Rebecca was more than slightly worried about the outcome of this scrutiny; however, I was not the least bit concerned. After all, I was well acquainted with both parties, and I felt in my bones that they would hit it off together famously. I was right.

Before the question of my going to another school the next year abruptly reached a climax, I had done considerable worrying about the effect on our plans while we were separated for a year before our planned marriage date. When the decision was suddenly forced upon me and Rebecca showed distress but no sign of wavering, I felt better. At the same time I realized that Rebecca would be concerned about her man wandering around alone for such a long time with no female companionship. I did everything possible to reassure her; told her that I had never in my life reneged on a pledge, stated that "my word of honor is worth a lot more than any piece of paper with signatures on it." This gave me some practice in allaying the concerns of Rebecca's father when I pulled out of 615 S Highland Ave. in June with some of Rebecca's most cherished possessions loaded into the car. The excuse for this transporting of these possessions was that it would save the expense of shipping them east later on. Both Rebecca and I knew better. We wanted to leave no stone unturned in establishing a firm bond between us.

When that fateful day arrived, that is, the day when Memur stepped off the train in the railroad yard which passed as a station in Oakland, it was love at first sight. Rebecca greeted her as Memur, said that she had heard so much about her that she was already qualified to call her by that name. We heard from several people, years later, that Memur had told them that by the time she got into my car she knew why the Lord had sent me so far away from home; it was to find Rebecca. Subsequent events certainly make it qualify as a plausible explanation.

While Memur was in Berkeley we took her to a restaurant in San Francisco, probably Leuca's, in order to generate the greatest sensation of novelty; took her for a drive in Marin County, including Muir Woods, and finally to Yosemite Park. Of course the trip to San Francisco involved the Berkeley auto ferry. I do not remember how we got to Marin County, but we definitely took her for a drive there, because when I stopped on top of the mountain in a place above San Quentin prison to take a picture, I remember a guard coming out and shouting to us with amplification that no stopping was allowed there—move on. Memur was a little shaken up, but there was actually no problem. At Yosemite, we stayed in a cabin just outside the park in a place beside the river. It was a two-bedroom cabin, so Memur and Rebecca roomed together. I think that was the time that Memur became convinced that the Lord really knew what he was doing. We drove around the park to the usual places the next day, then went back to Berkeley. We put Memur on the train, engaged in some loving after the absence of such for several days, then went to bed exhausted, but satisfied, with a mission accomplished. We drove to Fullerton the next day, with all my worldly goods loaded in the car; however, the most valuable part of the cargo was not a part of my worldly goods—and never would be, but was something more valuable.

Driving to Fullerton was uneventful, and we arrived in time for the nice dinner that had been prepared for us by Rebecca's mother, Rolena. Her father was named Rollin, but he was always addressed as Rollie. Since I knew that Rebecca's sister Marion and her husband Bob addressed Rebecca's parents by their first names, I decided, with Rebecca's concurrence, to start using their first names immediately. This worked out very well and probably increased the sense of familiarity between us. During the approximately ten days that I was visiting in Rebecca's home, we did numerous enjoyable things. Since I had never been swimming in the ocean before, I greatly enjoyed the several afternoons we spent at the beach at Corona Del Mar. I remember one incident that occurred when we went to the beach with Rebecca's parents. Rebecca and I were horsing around in several ways, and at one time I had her on my shoulders with my head between her legs and holding onto her thighs to keep her balanced. I forget where Rollie was when we assumed this position, but he came up behind us and yelled at Rebecca, "You get down from there!" I turned around and said, "What was that you said? My ears are stopped up by Rebecca's legs." Whereupon he went around to my rear and began paddling Rebecca's bare rear end. I decided it was time to kneel down and let her off. Of course Rebecca put on a show by dancing around and rubbing her rear end. This is illustrative of the rapport that rapidly developed between Rebecca's parents and me. It was quite gratifying, and contributed greatly to the enjoyment of my visit with the Marsdens.

During a period when Rebecca was menstruating, she got the idea that since Rolena knew that she was "out of season," she would let us go to the big international fair in San Diego, stay overnight in a motel and return to Fullerton the next day. Rolena agreed to the idea. Since Rebecca and I remained firm in our resolve not to engage in sexual intercourse prior to marriage, Rebecca's being out of season was unnecessary to prevent us from engaging in that act. Of course a skeptic might say that I am simply rationalizing our behavior in order to pump up my ego; however, I think this is not true. There were many instances when there was nothing to stop us except our determination that nothing interfere with the many years of happiness to which we were looking forward. After we spent more time at the fair the next morning, we drove back to Fullerton and told Rolena and Rollie about the things we had seen at the fair, but not about all the things we had done.

As time marched inexorably on, the time came when I must leave for Murfreesboro. Rebecca got the idea that she wanted to pack in my car as many things as the car could hold, in order to avoid the expense of shipping them after our marriage. Of course, these things had to be things which she would not be needing until the next summer, and hence included many of her most cherished keepsakes. This was just too much for Rollie. As I came out of the house, he was remonstrating rather heatedly with Rebecca on that subject. I could understand exactly what was worrying him. After some very fast and hard thinking, I suggested to Rebecca that she was obviously tired and should go into the house for a rest while Rollie and I finished with the packing of the car. Fortunately, Rebecca got the message and went into the house without any comment—and so I exhaled. I shook Rollie's hand and told him that I thought he was dead right in objecting to Rebecca's packing all these things in my car for me to carry away. I then told him that I would like to try to persuade him that he had no reason to worry about those things when dealing with me. I told him the things that my dad had told me when I set out for college, and that I had pledged to myself that I would never disappoint my dad by failing to do what was right. I closed by saying, "My word of honor is better than any piece of paper with signatures on it. I promise you that only death can prevent me from returning to marry Rebecca, if she still wants me; and I am dead sure that she will still want me." Rollie said nothing, but held out his hand, which I shook. I then went into the house and found Rebecca weeping, so I immediately told her that everything was A-OK, and that Rollie was waiting to help her pack the car. She kissed me, as meaningfully as ever before or since, then washed her face and went out to see Rollie. We both knew that the last possible hurdle had been cleared, and that we were going to be married. I do not know what was said between Rollie and Rebecca, and neither of us has discussed this matter since. It always generates a warm, comfortable feeling to remember that it happened.

My memory of the summer spent in Murfreesboro is almost blank. Before leaving Berkeley, I had correspondence with three universities, the University of Wisconsin, the University of Illinois, and Yale. In view of my interest in working for my degree in a chemistry department while doing research directed to biochemistry, I chose Yale. A professor at Yale, R. J. Anderson, was working on the chemical components of the capsule of the tubercle bacillus, Mycobacterium tuberculosis. This fit well with what I wanted, and I was especially intrigued by working with such tiny amounts of material. At that time the ability to do chemical analyses with as little as 3 mg. of material, termed "microanalysis," was very new, and I was eager to learn how to do it. Since my future for the upcoming fall was all set, I really had nothing urgent to do that summer—an experience which was entirely new to me. In thinking of what I might do to pass the time and be of some use, I decided to do heavy reviewing of both French and German. In those days, all major universities required a "reading knowledge" of both these languages as a part of the requirements for the award of a Ph.D. degree in chemistry. This was long before the English language became so dominant in scientific writings. In the research that I published prior to World War II, about one-fourth of the references cited in the papers were likely to be in German, with a much smaller number in French. French is a much easier language to read than is German, although anyone not born a Frenchman is likely to have trouble with speaking the language. Therefore, I spent most of my time studying German, especially learning the vocabulary for chemical writings. Since there was no library closer than Nashville where I could borrow German chemical journals or books, I bought a textbook used in German universities. It was Kurzes Lehrbuch der Organischen Chemie (Short Textbook of Organic Chemistry), by A. Bernthsen. I still have this book in my bookcase and have just gotten it out to check the spelling. Although this summer's activities left few items in my memory, it served me well. I was able to pass both the French and German exams during my first semester at Yale. This was almost unheard of; more often a degree was held up because of failure to meet the German requirement. Of course there was much correspondence between Rebecca and me during that sterile summer. It was so important in helping to keep our spirits up.

Fortunately, the ragweed allergy season was a little early in 1935, and so I was troubled only a little at the time I started out for New Haven. At the height of the season I was hit so hard that I went outdoors as little as possible. I enjoyed driving up the beautiful Shenandoah Valley, and stayed overnight in one of the small cities there. On the next day, I had a lot of surprises with the traffic layouts. Even with the route signs to help me, I had a really tough time getting through Washington. Finally I arrived in North Jersey, where I was confronted with a traffic circle, something which I had never seen before. After driving around the circle a few times, I finally decided which outlet to take to go toward New York. The Holland Tunnel was a new thing to me, and rather fascinating. I got onto the elevated roadway with no problem, but had a little trouble getting off it and on my way to New Haven. I had already rented my room in The Hall of Graduate Studies, and was able to go directly there without going to a hotel. Dad had sold the bus business by that time and was able to pay my tuition and room at The Hall of Graduate Studies. The price was not much more, and so I had chosen a single room in the tower with a private bath. Real luxury, especially when compared with the single room I had in Kissam Hall. There was also a dining hall in the building where one could eat for a fee which was based on the food bought, as in any restaurant. All the colleges at Yale had dining halls, so decent restaurants around the campus were few and far between, and I ate most of my meals in my dining hall.

For my first few weeks at Yale I was quite intrigued by the novelty of it all—large buildings with spires or towers in architecture reminiscent of pictures I had seen of England; a library of many stories, with a tower full of stacks of books and study crypts; a gymnasium with a tower of six or eight stories of squash racquet courts and indoor tennis courts, and a swimming pool with tiers of seats around it so that a spectator could look down into the water and see the swimmers; and vast expanses of very green, well kept lawns. The Hall of Graduate Studies (HGS) had a broad arched entrance with a window on one side where a guard was on duty night and day. After I had checked out my room at the business office, my next stop was to visit the guard and tell him my name and room number, as well as any visitors I might be expecting. The latter item was easy for me to cover. If anyone he did not recognize as appropriate entered he would call to him on his amplified speaker and inquire as to his business. There were no solicitors or peddlers in the HGS.

I had no way of meeting people except in the dining hall at the HGS, but I did get acquainted with a few people there. One of those I met early on was named George Waters. He was a new chemistry graduate student and lived in one of the rooms on the top floor of the Sterling Chemistry laboratory, but ate his meals at the HGS. This business of having rooms for graduate students to live in the chemistry building was just one of the odd features of the ancient Sterling Chemistry Laboratory. After eating a few dinners together, George and I found a very unusual common interest— we both liked well-done beef, a characteristic which frequently made me feel rather lonesome in most dining rooms. George and I remained good friends and did things together, continuing until after I married Rebecca. Another man I met in the dining hall was very helpful to me during those first few weeks, although I have forgotten his name. In a conversation about athletic activities in which we were interested, he stated that he liked squash better than anything else, and therefore greatly appreciated the plentiful supply of courts for that game in the Yale gymnasium. Since I was really hurting for lack of physical activity, I found out from him how to get a locker and how to reserve a squash court. I began playing with him, but he was so much better than me that I soon found other squash players among the chemistry graduate students, as well as one professor, whose name was Bob Coghill. I played with Bob occasionally during my years at Yale and later had some contact with him during World War II.

The Sterling Chemistry lab was only six or seven blocks from the HGS, therefore within easy walking distance, except in bad weather. It was up the hill on Prospect Street, next in line above the geology and physics buildings. Still further up Prospect Street was the Divinity School. The main campus with its quadrangles and Colleges was on the relatively flat ground at the foot of Prospect. Residential and commercial buildings surrounded the Yale campus on all sides. Prospect Street projected like a horn into the area of New Haven around it. In one direction, Winchester Arms Co. was one block away from Prospect Street. I rented a garage (shed) for my car three blocks away from the HGS. This sort of thing seemed strange to me, but I later learned that it is quite characteristic of old New England industrial cities.

The Sterling Chemistry Laboratory looked like a medieval castle, with stone stairs about thirty feet wide leading to the main floor. Several wrought iron gates closed off these stairs every night at 6 o'clock sharp, after which the laboratories could not be entered until 8 A.M. The library could be entered at night by way of a winding staircase that was surrounded by thick masonry walls. Since I was fresh from the College of Chemistry at the University of California, where everything was wide open, including the stock rooms, I was somewhat more than slightly astonished. I was even more surprised when I learned that I had to pay for everything I checked out of the stock room: every flask, every clamp for a ring stand, every bottle of reagent or solvent, every towel, everything. This alarmed me when I learned this, but it later developed that I would luck out and not have to put up this substantial sum of money.

I had already scouted out the territory before I came up the stone stairs on the first day of classes and went to the office of the chairman of the department, A. J. Hill.   I had been directed to consult him about getting going in my graduate work. He said that first year graduate students ordinarily took a laboratory course with two afternoons per week of lab work, but I might not have to do that since I already had an M.S. degree. He said that he would like to see my M.S. thesis. Since I had anticipated this, I had my copy of the thesis with me. I also told him that the advanced organic chemistry course that was listed on my transcript from Vanderbilt involved two afternoons per week of synthetic work for two quarters and one quarter of qualitative organic analysis for the third quarter. He glanced superficially at my thesis and declared that I did not need to take the course in experimental work. I breathed a deep sigh of relief as he went on to say that I would be required to take the course in advanced physical chemistry taught by Dr. Smith, and the course in organic chemistry taught by him. He noted that I had taken a year of thermodynamics at California, but that Professor Saxon taught a rather different course based more on the work of Willard Gibbs. He suggested that I should discuss that matter with Professor Saxon. I noted that he referred to Dr. Smith and Professor Saxon. I learned later that the Yale chemistry department had several rather unusual titles among their faculty, such as Professor of Freshman Chemistry, and Research Professor. Finally, Professor Hill said that I could start immediately doing research, and asked which professor I would choose for research. I told him that I had chosen Yale as my second graduate school in order to work for Professor R. J. Anderson. He seemed rather disappointed at that and asked me questions about why I had chosen Anderson. When he realized that my choice was grounded in considerable thought, he told me where to find Anderson's office and suggested that I talk to him right away and get settled in a space to work. I learned later that A. J. Hill had a rather unsavory reputation for picking off the most promising graduate students to work for him. My first weeks at Yale were filled with surprises. I was not surprised that Professor Saxon told me that I would have to take his course in thermodynamics.

When I went to talk to Professor Anderson, I had another surprise—this time a good one. Professor Anderson proved to be a tall, rather handsome grey-haired man who said that he would be glad to have me work for him. He then asked me if I had any kind of fellowship that would pay for my lab expenses. When I said that I had to pay for them myself, he replied that he always paid for the expenses of his graduate students and postdoctoral research assistants. He would advise the stockroom to honor all of the tickets for withdrawals that I signed. This took a big load off my mind. I hated to think of telling my dad that I would need still more money. Quite a change from my sensation of feeling rich when I was at Berkeley. I soon learned that "rich" is defined somewhat differently at Yale than at the University of California. Anderson took me into a very large laboratory with eight or ten rows of work benches with two students occupying each side of each work bench. I had thought that I was crowded in that little laboratory at Berkeley. My bench was on the first row at one end of the room, on the inside of the row; that is, the side away from the wall. At my end of the row of benches, directly opposite my bench, was a broad door into the next large laboratory where the rest of the first year students did their required experimental work before starting research. Thus, I was separated from the rest of the first year students during laboratory work, unless I chatted with them as I walked through their room on my way to the stock room. Of course, I also got acquainted with them in the classroom for the three courses all of us took. Also, the large lab I was in had students in it who were beyond their first year; however, all of them were already acquainted with each other. The entire setup worked out to make me feel rather isolated and correspondingly lonesome, especially when students in earshot were planning some kind of event for the weekend. I was not encouraged to forget how much I missed Rebecca whenever I looked through the door into the next lab at the rear end of an attractive young woman named Jane Garrett. By some sort of diabolical combination of circumstances, when I was standing at my bench and doing experimental work, the normal direction to look was forward. Under different circumstances, the view would have been attractive. Under the actual circumstances, it exacerbated my longing for Rebecca.

Living alone in the HGS did not help my loneliness. I became well acquainted only with George Waters, and had no interests in common with him. About the only fun and relaxation I had was playing squash occasionally, and that was tempered by the fact that all those I played with were much better than me. All these things added together to keep me unhappy, but I realized more and more that my real problem was that I wanted Rebecca. And so I began to think of such things as the reasons that we had decided to wait until next summer for our marriage. A final analysis came up with only one reason that we should wait: it would give Rebecca a chance to finish her last semester of college and get her degree. I began to ask myself why it was so important to get that degree right now, even though it kept us apart. Lots of people drop out of school without finishing, and either finish later or decide that the actual degree is not what is important. It is the college experience that is important. And so I finally decided that all of this thinking about possible events in the future was trivia compared to the fact that I wanted Rebecca now. And so I decided to go into action and find out if it might be possible for us to get married at Christmas. No matter how difficult it sounded, I decided that I was going to find out if it was possible.

My first move was to write Rebecca and ask if she would like to forget about finishing up her degree and get married at Christmas if that should prove to be possible. I received a prompt answer which was more enthusiastic than my fondest hopes. The next move was to write my dad and ask if he could afford to pay for me to go to California and get married during the Christmas holidays. As always, Dad came through like a champ. Among other things, he said, "I will find the money if I have to steal it." What a man! These few sentences communicate a lot of fiendish activity; however, the tempo rose rapidly. After a very few days, my mother wrote that she wanted to drive out with me and come back on the train by way of Kansas City, where she would visit relatives she had not seen for years. I responded that I would be very happy indeed to have her company. For one thing, I would be pleased to have my mother on the groom's side of the aisle at the wedding. Furthermore, it would be very pleasant to have her company on that long drive, and would probably ensure that I did not fall asleep and ruin everything. I mentioned that I had driven across the country enough times to last me the rest of my life. As a result of this wedding, there proved to be no reason for me to make that drive again. Of course I was insulated from the most fiendish activity of all, the preparation for the wedding by Rolena, Rebecca's mother. Rebecca was at a much lesser distance and by no means as well insulated, especially in the days after her semester at the University had ended so that she could go home and enter the festivities and activities. Somehow or other, everything held together.

Rebecca and I prepared for the wedding in connection with the important matter of proper performance in sexual intercourse and the use of contraception. To a reader today, this may sound rather silly. Contemporary youth learn all about this sort of thing in high school. To get away from historical reminiscing, Rebecca sought the advice of a medical doctor in Pasadena who was recommended to her by two lifelong friends who were registered nurses. This doctor gave her good advice and fitted her with a diaphragm. My brother, John, who had finished medical school by that time and was a practicing physician, gave me a small book to read and a tube of spermicidal vaginal cream to be used for the first week or ten days immediately after marriage. He said that if a woman had not previously had sexual intercourse, this procedure was reliable, and the diaphragm might prove uncomfortable at first and better used after a few nights. He also told me that he had never heard of a pregnancy occurring when the diaphragm had been used, which is more than can be said for condoms.

In addition to preparing for my final exams, I had a major job to do at my end of the undertaking. That was getting out of the lease to occupy my room for the entire semester, and finding a place for us to live when we came back. I started on both things at once, but first on the search for a place for us to live. The situation with apartments was really grim—poor accommodations and high price. I began reading and acting on the want ads in the newspaper. After a rather discouraging sequence of ads which I followed up, I finally went to an address on Chapel Street a few blocks from the Yale Yard on the side away from downtown New Haven. It proved to be a large three-story house, across the street from a large hospital. I was rather nonplussed at the appearance of the address which I proceeded to check against the newspaper I carried; however, I decided that I should investigate. In answer to my ring of the doorbell, a small withered man answered and confirmed the fact that I had the right address. He told me that he was a retired medical doctor named Sheehan, who owned and had lived in this house since graduating from medical school. He lived with his wife on the first floor and rented out the top two floors, usually to nurses at the hospital. He and his wife always spent the winter in Florida and returned to their home in June. When he learned that I was a graduate student in chemistry at Yale who was getting married and was now living at the Hall of Graduate Studies, he said that he would like to rent to me during the time he was in Florida. He charged a low rent because I would also have the job of maintaining the house for the renters, as he paid the bill, and would leave with me the names of tradesmen whom I would call in case repairs and/or upkeep should be needed on such things as the furnace. It later turned out that it was not accidental that he specifically mentioned the furnace. After my trudging of the streets for days, I was simply ecstatic about the place, and agreed to rent it on the spot. There was even a little wooden garage behind the house, approached by a very narrow drive between buildings where I could park my car out of the severe winter weather. He was leaving for Florida about five days before I wanted to leave for California. I would come to the house on the day before he planned to leave, get keys to the house, and pay the first month's rent. Truly a minor miracle, a bolt from the blue! I was so happy that I was able to bear up under my experience with Yale University in regard to defaulting on my year's lease at the Hall of Graduate Studies.

Concerning this lease, the very nice woman, whose name I forget, who was the manager of the HGS, directed me to discuss the matter with the man in charge of Yale's financial affairs; I forget what his title was, probably Vice President, Finances. He proved to be a stern old man who immediately adopted a belligerent attitude toward me, spoke down to me with the attitude of a lord addressing a serf. After a few minutes of increasingly heated discussion, he summed up his attitude by saying, "Young man, if you cannot afford to honor your agreement to lease your room for a full year, you should not get married." After sitting quietly for a few minutes while considering what to say, and rejecting the first few lines that occurred to me, I replied, "Old man, I know nothing about you, since I have been previously unaware of your existence; however, I have learned one thing about you. You are suffering from a weakness of intellect. Since I am a graduate student in chemistry and am good enough to have been admitted to the Yale Graduate School, the odds are good that I will earn more money than the average Yale graduate student. One thing which is just as certain as death and taxes is that Yale University will never be given one red penny of my money." My tormentor seemed too surprised to say anything, so I left his office and went over to the HGS to ask that nice lady what, if anything, could be done about the situation. She said that she was well aware what I would be told, but felt that it would be better to discuss the matter after I came back. She said that there were usually one or more students who would like to get a room in The Hall at midyear, especially if it were discounted some. Since I was the first one to want to vacate, I would be the one to sell his lease to the first applicant. If I came around a day or two before leaving, she would tell me if I had a customer, and I could clear out my belongings, leave my key with her, and pay her the discount on the transfer. I told her that I might not have enough money to pay the discount, so she said that she would take an unsecured promissory note for the amount, and I could pay it when I returned after Christmas. When I returned two days before leaving, she had a new tenant, I signed the note, and went happily on my way to head for Rebecca. What a glorious feeling; the improbable seemed started on its way. The woman at The Hall was so nice that I almost forgave Yale University for the behavior of the clown with an administrative title—but not quite, and I have never changed my attitude.

It was snowing when I pulled out of New Haven before daylight on the day after my last exam. I had started my car a few days earlier to make sure it would deliver, and was very happy that it did so after standing for a few weeks. On the day before leaving, I had checked out of my room at The Hall and loaded my belongings in the car. I had learned that my mother naturally wanted to travel in her car, and this worked out well for me to leave my car with my belongings in it in Murfreesboro. We could then bring back to Murfreesboro as many of Rebecca's belongings as she wanted to bring, and transfer to my car as much as it would hold of her clothes that she needed. Any excess of her things would be left in Murfreesboro to be dealt with as and when they proved to be needed. The snow was falling rather steadily, but the temperature was not low enough to cause it to collect on the road. This fortunate situation persisted until I arrived in the Shenandoah Valley. I stayed overnight in one of the small cities there and carried on to Murfreesboro the next day, where I arrived after dark. Memur and Dad were not worried about my rather late arrival because they knew that I was driving from New Haven in two days.

There was a document waiting for me to sign and have notarized immediately and returned by special delivery air mail to Fullerton. This document had to be filed a certain number of days before the marriage, and of course the wedding date had been set earlier. Unless the document arrived on time there would be a problem about the wedding date, and so it was imperative that the document be mailed the next day, and we had to leave before daylight in order to get to Fullerton for the wedding. This problem seemed easily solvable since Uncle Gent, husband of my Aunt Indiana, was a notary public. However, a problem developed. Uncle Gent had never been to his office after dark, and he was afraid to go downtown and into the building, which was deserted by this time of night. After much argument, and my promise to take a handgun with me, which I had customarily carried in the car ever since my initial trip to California, Uncle Gent finally agreed to go down to his office and notarize my paper. Another hurdle cleared!

It was still snowing when Memur and I pulled out before daylight and headed west. Starting in Arkansas, the highway all the way to Little Rock was through the swamp that occupied that area of Arkansas. The road had been elevated above the water by digging deep and wide trenches on each side of the road and piling the dirt in between the trenches. Thus, the road was between what appeared to be rivers on each side. Periodically, there was a short bridge across a connection between the rivers. Since the roadway across a bridge was out of contact with the earth and the water, most of the bridges had ice on them. After skidding a little on the first frozen bridge, I realized that I must hold a very steady steering wheel as I approached a bridge. I had not realized previously that Memur had some steel in her soul. She was probably helped by her faith in the Lord. She never told me to slow down or to drive carefully, even when I skidded a little on the first two bridges. For whatever reasons, she came through like a champ. As for me, I concentrated on the driving as I sang to myself the chorus from a song which was popularized by a singer named Johnny Carson at somewhat earlier times:

> Golden Gate, I'm coming to ya; Golden Gate, sing Hallelujah;
> I live in the sun, love in the moon, where every night is June.
> A little sun-kissed blonde is smiling my way, just beyond the
>   Lincoln Highway;
> Going strong now, won't be long now, open up that Golden Gate!

It didn't bother me any that the little blonde was currently displaced a little from the Golden Gate; I met and wooed her directly opposite that beautiful landmark.

We finally arrived at Texarkana a little before midnight. The snow let up near Little Rock, and there are no swamps west of Little Rock. We slept until after daylight and left after breakfast, with Pecos, Texas, in mind. The weather had cleared and remained sunny all the way across Texas. Each time I have driven across Texas, I am reminded of an infamous comment that General Sherman made after having served as military governor of Texas after the Uncivil War: "If I owned Texas and Hell, I would rent out Texas and live in Hell." After hanging onto the wheel all afternoon to hold a steady course against the strong north wind, when we stopped for gasoline I asked the filling station attendant, "Does this wind blow all the time here?" After a significant pause, he replied, "I don't know, I only been here five years." We got into Pecos at about 10 P.M. and drove up to the little hotel at the edge of town where I had stayed going both ways on my trip home at Christmas. It was dark all around it and there were no outside lights. Memur was really beat. She said, "I am not moving out of this car until you find out whether we can get a room in that hotel." I told her that we might be the only guests in the hotel. This was not quite true, but there was no problem about getting the best room in the hotel, with two single beds. It was actually a better room than we had in Texarkana, with a nice bath. We left Pecos later in the morning than on the previous day, for the drive to Tucson was not such a long one. After an uneventful trip to Tucson and on to Fullerton the next day, we pulled into 615 S. Highland Avenue in mid-afternoon. We received a hero's welcome, with Rebecca leading the charge. She had been waiting on the porch since lunch.

During the time between our arrival and the wedding, there was what might be called persistent frantic activity, which reached a climax on the night before the wedding. The Marsden home was a rather typical one story ranch house situated in an orange orchard. It had three bedrooms, counting the sleeping porch, and there was also a bedroom in a building known as the "tank house." Those who slept in the house were distributed as follows (to the best of my memory): the bride and Memur were honored with the best bedroom, Rebecca's parents occupied one bedroom, and her grandmother the third one; Rebecca's Uncle, Elwood Starbuck, slept in the tank house; I, my best man, Lou Blanc, and Rebecca's brother, Ralph, slept in the living room. This arrangement would have been easier to handle had it not been for a tradition of the choir of the Methodist Church, of which Rebecca was a member.

According to this tradition, when any member of the choir was married, the remainder of the choir gathered at the home of the bride at first daylight and sang the anthem, 'Tis Thy Wedding Morning. After the singing of the anthem, the choir was invited into the home to partake of coffee and toast. When Rebecca was a choir member, she thought that this was such a nice tradition that she always looked forward to each occasion. When she was on the receiving end, and three people had to be cleared from the combination living room and dining room so that coffee and toast could be served soon after daylight, she thought it was a pretty tough way to start her wedding day.

Rebecca's matron of honor was her sister, Marion Fry, and she also had two bridesmaids. My best man was Lou Blanc, a friend of mine from the year before at Berkeley and still a graduate student there. The wedding was at 7 P.M. at the Methodist Church, and followed a traditional pattern. One side of the church was for the family of the bride, and the other side was for the family of the groom. The side for the groom was unoccupied except for my mother and a few Marsden friends who sat there as a friendly gestur—that is until a few minutes before the music was to start.

Rebecca's brother-in-law, Bob Fry, who was an usher, led a young couple down to where my mother was sitting and introduced them as friends of the groom. My mother was considerably more than slightly surprised to look up and see Charles and Esther Travis. She had sent them an invitation because they were among the few good friends I had in Murfreesboro, but she did not dream that they would appear at the wedding because Charles had attended the Naval Academy at Annapolis at the same time that I went to Vanderbilt. Memur knew he was an officer aboard a ship but had no idea where the ship was. It so happened that his ship put into Long Beach just in time for him and Esther to make it to the wedding. My participation in this event occurred as Rebecca and I were standing in a receiving line after the wedding. After holding that bright cordial smile on my face for one person after another, I suddenly looked up to see a face that I had seen before. I restrained a whoop of joy, but I must have made some sort of noise because Rebecca looked at me and wondered what was going on. Charles and I held up the line for a while as we exchanged reminiscences. I remember only one other time that the diverse paths of Charles Travis and I crossed. I forget what the occasion was, but I remember his telling me, "I have sailed the seven seas, and never have I come so close to freezing to death as on one night in August that I was caught in San Francisco in my spring uniform."

After the wedding we returned to Rebecca's home where there was a reception. We changed to travel clothes and loaded all our belongings (mostly Rebecca's) into our car. Bob Fry stood guard at the car, which was behind the house, as a precaution against any activity of smart alec practical jokers. We spent our first night at the Del Mar Hotel, which was between Fullerton and San Diego, at a beautiful site on the ocean. We were dead tired, but not too tired to engage in the activity which, at that time, was traditional on the wedding night. I remember nothing about it—but I remember thousands of such that were destined to follow.

We required five days to make the trip back to Murfreesboro, one more than for the trip made by Memur and me. We had some minor problems, such as missing a route sign at an intersection and winding up at the Mexican border; however, there was nothing that could not be corrected. We arrived in Murfreesboro on a Thursday, and Memur was already back from her trip via Kansas City. Since the trip to New Haven was a two-day trip that I had already traveled twice, we stayed in Murfreesboro on Friday. This gave Memur a chance to invite a few of her closest friends to meet her new daughter-in-law, of whom she was obviously quite proud. Probably the most important thing about the one-day layover was the opportunity for my dad to become acquainted with Rebecca. It was another case of love at first sight. Also, I had a chance to have a long visit with Dad. Among other things, he told me that the money he spent to finance my trip to California was probably the best investment that he had ever made. I agreed with him.

The weather was good for our trip to New Haven. We were assisted greatly by the fact that we passed through both Washington and New York on Sunday. Not much snow had accumulated in New Haven, so we had no problem in driving our car through the narrow driveway to our garage. Since I was due to meet my thermodynamics class at nine o'clock the next morning, we unpacked the car and piled things in the middle of the floor, and left them for Rebecca to sort out while I went to my class on Monday. When I walked into the thermo class at 9:05 A.M. I was greeted by a standing ovation. Nobody thought that I could do it. I learned later that the members of the class had gotten up a betting pool based on the date of my return. The winner guessed Wednesday.

And so I settled down to doing graduate work, much less exciting and interesting, but less stressful—and never boring since I had Rebecca.

CHAPTER 6

YALE DAYS

After I got Rebecca with me, my outlook on life underwent a rapid metamorphosis. I began to enjoy life, and felt a return of self-confidence. I enjoyed the old fighting spirit; confidence that I could handle anything that might arise. We soon became oriented in our new surroundings and began to enjoy our new life together. We made friends with other married couples and enjoyed doing things together. Most of our entertainment revolved around the fact that Yale sold a student an athletic ticket for about $15, and sold his spouse one for about $10. Those numbers seem rather unrealistic, but they are not far off. These tickets included all sports, with rather good seats up high but near the 50-yard line for the big games with Princeton and Harvard. We became especially interested in ice hockey, which we had never had an opportunity to see before. We soon became a regular fixture at all the home games at the New Haven Arena, sitting right at the rail, dodging pucks and with Rebecca's feet freezing. We became so interested in hockey that we rarely went to a basketball game. Neither of us had played basketball in school, and had only a minor interest in it. These tickets were especially valuable because we had absolutely no spare money for entertainment. I recall only once that we had dinner at a restaurant during our residence in New Haven. When one married couple was invited to the home of another it was usually for playing bridge, with a very light dessert served.

The house I had rented for my bride was similar to others in the neighborhood, but very different from anything that we had experienced before.

It had three stories, with the first floor almost one story above ground level, so that the floor of the basement was only a few feet below ground level. It turned out that the basement was an apartment, which was rented to a young woman. We rented the first floor, which was called the main floor, and the second and third floors were rented to young women who were nurses at the nearby hospital. Our floor had some rather bizarre features, probably because it was not designed to have living quarters in it. In the front of our floor, which was directly on the sidewalk and touching the concrete of the walk, a narrow front room extended all the way across. The front wall of this room was a row of windows, so it was well lighted in the daytime. It was fitted with nice furniture, with a long couch extending under the front windows. This was a very nice place to sit and watch the world go by. A few days after we arrived, it began to snow soon after I went to work, and snowed all day. When I arrived home that night I found my bride on her knees on the couch in front of the front window. She had spent hours watching the snow come swirling down. It was a beautiful sight, especially to a person who had never seen snow fall. She had seen it on the ground in the mountains above Los Angeles, but had never seen any come down. I went down beside her on my knees, put my arm around her, kissed her a few times, then joined with her in watching the snow fall.

Behind this room, across the front of the house, was a sizable room probably used as a parlor, and next was a smaller room which was obviously a library, with lots of books along the walls. I did my studying in this room, at an ornate table in the middle of the room. There was a door in this room that opened to stairs which went down to the rented basement apartment, and another door which opened into the bathroom. This bathroom had a window in it which opened into the bedroom—that is correct, the only way to pass from the bathroom to the bedroom, or vice versa, was through this window, or walk into the library and then into the bedroom. Rather bizarre, but no further distance than is common between a bedroom and a bathroom. Beside the door from the library to the bedroom was a little room which was obviously designed as a closet, next to the bedroom. This was the kitchen. There was no door on the opening from the kitchen into the library because the cook had to stand in the doorway. There was a door from the bedroom that opened onto a landing on the stairs which went upstairs to the rented upper floors. There was also a door in the library that led into a little utility room which had a door to steps that went down to the back yard. This was my route to the little garage in back where I kept my car. Fortunately, there were a couple of snow shovels in the garage. We did a lot of snow shoveling. The narrow driveway beside the house accumulated only a little snow because it was sheltered by the buildings, and the short distance from the house to the garage was only slightly worse. Most of our shoveling was to clear a space to drive the car through the huge pile of snow that lined both sides of the streets soon after the heavy snows set in. The snow plows pushed the snow off the street onto these piles, which stayed there until the March thaw, except that when the downtown streets became overly filled by these piles of snow they were hauled to the harbor and dumped into the water. Shoveling a passage through the piles was the problem of the occupant of the house who owned a car. I don't remember anything about clearing the sidewalk while we lived on Chapel Street, so I presume that the city did that, just as they did for the streets. I do remember that there was a lot of snow to walk around in. For most of the winter and through the spring thaw there were streams of water flowing in all the drains at the edges of the streets. Every Yale student, and most of the rest of the people wore "arctic boots" for several months of the year. These were treated fabric boots about ten inches high, with buckles for facilitating frequently taking them on and off. Every true Yale man also wore pants whose leg bottoms stayed about four inches above the sidewalk. This avoided the nuisance of having to tuck one's pants inside the arctic boots to keep them out of the slush. Rebecca and I bought arctic boots very soon after our arrival in New Haven.

We soon began learning that the substitute landlord of this Chapel Street house had numerous duties. On the day after we arrived, just after I had gone to school, one of the nurses who rented the upstairs rooms knocked on the door from their stairway, and reported that they were in danger of frostbite because the hot water heat was not even getting to the second floor. After considerable exploration, Rebecca located the thermostat in the hall. She then set up communication with the nurse, who walked up and down the stairs, and finally learned where to set the thermostat to get heat to the top floor. This kept us nice and cozy—unless the furnace went out. About two weeks after our arrival, we woke up in the morning to find the house very cold. Examination revealed that the furnace was off and there was a pool of fuel oil on the floor of the basement. We called the furnace man whose phone number had been left with us by Dr. Sheehan. He came promptly, and removed the oil by dumping cement over it and shoveling the whole mess into a big bucket. He found that the furnace had failed to light, and the mercury switch that was supposed to cut off the oil flow in case of failure to light, had also failed. I watched this man carefully as he worked, and asked him a lot of questions so that I became able to handle the three mercury switches that controlled various things. In future months, I was able to save us and the nurses several days and/or nights of very low temperatures in the house.

There was another incident that was more easily handled than those just described. One night as I was studying at the library table, there was a knock at the door leading from the library to the stairs going to the downstairs apartment. When Rebecca answered the knock, the young lady who lived downstairs said, "May I please borrow your husband?" I jumped up immediately and said, "Of course." She had found a dead mouse in her bath tub, and wanted me to get rid of it for her. I did. After all, I had volunteered. We enjoyed good relations with this young lady. She worked for the State of Connecticut, and knew a lot about the operation of the state. For example, anyone who did not belong to the Catholic Church need not bother to apply for a job with the State of Connecticut. Later on in the spring, we began to notice a lot of people hiking around in the streets with crosses of ashes on their foreheads. Something about Easter . . .

During our residence on Chapel Street we became well acquainted with a young couple named Gordon and Marian Brown. Gordon was an immunologist who worked for one of the drug houses—I think it was Parke Davis. He was spending a year working on a project under Professor Anderson's direction. Since Anderson was my research director for graduate work, we met Gordon and Marian soon after our arrival. We spent several evenings with them playing contract bridge. We were in good agreement with them that a bridge game should be a social event rather than a rigid contest, and we had similar abilities. Since they were at Yale for only a year to work on a specific project, they were leaving at about the time that our rental on Chapel Street was to be terminated. When we played bridge at their place we found that they had a rather attractive attic apartment in a house in a very nice neighborhood on Whitney Avenue, which was out beyond the New Haven city limits and in the city of Hamden. Hamden was more a suburb of New Haven rather than a separate city. Since we needed a place to live when summer arrived, we inquired of the owners of the house if we could rent the apartment when the Browns left. Since the Browns had been good tenants, the owners of the house were pleased to have us succeed them as tenants. The owners were named Istas, of Belgian descent. He worked for the Winchester Arms Co. in New Haven. They had a grown son named Paul who had just finished dental school and who lived with them. Soon after we moved into the Istas's apartment, Paul married a girl named Olive, and the couple continued to live with the parents. For the next two years we saw a lot of the Istas family and enjoyed our association with them. We even did some gardening in their back yard, planted a lot of bearded iris from my mother which the Istases enjoyed for many years.

Yale University closed the chemistry laboratories for the months of July and August for reasons that were never revealed to me. So there was no reason for us to remain in New Haven for the summer, and there were several reasons for us to visit my parents in Murfreesboro during the period that the labs were closed. Of course we had to pay our rent while we were gone, but the trip to Murfreesboro cost less than our food for two months. A bunch of carrots cost only fifteen cents, but a gallon of gasoline cost about twenty cents. Naturally enough, the principal reason for our going to Murfreesboro during the summer was that my parents were anxious for us to do so. And both of us were eager to visit my parents and give them the opportunity to become better acquainted with Rebecca. As we had anticipated and hoped, the love affair between Memur and Rebecca blossomed, and Dad was obviously just as pleased. Both of them were proud of the wife I had brought home. Judging from fragments of conversations which I heard, I suspect that, in view of my rather unpromising behavior while I was growing up, there was some speculation about what kind of girl James would bring home from that notoriously wild state of California.

Rebecca suffered from the humid heat. There was no real relief from it, other than sitting under an electric fan when in the house; however, the downstairs in our house was relatively cool. The house had thick brick walls, and Memur would always open all the windows at bedtime and close them as soon as she got up, before the rest of us did. It was not always hot, but it seemed to Rebecca that it was. There were numerous events that attracted a lot of attention to Rebecca, and reactions to them were always positive. Rebecca got a reputation for being a "good sport"-not offended by trivial matters. I was proud of her. At about daybreak of our first morning, Rebecca woke me up to ask what was the horrible noise she was hearing, which seemed not to awaken me. After listening for a few moments, I heard the noise, and said, "That is merely a jackass braying." I explained that they were necessary for breeding to produce mules. After supper that night, Rebecca asked me what was the noise that was continuous and so loud that she could not hear what anybody was saying at the dinner table. That one stumped me; I could not hear a thing. After we went to bed, we had a session on "the noise." I realized that it must be something that I was accustomed to hearing much of the time. I had heard psychologists claim that there were many noises with which people were surrounded but did not hear because the ears learned to eliminate them and hear only desirable things. I asked Rebecca to tell me when the noise stopped, then tell me when it started. It was not continuous, but frequent. Finally it soaked through my head. It was the "dry flies," heard through most of the summer. I think it was a variety of locust. Whatever their official name, they make the noise by rubbing their wings together. It is a rather large bug that hatches out of a hard shell which remains stuck to the trees. As a child I gathered these shells, for some reason which I don't remember.

One of the most discussed events that was passed around among the "girls" in the Luncheon Club was amplified by the fact that the Luncheon Club had given us an expensive wedding present, a large silver tray. Rebecca had been alert to thank members of the Club whenever she met them. The occasion now being discussed happened soon after we had arrived, well before the reception that Memur gave for Rebecca. While Memur and I were away from the house the phone rang and Rebecca answered it. She told Memur that she was a little embarrassed by not being able to understand most of the conversation and asked the caller to spell her name so that she could report her call to Memur. She spelled out S M I T H. When Rebecca related the event to Memur, she said, "Oh, yes, I met her downtown and she told me she couldn't understand a word you said." During the reception for Rebecca, there was always a crowd around her; it reminded me of my problems as a teaching assistant when I first went to Cal. From all reports, Rebecca came through the reception smelling like a rose, even though she was so hot and sweaty that she wondered if she smelled like something else. Rebecca had not been properly oriented about carrying a little cane fan around with her to fan her face to prevent the sweat from dripping off her chin. The hot, humid weather in middle Tennessee in those days was the sort to "try men's souls." But Rebecca hung in there. She even agreed to go back to Tennessee with me when I accepted a teaching job at Vanderbilt University just before World War II. That decision was made a little easier by the fact that we were leaving Greencastle, Indiana. There were many times during those days when our love for each other was strained, but held firm.

There was not much for me to do during that summer, and the next one, but I did enjoy visiting with a few friends who were still in town, notably Kit Haynes, Tony DeGeorge and Henry Harrel. I also enjoyed the opportunity to get reacquainted with my parents. Dad and I enjoyed talking to each other on several evenings while sitting out in the front yard under a big maple tree. It usually cooled off enough to make it pleasant there after dark. Rebecca joined us occasionally after being anointed with Dad's "Skeeter Skoot." I remember Dad saying, "When a mosquito bites me on the neck, it makes my foot hurt."

I also did some carpentry work in Murfreesboro, using Dad's excellent array of carpentry tools. I made two little cabinets for storing chemical samples, both reagents used in my research and small samples of things I was working on. The latter type of sample was always small, kept in 2-4 milliliter vials. As these things became more numerous as I worked, I badly needed racks of some sort with holes for holding the small vials. With my crowded area in the Yale laboratory, the development of space became critical. Each of my boxes, equipped with a tier of narrow shelves and vial racks carried by the doors, measured about 12 x 18 x 24 inches. The front of the box, measuring 18 x 24 inches, was a swinging door with a latch on it. We had left the seat from the rumble seat in our car in New Haven, in anticipation of packing these boxes for transport to New Haven. These boxes proved very useful to me, not only for lab work but also as convenient storage for carrying samples of chemicals around from one lab to the next. I accumulated more samples as I progressed with my research. I carried these boxes from New Haven to Cambridge in the larger car we were to have by then; shipped them by van line from Cambridge to Greencastle, next to Nashville, and finally full circle back to Berkeley. In Berkeley, they were first deposited in the laboratory which also served as my office in the Old Chemistry Building. When Old Chem was demolished and the organic chemists moved into the new building named Latimer Hall, those two cabinets went with me to my new office on the eighth floor. In this final resting place, they remained until I was forced to retire, turned in my key at the college office, walked out leaving all my professional life behind me, and never looked back.

After we returned to New Haven, we rapidly settled into a very pleasant lifestyle based from our little apartment in the attic of the Istas's house in Hamden. This apartment was ideal for us; it even had a studio couch in the living room which could be used to accommodate a visiting couple. Bill and Laura Massie stayed overnight with us on one occasion, the first time that Rebecca had met them. I had not seen them since we went to the Chicago World Fair together before either Bill or I were married. All our recollections of this little apartment are pleasant-except for one sequence of a week or ten days, which seemed much longer at the time. There was a prolonged hot spell in New Haven, very hot indeed for that location, and our apartment was directly under the roof, with no insulation above us. We had good cross ventilation from an adequate number of windows, but in this very hot weather, by the time we finished a quick cold supper, the apartment reminded us of a tough day in Murfreesboro. Along with a significant percentage of the people on that side of New Haven, we fled to East Rock Park. This was (and presumably still is) a beautiful large area atop East Rock which juts several hundred feet above the surrounding flat land. We would lie on the grass under the trees, enjoy talking to each other, observing the life that went on around us. Some of this life was sufficiently interesting to keep us from being bored. I remember one event which we laughed about for days. A car drove up and numerous people piled out of it—we wondered where so many kids were stored in that car. Father and mother looked very harried. After everyone had gotten out of the car, father swung his arm around in a semicircle and yelled, "You kids scatter, and don't come back until midnight." We felt sorry for the man, but it was funny. Rebecca and I were able to avoid losing our sense of humor as we watched the surrounding scene. Except for this one hot spell, we greatly enjoyed our little apartment under the roof.

In the fall we enjoyed the football games. Yale had not yet succumbed to the idea of professional football, and going to the games was a lot of fun. We soon learned that Yale and Harvard had a mutual respect for each other, while each had contempt for Princeton. Some of the things done at the half of the game with Princeton were downright insulting, with nothing of the sort done at the Harvard game. During the second fall that we were there, the Harvard game was at New Haven. Rain was pouring down in sheets, and it was so cold that one wondered why the rain didn't freeze. Rebecca and I were wearing light overcoats—the only ones we had—and raincoats on top of them. Our seats were at about midfield as usual, at the very top of the stadium, which put us just below an entry portal. As we were huddled together waiting for the action to start, we heard a lot of loud talk behind us, and looked around to see what was going on. There was a row of five or six young people in rather common garb, topped by big coonskin coats and coonskin caps. As they surveyed the huge gathering of wet people, one of them announced in a loud voice, "I didn't realize that there are this many damn fools in the whole world." After guffawing loudly over this pronouncement, they worked their way down to their seats near the field.

In the winter it was ice hockey, which we had never seen before, and we really enjoyed — from seats at the rail. To hell with the flying pucks; we were good at dodging them. I doubt if we missed a single game during the two winters that we were in New Haven. In the spring came baseball, and this we had always enjoyed. During our last spring there, we sometimes attended the baseball games with George Waters, the first friend I had acquired during my days in the Hall of Graduate Studies. By this time George had gotten married — surreptitiously. His research director, Professor Harned, had a rule against his graduate students getting married. A rather ridiculous idea, but such crazy regulations were not uncommon in those days. As recently as 1950, the chairman of the chemistry department at Princeton, Hugh Taylor, ruled that no graduate student could be married because it detracted from the amount of work the man could do. A friend of mine who came to Berkeley on the teaching staff a few years after my arrival, Richard Powell, defied Hugh Taylor's decree. Taylor responded by taking his fellowship away from him. Dick did not tell me what he used for money after that. When Dick told me this story, I responded like a good Yale man, "Just what I would expect from Princeton."

Another thing that we enjoyed throughout the time we lived in Hamden was playing contract bridge with Joe and Bertha Hixon, who owned the house next door to the Istases. On the first day we arrived, Mrs. Hixon came over and introduced herself. After some conversation, she asked if we enjoyed playing bridge. When we answered in the affirmative she invited us to their house on the next Friday night to play bridge. This developed into a frequent occurrence which was always enjoyable. Dr. Hixon was a medical doctor who had retired after years of service in the Navy. He was currently serving as director of the Yale medical service, which was the unit of the university that took care of the students' medical problems. It was common in those days for universities to have this service, for which students paid a fee. Both Vanderbilt and the University of California had such services when I was a student. Bertha Hixon was quiet and friendly, while he was jovial and full of interesting stories—such as the one about having his automobile stolen. The insurance company had him fill out a questionnaire concerning the theft. One question was, "Was the car equipped with lock and key?" He answered,"yes," but did not tell them the key was in the lock. After all, they did not ask him. He had a little dog that looked like a tiny bulldog, a Boston Terrer, I think. His name was Andy Gump, named after a current comic strip character. Every night, at bedtime, Dr. Hixon let Gumpy out to attend to his business before going to bed for the night. Occasionally, Gumpy would not come back as soon as usual, whereupon Dr. Hixon would plead, with such as, "It's bedtime, Gumpy, come on in, precious." If Gumpy still did not appear, it became, "For crying out loud, Andy Gump, you come into this house right now." Gumpy always appeared. Dr. Hixon drove a big Cadillac, which sometimes would balk at starting on a very cold morning. First, he would come out with a tea kettle full of hot water and pour it over the carburetor. That usually worked, but sometimes it did not, and so he would hail me as I was coming out to go to work at the chemistry lab, and say something like,

"This big buggy of mine wants me to ride to work in your little Chevy." I was delighted to enjoy his company as we drove down to the Yale campus.

We enjoyed our two and a half years at Yale very much. In addition to things that have been described, we were involved in other things, such as ice skating, to a minor extent; however, at least three-fourths of my total hours awake were spent working at the laboratory on research directed towards obtaining a Ph.D. degree at the end of my third year. Some of this effort was directed to class work; however, the major amount of it was experimental work, all of which had to be done at the lab. This left Rebecca alone much of the time. For a few weeks she spent most of her free time searching for a job; however, the Depression was still in full force, and jobs were few and far between. She eventually located a job (from following newspaper ads, of course) which seemed ideal for her. It was clerking in a bookstore, and the job was still open when she arrived at the store. The woman who operated the store insisted that she needed a person with college education, and seemed about ready to hire Rebecca when she asked what work her husband did. When Rebecca told her that I was a graduate student in chemistry at Yale, that erased any hope of getting that job—and probably any other. The woman explained to Rebecca that so many people were unemployed that she would not feel right about giving this job to a person who did not depend on it for their daily bread. And so Rebecca had to find other things to occupy her time, and she did quite well at it.

Our first purchase with the little money we had available was a portable Singer sewing machine, which cost about a hundred dollars. Many years passed before we made another purchase of that size. Rebecca's mother, Rolena, was an expert seamstress, and taught home economics in high school. In those days, home economics meant just what the dictionary said about it. At the time we were married, Rebecca was an expert seamstress, hence the sewing machine we purchased with our nest egg. She repaired our clothes, and made all the new clothes she had during that period. She also made valuable Christmas presents at a low cost. She contributed a great deal to the comfort in which we lived—and continued to do so when the children arrived. That little machine has continued to be used , in spite of the fact that she now has a modern Singer.

Rebecca also enjoyed visiting with her friends, especially Mrs. Istas and Mrs. Hixon. She also enjoyed reading and listening to the news on our little portable radio. I helped a little by always coming home to have lunch with her unless the weather was very bad. On the days when she had the car, she would attend to her business in the morning and pick me up at the lab to go home for our usual lunch. We spent fifteen minutes of each lunch time with her curled up in my lap as I sat in our one big overstuffed chair, and we listened to a serial program that was on each weekday during the noon hour. The serial was called "One Man's Family," and we continued listening to an augmented version of it after we had been married for several years.

At about Christmas time during our last year at Yale, we became completely occupied with two things which consumed all our available time. One thing was my Ph.D. thesis and the concomitant typing of George Waters's Ph.D. thesis by Rebecca. The other thing was much less time consuming, but more important. Before Christmas, we began having serious discussions with ourselves concerning the question of when we should start attempting to have a family. We had concluded as early as our wedding date that we should not consider starting a family until: (A) we had enjoyed the bliss of married life together for at least two years, without the worries, responsibilities, and frustrations which inevitably accompany the raising of children; and (B) we had reasonable expectations of being able to support a family. Proceeding from these rather qualitative principles, we concluded that we should not defer the starting of the family any longer than necessary because of item B, on the grounds that this greatest of all tasks in life should be undertaken when one is young, strong, and self-confident. Next there followed the really difficult decision: Should we wait until we actually had a job that could support us, or should we proceed on the basis of confidence that I would be able to land a job immediately after getting my degree. At the beginning of my last year at Yale, I was notified that I had been awarded a fellowship which was assigned to the person in the graduating class who was regarded as ranking No. 2 in the class. Since the rumor mill had it that the No. 1 man had always been a Yale undergraduate, we concluded that if anybody got a job after graduation, it would be me. Therefore, we decided that the time had come to find out how good we were at reproduction. Rebecca became pregnant on first exposure. Roger's birth was in early October. In retrospect, I daresay that one reason we dashed ahead with self-confidence was my Dad's statement to me as I was preparing to leave home and go on the trip to California: "Whatever you do, please remember that I stand ready to assist you if you need help, to the best of my ability." As I have stated before, I have never forgotten those simple words.

As for the matter of Rebecca locating competent medical assistance, we lucked out again. Dr. Hixon was able to assist us, first by recommending a competent man in New Haven, and then by doing the same thing for that very important event, the delivery in Boston. It happened that Dr. Hixon had a nephew, Ben Cornwall, who was an obstetrician practicing in Boston. Obviously, having this sort of thing prearranged before we went to Cambridge took a load off our minds. We were to go to Cambridge because I had gotten an appointment as a post-doctoral research assistant with Professor Louis Fieser at Harvard.

The matter of getting a job that I wanted had begun to demand a lot of my attention at about the same time that Rebecca and I were occupied with our plans for reproduction. What forced me to consider this matter was that the chemical industry began sending their personnel representatives to the major universities to interview students who were completing their Ph. D. theses. I had decided that I wanted to do post-doctoral work in order to increase my leverage in getting a desirable university teaching position. A post-doctoral fellowship was not a prerequisite to obtaining a teaching position at a major research university, but it was so important that it amounted to a prerequisite because of the scarcity of university positions in those days of the Depression—even worse than for industrial positions. I had applied for a National Research Council (NRC) fellowship, one of the few available where the recipient could go anywhere he so desired, with no strings attached. In view of the scarcity of such positions, I also interviewed with industrial representatives. The first of these men to arrive was from DuPont, a man named Tanberg. I was aware that DuPont was regarded as the most desirable company for an organic chemist to work for. I was not aware that A. J. Hill, chairman of the department at Yale, had an understanding with Dr. Tanberg to "supply" him with the best organic chemist graduating in a given year. Having no powers of prophecy, I also was unaware that I was destined to have future relations with Dr. Tanberg which would cause me to have great respect for the man. In view of these things which I did not know, I was quite surprised to receive a telegram from Tanberg on about the fifth day after my interview with him. He offered me a job with DuPont, stating the salary and the laboratory in which I would work. He also stated that he required an answer to his telegram within forty-eight hours. I was really on the horns of a dilemma. I received the telegram at the laboratory in the early afternoon. After thinking about it for about a half hour while weighing a sample on the micro balance for an analysis, I realized that I should consult my research director, Professor R. J. Anderson, who had been particularly nice to me through the years. Soon after I returned with a wife, he invited Rebecca and me to a dinner at his house, to which his other research students had also been invited. As soon as I had explained my problem to him, he asked me where I would go if I should get the NRC fellowship. I replied that it would be with Professor Louis Fieser, for I was fascinated with his work on carcinogenic hydrocarbons. He told me that Fieser was well supplied with money to hire research assistants because of the importance of his work, and that he had hired another of his (Anderson's) graduate students a few years before, a man named Melvin Newman. He then asked if I would like him to telephone Fieser, in order to learn whether he would like to hire me as a post-doctoral assistant. Naturally, I said that I would be delighted if he would do this for me. He told me to go back into the lab and get to work while he telephoned and learned if he could contact Fieser. He would come to the lab and tell me what had happened. He knew that I would be on "pins and needles" while waiting, and that it would be best for me to be doing something. So I started the combustion analysis for which I had been weighing the sample when the interruption occurred. I have no idea how much time elapsed before Professor Anderson returned, but I do remember that I had just finished the analysis, and hence did not lose the result because of an interruption. When Professor Anderson returned, he wasted no time in telling me that Fieser had said, "Since you tell me that this man is as good as Melvin Newman, I will hire him. Tell him to make arrangements with me to come up here and talk to me as soon as convenient." WOW! I closed down my work for the day and went home to give the news to Rebecca. The next day I sent an apologetic telegram to Dr. Tanberg, explaining that after he had interviewed me I had been offered a job by Louis Fieser. I heard nothing from A.J. Hill about this matter until about two months later, after the interview season was over. He told me that if I had been unable to get an academic appointment there was a job that had come in with the Baker Castor Oil Co. in which I might be interested. I enjoyed telling him that I had a job with Professor Fieser. I had been alerted that I was really in the dog house with Hill, for having broken the commitment Hill had with DuPont to supply the best organic chemistry graduate to them.

At this point, I was unburdened by anything distracting me from cleaning up a few ends of my research, which were necessary for completion of the thesis, before launching full bore into thesis preparation. When George Waters learned that both Rebecca and I were good typists and were planning to type my thesis, he asked if we would be interested in Rebecca typing his thesis, at the going rate of pay, with me typing my thesis. Since my old portable typewriter, bought for me by Dad before I entered Vanderbilt, did not have very good type, such as a thesis ought to have, we decided to accept George's offer and thus raise the money to pay for a new portable typewriter. George was a physical chemist and would probably have numerous pages of tables in his thesis. Tables were such slow going, with the facilities available to a typewriter at that time, that typing each page of tables cost about fifty per cent more than was charged for other pages. Thus, Rebecca's income would depend on both the number of pages in George's thesis and also the number of tables. Based on George's estimate, we figured that the typing of his thesis would bring Rebecca about what the typewriter would cost. This turned out to be about right. At that time, there was no practical way of obtaining two copies except by use of carbon paper, and two copies of a thesis were required. Besides the ribbon copy, which went to the library, the author of the thesis naturally wanted a copy, as did the research director. These copies are the bane of a typist's existence—two carbon copies to erase besides the ribbon copy. One mistake was worth about a half page of double spaced typing. In our spirit of self-confidence and willingness to face a challenge, we decided that we could do it—and we were right. There were some frustrating times, especially with those tables in George's thesis, but we did it.

In organic chemistry theses, it was customary to have a rather long introductory section, followed by a discussion of results, and finally the specific details of the experimental work. In case papers based on the thesis were published, the research director's name appeared first, after the

title, and the names of any students who did the experimental work followed. This practice was ordinarily followed in the field of chemistry in
this country, and was reasonable. The research problem was proposed by
the professor and was often a part of ongoing research which eventually
involved many students and/or post-doctoral fellows. The research director always wrote the paper, and the experimental part of the paper came
from the thesis, frequently verbatim, or from the report made to the professor by a post-doctoral assistant. This system worked very well unless
the professor failed to keep in close touch with what the experimenter was
doing. There have been a few infamous cases in which the failure of the
professor to know what the experimenter was doing resulted in publication of fraudulent data. Of course, this sort of thing is more likely to occur
when the professor becomes famous and thus accumulates such large
groups of workers that he cannot keep in touch with what is going on. It
can happen to a Nobel Prize winner. Professor Anderson did not have a
large group, and kept "right on top" of what was happening in the laboratory. Two papers based on my research appeared in the Journal of
Biological Chemistry, and mine was the only student name on the papers.
The particular journal in which these papers appeared was inevitable since
R. J. Anderson was editor of that journal during the period I worked for
him, and for many years before and after my tenure there.

As is apparent, typing two theses on the same typewriter requires
some coordination. Since I had considerable library work to do in writing
the first section of the thesis, and physical chemists do not usually have
much in the way of the first section common in organic chemistry theses,
George began feeding copy to Rebecca before I started typing. After I started typing, I still spent considerable time conferring with Professor
Anderson. This eventually worked out so that Rebecca was able to finish
George's thesis before I finished mine. Thus, she was available to finish
typing my thesis. I had spent considerable time all along taking what I had
typed for Anderson to inspect and approve. Approval at this stage was
usually a matter of proofreading since the original rough draft of the thesis had already been worked over by Professor Anderson. No problems
developed which we could not handle, and both theses were turned in on
time for me to get my degree at spring graduation. This was important
since Memur had made the trip from Murfreesboro to attend my third

graduation ceremony—fourth if one counts my graduation from the McCallie School, where I delivered the valedictorian address. I cannot claim to remember it, but I daresay that she attended my graduation from the Crichlow Grammar School, where I was awarded a little medal for making the highest grade in arithmetic in the eighth grade. If there had been another graduation I am sure that she would have attended it. She covered my graduations coast to coast.

After the Yale graduation ceremony, Memur returned by train to Murfreesboro, and Rebecca and I attended to all formalities about filing my thesis. We then packed all our belongings into the Chevrolet coupe and drove to Murfreesboro, where we remained as in the two preceding summers. We were not expected at Harvard until the fall, for Harvard closed up their chemical laboratories during the month of September. We did not realize that this trip to Murfreesboro would be our last in the Chevy coupe, but we learned otherwise on the day after our arrival. Dad took us down to Jackson Bros. Garage, which was in a building rented from Dad, to show us the new Chevrolet four door sedan which he had bought for us. Among other things, he said, "Any man who has just been awarded a Ph.D. degree from Yale, and is expecting his wife to deliver a baby within a few months, deserves a bigger and better car than you have." We were surprised and rather overwhelmed. We had already been discussing how we would manage things when our child had grown larger than a baby. As usual, Dad came through like a champ.

CHAPTER 7

HARVARD DAYS

I was scheduled to go to work for Louis Fieser on October 1, since the chemical laboratories at Harvard were closed during the month of September. However, we left Murfreesboro several days before that to give us time to locate a place to live before I became occupied with working at the Converse Laboratory. When we contacted a real estate agent, we had several surprises. The most important surprise was that it was virtually impossible to rent a furnished apartment. This may have resulted from practices originating with Harvard students, but for whatever reason, it was necessary for us to first rent an apartment, then rent our furniture for a year. This proved to be less formidable than it sounded at first.

The first rental apartment that the real estate agent showed us was on a one block long street named Everett Street, which was adjacent to Harvard property on which tennis courts were located. The three or four story apartment building had been finished a few months earlier and was only about half rented, so the landlord was willing to make a one-time waiver of the rule against children which was in effect for this new apartment. A casual glance at Rebecca revealed that this rule would otherwise apply to us. Our rental agreement stated that we would not be allowed to stay after the original one-year contract. The apartment was only about three blocks from the Converse Laboratory, and there was provision for parking our car—I do not remember whether this was in a garage or outside, on land owned by the apartment owner. Naturally enough, I guess, we decided to look no further for an apartment. We had lucked out again.

There remained the matter of renting our furniture. The real estate agent advised us to consult Fournier, who was the kingpin of furniture rental. The address that we were given proved to be a large building about two blocks off Harvard Square, which gave the appearance of being a warehouse, which it was. We walked in the door to find a very large room with no obvious occupant; however, there were strains of beautiful violin music emanating from the rear of the room. Investigation revealed a man of obvious Italian descent who was really enjoying playing his violin. As a matter of fact, we also found the music enjoyable; however, we remembered our mission and interrupted the music. If this story sounds unreal, I will interrupt myself to report that Fournier was a venerable and respected institution, known by dozens of people scattered throughout the United States with whom we had chance encounters in subsequent years. When we told him the size of the apartment for which we needed furniture, he responded promptly with, "That will cost you $115 for a year, cash on the barrel head; I only rent for a one-year period." Since we had come to this unknown territory with most of the money we owned on our persons, we paid him the sum required on the spot. He then told us to look around and pick out everything that we wanted, and he would deliver it today if we so desired. We were pleased about that, since it would save us another night in the hotel; however, we were not prepared to present a list of what we wanted. Fournier said that we probably could pick out what we would need by looking around, but that he would not charge us for delivering one or two pieces later. It turned out that we had no trouble finding everything we expected to need. Some of the furniture was very good, some rather beat up and some in good shape. Having no powers of prophecy, we had no inkling of the bizarre future in store for that furniture. This future started only about six months later, when Fournier knocked on our door to tell us that if we paid him the $115 which a second year of rental would cost us, the furniture was ours. This time we paid him with a check which he accepted cheerfully, and signed a piece of paper saying that the furniture was ours. We gave away or sold pieces of that furniture to others who were remaining behind as we went on our nomadic way. Two chests of drawers came with us all the way to a final resting place in California.

On the day that I was due to start work with Louis Fieser, I went to his office in the Converse Laboratory at about 8:30 in the morning. He was already there. The first thing he did was take me down to the laboratory where I would work. It was a rather large room for only two workers, with an adjoining smaller room which contained apparatus, such as a low pressure hydrogenator, used whenever needed by anyone in Fieser's group. This side room also contained a glass-blowing table, with blow torches and other necessary equipment, which was destined to become very useful to me. In comparison with other places where I had done research, I felt like I had arrived in heaven. And this was before I had become acquainted with my lab partner, E. B. Hershberg, who came into the lab a few minutes after Fieser and I arrived. I learned later how he came to be known as "E. B." According to the story, when Hershberg came to work with Fieser, he was told that "we are rather informal around here; what is your first name?" The response was "Emanuel," whereupon Louis responded with, "My God, we will call you E. B." And so E. B. (pronounced Ebie with accent on the "E") it was, then and forever to all chemists. By the time that Ebie became director of research at Schering Corp. there were a great many chemists who knew how to pronounce the E. B. that appeared on a myriad of research papers. Besides the research papers, there was the Hershberg melting point outfit, the Hershberg stirrer, and other things that became regular items listed for sale by laboratory supply houses. Ebie was a better glass blower than the professional who worked for the Harvard Chemistry Department, and as good a machinist as the head of the machine shop. In addition to all that, he was the most skillful experimental organic chemist that I had the good fortune to know during my fifty years as a professional chemist. During my two years at Harvard, I learned more organic chemistry, especially experimental organic chemistry, than I had learned during all my previous years of study, which included work for an M. S. and a Ph. D. degree. This was due to several things: Louis Fieser organized and handled his group in such a way that its members were friendly with both Fieser and other members of the group, with a lot of information passing back and forth. Of course, I benefited more than most of the others because of Louis assigning me to be Ebie's lab partner. Fieser's international reputation was such that many promising young chemists came to work with him, and Louis made a particular point of learning whatever each of these people knew that would be useful to him. He lapped up information like a bee hunting for pollen. As will be reported later, he even managed to learn a few small things from me.

After Louis had shown me the lab where I would work and introduced me to Ebie, we returned to his office, and he outlined the specific problem on which I would work. When I visited him during the spring, according to his suggestion to Professor Anderson, he had formally offered me a job, but said that he had two different positions open, and I could choose whichever one I preferred. One position was to be a research assistant to him and work on whatever problem he decided to assign to me. The other was to manage the laboratory that was a part of the introductory course in organic chemistry which he taught. I had not expected to be offered this choice, but I wasted no time at all in saying that I wanted to be his research assistant. I knew what the ground rules in academia were: "Publish or perish." I knew that I could not possibly produce as much research working on my own as by working on problems developed by a prominent, experienced organic chemist. And having Louis Fieser's name on the paper ahead of mine meant that he was responsible for the validity of the work. I later came to learn that this was more important than I had realized at that time. The specific problem I was assigned was synthesis of the compound, 1',9-methylene-1,2-benzanthracene. This compound was used for testing for carcinogenic activity, needed for a comparison with similar compounds which had been established as carcinogenic. Thus, I became a part of the organic chemistry involved in establishing a firm basis for chemical carcinogenesis. I had asked Fieser to put me on problems in this field. Throughout the time I worked for Fieser, I was stimulated by the realization, promoted by Louis, that I was doing important work, which made it essential that I do it right.

During the period I worked for Fieser, interest in development of the basis for chemical carcinogenesis was at its peak. Several years earlier a group of scientists in England, which included biologists, chemists and physicists, had established beyond any doubt that the prevalence of cancer among coal tar workers was due to something in the coal tar, the gooey mess resulting from destructive distillation of soft coal. The numerous chemicals present in coal tar were the basis of a considerable portion of the chemical industry of that day. Eventually, a substance named benzpyrene was isolated in a pure state, identified, and shown to cause the appearance of malignant tumors in mice or rats a relatively short time after being painted on the skin in solution or applied by injection. There followed a period of synthesis of compounds having some feature or features of structure similar to the structural features found in benzpyrene. The principal workers in this field were synthetic organic chemists, and most of the work was being done in the laboratory of Louis Fieser or the laboratory of J. W. Cook in London. It was a very exciting time for all of us who worked with Fieser during this period.

Just before World War II cut off this research, as well as most other ongoing research in this country, Fieser was given the "Memorial Hospital Award for 1941" in recognition of his leading a significant part of the work that established a firm basis for chemical carcinogenesis. With behavior characteristic of the man, Fieser then sent each of us who worked with him during that period a silver plated letter opener, with an inscription indicating our participation in the work for which he received the award. I have this letter opener before me just now; it is inscribed as follows:

> To J. CASON
>
> Memorial Hospital Award for 1941
>
> L. F. Fieser

Before I started to work on compounds that were potentially carcinogenic, I received a briefing from the medical doctor doing the testing of the compounds produced in Fieser's laboratories. This briefing gave us details of how to handle these compounds without risk of becoming a cancer victim. There were just a few basic principles, which included the following:

1. In all transfers of solid compounds, work on a piece of black glass, a square about 24 inches on a side. The tiniest speck of dust or anything else is clearly visible on a well illuminated piece of black glass. Of course, the glass is kept clean.

2. In the case of solid compounds, never stir them around so as to flip fragments into the air. This prevents not only inhaling, but getting the stuff into one's clothes. We did not work in a forced draft hood for such transfers, thinking that a wind blowing around one while doing this kind of work is not a good idea, even if the wind is directed away from one. Eddy currents in a wind are treacherous; it is best to depend on a careful worker doing the right thing.

3. All glassware used for running reactions is handled only on the outside until it is placed with tongs into a bath of hot sulfuric acid containing nitric acid. There is no organic chemical that can hold together under that kind of treatment.

There was some prose amplifying these basic principles, but nothing significant was added. Compared to the kinds of precautions that are prescribed by law in the days of this writing, these procedures seem pitifully inadequate. No rubber gloves; no high capability filter masks, no changing of clothes after work each day. These things are no substitute for a careful, capable worker. As has already been mentioned, many of the people who were attracted to work with Fieser lived to become sufficiently prominent that it was usually possible to keep up with their activities by attending meetings of the American Chemical Society, reading the journals, etc. A pessimist might follow the obituaries in Chemical and Engineering news. I presume that there must have been an occasional person who worked with Fieser and later came down with cancer; however, I am unaware of any such. I am confident that if any of those who worked on these carcinogens with Fieser had developed cancer within a few years, all of us would have heard about it. Could it be that people who know how to protect themselves against cancer are unlikely to develop a malignant tumor? Could it be that the things that are really important in protection against cancer have become so buried in a torrent of prose that only a few highly informed people are able to dig out the gold? As is apparent, these important matters can be properly handled only in a full chapter devoted to them.

It saddens me—almost unbearably—to report that, some thirty-five years after he had worked on carcinogenic hydrocarbons, Louis Fieser developed lung cancer. He was a heavy cigarette smoker. I have forced myself to make this report in the hope that some people will read it and get the message as to what does cause cancer and what does not cause cancer.

After I had discussed my research project with Louis, been briefed on how to do the work without exposing myself to cancer, and done some library work, my next move, of course, was to check out from the stockroom the equipment needed for my work. Louis had told me to discuss with him any equipment that was not in the stockroom, and hence needed to be ordered. I had a few surprises in learning the difference between the

Yale and Harvard stockroom practices. Early in the process, I learned that the two stockrooms actually had different names for the same item of equipment. I needed a large burner in order to heat a large quantity of material. In every laboratory in which I had worked, from Vanderbilt to Berkeley to Yale, this item was known as a Meeker burner. The stockroom keeper advised me that they did not have a Meeker burner, and also advised me that it was strictly forbidden for me to look around in the stockroom for the item I wanted. On peering around on the shelves I could see from the stockroom window several burners which seemed to me to be Meeker burners. When I asked the name of the burner to which I pointed, the rather peevish answer was, "Those are Harvard burners." And so I checked out a Harvard burner and went on my way; I learned later that they also had something called a Harvard beaker. Within a few weeks, I had my equipment assembled and was turning out some work, more rapidly than I had expected because of the excellent facilities.

After only a few days spent assembling my equipment, the time arrived for the birth of our first child. As Rebecca and I were getting ready for bed, she discovered that she was bleeding. Since the obstetrician, Dr. Ben Cornwall, had advised her that she should go to the hospital when that happened, I took her to the division of Massachusetts General Hospital which was called Baker Memorial Hospital. This was for people of modest means, which included us since I had a job. At Baker Memorial, there was a set fee which included both the obstetrician and the hospital fees. I do not remember the size of this fee, but I remember that I had on hand $200 earmarked to pay this bill. Boston bluebloods and other rich people went for delivery to the hospital known as Phillips House, where the doctors could charge whatever they chose to charge. Those at the poverty level, which was poorly defined, went to the parent Mass. General Hospital. There were some other things about birthing in those days and at this place which were radically different from anything known today.

After I had taken Rebecca to the proper place for entering the maternity ward, I then went to the waiting room to await a report from Dr. Cornwall. After what seemed to me like a long time, but was probably less than an hour, Dr. Cornwall came in and told me that the birth was not imminent, that I should go home and get some sleep, and he would call me immediately after the baby was born. I got a call the next morning, but the report was that labor had not set in. Subsequent events are based on Rebecca's report. She was not in pain and had no contractions as she was kept in bed. When there had been no change on the second day, the nurses decided that something had to be done to generate some action. With one of them holding each hand, they had her run up and down the hall, and that did it. The diaphragm ruptured. As she went into labor, she was given medication so that "I was completely out of it; I can recall no great pain." Both of us feel thankful that she was not subjected to the practices that are in vogue today for birthing. Rebecca is almost willing to forgive them for keeping her in the hospital for twelve days after the birth, as was required in those days.

I visited Rebecca each day that she was required to stay in the hospital, and naturally took the occasion to take pictures of our newborn son, Roger. For Rebecca's roommate, who delivered on the same day that Rebecca did, this birth seemed to be about her third. Her husband was frequently there when I was, and so we became somewhat acquainted with each other. We walked out together on the last day before our wives were scheduled to go home, and he was filling me in on what to expect when the baby arrived at home. One comment he made was, "I should warn you that the first year is just hell." I felt sorry for him and the rest of the Catholics who are so abundant in both Connecticut and Massachusetts. The first year really is no bed of roses.

I think that the only thing on which Rebecca and I ever decided to disagree with my parents to the point of finally refusing to yield, was the naming of our baby if it should prove to be a boy. My brother had already had three girls, of which one had died as a baby, and so my parents only hope for a Junior was with us. I never discussed this matter with them on the grounds that an argument in advance of the necessity for such a discussion would be essentially open-ended, and provide unlimited opportunities to build up antagonism that might leave scars lasting a lifetime. On the other hand, if the basis of the disagreement is not known until after the fait accompli, the time available for argument is very much abbreviated. My grounds for feeling strongly about the matter were twofold: I am a Junior, and it proved to be quite a nuisance on various occasions. I encountered one such when I first drove into California, as has been recounted in an earlier chapter. Another problem was that my son could not be Junior, because I was already occupying that name. My son would have to be the Third, designated as III, and I would have had even stronger objections to that. Somehow, all the people I have known who had a III or IV hung onto their moniker were stuffed shirts or some kind of oddballs. This could be realistic because the name of a kid is very likely to reflect something about the genes inherited from those who applied the name. One of the most "unusual" people that I have ever known was named Isaac Croom Beattie IV. He was a rather likable guy, and I enjoyed his company as long as I did not get too much of it in one dose. At least twenty-five pages would be required to even begin to describe this guy.

Whatever might be the background of our naming our first-born Roger, we had principally in mind selecting a name that would not be disliked by its owner, and would be more likely to generate an advantage rather than a handicap. Not a name that is difficult to understand and spell; not a name that is also carried by a horde of people (when I was in a six-man squad in military school, three of us were named James—honest, that happened). So Rebecca and I examined various lists of names and considered the desirability of each on a competitive basis. When my Uncle Chicken wrote and inquired, "I guess Roger is an OK name, but where the hell did you dig that one up?" I replied, "We selected it from the names on a list of people attending the Junior Prom at Yale." That was the honest truth, but Chicken thought I was being facetious.

When I told Memur over the phone that her new grandson was named Roger, she responded in part, "I don't know whether I could ever love a little baby named Roger." After about twenty-four hours of taking care of "that little baby," Memur had completely forgotten about having ever said anything like that. As I noted previously, it pays to keep the time available for argument limited. Serendipitous events may walk upon the scene. As soon as I learned the day that Rebecca could leave the hospital, I advised Memur of it, since she had promised Rebecca that she would come to Cambridge to help her with the baby for a few days. I picked her up at the railroad station on the day before Rebecca's arrival at home was scheduled. We had already rented a bed from Fournier to put in the living room. Roger's crib was in our bedroom after Memur left, but while Memur was there I think it was in our little hall which had a wide door into the living room. Neither Rebecca nor I can remember whether Memur went to the hospital with me to bring Rebecca and Roger home. Both of us can remember how helpful Memur was until Rebecca got up to speed for doing hard work again.

Memur stayed to help us longer than originally planned, because of Rebecca developing mastitis, so that it was necessary to put Roger on a bottle. At this stage, we were already being advised by Dr. John Davies, the pediatrician recommended to us by our obstetrician, Dr. Ben Cornwall. I also telephoned my brother, John, who was practicing medicine as an obstetrician and pediatrician in Murfreesboro, to get his opinion about the merits of breast feeding versus bottle feeding. He responded that he had been unable to find any valid evidence against bottle feeding, other than the emotional impact on the mother. Ergo, if the mother is having difficulty with breast feeding, a shift to the bottle is clearly indicated. Roger prospered on bottle feeding, and so did Rebecca; after a few days she felt able to carry on alone, so Memur returned to Murfreesboro.

Not long after Memur left, Rebecca came down with a virus infection, which soon progressed to me. Unfortunately this was years before I became acquainted with the minor miracles that can be wrought by vitamin C. Both of us were rather sick, no doubt due to the strain under which we had been living recently—a strain on the immune system. Dr. Davies recommended an agency which helps in such situations, and they sent a middle aged woman to help us. She was truly a gem. She helped us to apply precautions against Roger getting the infection. Our efforts were successful, so we told our helper, after three or four days, that we could get along without her. But she showed up at eight o'clock the next morning, and said that we really needed her for at least one more day, and she would work without being paid. I told her that we would pay her, come what may. I kept thinking of a comment that my dad made on an earlier occasion, "I will find the money if I have to steal it." During our four and a half years in New England, both Connecticut and Massachusetts, we met so many people who helped us when we needed it. We have remained eternally grateful to all of them.

During our sickness, I missed several days of work. My problem was exacerbated by the fact that I had begun to have chronic asthma soon after we arrived in Cambridge. The problems of an asthmatic are always amplified if a virus infection is added. For alleviation of the symptoms, I followed the advice of my brother, who also had recurring problems with an allergy. The problem which interfered most with my efforts to live normally and stay at work was being awakened at night gasping for breath. In those days the only defense against allergy problems, other than alleviation of symptoms, was the long, drawn out procedure of consulting an allergist, who would engage in a search for the cause of the allergy. According to John, this procedure did not have a good record for solving the problem, so I decided to tough it out for a while by taking ephedrine when I was awakened at night, and taking a hypnotic to get back to sleep in spite of the effect of the ephedrine as a pressor amine. There was a prescription sold which put the proper dosage of ephedrine and Amytal in the same capsule. Of course, my getting up once or twice per night was not helpful to Rebecca during the period when she had to get up at night with Roger.

After a few months of this lifestyle, I decided that the time had come to consult an allergist. On the advice of friends I went to an organization called the Lahey Clinic, which bore a considerable resemblance to the modern day health maintenance organization (HMO). After a sort of general physical examination which had some painful aspects, I was told that I should make an appointment with their allergist. I paid up and said nothing, but I was thinking plenty, such as, "Thanks for nothing." At this stage of events, it finally soaked through my head that I should have asked Dr. Davies, Roger's pediatrician, for advice on consulting an allergist. Better late than never! Starting with my first meeting with Dr. Walter Burrage, my life was literally turned around. Of all the wonderful people that I met in New England, Dr. Burrage was the King. After listening to my story, he said that he would start on skin tests for allergens on my next visit to him, but that the most important thing for the immediate present was getting control of my symptoms so that I could stay at work without suffering a loss of ability by not sleeping properly at night. He gave me a prescription for 1:100 epinephrine (adrenaline), which is ten times the concentration used for injection, and a simple spray (not very different from the "atomizer" used for spraying perfume) to be used for spraying the epinephrine directly into my throat. I will never forget the sensation that flashed through my mind two minutes after I used that spray for the first time: "I am sure that I can make it now." A very important aspect of using this spray was that there was no systemic effect of the epinephrine, hence no interference with my sleep. Dr. Burrage was destined to become a very important man in my life for more than ten years. He never charged me much. During the early days, he charged me $15 per month, even if I visited him more often. He also made modest charges for the anti-allergy vaccine for year-round use to control my problems during the ragweed allergy season. He instructed me on how to make the injections to avoid the danger of anaphylactic shock, and also how to handle anaphylactic shock if I should make a mistake. He continued to prepare and send me the several strengths of material for years until I escaped the ragweed season by migrating to California. I cannot imagine, in the wildest flights of my imagination, a modern day medical doctor doing anything like that.

Before Christmas of 1938, the year I started working for Louis Fieser, I was able to get my personal problems under control. At this point, I shifted into overdrive, doing experimental work on the problems that Fieser assigned to me. I worked very hard, and for long hours, for at least two reasons which were probably of about equal importance in stimulating me. One reason, which was rather obvious, was that I was well aware of the ground rules which were applicable in securing a teaching job in a major university. Because the nation was still in the grip of the Great Depression, these jobs were scarce. I knew the papers that Fieser published that were based on my research would be a key factor in my getting a job in a major research university. The other reason was that, for all of my life, I found satisfaction and pride in doing the best job that I could do. Even if I failed, I was satisfied if I had done my best. This instinct controlled several of my actions after I became a professor at the University of California, and eventually resulted in my becoming one of a very small crowd of people who were able to defeat the Peter Principle. But that is a story for another chapter.

As has been mentioned previously, the first project which Fieser assigned to me was "Synthesis of 1',9-Methylene-1,2-benzanthracene and Related Hydrocarbons." The paper of this title was submitted to the Journal of the American Chemical Society (JACS) on 5/3/39, and was published in the July issue. The next paper was submitted on 12/18/39, the next one on 3/20/40, and the fourth one on 7/20/40. A fifth paper based on my work was published in the JACS about a year after I had left Harvard. The intervals of time between the submission of these papers is rather deceiving, for I was usually working on at least two projects at any given time. The project which received attention at a given time depended on several inter-related factors, such as: waiting for apparatus which had been ordered; waiting while searching for an industrial supplier of a needed chemical; working on one project while cogitating about another, or searching literature for clues.

The fourth paper in the above-cited sequence was by far the most difficult of all the work I did for Fieser. It was entitled, "Synthesis of 4',8'-Dihydroxy-1,2,5,6-dibenzanthracene and its Relation to Products of Metabolism of the Hydrocarbon." I started work on this project at about the same time that I started on the project which resulted in the third paper on the list. This work was done in cooperation with biologists in an effort to discover whether carcinogenic activity was due to the hydrocarbon or to some metabolic product from the hydrocarbon. This work was stimulated by the observations that different hydrocarbons resulted in different latent periods before the appearance of a tumor. In all the work with which Fieser and other chemists were associated, the potency of the carcinogen was assigned on the basis of how quickly a tumor appeared after application of the carcinogen. On this basis, one of the three most potent carcinogens was 1,2,5,6-dibenzanthracene, and it was chosen on the basis that it was most amenable to synthesis in order to identify the dihydroxy-dibenzanthracene isolated in the biological studies. In order to supply enough material to carry through a difficult multi-step synthesis to the desired end-product, I had to make about 150 g. of 1,2,5,6- dibenzanthracene, process it in several batches, and use it to carry through on subsequent steps of the synthesis. Since each step was synthesis of a new, previously unknown compound, it was necessary to select a synthetic method at each step, find out if it worked, and learn how to get the yield up to supply material for the next step. The next-to-last step in the synthesis was so difficult that I had to go back and prepare more dibenzanthracene.

This is why that was the last paper which Fieser published on my work before I left Harvard. As was the case for the other papers based on my experimental work, Louis wrote this paper on the basis of the report I gave him. When the paper appeared in the JACS, I noted that the authors were listed as James Cason and Louis F. Fieser, in that order. I later noted that the authors were listed in that same order on the paper published after

I had left Harvard. On page 4 of this chapter, there appears the following statement: "Having Louis Fieser's name on the paper ahead of mine meant that he was responsible for the validity of the work." I trust that no comment is needed concerning the significance of Fieser putting my name ahead of his on these two papers. This clear and unequivocal signal may well have had great significance in my eventually becoming a professor in one of the three or four most prestigious chemistry departments in the United States.

During all of my work with Louis Fieser, I had no qualms at all about the possibility of my becoming a cancer victim. The idea did not enter my head; I was too busy concentrating on doing the right things at all times. As a matter of fact, it was good training for the work with which I became involved during World War II: first high explosives, then poison bullets.

During the approximately two years that I was pushing hard to produce research, there were many hours of many days when Rebecca and I enjoyed various activities together. Unless there was something urgent developing, I did not go to the lab on Sunday. On Saturday I sometimes worked about half a day; sometimes a full day, sometimes none at all, depending on the pace of research at a specific time. During the week I frequently worked a few hours after supper. I had learned while working for my Ph.D. at Yale that a relatively long period for relaxing is much more effective than several short periods. Since Rebecca and I had a salary that was about two-thirds of the going rate in industry and still had help from my dad, even with the expense of the baby we were able for the first time in our marriage to spend money for relaxation and/or entertainment. Since we missed the athletic events that we had enjoyed at Yale, naturally enough we took advantage of our first opportunity to see major league baseball. This was long before the days of night baseball games; however, that was no problem for us. For that sort of attraction, I would even work on Sunday. Boston had teams in both leagues: the Bees (destined to become the Milwaukee Braves) in the National League; the Red Sox in the American League. The Red Sox had much the best team, with such legendary names as slugger Ted Williams, pitcher Lefty Grove (Old Mose), and manager Joe Cronin, who also played short stop. We saw a lot of Red Sox games, especially if they were playing archrival, the Yankees, whose drawing card was Joe Dimaggio. Dimaggio was famous for home runs over the "friendly" right field fence at Yankee Stadium. Fenway Park, the Red Sox park, had a very long right field. Whenever DiMaggio belted a long drive to right, which was easily gathered in by the right fielder, the fans would yell in chorus, "Wrong ball park, Joe." In spite of such attractions, we saw more Bees games than those of the Red Sox, for two reasons: since the Bees were far down in the standings, they used various devices to attract the fans, such as "Ladies Day" on a weekday about once per week, when ladies went free if accompanied by a man. Of course, this cut the cost of our attendance, but there was another advantage: since the crowds were small, we could always get a seat close to the field, right behind third base. The attraction of that location was the legendary Casey Stengel, who managed the Bees and always coached at third base. His antics, in our minds, were the principal attractions at those ball games, and fully justified taking off a weekday afternoon and working on Sunday instead. It was not surprising that we were quite interested in Casey Stengel and his antics at third base. When we first met in Berkeley, Casey was manager of the Oakland Acorns, and attracting attention with his antics as third base coach. We saw several games and always sat behind third base. Incidentally, Louis Fieser was a strong supporter of this sort of thing, and never asked me where I was if he was unable to find me in the lab on an afternoon. Occasionally I would tell him about some spectacular play in the game.

Of course, such activity as just described required finding a baby-sitter, but this proved to be no problem. As has been mentioned, times were hard. Following suggestions of friends we located a high school girl, Mildred Monahan, who proved quite satisfactory. We paid her $2 for an afternoon or evening, with extra pay at night if we failed to get home by eleven o'clock. We picked her up at her home to bring her to our house and returned her afterwards. She sometimes told us anecdotes about people she encountered as she pushed Roger around in his stroller. On one occasion, a group of boys seemed to look intently at Roger as they passed. Before they got out of earshot, one of them said, "It can't be hers, she's baby-sitting."

We met several friends with whom we enjoyed playing bridge. In the case of a couple who also had a child, we took turns being host, thus dividing the cost of a baby sitter, or coffee and cookies. In case the other couple did not have a child (outside the belly), we always played host. One couple with whom we always played host was Francis and Dorothy Carpenter, who were not connected with Harvard. Francis worked for Associated Press and was stationed at Boston at the time that we came to Harvard. They knew we were there on account of being alumni of Vanderbilt University and noticing in their newsletter that we were headed for Harvard. We kept in touch with them via Christmas cards until after we had been in Berkeley for about twenty years; Dorothy had died, and Francis was in the Bay Area to visit a daughter who was working, unbeknownst to us, for Equitec Financial Group, of which our younger son was chief executive officer. As has been often said, it is a small world.

An event involving our pediatrician, John Davies, is worth mentioning as an illustration of the character and behavior of Louis Fieser. Dr. Davies contacted me to ask if I could give him any assistance in acquiring a sample of a compound called homogentisic acid. He needed it for research he was doing in collaboration with some other people on the disease alkaptonuria, which causes a person's urine to rapidly turn very dark on standing. He had been unable to find a chemical supply house that sold homogentisic acid. I told him I would ask Fieser if he would object to my researching this substance and finding out if it was difficult to make. Louis responded that there was no objection at all to my becoming involved in things of this sort, and that Davies's research sounded interesting, so perhaps we could get together at his (Fieser's) house on a Sunday to discuss it. We did so, and Louis gave me the green light to make a sample for Davies if it did not prove very difficult. Louis felt that the synthesis should be relatively simple, which proved to be true. I supplied Davies with a sample. One afternoon after I had told Louis how I planned to make the substance, he stopped by my lab to make a suggestion about the synthesis. After Louis went out, Ebie Hershberg quipped, "I can't tell whether the boss is working for you, or you are working for him." I was a little uncertain how to take that comment of Ebie's, but I describe the event here in order to develop a picture of Fieser's natural behavior and his attitude towards his research group.

In Louis Fieser's research group, every day was likely to develop something exciting. I remember one event in particular that involved me. Louis was giving a paper at a national meeting of the American Chemical

Society, and he felt it would add a lot of interest if he could report the synthesis of a compound I was working on. By working all day on the day before he left, and into the night, I was able to finish the synthesis, and was taking a sample off the filter preparatory to putting it in the drying oven to get it ready for analysis, when Louis came in to tell me that he had told the analyst to give first priority to my sample so that I could telegraph the numbers to him before his talk at about two o'clock in the afternoon. A new compound, in those days, could not be reported as a valid new compound until the analytical results were available, showing the presence of the right amount of each element in the compound. Louis never showed any signs of doubting that my compound would turn out to give the right numbers, but I was virtually holding my breath when the analyst brought in his results the next morning. Of course, I had already calculated what the numbers should be. They turned out to be right, and so I went immediately to send the telegram to Louis. I was not at the meeting, obviously, but I was told what happened by several people. Louis was giving his talk when a man from the hotel desk walked in and handed Louis a piece of paper which was obviously a telegram. Louis called for a slide on the screen, waved the telegram around, and said, "Here's one that is hot off Jim Cason's bench."

Orchestrated? You bet it was! Not quite true in all details? No way! Working for Louis Fieser was a joy and a treat!

The Valentine's Day blizzard hit Cambridge during the winter of my second year at Harvard. We had been living in Belmont, a suburb of Cambridge, ever since our lease in Cambridge had expired. The snow started after lunch, and by the time I was driving home I could hardly keep the wide street located, and was barely able to get home through the snow already fallen. When I got to the driveway of our two-car garage, which was only about forty feet long, I discovered that Rebecca had been working for about two hours keeping enough ahead of the snowfall so that I was able to drive into our side of the garage. My first act after I got out of the car in the dryness of our garage, was to hug and kiss the person who had cleared my way in. The car of the man in the upstairs flat was already in the garage; he had gotten home earlier. He had not helped Rebecca in her fight to keep the driveway open.

When we got up the next morning, snow in the driveway was about level with the window sills on that side of the house. I knew that this meant that the snow in the driveway was about six feet deep. I learned later from newspaper articles that about half, or more, of the land area in a suburban city such as Belmont was occupied by buildings, and the situation was exacerbated by the fact that the space between the buildings where the driveways were acted as an eddy to the wind so that even more snow was dropped on the driveways. As soon as I finished eating a light breakfast, I went out, got the shovel from our basement which Rebecca had used, and started the challenging job of throwing snow from the driveway up onto the snow between the driveway and house. After a few minutes the man upstairs came out and demanded that I get the driveway cleared so that he could go to work. He knew that we paid a reduced rent in return for mowing the lawn and clearing snow from the driveway. I had already cleared the driveway a few times. I told him that I was not equipped to perform miracles, and that it would be at least mid-afternoon, probably later, before I could get that driveway cleared. He said that he had to get to work, and he got another shovel and started shoveling. I knew that he was a desk jockey at some business, and it was rather pitiful to see how he handled a shovel. I told him that there was no way he could get to work anyway, because the radio was full of the fact that the Boston area was paralyzed by the unprecedented amount of snow. Nevertheless, he kept on shoveling for two or three hours, then went in to go to bed—and got out of the bed two days later. As for me, five or six years at Elkhorn cabin had me still in shape to shovel all day—though slowly and with frequent resting. Rebecca also took over the other shovel for two or three hours; she had been much engaged in athletics for all her school years. Together we opened up that driveway, all the way to the street, just as it was getting dark—and just in time for the snowplow to come by and pile a six-foot bank sloshing all the way across our sidewalk. I took one look at it, then went into the house and said, "Let's eat." This remains a frequent statement between us. Before leaving this topic, I should mention that Roger was not yet old enough to get any fun out of all this whiteness.

After I cleared the snow bank thrown across our driveway by the snowplow, with Rebecca taking care of Roger in the snow, I decided to try to get down to Harvard. The radio had reported that many of the suburban streets had been cleared, and I would spend most of my time on a thoroughfare. All sorts of stories were going around about problems with the snow, or interesting things that happened on account of it. Naturally enough, the best stories were about Louis Fieser. On the day after the blizzard, essentially no professors were able to meet with their classes. The neighborhoods around Harvard were not conducive to attracting professors to live near the university. If a professor should fail to show up for a class by ten minutes after the hour, it was traditional for students to parade out singing a song, even if they passed the professor in the hall. Thus, after the blizzard the students would troop merrily out of class at exactly ten minutes after the hour and start throwing snowballs at each other. Not for Louis Fieser's nine o'clock class! At about five minutes after the hour, Louis walked into the room with his skis over his shoulder, parked the skis in a corner, got out his lecture notes from his briefcase, and started lecturing—well, after the tumult subsided, he started lecturing.

Another small story is about Louis and the snowman. This occurred on the second day after the blizzard. There was a parking lot a short distance from the Converse lab, so people normally came into the building from that side. Thus, the side for "the snowman" was on that side of the lab. Some graduate students had congregated very early that morning, still in a holiday spirit, and built the snowman, using various props besides just snow. I did not get there early that morning, because of having to open up my driveway; however, I saw the snowman when I did arrive, and it was a good likeness of Louis Fieser, especially his bald head, which had a characteristic shape. Since Louis was taller than most people, that bald head stood out in a crowd. According to the story that I heard, there were a few students around when Louis arrived, examined the snowman, and commented, "That is a helluva way for graduate students to spend their time instead of working at their research." Later on, Louis was observed taking pictures of the snowman from various angles and distances.

I have chosen a few events to illustrate that Louis Fieser was a splendid teacher, as well as a widely recognized research chemist. He had the talents for it, and he loved to exercise them. There may have been another college professor during my time who equaled or surpassed Louis Fieser in this dual role; however, I have not found him. Furthermore, Louis's treatment of me certainly indicates clearly that he was an honest and fair-minded individual, who could also be jolly good company. In retrospect, I cannot recall any instance in which I did not feel better after talking to Louis than beforehand. I will mention a final characteristic action which meant a lot to me. Before I left Harvard, Louis invited me to present the paper on the final difficult problem on which I had worked, at the national meeting of the American Chemical Society, which was at Detroit in September. This action was not as unusual as putting my name as first author on the paper—which, incidentally, had not appeared in print at the time of this meeting. I had already started my teaching job at DePauw University in Greencastle, Indiana and had to come up to Detroit to give the paper. I still remember what a miserable hotel room I had, and how far I had to walk to get to the building where the papers were delivered. When I came into the room where my paper was scheduled, about an hour before my paper was due, I noticed Louis was sitting in the seat on the aisle in the second row from the front. In this situation, the pressure on a young scientist who is looking for a job in a major American university is probably comparable to that on a young baseball player coming to bat for the first time in the big leagues. As I walked by Louis, he said "Give 'em hell, Jim." I knew that I could do it! Who could be a better judge of my capability than Louis Fieser?

At some time during my second year with Louis there developed a famous incident which I will call the Vitamin K Event. As a result of this event, a man named Doisy, who was a professor at a university in St. Louis, devoted a great deal of energy to spreading reports that Fieser was a disreputable chemist who was guilty of plagiarism. Since I was with Fieser at the time of the occurrence of this event, was contacted by him almost daily, sometimes more than once a day, I know what happened; there was no kind of intermediary between what Louis Fieser did and what I saw and heard. As to why Doisy did what he did, I have no way of knowing. Before this event, I had never heard of the man, and I have never seen him since. I can speculate that he was so disappointed at making a serious error in a paper which was otherwise an important contribution that he simply lost control. This may be too charitable an interpretation, but I have not heard an explanation which seems more probable. After I had been at Berkeley for many years, I had a somewhat similar experience involving a professor at Ohio State University whose name was Melvin Newman; however, there was a reverse twist on this one. Mel did not claim that I had done anything unethical, but he made claims of priority on work that I had previously done. I never allow myself to be upset about such things, for reasons that will develop in later reports on my life. I merely wrote the editor of the JACS, and explained the situation. I then made a point of not looking at Mel's paper when it was published, for I abhor controversy that accomplishes nothing. However, later events indicated that Mel was not very happy about what I wrote to the editor. (I had a long and friendly relationship with Mel Newman: as has been mentioned in an earlier chapter, he preceded me as a research assistant with Louis Fieser, and had a favorable effect on my getting the job with Louis.)

To return to the Vitamin K event, Louis came into my lab one morning and dropped on my desk a galley proof of a communication to the editor of JACS, which he had just received. These communications were—and probably still are—short reports regarded as sufficiently important to justify rapid publication so that the rest of the world can take advantage of the information. In this way research progresses more rapidly than it would otherwise. Naturally enough, I guess, there have developed, by the time of this writing, numerous instances in which a researcher who thinks he has a chance for a Nobel Prize withholds publication until he feels sure that he is sufficiently ahead of an investigator whom he fears is better than he is. There has been some disgusting public bragging about such affairs. Not in Louis Fieser's time, and not among Louis's associates whom I knew.

The communication which Louis dropped on my desk was a report from Doisy on the structure of vitamin K, a naphthoquinone derivative. Since Louis had been working in the field of quinones, especially naphthoquinones, for many years, it was natural that Arthur Lamb, the editor of JACS, would refer the communication to Louis Fieser. The editor of a chemical journal is expected to refer any manuscript that is submitted to a person whose own work qualifies him to judge the manuscript that has been submitted. This means, of course, that before a paper is published it has been submitted for evaluation to a competitor in the field. This system reduces to a minimum the likelihood that fraudulent or incompetent work gets published. It also generates violent arguments between author and referee, and places a heavy burden on an editor, for he must act as the umpire in such arguments. In the present instance, Arthur Lamb, editor of the JACS, would certainly have been open to criticism if he had failed to submit the manuscript to Fieser. Louis had done his graduate work under the eminent chemist James Conant, on oxidation-reduction potentials of quinones; later published papers on syntheses of condensed ring quinones such as vitamin K; and had recently written a series of excellent papers on quinones based on the beautiful work of a chemist named Samuel C. Hooker. After Hooker had retired as an industrial chemist, he set up a laboratory in his home and worked for years on quinones, excellent work which he recorded only in a series of notebooks, which he willed to Louis Fieser. Louis did his usual superb job of writing these papers; Hooker had known from reading chemical literature that there was probably no better writer than Louis Fieser. In summary, Lamb had no alternative but to submit the manuscript to Fieser as one of the referees.

The reason that Louis decided to talk to me about this manuscript was that I was the only one of his research assistants who had experience in working on natural products (refer to Chapter 6). As soon as Louis read Doisy's short report, he realized that the structure which Doisy had proposed was probably in error because it lacked a methyl group (consisting of one carbon and three hydrogen atoms) at a position where Louis knew, from his extensive knowledge of the literature, that a methyl group was nearly always present. There was no evidence against the presence of this methyl group except that the carbon and hydrogen analysis agreed well with the molecule that did not have the methyl group. Louis's question to me was: is the precision of the C and H analysis sufficient to distinguish the presence or absence of the methyl group? Since I had personally done many dozens of C and H analyses in my work under Professor Anderson at Yale, I was able to answer Louis's question at once and without equivocation: "In a molecule of that size, it is impossible to determine by C and H analysis whether there is present another methyl group; indeed, even if it were a question of two methyl groups, the distinction by C and H analysis would still be impossible." As soon as I finished talking, Louis stood up and said, "That is all I need to know, I will talk to Lamb immediately, and tell him that this manuscript from Doisy is hot stuff whose publication should be expedited. I will also tell him not to submit any more Doisy manuscripts to me for refereeing because I am planning to extend my work on quinones by entering this field." Before he hurried over to Lamb's office, which was in the Mallincrodt Laboratory, he also told me that he planned to start work immediately on synthesis of the molecule with the additional methyl group in it. In those days, the direct comparison of a natural product with a synthetic sample was the generally accepted method for positive identification of the structure of the natural product. Of course, the synthesis must start with a compound of known structure and proceed by way of reactions whose products have been reliably established.

At this point, a summary is in order: (1) Arthur Lamb, as Editor of JACS, properly discharged his duty by sending Doisy's manuscript to Fieser. (2) Fieser did his duty by immediately telling Lamb to expedite the publication of Doisy's manuscript, but not to send him any more Doisy manuscripts because of his decision to go to work in this field. (3) In any contest for priority in the synthesis of vitamin K, due to events over which neither Lamb nor Fieser had control, Fieser was put a few weeks ahead of the rest of the world because of the time elapsing between his reading of Doisy's manuscript and its publication in JACS. (4) Fieser was not given any time advantage over Doisy, for Doisy had known for a long time everything about vitamin K that Fieser knew after reading Doisy's communication. (5) The advantage which Fieser had over Doisy was greater knowledge and skill in the field of quinone chemistry, and much greater capability at inductive reasoning.

So why did Doisy spend so much energy and time in spreading around outright lies about Louis Fieser? It seems apparent that Doisy must have been painfully aware of the reality of items one to five above, and he simply cracked under the pressure. Subsequent events to be described are consistent with this interpretation.

Within minutes after Big Lou returned from speaking to Lamb and leaving Doisy's manuscript with him, he went into action on synthesis of the molecule which he had deduced would be the structure of vitamin K; i.e., the structure with the methyl group which Doisy's proposed structure lacked. When I say that Big Lou went to work, I mean that he went to work with his own big hands. I am sure that it did not even flash through his mind to assign the job to a research assistant. Only God knows how many hours per week Lou worked for several weeks, but it was probably at least eighty. Since it was impossible for me not to absorb some of Louis's excitement, I began working frequently until ten or eleven o'clock at night, checking occasionally on the light in Fieser's lab which was two floors above my basement lab. Occasionally, I went upstairs to satisfy my curiosity and asked how the work was going. I think I may have been a little worried that I might find Louis lying on the floor exhausted—I should have known better. Every morning when I came in at between eight thirty and nine o'clock, that light upstairs was already on. Once, I asked if he was sleeping in the lab, but he said not.

I have no recollection at all about elapsed time while Louis was driving at this pace. After all, I was working much more than usual on my research—no baseball games. Louis's spectacular performance was contagious. However that may be, Louis produced the synthetic sample with the structure which he felt was that of vitamin K. Ergo, he wrote to Doisy for a sample of vitamin K for direct comparison with his synthetic sample. This was routine procedure in those days, a part of the collegial spirit which was prevalent, and which made academia a pleasant place in which to work. During the years I worked on branched chain fatty acids, I sent hundreds of small samples to dozens of researchers scattered across the US and several European countries. This spirit has deteriorated rapidly in what might be called modern times. As for Doisy, this spirit deteriorated long ago. He declined to send Fieser a sample of his vitamin K. Big Lou did not show me Doisy's letter, which I appreciated. He told me that it did not make enjoyable reading.

In typical Fieser fashion, on the day that he received Doisy's letter he went to work isolating his own sample of naturally occurring vitamin K. He followed the procedure that Doisy had published earlier—up to a point. Part way through the isolation, he realized that there was a much better way to do the job, and finished the isolation in a few days. The isolated sample proved identical with the synthetic sample! For anyone who has not engaged in this sort of experience, it is not possible to understand the intensity of apprehension, followed by exhilaration.

It was during this drive to establish the vitamin K structure that there developed around the Converse Laboratory an expression which was applied in order to deprecate a particularly wild scheme: "Hell, that's not even Fieserble." The ultimate put-down; only one step below impossible.

Before concluding this communique concerning my Golden Days at Harvard, I will report several isolated events which will include things that may be of interest concerning particular individuals and/or their characteristic behavior. Incidents of fraud occurring in the scientific community have become distressingly frequent in what I refer to as modern times; however, such incidents were not unknown in the years preceding World War II. Perhaps the most famous of such incidents involved the chemist Fritz Kogel and his research assistant, Hannah Erxleben. They lived in the Netherlands, and in a series of papers extending over several years, they reported work on a plant hormone. These papers appeared interesting and well written, so they were widely quoted all over the world. I gave a report on them at the weekly Organic Chemistry Colloquium at Harvard. My report generated more than the average amount of discussion. Subsequent work in our country, appearing in part after World War II, reported inability to isolate a compound of the characteristics reported by Kogel and Erxleben. This work was confirmed in at least one other laboratory. By the time all this news broke out, Kogl and Erxleben had disappeared into Nazi Germany, never to be heard from again, so far as I know.

It is not known whether this fraud was due entirely to Erxleben; however, it is well known that the German professors, with very large groups working for them, had very little contact with the research. R. J. Anderson told me stories of the incredible occurrences that happened while he was working for his Ph.D. (or whatever the German equivalent was at that time) in the laboratory of Emil Fischer, who was sometimes described as the greatest of all organic chemists. A British chemist named Norman Haworth spent most of his life finally proving that the structure of sugars published in a series of papers by Emil Fischer was wrong. In two instances in my research, I encountered complete failure to reproduce what had been published in the German papers. That sort of thing could never happen in Louis Fieser's lab, for he was right on top of everything that was going on. I will relate a simple incident which illustrates this point. One morning, at about nine-thirty I was recrystallizing the product which I had synthesized the day before. Big Lou walked in the door, and immediately commented, "Hey, you were here plenty late last night." He was right. I was anxious to learn how my synthesis had turned out, and had worked until midnight.

I accidentally learned about a case of fraud that occurred in this country at about the time that I was working with Fieser. It involved a graduate student who had faked a Ph.D. thesis while working under Professor G. Bryant Bachman at Ohio State University. His thesis was so impressive and his recommendations so good that he was able to get a job as post-doctoral research associate with Louis Fieser. According to Louis's report to me, he began to be suspicious of this guy after he had been on the job for about a week. He could not seem to find him actually turning out synthetic work, and finally asked the man to show him a sample of the compound he was synthesizing. When he failed to do so, Louis accused him of being a fraud. The man disappeared that night without going back to his work bench, and according to the last report I heard, was never again located in chemical circles. But this was not the last time that I heard about him. At the same ACS national meeting at which I gave the paper on my last work with Fieser, I was listening to a paper being presented by a man named Bradsher, who was a professor at Duke University. At one stage of his presentation, he reported that one of the compounds which he had synthesized had a melting point differing by about fifty degrees from the melting point reported for the same compound in a paper by G. Bryant Bachman and a coworker. At this point, Louis Fieser, who was sitting in the same row with me but with several people between us, exploded like a volcano and yelled to me, "That is the crook I told you about." Louis explained, after Bradsher finished his paper, to the nearby people what his yelling was about. I think that he also cautioned that no one should confuse G. Bryant Bachman with Werner Bachman, who was among the most eminent of American chemists.

A final report in this hodgepodge of events is about a reaction that I was running in a sealed glass tube. Reactions on a small scale, which require high pressure, were frequently carried out in a very heavy-walled glass tube. One end of the tube was closed when it was manufactured, but the other end had to be sealed after the reactants had been placed in it. This seal had to be done in a way that avoided making the wall of the tube thinner at the point where the heavy tube was melted down to a smaller diameter preparatory to finally sealing off the smaller diameter tube. This was a rather delicate and tricky job which Ebie had taught me to do successfully. Failure resulted in an exploding tube. Of course, our tube furnace was arranged so that an exploding tube did not hurt anybody. I had sealed numerous tubes after Ebie had instructed me, with no explosions. The tube furnace, along with other hazardous equipment, was located in a large room which contained only one work bench for a researcher at the far end of the room. On this day, when I was heating a sealed tube, Louis was talking to a man from the medical school with whom he was working, and they were seated at the work bench at the end of the room, for that was the station of Ruben Sandin, a visiting professor from the University of Alberta who was involved with the project being discussed. At this inopportune time, my sealed tube exploded! I heard the noise in my lab at the other end of the hall, and I knew that Louis and the visitor were in that room. After a moment of panic, I realized that I had set up the heating of that tube so that nobody could get hurt if it exploded. The reaction had been described as generating a very high pressure. And so I sat and waited, with a little sweat popping out on my brow. After what seemed an eternity, Louis came rushing in and said, not quietly, "Jim, you must have goofed up the sealing of that tube; when it went off, that guy from the medical school damn near crapped in his jeans." Later, Rube Sandin told me that Fieser did not bat an eye when the tube exploded, but that the man from the medical school simply dissolved. When he recovered sufficiently, he asked Louis, "My God, does that happen often?" Louis's response: "No, not often; but it does happen occasionally. That is why we arrange the tube furnace so that nobody will get hurt when a tube explodes." I must report a happy ending concerning my reputation as a tube sealer. Ebie sealed one, with great care, as I watched, and it exploded. We solved the problem by using a longer tube, and a smaller charge, in order to keep the pressure down by providing a larger volume for a smaller amount of material.

As all things must, whether good or bad, my Golden Days at Harvard had come to an end. After searching for a job in a major university, I had finally decided that it was absolutely necessary that I get a teaching job— any teaching job—that would get me away from Harvard. The war clouds were gathering and, as much as I enjoyed working with Louis, I realized that if the war broke out while I remained at Harvard I would be stuck, probably for years, working as one of those in Fieser's group doing war research. At this stage in my career, being held essentially in neutral for several years could prove disastrous. If I could get a teaching job where I was independent, then whatever I might do would be registered to my credit. My Ph.D research director at Yale, R. J. Anderson, gave me some

much appreciated help in arriving at the best conclusion, as was supported by subsequent events. As things turned out, as the principal investigator for a contract at Vanderbilt University during the war, I became well
acquainted with all of the chemists in the older generation who had built
up organic chemistry in the U.S. These contacts were responsible, eventually, for my arriving at that "place in the sun," for which I had fought for
so long. In addition, Louis gave me very helpful advice, as well as the
equipment that I had to have in order to continue research at such a small
school as DePauw University, in Greencastle, Indiana, where I had finally
decided to accept a proffered job, in order to go out on my own.

A few days before my scheduled departure, Louis came down to my
lab to discuss the numerous things involved with my leaving. First, he
gave me advice on how to get along in the academic world, and subsequent events were destined to show that this was very good advice indeed.
I still remember vividly one item, approximately the following: "Many
people spend so much time trying to decide what research to do, trying to
find something important enough to justify their superior talents, that they
become discouraged before they ever get into action. The important thing
is to do something, do anything, but get moving. Once you are carrying
out chemical reactions, and following the chemical literature, you will find
plenty of interesting things to do, in contrast with those who sit and
think." That advice proved very useful to me on several occasions during
the early stages of my career. A few years later, after World War II, I was
reminded of Louis's advice, when somebody asked Vannevar Bush what
he thought of the Institute for Advanced Study, in Princeton, New Jersey,
where people would be given the opportunity to "sit and think." Bush
replied, "I know how to tell if they are sitting."

As a part of my last project with Fieser, which has been described previously, it was necessary for me to synthesize several dihydroxynaphthoic
acids. I had pushed ahead with the part of the work that was necessary for
inclusion in the paper; however, there was additional work to be done if
the work on the dihydroxynaphthoic acids were to be published as a separate paper. I suggested to Louis that I could finish this work, possibly during my first year at DePauw, and send him the usual report on the experimental part for him to use in writing the paper. After thinking a bit, Louis
replied, "I didn't really have anything to do with that part of the work;

why don't you write up the paper, in your name only. If you want to send it to me before you send it to JACS, I will be glad to criticize it for you." And so I was able to send my first paper to the JACS in less than a year after I started teaching. I had no trouble at all with the referees of that paper. How could I when the short paragraph just before the Experimental Part reads: "The author is indebted for many helpful suggestions to Professor L. F. Fieser, in whose laboratory a major portion of this work was performed." I do not need to be a mind-reader to know what Big Lou was thinking about when he paused for a few moments before telling me to write up the paper over my name only.

Louis did yet another thing that made it possible for me to do enough experimental work during my one year at DePauw to finish what was necessary to complete that paper. Furthermore, because of Louis's generosity, I was able to do much experimental work at DePauw for my second paper, my first entirely on my own, which was submitted to JACS on February 4, 1942. This date is approximately two months after the treacherous attack on Pearl Harbor by the Japanese, six months after my arrival at Vanderbilt University. I asked Big Lou if it would be possible for me to take to DePauw the Podbielniak fractionating column which I had built, with help on the glass blowing from Ebie. I asked about this specific piece of equipment because I knew that it would be absolutely necessary in order to start experimental work on my second paper. Louis replied, roughly: "Anything that you built, or apparatus that was built especially for you, is unlikely to be of much use to somebody else, so you are welcome to take it with you." Without that equipment, it probably would have been after World War II before I published my first paper. It makes me shudder a little to think about it. I owe it all to Louis Fieser, but that is not all that he was to do for me.

Naturally enough, I continued to have frequent contact with Louis, not only in correspondence but in meeting with him during national meetings of the American Chemical Society. The last time that I wrote him was soon after the publication of the first volume of the tremendous reference work entitled Organic Reagents. I wrote him a letter of congratulations, and also followed the suggestion he had made in the preface of the book about writing him regarding any errors or suggestions for additions to the next volume which was scheduled. I wrote a couple of pages of suggestions. Within a very few days, I had a letter back thanking me for the excellent suggestions and saying that he enjoyed hearing from one of the "heavy hitters" in the author index. He had counted the number of times that my name had appeared in that index. Louis Fieser retained his mental alertness and driving energy until severe illness took its toll. I count myself very fortunate to have known him as a friend, mentor, and benefactor.

CHAPTER 8

THE NOMADS

In moving from Belmont to Greencastle, Indiana, we had to arrange for a moving van to carry our furniture which we had bought from Fournier, as well as the valuable hoard of laboratory apparatus from Louis Fieser. Since we did not have enough belongings to come anywhere near filling a van, we had to arrange with a moving company to deliver our goods to the house that Jess Riebsomer, chairman of the DePauw chemistry cepartment, had rented for us, during a period of a certain number of days. We were able to resolve this dilemma by staying with my parents in Murfreesboro until we got the message from the van line as to when they would arrive in Greencastle. We brought the laboratory apparatus to our flat in Belmont, supervised the packing of it, and the loading of all our belongings except what Roger and we needed until we arrived in Greencastle. The van line came early enough that we were able to drive to Wilmington, Delaware, by dark. Fortunately good friends of ours, Gordon and Marion Biehn, who were working for the Du Pont Company, were glad to have us stay overnight with them. When I turned down the job offered by the Du Pont Company, in favor of going to work for Louis Fieser, the next in line for this most cherished industrial job was Gordon Biehn. Thus they tended to regard me as a benefactor. We kept in touch with the Biehns over the years via Christmas cards. On one occasion, when they were vacationing on the west coast, they stayed overnight with us at our house on our timber property in the heart of the redwood country. Although Gordon died a few years ago, we still exchange Christmas cards with Marion.

We enjoyed a few days of relaxing while staying with my parents, with everything provided to us without significant effort on our part. Rebecca was even relieved of most of the caring for Roger. Roger was upset by the dark skin of the cook, for he had never had experience with people who had a dark skin. Memur's faithful cook, Leilah, still relieved Rebecca of preparing Roger's food. She said, "Miss Rebecca, you take this food in to him, and he will never know that you didn't prepare it." She was right; Roger liked the food. He was too young to realize that he no longer had a home except for that Chevrolet sedan. That problem developed at a much later stage in our nomadic existence. He had a lot of fun running around in the large yard at my parents' home. After a few days we received the telephone call in late afternoon that the van with our furniture would be at our address in Greencastle, which we had never seen, at about 8 A.M. the next morning. We scurried around getting everything packed, and Roger bedded down in the hammock he slept in when we traveled. This hammock was very useful. It was supported by ropes with hooks stuck into the back window frames beside the glass. This placed him directly behind the front seat, a very good position in case of an accident- which we never had.

When we arrived at our Greencastle address the van was parked in front of the two-story, box-like frame house at that address. Apparently the drivers had slept in the van, so they were ready to start unloading imme- diately. We suddenly realized that we had no key to the house. No prob- lem; it was not locked, and there was nothing in it that anybody would want to steal. We had plenty of room for our meager supply of furniture. One item of furniture we had was a seat for Roger on the toilet. Since he had slept well all night, lulled to sleep in his swaying hammock, he was charging around the place, getting in the way of the movers. After the unloading got started Rebecca told the man who seemed in command that we were dead tired from driving all night and needed to have our bed unloaded. He yelled to the other man who was inside the van, "Hey, Joe, these people have been driving all night and are so tired that they are about ready to fall on their faces; get the bed and the kid's crib out of there and set them up." What a marvelous idea! We soon had Roger in the crib, and us abed. I don't remember much about what happened after that dur- ing our first day in Greencastle.

During our first few days in Greencastle we encountered numerous surprises, and these continued through the first few months. Some of these surprises were nice and others were not so nice. During our first day, before we had our meager belongings distributed to their places, a rather elderly gentlemen who looked and dressed like a minister introduced himself as the pastor of the Methodist Church. He had come to invite us to attend services on the coming Sunday. When we told him we were Presbyterians, he gave us a pitch for shifting to the Methodist Church since, after all, DePauw University was founded by the Methodist Church. We gave him a rather chilly turndown, but the incident worried me enough that I asked the chemistry department chairman, Jess Riebsomer, about it. He responded rather heatedly that this SOB was always pulling some such trick as that. He also said that he did not belong to any church and never intended to; furthermore, that I did not need to be impressed if the president of DePauw should tell me that faculty was supposed to attend the weekly chapel exercises and sit on the stage. From that day, my evaluation of Jess Riebsomer changed for the better, as my evaluation of DePauw University changed in the opposite direction.

After my return from Detroit, where I had presented the paper on my last work with Louis Fieser, I got my next surprise when Rebecca told me that the only source of pasteurized milk in town was from a dairy in Indianapolis, which was forty miles away. I was relieved to learn that such milk could be bought in Greencastle from that dairy or its local agent. She also told me that there was no such thing as a pediatrician in town, and that I would have to go to Indianapolis to get my eyes refracted for the new glasses I needed. She also gave me the further information that somebody she had met told her that only about half the houses in town had indoor toilets. In view of the appearance of our neighborhood, I felt happy that we had an indoor toilet. Of course, I realized that Jess Reibsomer would not have rented the house for us if it had been otherwise.

It was about the time of our arrival in Greencastle that Wendell Willkie was making a big drive to get nominated as a candidate for the presidency of the U.S. In a Time magazine article at the time, it was reported that Wendell Willkie had been born in some city in Indiana but had shown his intelligence at an early age by moving away from Indiana. I felt that to be a good basis for evaluation of Mr. Willkie. I had never realized what a progressive, modern, forward-looking state is Tennessee, the Volunteer State, until I moved to Greencastle, Indiana.

Not all of my early evaluations of DePauw and Greencastle were bad; indeed, most of my evaluations of DePauw ranged from good to very good. On the light-hearted side, I could not help but notice the constant parade of simply beautiful girls, even including those in my chemistry classes. When I communicated this observation to Rebecca, she said rather derisively, "You are just at that impressionable age." I suggested that she go over to the campus and look at the scenery. When she came back, she reported that I was right, and said, "What is going on around here, anyway?" After some inquiries and the passage of time, we learned about the local explanation of this phenomenon. Many years before, a person named Rector had willed to DePauw a substantial sum of money which had grown with time, to be used to finance "Rector Scholarships." Each recipient had to be a male student who had the highest scholastic ranking in an Indiana high school. By the time of our arrival, there was a substantial population of Rector Scholars on campus. That explained one thing I began to notice, especially by the end of the first semester. I had never enjoyed such good students, and not all of them were males. That takes us to the other side of the coin. There had built up, according to the story, a clique, or cult, of rich businessmen in Chicago who sent their daughters, especially beautiful ones who needed a husband to conserve the family fortune, to DePauw University to marry one of those brilliant Rector Scholars. Sound like a fairy tale? Consider this: in the year we were there, about 65 percent of the graduating seniors married each other. This was facilitated by the practice at DePauw to maintain about a 50-50 distribution of males and females.

When we were at DePauw, it was in the days of strict control of the morality of the students, especially girls. Every party of every kind had to have at least one faculty member chaperone. All the chaperones we encountered were married, but I do not recall whether that was a regulation. This put a substantial demand on faculty members, especially young ones. By the end of the first semester, we had developed a reputation for making "good" reports to the dean, so we had about as many parties as we could handle. I do not remember how we handled the baby sitter situation, but apparently older faculty members put us in touch with high school girls. The regulations required all parties to end by 10:30 P.M., except for one dance per semester for each organization. This one dance could go until midnight. Of course this was not very popular with the students, but it was quite popular with chaperones who had kids. We enjoyed getting acquainted with a variety of students, including many who were not in my classes. At dances, there was always one dance where students would tap us for a break and each of us would dance with a student. This was enjoyable for Rebecca, who had a great deal more experience than I had. I had never danced until Rebecca instructed me; however, I had learned during my instruction period to never take a foot off the floor, to slide it along and thus avoid stepping on my partner's foot. At first, I always apologized to my partner for not being experienced at leading, but later I became less self-conscious and more relaxed, thus the dances became more enjoyable. I have never danced since then, which is just as well, because of the demise of what we called ball room dancing.

Some of our experiences with students were interesting and/or enjoyable. At one dance with a Halloween motif, it was necessary to enter through a back door and pass through a dark room where various goblins and such were located. This resulted in our not being recognized or greeted when we came in, so we just went ahead and started dancing in the very dark room. At one point, as the dance ended, we heard a nearby student say, "I hope those chaperones are here, and have not gotten into that punch bowl at the end of the table." I spoke loudly enough to be heard at a reasonable distance, "Fear not, all is well." Another voice commented at once, "That southern accent; I did not pick it by accident."

At another dance, things did not start off well. When we arrived, there was a student with a microphone standing in an entrance hall, pretending to be announcing for a radio station. After he presented "Professor and Mrs. Jim Cason" to applause, we proceeded onto the dance floor. Since I was leading Rebecca, I got a step ahead of her at the point where there was a small step down from the hall, at which time I fell forward on my face and skidded across the floor. There was a rush of people asking if I was hurt. Being an experienced gymnast, I did not even lose my glasses. I motioned for the microphone and said, "I want you people to know that most of the time, I do not fall on my face when I enter the dance floor." More applause. I then suggested that something ought to be done about that step.

On another occasion, I was less conspicuous. This was a wiener and marshmallow roast in the evening, around a bonfire on a grassy slope. Since it was rather cool, Rebecca and I brought a blanket with us. After things had proceeded for a while with much hilarity, and it was getting crowded around the fire, we decided to take our blanket back from the fire, cuddle up together to keep warm, and watch the festivities. After a period, somebody called out, "What has happened to the chaperones; they definitely came." I responded at once that we were there, relaxing and enjoying the festivities. Whereupon somebody said, "We thought it was a couple of students pitching a little woo, so we naturally did not investigate."

As indicated in part by the above descriptions, we thoroughly enjoyed DePauw University and its very high-class student body. However, the miserable little town and the generally poor conditions that seemed to be prevalent in Indiana became more than we wanted to bear for a longer period than necessary. The proverbial straw that broke the camel's back came at the end of the first semester when all three Casons came down with a severe flu epidemic in Greencastle at that time. After the close of the semester, I spent two or three days lying in bed grading papers in order to get my grades turned in on time. At one point things got so bad that Rebecca and I would each take our temperature when Roger needed attention. The one with the lower temperature would get up and service Roger. The situation was exacerbated by the fact that we had no confidence in the Greencastle doctor. (There may have been more than one doctor in this town of about four thousand people, but I remember only one.) I telephoned my brother in Murfreesboro for advice, and we toughed it out as best we could with his good advice. Soon after I recovered from that siege, I filed my enrollment with the employment service of the American Chemical Society for the spring meeting which, happily enough, was at St. Louis.

On the second day of the ACS meeting, as I was walking down the hall on my way to check with the employment service to learn if anybody was interested in me, I met Professor A. W. Ingersoll, one of the two Vanderbilt professors who were my favorites. He said that he was quite interested in my enrollment with the employment service because he was at the meeting as the representative of the Vanderbilt chemistry department to search for a man who would fit the position the department needed to fill. This was a difficult assignment for him because of their need to have a man to run the laboratories of the upper division course in organic chemistry, and a man to do the same for the physical chemistry course. The problem was that their budget allowed them to hire only one man. At that point I realized that I had lucked out again. I knew that Ingersoll knew that I had a double major in physics and chemistry, so I was quite unperturbed when he told me that he would contact the chairman of the department, and would let me know the next day if Breckenridge would approve of me as the best choice for the job. I knew that the approval was inevitable. Professor Ingersoll was notorious for his solemn mien and unflappable behavior; he was known to the students as Iron Man Ingersoll. And so I started teaching at Vanderbilt University the following fall, but, if I may insert a metaphor, a lot of water flowed over the dam before I arrived at Vanderbilt.

I think it will be of interest to report on something I learned about three years later, during the war, when I was working as a principal investigator for the National Defense Research Committee's Division 8. Ralph Connor, a professor at the University of Pennsylvania, was the head of the division. According to Ralph's story at that later date, one of the reasons he had come to the St. Louis meeting of the ACS was to search for an organic chemist to hire at Penn. In a chance meeting with a friend of his, A.W. Ingersoll, he asked him for his opinion of a Vanderbilt graduate named James Cason, whom he was considering for a position at Penn. When Ingersoll told Connor that they had made Cason an offer to come to Vanderbilt, Connor decided that it would not be very fair to try and take the man away from Vanderbilt by making an offer from the larger and more prestigious university. This sort of collegial behavior was more common in those days than in what I am frequently calling modern times, for lack of a more appropriate simple expression. This particular situation, however, has an interesting twist to it. The man who was offered the job at Penn, and accepted it, was a chemist with whom I later became acquainted because we were both working on organocadmium reagents in organic synthesis. In later years, he reported to me during a chance contact at an ACS meeting that during the prewar and war years, the Penn chemistry department had deteriorated so rapidly that Ralph Connor had left to go into industry. On the other hand, Vanderbilt had proved better than I had expected, and provided me with some expensive items of equipment which made it possible for me to turn out some research in spite of most of my time going into the war effort. This, combined with continuing assistance from Louis Fieser, caused me to ultimately wind up in a "place in the sun" called Berkeley. I think that I have heard this sort of thing called poetic justice.

At some time near the middle of the spring semester, I received a letter from the college personnel representative of Union Oil Co., saying that he had heard from people at Harvard that I had an M.S. degree from the University of California and might be interested in a summer job working in the Union Oil research laboratory in San Pedro, California. When I answered in the affirmative, they offered me a summer job to start as soon as I could get there, and lasting until I had to return to my teaching job in the fall. By that time I had received and accepted the offer from Vanderbilt, so this generated quite a maneuver for us: shipping our worldly goods, except clothes, to be stored in Nashville until we returned by way of Los Angeles. We accepted the challenge without any hesitation. Again, it was "Golden Gate, I'm coming to ya."

Our final weeks at DePauw were uneventful, and I was able to get considerable research done on the first of a series of papers entitled "Branched-Chain Fatty Acids." This series was destined to extend to No. XXV, published in 1953. This first paper was submitted to JACS on Feb. 4, 1942, three days less than two months after Pearl Harbor Day, and about five months after my arrival at Vanderbilt University. It was made possible by the gift of apparatus from Louis Fieser.

Our departure from Greencastle involved a flurry of activity. We had to first decide what Roger, Rebecca and I needed while living in Long Beach for about three months, then pack that in our Chevrolet sedan, keeping things we would need for the trip accessible. Simultaneously we had to arrange for the moving van to arrive early in the morning to load our goods for shipment to Nashville and leave us enough time to make a little progress on our trip west. On that day of departure, of course we had to live on what we were carrying in the car, just as we would on the several days following. The complicating factor was our three-year-old son. My recollection of that day is largely a blur, but somehow or other we bedded down that night some place west of the Mississippi River.

Rebecca's mother, Rolena, had been able to rent a small house for us at Belmont Shores, a suburb of Long Beach built along the seashore. Of course we went to Rebecca's parents' home after our long trip with Roger. After resting up for a day, with Rolena to take care of Roger, we went the next day with Rolena to Belmont Shores to take possession of our rented house. This house belonged to a professor at Long Beach State College, who always took a vacation somewhere else during the summer and made some money by renting his house, complete with furniture. It was a small house, stuffed in between two similar houses, with a tiny front yard. It was only two blocks from a nice sandy beach that was open to the public, including us. This location proved to be ideal for us for the summer, and we felt quite grateful to Rolena for finding it for us. The beach was especially wonderful for Roger, also for Rebecca, because it made taking care of Roger a pleasure rather than a chore. Being a veteran beach bum from her early years, Rebecca was beach-wise and kept her very fair skin covered sufficiently to avoid problems with sunburn. I also enjoyed the beach, especially after I began to be able to work the swing shift frequently. The swing shift was from 4 P.M. to midnight, only eight hours because of being able to '"eat lunch on the job." I will develop this angle later, after I learned what my job would be. Suffice it to say that, on the swing shift, I would get home at about 12:30 A.M. and get a good night's sleep until about 8:30 A.M., have breakfast, then head for the beach with a lunch that Rebecca packed for us, return to the house, get a leisurely shower, and head for work at about three-thirty. What a vacation with pay! Especially since it followed about five years when ten-hour work days were sometimes routine for me.

For my first day at work I was instructed to report to the Union Oil office in Los Angeles. While I waited for a few minutes in the reception room, two other new summer employees arrived. One was named Black and was a graduate student at Princeton. I forget the name of the other one, but he was a graduate student at an upstate New York college, probably Rensselaer. Apparently Union Oil was seeking to enlarge the pool of Ph.D. chemists available to them by recruiting in the east. When the Union Oil personnel manager came in, the first thing he did was explain that demands on the refinery by the war in Europe were putting a heavy demand, in turn, on the analytical laboratory, which was integral to keeping the refinery running at over-capacity. As a result, he would appreciate it if any or all three of us would agree to shift to the analytical lab for the summer. I had done so much analytical work during my graduate work at Yale that I had, during my job-seeking at Harvard, applied for a job at Dartmouth teaching analytical chemistry. Fortunately, they turned me down and hired a physical chemist who was graduating from Harvard. I immediately volunteered to shift to the analytical lab. Black, the Princeton man, followed my lead, but the man from upstate New York demurred. During the next few weeks, a rather ironic situation developed. Due to the operation of the refinery at over-capacity, a hard push was being made in the effort to keep up with demand. Among other things, this involved throwing a lot of manpower into proceeding from a semi-works to a full production plant. This was a very critical and delicate operation, with every employee serving where he could do the most good. This resulted in the new summer employee from New York spending most of his time riding herd on the graveyard shift for the semi-works, which was being beefed up to full production. Of course this did not make this summer employee very happy, whereas Black and I were quite satisfied with our work in the analytical lab.

Before terminating our meeting in the Los Angeles office, we filled out some papers directed especially to two things: one was learning where each of us lived, and who had a car they were willing to use as a car pool vehicle, for a small fee. It turned out that the two people who came into the office with me lived between Belmont Shores and the refinery in San Pedro. I volunteered to pick up these two and take them to work. Occasionally I would get a telephone call to pick up somebody else, but after a couple of weeks the New York man disappeared into the graveyard shift. There was inevitably a lot of car pool juggling. For example, my riders had to be reassigned whenever I worked on the swing shift. This was rarely a problem because there were not many new employees except for the summer ones. The other minor matter that was settled before I left the office was getting instructions for getting something called a Social Security number, which I had never heard of before.

As soon as I actually went to work in the analytical lab, I discovered that Union Oil had a very enlightened system for operating the lab. They did not assign a certain procedure to one person and keep him on that specific procedure for a long period. The merits cited for that system included the expectation that the operator would become quite expert at his procedure, and hence be able to do a better and faster job. There is, however, another side to the coin. Neglecting the fact that the operator might become bored with his job and thus do it routinely and with no interest, this system can also generate scheduling problems since the variety of analyses varies from day to day. This variety of analyses was conspicuously present in the Union Oil lab. In any case, the foreman assigned certain procedures to each man at the beginning of the week, and changed the mix to accommodate the flow of work to the lab. Another thing I became aware of soon after my start, was the practice of shifting the swing shift from one man to another, because this shift was regarded as unattractive by a majority of the workers. For this same reason, trading between swing shift and regular shift was allowed as long as the person on the swing shift was able to perform satisfactorily all the analyses that came in from the refinery and the loading platform. The principal function of the swing shift was to keep the refinery and the loading platform operating around the clock. Since the beach was more attractive to my family than social activities in the evening, I became interested in the swing shift at once. I asked the foreman, who was a very nice chap, to give me assignments which would allow me to work the swing shift. This was quite agreeable to him, for it would solve his problem of finding enough happy workers for the swing shift. It also tended to make me popular in the lab. I worked hard to master the procedures assigned to me, and gave the foreman the word when I felt ready for another set of procedures useful for keeping the refinery and loading platform in operation. After about a month, I went onto the swing shift and stayed there for most of my tenure.

Knowing all the procedures necessary on the swing shift and working that shift made my work at the refinery quite interesting. By noting the analyses that came to me, I soon became familiar with nearly everything that went on in that refinery, from hot neck grease to the naphthenic acid still. Around the middle of the summer, they gave the summer workers a tour of the refinery, which was especially meaningful to me—learning where all those analytical samples came from. This was especially true because of some adventures I had on the swing shift. Soon after I started in this shift, I encountered an anomaly in the Indiana Oxidation Test, the monitoring of which was one of my duties. This test checked on the rate of breakdown in an engine oil under the operating conditions of high heat in the engine. At that time, once an oil started breaking down, depositing a lot of carbon and sludge in the engine, it then went to pieces rapidly so that the engine would be ruined unless the oil was changed. Changing the oil after one thousand miles was imperative. On this night the two or three dozen test samples began breaking down early in the evening except for four of the samples, which kept rolling along. Being new on this job, I telephoned the foreman at home, following directions I had received, and asked him if there was anything I should do about that behavior. He replied that there was nothing for me to do except to be sure to check those samples just before leaving. He would check them first thing the next morning. When I came to work at four the next day, the lab was buzzing with excitement. Those four samples were a competitor's engine oil, and they were still rolling along. I was pulled off the swing shift, and set to work finding out what was in that oil. By a twist of fate, I was working for the research lab for a while. I consulted the row of big books on the shelf above the hand-cranked calculators and asked the foreman some questions before starting to do experimental work. The foreman had an M.S. degree from the University of Illinois in analytical chemistry, and he really knew his business. After a few days I told him that the competitor's oil had an additive in it which was the barium salt of a phenyl monophosphate. Two people from the research lab appeared within a few minutes to question me about the basis for my conclusion. Interestingly enough, one of those who came to talk to me was doing post-doctoral work in the lab next to me when I was working for my M.S. degree at Berkeley. As a result of this furor, the direction of research for several people in the research lab was changed to searching for additives to engine oil that would prevent breakdown for a long period. Before I left for the summer, Standard Oil Co. of California had billboards spread all over California touting their marvelous new engine oil. I think it was called RPM Oil.

I had another adventure on the swing shift, of an entirely different sort. Early one evening I received a sample of naphthenic acids from the loading platform. This material was used for impregnating canvas to protect it from attack by mildew in the tropics. A tank carload was usually blended from two or more stills in order to meet required specifications. By the time of this event I had a good idea of the range of specifications set for these samples, for I had frequently received them. I noted that my numbers were different from what I expected, so I made a check by doing two additional samples. When I reported my numbers to the loading platform, the telephone receiver was slammed down hard. I had only a fifteen minute wait before I received another sample from the loading platform. The numbers were the same, so I again did a double check. When I reported these numbers, the man at the loading platform, after giving a lurid description of me and my ancestors, demanded that I check my results. When I told him that I had already run a duplicate check, and that all the numbers were the same as on his preceding sample, that telephone really took a beating. When I came to work the next morning, I was greeted with cheers. Apparently, this SOB at the loading platform was not popular with the analytical lab. He had turned some wrong valves in blending the load, so the tank car had to be unloaded and reloaded to meet specifications. Merely a two-day delay in a large shipment overseas.

As indicated in the above report of two selected incidents, I thoroughly enjoyed my summer of work at the Union Oil Co. However, Rebecca and Roger also enjoyed this summer. We still occasionally look at a picture that we have of our three-year-old son charging through the edge of the surf at the beach. That son is now retired and has spent the past few years sailing around the South Pacific in a forty foot yacht. How time flies! I also enjoyed, during this summer, getting better acquainted with Rebecca's parents, and they enjoyed getting acquainted with their first grandson. In addition, Rebecca and I attended to spending the extra money I had earned on some much needed furniture and table dishes.

In order to buy a table setting of Catalina Pottery, we left Roger with Rolena and took the boat from Long Beach to Catalina Island. It was a beautiful day, and we enjoyed the trip, especially me. I had never been to Catalina Island, and was fascinated by its unusual topography. At that time, commercial development had not really damaged the attractiveness of the area; I presume that has changed by now. We used some of my summer earnings to buy a set of pottery dishes which Rebecca selected. In addition, there was enough money left to pay for most of the set of Heywood-Wakefield furniture we bought for our bedroom and dining room. We had sold most of our furniture, which we had rented from Fournier in Cambridge, for a small sum to the person who succeeded me at DePauw. We bought our new furniture by mail from a discount house in Boston, which we had learned about while in Cambridge. We went to a Heywood-Wakefield warehouse in Los Angeles to select what we wanted, took the numbers off it, and sent our order to Boston. For this sort of thing the Boston area was ahead of the other places we had been. For delivery of the furniture in Nashville, we had to wait to get an address before we called for the furniture. This meant about a three week delay with no bed, so we bought a studio couch in Nashville. We still have that couch in our sun room in Berkeley.

When the day came for us to leave Union Oil, they offered us extra pay if we would stay a few days longer. The pressure on the analytical lab was increasing, so every day we stayed was a big help. By staying five more days, we got enough money to finish paying for the furniture, but that left us very pressed for time to get to Nashville. With two of us driving and Roger still sleeping in his hammock, we were on the road for long hours, and we made it with no days to spare. I was not especially worried about an unexpected delay making us late, for the first week of school involved only registration, no classes. By driving carefully, as we always have, and with a little bit of luck, we were not late.

My last day at Union Oil Co. involved the usual thing of first signing all the pages in my book where my data was recorded. This was routine as a precaution against needing such data in connection with patents or lawsuits. The final maneuver was to talk with the head of the personnel office. I had anticipated that I might get an offer of a permanent job with them, so I had thought quite a bit about what my answer should be. I liked working for Union Oil during this short period, and both Rebeca and I were anxious to get back to California; however, I had decided that it would be foolish for me to make any commitment. I would tell them that, in view of the war clouds becoming more ominous, I would have to think it over. I wasted my time thinking of that sort of thing. I did get an offer of a permanent job—as head of college recruitment for all of Union Oil Co. I wasted no time in turning that down. I have never been able to imagine why they should have offered me such a job. They obviously had a very poor picture of my character—a social introvert who abhors drinking ethyl alcohol.

In spite of feeling rushed, we had a good trip to Tennessee. On our drive to California, we did not let Roger drink anything except water in a restaurant or motel, and condensed milk, which he loved. He had been fed condensed milk since a few days after birth, and so he naturally liked the taste of it, which is pretty bad compared to fresh milk. In later life he rebelled against fresh milk. On the way home, with expectation of a more stable immediate future, we decided to let him have a cold soft drink whenever we stopped for gas or to eat. The weather was very hot all the way. After a day of this, Roger kept his eye on the gas gauge and frequently asked, "Daddy, don't you think we need gas?" We did stop more often than necessary, in spite of being rushed. We needed some Coca-Cola—to make sure we did not get sleepy while driving, of course. When we arrived at our destination, we did not stop at Nashville since we had no address there, but drove the thirty-two miles to Murfreesboro, where my parents were expecting us. They gave us a warm welcome, especially Roger.

Chapter 9

THE WAR YEARS

The day after we arrived in Murfreesboro I went to Nashville and to Vanderbilt, and then to Furman Hall, the old building where the chemistry department was located. Everything was exactly the same as it was when I left there seven years ago, so I knew where to find the office of the chairman, Professor Breckenridge. He welcomed me, and told me that I would have no duties until classes started next week, but suggested that I touch base with Professor Ingersoll to find out where my office (actually a laboratory) would be. I went to Ingersoll's office, found him in, and we discussed what I would be doing on the organic chemistry side. In addition to helping him run the laboratories in the elementary organic chemistry course, I would be expected to be in charge of the advanced organic chemistry course. I was not expecting this, but did not object, for there were no more than a dozen students in the course, just as when I took it seven years ago. At every step of getting reoriented there proved to be no change in anything. That changed rapidly after December 7.

Professor Ingersoll told me that he would alert Professor Bircher that I was aboard, since Bircher was not there that week. He then took me down to see Tom Marshall, the big colored man who was in charge of the stockroom, and was also in charge of such things as giving me keys to the building, library, stockrooms, and my office (laboratory). I did not know at that time that Tom was also the glass blower, the machinist, and actually in charge of running the department in terms of its physical aspects. He had a college degree in chemistry, and was something of a legend in the department. I rapidly learned that for anything I might want, including a major item of equipment, the first thing to do was to see Tom. It was natural, therefore, that it was Tom who would show me my laboratory, get it cleaned out, and help me supply it with laboratory equipment. From square one, Tom and I were destined to become close friends. He would even fix Roger's broken toys—and refuse pay for it.

Since my teaching did not start until two days into the next week, Rebecca and I left Roger with his grandmother, who had no objection to that arrangement, and began commuting to Nashville in search of a place to live. It was very important, indeed necessary, for us to find a place to live outside the bowl in which Nashville was located. Since soft coal was the principal fuel then available at a much cheaper price than electricity, essentially all space heating was done with furnaces burning soft coal. Prevailing winds, except in storms, blew right over the bowl Nashville was located in, leaving smoke and other pollutants for the inhabitants to breathe. The smoke was worst in the winter, because more soft coal was burned in colder weather. Forcing industry to eliminate air pollution from their smokestacks accomplished very little, and there was no way that residences, both apartments and single family houses, could be forced to eliminate the smoke coming from their chimneys. Installation of Cottrel precipitators in every house was obviously completely impractical economically, and no alternate fuel was available. This problem was solved after the war because of the building (to meet war needs) of a very large diameter pipeline to carry petroleum products from the Texas oil fields to the northeast industrial areas. Areas between Texas and the northeast tapped this pipeline to bring natural gas to the cities, so that inhabitants no longer had black lungs. The present situation in Nashville forced us to search for a place to rent, and the suburb on the side of Nashville where Vanderbilt was located was Belle Meade, probably the most upscale of the Nashville suburbs. This was not helpful to a person looking for a place to rent—all the Nashville suburbs were upscale. The city itself was populated mostly by those who could not afford to live in the suburbs, generating an obvious political problem, which we frequently encountered while living in Nashville (considering the suburbs as a part of Nashville). In spite of the deck being stacked against us, by luck and persistence, we found a place to live in Belle Meade.

The place we were able to rent had many good features, which were obvious when we rented it, and a few bad features which we discovered later. We were able to overcome the bad features as we encountered them, and we continued to feel very fortunate in being able to find such a nice place in such a nice suburb, especially after December 7. A problem we encountered immediately was the absence of a bus line anywhere near our location. Finding baby-sitters in this neighborhood was not something likely to happen. We usually used college girls whom we picked up near Vanderbilt and returned to their residences afterwards. This situation was alleviated by our having few social engagements during the year we lived in that house. Another problem we encountered at once was the little coal burning water heater in the basement. I learned how to manage it in order to prevent it from going out overnight, but I still had to carry coal to it and carry ashes away from it. Coal gives lots of ashes. The floor of the basement was dirt, which was not so bad except after very heavy rains, when a stream of water flowed through a crack in the foundation on the uphill side of the house. Of course, the water heater and the coal were stored on the side of the basement uphill from the little stream. After all, other people had lived in the house before us.

We encountered no delay in getting our belongings shipped from Greencastle and delivered to our new residence. After the studio couch had been delivered, we were ready to move to Belle Meade. Having all our belongings with us again was a great improvement. Both of us had to get adjusted to a lifestyle which was entirely different from anything we had encountered previously. The nearest bus line was a mile or more away, the nearest shopping area was much further; Vanderbilt was six or eight miles away, and we had one car. We worked things out as the situation developed, but one system took care of most things. All my afternoons at the university were occupied by afternoon labs. Thus I would stay home in the morning and take care of Roger while Rebecca attended to whatever was needed, such as buying groceries. I would then go to school after eating my lunch. Otherwise I ate lunch at the Kissam Hall cafeteria which was inexpensive and served satisfactory food. Since my brother was in Murfreesboro, thirty miles away, and we went there occasionally, we made no effort to contact a doctor immediately.

My teaching job was rather time consuming , but as soon as I had gotten oriented, I was able to spend a significant amount of time on research. I was especially anxious to be able to finish the paper which was then more than half done because of my work at DePauw. The most time consuming job I had to do in order to publish this paper resulted from the fact that I had made fourteen new compounds in the course of this work. A compound cannot be claimed as new unless there is an elementary analysis; i.e., the percent of carbon and hydrogen contained in the compound. This is not the only requirement for a valid report of a new compound, but it was the most essential one at that time. I did not have the funds for sending a sample of each of these compounds to a laboratory whose business was carrying out such analyses, and at that time Vanderbilt did not supply research funds for that sort of thing. I had done many such analyses during my research with R. J. Anderson at Yale, and with the assistance of glass blowing and machine work by Tom Marshall, I was able to build the combustion furnace required for such work. Fortunately, Vanderbilt had on hand a microbalance required for weighing the very small samples used. Apparently, that microbalance had never been used, and so it was especially fortunate for me that it was on hand; I encountered no competition for its use. There remained the matter of doing two analyses that check each other for each of the fourteen compounds. I finished building the combustion furnace a few days before December 7, Pearl Harbor Day.

I certainly had no powers of prophecy, but I did have a premonition that I should work hard to get this paper finished. I certainly was as astonished as everybody else at the events which forced us into the war. How could we have anticipated the most treacherous attack of all time? How could we have expected that this little country, Japan, would have leaders so stupid as to think they could conquer the U.S. militarily and take for theirs all that we had worked to build for one hundred and fifty years? The attack by the Japanese did not affect me directly and immediately; probably in part because we were so far from the west coast, and in part because it took some time for the government to get the wheels turning on such things as gasoline rationing. In any case, I poured on the coal and was able to send my paper to the Journal of the American Chemical Society (JACS) in time for it to be received on January 4,1942. My next paper was published in 1944, and this was made possible, in spite of distractions, by two things: my combustion furnace for micro-analyses continued to function like a champ, and I had no teaching during the summers.

Most of the events during the war years are a blur in my memory; partly, no doubt, because of a deliberate attempt on my part to erase them. Bad enough to have experienced these events; certainly no virtue in recalling them. Thus, this chapter will be largely a collection of scenes, rather like the situation in Chapter 1. After a flurry of rationing of everything from gasoline to toilet paper to food to shoes for a kid who wore them out rapidly, I remember our search for a house to buy. Renting in Belle Meade after the start of the war progressed from difficult to impossible. Thus, we had to buy a house unless we remained in the unsatisfactory house we were renting. I had enough money for a down payment—barely—saved starting at about the age of four by putting nickels, dimes, and quarters in a little bank which rang a bell each time we pulled the lever down to make a deposit. When the register reached $10, a slide in the bottom of the bank could be opened, and Dad would put it in a savings account. When this account, supplemented by cash gifts from relatives for Christmas and birthdays, finally got large enough, Dad would put it into a U.S. treasury bond. We cashed in these bonds to make the down payment on the house. Spending this nest egg made me very apprehensive, even though I kept telling myself that this is why my dad trained me to save money. I was made even more nervous about the whole thing because neither of us had ever borrowed money—and such an enormous sum. I also reminded myself that Dad would be there if I needed help. We were able to buy a beautiful brick house, with three bedrooms and two baths, and surrounded by about a half acre of nice lawn. It was not at all out of place in the upscale suburb of Belle Meade. We paid $9,000 for it. There were two reasons that an insurance company was willing to loan us enough money to supplement my nest egg and make up that large sum: first, I was employed by Vanderbilt University; second, the draft seemed not threatening to me; I was thirty and had a wife and one child, with another obviously on the way. In 1945, we sold that house for $13,500. That gave us enough to make the down payment on a beautiful home in Berkeley, with a magnificent view across San Francisco Bay. Price: $14,000. That left us enough to pay $1,500 for a vacant lot next door to the west of us to protect our view of the Bay. We still live in this Berkeley home, thanks to

Proposition 13; otherwise, we would be unable to pay the taxes on this property.

As has been noted above, Rebecca was pregnant when we started looking for a house to buy. We had decided, soon after we arrived in Nashville, that the time had come for us to try for another child. Roger would be four years old in October, and Rebecca felt strongly against a single child in a family; I was not averse to it. As happened before, one try was sufficient. The expected time of arrival was in October, the same month Roger was born.

Soon after Rebecca became pregnant, Roger became very ill. After a few days his temperature rose to about 105 degrees. Since it was impossible for a newcomer to find a doctor in Nashville during this war time, I telephoned my brother John, who was practicing medicine as a pediatrician in Murfreesboro, explained that Roger was very ill, and asked if he could help us. He replied that he would try to locate a doctor in Nashville who could call on us at once; if that should not work out within a half hour, he would set out for our house at once. After about twenty minutes, John called to report that he had found a competent doctor named Frazier Binns who would come to our house at once. There was only a short wait before Frazier Binns knocked on our door. He took one look at Roger, felt his forehead, and without doing anything else first, he wrote out a prescription for sulfathiazole, a recently introduced sulfa drug. He asked if I had enough gasoline to drive to the drugstore and back. When I answered in the affirmative, he said, "Take this prescription to the pharmacist and tell him it is very urgent. Drive carefully but not too fast. Give the child his first dose as soon as you get back. I will stay here and see what I can do about lowering his temperature." When I got back, Dr. Binns was gone, and Rebecca was ready with some water to give Roger the first pill (it could have been two pills). When I left for work the next morning, Roger seemed better; his temperature was down and he moved around a little. When I returned from work that night, Roger was jumping up and down holding onto the side of his crib, and yelling for food. Rebecca was standing in the door, weeping. My eyes were not dry as I put my arm around her and kissed her.

At this period in our lives, things were happening to us in a rather staccato manner. A few months after we arrived at Vanderbilt, on January 22, 1942, I received a letter from the editors of Organic Reactions, asking me to write a chapter for the third volume of that series of books. The plan was to publish a volume yearly, with each volume to contain about fifteen chapters, each chapter on a different subject and with a different author. My chapter, in volume three, would be entitled "Synthesis of Benzoquinones by Oxidation." It was apparent to me that Louis Fieser was obviously responsible for my being chosen for inclusion in this series of books, and that this would be a great asset to me in seeking a faculty position in a major university. Clearly, it would be a big mistake for me to decline this invitation, even if I were not vitally interested in writing such a chapter, I was pleased at being given the opportunity. It was not surprising that I had become interested in quinone chemistry when I spent two years of close association with Louis Fieser. I estimated that the time required to write the chapter would cause me to publish one or two less research papers, but that being an author in Organic Reactions would more than compensate for having a few less research papers published. Thus, I cheerfully accepted the invitation. It scares me a little to realize that if the timing of several things had been a little different, I might have refused the invitation, and this would have been a ghastly mistake.

After we had bought our new home, but before we had moved into it, I received a letter from Professor Homer Adkins of the University of Wisconsin, asking me to take a "war leave" from my job at Vanderbilt to become the group leader of a group of about six people working on high explosives at the Explosives Research Laboratory in Bruceton, Pennsylvania, just outside Pittsburgh. Adkins was head of Division 8 of the National Defense Research Committee (NDRC). NDRC was the civilian arm of the war research effort, and the business of Division 8 was high explosives. Of course I received this letter at the university. After staring at it for a while, and complaining to no audience about how the gods and the fates seemed to be zeroing in on me, I realized that I had to go. Not only would I become a disappointment to so many who had befriended and helped me all along life's way, but I would also have trouble living with myself if I declined. For anyone who did not have the experience of living in our country during those times, it is quite impossible to understand the sentiment that prevailed among nearly all the populace. Things that various people said became slogans or illustrations of determination, such as Winston Churchill's statement, in his famous "blood, sweat, and tears" speech: "We will fight them in every street in London, and we will never give up." I liked the story about the chaplain who was caught aboard his ship when the bombs began coming down. According to the story, he knew how to fire an anti-aircraft gun, and found a sailor to pass ammunition to him. At one point, he was reported to have said, "Praise the Lord and pass the ammunition; I just shot down that son-of-a-bitch." Many of those much younger than I must have heard the song in which variations of that comment appear. In any case, I went home and sadly broke the news to Rebecca.

As soon as we had the news that I was going to Pittsburgh to work for the NDRC, I took out term life insurance through a program offered by the university. This has proved to be the only time in my entire life that I have taken out any kind of life insurance. We never talked about it, but we both knew that I might not come back. About two days before I left, we went to a movie, "Holiday Hotel." It was probably the first movie we had attended since coming to Nashville. The song "White Christmas," sung by Bing Crosby, became something of a souvenir of our last night together before I left for Pittsburgh. We have numerous recordings which contain that song: first LP records, then tapes, and finally compact discs.

I had been in Pittsburgh for several weeks before I received word via a telegram that my second child was a son, named Marsden Starbuck Cason. His first name was Rebecca's maiden name and his middle name was her mother's maiden name. We had selected this name after long discussion and cogitation, for we had to deal with the strong ambition of my parents for a second son to be a Junior. They were deterred somewhat when I explained to them that it could not be Junior; it would have to be the Third (III). Since neither of us could bear to hurt my parents, we had to think of a name which a man would be proud to bear, but which would mollify my parents. Using Rebecca's family names did the job. We detected no sign of disappointment from either of my parents, which is more than could be said about Roger's name.

It was only after I returned from Pittsburgh that I got the full story about Rebecca's heroic performance at Mardy's birth. I already knew that she had some steel in her soul. Her mother had agreed to come from California to take care of Roger when Rebecca went to the hospital, as well as after the newborn returned to his new home. By good fortune, the obstetrician lived in Belle Meade in a location which made Harding Place, where we lived, on his route to Vanderbilt Hospital. According to the story, to which I listened enchanted, the obstetrician told Rebecca to telephone him after she had the car running and just before she left for the hospital. He then said, "If you should decide that you can't make it, pull just off the road and put on your blinker light. I will arrive in a very few minutes and take whatever action is indicated." She made it—with a little time to spare.

In contrast to Roger's neonatal behavior, Mardy did a lot of crying after he arrived at home. Rebecca decided that she was not giving him enough to eat, which would not be surprising under the circumstances. She made a telephone call to John, who told her to put him on a bottle at once. This cured the problem. After Rolena had left, Memur came from Murfreesboro for a few days. I was destined to come home in December, but this was not known at that time.

My trip to Pittsburgh by train was no more troublesome than normal for those times, when every railroad station was jammed with soldiers. Only high ranking military personnel were allowed to travel by air, and the NDRC was civilian. In time of war the military is in control of the country. That is why our Constitution wisely gives Congress the authority to declare war, but our President is commander-in-chief of the armed forces in peacetime as well as wartime. Following instructions I had received by mail from Professor Adkins, I checked in at the Webster Hall Hotel, which was in an area of apartment houses, the University of Pittsburgh, the Carnegie Library, and numerous other institutions. It was on the other side of "The Rock" from the confluence of the Allegheny and Monongahela Rivers. The Rock was a large promontory between the rivers, with a relatively small area of the industrial section between it and the confluence of the rivers. Early the next morning I met Homer Adkins and the others who traveled in a car to the Explosives Research Laboratory, which was located on property owned by the Bureau of Mines near Bruceton. Those besides me who regularly traveled in "the car" were Monk (Larkin) Farinholt, from a small college in Virginia, Frank Long from Cornell, and Louis Hammett, a pioneering physical organic chemist from Columbia. Any visitors were directed to register at the Webster Hall Hotel and meet the car there.

On arrival at the lab, everybody except me checked his ID badge with the guard and we proceeded up the hill to where the laboratories and offices were. I was turned over to the personnel director for introduction and equipping me with such necessities as my ID badge. The laboratories were in a long narrow building with a wide corridor extending the full length of the building. Each man's work space was in a bay opening to this corridor, with no wall separating the work space from the corridor. My office was the only small room set off by a wall with a door in it. The whole building was set up to minimize damage and allow rapid evacuation in case of an explosion. One of the first things my guide told me was that the roof of this one-story building was made very light so that it would be blown away by an explosion, with no danger of it falling on me. My reply: "Thanks, I will not worry about that sort of thing any more." This was my introduction to the crazy things which safety engineers do. They have two missions in life; one is to regulate everything the workers do; the other is to see to it that these regulations are followed. I have no sympathy for the difficult job these people have, for they would not be doing this job unless they liked it.

It became apparent to me immediately that this lab had been set up to do things regarded as too dangerous to be done near a populated area; however, I figured that it was my job to find out if I agreed with the safety engineers. My men were all working on a problem assigned by my predecessor, and so I did some work in the Carnegie Library in Pittsburgh on days when I secured leave to do this sort of thing. I learned a lot about types of compounds, such as nitramines, which I had never heard of before. It turned out that nitramines have some very useful characteristics, such as a high rate of detonation, which make them of great interest for use in aerial bombs.

After my first meeting with several technical representatives in Division 8, I learned that a major focus of interest just now was directed towards the explosive which we called RDX (British Research Department explosive) and the British called Cyclonite. In the early days of the German pounding of London from the air, an interesting thing had been noted. Most of the German bombs were loaded with TNT, which would blow a large hole in a modern building of reinforced concrete construction, but not destroy the building. TNT has a relatively slow rate of detonation, so the largest weight that can be fired simultaneously is some five hundred pounds. Any more present is simply blown around. But occasionally the

Germans would drop a bomb which completely demolished a large building of reinforced concrete. Eventually a bomb of this sort was found which had failed to detonate. It proved relatively simple, by use of x-ray diffraction and other analytical techniques, to discover the structure of this compound. Since this work was done in Britain, we called this explosive RDX. I was destined to spend a large amount of time working on RDX later.

After much library work and talking to other people at the lab, I was able to talk intelligently with my men about their research problems and reach any necessary decisions. Actually, only one of my men was doing what is properly called research. The others were doing very important things, however, such as seeking to learn why the explosive in anti-tank grenades had gone bad in the desert sun of northern Africa. This was the principal weapon expected to stop Rommel's tanks from rolling across northern Africa. Another man was experimenting to learn how much TNT was needed in a mixture with RDX to allow the mixture to withstand rifle fire without exploding (with the rifle using the same load used in aircraft guns.) The molten mixture was poured into a one by three inch pipe nipple which was capped at the bottom end, then capped at the top after filling. It was important not to have any of the explosive in the threads when the top was put on. We had a lot of trouble with the safety engineer on this maneuver, and finally had to fill pipe nipples with a lookout posted to warn of the approach of the safety engineer. I went out a couple of times to watch the testing of the pipe nipples by firing a rifle from behind a barricade at each of them, properly supported at the target. The results were reported in three ways: winner (no explosion); weak loser (occasionally explodes); EOH (echoed over the hill). This last was completely off the scale.

After becoming familiar with what my men were doing, I began to do some experimental work on nitro compounds which were not nitramines; however, I was not able to accomplish anything useful. I had to spend a lot of time writing reports and dealing with the safety engineer. My worst encounter with the safety engineer occurred when he came in to tell me that I was neglecting my duty of forcing my men to wear safety goggles. I responded by asking if he had tried seeing enough to do work in this hot, humid weather while wearing those safety goggles with side shields. When he responded that his job did not require wearing those goggles, I blew my stack, and told him that I would punch him in the nose if he did not get out of my lab and stay out of it. Five minutes later, my telephone rang. It was George Kistiakowsky, a Harvard professor with whom I had become moderately well acquainted during my Harvard days. After some conversation in which I described what had happened that caused me to lose my cool, George said, "Jim, I don't like this son-of-a-bitch any better than you do, but I think we are stuck with him, short of a real brawl; so how about cooperating with me as follows: I will tell him to not make unreasonable demands on your men, and if he has trouble with them to report the incident to me, not to you. As for you, I am now asking that you stay away from him unless he comes into your office, in which case I will not object if you punch him in the nose." I had no more trouble with that guy. Of course, I don't know what George told him, but things seemed to work out. After the war some reports worked around about what expert politicians the college professors who were running the NDRC proved to be. Somebody said, "After all, the politics in Washington is amateurish compared to what goes on at college campuses." That may be a slight exaggeration; however, it certainly was true that the academicians had a rough time of it with both the politicians and the generals.

A specific event will illustrate this situation. Homer Adkins made an appointment with a general to discuss a matter which Homer felt would interest the general. It turned out later that I was destined to be shifted onto this particular project, from what I was working on, because of its perceived importance by the military. When Homer arrived at the general's office, identified himself, and stated that he had an appointment, the orderly went back to the general's office to report Homer's arrival. The general declared, loudly enough for Homer to hear the comment clearly, "I am entirely too busy to talk to a long-haired son of-a-bitch such as this." When the orderly reported to Homer, "The general is very busy and does not have time to see you," Homer responded, "Will you please tell the general that I may be a son-of-a-bitch, but that I am not a long-haired son-of-a-bitch; I am bald-headed and clean-shaven." After the orderly controlled his laughter, he reported to the general, then came back to tell Homer that the general was ready to see him. Obviously, Homer spoke a language the general could understand. Is this diplomacy? I heard this story directly from Homer, when he gave me orders to shift my work to a new project. Whenever an NDRC man came back from Washington, he usually had new stories of frustration. An early description of this sort of frustration was SNAFU (Situation Normal, All Fucked Up). As things got worse, it was TARFU (Things Are Really Fucked Up). Finally, the peak was reached in the superlative, FUBAR (Fucked Up Beyond All Recognition). Fortunately, the war finally ended before the academicians cracked up. Among the professors who died a few years after the war were Homer Adkins and Werner Bachman, in whose laboratory the successful synthesis of RDX was developed.

During my few months in Pittsburgh I had no opportunity at all for doing anything that was fun. On one occasion, an industrial representative came to the explosives lab to talk to me about the formaldehyde he was selling to us, and he suggested that he take me to a movie that night. I accepted the invitation with pleasure. It was a good movie, named "Yankee Doodle," much better than the stage play of the same name which I saw much later. Other than this one incident, I recall nothing that could be called rest and relaxation. A major activity of the people that I was associating with at Pittsburgh was gathering in somebody's apartment to sit around and drink whiskey while discussing lab gossip and telling the latest dirty stories that had come by. Another type of event that was sometimes of interest was the daily lunch that we had at a rundown hotel in Bruceton. There was no better place to eat anywhere near the lab. Any visitors at the lab were taken there for lunch, and some of them were interesting in different ways. One day a visiting Britisher was lunching with us. After watching one of our group drinking a glass of milk, he commented, "The least you could do is put some gin in it." On another occasion, a visiting Britisher was in the Royal Air Force (RAF). Something in the conversation led him to tell a story about the German bombing of London. His girlfriend was a dispatcher who sat in front of a large board which showed the location of all the fighter planes in England that were ready to go up at a moment's notice to attack the German bombers. When bombers were located on the radar, her job was to select the best place to send up fighters. One night when she came to work, her board showed only fourteen fighters that were ready to go up against the bombers. On that night, the bombers did not come. It developed that Hitler had kept up a supply of bombers to pound London, but each time a bomber went down over England, the crew went down with it and was lost. Each time a Spitfire went down over England, the pilot bailed out, and went back up to fight again. Hitler ran out of bomber crews barely before England ran out of fighter planes. The outcome of so many things in this war seemed to hang by a thread.

During my associations while working with NDRC, I learned of many incidents which could not be entrusted to the news media for security reasons. Many of these incidents were so scary that broadcasting them would have been disastrous.

The thing that saved me from coming unraveled during my sojourn in Pittsburgh with so much spare time on my hands, was working on the chapter Synthesis of Benzoquinones, which had been assigned to me for the third volume of Organic Reactions. The nature of this work demanded my full attention, which did wonders in screening out bad thoughts. I spent many Sundays and Saturday afternoons (we worked on Saturday mornings) working in the Carnegie Library, gathering information for my writing. During the nights I organized tables and sections of the chapter, using my portable typewriter, which I had brought with me. My typing skill proved very useful.

When Homer Adkins visited the lab near the end of November, I asked to have a conference with him in my office. I explained to him the things about which I had been thinking. The work being done in this lab by my group was important work, especially two of the projects; however, it was not research; it was developmental or analytical. Since I had demonstrated some talent at organizing and directing research, as well as doing experimental work myself, I thought that my being there was a waste of an asset of the NDRC. As soon as I finished my prepared speech, Homer responded immediately, approximately as follows: "You are absolutely correct. Moreover, you have done the job for which we hired you and stationed you here." I was so happy that I was rendered speechless. Homer went on to say that he would arrange for my stint here to be terminated, and for me to become the technical representative for a contract between the Office of Scientific Research and Development (OSRD) and Vanderbilt University, to be activated at the first of the year. I should terminate my affairs here, including notifying the apartment where I was living, and return to Nashville as soon as I could arrange things. Due to the wartime conditions, my progress from then on was quite different from the speed with which Homer had acted. As a matter of fact, my recollection of everything that happened between that conversation with Homer and Rebecca meeting me at the train in Nashville is a blur. It is a fact, however, that I did get back to Harding Place in Belle Meade, and met my new son and stalwart wife before Christmas.

I was so happy to be back home that I was upset only temporarily by the way certain officials at Vanderbilt gave me a bad time over details of my returning to teaching. In view of the fact that I was involved in the present situation as a service to my country, which was at war fighting for the future of all of us, I regarded the behavior of the officials involved to be especially reprehensible. Just as when I was a student at Vanderbilt, I found the behavior of the faculty to be laudable in the extreme; that of the officials that I contacted to be disgusting. The person in charge of determining how my salary would be adjusted after my absence came up with the remarkable idea that I should lose half my salary since I returned at the end of a calender year. Actually, I did not have much trouble convincing this individual that since I had been away for one-third of the academic teaching year, I should lose one-third of my salary. I had a much harder time with my old enemy from my student days, Gerald Henderson, the business manager. He came flat out and said that he would not allow such dangerous work to be done in Vanderbilt buildings, since he did not even know what would be going on. After I reminded him of a few things, including the fact that we were at war, and how disgraced he would be if I decided to communicate some things to the newspapers, he reluctantly agreed to approve the contract if it included a statement that Professor Ingersoll could get a secret clearance so he would be knowledgeable of what was going on in our laboratory. Of course, Dr. Ingersoll, behaving in the manner characteristic of Vanderbilt faculty members, expressed no interest whatever in what Frank Prout and I were doing.

My contract allowed me to hire one or more research assistants, according to the requirements of the work. Franklin S. Prout was currently engaged in doing graduate work under my direction, so I hired him as my assistant. Since I did a lot of the experimental work, putting in about as much time as Frank did and Frank was such a good and hard worker, I never did feel the need for more assistance. In retrospect, I dare say that Homer knew what projects I would be assigned, and knew that they required more know-how than manpower. All the work that Frank and I did was assigned a Secret or Top Secret classification, so I will not be discussing any of it in any way that would reveal just what was going on. I will discuss one general aspect of our work which was related to the RDX project. I am sure that this aspect of the RDX work was publicized after the end of the war. As previously mentioned, the work on RDX was focused on a safe, practical synthesis of RDX. Because of the urgency of developing this synthesis, it had been assigned to several labs at the same time. As things worked out over the months, Frank worked on several projects as the need arose, while I spent considerable time working with a polarizing microscope studying crystallography; an unexpected development dictated by need.

As has been briefly mentioned, the Germans had occasionally dropped a bomb on London that did a great deal more damage than their TNT bombs. These bombs, which were dropped occasionally, were found to be loaded with a new explosive which came to be known in the US as RDX. Since very large quantities of RDX would be required for the intended use, its synthesis must be adaptable to a large scale, and safe enough to justify such large scale manufacture. This was a truly daunting assignment, simply mind-boggling, and the consequences of making a mistake were frightening. To add to the pressure on those doing this work, it was apparent from the beginning that the German chemists had a head start of several years. RDX bombs had been dropped on London before America (henceforth, I will refer to the United States of America as America) was forced into the war by the treacherous attack by Japan. Furthermore, it could be surmised, judging from the infrequency with which the Germans dropped RDX bombs, that they had blown up a few manufacturing plants as a result of their failure to discover "the secret." The fact which eventually emerged was that American scientists defeated the German scientists. One could philosophise about whether this result depended on the fact that American chemists are much better than German chemists, or alternatively that American chemists were working in a free country, whereas German chemists were working under a dictatorship. It is my opinion that each of those factors made a significant contribution to our triumph. Furthermore, this specific triumph made a significant contribution to our defeat of Germany in World War II.

Later in the heavily accelerated study of the synthesis of RDX, other smaller projects were assigned to support projects that had been started earlier. One project required research chemists who also understood the study of crystallography using a polarizing microscope. A survey of the country to locate such individuals came up with only four, with me being one of them. My proficiency at the use of a polarizing microscope was accidental. In my work on the chemical content of the wax of the bovine tubercle bacillus, I encountered a compound which could not be identified by methods then commonly applied: melting point and elementary analysis. All the candidates for the identity of this compound had exactly the same elementary analysis, and the compound did not melt on heating, it simply decomposed. There remained only the crystal structure of the compound for its identification. Each crystalline compound has a characteristic structure which is different from that of every other crystal structure. By identifying the characteristics of the crystals of my compound, I could distinguish between the several candidates for my structure by reference to the literature on the candidate structures. This was easy if one understood the use of a polarizing microscope. Ergo, I persuaded the geology department to give a course on the use of the polarizing microscope if I could supply four students to attend the course. This was a university requirement regarding small graduate courses. The course was in the catalog but had not been given recently for lack of students. I persuaded three other chemistry graduates to sign on for the course, and so we took this one-quarter laboratory course. Interestingly enough, the other three besides me who were located for the NDRC work had not taken the course with me.

As for the need for use of a polarizing microscope in connection with RDX synthesis, the story starts with an iconoclast who was in the graduate school at Cornell University studying for his Ph.D. degree. Unfortunately, I do not remember his name. He was working for his degree in the field of organic chemistry; however, in the course of that work, he had also become quite interested in crystallography. By the time he arrived at the point of submitting his thesis, he decided that the use of crystal properties was a better method than the common ones in use, especially elementary analysis, for identifying a chemical compound. No matter how clearly the iconoclast explained that elementary analysis was worthless, the director of his thesis work refused to approve his thesis, on the grounds that JACS would not accept the work for publication, and Cornell would not award a Ph.D. degree for a thesis that was not acceptable for publication in JACS. At some stage in this debate between entrenched customs and the iconoclast, Cornell University received a contract from the OSRD for work on RDX. As usual, all available scientific personnel were put to work, including the iconoclast.

Naturally enough, the first thing that The Iconoclast did was take a look at a sample of RDX under the polarizing microscope. His first reaction was that he had been given a mixture of three things. He was assured that this was impossible, for the usual criteria of melting point, elementary analysis, and other minor characteristics determined on several different samples, demonstrated beyond any shadow of doubt that this sample of RDX was a pure single compound. And this proved to be correct! Proceeding on such well established, venerable principles, the Germans had blown up several RDX manufacturing plants. But in the land of the free and the home of the brave, it was possible for the iconoclast to be heard eventually. A chemical compound can be polymorphic. This means that it can form crystals with different properties, such as sensitivity to detonation by mechanical shock. It so happens that RDX can crystallize in three different crystal forms, which were designated as the alpha, beta, and gamma forms. The gamma form was very sensitive to mechanical shock, almost as sensitive as the primary explosive used in caps, which are detonated by a blow from a hammer in a gun. This small explosion then fires the principal explosive in the gun. The alpha form was quite sensitive, but nowhere near as sensitive as the gamma form. The beta form; however, proved to be much less sensitive to shock than the other two forms. This is the "secret" that the German chemists failed to discover. This discovery by the iconoclast made possible the manufacture of many hundreds of tons of "bomb-suitable" RDX without an accident. It was subsequently learned that the rate of detonation of RDX was high enough to give simultaneous detonation of thousands of pounds in one charge.

After the iconoclast's discovery, it was necessary to work out a procedure for making RDX crystallize only in the gamma form. The first step in this investigation involved picking out, with a pair of small tweezers, the beta form of RDX from a sample of the mixture. This small sample was then carefully examined under the polarizing microscope to ensure that not a single crystal of the other forms was present. This sample was then used to "seed" a saturated solution of a production mixture of RDX. While in solution, there is only one kind of RDX; when any crystal goes into solution, there is no record of which form of the solid crystalline material existed before solution occurred—crystal form is a characteristic of the solid state. Conversely, when a molecule of RDX in a hot saturated solution encounters a crystal form, added as a seed, then the molecule separates from solution as a crystal identical to the seed that it encountered. This new crystal then becomes a seed for forming more of the same. As the hot solution cools, formation of the same crystal continues until cooling has caused deposition of all the RDX that was dissolved in the hot solution. If the carefully selected sample of the beta form of RDX is used, then the entire production of RDX is in the beta form, ready to be processed in whatever way is necessary for loading into bombs.

The complicated procedure required for conversion of RDX to the beta form was worked out before a satisfactory, economically feasible manufacturing process was developed. Anticipation of this development was responsible for assigning several laboratories to work on this synthesis at the same time, each keeping in touch with the others through monthly reports. As a humorous sidelight on this multi-lab operation, one of the reports from one of the labs made reference to use of the "hair-raising procedure" of Cason and Prout.

The laboratory that developed the procedure which was eventually put into a pilot plant, then a semi-works, and finally into large scale production, was that under the direction of Professor Werner Bachman, at the University of Michigan. He was the son of parents who had emigrated from Switzerland to the land of the free and the home of the brave. As soon as enough RDX had been manufactured to meet the requirement, it was loaded into a bomber fleet which went over Mannheim, Germany, one night. Not all of those planes came back to their home bases, but Mannheim was wiped off the face of the earth. Hitler's management officers had stupidly concentrated the manufacture of ball bearings in one place, Mannheim. More efficient that way; also can be destroyed more efficiently. It is difficult to operate an army without ball bearings.

At some time during the latter part of 1943, I received a letter from Homer, telling me that he was shifting me to an important project which had developed in Division 9 of the NDRC. My OSRD contract would be shifted to Division 9, but he would continue to direct this work. Arthur Cope, at Columbia University, was the Head of Division 9, and he had been sharing with Homer, previously, certain projects which would profit from such an arrangement. This project had no direct relation to organic chemistry, but it required a man familiar with the handling of firearms and capable of doing or directing machine work. By that time Homer and I had become so well acquainted he knew that my dad had given me my first rifle at age eleven, and that I had spent a lot of my time during my teen years in Murfreesboro messing around in the machine shop that was a part of Dad's garage. Thus, I seemed to be the best available fit for the unusual project being inaugurated, and organic chemistry was cast aside for the duration. The new project was Top Secret so I will make no further reference to it.

As a necessary conclusion to this chapter, I must report on my personal activities in pursuit of my profession as a college professor. I will refer to the other part of my life, my supportive wife and two attractive children, only as regards their impact on my professional life. In time of war one's family is pushed into the background; that is why married men with children were the last category to be drafted. At the least they were with their families; after all, families also needed support during these trying, sometimes traumatic conditions.

After my return from Pittsburgh to my beautiful home in Belle Meade, I worked very hard to sandwich in with the war research what might be called my personal professional activities. The leaders of the NDRC always encouraged the professors who were "drafted" into the NDRC to not abandon their personal professional activities. Partly because of the work I did in Pittsburgh on my chapter for volume three of Organic Reactions, when I had time on my hands, I was able to submit the manuscript for this chapter on August 6, 1943. I also submitted to the JACS, on September 9, 1943, the second paper in the Branched-Chain Fatty Acid series, and on August 16, 1944, the third paper in that series. This was the end of the line for my personal research at Vanderbilt. I became completely immersed in working on the project in Division 9.

On April 17, 1945, I received a letter from Wendell Latimer, Dean of the College of Chemistry, University of California, in which he stated, "We are now looking for several young men who will form the nucleus around which we may develop our organic chemistry staff. I note that you wrote in 1940 stating that you would be interested in a position at Berkeley, and I would be very glad to have you write me concerning your present availability." In a long letter dated April 21, 1945, I responded to Dean Latimer's letter. The essence of my response was: I am very much interested in a position at Berkeley, and I am very familiar with the situation in organic chemistry there; therefore, I am in a good position to compare an offer from Berkeley with any other offers I might get. I was a little worried about the preceding sentence, but decided that I should not reveal at this early stage of negotiations how anxious I was to return to California. I was simply enchanted to receive a letter dated May 5, 1945, from Dean Latimer, in which the first sentence was: "I found your letter most encouraging." The second paragraph read: "Subject to official approval of the university administration, I am pleased to offer you a position as assistant professor in our department for the year 1945-46". After my euphoria had simmered down a bit, I realized that I should not rush madly into accepting the offer without getting more information about the parameters of my position in the department, especially about how much respect the older physical chemists would have for upstart organic chemists. I spent many hours in a debate with myself, during which Rebecca was very supportive. She listened to this debate and sometimes made suggestions, but never once reminded me how anxious she was to return to the Golden State. She knew that I also was anxious to return to California, but was justifiably concerned that organic chemistry would always be a poor third cousin at Berkeley, and I might find it difficult to get enough money from the budget to buy what was needed for research. I knew that essentially none of the equipment needed for research in organic chemistry was there.

Caught on the horns of this dilemma, I decided that I should consult Homer Adkins, who had been so helpful to me all through these trying times. I telephoned Homer, reported the letter I had received from Dean Latimer, and asked for his advice. He responded by saying that he was already planning to have me come to Madison to discuss what needed to be done in closing down work on the project in Division 9. As usual, Homer was ready to help me. On my arrival in Madison, we spent an hour or so discussing the few things that needed to be done on the Division 9 project, then proceeded to my problem. I explained in detail the things which concerned me about the situation at Berkeley, in particular the possibility, or probability, that organic chemistry would always remain a poor third cousin there. Homer listened carefully to my long presentation and showed no visible reaction except for crossing his legs frequently, a maneuver for which he was well known. After I finished, Homer promptly responded as follows: "I would advise most people not to plunge into that den of narrow-minded physical chemists, but you are such a stubborn son-of-a bitch that I advise you to take the job. They will never be able to budge you." I knew exactly what Homer was thinking about when he gave this rather forceful description of my stubbornness.

A Canadian chemist named George Wright had recommended that a certain type of compound should be synthesized in Division 8, and Homer assigned the job to me. After consulting the literature, I advised Homer that this recommendation of Wright's was one lousy idea; the meager information in the literature showed that such compounds were quite unstable. Homer insisted on the grounds that he did not want to alienate the only Canadian in Division 8, and so I agreed to do it to the best of my ability, but I continued to insist that it was a waste of time. I set Frank to work on the problem and also worked on it myself. We took great precautions to protect ourselves in case of an explosion. Frank had an explosion, which did not hurt him much because of his protective clothing and goggles—only some powdered glass in his face around the goggles. I do not remember if face shields had been in use at that time. Eventually, I was able to synthesize a compound of the structural type desired, and it was too unstable to be of any use. So much for that project.

It was years later that I learned, during a conversation with Wendell Latimer, that Homer knew a great many other things about my offer of a job at Berkeley, but that is for a later report. Since I was very anxious to take the job, but consulted Homer as a precaution against my making a mistake because of ignorance of things I needed to know, I wrote Dean Latimer a long, cautiously worded letter in which the opening paragraph was: "I was quite pleased to receive the offer contained in your letter of May 5, but before reaching a decision I wonder if I can get some information concerning the teaching responsibilities and research opportunities in such a position." Among other things, I also stated: "I might as well admit that I am decidedly allergic to teaching anything other than organic chemistry." I included that statement in my letter on account of being familiar with the practice in the department of expecting everybody to help with the freshman labs. Subsequent events revealed that this statement in my letter was very important.

I spent a lot of time composing this letter, since I did not want to lose the job opportunity by appearing too greedy. Thus, I was so pleased to receive a very favorable letter from Latimer that I immediately wrote a firm acceptance, and then telephoned Rebecca: "There was a very favorable letter from Dean Latimer in the mail today, and so I have written him a firm acceptance of the job. Next year, we are heading back to that Golden Gate for permanent residence." I then held the telephone receiver out at arm's length to reduce the decibels of the scream that was coming through. Both of us knew that an assistant professor is not at tenure rank, but I think that Rebecca was just as confident as I was that I would make it there. I thought of lines from a song that came out near that time: "It's the same old story, a fight for love or glory; the will to do or die. The fundamental things apply, as time goes by." Even so, I was somewhat surprised, and quite elated, when I received notice in 1948 of my appointment as associate professor.

Finally VJ Day arrived. Japan surrendered the day after the second atomic bomb was dropped on Nagasaki. As one might imagine, there was a lot of printer's ink expended during the days following the release of the atomic bombs. I can recall none of it that did not revel with great exuberance. There were millions, in this great country alone, who now knew that their loved ones were going to come home alive. Compared to the emotions of these millions, Rebecca's joy at coming back to California was trivial. There was a flood of tears of joy, and those who knew what had happened as a long prelude to the development of "The Bomb" and the decision to drop it thanked God that President Harry S. Truman had the courage and the wisdom to issue the order to drop it. There were numerous estimates of how many human lives were saved by Harry Truman's decision. The estimates ranged between one million and three million. During recorded history, there have been a few people who might have been able to claim that they were instrumental in killing a million people. How many people are there who can claim that they were clearly responsible for saving the lives of a million people? And yet, in modern times, it has become respectable for self-appointed "authorities" to debate at great length the moral principles involved in the whole affair of the atomic bomb. To people who were putting their lives on the line, and their loved ones, such debates are not only futile but positively contemptuous. In war against such as the Japanese warlords and Adolf Hitler, there is only one thing that counts: winning the war. Losing would have been the end of everything as we know it, so what is the debate about? About as important as the debate among ancient priests about how many angels can stand on the head of a pin.

In the final orders for closing down our contract with the OSRD, we were instructed to destroy everything that could be linked to the research that we were doing: papers, tools, chemicals, safety equipment, everything that could possibly be connected to our research. This was not a problem with most things, for they could be burned, but there was one thing which was a small problem and one larger problem. The tools that we had fabricated or had made, I buried in my parents' garden. Even if someone should some day be plowing deeply enough to hit this mass of pieces of rusting metal, no connection with anything could be deduced. A pound or two of various samples of high explosive was another matter. If we should call in the army to do it, the cost might reach a million dollars and several pounds of paper would be generated. And worse, we might be prosecuted because we failed to protect the top secret clearance involved. We finally decided to come down early on a Sunday morning and burn it. We judged it impossible for a pound or two of high explosive, spread in a thin layer against the ground, to detonate. And so at the crack of dawn, but not early enough to need a light which might attract attention, we spread it out in a bare spot behind Furman Hall and set a long line of wick material which we had bought and paid for with cash. After lighting the wick, we got behind large trees at a great distance. Our strategy worked perfectly; there was no detonation, but that blinding flash of light came near to causing us to crap in our jeans. We waited around for a while, but nobody showed up to ask any questions. We had judged correctly that foot traffic on that part of the campus at dawn on Sunday would be light.

And so those dreary days of the war, some periods worse than others, finally passed into history which I would be glad to forget.

CHAPTER 10

ORGANIC CHEMISTRY COMES TO BERKELEY

Since we had the opportunity to sell our house if we vacated it by August 1, we could not afford to decline the offer. The buyer would accept our loan as down payment, and pay the remainder in cash. We had paid on our loan for about four years, and had also sold a house in Murfreesboro, which my Dad had given me years before, to augment our equity in the house. Thus, we were in good shape to pay our moving expenses and make a down payment on a new home in Berkeley, unless that down payment should prove to be larger than expected. Ergo, we put our furniture and other impedimenta such as kids' toys in storage. We packed our clothes and what we expected to need for our trip to Fullerton in our car and migrated to my parents' home in Murfreesboro. As in our previous migrations, we were using our respective parents homes as terminals for a change in direction. We encouraged each other at this time by expressing determination that our wanderings would end in Berkeley. In order to complete my contract with OSRD, I commuted from Murfreesboro to Nashville by bus, and also took a bus back and forth from the bus terminal in downtown Nashville. The trip back to Murfreesboro in the evening was not so bad, but the morning trip to Vanderbilt was jammed every time. I can recall no trip that I did not stand up in both buses in the morning. I learned a lot about commuting. When I set out to buy a house in Berkeley, while the family remained in Fullerton, item one on my marching orders was: "The house must be in Berkeley or no more than 100 yards from the Berkeley line".

The schedule in effect at the University of California at that time was still the "war schedule," which set the fall semester to start in October, so we had enough time to take a leisurely trip to California; however, the trip was not leisurely, only slow. We were riding on tires that had been recapped twice with "ersatz" rubber (synthetic rubber). Ersatz is a German word whose equivalent in English is replacement, or substitute. Thus, this word crept into the English language with the meaning, "really bad substitute." We were advised before leaving for California that driving faster than 45 miles per hour would be likely to cause blowouts, so we followed that advice faithfully. We could not bear to even think of the consequences of acting otherwise, with the two kids in the car. The two kids fit well into the car. Roger was in the hammock that he had traveled in previously, and Mardy, age 3, slept on the back seat. Roger, in the hammock, was pulled down low enough to block Mardy from flying forward in case of a sudden stop or collision. I have no recollection of how many days were required for our trip, but driving from Tennessee to California at 45 mph is a very long trip. I also do not recall what route we took, or what towns we stopped at for the night, only events that were difficult to forget. The kids were old enough to go together to the rest room while Rebecca used the other one, and I took care of servicing the car, then followed the kids. At some town in Oklahoma, when Rebecca came back to the car before I had returned, she found a man doing something to one of the tires with a piece of wire and a pair of pliers. On inquiry, she was told that we had a slow leak around the valve stem, between it and the rubber cover. When Rebecca told him that we had a ration coupon for a new tire he advised against using it now, even if she could find the tire in town. He said, "I was real careful about twisting the wire so that it will hold but not bite into the rubber. It may last longer than the rest of the tire." When I came back from the restroom, and asked how much we owed for his assistance, he declined to accept any pay. A bright spot on our trip was that everywhere we stopped, people were very helpful to us. They probably felt sorry for a young couple traveling across the country with two kids, but it was also true that, with times as tough as they were for four years, people had learned the virtues of pulling together to help each other.

There were some incidents on the trip that we still recollect with pleasure. During the day, Roger's hammock was down and the kids engaged in various things besides looking at the constantly changing scenery. One thing they did was count the number of cars of a certain make, such as Chevrolet (we were still driving the sedan Dad gave us in 1938). Roger taught Mardy how to count; that took a lot of time. Early in the trip, after we had stopped for gas a couple of times, I became aware that Roger was looking over my shoulder now and then. I knew that he was up to something, but made no comment; I thought maybe he was looking at the speedometer, to see if he could catch me going too fast. After a while we learned what was up, via a comment from Roger: "Daddy, isn't your gasoline getting kind of low?" Every day was hot and got hotter as we started through Texas, so we always bought a cold drink for each of us at every stop. No danger of running out of gas!

The trip continued, with some levity and some worry, and with our tires holding up—until we were about fifty miles from Fullerton. We began to hear a thumping noise. Investigation revealed a "goose egg" protruding through a split in one poor old double recapped tire. We decided to let a little air out of it, and proceed at 35 mph until we reached S. Highland Avenue, or it blew out, in which case we could hardly be very far from a phone in such populated areas. The tire held out, and we limped home—quite a contrast to the arrival of Memur and me when we arrived before the wedding, but the kids and grandparents made it almost as lively.

The first thing the next morning Rollie took me down to his garage, and we bought a new tire, and also had the inner tube with the wired valve stem replaced, since that did not require a coupon. Later that day we received a telegram from Dean Latimer, stating that it had proved impossible to rent a place for us, and so I should anticipate the necessity of buying a house before bringing my family to Berkeley. Too many war workers were still living in the Bay Area. Thus, I made arrangements with Dean Latimer to come to Berkeley the next day. He said that he would meet me at Shattuck Square on the University Avenue side. I told him the flight I intended to take to San Francisco, and got his phone number so that I could phone him when I arrived at the Key Train station in San Francisco.

Rebecca was very much engaged with getting Roger enrolled in the second grade at grammar school, since we expected a significant delay before Rebecca could come to Berkeley with the kids. This was complicated by the fact that Roger had become worried about having no home other than that Chevrolet sedan. With help from Rolena, she was able to handle the situation.

Dean Wendell Latimer picked me up at Shattuck Square and took me to his home where I stayed for that night. His wife was returning from vacation the next day, so he had arranged for me to stay in a little apartment at Professor Calvin's house, beginning the next night and for as long as I wanted to stay. Many homes in Berkeley had been remodeled to put little apartments in the basement or attic, as a part of the effort to find housing for the overwhelming influx of war workers. I was rather overwhelmed by this royal reception by the dean of the College of Chemistry, a sensation that increased steadily and rapidly. The next morning he took me to his office in Gilman Hall, and soon after our arrival there he handed me an unsealed envelope, commenting that this was for me. Opening the envelope, I saw that it contained money, several bills. I was so astonished that I had trouble collecting my wits. Finally, I handed the envelope back to him, and said, "I really should not accept this money from you." He replied that it was not his money, that the College of Chemistry had a fund, called the Gilman Hall Fund, which was used in situations where a faculty member or a graduate student was in need of temporary assistance, such as helping to pay moving expenses. At that time, the university paid none of such expenses. After leaving the dean, I looked at the contents of the envelope and found five one hundred dollar bills. This was the beginning of a warm personal friendship between Dean Wendell Latimer and me, and also the beginning of my frequent contributions to the Gilman Hall Fund.

The dean then took me over to the "Old Chemistry Building" and showed me the room which had been a laboratory accommodating two graduate students, but now would become my office. I noted with pleasure that this room was much better than the room I had at Vanderbilt, and about twice as large as the space which I had used as a laboratory for my graduate work. We then went back to his office, where he instructed Miss Kittredge to give me keys to my office, the Old Chemistry Building, Gilman Hall, the library, and the organic chemistry stockroom. Thus I had a home base for my short stay at that time where I could start stocking my laboratory (office) while getting a place to live with my family. I was planning to land running in my new job. A final item to receive attention on that day was leaving my bag with a few clothes in it at the dean's office and arranging to meet Professor Calvin later in the afternoon to go to his house for the night. In so doing, I met his charming wife, Genevieve.

The next morning, after breakfast with Melvin and Genevieve, I went to the real estate office of Mason, McDuffie, the largest realtor in Berkeley at that time. An affable, elderly woman named Mrs. Bonsall was assigned to showing me around, and I spent the rest of that day riding around Berkeley in Mrs. Bonsall's Model A Ford. As to what kind of house to buy, I had my marching orders clearly delineated:

1. The house must be in the City of Berkeley, or in the immediately adjacent area in Contra Costa County which was east or north of Berkeley; not in Oakland or in the hot area to the east, over the hills. Having been in Berkeley for a year while I was in graduate school, we knew what to seek as well as what to avoid. We remembered vividly what it was like on an August day to drive from Berkeley through the tunnel into Contra Costa County—from an ice box into an oven. As has subsequently developed, there are many people who enjoy living in an oven rather than an ice box, but not us. Even with air-conditioning, not available in those days, we prefer the ice box. There was no discussion about what should be item No. 1 on my marching orders.

2. The house must have a good view across San Francisco Bay. How could it be otherwise? There must be constant reminiscing about those nights we spent loving each other in my Chevrolet coupe and making plans for our future together. And not only that, but such a view was sure to be worth big money in future years.

3. The house must have at least three bedrooms; one for us and one for each child. A fourth bedroom was highly desirable, but two was acceptable only if long search failed to find a house which met requirements one and two and had three bedrooms.

I looked at several houses that first day, most of which did not meet two of the criteria. One house met all the criteria, but had a characteristic on which I did not need any advice. It was built at the top of a lot which was so steep that stairs with a normal rise per step followed the terrain. Those steps were the equivalent of at least three floors, and the tiny garage at street level would accommodate only one car. I decided that only a fool would buy that house unless an escalator was planned.

On the second day, Mrs. Bonsall had more houses to show me, ones that were listed with another agent. The first two had a beautiful view of the Berkeley Hills or Tilden Park, but simply did not qualify according to my marching orders. Finally, she showed me a house on a very steep hill which Mrs. Bonsall's Model A was barely able to climb. There was a backyard much larger than any I had seen, but even steeper than the street in front of the house. But the front door was only three steps above street level, and there was a garage which could accommodate two cars only if one of them was smaller than our 1938 Chevrolet. There was a sweeping view of the whole bay, and so I told Mrs. Bonsall that I would like to see the inside. Everything looked OK, although the big window in the sun room had obviously been leaking badly during rains, and the furnace had no thermostat on it; it was controlled by hiking down to the basement and setting a valve by hand. The price was $13,500, significantly higher than all but one of the other houses I had looked at. I had not become accustomed to such large sums of money, and so I told Mrs. Bonsall that my present mood was to buy this house, and I did not want to look at any more houses, but I wanted to think it over. I would call her the next day. The house definitely met all the criteria in my marching orders. It had two baths, one on the main floor and one on the upstairs floor. It had not just three but four bedrooms, two upstairs, one on the main floor which was rather small but immediately adjacent to the bathroom, and one on the basement level. We were destined to learn much later that a bedroom on the main floor level and adjacent to the bathroom is a very important asset to any house. This sort of thing is appropriately called serendipity, since we had no clue about its importance until more than fifty years later. Since no other house I had looked at had all the features specified in my marching orders, I decided that this was the house for us. Things like leaking windows and an old furnace without a thermostatic control could be fixed, but lack of a view across San Francisco Bay was not fixable.

Since Wendell Latimer was my only available confidant, I went to his office the next morning, found him there, and asked for his advice. I told him that this house was so much better than any others I had looked at that I was not inclined to bargain for a lower price, even though the price was somewhat higher than the others I had looked at. Was I making a mistake? Judging from my later dealings with Wendell Latimer, I dare say that he knew I was angling for some indication of his current opinion about the likelihood of my reaching tenure rank at Berkeley. In any case, after shifting his cigarette from one side of his mouth to the other, using only his tongue, a maneuver which I later learned was famous, he stated: "In view of the instability of these times, and the fact that you have been unable to find another house that you like, I think that you should offer to buy it at the offered price. The real estate market is likely to become more active soon, so you probably will be able to change houses later, if necessary. Your immediate job is to get a place to live so that you can bring your family here to live with you." This was the first of many comments from Wendell Latimer that made me very happy and was proven by later events to be very wise indeed.

I entered into negotiations to buy the house at once, and had no trouble with making the down payment and arranging a loan from the Bank of America for the remainder. I had already opened an account with B of A, using the five hundred dollars in that envelope, and I had my bank book from Nashville which showed the considerable sum of money representing most of the net proceeds from selling our house in Belle Meade. I then arranged to meet the MacIntoshes, the sellers, arrange for the date for us to take possession, and get the keys to the house. Next was contacting the moving company where our furniture was stored and arranging for them to deliver on a specific date. As soon as all this was settled, of course I telephoned Rebecca. She was very happy to receive the news, but so beaten down that she could not muster much exuberance, but showed much relief. Her family helped her with her problems, but there was a big problem with Roger going to a strange school, with no Daddy on hand and no home except that Chevrolet sedan. He was seven years old, just the age when a protracted lack of a home was difficult for him to deal with.

Fortunately, we were able to take possession of our new home in just a few days. I stayed in the little apartment at the Calvins, which was in easy walking distance from the campus, so I was able to keep busy at outfitting my laboratory by moving things from the storeroom, arranging for the glass blower to build items of apparatus I would need, and asking Miss Kittredge to have some items of furniture delivered to my room so that I would have something to sit on and something to write on. I spent some time attending to the matter of getting friendly with the men in the machine shop, the glass blowing shop, and the woodworking shop. That sort of thing was important. The movers arrived on schedule with our furniture and other belongings, including the laboratory apparatus from Harvard which I had brought via Vanderbilt. I worked late into the night getting essential things unpacked for the arrival of Rebecca and the kids. I got a flight to Los Angeles the next day, where Rebecca and the kids met me at the airport—the last emotional reunion before we hit the end of the nomadic trail.

Naturally enough, we were anxious to get to our new home, with Roger not the least anxious, and so we delayed only a couple of days to get rested up for the overnight drive. Although an overnight drive with two kids is strenuous, we had concluded that it has some merit over a daytime drive. After an overnight drive the parents are dead tired, but on finally arriving at home the adrenaline in their system generally keeps them going until it is time for the kids to take a nap. It takes awhile to get beds made and prepare food, and get out essentials to prepare for living in the new place. It was long before anything resembling freeways had arrived, and so we had to plow through Oakland to get to Berkeley after we got off the highway. Coming from the south, the best route to Berkeley was up Telegraph Avenue. At a certain point the campanile is visible dead ahead, centered in the view down the street. I was driving and Rebecca was sleeping. I yelled what I had been planning to say: "Look, Rebecca, there is the campanile; we have finally arrived at our place in the sun." She was so beat that she looked up, said something that sounded like "Uh," after which her head fell back on her chest as she continued sleeping. At this point, Roger whacked her on the head with a stuffed rabbit and said, "Wake up, Mommy, there is the campanile." And so Mommy finally woke up enough to enjoy that historical event.

On the next day after our arrival, Rebecca went down to the Cragmont School, which was about a quarter mile from our house, to attend to Roger's late enrollment in the second grade. Since the fall semester at the university did not start until October, for several days I was always available to take care of Mardy while Rebecca attended to the numerous things which were a part of her "job." Thus, the events regarding Roger's enrollment in the second grade are based on the account given me by Rebecca. The grammar school principal, whose name was Horning, was not at all agreeable to Roger entering the second grade. It was bad enough that he was a couple of weeks late; his being from such a "backward" school as those in Tennessee was just too much. After a heated debate, Rebecca demanded that before they argue any more, the teacher whom Roger would have in the second grade should be called in to evaluate Roger's reading ability in terms of his being qualified to be in the room where she would teach. Horning agreed, obviously thinking that this would be a good way to get rid of this pesky woman. So the second grade teacher took Roger off to another room in order to test his reading ability. After a few minutes, the teacher and Roger returned, and the teacher reported, with a baffled expression on her face: "This kid reads better than anybody in my class."

So much for Horning's insults to Tennessee. After Roger had been in school for a few weeks we learned why he was such a good reader. Tennessee was indeed a backward state—in terms of getting with the new fad of reading English as if it were a picture language. When it became Mardy's time to go to first grade, we learned just how bad the "new reading" was. We had to teach Mardy at home, but that traumatic experience did not hit us until three years later.

A few days before the opening of the fall semester, I was working at my desk (table), making some plans for teaching at this new place, when a man walked in and announced, "I am Dauben, the new instructor in organic that Dean Latimer has hired to work with you." Whereupon I jumped to my feet and said, "The hell you are, I happen to be acquainted with Hyp Dauben; we were at Harvard together." Instead of fleeing, as I rather expected he would, my visitor smiled and explained that there were two of those Dauben boys who did graduate work at Harvard, and this one was Bill. I was to learn later that both the Daubens had applied for the job at Berkeley, but Dean Latimer had chosen Bill because he had worked with R.P. Linstead and Louis Fieser at Harvard. Depending on some things that he had learned from associations with organic chemists during the war, Latimer knew that he needed a synthetic chemist. Hyp Dauben had earned his degree working with Paul Bartlett, one of the leading physical organic chemists of that time. Subsequent events were to reveal that Latimer's pick of Bill was the better choice by an order of magnitude. As

far as functioning in a university setting, Hyp had some fatal flaws, whereas Bill was excellently adapted.

During the days before the semester started and we became occupied
with our assigned teaching duties, Bill Dauben and I conferred with each
other frequently and at length. Since both of us had most of our indoctri-
nation from Louis Fieser at Harvard, we agreed on everything involving
equipment or protocol, hence we wasted none of our time in debates. Both
of us were at non-tenure rank, and we knew the ground rules. So far as our
future at the University of California was concerned, we must produce
research that was worth publishing in reputable journals, preferably the
Journal of the American Chemical Society (JACS). It was also apparent that
we must deliver the goods in that respect if organic chemistry was to come
to Berkeley just now. It was two or three years later that I learned from several sources, especially from Wendell Latimer, that I had been "chosen" for
that job. I was unaware of that at the time that Bill and I were setting up
our battle plans.

At the time that Bill and I arrived at Berkeley, Melvin Calvin had just
been promised substantial money from "The Radiation Lab" to organize a
research unit for utilizing the recently available carbon fourteen (C14) in
studying the mechanisms of organic chemical reactions. Melvin invited
both Bill and me to join his group, a logical maneuver since we were the
only synthetic chemists available. I had already turned down an offer,
received immediately after arriving at Berkeley, from those extending the
work of NDRC for a period after the war. The offered contract contained
substantial sums of money for buying equipment, hiring research assistants, and paying me extra money beyond my salary if I worked on the
project directing my assistants, during the summer. The letter I received
also broadly implied that this could mean the nucleus of continued
expanded activity in the future. In short, a gold mine handed to me on a
silver platter. The only apparent string attached was that the project would
be initially directed towards synthesis of a certain synthetic anti-malarial
drug with a C14 atom in its structure. In other words, I would work on
what was decreed by somebody in Washington. Subsequent events
revealed that many chemists were to be provided much government
money via this route. However, I had learned a lot working with the
NDRC during the war, and I didn't like most of what I had learned. So I

turned down this offer, and thus became a loner, a rare species which rapidly became more rare. I soon began to apply for support by the federal government to work on projects suggested by me as a part of the grant application. I think that one reason I elected to travel that route was that, even at that relatively young age I had an instinctive opposition to becoming a "great man." Years later, I had to face this issue squarely. So I turned down Calvin's offer—to his considerable annoyance. His attitude towards me was considerably softened, however, by the fact that Bill Dauben accepted his offer.

Due to the fact that Bill was just starting out as an independent researcher and desperately needed to work on a project that was popular to the point of being fashionable, he worked very hard indeed, and a "communication" was submitted to JACS on August 15, 1946, slightly less than one year after his arrival in Berkeley. A communication is a short paper deemed of such current interest that its publication is expedited. The names on the paper, in the order listed, were: Wm. G. Dauben, J. C. Reid, Peter Yankwich, and Melvin Calvin. Bill did all of the experimental work on the paper, except for some help from Reid whom Wendell had assigned to Bill as an undergraduate senior research student. Bill also wrote the short manuscript for the publication. Yankwich was a physical chemist, and so it is reasonable to assume that he did the measurements of radioactivity in the compounds that Bill synthesized. This is the sort of thing that was done by a technician after the use of C14 became more established. The unusual feature of this sequence of authors' names was the listing of Calvin's name last. Since he was the head of the research group and responsible for bringing in the money, it was common practice for his name to be listed first.

Prior to publication of this communication, Bill had complained, with me as listener, about Calvin wanting his name first on the communication, but I was unaware that this matter had reached the stage of a confrontation until Wendell called me into his office to discuss the matter. He wanted my opinion about whether he should follow Melvin's suggestion that Bill Dauben's appointment as an instructor should be terminated at the end of his contract. Melvin's complaint was that Bill was adamant about his name appearing first on the list of authors of the communication. I pointed out the basis for the disagreement. Melvin was anxious to have his name first to encourage getting more money for his group; this sort of thing was commonly done. Bill knew that it would accomplish little, if anything, for his name to be one of those accompanying the head man. He had worked long and hard to produce this paper, and felt he would be robbed of any reward if Melvin's name was first. I suggested that, although Bill had been very foolish to engage in such an argument with a tenure professor, it would be overkill to fire him for the error. I added that Bill had demonstrated that he was a hard worker, and my estimate of him was that he was not only competent as an organic chemist but skillful at experimental work. He might prove to be an asset to the department. I added that both Bill and Melvin were working under very high pressure, and that it is common for people to make mistakes in the heat of battle. Wendell used his usual tactic, which I later encountered on several occasions; he told me that he appreciated my advice and would consider it carefully in making his decision. I never received any further information as to how things worked out so that Bill's name was first on the communication.

The next publication on which Bill Dauben's name appeared had several interesting aspects, especially to me. The names on this paper, in order listed, were: Charles Heidelberger, P. Brewer, and William Dauben. There was no mention of either Yankwich or Calvin. Obviously, several things had been settled between this publication and the preceding one. This publication was devoted entirely to synthesis of the very potent carcinogen, 1,2,5,6-dibenzanthracene, containing one atom of C14. There was nothing whatever original in the synthesis, typical of numerous publications in those days. This is why I had refused to accept a contract for doing this kind of work. As for the people whose names appeared on this publication, each racked up one entry in their bibliography. Charlie Heidelberger was a Harvard Ph.D. whom Melvin had hired to do synthetic work for his group. He ran the Elbs reaction which gives the desired DBA. Bill Dauben synthesized the starting material for the Elbs reaction, with assistance from Phyllis Brewer. Phyllis was working for Calvin to earn some money before she entered graduate school, and she did her Ph.D. work with me. As I just mentioned, all this work was repetition of work that had already been published. As a matter of fact, the only difficult step in the synthesis was the Elbs reaction, a high temperature pyrolysis which gives a yield of 25-30% of a highly carcinogenic product which must be separated from a lot of tar. I had to make about 150 grams of this stuff to be used as starting material in further syntheses involved in the last paper I published with Louis Fieser. In a chapter on the Elbs reaction which Louis wrote for a volume of Organic Reactions, he used my report on synthesis of DBA as a good illustration of the Elbs reaction. Thus, Charlie Heidelberger was making DBA by following a procedure that had been published in the primary literature (JACS), and then published in the secondary literature (Organic Reactions). But Charlie decided that he would have to improve that lousy yield before he expended C14 for the synthesis. He kept at it for several months, frequently consulting me for advice on improving the yield. I told him that when I wrote up that procedure after doing it six or eight times, and Louis Fieser was well enough impressed to use it as an illustration of the Elbs reaction, the chances of his improving the yield approached zero.

A rather grisly commentary as an aside to this sequence of events: After Charlie Heidelberger and I had each worked for many weeks with DBA, separating it from twice its weight of tar, neither of us showed any symptoms of cancer for many years subsequently. We used the simple precautions described in Chapter 7 to protect ourselves, since we worked with DBA, one of the three most potent carcinogens known. Yet our country and other countries are spending billions of dollars annually to protect ourselves from things which "may" be carcinogenic. As a final part of this report, about thirty years after Charlie Heidelberger had worked with DBA, he became a cancer victim-and died in misery and pain after being "treated" with a chemotherapeutic agent, of which he was a patent holder.

About the nicest thing that can be said about the events described in the above paragraphs is that there is something drastically wrong with the current theories regarding carcinogenesis, and about prevention and therapy of cancer. More on this subject in a later chapter.

Let us return to my main theme, regarding the alacrity with which Bill and I produced publications. Thanks to my sophistication, which kept me out of entanglements, I worked hard and long to produce my first paper from Berkeley, which was received by JACS on June 27, 1946. The title of this paper was "A Further Study of the Preparation of Ketones and Keto Esters by Means of Organocadmium Reagents". I was the only author of this full length paper. An anecdote may illustrate the kind of effort that went into the production of a paper in that length of time. I was working in my lab in the evening of December 24, 1945, finishing the fractional distillation of one of those keto esters mentioned in the above title. At about nine-thirty, the telephone rang; Rebecca reminded me that I had promised to help decorate the Christmas tree for the kids to see when they awoke in the morning. I told her I was finishing the distillation, and would definitely be home by ten-thirty. I then asked her what was the yelping noise that I heard after answering the phone. Her answer: "That was probably that switchboard operator who gave me such a bad time about ringing your phone; she claimed that she and a couple of police were the only people on campus at this time." Incidentally, I made it home by 10:15.

My next publication was a thirty-two page review article, written by invitation from Chemical Reviews. I was the only author. It was received by Chemical Reviews on August 26, 1946, and appeared in the February, 1947, issue.

My next article involving experimental work was a communication entitled, "Rearrangement in Preparation of Ester Acid Chlorides." Again I was the only author. It was received on May 26, 1947.

As is apparent from the above paragraphs, I concentrated heavily during the first two years at Berkeley on turning out publishable research, and this no doubt contributed heavily to my being promoted to tenure rank in 1948. However, I spent as much time as was practical, beginning at the start of 1947, in working to improve the courses being taught. Wendell also applied for and secured permission from the Academic Senate for the chemistry department to install an essentially new curriculum in organic chemistry. I will discuss this development before getting on to the matter of improving the manner of teaching the courses, especially the laboratory part of the courses.

As the first step towards a new curriculum, Wendell appointed a committee of three professors whose charge was to study organic curriculums across the country, then recommend a new program for Berkeley. These three were Branch, Calvin and me. By this time in his life, Professor Branch had no interest in anything except playing hearts at the faculty club, so he was an ideal third member of the committee—causing Melvin and me no trouble at all. At that time, the "Illinois Group" was essentially in charge of the development of organic chemistry in America, dating back to World

War I when the supply of organic chemicals from Germany was cut off. This group included Minnesota, Wisconsin, Iowa State, and Penn State. Although Melvin's Ph.D. was in physical chemistry, he knew what an organic chemistry curriculum was like because of doing his graduate work at Minnesota. Furthermore, he had saved for posterity Professor Branch's "new ideas" regarding physical organic chemistry by writing a textbook based on the lectures Branch was giving in Chemistry 103. This textbook became known as Branch and Calvin, but was not used in a significant number of places because of competition from the textbook entitled Physical Organic Chemistry, written by Professor Louis Hammet of Columbia. It is probable that the dominance of Hammet's book derived from the essentially total absence of traditional organic chemistry at Berkeley; however, there was another problem with Branch and Calvin's theory of organic chemistry. Due to a total ignorance of classical organic chemistry, Branch had chosen a very cumbersome basis for his theory. In any case, Melvin was in an excellent position to set up a curriculum adapted to the expected inroad of physical organic chemistry. In contrast to Melvin, I was saturated with the philosophy of the Illinois Group regarding classical organic chemistry. My professor of organic chemistry at Vanderbilt, Arthur W. Ingersoll, was an Illinois graduate. The crux of the Illinois curriculum was at least a half year of qualitative organic analysis. This was wholly different from the year of inorganic quantitative analysis commonly required in the sophomore year of the chemistry curriculum. Qualitative organic analysis not only taught a lot of general organic chemistry, but provided experience with inductive reasoning, which is the heart of much of organic chemistry.

Another factor I was able to supply was knowledge of the growing importance of heterocyclic chemistry. Much of my work during the war, including a lot of literature searching, involved heterocyclic chemistry. For two years, my contract at Vanderbilt was involved with RDX, which is a heterocyclic nitramine. Thus, I had alerted Wendell immediately after I arrived at Berkeley that we needed a heterocyclic chemist to round out our group. Sometime around the beginning of the next year (1946), Wendell called me to come to his office to discuss a new man he was thinking of hiring who was working in the field of alkaloid chemistry. This man was Henry Rapoport, who had gotten his Ph.D. working with

Morton at M. I. T., worked in industry during the war, and was now a research assistant to Lyndon Small, editor of the upstart Journal of Organic Chemistry. I said that I knew nothing about Rapoport, but that it should not be assumed that he had learned anything by working under Morton. Wendell replied that what Rapoport learned as a graduate student was unimportant compared to the fact that Lyndon Small said he was a good man. Since Rapoport was involved with heterocyclic chemistry, I immediately agreed that he was a good man to bring aboard. As time went by, I learned that Wendell Latimer was a man who could reach the right decision on the basis of very little information. He could figure out which information was the right information to use.

After several meetings, and seeking information occasionally from other people we knew, Melvin and I submitted our recommendation for the new curriculum in organic chemistry. Wendell then called a meeting of the tenure faculty to consider the new curriculum recommended by our committee. I was invited to the meeting since I was a member of the committee, but I made a point of not saying anything. Melvin was our only spokesman, and he was an associate professor. The manure really hit the fan. Everything said was against the new curriculum except for an occasional rebuttal by Melvin, defending against a specific statement. Joel Hildebrand was simply beside himself at the idea of requiring a five unit, full year course with laboratory for all chemistry majors. What use is all that pot boiling to physical chemists, who make up nearly all the student body? Ernest Gibson sputtered, "Gilbert Lewis would never have tolerated such an outrage." After most of the sputterers had said about everything twice, Wendell used his usual ploy: "Gentlemen, I want to thank you very much for taking the time to give me your opinions on this complicated subject. You may rest assured that I will carefully consider everything that has been said here before I reach my conclusion as to what to do." Meeting adjourned.

Wendell then appointed the only three people in the department who could possibly have approved our recommendation: Wendell Latimer, chairman; Axel Olsen, and G.K. (Rollie) Rollefson. Axel and Rollie were the two final appointees by Gilbert Lewis. Rebecca and I had already become aware that these two people were clearly not a part of the clique of "old boys" who spent a lot of time playing hearts at the faculty club, and spent more time away from their offices than in them. As was related in Chapter 4, I had already encountered an incident which gave me a clue, in 1934, as to about what went on in the College of Chemistry faculty. Soon after Rebecca and I arrived in Berkeley, Axel and his wife invited us to dinner. Rollie and Nellie Rollefson gave a bridge party for all the new arrivals in 1946. Wendell did the same. During my first years in Berkeley, I do not recall any social contact with the old guard; however, in later years we had a large amount of social contact with Joel and Emily Hildebrand. Joel taught both of us how to ski when we were about 40 years old. After Kenneth and Jean Pitzer came back from Washington, we had closer association with them than anyone else in the department. Eventually Ken persuaded me, with difficulty, to hold the fort as acting dean so that he could take a well-deserved sabbatical leave.

The Committee on Courses of the Academic Senate gave immediate approval of the recommendations of the Committee on the Organic Chemistry Curriculum, which had been approved by a departmental committee and forwarded to them by the dean of the College of Chemistry. I am sure that no one would even think of opposing the powerful dean in chemistry on his recommended curriculum; however, I also learned that the biology departments had long been criticizing the chemistry department for not doing something for biologists in their undergraduate teaching. Hence, organic chemists were welcome. Bill, Rap and I had long lasting and permanent good relationships with the several biology departments that were on campus at that time.

I think that anyone cognizant of the events previously related in this chapter would be unlikely to disagree with the statement: Wendell Latimer brought organic chemistry to Berkeley! The rest of us were his hard-working lieutenants whom he always supported to the limit. It is not surprising that the organic chemists were very active in the campaign to name Latimer Hall as it was named. Possibly it all goes back to my days at Harvard when Louis Fieser seemed to progressively adopt a rather paternalistic attitude towards his hard-working assistant who produced five papers in two years, one of which was on a really tough problem. When I left, he gave me quite a talk on how to get along in the world, as described in Chapter 7. Furthermore, he suggested that I finish a problem which was about half done, at DePauw or later, and publish it in my name only; he would be glad to look it over and give me advice. Never did I have a paper sail through the referees as smoothly as that one did. He had already put my name as the first author on that tough fourth paper. He gave me thousands of dollars worth of apparatus, including the Podbielniak fractionating column and the Hershberg melting point outfit. Without this array of apparatus, it would have been impossible for me to publish a paper during the one year at DePauw and publish three papers and send a chapter to Organic Reactions while heavily engaged in war research for the NDRC during four years at Vanderbilt. There were no other authors on any of these papers. Another item floating around in my memory was that comment from Homer Adkins: "you are such a stubborn son-of-a-bitch that I advise you to take the job. They will never be able to budge you." I was unable to decide whether that comment was complimentary or derogatory, but I didn't really care because I was so happy to get the advice.

It was on a Sunday morning sometime in 1947 during a chat with Wendell that I suddenly was able to put the picture together. During that period, I frequently worked in my lab on Sunday mornings, and Wendell was usually in his office, so I sometimes stopped by to chat with him regarding anything that was appropriate. By that time, I had become quite fond of Wendell and enjoyed talking to him. On this occasion, for reasons I do not remember, I asked him why he had picked me to come to Berkeley. I had continued to be curious about the whole thing; I had a feeling there was something I did not know. Wendell responded by saying, among other things, that he had become acquainted with several organic chemists whom he consulted for advice. To my, "such as," he responded: "Ooooh, Homer Adkins." A bright light flashed through my cyberspace; now I could understand many things. Some of the "old guard," certainly including Homer Adkins and Louis Fieser, had decided that something had to be done about the complete absence of organic chemistry at such a prestigious university as Berkeley. Of course, there is no way of knowing at what stage Wendell Latimer became involved, but the evidence is clear that he did. I was very closely associated with Homer at the time, because of a "top secret" project to which I was shifted during the last half of my work for NDRC. Thus, it was logical that Homer would be elected to make sure that I accepted the offer of a position at Berkeley. Is all this just cerebral ramblings? I think not. It explains a lot of things besides those just mentioned, such as the royal welcome given to this new recruit by the dean of the College of Chemistry.

Concurrently with the activities described above, I spent a lot of time trying to discover some way to stop the widespread "dry labbing" which I knew to be occurring in our undergraduate organic courses. During my first semester as a graduate student at Berkeley in 1934, one of the labs assigned to me as a teaching assistant was an organic lab. From casual observation of what was going on in my lab section, I quickly became aware that there was a persistent light attendance at the lab, yet students presented me with notebook reports on schedule. I began to require that each student show me a preliminary write-up of the experiment which I signed, before he could get his starting material for the experiment from the stockroom. I had the stockroom stamp the notebook before issuing the starting material. I had been given no directions whatever on how to run the lab, so I instituted the system used by Professor Ingersoll at Vanderbilt. The students in my lab section complained bitterly about my conduct of the lab, so I was removed from heading an organic lab section in the second semester and assigned to grading papers instead. This required less time on my part, and I had already decided to not return to Berkeley for the next year, so I registered no complaint and made no inquiry about why my assignment was changed. Having no powers of prophecy, I had no way of knowing that this matter of dry labbing would come back to haunt me more than ten years later.

By the time our new curriculum was installed, either Mel Calvin or I would be in charge of Chem 12A or 12B, the organic courses required of all chemistry majors, and give the morning lectures. When the new curriculum first started, Mel chose the textbook and gave the lectures for Chem 12A, and I was in charge of the laboratory part of the course. In the following semester, I gave the lectures for Chem 12B, continuing the pattern established by Mel at the outset. When I lectured, Henry Rapoport, who came to Berkeley in 1946, was in charge of the lab. Wendell had put Melvin and me in charge of the two-semester course, with each of us responsible for the part of the course where our expertise lay. Rap continued operation of the lab in the manner that I had developed, just as I had followed Melvin's lead for the lectures.

Rap and I had a tough time developing a system of stopping the dry labbing. The students were very clever, as they should have been since they represented the upper 12 percent of California high school graduates, and kept one step ahead of us at stopping the dry labbing. After all, they were following a venerable, well established tradition. Also, we were handicapped by wanting to stop the dry labbing, not penalize people for doing it. We would report students for cheating as a last resort. Finally, the problem was solved in a rather unexpected manner. A part of our system was to have the stockroom issue a weighed sample of the starting material for each synthesis to each student, and stamp the student's notebook as evidence that he had received the sample. I will not waste time describing the various ways that students were able to circumvent this system. Suffice it to say that the stockroom made a mistake in issuing about twenty bottles that were supposed to contain castor oil, but actually contained cyclohexanol. Cyclohexanol is a colorless viscous substance when pure, but commercial samples are likely to be dark enough to give the appearance of castor oil. In the experiment in which the castor oil was used, it was put through a two-step process that yielded azelaic acid, which melts at 105 degrees. Our first signal that something was wrong occurred when several students reported that they got a compound melting at 153 degrees. A typical comment: "I went through that long miserable procedure and got this beautiful product as expected, but the melting point is 153 degrees." A small amount of qualitative organic analysis revealed that the compound melting at 153 degrees was adipic acid. The plot thickens; investigation in the stockroom revealed that the material issued to a few students by mistake was cyclohexanol. Of course, I realized at once that putting cyclohexanol through "that long miserable procedure" would yield adipic acid, which melts at 153 degrees. The final step was to learn from the stockroom how many bottles of cyclohexanol had been issued; it was about twenty. Inspection of the samples turned in revealed that it was easy to distinguish between the two compounds by visual inspection; no need to take melting points. Of about fifteen bottles of adipic acid, excluding those turned in by the students who had complained, all but two of them had m.p. 105 degrees on the label, the m.p. of azelaic acid. And so we also got a rough idea of how many students actually took the melting points and recorded them on their labels.

We wrote up a report on this event, and passed out a copy to the entire class. We commented that there might be other such errors by "the stock-room," also that we might check the melting point reported on the label. Apparently, the students were jolted considerably by this unconventional behavior. When we had the stockroom pass out six "wrong" samples of starting material a few weeks later, only one student fell into the trap. I called him into the office, told him I was giving him a zero grade for that experiment only, but if it happened again, it would be a zero grade for the course. He seemed relieved by the light penalty, and made no comment about being "trapped." During the next few years, we occasionally passed out "wrong" samples, and caught about one student in two semesters. Concluding that we had gotten the message across, we discontinued the procedure.

During the five or six years that Melvin, Rap and I were directing much attention to developing an organic chemistry curriculum and learning to teach it properly, we were also continuing to bear down on producing results in our research. Melvin was so immersed in developing the program that made him a "great man" that the development of our organic curriculum was done largely by Rap and me. I am not including Melvin's large research program, with essentially infinite backing from the Atomic Energy Commission, with "organic chemistry coming to Berkeley." Except for Bill Dauben's first two short publications, Melvin's operations were completely dissociated from and physically separated from organic research carried out in the Old Chemistry Building and "The Rat House."

There is some difference of opinion about the origin of the name Rat House; however, it was probably originally applied during a period early in this century when it was used as an animal house by biology departments. In any case, by the time that I arrived in Berkeley in 1934, the name Rat House, was an established tradition. I think that its official name was the "Chemistry Annex," but I do not recall seeing that name in print. The Rat House was a small three-story wooden building occupied by physical chemists when I arrived in 1945. With the completion of Lewis Hall, the physical chemists moved into their new building and the Rat House was inherited by the upstart organic chemists. The Rat House was about the minimum that could be called a building, and was clearly a cast-off allotted to the newcomers; however, there was no place else for the expanded organic research to go. Furthermore, this old building proved to be a real asset to the "organicers," for Wendell Latimer saw to it that we got everything that we asked for. After we had Grounds and Buildings clean up about ten kilograms of mercury that the physical chemists had left in floor cracks and sink traps, the next step was installation of a sprinkler system and a few fume hoods. Beyond that stage, our graduate students did the plumbing and wiring, with all the help we asked for from the woodworking shop, which also did welding. This activity built up a pronounced esprit de corps among that first wave of graduate students, who "built their own laboratories." One of the students who was among that first wave, at an American Chemical Society meeting twenty years later declared to a meeting of a group of Rat House Alumni, that this building should not be torn down to make way for new construction of a very modern building. Her suggestion was that the Rat House should be made a National Historical Monument, and preserved forever.

Whatever may have been the numerous things involved, those students really poured on the coal. And so did Bill and Rap and I. In retrospect, I think there was a general feeling of being involved in history. As far as production of research was concerned during those first years, I had a significant advantage over Bill and Rap in that I came aboard with a viable research program in full swing. I also had other advantages. Since I was an assistant professor, I was able to take on graduate students under my direction immediately upon arrival, and Wendell told the only two new graduate students in organic chemistry to sign up to work under me. In those days new appointments were ordinarily appointed as instructors unless they already had an assistant professor title in their previous institution. Thus Bill and Rap were instructors. I also had the advantage of lecturing to the introductory organic chemistry course during the second semester of that course, required of all chemistry majors, and taken by some of the better premedical students. Melvin not only lectured to the first semester of that course, but also could hardly have been less interested in working with undergraduate students. Was this beautiful set-up for me just good luck? I think that Wendell Latimer had more influence on it than did the gods and the fates.

The paper I published in 1946 was selected from three or four other options on the grounds that it was most likely to produce a publication the soonest. Besides the Chemical Review article, written by invitation (I wonder who was responsible for that invitation?), a second article that I published in 1947 also had no co-author. The first article that I published in 1948 had two co-authors who were senior research students; therefore, I had two capable students doing experimental work for me to publish. During the period 1949 to 1952 inclusive, I published 29 papers, all of which had one or more co-authors. Three of these had one co-author who was an undergraduate senior research student; two of them had two senior research students as co-authors; and two of them had one graduate research student and two senior research students as co-authors. The remainder of these 29 papers had one or more graduate students as co-authors. None of these papers had a post-doctoral research assistant as a co-author. My first paper with a post-doctoral research assistant as co-author was published in 1953. It was No. XXVI in the Branched-Chain Fatty Acid Series. That was the time at which I began to apply for grants from the National Institute of Health, initially to pay for having cultures of tubercle bacillus grown. I had started an investigation to separate and identify the structure of the very unusual branched-chain fatty acids produced by this bacillus. This was an extension of the graduate work that I did under the direction of Professor R. J. Anderson at Yale. I continued to be reluctant to apply for research grants in order to hire post-doctoral research assistants. There were several reasons for this attitude, but probably the strongest one was my powerful inhibition against allowing incompetent scientists with political appointments in Washington to dictate to me what research I could do. This was one reason that the rate of production of my research began to drop off after 1953, but this complicated affair will be discussed in at least one subsequent chapter in this chronicle.

In view of the events discussed in this chapter, it seems apparent that by 1953, organic chemistry had come to Berkeley, for both undergraduate and graduate instruction. Furthermore, our output of research had resulted in the fact that major universities such as the University of Illinois and Massachusetts Institute of Technology had begun sending some of their undergraduates to Berkeley for graduate work in organic chemistry. A major factor involved here was our sending top-notch students from Berkeley to do graduate work in organic chemistry at such universities as just mentioned. My publication of several papers based on the experimental work of senior research students certainly speaks well for the caliber of the undergraduates we were training; however, there is other independent evidence. In one year, we sent our three best graduates to MIT. They were Douglas Applequist, Ronald Dean Smith, and Bradford Walker. When Art Cope wrote me after the end of that year that our three students were rated one, two, and three in overall standing among the new organic graduate students, the emotional impact on me was great. I knew that we had it made in the shade.

Among the excellent undergraduate students who did research with me, Norman L. Allinger, known as Lou to his friends, has become the most prominent. At age 68 in 1996, he received from the American Chemical Society the ACS Award for Computers in Chemical and Pharmaceutical Research. In the Chemical and Engineering News (C & EN), there was a regular laundry list of other awards he has received. He is director of the Computational Center for Molecular Structure & Design at the University of Georgia, and they have built or are building a new building for the exclusive use of Lou's Center and another Center called the Center for Computational Quantum Chemistry. By a twist of fate, this latter Center is headed by Fritz Schaefer, seduced to leave UC Berkeley to take the job as the Center's Director.

Lou entered UC in January, 1948, and immediately showed great interest in instrumentation; was seduced into doing senior research with me, partly because we were using a lot of spectroscopy at the time, somewhat ahead of most places. He proved so phenomenally productive that his name appears as co-author on four papers with me, after working for one year and one summer. He was really crowded at getting his report written for me because he had to play several nights with his jazz band in order to make recordings before he left. He then went to UCLA and earned his Ph.D. degree in three years working for Don Cram, who has recently won the Nobel Prize for his work in synthetic organic chemistry. Lou's feat in getting his degree in three years under Cram was unprecedented. A unit of work at that time at UCLA was a Cram, but this unit was so large that the operating unit was the Millicram. After post-doctoral work at Harvard and a teaching stint at Wayne State University, Lou went to Georgia. In view of Lou's rapid rise, one might wonder how much credit I deserve for the four papers on which Lou was a co-author; however, I do want to report that there were other co-authors on all four of those papers.

Although Lou rose rapidly to be head of the Center mentioned above, he also kept alive his interest in music. In a letter to me dated 4/14/96, he mentions the occasion when he reluctantly agreed to give a concert at a big birthday bash for somebody involved in computational chemistry. He said, "I practiced quite a bit for about a month, and I was surprised at how well it went." He played for forty-five minutes, but the audience refused to let him go, so he played another forty five minutes. "They loved it." Let us now return to development of organic chemistry at UC.

My report thus far has been directed to the work of Cason and Rapoport, on account of their involvement in developing the undergraduate curriculum and Cason's arrival as an assistant professor with a well-developed research program in place. However, Dauben had only four less publications to his credit than Cason and Rapoport combined. Moreover, Don Noyce arrived at Berkeley in 1948, and Andy Streitwieser in 1952. These two worked very hard and effectively in developing research programs which also contributed to bringing organic chemistry to Berkeley. I have devised a method of comparing the output of research by all of the young organic chemists with all of the young physical and inorganic chemists who came to Berkeley in 1937 or later. The physical and inorganic chemists of those days were so difficult to distinguish from each other that the most useful comparison comes from combining the two types. The time period chosen for the comparison is the years 1953 to 1958 inclusive. This period is centered about ten years after the arrival of the first of the new generation of organic chemists, and hence gave them a chance to get organized and up to speed. There is also a fair comparison with the physical chemists, for Pitzer had a chance to start after the war with a well-organized research program at hand as did Cason. Connick and Gwinn were appointed in 1942, but it seems reasonable that they had very little opportunity to organize a research program prior to 1945. For obvious reasons, no one will be included who was first appointed during the comparison period. Also for obvious reasons, no one will be included who had an appointment in the Radiation Lab. The comparison will be made of the total amount of publication in prominent chemical journals, on each side, divided by the number of researchers on each side. Secondary publications, such as talks at scientific meetings, reports to a governmental agency, review articles, articles published in such publications as Organic Syntheses, Organic Reactions or Annual Reviews of Physical Chemistry will not be counted. In case of more than one faculty member appearing on a paper, which is not an infrequent occurrence in these data, credit is given to the faculty member whose name is listed first for the first time, whether chronologically or alphabetically. This system may occasionally under-credit one person and correspondingly over-credit another; however, it cannot count a paper more than once. Ordinarily the lead professor's name is placed first, but in nearly all cases where I encountered this problem, the second listing of the paper placed the name of the "other" professor first. Since three of the people involved in this practice are dead, I cannot think of any better system than what I am using. There is one notable exception to the statement above that the first-listed name is normally the leader of the research. This exception is: if the paper is based on one or more of the professor's students who are working under him for their degree (graduate or undergraduate), the professor's name may appear last. With the presently considered data, there is no problem with identifying the professor, for I know them all. They were my colleagues during the entire six-year period which is tabulated.

I am greatly indebted to Professor Clayton Heathcock for making it possible for me to gather the data required for making this comparison. These data have been obtained from the reports of the American Chemical Society, issued at two-year intervals, of all publications by each faculty member in each chemistry department recognized by the ACS. The ACS gathers these data by requesting each faculty member to make a yearly report of his publications. Some people have criticized this system of gathering data by pointing out that if a professor fails to report all his publications he will be under-credited for work actually done. As far as can be determined by notating these data, as I have been doing, the ACS recognized this possibility by allowing a person to report publications from an earlier year that had not been previously included. As is apparent from examination of my tabulated data, which is included in two tables presented on page 227 as an Appendix to this chapter, this system opens a Pandora's Box of flagrant abuse. I spent many hours leafing back and forth, in order to make sure that no paper is counted more than once in my data.

Many interesting things are revealed in these data; however, the part that is most interesting to me, as would be expected, is comparison of the data on organic chemists with the data on physical and inorganic chemists. My motivation in spending several days in notating this data was primarily due to a hope that these data would show that the organic chemists would make a decent showing, if their start at zero is considered. As the results unfolded, revealing that the organic chemists had published more than twice as many papers per chemist as had the physical and inorganic chemists, I was so incredulous that I did the laborious task of rechecking the data. No change. I dare say that critics might try to rationalize the accomplishments of the organic chemists by saying that we had good luck in getting Bill Dauben on our team. That was not good luck, that was Wendell Latimer, as related earlier in this chapter. Moreover, if one simply deletes Dauben from the organic list, leaving us with one man who did not arrive until 1952, and dividing the 83 remaining publications by four, we get 20.75 publications per chemist. Let us consider the record of Andy Streitwieser, who arrived at Berkeley the year before the start of the six-year period being compared. He had 18 publications, one of them in 1953 and eight of them in 1957. For the physical and inorganic chemists, only two of them had more publications than Andy Streitwieser: Pitzer with 34; and Pimentel, who came aboard in 1949, with 22. Pimentel did his thesis work under Pitzer. The only other physical chemist who had more publications than the organic chemist who is the lowest in his group is O'Konski, with 18 publications, just equal to Andy Streitwieser. Regarding Chester O'Konski, I should point out that it would be appropriate if I had omitted him from the group of physical and inorganic chemists, for Chester is a biophysical chemist. He was the forerunner and original nucleus for the several competent biophysical chemists who came aboard during subsequent years. If one omits Pitzer, O'Konski, and Pimentel, about the best that can be said for the six remaining physical and inorganic chemists is that their performance is disgraceful. Not only has organic chemistry come to Berkeley, but it is dominant in any prestige that accrued to the chemistry department at Berkeley by 1960. Wendell Latimer made it possible. The organic chemists developed an esprit de corps while working hard to justify Wendell's steadfast support.

Examination of the data in the tables reveals a remarkable difference between the organic chemists and the physical and inorganic chemists.

Among the organic chemists, with the exception of one instance of repeated submission of a paper which could be regarded as accidental, only one faculty member reported six instances of repeated submission of a paper for listing by the ACS publication. In vivid contrast, each of the physical and inorganic chemists reported more than two resubmissions. The two people with the highest number of publications have by far the smallest number of resubmissions, considered percentagewise. Three members of this group have twice as many resubmissions as papers actually published. This becomes possible if all published papers were reported during the years 1953 to 1956, and each was resubmitted during the two reporting years of 1957 and 1958. It is also notable that the physical chemist with the third from highest publication record, Chester O'Konski, made no resubmissions until 1958, when he reported no new publications, but nine resubmissions.

Blaming these facts on being absentminded is irrational, and a rational explanation of these data is difficult. Could it be that the physical and inorganic chemists, becoming well aware that the upstart "organicers" were charging ahead while they were relying on the past glory of the Gilbert N. Lewis era, became desperate enough to do irrational things in order to attempt concealment of the facts in the case? Who knows? Six of the principals involved are dead at this writing, while only one of the organicers has passed on to the Great Beyond. Thus, only three out of nine physical and inorganic chemists considered for this comparison are alive in March 1998, while four out of five organic chemists are alive at this same date. Why would organic chemists live so much longer than physical chemists? I have an idea on this subject which I will not present!

Publication Report for Organic Chemists

Papers Published each Year (repeats)

Name (yr. first appointed)	'53	'54	'55	'56	'57	'58	Totals
Cason (45)	7	2	3	5	2	5	24
Dauben (45)	3	10	13	10	6	6 (1)	48 (1)
Rapoport (46)	2	3	10	4	3	6	28
Noyce (48)	1	2	4	1	1 (4)	4 (2)	13 (6)
Streitwieser (52)	1	0	4	3	8	2	18

Grand Total (7 repeats) 131

Publications per professor 26.2

Publication Report for Physical and Inorganic Chemists

Papers Published each Year (repeats)

Name (yr. first appointed)	'53	'54	'55	'56	'57	'58	Totals
Pitzer (37)	5	1	5	9	4 (3)	10	34 (3)
Connick (42)	2	1	0	2	3 (3)	4 (2)	12 (5)
Gwinn (42)	2	2	1	1	0 (6)	0 (6)	6 (12)
Orlemann (45)	2	0	1	1	0 (2)	0 (3)	4 (5)
Jura (46)	2	3	0	0	0 (5)	0 (5)	5 (10)
Powell (46)	0	3	0	0	0 (3)	0 (3)	3 (6)
O'Konski (48)	2	1	7	3	5	0 (9)	18 (9)
Pimentel (49)	0	3	5	6	3	5 (5)	22 (5)
Myers (51)	0	1	0	3	1	0 (4)	5 (4)

Grand Total (59 repeats) 109

Publications per professor 12.1

THE PETER PRINCIPLE AND ME

Chapter 10 was devoted to my impact and that of others on the historical event described as organic chemistry coming to Berkeley. The present chapter is devoted to historical events affecting my life, whether or not those events are directly involved with organic chemistry coming to Berkeley. There will inevitably be some overlap of these two categories in the same time period. The categorizing of these events may be made in another way: Chapter 10 is focused primarily on my impact on events, whereas Chapter 11 is concerned with the impact of events on me and my efforts to contend with same. As will be developed, this difference has a pronounced influence on my pleasure in writing the two chapters. Chapter 11 contains several events which I would rather skip, for I prefer writing about things in which I enjoyed being a participant. After considerable cogitation, however, I concluded that I must cover all events which exerted a significant impact on the history being reported. Otherwise, I cannot convince myself that I am an honest historian.

The most frightening event of my academic life occurred during the summer of 1947, less than two years after my arrival in Berkeley. It involved paper No. VI in the Branched-Chain Fatty Acid series. Soon after my arrival in Berkeley, I began working very hard on this paper, for it would be my longest and most sophisticated paper since my arrival, with much of my own experimental work, since there was no co-author. I sent the paper to JACS, where all my previous papers, except a review article and two papers on my thesis work at Yale, had been published. I was rather upset when I received referees' reports which were the worst I would ever receive in my future career. One referee stated approximately as follows: "I recommend that pages 7-18 should be deleted entirely." (There were about 30 pages of typescript in the entire paper.) After some cogitation, I decided to learn whether Lyndon Small, editor of the upstart Journal of Organic Chemistry, which was bankrolled by Morris Kharasch, would be interested in considering the paper for publication. In connection with the hiring of Henry Rapoport, Wendell Latimer made the decision that Henry would be a good man, because Lyndon had said that he was a good man. I figured that if Small was that good a judge of chemists, maybe he would be good at judging papers by chemists. I wrote to ArthurLamb, the JACS editor at that time, and said that I could not meet the referees' objections without destroying the paper; hence, I was withdrawing the paper. I do not remember if I returned the paper with my letter, but presume that I did not, since two copies were required on submission. It turns out that I should have asked for the return of the second copy, but I was much too unsophisticated to think of such things. I may have used the copy that was returned to send to Lyndon Small, since making copies was not simple in those days. In any case, I sent a copy to Small, explaining the situation, and noted that I realized the format was different for JOC, but I would like to know if he regarded this paper as the sort of thing he would consider for publication. If his decision should be favorable, then I would rewrite it in the JOC format.

After a period of time, I received a very short letter from Al Weitkamp, who was the first reference on my paper. The entire letter was approximately the following: "I will appreciate it if you will explain to me as briefly as possible and clearly, why I have received the same paper authored by you from two different chemical journals." I was somewhat acquainted with Weitkamp, had met him at an ACS meeting, and exchanged some correspondence with him. He was working on a different kind of branched-chain acid, and had devised a new type of fractionating column for vacuum distillation of high boiling compounds. Of course, the only thing I could do was write Al and explain the situation. After he received my story he seemed to shift his animosity from me to Lamb. He sent me a copy of his referee's report that had been sent to JOC. It was very favorable and contained a statement: "I especially liked pages 7 to 18."

After a few days, I received a letter from Lyndon Small saying that the paper was accepted as is, because of the favorable report from a referee. I don't know what Al wrote to Lamb, and I did not ask him, but it certainly put Lamb into orbit. He wrote me a scathing letter, containing statements such as, "In all my years as editor of the Journal, I have never encountered such reprehensible behavior as displayed by you." He must have scoured Roget's Thesaurus to accumulate some more words for his vocabulary. As a non-tenure professor in his second year in a new job, I was quite frightened. I could think of nothing to do except reiterate that I had withdrawn the paper. I did not even have a carbon copy of my letter of withdrawal. I thought I was through with the affair, since I had withdrawn the paper. After a few days I received a reply from Lamb in which he stated that his action had resulted from the fact that he had not reviewed the file on my paper, which had been handled by Dr. Warren Lothrop while he was on vacation. Lothrop was a close acquaintance while he worked with Professor Anderson for a year at Yale during my tenure there. He was one of those we had invited to a Thanksgiving dinner one year; he had liked the skin of the turkey. Warren probably felt sorry that his old friend had been treated so badly and decided to try another referee. Being rather inexperienced in such matters, it might have been natural for him not to notify me of what he was doing. Whatever parts of this scenario I do not know about, it seems clear that the actions of two of my friends who were "helping" me really sent Arthur Lamb into orbit and scared me stiff. It is also true that Lamb's final letter included nothing that could be called an apology, or even an expression of regret.

After one or two years had passed following the above described scenario, I had another encounter with Arthur Lamb that caused me to conclude he could learn a lot about how an editor should behave by having some instruction from Lyndon Small. Somewhat to my surprise, I received a communication from Lamb, with a routine request to act as referee. This communication was by Einar Stenhagen, the Swede who was a prominent pioneer in applying mass spectroscopy to rather high molecular weight compounds. I had sent him many of the branched-chain acids or esters that he had used in his early studies before his wife Stina, who was an organic chemist, began to supply many of the compounds he needed. I reported that this was an excellent manuscript quite worthy of being published as a communication, since a variety of organic chemists in several fields would profit from expedited publication of the information. I added that there was a minor error in the manuscript which had no impact on its importance, but I was confident that Dr. Stenhagen would like to correct it before publication, hence my mentioning it. The paper appeared with the error intact. After some cogitation, I decided not to write Stenhagen, but to write Lamb. I went to great effort to write Lamb a very polite letter, saying that the matter was not important, but I was curious about whether Stenhagen had disagreed with the statement I cited as being erroneous. The first sentence in Lamb's reply was, "This time you have me."

I don't remember what else was in the letter, but it reminded me of some things that Homer Adkins told me about his problems with JACS when he was a young man trying to introduce the concept of high pressure hydrogenation on a laboratory scale. He later discovered accidentally that Lamb was sending his papers to Hugh Taylor, a physical chemist who was chairman of the chemistry department at Princeton. This was the same individual who took away Dick Powell's fellowship because he got married in violation of Taylor's rule against graduate students getting married—"Takes too much time away from their research." I was also reminded of the instance in which Doisy slandered Louis Fieser publicly and at length, claiming that Fieser had stolen information which he had sent to JACS as a communication, and used it to completely defeat Doisy in proving Doisy's structure of vitamin K to be wrong. I was very close to Louis at the time, and gave him some information that made it possible for him to immediately recognize that Doisy's structure was wrong. (I have given a full account of this "vitamin K affair" in Chapter 7.) I do not remember anything that Lamb did to cut off this slander, in spite of the fact that Lamb was being included in Doisy's allegations. Apparently, many people were not aware of the facts in the case. Max Tishler was appointed to write the In Memorial resolution for Louis Fieser after his death. He asked me to supply him with information about Louis's teaching and his fellowship with his graduate students and research assistants, and made a separate request to tell him what I knew about the "vitamin K affair." I became rather well acquainted with Max when we were on the Organic Syntheses Board of Editors. We sometimes enjoyed swapping stories about events at Harvard, especially the time that Max was hanging by his fingers from a third story window in Converse with a raging fire in the room. I wrote several pages in response to his request, and he promised that he would send me a copy of the In Memorial, but I never did see it. He commented that I should have been writing the In Memorial. Of course this was impossible; he was merely complimenting me. The National Academy of Sciences would never tolerate a peasant outside the fraternity writing an In Memorial.

My final encounter with JACS editors—thank God—occurred during the period when W. A. Noyes, Jr. was the editor. It involved a paper in the Branch-Chain Fatty Acids series, and was probably in 1954 or 1955, for Wendell Latimer was still alive. As with most of the papers in this series, several new branched-chain acids were reported. With such compounds, the elementary analysis (carbon and hydrogen in this case) is of no value for characterizing the compound, for compounds differing by as much as two carbon atoms give elementary analyses which are unable to distinguish between the two compounds, due to limitations on the accuracy of such analyses. I received this particular paper back from the editor after the referees' reports. The referees raised no objections, but the editor said I must furnish elementary analyses for three of the new compounds before the paper was acceptable for publication. I replied by explaining that the elementary analyses had no value, whereas the values for molecular weight which I supplied were clearly able to easily distinguish between the compounds in question. I then added a comment that Art Cope told me later was my big mistake. He said that it is necessary to humor these people regardless of whether they are right or wrong. My erroneous comment was, approximately as follows: "It seems to me that a modern, world famous chemical journal such as JACS should abandon practices which were important and necessary in the days of Justus Liebig, but are outmoded in days of modern technology such as spectrometers." In order to make sure that everyone understands why this comment might be regarded by W. A. Noyes, Jr. as offensive, I will note that Justus Liebig founded a famous chemical journal before the middle of the nineteenth century. Noyes's response, however, made Lamb's behavior seem mild, especially since Lamb had good reason to think, when he wrote the letter to me, that I was a bum. In contrast, my only offense against Noyes was disagreeing with him and using some language which emphasized my point; no exaggerations or superlatives. Nevertheless, a few days later Ken Pitzer, my chairman and dean asked me to stop by his office, and when I walked in, handed me a letter to read. Among other things, I remember one sentence which was approximately as follows: "As editor of the Journal of the American Chemical Society, it is my duty to inform you that a member of your teaching staff named Cason is so emotionally unstable that he is likely to go off the deep end at any time." I handed the letter back to Ken and asked if he would like to see my entire file on recent correspondence with Noyes. He responded that he had more important things to attend to than reading such stuff and he would dictate a short letter to Noyes advising him he did not need advice from him on how to handle his teaching staff. As I walked out of Ken's office, I met Wendell Latimer in the anteroom. He said, among other things, "Don't let it worry you; W. A. Noyes has outlived his usefulness." I thanked both Wendell and Ken warmly, and to myself I thanked God I had been recently promoted to full professorship. I often think how fortunate I have been to have met and dealt with so few people who are real jerks.

The period during which I had distasteful encounters with editors was also the period of my highest rate of publication. During the period from 1948 to 1953 inclusive, I had 40 publications. There may have been a purely statistical connection between these two items; however, I think that a major factor was my determination to do all that I could to help bring organic chemistry to Berkeley. I was more interested in that event than in promoting my professional standing. Several things happened that caused me to feel secure about Berkeley's position in the organic chemistry world, and hence caused me to ease up on emphasizing production of publications. One of these things which remains vivid in my memory occurred during 1955, a few months after I started serving as acting dean of the College of Chemistry, so that Ken could take a well deserved sabbatical leave. A Du Pont official was visiting the college regarding the generous gift Du Pont gave us each year, so he naturally came to talk to the dean. As soon as he came in the door, before he sat down, he looked at me, smiled broadly, and said, "I never expected to live long enough to see an organic chemist sitting in that chair." I assured him that it was only temporary, so that Ken Pitzer could take a sabbatical leave; however, that comment caused me to think of several things. First and foremost was the thought: "It was worth the struggle."

Even during the period of my giving first priority to publishing papers, I was also becoming more and more interested in teaching undergraduates, much to my surprise. I had come into teaching almost entirely because of having an ambition to do research on anything that interested me, hence the drive for a professorship in a major university. As I related earlier, this idea fitted in perfectly with developments that resulted from my contacts with Louis Fieser and Homer Adkins. However, I soon learned that association with people of college age can be quite rewarding, especially when the young people are obviously anxious to learn what I am teaching them. This led first to my publishing several papers based on the work of senior research students, and eventually to publishing of textbooks; however, the laboratory textbook with Rapoport was the direct result of my being encouraged by Wendell Latimer. He came into my lab one day and said that he had learned that I had written several experiments for laboratory work which had been favorably received by the students. After I responded that I enjoyed working with students on that sort of thing, he suggested that perhaps I might like to write a laboratory manual. He then told me that he was chemistry editor for Prentice-Hall and could arrange a contract with them if I so desired. I told him that I would probably prove to be interested, but would need to think about it, especially to learn whether one of my colleagues would be interested in joining me as a co-author.

Since Henry Rapoport had worked with me during most of the time that the laboratory part of our new course was being developed, I naturally approached him on the idea of writing a book based on our developments. I told him that Wendell had broached the subject and said that he could arrange for us to have a contract with Prentice-Hall. Rap was enthusiastic about the project, and so we proceeded to get organized and under way. As our plan developed, we decided to model the book after Louis Fieser's lab manual; i.e., put in some discussion of the experiments. We planned, however, to go much further than Louis did by putting in a significant discussion of why the synthesis was done as it was, and including a tabulation of reactants and the ratios between them, so that a student would finish the elementary course with knowledge of how to set up an experiment in the context of doing research. This meant that the *cookbook* part of each chapter was usually much smaller than the discussion which presented the theoreticals involved in setting up a synthesis. Ergo, we named our book, Laboratory Text in Organic Chemistry. I believe this was the first laboratory manual for elementary organic chemistry organized in this manner, and we wanted the name to properly describe the nature of the book.

Rap and I were able to develop a good variety of synthetic procedures for our book, as well as a suitable number of other procedures not involving synthesis. As time went by, and the book went into a second and third edition, the non-synthetic procedures became progressively important. We introduced such topics as gas chromatography, paper chromatography, and nuclear magnetic resonance. In the latter topic, the discussion was the entire presentation. Even in research using this topic the experimental work was done by a trained technician with elaborate and expensive equipment. And so our foresight made it possible for our book to keep up with progress in the teaching of organic chemistry. Each of us had senior research students, and we set them to doing certain of the more difficult experiments before entrusting them to a large class. On a few of the experiments Rap or I made one or more runs after the procedure was written, before we turned it over to a senior research student. I think that it is safe to claim that there has not been a laboratory text before or after ours in which the syntheses all "worked." We also set schedules for ourselves, and produced the book relatively promptly. The initial publication was in 1950, five years after my arrival in Berkeley and four years after Rap's arrival. The second edition was published in 1962, and the third edition in 1970. It was printed in an Asian edition in English, and in an Israeli edition in Hebrew. There was also an "outlaw" edition in Chinese, of which I received a copy of the preface, which was in English, from Harold Chen, one of Rapoport's earlier graduate students. I think that it is fair to say that this book made a very significant contribution to spreading the word that organic chemistry had come to Berkeley. During the first five years after publication of this book, it may have had a greater impact on Berkeley's reputation in organic chemistry than the research publications appearing in that particular period. Rap and I worked hard to produce a good book as rapidly as was practical, but it should always be remembered that it was possible because of Wendell Latimer, who knew exactly what he was doing, as usual, when he broached the subject of a book to me. Using the jargon of a currently popular sport, one might say that Rap and I carried the ball, with Wendell quarterbacking. It is also fair to say that Prentice-Hall did a splendid job of marketing the book. It is sad that I must report the degeneration of Prentice-Hall which occurred a few years after Wendell's death.

Our relationship with our publisher, Prentice-Hall, during the initial production of the book and its marketing was quite good. We enjoyed all of our contacts with the Prentice Hall employees. By the time production of the third edition got under way in 1969, however, things began to unravel. In retrospect, this probably occurred for a combination of reasons. Wendell Latimer, the chemistry editor, who had introduced us to Prentice-Hall, had died in 1955. One of the founders of Prentice-Hall, named Ettinger, who had guided the company through its rapid expansion, either died or retired and his son, who had no interest in the publishing business, appeared to allow the company to be taken over by inept people. Our trouble with the third edition, which was published in 1970, began at the beginning. When the manuscript was returned to me after editing, I discovered that our copy had been drastically rewritten—unheard of for a third edition. Among other things, all of the experimental directions had been rewritten in the imperative—completely unacceptable. All directions for experimental procedures in chemistry, whether in The Journal of the American Chemical Society or textbooks, were written in the passive voice. After some thought and inspection of the returned copy, I wrote the editor and told him that there was nothing that could be done with this copy except to throw it away and try again with another copy editor. After that start, things did not improve any; however, we finally got the book published. It was in paperback, and after a book had been opened a few times the pages began to fall out of the binding. Everything that had been sold had to be replaced. Perhaps it is redundant to report that the book did not sell well. I did not realize that we had been deliberately sandbagged until about a year later. I received in the mail an advertisement for a laboratory manual published by Prentice-Hall entitled Laboratory Text for Organic Chemistry. It was not the same title as our book, which they were supposed to be selling;

one word, a preposition, had been changed—"in" replaced by "for." What could we do about it? Nothing!

My becoming involved in writing a textbook for the elementary organic course without a co-author, resulted from an entirely different sequence of events than was the case with the laboratory text. After several years had passed since Wendell had put Melvin and me in charge of developing our elementary course in organic chemistry, Don Noyce and Andy Streitwieser had been added to our teaching staff. Melvin and I began to teach the course less often, especially Melvin, who had become quite involved with becoming a famous man. Thus, a meeting of the organicers was held periodically to determine what textbook to use, rather than to continue with Melvin's original choice, which was Conant and Blatt. Eventually it was decided, with me abstaining and Melvin absent, that the new textbook would be a recent one written by Fieser and Fieser, which was being widely used. On the first occasion that Melvin taught the course using the newly selected textbook, he came into my lab under a full head of steam, tossed this big book on my desk, where it landed with a loud bang!, and said, "When you last taught this course, did you use this book as the text?" When I answered in the affirmative, he said, with much emphasis, "How did you do it?" I explained that I had found the sequence of topics so difficult that I had simply continued with the system that we had previously used. I also told him that students had complained bitterly about my prescribing a textbook which cost a lot of money, then paying no attention to it. The upshot of all this was that Melvin and I had a conference, sometime in 1953, to decide what to do about the textbook.

The first thing that we decided was that, since Wendell had assigned us the responsibility for developing the elementary course in organic chemistry, we had been premature in turning over the choice of textbook to people with no experience in teaching. Consequently, we examined available textbooks and found none in which the sequence of topics at the beginning of the book was similar to that of Conant and Blatt. This book was, admittedly, rather out of date in other respects, so we reached the conclusion that one or the two of us must write a book if we were to continue to teach the course in the way that we wanted to teach it. The most important part of our method—really Melvin's method—was to start the course with a discussion of chemical bonding, the distinguishing characteristic of organic chemistry. As soon as I had taught the course for the first time, I realized that this system was distinctly superior to any other I had used in teaching or had studied under. Moreover, students seemed to be very interested in specializing in organic chemistry when taught by this system, if judged by the number of senior research students who selected organic chemistry as their field of specialty. In addition, by the time of our conference in 1953, many of our graduating seniors had gone to graduate school at major universities and had proved to rank higher than students from other colleges or universities.

In view of Melvin's being rather submerged in his campaign to become famous, I would have to write the book. I reluctantly agreed, with the stipulation that I would start writing immediately if Melvin would follow my writing on the next occasion that he taught the first semester of the course. He would review everything that I wrote before he would use it as a basis for his lectures, and we would have a discussion of everything that seemed to justify a further discussion. After the lectures had been delivered, periodically we would discuss further any indicated revisions. Our system worked out well, although it sometimes caused some crowding of my time during the initial application of the system. I had only a few weeks to get ahead of Melvin before he started giving the lectures, and writing text for one lecture would take several days, or sometimes two or more weeks. Since I had the general organization well in mind, I got along better after the first couple of chapters, but on several occasions I had to forego my usual practice of relaxing by working in our yard on Sundays. One thing that helped me was that there was no need for clean copy for Melvin to use, just copy that he could read, and I was a good typist while composing. Of course Mel made no pretense of following my copy; he delivered the same thoughts in his own lecture style. As a matter of fact, I later did a lot of revising based on Mel's suggestions.

After what seemed like a very long time, I finished the writing and submitted the manuscript in time for a publication date of June 1956 for Essential Principles of Organic Chemistry. Considering the major difference between this book and all others on the market in the same field, it did fairly well. There was a second printing in March 1959. In any case, it provided a suitable textbook for Melvin and me to use in teaching the elementary course in organic chemistry in the manner that we preferred. This book was published by Prentice-Hall after Latimer's death in 1955, and Dean Kenneth S. Pitzer was listed as the chemistry editor for Prentice-Hall. I published a second textbook with Prentice-Hall in 1966, entitled Principles of Modern Organic Chemistry, in order to carry on the tradition of the Berkeley system of organizing the presentation of topics in a different way. This book encountered competition from the most successful textbook ever published for organic chemistry, written by Morrison and Boyd. It was inevitable that my book would not do well, although this was before the disintegration of Prentice-Hall, which I discovered during publication of the third edition of our lab book. Fortunately, the tradition of a modern, successful elementary organic textbook from Berkeley was carried on by Streitwieser and Heathcock, who published an excellent book that was widely used. The second generation of organic chemists at Berkeley carried on splendidly as the first generation was phased out.

Sometime after Rap and I had finished writing our lab book, probably before I became immersed in the lecture text, I received a letter that made me face the fact that the time had come to reach a decision about what I intended to do with my life. Heretofore, I knew what I was trying to accomplish: first, to build a reputation that would bring a tenure position for me in a major university; second, as a result of the success of the first item, to bring organic chemistry to Berkeley. Since both of these objectives appeared to have been accomplished, what was I planning to do now? The letter was from Edgar Lederer, a prominent organic chemist in Paris. He was inviting me to be one of the speakers at a symposium in Rome on bacterial lipids. I realized at once that my invitation to such a symposium was inevitable. Lederer, Einar Stenhagen in Sweden, and I were the leading workers in the field. My series on branched-chain acids had gone well above twenty papers, some of which had been devoted to an extension of R. J. Anderson's work on isolation of lipids from the tubercle bacillus and the study of the structures of the branched-chain acids in them. By use of infrared spectroscopy I had discovered a structural feature of these compounds which had not been recognized previously. In addition to the inevitability of my receiving the invitation, it was just as inevitable that I would not want to go to Rome for this symposium. And so why would most people revel over such an opportunity? I knew the answer to that one; I had figured it out long ago. I had refused to join a fraternity upon entering college, in spite of receiving a flood of invitations to do so, and with the knowledge that at least 90 percent of the male students at Vanderbilt University belonged to fraternities. There is no reasonable doubt that most people would be ecstatic over receiving an invitation to speak at such a symposium, but not most social introverts. I had frequently taken comfort on previous occasions by recalling the story about the famous ichthyologist at Stanford who declined membership in the National Academy of Sciences on the grounds that, "It would inevitably expand the circle of my acquaintances, and my experience is that every time I learn the name of another person, I forget the name of a fish." With my run-ins with the "powers that be" in the ACS, that is a problem with which I would never be confronted. I had refused to drink alcohol, except under extreme social pressure, after my ninth friend had turned up dead because of said chemical compound. I despise undercooked beef, so what would attract me to Rome? Surely not an opportunity to explore the upscale whores in Rome. I would rather sleep with my wife, and help her with the big problem of raising our kids. I recalled the time that a beautiful little blue-eyed blonde got up close to me and said, "Isn't there anything I can do to get my grade raised?" I explained to her gently but clearly that a man with a wife like mine would be a damn fool to even think of exploring with other females. And so what was it that would make me want to go to Rome? I would have to be so anxious to become a famous chemist that I would be willing to pay the price that it would cost me. I would have to join what Nobel Laureate Bob Woodward once called "The Traveling and Speaking Society." My conclusion had to be, "No Sale." And so I sent my regrets to Edgar Lederer, which annoyed him considerably more than somewhat.

Not long after I arrived in Berkeley, I began to get involved with campus politics and campus administrative work. About three years after I arrived in Berkeley, Ken Pitzer dropped by my lab to inquire if I would be interested in becoming the secretary of the local Sigma Xi chapter. I replied that I had been active in forming a chapter at Vanderbilt while I was teaching there, and would be glad to serve as secretary of the Berkeley chapter. I rather enjoyed getting acquainted with others on science faculties, which proved useful in later years; however, the work consumed more time than I had anticipated. I learned that others who had held the job felt as I did about the workload. After a few meetings with the rest of the officers, I wrote a new set of by-laws, which was readily adopted. The difference in the new by-laws was that there were two secretaries: corresponding secretary and membership secretary. I continued for a second year as the membership secretary.

At Berkeley at that time, senate committees and the chairmen thereof were appointed by a committee on committees which was elected by vote of the entire senate membership. At the time of my arrival, this powerful committee was pretty much controlled by the science faculty, led by chemists. The heritage from G. N. Lewis, followed by Joel Hildebrand and Wendell Latimer, followed by Kenneth Pitzer, gave the chemistry department great influence on the campus. Years after my arrival, when Glenn was appointed chancellor of the Berkeley campus, President Robert Gordon Sproul was reported as saying, "The chemistry department has long been dominant on the Berkeley campus; now they own it." Even at that late date this was only a slight exaggeration. I began to learn rapidly about the modus operandi on the Berkeley campus, both by appointments such as to Sigma Xi, and appointments by the committee on committees. While I was still working for Sigma Xi, I was appointed to the committee on undergraduate scholarships, which I found very interesting because of my growing interest in undergraduate students. Somebody—probably Ken—had no doubt told the committee on committees that I was a good candidate for the committee on undergraduate scholarships. The chairman of that committee was Gerald Marsh, chairman of the speech department, who did an excellent job as chairman of this large committee; as I recall, it had about twenty-five people. A large committee was required because each candidate for a scholarship had a fifteen minute interview by a member of the committee, which counted about 15 percent of the score as finally accumulated in several categories. Because of Gerry Marsh's concern that this interview was more important than recognized, and my enthusiastic support of him, the credit assigned to the interview was increased as the credit assigned to the grade point average was decreased. I was sorry to hear later that the interview was eliminated because of the faculty feeling that it was too much like work, and it was unfair because different committee members would give different scores—an objection that can be raised against anything involving mere mortals. In any case, Gerry Marsh and I worked together on several subsequent occasions, especially while I was working in the chancellor's office.

I rose to the apex in 1953, the year after I was appointed full professor, eight years after my arrival in Berkeley. I was appointed as one of the seven members of the budget committee, the most powerful committee in the Academic Senate. It makes recommendations to the chancellor for every new appointment to the faculty, every promotion, the salary of every faculty member, and the budget of every department. The load on this committee is so heavy that each member is relieved of one-half of his normal teaching load, and this was woefully inadequate. By working on this committee, I learned a lot about how to accomplish a great deal with a committee. Too bad politicians in Washington can't learn how to operate in the manner of the budget committee at Berkeley. I hope that this committee is still operating in the same way.

The modus operandi of this committee was as follows: each member, except for the chairman was assigned a group of departments whose business he should be able to understand well enough to properly judge items related to their business. Of course, no member had his own department in his assigned group. Each member then wrote his recommendation to the chancellor for each item under consideration in one of his assigned departments. This was done without any consultation with anybody; in fact, most of this work by me was done at night when there could be no distraction. Even when one or more other members was present with me, there was no tendency at all to engage in conversation. Nobody in his right mind would come from home to the university to engage in socializing. The entire committee would review each recommendation, with any member making any comments he regarded as appropriate. It was uncommon for significant discussion to result. In rare cases where much discussion was indicated, the person who had written the recommendation was likely to welcome input from the other members.

On account of the training and experience necessary for a person to function properly on the budget committee, it was common for a member to serve more than one year, frequently to become chairman eventually. In my case, my tenure was only one year, for Clark Kerr asked me to become faculty assistant to the chancellor for the next year. This was the second year that Clark was chancellor, having replaced Bob Sproul who had previously functioned as chancellor at Berkeley as well as president of the University. In view of Bob Sproul's long and distinguished service as president during the very rapid expansion of the University to new campuses, it is easy to understand why he would be reluctant to let go of the reins at Berkeley. His task of cutting loose was made more difficult by the fact that he was deservedly very popular with students and faculty alike. The upshot of this situation was that Sproul did not take kindly to being replaced by Kerr as the chancellor at Berkeley, and vigorously resisted giving Kerr any assistance at running the campus which he, Sproul, had not had. Why should this newcomer in the chancellor's office require the assistance of vice chancellors? One result of this was that my title was faculty assistant to the chancellor, with a rather minimal stipend in recognition of my service in the chancellor's office. My service in this office lasted only one year and a summer, for reasons to be related later, and my successor had the title of vice chancellor, student affairs.

This situation in the chancellor's office made my position a rather delicate one at the beginning, for I had many fond memories of associations with Bob Sproul, especially during the year that I was on the steering committee for the All University Conference, which Sproul had organized to try and get the faculty on the several campuses acquainted with each other and willing to work together. With advice from the steering committee, Sproul selected faculty members to be invited to the All University Conference, and he exercised great care to ensure that the faculty members invited were spread over the range from recent arrivals to old timers such as Joel Hildebrand. During my second or third year at Berkeley, I received an invitation to attend the conference. Knowing nothing about it, I asked Wendell Latimer what it was about. After explaining the basic function of the conference, as advertised, Wendell then added, "Bob Sproul is a very smart and perceptive guy. He is entirely aware that there is nothing an average university professor enjoys so much as orating before a large captive audience. That is the real function of the All University Conference." Truer words were never spoken; however, I found that these conferences were also quite enjoyable, and did accomplish a great deal along the lines of the stated objectives. I became a member of the steering committee in 1953, and thus was quite active at the conference that year. At one session where I was serving as secretary, and thus recording the motions that were submitted for voting, I became completely snowed while trying to keep up with a long, complicated motion being presented. When I asked the man presenting the motion for a repeat, presented more slowly, Bob Sproul, sitting next to me, boomed out, "While you were asleep, Cason," and then stated the motion word for word before the submitter of the motion could get his mouth open. Bob Sproul really enjoyed such things, and rarely missed an opportunity to demonstrate his capability. The spirit that Sproul was able to develop in such situations was such that everyone was amused, Bob's prestige was increased, and no one thought any less of me. Indeed, I got the impression that my standing had increased. Judging from comments I received, I concluded that this event established me as a confidant of Bob Sproul—a position which I enjoyed. Two things that all of us remember about Sproul are his simply phenomenal memory and his booming voice. At the time of this writing, there would probably be reference to "The Magic of Bob Sproul." Magic he had.

In spite of the fact that my relations with Clark Kerr seemed to offer a threat of being rather fragile, nothing at all threatening developed. Indeed, I began to suspect that my activity at the 1953 All-University Conference resulted in my being in the chancellor's office in 1954. In any case, I enjoyed my year in the chancellor's office, even though it was rather harrowing at times. I suspect that this good relationship between Kerr and me was due in some significant measure to personal characteristics of Kerr which made him a good labor arbitrator. I remember one situation when I was able to settle a serious dispute between the residence halls supervisor and the students in one of the residence halls. I received in the office mail a characteristically cryptic note from Clark, written on a small piece of paper in his virtually illegible handwriting: "Congratulations, are you ready to take on Harry Bridges?" Soon after I arrived at my post in the chancellor's office, I began to realize that I enjoyed working there and being a part of such a congenial office force. A major factor in this congeniality appeared to reside with the three women who ran the office: Virginia Norris, Gloria Copeland, and Fran Essig. Virginia and Fran were married, while Gloria was not. These three differed from each other about as much as three people could, and each was very highly adapted to the job they were doing. Virginia and Gloria took care of all the paperwork involved in running the office. It was not clear to me how the work was divided between them, but when Clark received the offer to succeed Sproul as president, a rumor circulated that he had said that he would not take the job unless Virginia moved with him. On the other hand, years later, after Virginia had retired, Gloria became a vice president in charge of some entity. Fran was a very different kind of person, a rather tall, buxom woman whose voice could pack a lot of decibels. Her principal job was sitting at the desk in the reception room and filtering out people who should and should not see Kerr. She also decided which nuts she would send to me. She seemed to enjoy this part of her job. Although these three women were the leaders of the crew, an additional factor in the congeniality was the interplay between members of the group, both male and female. Some of the things that made the surroundings pleasant could not be realized in the days of this writing, on account of the litigious relationships that have developed in our society. Some of these additional factors are trivial when considered in isolation, others are important; but taken as a whole, all are important. A few events or incidents, chosen from many, which loom prominently in my cyberspace, will be reported.

On the second day after occupying my desk, a gorgeous young woman came into my office, carrying a satchel full of papers. She deposited some of these papers in my IN basket, then commented, "I am your mail girl." Responding to a normal biological instinct, I looked her over carefully from head to toe, then responded, "You don't look male to me." She flashed me a big smile and pranced out. I learned later that she had spread the word that the new arrival was an OK guy. Another occurrence of the trivial sort involved the word that got around after I had been there about eight months, to the effect that Fran and Virginia were engaged in a contest to see which one could become pregnant first. If I were a betting man, I would have bet on Fran. I would have been wrong. One day, sometime in the spring, I came back from lunch, coming in the door from outside that was about fifty feet from my office. Before I reached my office door, Fran Essig came out of the chancellor's reception room, which was about seventy-five feet farther down the hall. As soon as she spied me, she bellowed, with quite an output of decibels, "Jim, Virginia is pregnant." I quickly looked around to see if anybody was in the hall behind me and was quite relieved to see that no one was in sight. I could vividly imagine the headline in the Daily Californian if some wrong person had been on hand.

Congeniality in the chancellor's office sometimes caused a small problem, such as one that developed in the small coffee shop in Dwinelle Hall for use by the people who worked or had offices in the building. When I worked on the budget committee, we sometimes went in there to "build up our blood sugar." I remember one day when the budget committee walked into the coffee shop, a rather indelicate person said in a scornful tone, "Behold, the powers that be on this campus." It was not a large room, so this sort of comment was likely to be heard by most of its occupants. Similarly, when the crew from the chancellor's office descended on this room for their coffee break, the prevalent congeniality generated quite a clatter. On one occasion, a young professor in the mathematics department wrote Clark a letter of complaint about the noise which his crew generated when they invaded the coffee shop. At one point in this letter, he commented, "Even on New Year's eve, I don't get that happy." As I recall, this individual was well known on the campus for his unattractive personality, and the matter was settled by Clark having a letter sent to the man, saying that he was asking the crew to quiet down. He also warned the crew to watch for this guy and clam up if he walked in. I forget the name of the older woman who wrote most of Clark's letters. I wrote a letter for him only rarely, when something in my area of expertise developed.

Most of the students Fran referred to me did not generate a problem, such as the young man who wanted the chancellor to excuse him from passing the exam in the college math course, because "I just can't do math." The math course in question was required for graduation, but not for admission to the university. I think that was changed later. After I explained to this individual that if the chancellor granted such a request it would open Pandora's Box for an unmanageable flood of requests for all kinds of things, he went on his way. Another man who came in to see me was a very different case. He was a graduate student in biochemistry and explained without delay that Professor David Greenberg, chairman of the biochemistry department, was ruining his chances of success in life by writing poor recommendations for him to the places where he was applying for a job. After my inquiring regarding his evidence of Greenberg's misbehavior, and receiving no intelligible answers, he became more excitable and finally announced that if the university persisted in doing nothing to help him, he would have "to take matters into my own hands."

At this point, I told him that I would need an opportunity to investigate this serious matter, so I wanted him to come back to see me the next day at three o'clock. I immediately got in touch with Professor Douglas Kelly, psychiatrist in the School of Public Health, who was retained by the chancellor's office for advice on such matters. I reported my conversation with the graduate student, and said that he seemed to me to be crazy, and I was afraid he might murder Dave Greenberg. Kelley responded, "He's crazy all right, nutty as a fruit cake.".He then explained that paranoid psychotics who are males often become violent, but things are such a blur in their brain that they are about as likely to attack one person as another, so Greenberg was not necessarily the most likely target. He said that he would alert Greenberg, and tell him not to be unduly concerned, but to avoid direct contact with the man. He advised me not to be sympathetic with the student's problems because paranoid psychotics had been known to attack a benefactor, as the person who is conspicuous in the blur in his brain. At that point I responded rather emphatically, "That doesn't make any sense." Kelley replied, "Of course that doesn't make any sense to you; you are not crazy." He then said that I should tell this character clearly and forcibly that he had no reason for thinking that Greenberg was persecuting him. I was so uncertain about the approach recommended to me that I called a friend, Alex Sheriffs, a psychology professor, to get his advice. As soon as I gave Alex my story, he replied, "You better believe what Doug is telling you; on a recent occasion I came near to getting killed by ignoring such advice, and I should have known better."

In spite of so much professional advice, when I went to my office the next afternoon I took with me a paper weight which I had kept for years on my desk in chemistry. Rebecca and I had long been rock hounds, and my office was loaded with all kinds of polished rocks. This paper weight was fabricated from a nice piece of agate, a cube about three inches on a side, except that one corner had a sharp spike which projected about an inch. I had sometimes commented jokingly to a visitor that this was my protection if attacked by a student who objected to his grade. Little did I even dream that I might actually need to use this paper weight as a weapon. When my visitor arrived, I asked him to have a seat, and I would explain things to him. I had put the chair only about a foot and a half away from me, in case a weapon should be produced. He sat down at once, and I explained in a quiet tone that I had investigated his affair with Professor Greenberg and that I must tell him that I could find no evidence whatever that Greenberg was doing anything to damage him. He looked at me intently as I talked. When I paused in order to give him a chance to react, he stood up, said excitedly, "You are just like everybody else; you think I am crazy," and then walked out. After I sat there for a while in order to unwind, I walked up the hill to my office in chemistry. An interesting experience to have had, but not one such that I would yearn for a repeat performance.

To close this account of my experiences in the chancellor's office, I will report a more light-hearted matter. For a few years before I went to work in the chancellor's office, I had been on a kick of wearing corduroy coats. This was initiated by Rebecca's making me a nice corduroy coat which I enjoyed wearing. In order to not present the same appearance day after day, I bought other corduroy coats and wore one of them most of the time. After a few months in the chancellor's office, I began to notice other people in the office wearing corduroy coats, including some women. My only reaction to this observation was to think it was rather reasonable for people to choose such a utilitarian garment with low cost and low upkeep—a vindication of Rebecca's introducing me to the garment. By the time that I began to feel hemmed in by a crowd of people wearing corduroy coats, my instinct against following the crowd, especially regarding fashions in clothes, asserted itself. And so I bought myself a nice blue blazer with brass buttons. On the first day that I wore it, I went down to the chancellor's office for some reason—possibly a pretext. When I walked into the reception room, Fran Essig looked up, visibly recoiled, and addressed me with her normal emphasis, "Jim, after you have established the fashion for dress in the chancellor's office, how could you walk in here wearing that blue blazer?" I told her that I liked a change of scenery now and then, and related to her the story about my not wearing a tuxedo to my initiation into Phi Beta Kappa. She was not mollified, and suggested, "Why don't you go home and come back here wearing one of your nice corduroy coats." Admittedly, I was fishing for a reaction from Fran, so I didn't say anything, but went out, walked up the hill to my chemistry office, took a corduroy coat out of my locker where I had stashed it that morning, exchanged coats, then went down the hill to Dwinelle Hall and went to work in my office. At quitting time for the office force, my door opened. I did not look up from the papers I was reading, but flicked an eye up enough to see Fran stop halfway in the door and then leave. I heard no more conversation about coats, and did nothing to precipitate such a conversation.

The above described event happened after I had already learned that I would not be working in the chancellor's office at the start of the fall semester. I had already agreed, reluctantly, to serve as acting dean of the College of Chemistry. Since there had been a discussion of this between Clark and Ken, Virginia probably knew about it, but there was no gossip about it among the office force. Another change of plans for me had already developed. My appointment in Clark's office was for a year, beginning with the start of the academic year on July 1, hence ending on June 30, 1955. There occurred, however, a change in Clark's plans. He had agreed to give one or more papers at a conference in Germany on something or other, probably either labor relations or university administration. Because of Sproul's limiting of Kerr's staff, I was the senior academic administrator in the office, so Clark asked me to stay over the summer before starting to dean in chemistry. After answering a number of questions from me, he assured me that I would have few, if any, duties to discharge other than being in the office. Virginia and Gloria would run the office just as they always did, show me where to sign any necessary routine papers, and defer anything that was not routine. Clark's and my confidence in Virginia and Gloria proved justified, and everything went off so smoothly that I was able to get a couple of papers written for publication in the Journal of Biological Chemistry while working at a desk in the chancellor's office. After Clark's return, he wrote me a usual illegible note and sent it through the campus mail this time. He said that "the women" in the office gave me high marks for my work in the summer; I did everything I was told to do, and was pleasant to work with. He thanked me for my assistance in the summer, and hoped that I would enjoy working in the College of Chemistry.

At some time during the spring, Ken called and asked me to come to his office for a conference. I was somewhat surprised when he asked me to be acting dean so that he could take a sabbatical leave. I replied that I certainly agreed he deserved a sabbatical leave, but suggested that Bob Connick would do a better job than I would. He replied that he had already asked Bob to do the job, and Bob had suggested that I would be a better choice. This surprised me still more, but I was not worried at that point, and invoked the fact that Clark would have to get a replacement for his office after only a year. The biggest surprise then came when Ken said that he had talked to Clark about bringing me back to the College of Chemistry where I was badly needed. Since there had been numerous occasions when Clark had praised me, both privately and publicly, I realized that I was facing a big problem. I was left with no choice but to invoke my long-standing dislike for administrative work. Among other things, I noted that I had decided to go into university teaching so that I could spend my time, divided as I should choose, between teaching courses to undergraduate students and doing research on whatever I should select, either by directing graduate students or doing experimental work myself. Ken responded by saying that he was anxious to take his first sabbatical leave ever, but would not enjoy it if he had to worry about College of Chemistry affairs going to hell in a handbasket. At that point I suggested that there were several young people in the department who could do the job and enjoyed being in charge of things. Ken cut in to say I should believe him when he told me that I was wrong about what I had just said. Having no powers of prophecy, it was more than forty years later, soon after Ken's death, when I was writing Chapter 10, that I realized how right Ken was when he said I was wrong. And so we wound up a long discussion by my agreeing to talk to Bob and try to reach an agreement about which of us would agree to being acting dean.

One night after dinner at the faculty club, we met in Bob's office in Gilman Hall and sat down for a long discussion beside a stack of issues of Chemical Abstracts which was piled on his desk. I remember asking Bob if the stack of CA was piled on his desk because he was searching for something in the literature. He replied that he just had not gotten around to looking through them yet. In retrospect, I should have gotten a message from this seemingly trivial event , but my sophistication had not reached a level where I could learn something from that sort of thing. After a prolonged discussion, we finally decided that he would tell Ken, since his office was adjacent to the dean's office, that whichever one of us he picked would serve. As nearly as I can remember, I agreed to such a conclusion partly because I was tired of pursuing an obviously futile discussion, and partly because it was a one-year appointment which was involved. As I expected, Ken chose me to be the acting dean for a one-year appointment.

Subsequent events revealed that in all probability Ken Pitzer and Clark Kerr had some long-range discussions about which I had no way of even guessing. I was still battling to defeat the Peter Principle and, again, was handicapped by having no powers of prophecy.

During the first summer of my deaning, I was one busy man, getting two research papers written while starting the job of being chemistry dean and holding the fort for Clark Kerr in the chancellor's office. The situation was manageable for two reasons: first, as Clark had promised, I really had nothing to do in the chancellor's office except be there a few hours per day because Virginia and Gloria did all the work. While there, I was insulated from chemistry and got the papers written. Second, Mabel was accustomed to doing most of the sorts of things that came up during the summer, and she was very good about not calling me in the chancellor's office unless for something that could not wait until tomorrow. First thing each morning, I came by the chemistry dean's office and cleaned out the IN basket. There were no problems during the summer that have remained in my memory.

I was rather nervous while holding a staff meeting early in the fall semester, but I had no demands—at that time—for doing various things for various people. I pointed out the obvious by commenting that I had no experience at being a dean and hence would appreciate receiving advice whenever I needed it. I was quite reassured at the start of the fall semester by the knowledge that Wendell Latimer had his office just down the hall from the dean's office. Also, my best friend among the older generation, Rollie Rollefson, was also available. My first shock came when Rollie had a heart attack and died while attending a dinner for a visiting notable at the faculty club. Soon after that, Wendell also had a fatal heart attack. Fortunately for me, Ken was still present; he had not yet left for his trip to Europe.

I had a few problems with people wanting me to appoint some friend to a faculty position. The first one was a strong recommendation from Leo Brewer that I hire at least one of the top-notch physical chemists who were unemployed because of closure of the "Flame Laboratory" at Johns Hopkins University. There was a lot of this sort of thing occurring because of closure of facilities that had been set up during the war. I got out of this by saying that I had no intention of even suggesting hiring anybody while Ken was away, except for positions mentioned in the memo he had left for me. I was not able to dispose so readily of an organized effort by several people to explore the possibility of hiring Nobel Laureate Willard Libby away from Chicago. After all, Libby had started out as an instructor at Berkeley. I had a vague recollection that I had heard Glenn Seaborg express something less than enthusiasm over the work for which Libby was awarded the Nobel Prize. Furthermore, I thought that the work demonstrated no great brilliance and was not very important. Thus, I consulted Glenn and expressed my dubiety about the whole idea. I remember one statement from Glenn's reply, "I can think of hardly anything that we need less than having Bill Libby on the Berkeley faculty." So much for that problem.

I had a different kind of problem when Linus Pauling tried to steal Rollie Myers away from us. Before Ken left for Europe, he had invited Linus to spend a week as a visiting professor and give a couple of lectures, with the idea of giving graduate students an opportunity to talk with and become acquainted with the famous Linus Pauling. Before Linus came, he received instructions from the treasurer's office that he would have to sign the famous "loyalty oath" before he could be paid as a visiting professor. I was rather well acquainted with Linus because he was a consultant at the Explosives Research Laboratory when I was working there during the war. Thus, he wrote me and said that he was not about to sign any loyalty oath. With Mabel's help, I was able to devise a type of appointment that did not require signing that damn oath, and so Linus arrived on the appointed day in the morning before he was scheduled to lecture that afternoon. I was getting a little jumpy because Linus had not arrived, and had gone down to the street beside the Old Chemistry Building and Gilman Hall, when Linus drove up in his Porsche. Before he got out of the car, he looked at his watch and said, "I left Pasadena exactly three hours and forty minutes ago." My response, "Thank God I was not with you." We had a chat in my office before we went to the faculty club for lunch, and he gave his first lecture at four o'clock that afternoon.

At some time the next day, Rollie Myers, who was a recently appointed assistant professor at the time, came into my office to report that Pauling had offered him a job as associate professor at Cal Tech. Rollie's undergraduate degree was from Cal Tech. He said that he had not given Pauling an answer, but would probably accept the offer, since he was not of tenure rank at Berkeley. I told him that, as an acting dean, there was nothing I could do at once, but that I would get in touch with Pitzer and find out what could be done. Would he hold off on making a commitment to Pauling for a few days? He agreed to do so. I got on the phone at once, explained the situation to several people, including Bill Gwinn, Bob Connick, Bill Giauque, and Glenn Seaborg, and asked them if they would be willing to call Rollie and tell him how much we would hate to see him go to Cal Tech. As has been reported in Chapter 10, Rollie is still with us. Since I was previously acquainted with Linus, and since we had a chat before he made the offer to Rollie, and since he knew that Pitzer was in Europe, I think that Linus Pauling played a dirty trick on me by trying to steal Rollie Myers.

I had another problem with holding one of our important technicians whom Dow Chemical Co. sought to lure to work for them by offering a higher salary than the College of Chemistry could pay. The target in this instance was Vazken Tashinian, our microanalyst, who was probably the best microanalyst in the Bay Area. I was well aware that Tashinian was very good indeed, so I was not surprised that a chemical company might try to take him away from us. I was, however, entirely unaware of the complicated history of the development of our microanalytical laboratory. Since the microlab was so important to the organic chemists, I naturally launched an investigation. I found that Tashinian was at the top of the wage scale for his job title, and that the personnel department for non-faculty employees would do nothing for me in terms of changing Tashinian's job title to one carrying higher pay. In this emergency, I naturally sought the advice of Mabel Kittredge, who was able to find a suitable academic job title which would make higher pay possible. I had some trouble with the head of the non-academic personnel office about changing Tashinian out of his realm; however, I finally succeeded in persuading him by referring to my friendship with Bill Monahan, the business manager, with whom I had frequently worked while in the chancellor's office. It was after I had resolved this relatively minor problem that I learned about the very complicated history of the microanalytical lab. It was probably fortunate that I did not know about it until after this problem was resolved.

This microanalytical lab was so important to the success of organic chemistry coming to Berkeley that the reporting of its history at this point is in order. The man who gave birth to the microanalytical lab was Charles

William Koch, known as Charlie to everybody, except his family who called him Bill. Charlie was an undergraduate at Berkeley in the years prior to World War II. By his senior year (1940-41), he had taken two courses in microchemistry under famed microchemist Paul Kirk, and was also engaged in doing a year of senior research under Kirk. He was also working part-time in the part of the chemistry stockroom known as the solution room. He had become acquainted with Wendell Latimer, who was appointed dean of the College of Chemistry in 1941. Latimer knew of Koch's extensive training under Paul Kirk, and asked him if he would help Professor Blasdale set up a microanalytical lab capable of doing any elementary analyses the department might require. Professor Blasdale, long-time teacher of inorganic analytical chemistry in the days of macroanalysis, was about ready to retire, and had been asked to set up the newly required microanalytical lab because no one else was available. As soon as Charlie's capability became apparent, Blasdale cheerfully retired from any further struggling with the lab, and Charlie was left in charge at about the time of his graduation, with a B.S. in chemistry.

At this early stage in the history of the microanalytical lab, Professors Branch and Calvin were the only organic chemists whose graduate students required elementary analyses, so the demand for Charlie to provide microanalyses was relatively limited; however, he continued to work full-time for the department during the war years of 1941 to 1944, developing the lab and doing any analyses required. He worked full time for the Manhattan District from 1944 until the fall of 1946. With the war ending in 1945, he returned to full-time work for the department, and revitalized the microanalytical lab. He was stimulated by the arrival of the organic chemists, who were pouring on the coal and producing work for the microanalytical lab. The whole development was fortunate for the organic chemists, including the next step in this scenario. In view of the shortage of new graduate students immediately after the war, and the concurrent influx of hordes of undergraduate students, Charlie was appointed a teaching assistant in Chemistry 5, the sophomore course in analytical chemistry. This was a very large course since it was a requirement in several majors, and hence felt the greatest impact of the influx of undergraduates. More serendipity walks on the scene. One of the students who happened to be taking Chem 5 at that time and who happened to be put in

Charlie Koch's lab section was named Vazken Tashinian. Charlie noticed at once that this man was not only a good student but unusually adept at experimental work. And so he asked the department for permission to hire Tashinian part-time while he continued as a student. By the time that Tash graduated two years later, he was rated by Charlie as better than any microanalyst in the Bay Area with whom he was acquainted. This development was just on schedule for meeting the rapid increase of requirements for microanalyses generated by the upstart organic chemists. With things so good for the organic chemists, perhaps it was inevitable for others to take notice. We were threatened with losing not only Tashinian, but also Koch. A really scary situation.

At the time of Tashinian's graduation (the fall of 1948), the chemical industry was operating at the peak of the rapid expansion after the war. Jobs were readily available, especially for people with training in a hot field such as microanalysis. Tashinian had a good record as a student from a chemistry department with a top-notch rating. Charlie Koch had a good job offer from Chevron, but Charlie wanted to stay at Cal if Tashinian could be held. He had a number of inquiries from industry, including Chevron, about getting microanalyses done at the university. When the situation seemed to be getting out of control, Charlie decided to ask Dean Latimer about the possibility of he and/or Tashinian using the microanalytical lab facilities in order to do work for industrial labs and be paid by the industrial companies, thus increasing their incomes without any cost to the university. There was a regulation at the university at that time that employees could not do outside work for pay unless the industry was having trouble getting the work done otherwise. The dean decided that the kind of salary being offered microanalysts by industry was a clear indication that Charlie's proposal was acceptable, especially since failure to accept the proposal would cripple the organic chemists' ability to continue their demonstrated ability to turn out good research. Of course, a part of the agreement was that outside work would always be done only when no work for the organicers was immediately on hand. Furthermore, any supplies used for outside work would be replaced at the expense of Charlie and Tash. I had noticed how remarkably quickly I usually got the results of an analysis after I submitted the sample. I did not know that Tashinian often worked on weekends if necessary to keep the regular work days clear for our analyses. As years went by, the system worked perfectly, to everybody's advantage: the department was able to hold the best microanalysts in the area; the organic chemists had very fast and accurate analytical work done for them; Tash and Charlie were able to get enough income to stay at the job which they loved and wanted to continue pleasing those they worked for. All of this was at no cost to the university, paid for by the outside industrial companies, who were grateful to the university for helping them to solve an intractable problem. Once again, when the chips were down, Wendell Latimer came to the assistance of the organic chemists. How unfortunate that when Harold Johnston became dean, he decided to dismantle the system.

Immediately after I became acting dean, I learned that an important function of the dean's office was basically a social one—entertaining visitors of all sorts, frequently referred to as "Visiting Firemen." These people were divided into two classes which were quite different; one class consisted of representatives from industry who came to interview students at both undergraduate and graduate levels; the other class consisted of visiting notables, nearly always invited and scheduled to deliver one or more lectures while here. The lectures were paid for either by a fund established for the university, or by an industrial company eager to increase their leverage in hiring the best of our Ph.D. graduates. The first class of visiting firemen were not a great problem for the dean's office, for the industry visitors invited both professors and deans to lunch or dinner, again to increase their leverage in hiring the best Ph.D. candidates. Principally because I was a professor, I became good friends with some of the personnel from industry. In one case, Karl Folkers and I continued to exchange Christmas cards for many years, until both of us were retired.

In the case of the other class of visitors, entertainment was definitely up to the dean's office, and was handled in a professional manner by my capable wife, Rebecca. In instances where a larger dinner or lunch was needed, we usually turned the whole affair over to the faculty club. The event which I remember most vividly was the visit by Nobel laureate Richard Kuhn, from Germany. We had a rather large dinner at the faculty club to which the organic chemists and biochemists and their wives were invited. In addition, Rebecca invited Professor Kuhn, his Swiss wife, and his daughter, who was a graduate student at UC Davis at the time, to dinner at our home. When the Kuhns walked in our front door, the professor declared in his stentorian voice, "I have been told that if I should have the good fortune to come to this home, there are two things which I should make sure to see; one is the magnificent view from your window." As he spoke, the trio of them were walking towards the window in our sun room. Fortunately, it was a clear day and the sun, at that season, was far enough to the north so that there was no interference with the sweeping view across San Francisco Bay to the Golden Gate. As they stood and looked around as if hypnotized, there was frequently heard the word, "Wunderbar." I had felt the same sentiment—in English—hundreds of times since I first looked out that window in 1945.

After the ceremony at the window, Professor Kuhn said that he now wanted to see, before dinner, the dog that sneezed on command. Our sons had worked for months teaching Xylene to sneeze on command—using a cookie of course. Not being satisfied with that, they then taught her to sit up, not an insignificant feat, in view of the size of the shoulders of a boxer dog. As I went to get Xylene out of the small room that we called the den at that time, I kept thinking, "I hope that Xy can perform before such an audience." With cookies in my pocket, which Xylene could smell, of course, I took her into the dining room where there was a space by the head of the table, got her into a good position, and said "Sit up Xy." She did so at once, with her front legs hanging in front of her barrel chest. I then said, with my voice trembling a little, "Now sneeze, Xy." She came through like a champ, sneezed so hard that she fell over onto the floor— and looked up at me with a disappointed expression. I patted her head, told her she was great, and fed her five cookies. Needless to say, Xylene dominated the conversation for quite a while, as she sat on the floor beside Rebecca at the head of the table. This was a special treat since she had been trained to stay away from the table until dessert time, at which time she also had her dessert, usually a few cookies. There were so many stories about Xylene available that there was a lot of laughter for quite a while. I will report here only about the time that we first realized that Xylene understood the English language. We were taking our sons to a Gilbert and Sullivan Operetta in San Francisco, as we frequently did when the D'Oyle Carte group was in town. As all four of us were leaving Xylene sat looking at us so sadly that I said, "We are sorry that we must leave you all alone, so you can have the special privilege of sleeping on the sofa tonight." (She was not allowed to sleep on the furniture.) When we returned at about midnight, Xylene was stretched out full length on the sofa, and made no effort to move when we came in. As Rebecca and I looked at each other, and our sons laughed, I said, "Well, it seems to be rather clear now that she really does understand the English language. I wonder if she could learn German."

Xylene came to us as a stray, following one of our sons home. When she died about ten years later, Rebecca was so broken up about it that we vowed to never again have another dog. Its demise could be too painful, considering the short life of a dog compared to ours.

Before vacating the dean's office, I wrote a long memo to Ken, reporting on my administration of his deanship. Among other things, I suggested that with the current size of the department and the rapid growth of chemical engineering, it was really too heavy a load on the dean to also be chairman of the chemistry department. A few days after Ken had gotten back into the swing of things, he phoned and asked me to come over to his office for a conference. He said that he had decided to follow my suggestion about separating the chairman of the chemistry department from the office of the dean. He continued by asking me to serve as the first chairman of chemistry. In retrospect, I should have known that this would happen, but somehow it had never entered my mind. Since I was just now feeling a little relaxed after three years of administrative work, apparently I came completely unglued, and told Ken that I wanted no part of any more administrative work. This obviously was a great disappointment to Ken, for he also crumbled and finally invited me out of his office, and to go over to my office where he could not hear me. Never before had any cross words passed between us—our families had gone skiing together. As I walked very slowly back to my office, I was filled with recriminations: I handled it stupidly; I should have said that I want to think it over; etc. When I arrived at my office, the phone was ringing. It was Ken who apologized at length for hitting me so suddenly with this; he should have invited me to discuss the matter; etc. After quite a lot of each of us apologizing at length, the conversation finally ended, without any mention of whether or not I might reconsider taking the job. Ken and I remained on friendly terms, but our relationship was never quite the same, even after he returned from a stint as president of Rice University, followed by the same at Stanford University. It took him longer than it did me to get the message about administrative work. Obviously, I will never know what went on between Clark Kerr, Ken Pitzer, and Bob Connick, but I am suspicious that my determination to defeat the Peter Principle demolished some plans that they had developed. In retrospect, from this distance, I am not sorry that I did it.

Ken appointed Isadore Perlman as the first chairman of the chemistry department. Since Perlman was located primarily in the radiation lab and had no office in the chemistry buildings on campus, it was never made clear to me why Ken made that choice. I assumed that it was a political matter, involved with relations between the rad lab and the chemistry department. With Wendell Latimer gone, the relations between these two units were in a state of flux. In view of Perlman's inexperience in the chemistry department, Ken asked me to take over the selection of new teaching assistants for the next year. In view of the situation, I could hardly refuse, and so this caused me to spend considerable time in the chairman's office, sorting over applications by students applying for graduate work in chemistry. Normally, all new graduate students were either TA's or had a scholarship or fellowship with outside money, such as a National Science Foundation fellowship. The secretary for the chairman was Lucille McCormick, who had been employed by me soon after I became dean, because she was a very accurate and high speed typist. She had a college education and had been employed as secretary to a prominent chemist at the University of Chicago, so she was soon shifted to being an administrative assistant, and was clearly in line to be the secretary to the new chairman.

After the first of the year, when new student applications began coming in, I was frequently in the chairman's office, sorting through applications, searching for top-notch applicants to whom we would want to immediately send an offer to be a TA. The idea was to get them before somebody else skimmed off the cream of the crop, and so I wanted the "offers" to go out promptly. I had been through all this the year before when I was both dean and chairman. The offers had to be signed by the chairman, and Perlman was not in the office at all regularly, so I was the only one to keep tabs on whether Lucille was getting the offers out. I was accustomed to running a tight ship with Mabel Kittredge at the helm, so I had occasion now and then to badger Lucille about keeping the paper moving. When Mabel told me I was making Lucille cry, I told her that I would not do that any more. And so I said to myself, "To hell with it; I am going to get caught up on paper writing." My publication rate showed an improvement.

And so there comes an end to the Pitzer Era, with Latimer Hall being built; the Old Chemistry Building and the Rat House being torn down; Pitzer leaving to become president of Rice University; and an assortment of deans and chairmen serving in chemistry. When my long-time friend— since 1934—Glenn Seaborg was appointed chancellor of the Berkeley campus, to succeed Clark Kerr who had been appointed president of the university, I knew that Ken Pitzer would not be long for the Berkeley campus. I knew that Pitzer was Clark Kerr's favorite Dean—and for many good reasons. And so I judged that Kerr had lost control over appointment of his successor. Whatever was involved in that decision, as subsequent events have proven, it was a sad day for Berkeley. The College of Chemistry was never the same again.

CHAPTER 12

SUNSET AND EVENING STAR

Chapter 11 was devoted to the effect of events on me and my reaction in seeking to influence the development of those events by serving in various administrative capacities. In a few key situations, my determination to defeat The Peter Principle caused me to decline acceptance of administrative positions and invitations of a sort that would be likely to promote my prominence as a research scientist, but have no other functions regarded as useful or desirable by me. During that period, much of my energy was directed towards activities that would increase the prestige of organic chemistry at Berkeley. This involved not only publication of good research, but also the writing of textbooks. Administrative work had the inevitable effect of reducing my research output, which is noticeable in the tabulation reported at the end of Chapter 10. I regarded this as entirely acceptable for several reasons, until things reached the point where what I regarded as the tail began to wag the dog. So I blew the whistle, or did I pull the plug? or was I simply acting in a characteristic manner as a "stubborn son-of-a-bitch?" Paraphrasing an utterance of The Lord High Executioner in the Mikado, I will leave that choice up to you.

A few years after I had managed to get out of administrative work, changes in academia affecting physical and biological scientists reached the point where a nuclear chemist would refer to "critical mass", the weight of material which will explode if packed together. The seeds for this change were planted during World War II when contributions by academic scientists had such an obvious and enormous impact on the Allies winning the war. The atomic bomb, which was responsible for saving millions of lives, was the centerpiece of academia's efforts; however, other less conspicuous things such as radar and the RDX bomb were very important in making it possible for the Allies to hang in there until the bomb was ready for delivery. In any case, both the public and the politicians became quite aware of the importance of academic scientists to the welfare of the country. This development was obviously good, and certainly added a great deal to the rapid rise in the prestige of American scientists, as well as to the prosperity of the country.

Since both the public and the politicians were convinced of the importance of science in academia, there resulted a veritable gusher of financial support for scientists. This sort of support was especially welcome because the introduction of instrumentation such as spectroscopy and gas phase chromatography made it easy to accomplish research rapidly, which had previously been either impossible or very slow and tedious. I remember some striking illustrations of this situation. Bill Gwinn, a physical chemist in my department had earlier gotten his Ph.D. degree working under Kenneth Pitzer. One day in 1965, Bill came to lunch at the faculty club with a rather peculiar, rapt expression on his face. After looking around, he made the comment, "I just learned that, using a computer, I can do in about one week what I did for my Ph.D. degree in three years." In my own research on the lipids of the tubercle bacillus, where I had to work with very small amounts of material, I had shelved two interesting problems in the early 1950s, because I judged them to be impossible with the small amounts of material available. In the early 1960s, I revived these problems and published papers on them. With gas phase chromatography to separate amounts of material which were just enough to see, and identification of such samples by the use of mass spectroscopy, truly amazing advances in chemistry and biochemistry resulted. In order to take advantage of this revolution in scientific endeavor, it rapidly became necessary for scientists to devote as much energy as necessary to secure access to the megabucks needed to buy and operate the instrumentation.

In about 1962, Bill Dauben, Henry Rapoport and I went together and applied to the National Institutes of Health for about $120,000 to be used to buy a mass spectrometer. Our application succeeded, and we were faced with the problem of deciding how to spend our money. Since I had more knowledge of such instruments than my colleagues, due to having a double major in chemistry and physics as an undergraduate, I was elected, by default, to be in charge of the mass spectroscopy lab. My first task was to decide which instrument to buy. There were two types of these instruments on the market at that time; one termed a time-of-flight instrument and the other a magnetic deflection instrument. As a start in my investigation, I consulted Professor Harold Johnston, who already had a time-of-flight instrument in use with his research group.

Hal had been appointed to our faculty as a full professor in 1957. Melvin Calvin and I were the two department representatives on the ad hoc committee which reported to the budget committee its recommendation about whether the appointment should be approved. If appointed, Hal would be the first person in modern times to be appointed at a tenure rank in the chemistry department at Berkeley. All others had started in a non-tenure rank, as I had. Most of the appointments were of people who had received the Ph.D. degree from the Chemistry Department at Berkeley. They were home grown. This led to the situation which was described to me by Homer Adkins (see Chap. 9) as a "den of narrow-minded physical chemists." Ergo, I put up a "stubborn" fight in order to convince the other members of the committee to send a favorable recommendation to the budget committee for Hal's appointment. Since Melvin's background was so different from mine, he remained neutral in this debate. Little did I dream that the day would come when I would be fighting to prevent Hal Johnston from taking away what Wendell Latimer had done for the organic chemists. As I have previously quoted Robert Burns, "The best laid plans o' mice and men gang aft agley."

When I consulted Hal about what type of spectrometer to buy, he strongly recommended that I buy a time-of-flight instrument such as he had. I knew enough about physics to have some misgivings about the ability of the electronics technicians to generate sufficient accuracy in measuring the time of flight to determine a molecular weight accurately for high molecular weight compounds. Organic chemists are very frequently working with "high molecular weight" compounds such as the lipids from the tubercle bacillus with which I had been working ever since my arrival at Berkeley. I also knew that Einar Stenhagen in Sweden, a pioneer in applying mass spectrometry to high molecular weight compounds, used a magnetic deflection instrument. In fact, I had sent him many compounds for use in his work. Eventually, I decided to get in touch with the Bendix Corporation, manufacturer of the time-of-flight instrument, and ask them if they would determine the molecular weight of a compound I would send them so that I could decide if the accuracy was sufficient for our purposes. They complied, I sent them a sample, and they sent me a report that the molecular weight was between 376 and 378. Our requirement was for an answer which specified one number; a range we could get by old-fashioned methods. So much for Professor Johnston's recommendation.

By this time I was convinced that we should buy the magnetic deflection machine, but there remained the problem of acquiring someone, either a technician or a faculty member, who was capable of cooperating with the manufacturer in setting up the machine and then putting it into operation. In the day of expensive and complicated machines, it is always necessary to have an operator to whom the researchers take their samples. I was slightly acquainted with a professor at the Massachusetts Institute of Technology (MIT) named Klaus Biemann. My contact with him derived from the fact that he was an Austrian. A good friend of mine, Peter Tavs, one of my former post-doctoral research assistants, was also an Austrian. In my search for someone to help us with establishing a mass spectrometry lab, I contacted Klaus Biemann, for he was a leader in developing mass spectroscopy in this country. This contact proved to be very fortunate. Klaus first told me that we were fortunate in choosing the magnetic deflection machine; he had tried them all. He also told me that Consolidated Electrodynamics Corp., manufacturer of the machine we were to buy, also was the best manufacturer worldwide, of the "high resolution" mass spectrometer, which was capable of determining a molecular weight much more accurately than just to a single whole number. He also told me that he had an excellent graduate student named Alvin Burlingame who was graduating soon and would probably be interested in an appointment as assistant professor at Berkeley. With the cooperation of Bob Connick, who was dean of the college at that time, we were eventually able to appoint Al Burlingame as assistant professor, and he was aboard when our new mass spectrometer arrived. As the final step in this long process we were able to hire a very capable student, Sherri Firth, who was just graduating with a B.S. degree, as the technician to work under Al Burlingame. I was acquainted with Sherri, because she was an "A" student in one of my classes. While I was desperately looking for a person to work under Al in the mass spec lab, Sherri walked into my office to report that she did not like the idea of working in industry, and wondered if I had any alternate suggestions. I did have one.

During the period when I was devoting considerable energy to getting the mass spectrometer installed and in service for turning out mass spectra, there was a considerable overlap in time with construction of our new building, Latimer Hall. As soon as Latimer Hall was ready for occupancy, there followed demolition of the Old Chemistry Building. When the big crane with a big clamshell arrived, I went down from my new office on the eighth floor of Latimer Hall to watch the demolition from a site near the bridge across Strawberry Creek. There were others there besides me whose eyes were not dry. When the clamshell came down for its first bite, I realized that it was heading for my former laboratory (office). I watched with a mixture of fascination and despair as the walls and everything between them disappeared within five minutes: the table with shelves built on it which I used as a desk, the work benches, including the glass-blowing station; the two fractionating columns which I had built with such care and used so frequently; everything—gone forever.

The move from Old Chem to our fine new building, Latimer Hall, involved a great deal of labor for all of the organicers; however, it was especially difficult for me. I knew that I had spent the best years of my professional life in that old building, and I also knew that life for me in Latimer Hall would never be the same. Whereas the others were stimulated by looking forward to a future of research in the fine new building, the principal view of research in my future was looking into the sunset. During the period when I was working on acquisition of the mass spectrometer, I was forced to realize that the scene in academia was becoming more and more distasteful to me. In a major university, the most important activity of a professor had become the acquiring of money to support his research. This research, in return, was the principal consideration in hiring new faculty; for it was a key factor in the prestige of the university. And this prestige was the principal interest of the upper echelon of administrators. The research grants, usually from the federal government, carried large "overhead" charges, in some cases more than 50 percent of the money in the grant. In reality, this "overhead" was a grant directly to the university. As time went on, this money became a larger and larger fraction of the total money spent for research in the university. It was sometimes used for construction of buildings and maintenance thereof, for development of a "research institution." And it was the professors who were bringing in this money. Inevitably, famous professors tended to become free-lance operators, selling their services to the highest bidder. Even rather young professors, who showed great promise of being able to bring in lots of research grants, were sometimes attracted to another university which offered them a position as head of a research institute. A younger friend of mine at Berkeley was the recipient of such an offer. He did not want to leave Berkeley, but he had to go. He told me, "I cannot refuse the offer; I would be betraying my family and all those who recommended me so highly."

This situation became more far-reaching than I had expected, although I had become well aware of what was happening, first when I was on the budget committee, then working in the chancellor's office. It was normal, inevitable, and desirable that a professor would seek to improve his professional status and/or satisfy his personal ambitions; therefore, he wanted to get research grants. A major requirement for money in doing research is the hiring of assistants to work for him. And, of course, he must pay the salary of his assistant. Much of the research was likely to be carried out by post-doctoral research assistants, such as the position which I occupied with Professor Louis Fieser at Harvard. This was an important factor in training competent research scientists. However, the cost of supporting a post-doctoral assistant was much greater than the cost of paying a graduate student as a research assistant while the student was getting the research done that would lead to his Ph.D. thesis. This was probably the best and most important feature of the system developed for academic research. It had numerous obvious advantages: it made it possible for a person who was capable to get a Ph.D. degree while being supported financially. It gave a very effective method for sorting out the most capable people, depending almost entirely on performance actually delivered over a period of three years or more. The students involved would work very hard in most cases, for they would become eligible for a high paying job as soon as that coveted degree was received. There is no free lunch, however, for it was inevitable that there would develop fierce competition between universities for the best graduate students, as well as competition between professors for the best graduate students. It is probable that any system which produces good results must involve competition. This system was certainly very important to the dazzling advance of our country in science, which was in turn responsible for the spectacular increase in the general prosperity of our country. Nevertheless, I was soon to encounter another serious side effect of this "system."

Although I was well aware of the virtues of the system being used to support academic research, and had taken full advantage of it, by about 1960 I began to feel rather discouraged by the authority bestowed on people in Washington to have what sometimes amounted to control of the research I did. An integral part of the system of awarding grants was to place the taxpayer's money where it was expected to do the most good. It seems clear that such a system must be judged as good; however, there were side effects which were undesirable, and I was directly impacted by one of them. By 1962, I had published more than forty papers on various aspects of our study of the branched-chain fatty acids from the tubercle bacillus, and there was no reasonable doubt that I, the Stenhagens in Sweden, and Edgar Lederer in Paris were the foremost authorities in this field. For years I had been in close contact with the Stenhagens, as has been previously mentioned. By about 1962, we had agreed that problems related to this field had been solved, or else had become of little practical interest because of the introduction of antibiotics in therapy for tuberculosis. Since I had published about as many articles in several other fields, so that the total was about equal to the articles in the branched-chain fatty acid field, I naturally decided to direct my attention to other fields, especially the study of the effect of steric hindrance on the direction of reactions of organic compounds. I had published some papers in the field, which seemed well accepted, but I certainly could never be rated as an authority, especially with people in the field such as Herb Brown at Purdue, who subsequently won a Nobel Prize. Therefore, I applied for a research grant to work in this field. The application was denied on the grounds that I was not a very prominent researcher in this field. I got the message. A part of the message was that a prominent researcher in a field was destined to become more prominent, unless he decided to abandon the field or a competing researcher in the same field outdid him and took over as the prime recipient of the research grants. Several situations could develop, and some of them did. If one researcher became so prominent so rapidly, he could become essentially the owner of the field and build up such a large organization that he became out of touch to the extent that fraud developed, with the eventual development of court cases, with the National Institutes of Health or others, accusing the Great Man of fraud. In other instances, two or more researchers became competitive on rather equal terms, with the result that one researcher withheld publishing his data in order to make sure that a competitor would not be able to outdo the creator of the data. In one case, the man who withheld some of his data publicly bragged about the way he had outmaneuvered his competitors. This appears to be legal, but in the mind of a researcher who did his work in a collegial atmosphere, it certainly stinks.

In any case, after I had been cogitating for several months, I decided that I should phase myself out of doing research with graduate students and make way for our younger faculty in organic, who were making it clear that they were adequately capable of carrying the ball for organic chemistry at Berkeley. This decision carried a lot of serendipity, including elimination of the need to compete with my friends for graduate students. In view of this decision, I stopped applying for research grants from government agencies and did not accept new graduate students to work with me. I applied to other agencies for small grants to continue research with a few undergraduate students and to phase out research involving mass spectroscopy. By this time, the department provided only a rather meager sum of money to pay for the expenses of doing research. Any expenses beyond that meager sum must come from grants or out of the professor's pocket. The tables were turned! Instead of the university supporting the research of the professors, the grants of the professors supported nearly all the research done in the university, as well as significant support to the general budget of the university. As mentioned previously, this latter item was called "overhead" and charged to the grant to pay for the expense to the university of managing the research. It was not uncommon for all or some of the space used by the research to also be rented to the research grant. Small wonder that universities are so fond of professors who can "bring in grant money."

As I became more disenchanted with the mechanics of doing research in academia, I became more interested in teaching and administrative affairs in the College of Chemistry and the Department of Chemistry. Concerning administrative affairs, I was saddened to learn that Ken Pitzer was dead right when he told me that I was wrong when I said that there should be an adequate supply of people on the teaching staff in chemistry who could do a good job of administration and enjoy doing it. By the time that I reached retirement, which was mandatory in those days with no bribery necessary, I began to wonder if the gods and the fates were punishing me for declining to accept Ken Pitzer's offer to be the first chairman of the chemistry department after that post was separated from the deanship, on my recommendation. If I should rate the performance of our administrators in the post-Pitzer era, in both the College and Department of Chemistry, with two exceptions I would have to assign grades in the range between B- and F. As Wendell Latimer pointed out to me a few years before his death, the problem with administrators is that nearly all of them are afflicted with "administrator's disease," characterized by love of brandishing authority, and love of glorifying oneself. I have had considerable contact with the damage done by administrator's disease in industry, as well as in non-scientific areas of academia; however, I do not claim expertise in other than scientific areas in academia. I believe that scientists are particularly susceptible to administrator's disease for several reasons. One is that they are hired, at least in major universities, on the basis of their competence in research, not on the basis of their competence in administration. If a given individual is competent at both scientific research and administration, that is good luck. If the individual is highly competent at research, but totally incompetent at administration, that is bad luck—especially for those who must suffer under his authority. The College of Chemistry had bad luck in suffering for four years under Dean Harold Johnston.

When Ken Pitzer left Berkeley in 1960 to become president of Rice University, Bob Connick was chairman of the department of chemistry. Bob had done an excellent job as chairman, and so everybody was pleased when he became dean. His service as dean was as good as had been expected, so good that the College of Chemistry suffered the same fate as when we lost Pitzer. Bob Connick was taken away from us, this time by our own university, to become vice chancellor of the Berkeley campus. This occurred in 1965 at the height of the campus rioting around the country. Berkeley got very bad press regarding this rioting because we were the first to be picked by the Communist Party as a target. Actually, there were at least five other universities that had much worse problems than Berkeley, in terms of property damage and/or people killed. However that may be, before things had quieted down our chancellor left, for reasons which I do not remember, and in the emergency Bob Connick became acting chancellor. This left the College of Chemistry with our two good administrators gone, one lured away and one conscripted. This generated quite a number of conferences directed toward choosing a new dean, as Richard Powell served as acting dean for a few months. I was completely helpless in blocking the choice of Harold Johnston, who was chosen because he was a member of the National Academy of Sciences. I had already had a serious problem with Johnston in connection with his use of our mass spectrometer. This event had made it clear to me that the man was not a capable administrator, but there was nothing I could do about it. The gods and the fates were really picking on me. I did not dream at this stage just how tough things were going to get.

The trouble I had with Johnston in connection with our mass spectrometer occurred in late 1964 or 1965, before he had become dean. Al Burlingame had just gotten our spectrometer up and running and was turning out spectra for the organicers. It was before I hired Sherri Firth to operate our spectrometer, and so Al was the one turning out the spectra. One of Johnston's graduate students brought a sample of a gas to Al and asked him to run a mass spectrum on it. Apparently, Johnston's time-of-flight spectrometer was not working at all well. (This was the machine that Johnston had tried to persuade me to buy.) Al agreed to run the spectrum, but explained to the student that all the samples from the organicers who owned the machine were solids or liquids. Thus, it would take him a while to build a suitable chamber for running gases and, even after the suitable container had been fabricated it would take an hour or so to change from a solid to a gas or vice versa. When the sample turned out to be air, Al was more unhappy than before he made the run. After Al had run two more samples of air from the same student, he lost his cool and told the student that if he brought in another sample of air he would never run another sample for him. And then another sample came in that proved to be air. Because our spectrometer was housed in a room about fifty feet down the hall from my office, the explosion was not loud enough for me to hear. The first I knew of the affair was when Johnston telephoned me and complained bitterly. I told him that I knew nothing of the affair but would investigate. When I talked to Al, I heard a different story than the one that Johnston gave me as the report from his student. I told Al that I would back him up in case any such situation should arise in future. I knew the futility of engaging in any discussion with Johnston about his student not giving him the true story in order to protect himself from having to report to his research director that he had made some stupid errors. I had already learned that Johnston had no ability to deal with any matters requiring competence at the administration of anything. Thus, I merely explained to him that Al was getting pushed rather hard to keep up with running spectra for the organicers at the same time that he was getting familiar with a machine that was new to him and was afflicted with the usual number of bugs.

I made no effort to explain to Johnston just how great a head of steam Al Burlingame was working under. I am sure that Al's response to that student's continuing to bring him samples of air was greatly restrained because of his ambition to make a good impression that would contribute to his eventually getting promoted to a tenure rank. I knew that Al was working extraordinarily long hours. On any night that I came to the lab after supper, Al was there. Also, I rarely went home before six o'clock in the afternoon, and Al soon observed that. He would frequently come into my office at about five o'clock, go to my chalk board and start trying to learn how his data would solve the structure of the compound on which he was working. As he talked out loud explaining things to himself, but addressing me, I learned a lot about structure determination by use of mass spectroscopy. My education was amplified by the fact that Al always answered patiently all the questions I asked. I certainly knew more about structure determination by use of mass spectroscopy than anyone else in the department. Five of my papers published in 1964 or later could not have been published in the absence of mass spectroscopy. I also passed much of this information to Charlie Koch, who became in charge of our mass spectroscopy lab when the high resolution instrument was acquired by the department. The high resolution instrument was sufficiently complicated that Charlie Koch was given one year without teaching duties in order to supervise setting up and learning how to operate the instrument. In addition to the above-cited five papers, I published two additional papers in which mass spectroscopy was sufficiently important that Koch's name was listed among the authors.

From this point onward, Charlie Koch spent the majority of his time developing the mass spectrometry laboratory. This included persuading the department to buy the British-manufactured instrument, from which Calvin's group had never been able to get satisfactory results, for a small fraction of the original cost of the instrument. Under Charlie's direction, David Gee in our electronics shop completely replaced all of the original components in this machine with solid state components. After this infusion of new blood, the machine worked excellently. Concurrently with Gee's rehabilitation of the British machine, Charlie persuaded the department to engage a newly started company to devise software to make it possible for a mass spectrometer to send its output to a computer which would print out the results. This would save much time in interpreting each mass spectrum. The start-up company agreed to provide the required software by a certain date if they could use one of our spectrometers to do the development, working at night and on weekends. In the drive to meet this deadline the software man nearly went crazy, but after we granted a delay he finally came through, and we got our computer output at a very low price. It was quite a gamble, and it was hard on Charlie's emotional equilibrium, especially because of an occasional failure of the department to cooperate cheerfully; however, it eventually paid off. At this point, the organicers were set up for smooth delivery of mass spectra via the computer, and so I did not follow Charlie's further adventures with this high resolution instrument. The instrument bought by Bill, Rap, and I about ten years earlier, which introduced modern mass spectrometry to the department, had become obsolete and was retired. During the electronic revolution time moves at a dizzy pace. I recently read a story by a computer expert who sought to keep strictly abreast of all new developments. One comment he made: "Before I can get a new computer out of the box, the damn thing is obsolete."

I have no way of knowing whether the problem involving Johnston and our mass spectrometer was responsible for his attitude towards organic chemists after he became dean. However this may be, his damaging actions appeared to be focused on organic chemists. Most serious for the organicers was Johnston's attack on the microanalytical lab, which had been a critical component in the rapid build-up of organic chemistry at Berkeley. As has been described in Chapter 11, Dean Wendell Latimer had authorized the operation of this laboratory to include doing analyses for outside industry, with the payment for same going directly to Koch and Tashinian. These two were doing the analyses at that time, but were receiving very attractive offers to go to work for industry, which would have been a disaster for the booming organic chemists. Koch and Tashinian would use the facilities which Koch had built up for the university, but would pay for any consumable supplies used. They would also never keep a request for an analysis from a faculty member waiting while an analysis from outside was done. This arrangement would probably cause both Koch and Tashinian to accept a significant reduction of income, but they were willing and anxious to do so because of love of their work and associations in their present position. As explained in Chapter 11, this arrangement could be authorized by a Dean in case the arrangement would supply industry with results which they could not get otherwise. This situation obviously existed, in view of the kind of salaries that were being offered to Koch and Tashinian. This setup was developed and put in place by Wendell Latimer, a chemist so highly respected around the country that he was awarded the Perkin Medal, awarded annually to an elder statesman among chemists, for his long service to the chemical industry.This arrangement was next approved by Joel Hildebrand when he was dean for two years awaiting return of Kenneth Pitzer from his position as Director of Research for the Atomic Energy Commission. The arrangement for Joel to hold the fort until Ken's return resulted from a letter to President Robert Gordon Sproul requesting that action, and signed by every non-tenured faculty member in the department. On his return, Pitzer also approved the policy. As a final comment, it may be in order to point out that this arrangement is not different from a policy that has been in effect for many years, and practiced by thousands of faculty members who have consulted for industry or worked as editors of scientific publications. They certainly use university facilities such as a telephone, office, and even secretarial assistance until recent years. Organic Syntheses certainly did not pay anything to the university during the years that I was on the editorial board, and editor-in-chief during my final year.

I trust that the above paragraph makes clear the nature of the arrangement which Dean Harold Johnston demolished. At the time of Johnston's action I was not able to discover any reason for it, but I later learned that he had fired our long-time business manager, Bob Anthonison, because he discovered him doing business as a real estate salesman, using his office telephone. Since that could hardly be ascribed as an attack on the organicers, one is at a loss to explain his actions unless he was motivated by a message from heaven to cleanse the College of Chemistry of sin. I first learned of the attack on the microanalytical lab when Johnston summoned me to his office to inform me of what was already done, a fait accompli. I asked him if he thought he was wiser than Latimer, Hildebrand, and Pitzer combined. His response was that the system was wrong and against University regulations. I realized that there was no object in discussing something that was basically a religious principle. And again, there was absolutely nothing I could do about it except appeal to the chancellor or an academic senate committee. Of course, I was interested in building up the College of Chemistry, not tearing it down.

In order to summarize the impact of Johnston's action, I will outline what he did and the consequences thereof: Koch remained in charge of the microanalytical lab but received no extra compensation for the outside work done. Tashinian was reduced to receiving $300/month from doing thousands of dollars worth of analyses per month; and money paid by the outside industry went into the budget of the College of Chemistry. As a final blow, the organicers were required to pay from their research grants a fee for each analysis that they had done in the microanalytical lab which Wendell Latimer had built for us. Somehow or other, this arrangement seemed to be OK, free of sin, if the university got the money instead of those who did the work. In retrospect, maybe this is not a question of religion, but of greed or jealously. When Johnston was explaining to me what he had done, he dropped a rather careless remark. He said it was outrageous that Koch should have a higher total income than that of the dean of the College of Chemistry.

While dean, Johnston took an action against a specific member of the organic faculty which reveals the focus of his attention on the organicers.

Without any previous discussion, he wrote Henry Rapoport a letter in which he said that Rap was accepting entirely too many graduate students to do their thesis work under him. If one should examine the literature in order to note the papers published by Johnston compared to those published by Rapoport, one might conclude that Johnston was motivated by jealousy. There has been some propaganda in the news media recently to suggest that Johnston may have been having some dreams about a Nobel Prize. However far-fetched these speculations may or may not be, there are some serious violations of protocol involved in Johnston's writing such a letter to Henry Rapoport. In the first place, at the University of California, the dean of a college, in a formal sense, has authority over the faculty and students in the undergraduate curriculum, not in the graduate school. Affairs of the graduate division are under the authority of the dean of the graduate division. I am familiar with these regulations from having been a dean of a college and chairman of a department for a year, as well as associate dean for research, in the graduate division for four years. I always try to make sure that I am familiar with the duties and responsibilities of my job. Even if Johnston did have authority to regulate the number of graduate students a professor accepts to work under him—as the dean of the graduate division does have for a department as a whole—a wise and/or capable dean would make a phone call and suggest a discussion of the matter. Could it be just a coincidence that George Pimentel, who insulted me so raucously, as will be described later, was appointed chairman while Johnston was dean?

Before proceeding to more interesting things, I will complete my references to Dean Johnston by reporting an event which cannot easily be interpreted as targeted toward either an organic chemist or organic chemists. However, it certainly stirred up opposition from an organic chemist who has demonstrated interest in many things, including the welfare of the College of Chemistry and the welfare of the Berkeley campus of the University of California. There is an interesting arrangement at Berkeley whereby a student majoring in chemistry can graduate with a B.S. degree in the College of Chemistry, or alternatively with an A.B. degree in the College of Letters and Science. This versatile arrangement proves to be very useful to students. For example, the A.B. in chemistry is chosen by many premedical students because it allows them to elect a wider variety of upper division courses than is sometimes possible in biology majors. While advising Letters and Science chemistry majors, I encountered a variety of interesting people, including: several students headed for law school, with plans to work on legal problems in scientific industries; one woman who was already working for an advertising agency, who told me, "You might be surprised to know how big an advantage it gives me to know what the real facts in the case are"; two students who went to graduate school in Public Policy; and several others scattered about. Conversely, several premeds took a B.S. in the College of Chemistry, usually because chemistry allowed as much as 10 units of lower division biology courses among the upper division units of courses other than chemistry, which were required. This was done with the approval of the biology departments to compensate for fragmentation among the departments. This may have changed after the much-needed consolidation of the biology departments under the guidance of Dan Koshland.

For reasons which were never made clear to me, Dean Johnston decided that it would be nice to move the A.B. degree in chemistry from the College of Letters and Science to the College of Chemistry. Among other undesirable results of this transfer would be that the chemistry faculty would no longer be members of the faculty of the College of Letters and Science. If one considers the recent history of events that had occurred in L. & S., a combination of the large and influential faculty in chemistry and physics stopped a lot of nonsense there. When Johnston called a meeting of the tenure faculty of the College of Chemistry in order to announce this plan as fait accompli, without any previous discussion, only two other faculty members besides me raised objections to the plan. One was Sam Markowitz, and I cannot remember who the other one was. Although the plan had thus been approved by the tenure faculty of the college, there remained the necessity for the dean to get it approved by vote of the full membership of the academic senate.

I did my homework and prepared my pitch to be presented to the senate meeting. I was apprehensive about being able to secure the floor and present my pitch before Johnston's cohorts were able to get the floor and throw up a smoke screen to confuse the issue. I was especially worried because the chairman of the senate, who was chairman of the meeting, was Dick Powell, who knew my position since I had stated it loudly and clearly at our college meeting. I went to the senate meeting early to insure being able to get a seat on the aisle about eight rows from the front. After Johnston made his motion with usual recommendation for passage, before Dick could get his mouth open to call for comments, I strode rapidly to the front while calling loudly, "Mr. Chairman." Dick sputtered a little, but realized that he could not deny me the privilege of the floor because I had asked for it first. I caught him flat footed! The senate operates by Roberts Rules of Order, with which Dick was just as familiar as I was.

I started my presentation by first making a statement which was approximately the following: "I find myself in a rather unattractive position, in that I am opposed to the motion made by the dean of my college, which is supported by an overwhelming majority of the faculty of my college. Nevertheless, I am undaunted; I will press my opposition to this motion to the best of my ability, for I am convinced that this motion is against the best interests of the College of Letters and Science as well as the best interests of the College of Chemistry." I continued my presentation with the following items, among others: I have been unable to find any college or university in this country which has a College of Letters and Science which has no department of chemistry in it. Since we have a College of Chemistry at Berkeley, if the major in chemistry is transferred to that college, then I and all my colleagues in the chemistry department will no longer be members of the faculty of the College of Letters and Science. I think that the record is clear that members of the chemistry department have been quite active in promoting what they regarded as the best interests of L & S. I would definitely feel disenfranchised. I then noted that there were approximately fifteen majors on the Berkeley campus which require more than one year of chemistry. All of these majors would be completely helpless in having any authority over the chemistry department giving courses suitable to their needs. The bad situation which now exists would become worse. As I walked back to my seat, I was encouraged by hearing some applause, an occurrence which was not very common in senate meetings. Before I got back to my seat, Walt Knight, Professor of Physics, then dean of L& S, seized the floor by using the tactics I had used. He stated that he had told Dean Johnston that he did not like this proposal to deprive L. & S of a department of chemistry, but would not oppose it in order not to damage the long-time excellent relations between the

departments of chemistry and physics. He then stated that he was changing his mind. "I am opposed to this motion." More applause. There were a
couple of the chemistry faculty who made rather pitifully weak arguments
in favor of the motion, and Johnston attempted to rebut my arguments;
however, there were not any interesting developments, and there soon
were calls from the floor: "Question"; so Powell had to call the question
without further ado. The vote on the motion was so heavily against it that
no count was made.

I lost every argument with Dean Johnston where the item under discussion was within the purview of the College of Chemistry; hence,
Johnston had authority, and I had no practical recourse. On a level playing
field, the score was lopsided in my favor. This did not make me feel particularly good, for I could not get out of my mind the disagreement with Ken
Pitzer in which I was wrong. Furthermore, writing about the presently
reported event has caused me to do much re-thinking about my disagreement with Ken Pitzer's statement that I was wrong when I said that there
were plenty of people in the College of Chemistry who would be satisfactory administrators. Soon after that, Ken was appointed president of Rice
University. After a few years at Rice, he became president of Stanford
University. After a period as president of Stanford, he announced his resig-
nation and eventually returned to Berkeley as a professor. He appeared to
live happily in that capacity until his death in 1998. Before my retirement in
1983, I sometimes had lunch with Ken and he behaved exactly as I remembered him from earlier, happier days. It is apparent that Ken was one of the
rare individuals who are able to defeat the Peter Principle at a very high
level. I dare say that he was also one of those described in the ancient saying, whose origin I cannot identify: "A prophet is not without honor save in
his own country." I cannot help but speculate occasionally about what
entirely different sequence of events would have transpired if Ken Pitzer
had been appointed chancellor at Berkeley, or if I had not declined to be the
first chairman of chemistry, after the separation of that office from the
dean's office. I do not enjoy thinking about these eventualities.

My problems with administrators in the department and College of
Chemistry were not confined, by any means, to the dean of the college.
Partly as a result of Johnston's effort to transfer the chemistry A.B. pro-
gram from L & S to the College of Chemistry, there was more discussion

than usual of the unwillingness of the chemistry department to offer any freshman chemistry course except the one designed specifically for the needs of chemistry majors. Since the existence of the A.B. program in chemistry in the College of Letters and Science seemed secure, I decided to make an effort to create a first-year chemistry course adapted to the needs of majors in fields other than physical science. I found it easy to co-opt my friend, Charlie Koch, now in charge of all the mass spectrometers in the department, into forming a partnership to explore the possibility of such a course. Charlie was a physical chemist, but had primary responsibility for developing the course in quantitative inorganic analysis which was still being taken by premedical students. We made a good team to develop a freshman chemistry course which presented the principles of physical chemistry by applying them to organic chemistry. This also made it easy to introduce the concept of covalent chemical bonding into the Freshman course where it belongs. This type of bonding is at the heart of organic chemistry, hence also biochemistry. Outlining the chapter titles for such a one-year course proved easier than we had expected, for it was such a natural way to teach chemistry to introductory students; much attention to the appearance and shape of molecules, with minor use of mathematics, nothing beyond simple algebraic equations. And so we put together such a course outline and took it to the chairman of the department at that time, David Shirley. We expected opposition and we got it. Although David did not say so, it was clear that he dreaded having a freshman chemistry course which would be allowed to compete with their traditional narrowly constructed freshman course, on a student choice basis. For starters, David chose to stall us to death, said that he would not even look at our exhibit until we had cleared it with a suitable number of biology departments. We expected this, and so we proceeded to do just that. I had friends in most of the numerous biology departments on campus. We arranged a meeting with representatives of the more important biology departments, and all of them were enthusiastic about the proposed course; it would be only a slight exaggeration to say wildly enthusiastic. And so we came to David Shirley with our approval from biology. He then said we would have to clear this with the dean, David Templeton, one of the better deans in the post-Pitzer era. Templeton said that this was strictly a problem involving an undergraduate course, and out of his purview. Shirley was beginning to feel quite annoyed by this time, and was digging pretty deep for a reason not to let us try such a course, which would be limited to about fifty students. After some muttering, he finally said for us to give him a couple of days to study the matter. After this study, he decided that he could not spare us from teaching the important courses we were then teaching. When we volunteered to take on this course as an extra assignment without any diminution of our regular assignments in teaching or advising students, he simply said "NO." And so I was again left with nothing practical I could do. I felt unwilling to face my friends in the biology departments and tell them that we had been turned down, so I wrote a memo and sent it to them in the campus mail. One man who felt very strongly about the absence of a suitable freshman chemistry course telephoned me and said that after he read my note he sat and cried for a while. The response of the chemistry department to the flak which I presume that they got was to set up a course with a number larger than one, restrict enrollment to students who passed an entrance exam, and term this an honor course which was more narrowly designed for chemistry majors and involving much more mathematics. I have heard nothing about this matter since I retired, so I do not know whether the reorganization of the biology departments has had any effect on the freshman chemistry course.

This same chairman, David Shirley, was involved in another incident which did not really involve me directly, but was one for which I had strong feelings. At the time of this event, which was in the first half of the 1970s, there had developed in the physical chemistry community a great interest in the study of events which occur when a high velocity ion collides with another molecule. The instrumentation for this study, which was commonly called molecular beam chemistry, was similar to that used in mass spectroscopy, but attention was focused on specific aspects of a specific chemical reaction rather than on how a large molecule is broken into fragments, as in mass spectroscopy. In general, each investigator had to have an instrument custom built for his use, so there were only a few laboratories in large universities where such investigations were being carried out. One university where the study of ion collisions was being carried out was Harvard, with Dudley Herschbach the leader of the group; another was Chicago, with a man named Yuan Lee the leader of the group; and another was Berkeley, with Bruce Mahan the director of the group.

These people were well acquainted with each other. Herschbach had started his teaching career at Berkeley, but was seduced to return to Harvard, where he did his graduate work. Berkeley was unable to hold Herschbach, who was being classified as one of those likely to win the Nobel Prize which was anticipated in this field. Yuan Lee had earned his Ph.D. degree at Berkeley several years earlier, as a graduate student under Bruce Mahan. Yuan had become famous for his rapid rise at Chicago. Since Bruce Mahan had become afflicted with Lou Gehrig's disease in 1966, Berkeley had hired Ronald Herm, who got his Ph.D. degree under Herschbach at Harvard, to continue to lead this field at Berkeley. So much for the background to this exciting event.

The reason that this event was exciting was that there had developed a conviction among physical chemists that a Nobel prize was going to be awarded in this field; hence, frantic jockeying among the contesting universities to hire the winner. After many telephone calls, many conferences, and many letters (no E-mail in those days), our chairman, David Shirley, decided that the prize would go to Yuan Lee, the Berkeley product now at Chicago. There was another problem, however, we already had on hand a professor in that field who was not expected to win the prize. The only solution was to fire Ron Herm, an assistant professor, thus not of tenure rank and therefore, fireable. To put it another way, his appointment would not be renewed. So Shirley called a meeting of the tenure staff in chemistry in 1973 to explain the situation. Bruce Mahan attended in his wheel chair; it was the last time I saw him. There followed much discussion about whether to fire Ron Herm. Among those who spoke against this action were all those present who had previously served as chairman of the department. This group included Jim Cason and Bruce Mahan, one of whose former graduate students was Yuan Lee. Finally, Shirley decided to take a written ballot, each person writing on a piece of paper either yes or no, and passing the pieces of paper to the secretary of the department to be counted on the spot. No cheating on this vote! About 60 percent of the votes were against firing Ron. And so Shirley stated that he would not be influenced by such a close vote, and adjourned the meeting. We learned later that Shirley had fired Ron Herm. Yuan Lee was appointed in 1974.

Yuan Lee later won the Nobel Prize, and became quite a big man around the world. The university, in the years after I retired, decided that

they had to clean out all the old professors to save money, and simultaneously clear the tracks for hiring young blood more likely to bring fame to
the university. They adopted a policy widely used in business, of bribing
professors to retire. They could not do this legally without offering the
same inducements to all members of a group on the same terms; the same
problem industry encountered when "downsizing." The results were particularly disastrous in regard to science teachers. There are so many publicized ways, which can be easily used by a layman, to distinguish between
phenomenally good, very good, good, etc., professors. This problem no
doubt occurs in industry in regard to hiring top executives, but usually the
information is not publicly displayed. In any case, Yuan Lee accepted the
bribe to resign, then went on to another high paying position elsewhere.
Did Shirley do the university any good by firing Herm and hiring Lee? I
do not know the answer to that question, but I do know that Shirley's
action was hard on Ron Herm, and I also know that his action was
opposed by all previous chairmen and the majority of the members of my
department. Thus, it seems that a majority of my colleagues was somewhat less than enthralled by seeing our university act more and more like
the average business. As this scenario was playing out, for the first time, I
began to approach retirement with less apprehension. But little did I know
how great the emotional impact of retirement would be.

I greatly enjoyed teaching during my last ten or twelve years before
retirement. During several years prior to 1966, I had been doing most of
my teaching by giving an advanced laboratory course in experimental
organic chemistry for undergraduates, and a lecture course which was
given to all new organic graduate students. I enjoyed both of these courses, for they kept me in touch with both undergraduate chemistry majors
and new graduate students. As previously mentioned, I was no longer taking new graduate students for thesis work. With the appointment of
George Pimentel as chairman of the chemistry department, my smooth
sailing began to hit some whitecaps.

When Melvin Calvin announced that he was taking a sabbatical leave,
it became necessary to assign someone else to the teaching of Chemistry
8A and Chemistry 8B, for Mel had been teaching that course since the
retirement of Dale Stewart several years earlier. Without warning, I
received a letter from Pimentel which stated that he had assigned me to

teach Chemistry 8A and B during Calvin's absence. Since no change of assignment of teaching in organic courses had ever been made without a conference of the parties involved, I telephoned the chairman's office and asked for an appointment to talk to him about my teaching assignment. I received an appointment for a few days later, and arrived at the appointed time to find that the chairman was not in his office. After a search by his secretary, Pimentel arrived. I explained to him that I was not a good choice for substituting for Melvin, because of the history involved in the choice of the content of the course that would be used to replace the course that Stewart had taught for many years. During this period, when Stewart owned the course, its content had become badly out of date, so Ken Pitzer called together all the organic staff for a conference on that subject. There proved to be two divergent opinions as to what the course content should be. Melvin and I were the authors of the two divergent plans. This was in marked contrast to the situation when Melvin and I were assigned by Wendell Latimer to develop the content of the course for chemistry majors. After having developed that course in perfect harmony, neither Melvin nor I had any interest in debating the development of the "new Chemistry 8," and so we asked Ken to decide who should teach this course in the near future. Ken decided in favor of Melvin and that was entirely satisfactory to both of us; however, there was a spirit of competition involved. In view of this history, if I should teach the course while Melvin was away, it would be unnatural for him not to assume that I had volunteered to teach the course in order to install my ideas on what should be taught in it. I did not want to spoil the good relationship between Melvin and me. Pimentel was rather inattentive during my monologue. As soon as I paused to get his reaction, he said he had another appointment and could not spend more time on my complaint. I asked him if he had consulted the other organicers about appointing me. When he answered in the affirmative, I asked which ones. He answered Dauben and Noyce, then left.

I next consulted Dauben, who told me that he told Pimentel that I was the worst possible choice to teach the course because of the danger of generating conflict between me and Calvin. When I consulted Noyce, he told me that Pimentel had asked him if I would do a good job of teaching Chem 8 while Calvin was gone. He said that he had answered Pimentel in the affirmative. In view of these developments, I wrote Pimentel a letter, saying that I would appreciate his discussing the teaching of Chem 8 with the entire organic staff before I accepted the assignment. After some delay, he responded with a short letter in which he said that he did not want to waste his time in debating his assignment of me to teach Chem .8, and he wished that "I would stop crying and get on with my job." I had never been treated so rudely by anyone with some authority over me. My only recourse was to appeal Pimentel's ruling to the dean, which would accomplish nothing useful and generate turmoil in the college. I had no instinct whatever to do that sort of thing; I wanted to support this college which I had worked so hard to build up. I taught the course, and did the best job that I could, as I always did. Apparently I succeeded in doing a satisfactory job, for I received compliments from students. Calvin's long-time, competent secretary told me that her son—or it may have been nephew—enjoyed taking the course with me. After Mel's return, we never discussed the matter, but I was saddened by detecting some coolness in our relationship. No Sherlock Holmes is required to deduce the identity of one administrator to whom I would assign a grade of "F".

A few years after my experience with Pimentel, Mel Calvin retired from teaching Chemistry 8, because of the pressure of other duties, especially those resulting from his appointment to the prestigious position of University Professor. There were very few of these appointments, which were heavily weighted with Nobel Laureates. The idea of this position was that the recipient of the title was possessed of characteristics so useful to the university and its faculty and students, that such a professor should be shared with all campuses of the university, not restricted to his "home" campus. In the case of Melvin Calvin, the assignment of the title University Professor was quite appropriate, due to his personal characteristics. However, his retirement from teaching Chem 8 generated the necessity for finding a teacher for it.

Against my advice, Henry Rapoport was selected to teach Chem 8. Other than my advising against assigning Rap to teach the course, I know nothing of what, if any, discussions were held regarding this appointment. From my close association with Rapoport since he came to Berkeley, I was well aware of his characteristics as a chemistry teacher. I heard many students comment favorably on his excellent teaching of the course required for chemistry majors. However, I also knew that the same characteristics which tended to draw approval from students who were majors in chemistry would be unlikely to go over well with premedical students. Sure enough, the students complained to the chairman about Rap's teaching of Chem 8. The first I knew of these developments was when Clayton Heathcock, who was vice-chairman of the chemistry department at that time, came to my office to ask me to take over the teaching of Chem 8 next year: "You advised us against this appointment; how about you taking it over." My response was several levels below enthusiastic, something such as the following: "After Pimentel brutally bulldozed me into teaching that course for a year, you are now asking me to teach it again, presumably on a recurring basis; GET LOST!" Clay's response was very mild: how happy the students were about my teaching the course; several indignantly demanded to know why I was taken off the course; I should not allow Pimentel's misbehavior to cause an impediment to teaching Chem 8, which affects hundreds of students who don't deserve to be penalized by my feelings about Pimentel, etc. Finally, he got the message across to me. I agreed to teach the course for a year, with the understanding of two qualifications: I would teach Chem 8A and then 8B in the fall and winter quarters when the enrollment was heaviest; then in the spring quarter I would teach the upper division course in organic synthesis. If I should find teaching Chem 8 so unattractive that I would like to get out, then a decision would be made in a meeting of all the organicers as to who would try it next. Clay agreed immediately. Nothing was put in writing, and neither of us even thought of such a thing. This agreement turned out quite differently from the agreement of years before when Bob Connick outmaneuvered me as to who would take on the deanship so that Ken could take a well-deserved sabbatical leave. Soon after the start of my teaching Chem 8A, I realized that I was enjoying this experience; probably because students in the course seemed to like what I was doing. I was grateful to Clay for two things: first, for acquiring the information needed to convince him that Chem 8 was the best slot for me; second, for showing the administrative skill necessary to convince me without bulldozing me. The latter was the hard part.

One of the things that worried me about taking over Chem 8 again was the fact that, when I taught it while Melvin was away, I was unable to find a textbook which presented anywhere near what I wanted. I wanted a book which presented things in the sequence Mel Calvin worked out with me, for the chem major course. In examining the second textbook I had written, I realized a book could be developed that would cover the fundamental theory of chemical bonding, which is the heart of organic chemistry, but would treat organic synthesis sufficiently lightly and non-exhaustively so that time would be available to emphasize things with specific applications to biochemistry and medicine. Since no book was available that was applicable to that kind of organization, I decided to use my textbook written for the chem major course and supplement it with frequent "handouts." By the middle of the first quarter, I had decided what Mel and I had decided long ago for the chem major course: to write a textbook. Only this time it would be different, I would not write the book for publication by a book company, but exclusively for my teaching of Chem 8. The physics department had an office devoted to handling such publications, presumably because they frequently used syllabuses in teaching their courses. The chemistry department agreed to pay for the initial publication, and the proceeds from selling the book, minus the costs of handling, were submitted to the department. Thus, the net effect of this system was furnishing the students with a book at less than one-half what the cost would be if the book were produced commercially. The professor donated his labor as a part of teaching the course, and the department paid the dollar cost of producing the book. The students were the beneficiaries and they knew it. I don't recall having ever heard a complaint from a student about the book I wrote for Chem 8. Two students who were English majors complimented me on my writing style which was in marked contrast to the dull writing in most science textbooks. I told them that any proficiency that I showed in writing should be ascribed to my good luck, as a freshman at Vanderbilt University, in drawing a professor named John Crowe Ransom as the teacher of a required full year course in writing. They immediately recognized the name, John Crowe Ransom, on account of his having been the last editor of the Kenyon Quarterly Review. They were incredulous that I could have had such a teacher in a freshman English course. I told them that things were different in those days. The famous Eddie Mims lectured to the large class once per week, and professors taught the writing class two days a week in sections of about twenty students. When I was teaching from a published textbook that I had written, the normal attitude of students was rather different. Snide remarks were not uncommon about my picking this book because I had written it, which was true. I never made any effort to explain that I wrote textbooks for other reasons than they were assuming. I did comment on one occasion that if I were channeling my efforts toward making money, I would be studying the stock market rather than writing textbooks. That went over like a lead balloon, so I did not try to be facetious any more.

As to why I rapidly became aware that I enjoyed teaching Chem 8, whereas nothing of the sort happened in my earlier contact with the same course, I am sure that a normal explanation would refer to the fact that I was not forced to teach the course on this second occasion. I presume that this sentiment was involved; however, I am confident that other factors were more important. For one thing, when I was teaching the course for only a year, I had no inclination to try and improve the course; indeed, I was careful not to make any conspicuous changes, in order to avoid damaging my friendly relationship with Mel Calvin. In addition, I had a lot of empathy with the problems faced by premedical students in the highly competitive situation which existed in those days concerning entrance to medical school. In many cases which came to my attention, this problem was exacerbated by incredible pressure from parents who were medical doctors. This pressure frequently resulted in a fierce—if not frantic—determination by these students to see to it that they were graded fairly. Not only were the grades of paramount importance in a direct sense, but also as an influence on the very important recommendation to medical schools. I took steps to deal with both of these problems.

According to my analysis, there were two problems related to an effort to make the grade reflect the actual merit of the student's performance, and both of these problems are different aspects of cheating. I will consider first the matter of cutting off fraudulent excuses for missing an exam. This applies to midterm exams, for missing a final exam is surrounded by so many difficulties that the cheater is more likely to attempt cheating on the grade received on the final exam, rather than cheating by getting a deferral of the exam. On the other hand, getting a midterm exam deferred offers the chance to take it later and thus get more time for last-minute cramming. The regrettable prevalence of last-minute cramming makes deferral of midterm exams the most damaging and insidious form of cheating. Many teachers save themselves the bother of solving this problem by simply allowing deletion of an exam missed, and basing of the total grade for midterm exams only on midterm(s) actually taken. I regarded this latter system as especially obnoxious, because it has absolutely no merit other than saving the professor—or the TA to whom he has shunted the problem—from expending the time and effort required to use a better system. So, I searched for a fair system, one that would protect the honest premeds from the cheaters. As one premed told me, "My opportunity to spend my active lifetime in a high-paying respected position in society is on the line." I finally came up with a system that satisfied me and was eventually endorsed by the Senate Committee on Courses. I have no idea whether it was ever used widely.

My determination to solve this problem was brought to a climax by a series of events. I will describe three of them; the shortest one first. A couple of days after a midterm exam, a student brought me a doctor's excuse for missing the exam; he had an impacted wisdom tooth removed. In response to my question, "Was it necessary to have that tooth extracted exactly on the day that would give you a deferral of the exam?" he answered: "No, but I did." He knew that I could not do anything about it. I laughed because it was funny, but I was filing the event in my memory to use for later reference. The next scenario had no saving grace of humor. A young man came into my office and presented me with a sickness excuse for the midterm he had missed. It was written on a doctor's prescription form, and I noted that the name of the doctor was the same as that of the student. I looked at the student, pointed to the prescription form, and said, "Your father?" The student looked at the floor and said, "I guess you don't think much of my excuse." I replied, "I did not say that I think your father was lying in writing this prescription. The prescription is legal and valid, so you are excused from the exam." He left without further comment. I felt very sorry for him, for I could imagine the kind of pressure that a doctor parent was probably applying to his son. On the same day that I had received numerous excuses for missing the midterm, including the one just described, I had one that really got to me. A student walked into my office, looking as if he were marching to his execution, and said, "I was so sick during the night before that exam that I thought I was going to die; I could hardly get out of bed." Having heard so much of this sort of stuff that day, I responded, "Now that is very touching; let me see your excuse."

He took a piece of paper out of his pocket, which had been torn off a tablet, and handed it to me, saying that it was all he had. It was from his roommate, Joe. Written on the piece of paper with a pencil was something like the following: "Tom was real sick; he kept upchucking; finally I went out and bought him some oranges, which he began to eat slowly, and finally he stopped upchucking." It was signed "Joe." As I looked at that rather wadded up piece of paper, I realized that it was probably the only legitimate excuse I had received all day. I told the student that I was sure Joe was telling the truth, and that he was excused from the exam. I immediately went to work setting up a "System" to stop the extensive and egregious "system" of cheating by securing deferral of exams.

The system was basically simple. I gave three midterm exams, but the final grade was assembled by counting the two exams with the highest grades. This meant that the lowest grade was discarded, which effectively selected a missed exam for discard. There were no excuses for a missed exam—none, of any sort. The total points counted for the two midterm exams were based on the two exams with the highest scores. For determination of the grade, I had no interest in why a student was absent from an exam, no matter whether he went skiing or was critically ill, or was suffering from a hangover. The System was designed to eliminate fake excuses, and it clearly did so. Nobody disputed that point. The System was explained in great detail, with explanation of why it was adopted, on a printed sheet which was passed out in class at every midterm exam. Several good students praised me highly for eliminating the necessity for them to compete with cheaters in order to get into medical school. Some of these good students were very frank and admitted that the large amount of cheating in this way was a severe temptation to them to cheat in one way or another. "After all, my lifetime of happiness and helping sick people is on the line!" But this was not the story I heard from everybody. It was during the second term that I was applying this system when I encountered a really contentious young man who declared loudly, belligerently and at length that my system was unfair. I reminded him of how I had explained in detail on the printed sheet he received that this system had been developed with the objective of giving the most advantages to the most people, with the least number of concurrent drawbacks. After considerable repetition by both of us, he announced that he was taking it to the ombudsman, and I agreed heartily. I did not tell him that this was the ombudsman's job, not mine, for that would add nothing to the discussion. I had a few contacts previously with the ombudsman, which were uniformly satisfactory, but the English professor who called me this time was a different kind of person. I had no more luck with him than with the student. He persisted in repeating matters of principle which made no contribution to the evaluation of the worth of my system. Finally, he declared with a flourish that he was taking this matter to the Committee on Courses, which has jurisdiction over whether a course is being handled properly. After a few days, I received a note from this committee notifying me that they had heard this case and ruled in my favor. A second paragraph stated that they were circulating a memo to the members of the senate suggesting that they give serious consideration to adoption of the system used by Professor Cason to curtail cheating in deferral of midterm exams. There was a CC on the memo to the ombudsman. I knew several people on the Committee on Courses, and knew that a biochemist was chairman, so I was not worried—much, but I was relieved to get their report to me.

Another very effective method for cheating was to return a graded exam along with a note pointing out that the grading was in error—which usually proved to be the case. The student had written the exam in such a way that there were blank spaces at appropriate locations so that the meaning could be changed by use of a few well-chosen words or numbers. I struggled for some time with requiring the TAs to mark through all open spaces. This was a damn nuisance, to put it mildly, and also it did not work, as one student demonstrated to me. He brought in his exam, and his pen, wrote over the line drawn by the TA, and asked me if I could tell whether his line was on top of the TA's mark or below it. I had to admit that I could not tell. He then showed me another place where he said the TA had written over what he wrote. Improbable? Yes. Impossible? No. So much for that system. We were saved by the Xerox machine; is that machine properly described these days as a copying machine? In any case, I devised a system which not only saved grading time but also stopped cheating. I typed the exam on four sheets of regular typing paper, and had the typist set up these four sheets to be four pages on an 11 X 17 sheet of paper folded in the middle. Page 1 is the front page of the folder, pages 2 and 3 are the inner pages, and page 4 is the outside back page. The TA copied both sides of one 11 X 17 sheet, and there is no way to get pages of one paper mixed with another paper. It is probable that the time required to copy the exams before returning them is less than the time saved in the grading. In this system, the person who writes the exam must spend some time deciding how much space to leave for an answer, which is likely to cause him to ask questions which can be answered without the necessity of an essay. When first starting this system, I wrote a few answers to get the feel for the space required; I sometimes decided to ask somewhat different kinds of questions, all of which would be a blessing to the TAs who were grading. But still more time and tedium is saved by the fact that the student is limited in the space allowed for his answer. This generates a lot of complaint from poor students: "I write big." "You will have to learn to write smaller or write less." "I spend all my time trying to make my answer short enough." Translation: "I can't write a lot of stuff that is more or less related to the question, in hopes that the TA will find something that applies at least a little bit." Lots of such stuff of all kinds, which adds up to faster, more reliable grading. A final important point is that all papers which were returned for regrading go to me, with a written statement of what is graded incorrectly. No other route of return for regrading was accepted. I did all the regrading, not the TA who did the grading. Thus, the regrader was not prejudiced in favor of the original grading. It is reasonable to assume that this had a significant effect on the quality of the grading, and the results which I observed supported this assumption. Since a given question on all the papers was graded by the same TA or TAs, this eliminated the possibility of a TA favoring his friends or the students in his lab section. In case a student should be not satisfied with my regrading, he was invited to resubmit the paper to me for a full discussion. I rarely had a paper that went to this final step, and none that was not satisfactorily resolved; occasionally by a compromise in cases where there was some uncertainty as to whether another answer would fit the question. In one instance, the student convinced me that I was wrong. When I told him that he was right, and apologized for putting him to so much trouble, he said that he hoped this incident would not affect my recommendation of him to medical school. I responded that it would affect my recommendation; I would make it stronger than could have been justified otherwise. I told him that his action required both a sharp mind and courage of his convictions, which are important characteristics for a medical doctor. As I expected, this event got around in the scuttlebutt; however, it did not cause any ripple in the rate of return of regraded papers. In case anyone reading this scenario thinks that this system does not stop this type of cheating, I will report a story related to me by a faculty member who was a member of the Committee on Student Conduct, which holds hearings on cases of cheating and makes recommendations to the appropriate dean. This committee also has students on it. According to this report, as they were holding a hearing on a case of cheating, a student on the committee spoke up as follows: "If all professors would use the system that Professor Cason uses, it would probably eliminate hearings on cases such as this." The reason that my informant contacted me was that he wanted copies of the printed sheets I passed out on all aspects of cheating. I supplied them, but I never did learn if my system came to be used by a significant number of professors. I suspect that this did not happen; it takes too much of a professor's time, and there really is no reason why a professor should be expected to act as a warden to the students in his class. I suffered under that concept at Vanderbilt University, which had an "honor system" at that time, where the professor was not even burdened with having to stay in the room during an exam. As for the student body, this system was commonly referred to in the following manner: "The teachers have the honor, and the students have the system." Whatever may be the faults of my system, it does eliminate this type of cheating.

As regards "classical," or old-fashioned systems of cheating, I dealt with those in a rather straightforward manner. For final exams, there was no problem with rooms being assigned that were large enough to give alternate seating to all students. For midterm exams, my large class met at 8:00 A.M. in the Physical Sciences Lecture Hall, which had a seating capacity of more than 500. Frequently the enrollment was more than 250, in which case we were able to get the use of another large lecture hall because there was no great demand for the large halls for 8 o'clock classes. I proctored one room and the instructor in charge of the laboratory proctored the other. We communicated between the rooms by use of walkie talkies—modern technology to the rescue. Every TA was required to attend the midterm exam (as well as the final), with his roll book. The students in each lab section were pre-assigned seats that were contiguous, and the TA checked each body present in his area. In case he did not recognize a particular body, he inquired as to identity. Usually, the student was sitting in the wrong place, and that was corrected even if it meant going to another room (we were quite familiar with the standard practices). Occasionally, inquiry resulted in the student's hasty exit, without looking back (we were very familiar with the practice of sending a professional, such as a graduate student, to take the exam). We also interfered with that practice by passing out our preprinted sheets just as the exam started, and requiring the student's signature on the paper. Finally, papers were passed in to the TA, who counted them and kept them in his possession until all were in, refusing to talk to anybody as long as papers were coming in. Sound like overdoing it? Not after a colleague had five exam papers stolen as they were coming in. The professor was busy talking to students as the papers came in. The turmoil generated by that simple trick was gargantuan. We had a lot of ingenious devices used in the effort to defeat us, but we never had evidence that we failed to nail the offender and give him a zero on the exam, which effectively got him or her out of our hair. In teaching a class which is composed of 30 to 50 percent premedical students, one should never underestimate the ingenuity he will encounter in trying to prevent cheating. Premeds—in those days, at least—who survived long enough to be taking organic chemistry, were likely to be in the upper 10 percent of the student body. The selection of that student body, with the exception of a very few selected on the basis of brawn or genetic origin, was designed to choose the upper 15 percent of high school graduates in the state. The message is clear. I was dealing with a very select group of people.

I have little doubt that a major reason for my enjoyment of the last years of my teaching was the caliber of the students who populated my classes. These people were not only good students, but many of them were the sort with whom it is a privilege to be associated. From certain of these students I learned a great deal, things which later proved of much use to me. I do not cite any recollections of these people at this time, partly because it would be an injustice to those whom I did not mention. I am likely to refer to a few of these people in other chapters of this book.

Most of the experiences reported in future chapters of this book are concurrent with events reported in Chapters 11 and 12. These chapters deal with things which began to happen after I had been in Berkeley long enough to get my mind off the one-track, non-skid fixation with doing good research and writing papers on it. I judge that intermingling these two types of things would result in a rather disjointed presentation. So I have arrived at the point where I must terminate my report on my professional life. I did not die; only about half of me died. There was still my family, but our sons had long since established a vigorous life of their own, proceeding from the education we had encouraged them to get as we supported them financially. Rebecca and I have followed my retirement by doing many things which were quite different from the activities of nearly all our friends. We have not done things such as extensive foreign traveling where the retiree is a recipient of stimuli, but rarely does any putting out, other than keeping up with a travel schedule or managing the finances in the easiest and safest way. In contrast, we have done such things as buy significant holdings of timber property, which we have called Camelot; or buy and operate an almond orchard. This latter activity involved not only a lot of putting out, but a lot of receiving of things which came as a big surprise to us, such as the amount of expensive red tape involved in running a business. By the time our orchard was destroyed by a tornado in 1995, we were ready for relief. When the gods and fates began to help the various levels of government in making our lives difficult, we tossed in the sponge for that aspect of our post-retirement activities. In later chapters, there will be more about these activities, which were undertaken in order to give me something to do besides sit on my dead end until I die.

In any case, I gathered a few things I wanted to take home from my office: a few of the many books that were on my shelves, such as a copy of Roget's Thesaurus; polished stone bookends that I had made; a few keepsakes from my files, such as about an inch of notes of appreciation from students. Everything else was left: dozens of scientific books; several feet of all the issues of several chemical journals; about ten feet thickness of notes culled from the chemical literature on projects on which I did research; items of chemical apparatus that had come all the way from Louis Fieser's gift at Harvard; everything accumulated during about 45 years of professional activity. Rebecca helped me a lot in selecting things to keep and carrying them to our car. I wrote a letter to the dean, informing him that all personal property left in my office was now the property of the department.

I have never had any instinct to hang around as a spectator in any circumstance where I no longer had any function, no reason to produce. I walked out into the hall, locked the door, took my last card off the little bulletin board beside my door, turned in my keys at the college office, walked to my car, and never looked back. By that time, both the university and the College of Chemistry had begun to treat emeriti so badly—a small desk in a room with some other people—that there was no incentive to return to the campus. I have been on the campus only once since, when I went down to make a tape of a conversation with Bill Jolly, who was writing a book on the history of the College of Chemistry.

It took me only about ten years to recover—in part, anyway.

Chapter 13

THE CASONS OF BERKELEY

Chapters 10, 11, and 12 of this chronicle have been devoted largely to my professional activities. Although these activities were necessarily predominant in my life during that period, they were a long way from being all of my life. Indeed, as is clearly described in those chapters, my personal life and my family life remained the guiding principles by which my professional activities were directed. When we arrived in Berkeley, Mardy was three years old and Roger was seven. Roger was at the age where he required a lot of attention from Rebecca. From that time forward, until our sons had become adults ready and able to make the decisions necessary to produce a happy and useful life, Rebecca and I spent many hours formulating plans for making the decisions which we must make for our sons. Early on, we decided that the most important principle in raising children was with regard to the amount of money supplied to the children. We agreed at the outset that we would not supply any money to our sons, other than at such times as Christmas and birthdays, except as a reward for work done. In other words, we decided to train our children starting at square one, that there is no such thing as a free lunch; the more you work, the more money you have. When they were very young all the work was for us, of necessity, and we had plenty for them to do as we were busy developing our hillside yard with terraces and walks. At first, I ran the concrete mixer and hauled the concrete to the site where I was building something. Later, Roger ran the mixer and I carried the concrete; still later, Roger mixed and carried the concrete. Mardy followed along in the same sort of pattern for various jobs. When Mardy was in school at San Francisco State University, he sometimes came home on weekends and built a concrete wall for me. A matter of serendipity that developed during these activities was the opportunity for parents and children to get acquainted with each other. This pertained to one son getting acquainted with the other son, as well as with both parents.

As our sons got older they began to work for other people. Each, in succession, worked a paper route for the Oakland Tribune, an excellent paper published in the East Bay at that time. Roger started his route as soon as the law allowed it for his age. Four years later, Mardy took over, and so the Cason family was in the newspaper delivering business continuously for a span of eight years. Our smart and faithful dog, Xylene, always accompanied the boys on their paper routes, especially when they were collecting for their delivery. On one occasion when Roger was collecting at the door of a house, Xylene started into the house; Roger said, "No, Xylene, you stay outside," which Xylene did at once. The man from whom he was collecting asked, "What is the name of your dog?" When Roger repeated his dog's name, the man laughed and laughed, according to Roger's story. Roger asked me why the man laughed so much when he told him Xylene's name. I told him that the man worked for Standard Oil of California (SOCAL, now called Chevron), a major supplier of the chemical named xylene, so the man thought it was funny to have a dog named for a chemical, especially one produced by a company for which he worked. I also suggested to Roger that if anybody on his route should ask him the name of his dog, he should tell them, "Xylene, meta isomer, of no commercial value." I wrote it out on a card for Roger to carry so that he could have it memorized. I didn't tell Roger anything more at that time, except to say that if the man laughs he works for Standard Oil. I knew that several of the Standard Oil chemists lived in our neighborhood, probably because of the ease of commuting from Marin County by way of the San Rafael-Richmond bridge. Believe it or not, several months later Roger came in from his paper route with a story about a man who asked for the name of his dog. "When I told him 'Xylene, meta isomer, of no commercial significance," he laughed so hard, and called in another man to tell him my dog's name, then the other man laughed even harder". At that point, I explained to Roger about the three isomers of xylene, and that they could be made cheaply only by making all three at once. Two of the isomers have great value for making several important chemicals, but the meta isomer has no significant use, and hence keeps piling up in their storage tanks. Some of these people who laughed about Xylene's name may have been assigned the job of figuring out what to do with all that meta-xylene that had accumulated.

Mardy also had adventures on his paper route with Xylene. There was a particular problem with a house on Vassar Avenue where a Dalmatian was prone to run out and start a fight with Xylene. According to Mardy, Xylene usually disposed of the Dalmatian by swinging a right to the head and knocking him head over heels. Maybe that is why they are called boxers. Even after the Dalmatian gave up on attacking Xylene, it and another dog on Vassar barked when Mardy and Xylene came by. For this reason, we stopped letting Xylene go with Mardy on that part of the route on Sunday when the paper was delivered in the morning, to avoid disturbing the neighborhood by the barking dogs. We let Xylene go when Mardy came by at the far end of Kentucky Avenue where she could see Mardy. Xylene would sit at the front window until she saw Mardy go by, then she would rush to the door to be let out. She then charged down Kentucky to meet him. There were many antics by Xylene which injected a lot of humor into our lives, but this is enough for now.

I have already reported in Chapter 10 on the difficulty that Rebecca had with getting Roger into the proper grade in grammar school. After a few weeks in Berkeley, I asked Roger how he liked the school. His response, "The school here is just great, better than the one in Tennessee." When I asked him why he liked the school here so much, he responded, "We have lots of recesses here; lots of time to play with the other kids." I began to wonder if there were some connection between the number of recesses and Roger's ability to "read better than any kid in his class." (Refer to this quotation from his teacher, in Chapter 10). We learned a few years later, when it became Mardy's time to learn to read, that there was another factor involved with Roger's reading ability that was probably more important than the number of recesses.

When Mardy reached the age to attend school, it became apparent that his interest in school was less than Roger's was; however, our first clear signal was received when the time came for Mardy to be promoted to the fourth grade. About two months before the end of the school term, we received official notice that Mardy was unable to read well enough for promotion to the fourth grade on a scholastic basis, but would be promoted to the fourth grade anyway on a social basis. Our investigation revealed that, for all practical purposes, he could not read at all. We were not pacified when we learned that the parents of twenty-two of the thirty children in Mardy's room had received the same notice. Indeed, we were rather alarmed by the situation, but decided that our first obligation was to our own child. After some discussion, Rebecca and I decided on a plan of attack. We decided that each afternoon she would work for one hour teaching Mardy to read, and I would work for the same length of time each night. We felt that an hour would be about all that we could handle, at least at the beginning. How right we were! We started teaching him according to the methods by which we had learned to read. I suspect that Miss Eliza Ransom's methods were involved, especially the strict discipline. About three weeks after initiation of our efforts, when Mardy was doing more complaining and whimpering than anything else, he looked up at me and said, "You are frustrating me." I wondered where he learned that expression. I decided that he probably knew the meaning of that big word, so I responded with, "If you don't start immediately trying harder at learning to read, I am going to frustrate you a lot more by warming up your rear end with my slipper. Your mother and I probably enjoy this a lot less than you do, but we are determined to teach you to read. Otherwise, your entire life will be ruined, and you probably won't be able to do anything about it." Perhaps it was the excitement in my voice—or the apparent frustration exhibited, in any case, he seemed to start shaping up. He may have also been favorably impressed by how much better things were when he could read.

Whatever combination of events was involved, near the end of the school year we decided that he was able to read well enough for Rebecca to take him down to the school for a reading test. This experience proved to be a replay of her experience with Roger in the first grade. This time, the principal was adamant; it was ridiculous to think we could have taught him to read in two months. Rebecca finally threatened to take the matter to the school board, at which point the principal gave in and summoned the teacher who would be teaching Mardy in the fourth grade to see if he would be able to compete in that group. He told her to bring along the book which she would use for this group at the beginning of the school year. He probably thought that this would be the easiest way to get rid of this proud mama. He was right! Mardy came through like a champ, and so again the teacher and the principal were nonplussed. Rebecca didn't tell me whether she gave Mardy a hug or just took him to town for a campanile sundae. In any case, Mardy caused no more serious problems of this sort until he reached junior high school. He continued all through grammar school and high school to show much less interest in scholastic achievement than did Roger.

Roger's good performance in both grammar school and high school may have been due, in part, to the good start in reading he had. As has been previously reported, he was instructed in the first grade according to the "old fashioned" methods being used in Tennessee at that time. For whatever combination of reasons involved, it is also true that Roger showed a great deal more interest in the Boy Scouts than Mardy did. Roger's interest in scouting was no doubt amplified by a few fortunate circumstances. The scoutmaster of Troop 23, the troop in Berkeley, was Vincent Clemens, who not only devoted a lot of time to the troop, but also did all the right things that make boys into men who are responsible citizens. Clem had been guiding the troop for years by the time Roger joined the troop, and we never inquired about why he first became involved. It seems probable, however, that he became involved when his older son was at the age to become a Scout. This son had "graduated" by the time Roger joined the troop, and Clem's younger son, who was younger than Roger, was in the troop. I have not been able to keep up with the eventual behavior of Clem's younger son, but his older son, Bill, certainly provided evidence that Clem's ideas of making men out of boys were the right ideas. And I judge that it is harder for a father to sell these "right" ideas than it is for a scoutmaster to do so. In any case, Bill Clemens pursued his education to the point of earning a Ph.D. degree in paleontology, was soon appointed assistant professor in that department at the University of California at Berkeley, and rapidly advanced to become a full professor. By the time of this writing, Bill had become internationally prominent in his field.

Among the assets of Troop 23 was a cabin in the wilderness area of the

High Sierras on the shore of a small lake named Lake of the Woods. The scout troop rented this site from the federal government, which owned the land and, of course, the rental also carried permission to pass over the land to reach the cabin. The cabin was the only structure at the site. It was used as a kitchen when the Scouts were there, and was used to store their equipment, mostly cooking equipment, when they were away, which was most of the time. The summer camp lasted about six weeks. During the winter the cabin was left unlocked, as was common at that time, so that anyone lost in a snowstorm could find refuge. I was told that at least one person's life was saved by taking refuge in this cabin. The site of this cabin was not chosen with sissies in mind. The nearest approach to Lake of the Woods which could be reached by motor vehicles was several miles distant. From there on supplies were carried in on pack animals, and people carried their belongings in a backpack. There was a ridge on the trail to the Lake of the Woods which was the high point of the route. This uphill slope to the top of the ridge generated an appropriate name by the Scouts: Poopout Ridge. I trust that this brief description justifies the preceding statement that this site was not chosen with sissies in mind. A follow-up of the fate of several members of this troop reveals a dearth of sissies. After all, there were other troops in the area that could be joined by those who did not relish the rugged life.

I never did feel motivated to hike to the Lake of the Woods, and this posture was shared with the other fathers; however, the stories told by Roger suggest that the boys had a lot of fun during this camp at the same time that they did a lot of growing up. There were many games played at the camp, but everybody also had responsibilities to keep the place clean and not to engage in activities that would annoy others, such as making noise during the night. The rules were laid out, and violators were punished—usually by "laking." This procedure consisted of two Scouts picking up the offender, one holding the hands or arms, the other holding the feet, and throwing the offender, with his clothes on, off a bank a few feet high into the lake. From what I heard, this system was quite effective. No one enjoyed being the source of great hilarity, which always accompanied a laking. It goes without saying that those who could not swim were not among those participating in this camp.

The summer camp was the focus for Roger's greatest interest in the

Scouts; however, his interest persisted throughout the year. Soon after he became a Scout, he started to work on merit badges, and pursued that interest to the point that he earned two additional merit badges after he became an Eagle Scout. During his last year at the camp he acted as Clem's assistant in keeping things running with an acceptable amount of boisterousness. I think he was called a counselor. During the years that at least one of our sons was attending the camp, on several occasions we drove a carload of Scouts up to the camp and brought them back when the camp was closed down.

Mardy did not take as much interest in the Scouts as Roger did, partly, perhaps, because he felt eclipsed by his brother's prominence in the Scout troop; however, he attended the summer camp for two years. The principal focus of Mardy's interest during grammar school days was baseball. He started out in Little League as soon as he was old enough, and continued in the higher leagues as he grew older. It was difficult to convince him that anything besides baseball was worthy of his serious attention. After all, the news media does an excellent (or should I say lousy) job of selling the glamour and wealth that results from playing baseball. Nothing is said, of course, about the misery of playing in minor leagues, or the fact that one aspirant in a thousand reaches the major leagues. I must also admit that any efforts on our part to deglamourize baseball were handicapped by a factor that was well known to Mardy.

Rebecca and I were stockholders in the National Exhibition Company, which owned the San Francisco Giants at that time. To make matters worse, major league baseball had recently come to the west coast, so the sports sections of the local newspapers were persistently overcharged with baseball. As for our interest in baseball, that dates back to long before we were married. It has already been related in Chapter 1 how my Dad drove John and me to Nashville, thirty miles over unimproved roads, to see the Nashville Vols play baseball in the Southern League. At about the same time, the front page of the Fullerton newspaper carried a box entitled. "What Arky Vaughan did today." Arky Vaughan, with the Pittsburgh Pirates, was a top star of the day, although not competitive with such as Babe Ruth and Lou Gehrig. The difference was that Arky Vaughan was from Fullerton! A major factor that drew Rebecca and me together after our unpropitious first meeting at the International House was our mutual interest in sports, especially baseball. Early on, we began to attend games of the Oakland Acorns at their rather primeval ball park in Emeryville. Sitting on those plank seats was worth it just to see Casey Stengel putting on antics as he coached at third base. I presume that a critic might tend to lay the blame on us for Mardy's mediocre performance in grammar school and high school; however, I proclaim innocence, on the grounds that Roger reacted entirely differently to the same behavior on our part. Furthermore, whatever influences may have been applicable during Mardy's early years, he went on to eventually graduate with honors from San Francisco State University. Later on, he became a significant donor to the Business Administration School at San Francisco State.

In 1952, I was chatting with a group including Joel Hildebrand at the spring meeting of the American Chemical Society, which was at Buffalo that year. At one point in the conversation, for reasons which I do not recall, Joel said to me, "Jim, I believe that you are about forty years old now, the age at which I learned to ski, and so you ought to be sufficiently mature to learn to ski. If you want to accept this challenge, I will teach you." By that time, I was well enough acquainted with Joel to realize that he was not kidding me. I had heard him say on several occasions that he enjoyed teaching as much as anything that he had done in life. Therefore, I accepted the challenge. This occurred in March, and Joel said that there was not much snow left on the slopes, but that there was enough around "his" ski lodge for him to give me a lesson that would get me started properly in skiing; for example, always keeping my skis parallel, not snow-plowing the way that many instructors were starting people who were learning to ski.

I had already joined a group of people who, during the summer, had spent a few days at the ski lodge which Joel usually referred to as "his." This designation was proper because of the rather unusual terms of the agreement under which Joel and a group of other professors at Berkeley had built this ski lodge. According to my recollection of the story Joel told me, a group of some fifteen to twenty professors at Berkeley in various departments drew up a document which could be called "Articles of Agreement." The important features of this document included the following: (1) The proposed building would be built and owned by the entire membership in the group, with no member having a separate ownership of anything. (2) Membership in the group could not be sold or transferred in any way to anybody else. This included a specific statement that membership in the group could not be passed by inheritance to anybody, including the heirs of a deceased member. (3) When a member of the group died, the property would then become owned by the surviving members. (4) If at any time the property was sold or transferred in any way, this could result only by unanimous agreement among the members.

Joel explained these Articles of Agreement to a group of six or eight of us, all of whom were professors of chemistry. We were staying in the lodge as a wood cutting crew in a summer trip to the lodge. (More on this appears below.) Naturally enough, I did not ask any questions about the novel features of this agreement when Joel was our host. By the time that I and several others had made several trips to this lodge, either for wood cutting in the summer or skiing in the winter, Joel had become the only surviving member of the group except for one other who had become mentally incompetent. At an age greater than eighty, Joel decided that his days of using the property were history. Thus, the decision resided with one octogenarian about what to do with this property, which was probably worth more than half a million dollars on account of the amount of land owned in connection with the building. After much cogitation with his family and others, Joel decided to give the property to the Associated Students of the University of California, who owned a ski lodge adjacent to "Joel's lodge."

It was a large building, about one hundred by fifty feet in size, which consisted mainly of one large room. The only ceiling of this room was the roof of the building, a triangle with very steep sides rising to a point; i. e., an arch, except that the top was not rounded but was a peak. This large room, which could easily accommodate two dozen sleepers, had a huge wood-burning fireplace about thirty feet from one end, with a stone chimney extending to the peak of the roof. This fireplace was the only facility for heating the building except for a wood-burning cookstove in a little room to one side of the fireplace and between it and the end of the building. This kitchen was separated by a wall from the "big" room, but had no ceiling other than the roof of the building. There was another, smaller room at the end behind the fireplace which contained a shower—never used when I was there—and two toilets which faced each other with about six feet between them and a single swinging door, which could be placed between the toilets but which had to be moved whenever anyone visited or departed from either toilet. There was a small loft, partly behind the fireplace and extending to the end of the building. This loft was approached by ladder-like stairs, and had a railing across the side towards the rest of the room, but no wall except one about eight feet high on the side behind the chimney. The other side of this loft was the steeply sloping roof of the building. This loft was for use by any women who wanted a little "privacy." As Joel once commented in explaining the reasons for such a novel construction, "We don't attach much importance to privacy around here." More true words were never spoken! They also did not attach much importance to heating the building except for keeping the temperature above freezing so as not to freeze the small amount of plumbing. The only other addition to this building was a shed-like room about twenty feet wide, attached at the middle on the uphill side and extending some thirty or forty feet from the big room. This extension had a very strong roof designed to support several feet of snow in the winter. The only entrance to the building was via this extension. In the winter, a deep cut through the snow bank had to be made before the building could be entered. As is apparent, a lot of wood was required to keep the temperature in the main building above freezing in the winter. This wood was stored in this side extension. There was no insulation in either walls or roof. The object of summer expeditions was to cut firewood, with a two-man crosscut saw, an axe, and wedges driven by a sledge hammer. Since my visits to Joel's ski lodge were made many years before we bought the land at Camelot, I did not realize how underprivileged we were in cutting firewood with such antiquated tools.

Soon after I had returned from the ACS meeting in Buffalo, Joel contacted me and said that he was ready to take me down to the ski shop and advise me about buying my equipment. He said that this should be done promptly before the little remaining snow had melted. I said that there is no time like the present, and so we went down and bought my equipment: skis, poles, parka, boots and pants. I can hardly believe it, but my recollection is that this array cost me $85. Of course, the price was reduced at the end of the season. As a final trip for the winter, Joel took three other people and me for a weekend at his ski lodge. While Joel was teaching me some fundamentals of the art of skiing, the others enjoyed the ski lift at the Sugar Bowl, which was nearby.

Since my initial contact with skiing had proved satisfactory, Rebecca decided that she would like to get her outfit and get equipped for taking our sons skiing during the next winter. We went to the same place where Joel had taken me to buy my equipment and bought similar equipment for Rebecca. Our benefactor, Joel Hildebrand, during the ski season the next winter invited Rebecca and me, as well as Kenneth and Jean Pitzer, for a weekend at his ski lodge. Rebecca and Jean found the lack of privacy as they slept in the loft rather unattractive, but they benefited from Joel's instruction so that both Rebecca and I felt ready to take our sons skiing. After the ski season that winter, when prices were low, we shopped around for skis for both sons. Since the length of skis depends on the height of the skier, they can be outgrown like other things for kids. We shopped more for economy than for the quality of the equipment. We assembled equipment which was satisfactory for a couple of years, at which time the entire set of equipment had been outgrown. There were numerous small items of equipment which had to be purchased, such as mittens, goggles, silicone preparation to prevent goggles from fogging up, ski wax, etc. Our financial situation remained solvent, being assisted by my promotion to full professorship at about that time. Mardy was ten years old and Roger was fourteen when they first went skiing. This was probably a little young for Mardy, especially when his brother was four years older, but we all managed to retain good relations with each other, and the whole family became mutually better acquainted.

After some trial and error we found a satisfactory motel in Truckee where we stayed most of the time. It was quite convenient to the Squaw Valley ski area, and was also satisfactory for going to Soda Springs when the weather was not bad. For about eight years we took several ski trips each winter, on weekends except for Christmas and spring vacations. During the two years that I was working first in the chancellor's office and then as acting dean of the College of Chemistry, our ski trips were limited almost entirely to vacation times. We continued to frequent the motel in Truckee until the time of the 1960 Winter Olympics. Since we were old customers, the elderly couple who operated the motel did not charge us ballooned rates during the Olympics. We did very little skiing after 1960.

Roger was near to graduating from the University of Michigan with an M.B. degree in accounting. Mardy was in his last year in high school, which was followed by a year in college away from home. Finally, it was not long after that when I discovered that my arthritis had gotten to the point where skiing was contraindicated.

During these years most of our ski trips were uneventful, except for minor problems in dealing with snowstorms, and the whole family spent its time during the winter looking forward to and planning the next ski trip. Our most eventful trip occurred during the last half of the nineteen fifties, during the spring vacation period. Only Mardy went on this trip with Rebecca and me because Roger was in college at the University of Michigan. It was snowing in the mountains when we left Berkeley, and we had to put on chains at Baxter; however, it did not occur to us that we might have any big problem with snow, for it was late in March and there had been no ominous forecast. By the time we reached the short side road to Soda Springs, which was near the highway, it was snowing hard, but this did not deter us from going over to the ski area for a little skiing before going on to our motel in Truckee. We did not ski for very long. With the snow falling and the dead white reflecting surface, it was difficult to see anything ahead. On my second run, after I had plowed into a mogul which I simply could not see and went head over heels, I blew the whistle for "quitting while we are ahead."

When we got out to the highway, a two-lane road over Donner Summit in those days, we noticed that there was no traffic on the road coming from the east. By some sort of wishful reasoning and since light traffic was still coming from the west, we decided to continue to Truckee. After all, we were very close to the summit, so our track would be downhill after a short distance. There was a lot of snow on the road, but we had chains on, so we had no trouble in getting to the summit as far as traction was concerned. We had big trouble, however, in seeing well enough to stay on the road and not plow into the snowbanks on each side of the road. We soon developed a system which kept us on the road. There was no hope of seeing anything through the windshield, so we drove with the front windows open. I watched the left side and kept inside the snow poles which were at the edge of the snowbanks, and Rebecca watched the right side. Rebecca warned me when I got too close to the right side. Mardy in the back did nothing but put on his heavy coat and shiver as the snow blew in on him. We were saved by the absence of traffic coming towards us. We finally got to the motel, and were happy to see that the owners had cleared enough snow so that we could get to the entrances to the units. There were five or six units in this small motel, and we were the only occupants, so the owners were happy to see us arrive. They had not expected any customers at all.

When we got up the next morning, it was snowing about as hard as it was when we arrived on the night before. Of course, we did not expect the snow to continue at this rate since there had been no forecast of it. The fact, however, was that the snow continued coming down heavily for the next five days. Every time we looked out the window, it was the same white blur we had seen the preceding time we had looked out. Since we had no alternative, we proceeded to occupy ourselves as best we could from day to day. One thing we had to do was get food from the little store that was about a quarter mile down the road towards the center of Truckee. Since the snow removal equipment had given up on keeping the road open, Mardy and I went to the store on skis to get food which could be prepared without cooking facilities. I have a picture of Mardy skiing down the road beside a sign which projected just above the snow and which read: "Speed Limit 25."

We played a lot of cribbage, but that got old after the second day. We had brought a lot of reading material, which Rebecca used for many hours, but Mardy and I wanted some action. We began touring around in the snow on our skis, which had bindings adaptable to either downhill or touring. We were having a lot of fun until the time I looked ahead for Mardy, but he had disappeared! Remembering my experience at Soda Springs plowing into a mogul becaise of the continuous reflecting dead white surface, I proceeded with caution and soon heard Mardy yelling, "Get me out of here." He had skied right into a gully which was partly full of loose snow; only his head and shoulders were above the snow. After Mardy passed his poles to me, so as not to lose them in the soft snow, I packed down a place to give my skis a firm base. I then extended a pole to him and pulled as he packed snow beneath his skis to allow him to slowly climb up. Finally, he got out of the gully. We decided not to do any more touring and went back to the motel.

As time crept by, I became concerned about getting back to Berkeley in time to meet with my class on Monday. Of course, one or more of us was listening continuously to our battery operated radio. The radio spent most of the time on the consequences of the March blizzard. People were snow-bound all over the ski areas, and there were frequent reports on the condition of US Route 80 over the Sierras. This was before this route became I 80. The opening of Route 80 remained in the future, but on Saturday afternoon a report came in that the flooding on one part of the Feather River route had receded and the road was open, with chains not required. This route has the lowest elevation at the summit of any trans-Sierra route. Apparently, since the snow throwing equipment was unable to contend with the problem on Route 80, efforts had been diverted to the Feather River route so that transcontinental trucking would have a way to reach the west coast. Ergo, we got an early start on Sunday morning and arrived in Berkeley after dark, following a tedious trip. After unwinding with a long night's sleep, I made it to my class on Monday. This may not have been the most disappointing vacation I had ever had, but I don't remember any that was as bad. Actually, we continued to think of how fortunate we were to arrive home without any significant accident.

Our last trip to the snow country for a period longer than a weekend was to attend the 1960 Winter Olympics at Squaw Valley. I was able to get away from the university for a week, but Mardy was in high school, so we allowed him to cut only two days at the end of the week, so he was able to see three days of the races and the closing ceremonies. Roger was at the University of Michigan, so he was unable to attend this event. We stayed at our usual motel in Truckee, and this proved to be a very convenient location. During the two months before the scheduled opening of the Games, there was a pronounced dearth of snow. This resulted in much weeping and wailing which was transferred into print; however, about two weeks prior to the scheduled opening of the Games, storms began to come in one after the other so that there was an abundance of snow for everything requiring it. However, this generated a problem about parking for so many automobiles. It was resolved by packing down the snow with tractors over large areas for parking. This worked rather well for the duration of the Games. There were fewer problems than I have heard about in the news media for other Winter Olympic sites. A common problem, which was easily solved, occurred on sunny days. The dark tires on most cars absorbed heat from the sun so that snow melted under the tire and left it in a significant hole. This was easily solved. Whenever a car was unable to pull out of the hole (no chains were required during our stay at the Olympics), enough people would drop out of the passing crowd to easily push the car out and on its way with a wave. Our Corvair, with the weight of its air cooled rear-mounted engine, easily pulled out of such holes, but this did not deter us from helping others as we walked to our car. For some reason, for which there was much speculation in the news media, this spirit of cooperation and friendliness pervaded throughout these Winter Olympics and certainly added a lot to our enjoyment, especially since there were so many people of different appearances and so many native tongues involved. Since I was able to read French and German, and speak a very little German, I gave assistance on a few occasions. According to the news media, this behavior of people at Squaw Valley had a very significant effect on discussions which developed at that time regarding the advisability of continuing the Winter Olympics.

On the opening day of these Olympics, with all the pomp and ceremony and special events, it was snowing very hard before the actual opening events. There was a large area along one side of the parade route on an uphill slope which allowed an excellent view of things. The snow was driving directly across the parade route from a direction which put it in the faces of the spectators. We were standing with our backs to the driving snow and our hoods over our heads when the bugle signifying the opening of the 1960 Winter Olympics sounded. As I turned around I realized that the snow had stopped. Soon the dense cloudy overcast had cleared. The event which I remember most vividly was when Andrea Mead Lawrence, gold medalist in the ladies' slalom at Oslo in 1952, and about five months pregnant, came sailing down the mountain in the glare of the lights, bearing the Olympic Torch. Her descent was flawless.

We enjoyed many other features of the opening ceremonies, which we watched in brilliant sunshine. When the last parts of the parade were approaching, I realized that the sun had become obscured with clouds. As we were walking back to our car, stopping to push someone out several times, it began to snow. It had cleared by the next morning, and there was no more snow during these Winter Olympics. Of course the news media was full of the remarkable sequence of weather. I particularly remember the story about the Russian delegation, which was asking everybody how the Americans had learned to control the weather. If I had not seen it, and seen all these other people who declared that they also were looking at it, I might not have believed it. However, being a scientist, I was not inclined to believe that the U.S. had learned to control the weather.

When the time came for Roger to go to college, naturally enough there was considerable discussion of the matter between Roger, Rebecca and me. Early in this discussion, Rebecca stated that she would greatly discourage Roger from going to college at Berkeley. In high school she had been the daughter of a faculty member, and she felt that this had been a handicap to her enjoyment of high school. Anything she did that was good went unnoticed, but anything she did that was even slightly out of line with current norms for social behavior would attract attention. I certainly endorsed that point of view. In a place the size of the University of California at Berkeley, the son of a faculty member named Smith or Jones or Wong might escape notice, but for a name like Cason, there would be no hope; I found that out when two of our grandchildren attended Berkeley. One of my contributions to the discussion was to recommend strongly that Roger go away from the Bay Area to college, preferably away from California. The Bay Area of California is so unique as to climate, flora and fauna, and especially social and political customs, that a person growing up there matures in ignorance of what the rest of the world is like. I also added, however, that any place he wanted to go and was accepted I would pay the freight, unless he chose Harvard, in which case I would forbid it. I explained that I was not adopting this attitude because I was a Yale alumnus at the graduate level, but because of what I learned about the undergraduate college at Harvard when I was a research fellow there for two years. I found that an undergraduate could enroll at Harvard either in the degree program or the honors program. The degree program appeared to be principally for those whose principal interest in college was a degree from a prestigious school, especially their father's alma mater. The honors program was for those who wanted to get an education, but it had two faults. One was that no grades were given that carried any significance in terms of evaluating the caliber of the student. I learned about this during the years that I was in charge of picking new teaching assistants at Berkeley. The other difficulty was that it was almost impossible to flunk out of Harvard.

After consideration and discussion had evolved to application for admission, I had an interest in two of the schools to which Roger applied. This interest was developed largely from information which I had gathered over the years from professors with whom I had become acquainted. In some instances, however, I had gathered useful information by happenstance in conversations with Berkeley students who had transferred from other universities. One university to which Roger applied was the University of Michigan at Ann Arbor. It had such a good scholastic reputation at that time that it charged a rather high tuition to out-of-state students to protect itself from a horde of students from New York State, which had no state colleges of good reputation for producing outstanding alumni. Michigan and Illinois were the two state-supported universities with whom Berkeley compared itself when requesting higher salaries for teachers in order to avoid falling behind comparable universities. I had heard from one transfer student that Michigan had rather strict regulations about the behavior of undergraduate students. I did not discuss that matter with Roger for two reasons: this was one report from one student, and I felt that Roger would be rather surprised to hear that kind of report from me. He might even wonder if I did not want him to go to Michigan.

The other university to which Roger applied, and in which I had an interest, was Stanford. My interest there was in stark contrast to my approval of Michigan. I had learned from several people, including one person on the admissions committee at Stanford, that Stanford's outstanding reputation as a university carried certain burdens. According to this report, Stanford had several times as many applications for admission to the freshman class as there were spaces available. Furthermore, Stanford had numerous criteria for admission besides grades in high school, such as extracurricular activities, including athletics; and recommendations from important people such as wealthy alumni. In view of these considerations, it was easy to pick as many of certain kinds of people as desired. This meant that the number of those left to be admitted was so small that they were likely to be very unusual people, including various kinds of nuts. I concluded that this does not prove that all the residual group of those admitted are nuts; it would be likely to include some very highly talented people, the sort who would become famous politicians, or movie actors, or those who would lead a rock band. However, it would also include some bona fide nuts such as paranoid psychotics. In any case, I was not anxious for my son to be growing up associating with the kinds of people indicated by this information. I was mindful of the problems which I had with being classified as some kind of nut because of the grades I was making. I also recalled a comment made to me by a graduate of Reed College who was doing his graduate work for a Ph. D. degree in chemistry under my direction: "Now don't think that Reed College turns out only odd balls, but if you've got it in you, they'll bring it out." These considerations caused me to worry a little about Roger, for he was an Eagle Scout with two palms, and had won an award in some kind of speaking contest. My concern was somewhat increased when Roger received his admission papers to Michigan before hearing anything from Stanford. This consoled me somewhat, since I would at least have a chance to try and influence him without issuing any orders. After a period of time, Roger came in to where I was working at my desk wearing a very disappointed expression on his face: "They turned me down at Stanford. I am on the waiting list." In offering condolences, I think that I concealed my joy rather admirably. There was no discussion about whether he would wait and hope; he was smart enough to want to get the thing settled. Of course, I don't know whether he and I lucked out, or if I gave good advice. Whatever the answer, things worked out well.

When Roger was a senior at Berkeley High School he had the good fortune to have an excellent chemistry teacher who aroused his interest in chemistry. I had been very careful to avoid acting like a medical doctor who, so typically, is anxious to have his children become medical doctors. I had frequently told him of things which I knew from being a chemist, but avoided any attempt to sell him on the profession. When he began to ask me questions about chemistry, I always explained fully, and tried to add any pertinent facts that seemed of interest to me. When he decided that chemistry was what he wanted to study in college, I suggested that he seriously consider chemical engineering, since a chemical engineer with a B.S. degree could earn good wages as an engineer and would often get into administrative positions, because engineers usually took courses in business administration in college. If he desired to go beyond a bachelor's degree, he could go to graduate school in either chemical engineering or chemistry. At Berkeley, we usually had a few graduate students in chemistry whose undergraduate degree was in chemical engineering. In contrast, chemistry students with a B.S. or A.B. degree were likely to find that they could not advance beyond doing analytical work or the equivalent unless they did graduate work, usually for the Ph.D. degree. At Berkeley, we usually had a few students working for a Ph.D. degree who had spent a few years in industry. Roger bought all of this and enrolled in the Engineering School at Michigan.

After enrollment at Michigan Roger encountered a few surprises, most of which were surprising to me. By good fortune, most of the regulations concerning student behavior were regarded by me as desirable. All freshman were required to live in the residence halls during their freshman year, and later were allowed to join a fraternity only with the written permission of their parents. Also, no student was allowed to own an automobile or drive one on or near campus. Whatever the reason for this requirement, it certainly solved a lot of problems for the university, the students, and the city of Ann Arbor. In view of the size of the city, and the size of the student body, if a ratio of automobiles to students were the same as was prevalent in large universities in those days, intolerable traffic jams would have developed.

When we visited Roger at Michigan after he had been there for two or three months, we immediately encountered conspicuous evidence of the rule about no automobiles for undergraduate students. Each classroom building was surrounded by one or more acres of bare ground, except that this ground, at about 10 A.M., was covered with bicycles lying on their sides, sometimes on top of each other. We now understood why Roger had asked for money to buy a bicycle immediately after he arrived at Ann Arbor. Our next surprise came when we visited Roger's room at the residence hall. Hanging in his closet was a not very clean white shirt. When we asked why he had this dirty white shirt in his closet, he replied that this was his "dinner shirt." On certain nights each week they were required to wear a white shirt, tie and coat to the dining hall. This shirt was quite soiled inside the collar, but Roger said that this did not cause him to fail inspection because only what showed with his coat and tie on counted.

When Roger was home during Christmas vacation, I learned some things about the engineering school at Michigan which did not please me. They had a system of selecting a group of freshman students to be in the honors program, based on their grades in high school. When Roger was advised that he was eligible for this program, he was pleased at being in that group and gladly accepted. As he became acquainted with other students in the engineering school, he learned that grading in the honors program was much more severe than with the rest of the students. Rumor had it that only a small percentage of the students in the honors program were awarded "A" grades. The theory seemed to be that this program was so highly regarded in industry that lower grades were no handicap in getting a job. I had fought for years at Berkeley to prevent a different grading scale from being applied to students in a separate freshman chemistry course to which admission required passing an exam with a certain grade. Since I had no connection with teaching freshman chemistry, by my own demand at the time I accepted my appointment to an assistant professorship, my arguments were ignored. My acquaintance with students resulted in several of the premedical students telling me that many of the premeds avoided the course because of fear that it would lower their all-important grade point average. I had also learned that in several departments the honors course was of principal advantage to the professors who taught it, who were also the ones who promoted such a course. After all, most professors would rather teach good students instead of poor ones. I told Roger that if he should be told that he would be regarded as a poor student for dropping out of the honors program, that statement would probably come from a professor who enjoyed teaching in the honors program, and hence would be resistant to anything that might cast doubt on the desirability of having an honors program. I also told him that a certain professor named Cason would not lower his opinion of a student named Roger if he should decide to drop out of the honors program. I did not tell him that if he should drop out of the honors program, that act would confirm my high opinion of his intelligence and scholastic capability.

From the start, Roger's scholastic performance at Michigan fell short of what seemed to me to be reasonable expectations, based on years of teaching. He did drop out of the honors program at the end of his freshman year. That may have been the earliest that one could drop out. It seems probable that this discouraging start had a significant impact on Roger's early performance at Michigan. For whatever reason, his scholastic performance continued to go downhill. Eventually, I advised him that it would be more graceful to get out of the Engineering School before they decided to kick him out. He told me that the business administration courses he took in Engineering School interested him more than any of the other courses. He made the transition to the School of Business Administration in his junior year, and graduated with a B.S. in business administration after five years total at Michigan. His final record was good enough that he was allowed to enter the M.B.A program, and he graduated with an M.B.A after one more year. He told us that he was the "top man" in his class, and when we got the official record from the graduate school, we noted that he was, indeed, the top man in his class. We also noted, however, that the top student in his class was a woman—or should I say "lady"?

Roger was married to Priscilla Phillips during the summer after his fourth year at Michigan. Priscilla was a native of Michigan and a student at the university during the period that Roger was a student. A daughter, Kristen, was born to them during his graduate work. Roger and Priscilla did not lead the nomadic life that Rebecca and I did during the first years of their married life, but they moved around quite a bit, although not for such long distances for most of their moves.

Roger had worked for an accounting firm during the summer before his graduate year, which increased his contacts with the profession and with the recruiters who were searching for promising young accountants. This factor, coupled with his outstanding record in graduate school, resulted in his receiving several offers of employment. The position which he accepted was with L.H. Penney and Co., a small firm with its headquarters in San Francisco and with only two branches, both on the Pacific coast. When I asked him why he accepted the job with such a small company, he replied, "You told me that I should attend college at some place remote from the Bay Area, so that I could find out what the rest of the world is like. I followed your suggestion, and what I learned was that I do not like the rest of the world. I prefer the West Coast, and L.H. Penny can't send me to Kansas City or New York City." I assumed that he was citing the worst places with which he was familiar, and had, therefore, neglected to mention either Buffalo or Houston. Little did he realize what the gods and the fates had in store for him.

Roger rose rapidly in his position at L.H. Penney, partly because of his competence in his profession, as was well documented in later years, and partly because of an assist from a fortunate combination of events. Not long after his arrival at L. H. Penney, he was assigned to audit the books of a company in Sacramento. This was somewhat early in the invasion of business by the computer, and this company had only two people who were computer-wise. When Roger reported to the management that he was finding discrepancies in the computer records, they advised him of the fact that all computer work was done by two people. Roger asked them for the dates of any recent vacations of these two individuals, and for permission to work at the computer at night when no one else was around. Due to his background in electrical engineering, Roger had worked for one summer as a programmer for Ted Vermeulen, a friend of mine who was a professor of chemical engineering at Berkeley. Therefore, he knew exactly how to handle the situation he had encountered. He found that there were no discrepancies when one of the two computer workers was on vacation. The cheater was detected, and the company was very grateful to L. H. Penney for sending them such a helpful man. From that time onward, Roger was assigned to any company which suspected dishonesty of any of its employees. Since Roger continued to deliver sterling performances, his advancement was rapid.

Having reported on Roger's activities until the time of his launching his career into the cruel world, I will return to the activities of our younger son before his flight from the nest. As has been mentioned earlier, Mardy's scholastic activities were in marked contrast to those of Roger; however, he finally ended up quite successfully. Both of our sons were what has been classified as "very active" children. I am reminded of an event in Berkeley when our sons were between six and ten years old. A neighbor, who was a professor of law, and his wife were taking a walk with their two children and stopped by to have a chat with us as we were working in our yard. Our four children were tearing around in our terraced hillside yard, as I was yelling for them not to run through our flower beds or fall off a wall. My friend, the law professor, observed, "I have heard and read that problem children frequently grow up to be successful citizens who contribute a great deal to society. I certainly hope that is correct." There followed quite a discussion, most of which I do not remember, but I do remember that we both enthusiastically agreed that parents of "highly active" children should get a lot of credit if the children succeed.

Mardy's travels through his school years continued to remind me of a line from a song that came out before World War II: "You may have been a headache, but you never were a bore." When he was in the fourth grade he encountered a teacher named Mrs. Hardester, who was not equipped to deal with highly active children. After she had called home at least once before, I happened to be there when she called and Rebecca was away. I told her that I would be glad to substitute for Mardy's mother if she so desired. I gave her quite a lot of suggestions regarding how to handle such highly active children; above all to try and keep her cool under trying circumstances. I made no effort to defend the behavior about which she was complaining. I dealt only with how to contend with such behavior. Finally, I said the following: "When you are feeling rather frustrated and worn down, just remember that when this term is over you are unlikely to ever see Mardy Cason again. Just think of me; I must continue living with him, and I like to do as much as I can to help him because he is my son and I love him." This seemed to get through to Mrs. Hardester, for Mardy commented that she was not as bad as he thought she was. I almost sprained my arm patting myself on the back.

The next problem that Rebecca solved involved a practice prevalent in the junior high school Mardy attended. This practice involved separating the students into several groups according to their records in grammar school. It seems that somebody had been able to sell the idea that this would make it possible to give each group the "specific attention" that each needed. This system has a host of serious flaws; however, it is probable that the worst flaw was labeling each student publicly about how he was regarded. In view of his grammar school record, Mardy came out in the lowest group. As might be expected, the lowest group was mostly boys and the highest group was predominantly girls. This did not help any with the discipline problems in the lowest group. When we received a letter from the school on this subject, Rebecca went down to investigate. It was apparent to her that a "highly active" kid in this group would be a problem. He had no work to do to keep him interested instead of stirring up a commotion. The principal finally agreed to do what Rebecca demanded; put him in the next to top group and see how it worked out. The principal assured her that this would blight Mardy's life and it would be her fault.

It turned out that Mardy began to do his school work and changed his attitude towards the school. I don't remember hearing about any subsequent communication between Rebecca and the principal.

Mardy's performance in high school was the sort that might be called adequate by his parents, and termed mediocre by his critics. The facts in the case were that he did nothing particularly outstanding. When the time came to consider college, Rebecca, Mardy and I agreed that this would be a college in California. I would not attempt to psychoanalyze Mardy regarding the reasons for his decision, but Rebecca and I agreed on that decision for several reasons, one of which was expense. When we considered the results of Roger going to college outside of California, and applied the results to Mardy's situation with regard to rapidly increasing expenses and Mardy's less than outstanding record, we decided that the reward-cost ratio was not high enough to justify sending Mardy out of state. Mardy's scholastic record was good enough to attain admittance to what might be called the second tier of good colleges. After we had considered several prospective colleges, Mardy chose the University of the Pacific to visit. We did not accompany him on this visit or any other. We told him that he was an adult now and able to make his own decisions; we would be glad to offer advice whenever he asked for it. He did ask for advice on several occasions, and once asked us to get information he needed. Mardy did not like UOP for several reasons, especially its location in the hot Central Valley. He later visited the California State University at Chico, which is just at the edge of the Sierra Nevada mountains. The campus is on a sizable creek that runs through the city, and is rather nice. When he asked me what I thought of Chico State, I told him that my knowledge was limited to the chemistry department. From my acquaintance with faculty members in chemistry there, and considering the performance of transfer students to Berkeley, I would rate Chico as a good state college. I was a little concerned about the proximity of ski areas; however, I decided that it would be poor policy to mention that subject. I was well aware that he knew about the location of all ski areas in California, and that anything I said on that subject might be subject to misinterpretation. Since I was responsible for getting him hooked on skiing, my position was obviously a delicate one. In any case, Mardy chose Chico for launching his college career.

The year that Mardy spent at Chico was largely a total loss. There were so many factors involved, many of which were probably unknown to me, that any kind of analysis is probably a waste of time. I know, however, that the roommate he had could be properly described as impossible, and I don't remember whether he was able to get rid of that obstacle for the second semester. In any case, he got a notice soon after the end of the school year that he would not be welcome to return to Chico. Naturally enough, he was greatly depressed by this development. We had a long conversation while sitting on his bed. I introduced the conversation by saying that I had already had many years of experience in dealing with people of college age, had advised them on just about any topic imaginable, including how to avoid break up of a marriage that was endangered, how to deal with parents who were interfering with their career, how to handle an obnoxious professor, just about anything that came along. Frequently, a student whom I had never seen before walked into my office and said that his roommate or somebody else had told him he ought to talk to me about a problem he has. I concluded my monologue with the following: "In view of these things, I hope that you will believe me when I tell you that I can recognize a smart guy when I become acquainted with such. Now, I am well acquainted with you and I think that you are a smart guy. I know about the problems you have had in school, and I know that some of them are because you are a smart guy, but have inherited certain other characteristics from me that have caused you trouble sometimes. You are at a tough period in your life just now, and you must solve it by doing something; at first, just anything so long as it is something besides moping around and feeling sorry for yourself. Go out and hunt for a job, any job so long as you are employed and get paid for doing the job well." Only slightly to my surprise, Mardy said nothing, but went out and started hunting for employment.

For the first few days, Mardy was discouraged by not finding a job, but he then found and accepted a temporary job as stock boy at Montgomery Ward. He worked hard at hauling around boxes and doing other laborious jobs, and was told after the first few days that they would like to make his job permanent, and asked what his plans were. When he told them he was planning to go back to school in the fall, they approved of that and said that they would probably rehire him later if he wanted a job with them. When Mardy told us about this event, it was the first time that we knew that he had decided to go back to school at once. Of course we were pleased about that. At some time near midsummer, while we were having dinner, Mardy told us: "That man I am working with is married and has two kids, and his pay is not much more than mine. I don't understand why he is willing to work at such a job." Since I had been doing a lot of thinking about such things for a long time, as described near the beginning of this chapter, I responded at once with something equivalent to the following: "In this land of the free and home of the brave in which we have the good fortune to live, our Constitution was designed to develop a country in which any individual who works hard and well will be rewarded for it. This principle does not always work out, as you well know from reading or listening to the news; however, it does work often enough that several million people are clamoring, at any given time, to get into this country. A great many of those who cannot get into our country legally, are so anxious to get in that they will risk their lives in the effort to get in illegally. This is one of our problems which is most difficult to solve. We understand why such hordes want to share such privileges with us, but we cannot allow them to overrun and destroy these things for which many of our ancestors have fought and died to defend." I do not remember what followed this monologue, but I think that there were more than a few moments of silence.

Mardy decided to restart his college career by attending Contra Costa College, a junior college which was sufficiently close to our home to allow practical commuting. He lived at home and we supplied adequate money for anything that he needed or wanted to do, this being an appropriate reward for doing his job well. We emphasized that we did not want him to draw any money from his savings account, where he had deposited most of the money he had earned from delivering papers or doing any other jobs for us or others. His grades were passing or above for his first semester at junior college, and rose rapidly during his second semester. During his second year, he was in the Honors Group, and he transferred to San Francisco State University for his final two years of college. He graduated with honors. As before, we supplied adequate funds for him to live comfortably. He lived in a small, rather unsatisfactory apartment initially, but lived in a room in a private home for the remainder of his time there. The latter seemed rather satisfactory, and he became friendly with the woman who owned the house. According to Mardy, on one occasion she asked him for advice on how to handle her teenage son so that he would grow up to be like Mardy. Happily enough, Mardy's tenure at San Francisco State ended just before the much publicized rioting which occurred there during the nineteen sixties, but he made himself unpopular in some circles with his "far right" political stance.

Even though Mardy graduated with honors from San Francisco State, he encountered a problem with getting a job because of his age putting him in the cohort highly susceptible to the draft that was in effect at the time. With a typical Marsden display of intelligence, he went down to the appropriate office and enlisted for service. In filling out the forms, he reported that he was afflicted with chronic asthma, which was true. He was required to get a report from his family doctor as to the reality of the chronic asthma. Our family doctor since 1948, Peter E. Patch, was very familiar with Marsden S. Cason, for Mardy was his first Cason patient, while he was still a resident physician at Alta Bates Hospital. He put twenty-one stitches in Mardy's face after he had dived headfirst into the big glass window in the front of our living room. Dr. Patch consulted his records and reported that Marsden S. Cason was afflicted by chronic asthma. Thus, Mardy was classified as 4F, and became able to get a job. Naturally enough, Mardy did not tell the draft board that after several years of fighting chronic asthma, he began following the example set by his father, and started eating several grams of vitamin C per day. Amazing stuff! It has enabled two members of the Cason family to become useful and happy citizens.

Mardy's first job was with Koret of California, the small company which held the early patent on permanent press clothes. He worked hard and enthusiastically, as he always has, and soon was assigned to the job of traveling about the country to try and prevent companies from using the process without paying royalties to the patent holder. After a period of time, Koret made an initial public offering (IPO), and Mardy got sufficient funds to enable him to get started on his business career.

In this chapter, there have been chronicled the activities of our sons, Roger and Mardy, up to the point where each had established a successful career of his own. Since the chronicle that I am writing should be classified as my autobiography, although an unusual one, it is not appropriate to continue to include in this document the current activities of our sons, except as they have significant impact on the lives of Rebecca and me. They are living their own lives, and I will mention them in this chronicle, which is directed to my life, only as appropriate for specific reasons. Of course this line of reasoning does not apply to my wife of sixty-four years, since she touches my life constantly, day by day.

CHAPTER 14

VITAMIN C AND ME

As has been described in Chapter 1, one of the earliest recollections in my life was a scene in which I was propped up in bed at night gasping desperately to pull more air into my lungs. That was the earliest memory of my struggle with asthma, which lasted for about forty years. During my early years I normally had no difficulty unless I was also afflicted with a virus infection (a "bad cold," or "flu," depending on the severity), or severe allergy symptoms encountered during the ragweed season in August and September. As far as I am able to recall, there was little, if anything, really useful known about avoiding the spread of virus infections, and treating them was just as poorly understood. The flu epidemic during World War I frequently led to pneumonia, and claimed many lives. The only way to avoid the ragweed allergy season was to go to a climate where ragweed did not flourish. It was indigenous everywhere east of the Rocky Mountains, except for the northern peninsula of Michigan. The rich people on East Main Street who were sensitive to ragweed went up there for about six weeks during the height of the ragweed season. This long a vacation in a semi-resort area was too expensive for my family at that time, so my brother, John, and I had to tough it out in Murfreesboro, staying in the house as much as practical. The worst of the ragweed season was usually over by the time grammar school and high school started in September, and Vanderbilt started a little later, which was a major advantage.

Until about the time of my graduation from college, I had not spent significant amounts of time anywhere away from middle Tennessee, and I had not developed allergy problems other than during the ragweed season. Thus, I was troubled with asthma only intermittently, during the ragweed season and during virus infections. Actually, I was not usually affected during a virus infection, only when the infection was severe enough to be classified as flu. In prep school and college, asthma did not interfere with any of the things I wanted to do, including vigorous participation in athletics and spending the summers in the woods and by streams, as described in earlier chapters. I and my prep school roommate, Bill Massie, did not smoke cigarettes or anything else, did not drink alcohol, ate good food, including lots of fruit and grains, and engaged heavily in athletics. We were known as "health nuts," sometimes by less complimentary sobriquets. Perhaps it is not surprising that I never missed an examination throughout high school, prep school, and college. Clearly, asthma was not a significant handicap to me in any kind of activity in which I engaged. However, it certainly was a significant factor in causing me to go to graduate school in California, where there was no ragweed. Since meeting Rebecca Marsden at the International House in Berkeley was obviously the most important single event in my long life, it follows that asthma was a very important factor in shaping my life and career. It is also true that asthma later came near to sinking my career, as has been described in detail in Chapter 7. Dr. Walter Burrage, a saint who actually walked on this earth, came to my rescue.

The onset of chronic asthma occurred very shortly after my arrival in Cambridge to work for Professor Louis Fieser, so it was not surprising that I should attribute the persistent attack of asthma to something in my new environment. By "persistent," I mean that I was awakened gasping for breath nearly every night, and had to take ephedrine to dilate my trachea, accompanied by Amytal so that I could get some sleep and be ready for the next day's work in spite of the ephedrine. A rather stressful and unstable way to live. As described in some detail in Chapter 7, Dr. Walter Burrage saved me by introducing me to the adrenaline inhaler. Dr. Burrage told me that it was quite unlikely that my trouble with asthma would go away when I left the Boston area, and that was confirmed when Rebecca and I went to visit my parents in Tennessee when it was not in the ragweed season and I did not have a virus infection. As long as I stayed in the Boston area, I visited Dr. Burrage as frequently as he recommended in a search for the cause of my allergy. As already noted in Chapter 7, he did not charge me much for all this investigation. For one thing, this was an era of a different modus operandi in the practice of medicine. In addition, Dr. Burrage knew that our son, Roger, had been born at Baker Memorial Hospital, where both the obstetrician's fee and the hospital fees were specifically limited. Rich women went to Phillips House for delivery of their babies, where both the doctor and the hospital could charge whatever they pleased. Dr. Burrage also seemed to take a specific interest in me, for the usual approaches to discovering the cause of an allergen had failed to reveal anything. He was the editor-in-chief of a book on allergy, and was also writing more than one chapter in the book. At one point, he decided that he should get a basic metabolism test on me because there had been reported some cases in which asthma had been related to low metabolism. I assured him that there were indications that my metabolism was quite high, but he needed some quantitative data. So I came in early one morning after no breakfast, rested about a half hour, then had the test. It turned out to be quite high. Dr. Burrage worried that I was fretting about getting to work instead of resting, which I was, and so he needed another test. When I resisted on the grounds that the test would be high again, and would take time away from my job, he said that he would not charge me for either test if the second one was high. I agreed, since I did not relish arguing with my benefactor. While I was resting, the nurse chatted cheerily and played some nice music on a record player. The test results were nearly identical with the first results. Dr. Burrage cheerfully responded that he now had some really reliable data for his book on a difficult case to diagnose.

At the beginning of Burrage's examination, he did what he termed routine tests for allergens, which could be detected by the use of test patches on my skin. He put two or three spreads of patches on my back. The only thing to which I proved to be quite sensitive was a mold called Alternaria. This was included in the immunization injections against ragweed, which Dr. Burrage prepared for me and I immediately began injecting under his guidance. This immunization program proved unusually effective and gave me almost complete relief during the ragweed season, and thus meant a considerable reduction in the frequency of my use of the adrenaline spray during that season. This, in turn, reduced the frequency with which I awakened Rebecca, who was already burdened enough with getting up at night to take care of Roger. Furthermore, Dr. Burrage also continued to supply me with these injection materials during the four war years that I spent in Nashville.

So far as my problems with asthma were concerned, I stayed in a relatively stable condition as the nomads (Chapter 8) wandered first to Greencastle, Indiana, next to Long Beach, California, and finally to Nashville, Tennessee. Of course, this remarkable stability of my asthma symptoms made it clear that the trouble was something involved directly with me, not my environment. In some ways, this simplified my search for the cause of my asthma; as long as Dr. Burrage kept sending me my injection material, I did not have to worry about the environment. In another way, this complicated the investigation, since the human body is as complicated as anything can get. Furthermore, at this stage the adrenaline spray began to get less effective. At this point a big advertisement appeared in some magazine, or perhaps the Nashville Banner, touting a miraculous new relief for asthmatics. This was an uncommon event in the days before the electronic revolution. We were not bombarded daily with a "cure of the month" for whatever ails you, with heavy coverage for both allergy and arthritis. Ergo, I used the telephone to investigate.

A nice young man came out to our home in Belle Meade with his marvelous device for relieving asthmatic gasping for breath. To my astonishment, he had a nasal spray loaded with adrenaline, essentially the same device Dr. Walter Burrage introduced me to in 1938. As might be expected, there were a couple of minor improvements. For one thing, DL-adrenaline was used instead of the L-adrenaline which is used for injection. The use of the DL material, which is one half the inactive D-isomer, proves satisfactory for use in a spray where the solution sprayed is ten times the strength of the solution injected. Separation of the inactive isomer is expensive, so the DL material is cheaper than the pure isomer required for injection. At that time, the DL material did not require a prescription for purchase; hence, elimination of the need for intervention of a medical doctor and the cost thereof. Fortunately, at the time of this writing I have had no need for this adrenaline spray for about forty five years, so I do not know whether the solution sprayed remains free of the prescription requirement.

The other difference from my equipment, which was purchased with direction from Dr. Burrage, was a minor change in the geometry of the spray, which made it easier to clean out the dark material resulting from exposure of adrenaline to air. The salesman showed me how to clean out the spray with Clorox. Use of the spray that night gave me instant relief- another unforgettable event. Furthermore, when I cleaned out my "old" spray, it worked just as well as the new one. This sequence of events tended to generate some food for thought. During the intervening five years after I first used this spray, I had never received any other information about it. Furthermore, I have informed several people about this system of asthma relief, extending up to the time of this writing. In each case, the person I informed expressed previous ignorance of the device, and later reported enthusiastically about their good results. How can this sort of thing happen? I can think of a few possibilities: (A) The official publications of the American Medical Association failed to spread the news as they should have, for any of several possible reasons. (B) The developer of this simple device failed to push its advertisement; in the days before World War II, this could happen. (C) A business company or an individual, either within or outside of the medical profession, bought the rights to the device in order to withdraw it from the market and thus protect the sale of another device which was less effective, but more profitable to the seller. I have been involved in one way or another with two such situations involving instruments used in chemical research or the fiercely competitive copying industry. Of course, I have no reliable information on just how many, if any, of these simple devices, which are a blessing to an asthmatic, are in actual use. Since the device actually saved my career, I might be overly impressed with how many people need such a device. The advertising industry is much too busy, in modern times, spending big money pushing things where there is the potential for big profits.

My next encounter with a method for the control or elimination of asthma involved what has become widely promoted as "alternative medicine." However, this method was not widely advertised at that time; indeed, I learned of it by accident. One morning in 1952, as I was working at my desk (table) in my office (laboratory), there entered a well groomed man whom I did not recognize. He introduced himself as a DuPont chemist named Kvalnes. I recognized the name, because, while working for Louis Fieser, I had occasion to repeat some of the work that he had done for his Ph. D. degree at Minnesota. I told him that I had found his work reproducible in every detail, and found that a relief after trying to repeat some German work that was not reproducible. In answer to my inquiry about why he was in Berkeley, he said that for many years after he started working for DuPont he had been afflicted with chronic asthma. A fellow sufferer! He said that for the past two or three years he had been taking an occasional leave without pay, in order to live for a period in different locations in the hope that he would find a place where his asthma was not so bad. He was living just now in San Francisco, and had come to Berkeley to visit with the organic chemists and use our library. When I asked how his asthma was in San Francisco, he replied with a rather dejected air that it was no better, just as was the case in every other place he had lived. I then told him that I had the same experience while living in several places for longer periods of time, and that my allergist in Boston, Dr.Walter Burrage, had predicted that I would not find relief by changing my environment. I also said that this shows that there is something out of adjustment within me and within him; hence, nothing could be gained by searching for a more compatible environment.

After about a year, I met Kvalnes at a National American Chemical Society meeting. After a bit of chitchat, I got around to, "How is your asthma?" To my utter astonishment, he replied, "I don't have it any more." After his assurance that he would never kid me about such an important matter, he said that he had started eating two or three grams of vitamin C per day, and soon stopped having asthma. On my comment that 2 to 3 grams of vitamin C was a helluva lot of acid to dump in the stomach, he responded: "Come on, Cason, you know as well as I do that the stomach is about a tenth normal with hydrochloric acid, and so a weak acid such as vitamin C will have no effect on the acidity of the stomach." All that I could reply was, "Touché." I had made a stupid comment that I hoped none of my students would hear about—I blamed it on the stress and surprise at the information he gave me. I had tried many things that were supposed to help asthma and none of them did anything for me, so I was not impressed that Kvalnes success would endure.

In spite of my skepticism, I bought a bottle of crystalline ascorbic acid at a drug store, weighed out a gram to get a rough idea of how much a gram of the white powder was. It is very sour stuff, so I put it in a spoon, scraped it off against the roof of my mouth, and drank some water to immediately get it out of the region of my taste buds. After I had repeated this routine for several weeks, absolutely nothing happened regarding my asthma. I was disappointed, but not surprised. At the next ACS meeting, about six months later, Kvalnes was there, so I hunted him up, and immediately asked that same question, "How is your asthma?" I expected to hear that the asthma had returned to plague him. But the reply was, "I told you that I don't have it any more." He then added that maybe I would require a longer time to get the benefit. He had required at least a month of taking the vitamin C before he noticed an improvement. At this point I realized that I should find out why Kvalnes started taking such a thing as vitamin C for the improvement of asthma. He said that he saw a paper in some not very prominent chemical journal by Harry Holmes, a professor at Oberlin College, who referred to something he had read by a man named Irwin Stone. Stone was a biochemist who had been involved with promoting the worldwide use of ascorbate (vitamin C) for stabilization of food against deterioration from air oxidation. The widespread use of this process was no doubt a major factor in eliminating frank clinical scurvy in developed countries.

Kvalnes did not remember where he had read this paper by Professor Holmes, in which some ideas attributed to Irwin Stone were referenced. A somewhat more vague report than several I had read which proved groundless. Nevertheless, since Kvalnes was a living demonstration of the fact that something had cured his asthma, and said cure had lasted for more than a year, I decided that I would continue eating vitamin C unless some unpleasant development occurred. Being a chemist, I also knew that a healthy person eliminates vitamin C from the body rapidly, so I divided my 2 to 3 grams per day into at least four doses dispersed over my hours awake. Nothing happened month after month; I needed to use the adrenaline spray at least once during nearly every night. After many months—I remember estimating that it was less than a year—I seemed to be getting up at night less. One morning I asked Rebecca, "Does it seem to you that I am bothering you less with my inhaling of epinephrine during the night?" Her reply: "As a matter of fact, I think that your flouncing around during the night has been considerably less." After a few months, the asthma was gone—simply evaporated. It is difficult to imagine the emotional impact this made on me. After two or three years, I ceased to be apprehensive that the asthma would return. After more than forty years, it has persisted in not returning.

A few years after the end of my asthma, I was talking about it with Karl Folkers, a friend of mine who was at that time Director of Pioneering Research at Merck and Co. After hearing my story, Karl said, "Now Jim, if you treat this affair as a respectable scientist should, you will now knock off those megadoses of vitamin C for a period of time and see what happens to your asthma." Since I had already thought a great deal about that concept, my response was without delay: "To hell with that idea, Karl; you have had enough experience with biochemical research to know that pursuit of research on animals, such as humans, without adequate control of parameters which influence the research, is a good way to load up the literature with junk science. Look at the mess that cancer research is in. Furthermore, I am not interested in research on this subject just now; I am interested in keeping asthma away from me, and so I am not interested in willfully changing any known parameters. I only hope that there does not occur a change in some controlling factor which is unknown to me and which messes up my sand pile." When I finally paused to catch my breath, Karl responded, "Touché."

Although I was not interested in research on vitamin C, I did communicate my findings on asthma to various friends, and a few of them tried the megadoses of vitamin C. I remained in contact with only two people for the year or more necessary to know if they had favorable results. One of these was Bill Gwinn, a friend who was a professor of physical chemistry in my department. His asthma was so bad that I was not at all convinced that he had stuck to that routine of eating the little pile of white powder four times per day for a significant length of time. After asthma attacks had hospitalized him more than once, he was finally saved by use of a different inhalant which his doctor was able to get for him from England. The FDA, proceeding according to its usual modus operandi, had not approved use of the substance in this country.

It was easy for me to keep in touch with the other person to whom I communicated information about vitamin C. His name is Marsden S. Cason, and he is my younger son. One thing that he inherited from me was asthma. Since he was born in 1942, he was able to take advantage of my experience with vitamin C. He graduated from college with a major in business administration at just the time when young unmarried males were at high risk for being drafted to go to Vietnam, so he had trouble getting a job. Ergo, he went to the draft board and volunteered. Being a truthful lad, he noted on his registration card that he was afflicted with chronic asthma, and later supplied the requested notice from his family doctor that he was indeed an asthmatic. His classification was 4F. Mardy went on to become a business executive, and became known as the nut who kept a dish of chewable vitamin C pills on his desk, and was likely to offer a visitor as many as he wanted to eat. On one occasion, a departing visitor asked the receptionist, "What gives with that guy Cason and his dish of vitamin C pills?" As I heard the story later, the receptionist said, "He says that his dad claims that vitamin C is simply marvelous stuff—good for whatever ails you." At that time I had begun to realize that such a statement is only a slight exaggeration.

I think that the sequence of events described above caused me to recall an event which was reported to me several years earlier by my former prep school roommate, Bill Massie, who had become a prominent orthopedic surgeon. It was probably while I was working for Louis Fieser at Harvard and Bill was an intern at Massachusetts General Hospital that he related this story to me; we saw each other frequently during that period. Bill's report was about an occurrence in the Senior Research Seminar at the Harvard Medical School. Each senior student was expected to present to the seminar some report from the literature which suggested an interesting research project. The interesting project which Bill reported to me was presented by his roommate; since I do not remember this man's name I will refer to him as BR (Bill's Roommate). When BR's turn to report to the seminar arrived, he requested that a surgeon make a small incision on his back in some place where it would do no damage, and give it a normal aseptic dressing. BR gave no explanation of what he was about, but said that he would want to examine the incision at weekly intervals when the seminar met.

On removal of the bandage after the first week, examination of the incision revealed that it had not healed at all. BR seemed pleased and said that he was uncertain what would happen the next week. The next week was a repeat of the first, and BR still seemed satisfied but not relaxed. (I do not remember whether the climax was reached on the third inspection of the incision or a later one, but I will report the climax as at the third inspection.) When the bandage was removed for the next inspection, a gasp went up from the audience; the wound was completely healed, so that the incision was just visible. At this point, BR revealed that he had found some information in the literature which suggested that wounds would heal rapidly in presence of large amounts of vitamin C (usually called ascorbate in the chemical and biochemical literature). So he had deprived himself of any food known to be high in vitamin C, such as tomatoes or citrus fruit, for a period of time before the incision. Immediately after the incision was made, he ate heavily of oranges and tomatoes, and kept stepping up the intake of such foods until the incision proved to be healed.

Since this seemed to me to be a rather spectacular experiment, I later asked Bill if it had been followed up, and/or published. He said that he did not know the answer to that question, and had not heard from BR since the war. The war had interrupted any medical research at least as badly as was the case with chemical and biochemical research. In view of things to be reported soon in the present writing, I am now inclined to wonder if the literature regarding vitamin C which BR had found was also information originating with Irwin Stone. It is possible, although improbable, that Stone could have been that active in publication during the late 1930s.

During the 1960s, I rapidly became aware of a veritable gusher of information in the news media about vitamin C. This was due to the truly spectacular showmanship of Linus Pauling. Only a few scientists are endowed with this kind of ability, and those who are so endowed sometimes direct this ability towards self-glorification rather than for the benefit of society. By the 1960s, Irwin Stone had been engaged in important, well organized research for about thirty years. In spite of my well-justified interest in vitamin C, I had heard of Stone only orally and indirectly, as I have just now reported. When Stone talked to Pauling, things became very different. Linus Pauling was awarded two Nobel Prizes, one in chemistry and one for promotion of Peace. In my opinion, the most important thing that Linus ever did was recognize the importance of Stone's work, and proceed to publicize it for the benefit of society. He never failed to emphasize the fact that Stone was the pioneer. This situation is nicely summed up in the introductory paragraph to the description of Stone's work which appeared in the winter issue of the newsletter published by The Linus Pauling Institute of Science and Medicine:

"Linus Pauling's interest in vitamin C was originally aroused by Irwin Stone in April, 1966, when he was persuaded to try Dr. Stone's high-level ascorbic acid regimen for good health and longevity. The success of this regimen, along with other studies, encouraged Dr. Pauling to examine the matter of vitamin C and the common cold, and to publish his first book on that subject in 1970."

I have a suggestion for anyone, especially a medical doctor, who is attempting to reach an honest conclusion concerning the merits of Pauling's claims concerning the health benefits of vitamin C. Pauling's conclusions are based on experimental evidence acquired by him or those working with him. What is the factual basis on which the criticism of Pauling's assertions is supported? I have been unable to find such a basis in the real world. The only support seems to be in the cyberspace generated in the minds of numerous people whose credentials are suspect.

At this point, I will conclude my report concerning the key contributions of Pauling and Stone to development of public awareness of the health benefits of vitamin C in respect to the common cold and flu. This is actually only a narrow facet of the much larger benefits which are derived from vitamin C. Much greater benefits devolve from the same basic characteristic of vitamin C which renders it effective against a cold or flu. It is a radical scavenger; it has a chemical structure which makes it able to destroy a free radical on contact. Free radicals (please, they bear no resemblance to a communist; even the most far left politician loves things which destroy biologically active free radicals) are responsible for many of our most serious ailments, both from infection and from degenerative diseases which plague those who have grown old. Irwin Stone has published interesting material on the subject which he terms "hypoascorbemia." He correlates many of our human ailments with this basic concept of the fundamental cause of many of these ailments. At this point in my story, I will also defer further comment concerning Linus Pauling, for his work on vitamin C caused him to become involved heavily in the controversy concerning therapy and prevention of cancer, which is the subject of my next chapter.

When Pauling's book dealing with prevention and/or cure of the common cold appeared about 1970, it naturally caused me to review my recent experiences since I began taking 2 to 3 grams of vitamin C per day in 1953. After consulting with Rebecca, I concluded that I had only one severe cold or flu since 1953, whereas she had more than one severe cold plus the flu that both of us had at exactly the same time. This severe illness that both of us experienced in 1965 was a case of the "Hong Kong Flu," which was noted for its severity. We had our eyes examined by an optometrist on a Saturday morning, one after the other. On Monday morning, each of us came down with a sudden severe attack of flu at about nine o'clock. I was in the midst of a lecture which was finished at nine thirty, and I began to feel ill so rapidly that I had trouble getting home. I found Rebecca moaning in bed. We learned later that this optometrist, after examining us, went to the hospital at once and was not discharged until a week or more later. Apparently, the intensity of our exposure to a particularly potent virus was too much for the vitamin C. By this time "time delay" pills were available and we began taking them. Rebecca continued to take only one gram per day until after she had a couple attacks of flu which I did not have. She then went to two grams per day, and has been just as free from this kind of infection as I have been. We increase the dose when an epidemic is in the news, but about four grams per day is our limit without getting diarrhea. Linus insists that he can eat 6 to 7 grams per day without getting diarrhea. Either he happens to be quite resistant to this effect of vitamin C, or else has built up a tolerance to it. I have been told by a few people that they have experienced diarrhea at 2g./day of time delay vitamin C. It seems to have been well established by the time of this writing that time delay pills or capsules are always more effective, including the development of side reactions. Since 1970, neither of us has had a severe virus infection. On several occasions, when one of us would get that characteristic feeling in the throat which presages a virus attack, he or she would step up the vitamin C intake to three or four grams. On some occasions, the portent of the "rough" throat would not be realized at all; in others a light cold developed, without a hangover of heavy phlegm in the throat. One might argue that reporting the experiences of two people has no significance. Certainly, the FDA would derisively dismiss such a report as "anecdotal" in the extreme. I have no respect for the attitude of the FDA, and I suspect that many people will enjoy "relating" to such a report.

I believe that I should not conclude this chapter without presenting some discussion of what has become "alternative medicine." The rather frightening growth of alternative medicine has no doubt been influenced greatly by the fact that literally millions of people have experienced obvious, unmistakably good results from the use of vitamin C. A typical reaction might be: "If the medical profession, including my doctor, tells me that vitamin C is junk medicine, and I know that it helps me, I am going to investigate some other alternative medicines." The odds are reasonably good that a given individual may find another alternative medicine (AM) that helps him. Even if the AM did not help him, but did not hurt him, he is likely to think he is better and continue to use the "cure" indefinitely while searching for still more good AMs. After all, in the vaunted double blind placebo tests in which the FDA has such great confidence, I have frequently noted at least 20 percent positive results from those receiving placebos, as well as all kinds of weird negative results. If one should have the kind of experience I have had with the FDA (Chapter 16), which cut off my access to a therapy which gave great relief to my arthritic pains, perhaps one can understand why AM is so popular. I recently read in the magazine called Arthritis Today, published by the Arthritis Foundation, that the number of patients being treated by those practicing alternative medicine is greater than the number of patients treated by all varieties of orthodox medical doctors.

And yet the medical profession has held firm in refusing to endorse the use of vitamin C for the prevention and/or alleviation of the miseries of a cold and flu. I continue to harp on this specific aspect of the failure of the medical profession to recognize alternative medicine, because the facts involved here are so simple that they can be understood by anyone who can read. This behavior of the medical profession cannot be ascribed to the fact that they are collectively stupid. The fact is that they are collectively very smart indeed, as is appropriate for a profession which deals continually with matters of life and death, and on which all of us must depend. Since my three oldest and best friends, one of them my brother, were medical doctors, and since my last ten or twelve years of teaching at the University of California were involved with teaching large classes composed of more than 50 percent premedical students, I think that I am qualified to state that the average intelligence of medical doctors is probably above that found in any other profession. So how could the profession offer such a united front in failing to recommend the use of vitamin C for prevention of illness? Again, I am offering this niche as a simple example of the much larger problem. According to the work of Irwin Stone, which has been mentioned briefly, the impact of vitamin C extends far beyond what has been proven by firmly established facts. But I am not considering at this point that which I believe, as a scientist, will be eventually proven and will be of great benefit to our society. I am now considering what can be understood by anyone with a high school education, but which seems to be ignored by the medical profession.

This problem has been developing in our society for some twenty-five years, and its evolution has no doubt been accelerated by the rapid increase in the percentage of medical practice that is contracted medical practice. Most conspicuous of the organizations which practice medicine by contract are the organizations, operated for profit, which are known as Health Maintenance Organizations, commonly referred to as HMOs. At present in California, as well as elsewhere, several HMOs are public companies owned by stockholders, and the shares of stock are publicly traded. Thus, the owners of the company need have no interest in the company except for whether it makes a profit. The officers of the company may or may not be medical doctors, and so they also may not be interested in anything except the profit which the company shows. The doctors who serve the patients are the only ones who are likely to have the welfare of the patients as their prime interest, and that interest is often severely curtailed by regulations instituted by the businessmen who are in control of the company. California has passed some laws and is considering others to limit control of the medical doctors by businessmen. Recently, in southern California, an HMO was sued for a few million dollars on the grounds that the company had forbidden an operation which had the potential to save the patient's life. The HMO lost the suit. Included in the evidence presented at the trial was the fact that the salary of the chief executive officer of the HMO was in excess of one million dollars..

At the bottom of the pyramid, which has wealthy people on the top, we find the suffering patients. All of the patients who work for a large company have no choice except to "use" the HMO with which the company has a contract, and this contract is likely to go to the HMO which charges the company the lowest fees. A few companies will have contracts with more than one HMO, and give the employees an option. The University of California is one such company, and Rebecca and I have profited greatly by using our judgment to choose a very good company which was not an HMO. It has served us well as Medicare supplementary insurance during the twenty-three years since we reached age sixty-five. We can choose any hospital or doctor that we desire to choose. Judging from the news media, one of the hardest-nosed companies in bargaining with the HMOs is the California Public Employees Retirement System, known as Calpers. It is the largest pension organization in the country, and frequently uses its muscle to tell large companies such as General Motors how to run their business. It is easy to believe that Calpers, like every other company, is interested in getting the cheapest rate for the benefit of the pension system rather than the HMO which provides its members with the best service.

In summary, this system is hardest on the patients, which is all of us, next hardest on the medical doctors, most of whom are hard-working and conscientious. The profit goes to businessmen who are trading in a commodity—the health of the citizens. As Mr. Lilly said, when he announced that Eli Lilly & Co. would do all blood processing at cost during World War II, "Blood is a hell of a thing on which to make a profit." As I recall it, some other companies were not very happy about Mr. Lilly coercing them to process blood at no profit. What we need is lots of Mr. Lillys, but all that we have are ordinary businessmen, and I have not met very many of them who bear a significant resemblance to Mr.Lilly. Perhaps a hard-working conscientious core of medical doctors could combine with a wave of public opinion and generate a real restructuring of our society. But I am not holding my breath waiting for such a thing to happen.

Chapter 15

THE CANCER CONTROVERSY

Either because of good luck or good judgment, or some combination of both, I have not been personally and directly involved with the affliction commonly known as cancer. Among professionals in the field, whether medical doctors or research scientists, a malignant tumor is commonly called a carcinoma. For many years, I have been closely associated with this field as a research chemist. For two years, starting in 1938, I worked as a research assistant for Professor Louis Fieser at Harvard. This period was the height of activity directed towards discovering the chemical structures which were the most potent carcinogens. The leading laboratories in this investigation were those of Louis Fieser at Harvard and J. W. Cook in England. As has been briefly described in Chapter 7, nearly all of my work with Fieser involved synthesis of compounds for testing for carcinogenicity, or for study of the metabolism of compounds known to be potent carcinogens. Of course, the biological work was carried out by cooperating biologists. I and the other people who did this work, before starting, were given a course of instruction for several hours in how to handle these compounds without endangering ourselves to developing a carcinoma. As noted briefly in Chapter 7, these precautions were rather simple and sensible. In comparison with the precautions that we used, present day precautions required for such work may be aptly described as the hunting of mice with an assault rifle. Moreover, the compounds that we were working with were carcinogenic, not "may be" carcinogenic. The potency of the carcinogen was related to the length of time that elapsed before a mouse developed a tumor after an area of his skin had been painted with a solution of a fraction of a milligram of the compound being tested. In a sample of about ten mice, if no tumor had developed after a period of time chosen on the basis of experience, the compound was declared to be inactive.

As has also been noted in Chapter 7, many of those who worked with Fieser on these compounds became sufficiently prominent as research chemists that it was easy to follow them as time went by, in chemical journals, meetings of the American Chemical Society, and the news media. I have no written records that show whether any of these people developed a carcinoma within ten years, but no news of it came to me. One of those associated with this work from the start did develop lung cancer about thirty years after this work was completed. That was Louis Fieser, a chain smoker, but also a big, vigorous, very healthy man. A second man who developed a carcinoma some twenty years after handling large quantities of dibenzanthracene, one of the three most potent carcinogens, was Charlie Heidelberger. He worked with synthesis of this compound for several months in 1950, at the University of California. Since he was attempting to improve on the synthesis which I had developed at Harvard, he frequently consulted with me and we became good friends. Thus, I was saddened to hear that he died of a malignant tumor some time after 1970.

I believe that I am justified in stating that the brief preceding report develops a very strong suggestion that there is something radically wrong with current concepts concerning the cause of cancer. Inevitably, this error permeates the practices used in cancer therapy. The basic error involved flashed through my mind like a brilliant light during a lecture on cancer which I heard in Berkeley some time in the early fifties. The lecturer was Michael Heidelberger, father of Charlie Heidelberger, and a professor at one of the universities in New York. I do not remember what he said that caused that flash of light, but I remember exactly what I thought at that time: "The cause of cancer is NOT what we are exposed to in the environment, but what we are NOT exposed to in the environment." Sounds simple, but selling it is not simple. During this chapter, I will attempt to develop in detail some of the experimental facts I have encountered and the logical analysis of this information.

I must note at the outset that this controversy has become so bitter, so persistent, and so widespread over much of the world that I must confine myself mostly to those aspects of the controversy to which I personally was in direct contact. In addition, I must give enough of the background of said controversy, and the specific details of it, in order to allow an understanding of just what is involved. Almost everybody, including many of the professionals involved, regards the question of the best way to treat cancer as an issue which must be resolved because of its importance. This is obviously true; however, it is also true that about 1 percent of our population is afflicted with cancer at any given time. It follows that everybody, except those afflicted with cancer and their families, is most interested in not becoming a cancer victim. Fortunately, these two aspects of the cancer problem fit together because of the nature of the true cause of cancer. Another aspect of this controversy is that it has become so bitter, so prolonged, and so entwined with politics that it threatens to undermine the confidence of the public in the ability of those who have been entrusted to resolve the problem. In a chronicle such as the present writing, it is apparent that I can do little more than present a picture of the problem and present some opinions of myself and others who are more important than me. During this writing, I have referred to a stack of paper more than one foot high. And there is a larger stack that has been discarded or reserved on the grounds that it is much less important than the stack in use.

At the time I experienced that flash of light during Michael Heidelberger's lecture, I had no inkling of the violent warfare that was developing between the Food and Drug Administration (FDA), with the cooperation of the California Medical Association and the California Health Department, against a group of people who were frantically attempting to establish an alternative medical procedure for the prevention of cancer, and consequently cancer therapy. The group of three political organizations just mentioned, together with the American Cancer Society, have usually been referred to as the "cancer establishment" by those who are fighting for recognition of an alternative medical procedure for therapy and/or prevention of cancer. For reasons which need not be considered at this point, those who support the alternative medical procedure refer to it as the "metabolic therapy" of cancer. The cancer establishment normally refers to this same therapy as "Laetrile therapy." This establishment, as well as the overwhelming majority of the news media, routinely refer to Laetrile with accompanying snide and derogatory adjectives, phrases, and/or clauses.

The largest and most successful group in support of metabolic therapy is known as "The Committee for Freedom of Choice in Cancer Therapy" (the Committee). This Committee publishes a news letter called The Choice. There were other groups assembled in California during the 1960s or earlier with approximately the same objectives as the Committee, but none of them proved to be as durable and effective as the Committee. The most durable one among the other groups ultimately became known as the Cancer Control Society. However, the Committee developed rapidly and soon became the dominant organization in the country in the fight against the cancer establishment. There is little doubt that the spectacular success of the Committee should be ascribed to the leadership of Bob Bradford.

At this point, I must report that most of the information in this chronicle regarding the history of the Committee and the atrocities committed by the FDA and the California Health Department have been taken from eight Rorvik newsletters on "The Politics of Cancer Research." As a footnote on the first page of each newsletter, the following appears:

"David M. Rorvik, a free-lance writer, is an Alicia Patterson Foundation award winner. He is studying the politics of cancer research in the United States and elsewhere. This article may be published with credit to Mr. Rorvik as a Fellow of the Alicia Patterson Foundation. The views expressed by the author in this newsletter are not necessarily the views of the foundation." It is rare that I use an exact quotation from the newsletter, and so quotation marks will be used only as appropriate.

Co-founders of the Committee were Bob Bradford, president, and Frank Salaman, vice president. Their objective in founding this committee was prevention of the FDA and the California Health Department from jailing John Richardson, M.D. Everything that I have been able to find indicates that these two men entered into this venture for purely idealistic reasons. They simply could not bear to sit idly by and see a benefactor of our society such as John Richardson be prosecuted as a criminal. The more they investigated, the more determined they became to stop this travesty. They are the sort of people who cause a real change in our society. They fight to the finish, even when they are pitted against the federal and state governments. I fervently hope that what they have started will some day lead to the solution of a very important and very intractable problem. I did not have the privilege of becoming acquainted with Frank Salaman, but I learned that he was a wealthy northern California businessman. I had the good fortune to have considerable association with Bob. Ironically enough, Bob's father was a medical doctor. He served with the U.S. Air Force during the Korean War, and graduated from Georgia Tech in the field of electronics and missile guidance systems. His work in electronics, first with the Air Force and then with General Electric for ten years, attracted enough attention that he was invited to join the group that built the Stanford linear accelerator. He continued working at Stanford during his first years as president of the Committee, but eventually became so absorbed with the battle against the cancer establishment that he gave up his job at Stanford. I have been told that both Bradford and Salaman devoted substantial amounts of their personal fortunes to the activities of the Committee.

Having developed the picture of the scene of battle, and presented the most important early performers, I will proceed to the point where I entered the picture.

One morning while I was working at my desk at the university, my telephone rang. It proved to be my prep school roommate of years before, Bill Massie, who had become a rather prominent orthopedic surgeon. I had become accustomed to getting letters from him from places such as Bangkok, where he would be demonstrating his device known as the Massie Nail, used in hip replacement. This time, however, he was calling from his office in Lexington, Kentucky. After some chitchat about our kids, Bill asked what I knew about Laetrile. I replied that the word did not sound familiar, and that I knew nothing about it. He expressed surprise that I had not heard of the Laetrile controversy when I was located a few miles from the center of said controversy. I remember a comment about "living in a cave." That was before I had become aware of the fact that the entire Bay Area news media would clamp a lid on anything of which they disapproved, especially local politics or new ideas. Bill went on to explain that he was trying to get all the information available on a new cancer therapy utilizing a substance called Laetrile, but was being frustrated by the fact that there was absolutely nothing about it in the medical literature. He asked me to gather all the information that I could on the subject and pass it on to him. He was my oldest and best friend, and I knew that both he and his sister were afflicted with cancer. I could not refuse. Little did I realize what I was diving into. I made no written record of when this conversation occurred, having no reason to do so, but I have been able to locate it as occurring in about 1975 by relating it to events described in dated articles published in the news media.

Since there was no point in looking at orthodox scientific literature or the local newspapers, I began inquiring of friends and acquaintances. One colleague on the teaching staff in the chemistry department, Charlie Koch, some of whose activities are described in Chapter 12, had some information for me. He referred me to a man named Mike Culbert, editor of the Berkeley Gazette, which was a very conservative newspaper published in Berkeley at that time. He had become acquainted with Mike through their mutual interest in a Sister City program with a Japanese city. He said that Mike had recently become preoccupied with a trial about Laetrile in the local court. When I asked how I could meet Culbert, Charlie volunteered to invite Rebecca, me, and Culbert to his home for an evening of conversation.

Mike told about the trial at which the FDA and the California Health Department were seeking to have Dr. John Richardson jailed for breaking the California law against the use of "quack" medicines, especially Laetrile. A high point of the trial was reached when Richardson's lawyer called a typical "little old lady" to the witness stand, explained to her that Dr. Richardson was on trial for being a criminal, and asked her, "Do you think that Dr. Richardson is a criminal?" According to Mike's report, the little old lady erupted like a volcano: "OH NO, I think he is an angel!" When asked why she thought Dr. Richardson was an angel, she related a story that has been told many times since that first trial. She was diagnosed as a terminal cancer patient (her clinical record was at hand), so she decided that she had nothing to lose by trying this unorthodox method she had heard about. She was now enjoying good health and living happily. That was the beginning of the end of that prosecution. The FDA tried again, with the same result, and also a third time, but the judge threw it out of court on the grounds of harassment.

As for the destiny of Mike Culbert, he wrote an editorial about the Richardson trial, which resulted in the Gazette informing him that he would be fired if he put out any more such nonsense. Mike said that he did not know whether he quit or was fired; hard to tell which one came first. And so Mike became full time with the Committee, edited their publication called The Choice, and joined with Bob Bradford in spreading The Word. They have worked in several foreign countries. As time went by, some goals were attained, and some seemed hopeless. Eventually, they began to lose specific interest in cancer, and became the Committee for Freedom of Choice in Medicine—at least this was the situation in 1992, ten years after I retired from teaching and dropped my subscription to The Choice.

Proceeding from information supplied by Mike Culbert, I contacted Dr. Richardson and Rebecca invited him and his wife to have dinner with us so that we could get acquainted with his work. This proved to be an enjoyable but rather emotional evening. I knew of the tribulations suffered by Dr. Richardson at the hands of the Cancer Establishment, so I deliberately kept that out of the conversation. I did, however, ask him how he happened to become involved in the cancer controversy. I will relate his story, according to my memory of it, using the first person to indicate that Richardson is the narrator. However, it is apparent that I cannot remember the particular words that Richardson used, so I do not use quotation marks.

I first heard about the substance called Laetrile from Ralph Bowman, who is now my office manager. At that time, he was employed by a book company to coordinate the wholesale marketing of books. My friendship with Ralph originated because both of us were active members of the John Birch Society. We usually had lunch or dinner together each week. On one occasion Ralph was rather excited about a book he was selling, which reported the use of a substance called Laetrile for therapy of cancer. Since I had been frequently frustrated by being unable to do anything to help cancer patients, I asked for a copy of the book. I was so impressed with the claims that were made that I decided to try the protocol recommended by the book on my cat, which had developed a malignant tumor. To my surprise, the tumor remissed and the cat recovered. I naturally talked to my office staff about this remarkable event. Later, Charlotte Anderson, a nurse on my office staff, told me that her sister, Mildred Seybold, had been diagnosed as a terminal cancer victim and wanted me to give her the treatment which the cat had received. I was vaguely aware of the California "anti-quackery" law, but after Mrs. Seybold had personally pleaded with me, I decided to give her the treatment. Among the things which I considered were my Hippocratic Oath and my moral obligation as a human being to do what I could to alleviate pain and suffering.

This is the end of John Richardson's report to me, as we sat on the sofa in my living room. I will add that the malignant melanoma on Mrs. Seybold's left arm remissed and she lived for many years after her attending physician had told her that her only hope for living more than a few months was to have her arm amputated, in the hope that the melanoma had not metastasized.

I have presented the above report to illustrate the kind of people who have been vilified by the cancer establishment for about thirty-five years, using every derogatory adjective that could be accumulated by searching Roget's Thesaurus. Many of the derogatory expressions used by officials of the American Cancer Society were new to me. I will not clutter up this report by entering pages of quotations from this source. Anyone with the morbid instinct to enjoy such statements may find many pages of them in the Rorvik newsletters. I will, however, include here about one page of the report on Richardson's arrest, which appears in Chapter 1 of the book published in 1977 written by John A. Richardson, M.D. & Patricia Griffin, R.N. A total of four pages were required to make a brief report of this outrageous and clearly illegal affair.

"The inevitable finally happened at ten in the morning June 2, 1972. Without warning of any kind two police cars and two unmarked government cars screeched to a halt at strategic points around our clinic. Uniformed officers surrounded the building and, with guns drawn, nine men and one police matron burst through the front door, flashed a search warrant at the receptionist, and pushed their way on through to the clinic itself. I was thrust against a wall and frisked for a concealed weapon. The nurses were confined to their station, and the patients, with one exception, were told to go home.

"I was told by Inspector Jackson of the California Health Department that I was under arrest for violation of the California 'anti-quackery' law, and that his warrant authorized a search for any and all Laetrile as well as literature pertaining to it. By this time, agents were everywhere: looking in cupboards, pulling out drawers, checking the contents of closets, even examining the books in my medical library to see if there were any hollowed-out secret compartments.

"I refused to answer any questions until I had called my attorney. I was denied that right! I then asked for permission to call my wife. That, too, was denied. (Later, when my wife tried to reach me by phone, she was told that I could not speak with her.) There being no alternative, I sat in silence as they rummaged through every drawer and shelf at the clinic."

I will next enter a short paragraph which occurs about two pages later:

"When I completed my work on Kerry's leg and sent her home, Jackson informed me that he was taking me to jail. Along with my two nurses, I was marched out the front door past TV cameramen and put into a police car. The cameramen were there almost from the start."

It is no doubt redundant to note that this incredible humiliation of a handsome ex-marine and highly respected medical doctor with hundreds of patients was designed to discredit metabolic therapy. Dr. John Richardson was merely the most attractive target for their wholly reprehensible tactics. The outcome of these tactics has already been reported earlier in this chapter. I dare say that there is no object in my seeking to cover any significant fraction of the documented cases of such behavior by various units of the cancer establishment, but I think it serves a purpose to present a few of the more egregious cases of such behavior.

Since the California "anti-quackery" law has been very useful to those wishing to discredit Laetrile therapy and its practitioners, I believe it serves a useful purpose to examine the character and motives of those responsible for persuading the legislature to enact this law. The problem dates back to a report issued in 1953 by the Cancer Commission of the California Medical Association, published in California Medicine 78 (4) April, 1953. This was republished in 1963, perhaps because that would make it seem more modern as evidence in support of the "anti-quackery" law. As is documented in No. 2 of the Rorvik newsletters, there was nothing right about this report. Among other things, the amount of Laetrile given during the full course of a treatment was less than used in a single injection in the treatment developed by Dr. Richardson. Another interesting item: In the original report issued in 1953, it was stated that six pathologists who examined tissues of the Laetrile-treated patients were of the "unanimous opinion" that "in no instance could any recognizable effect of a chemotherapeutic agent be observed in the histology of these various neoplasms." When the raw data was attached to the 1963 report, it turned out that some of these pathologists had indeed commented on possible Laetrile-related chemotherapeutic effects: e.g. "-hemorrhagic necrosis of tumor is extensive—an interpretation of chemotherapeutic effect might be entertained-." Nevertheless, according to Mr. Rorvik, there is no better evidence in support of the "anti-quackery" law.

So let us examine the character of the two medical doctors who were responsible for the report which resulted in condemning Laetrile to the American Cancer Society's "unproven" column. Dr. Ian McDonald, a prominent cancer surgeon, served as chairman of the commission which produced the report, while Dr. Henry Garland, a famous radiologist, was its secretary. Both of these men directed considerable effort towards discrediting the evidence that was beginning to accumulate against cigarette smoking. The August 2, 1957, issue of U.S. News and World Report carried a picture of this same Dr. McDonald, smiling, with cigarette in hand, as he declared that smoking may be "a harmless pastime up to 24 cigarettes per day." He also suggested modifying an old slogan to read: "A pack a day keeps lung cancer away." After all that I have read about the character and tactics of those in the cancer establishment, I am even willing to believe this story. Those who have become less numb than I am might be able to secure an issue of that U.S. News and World Report. The article to look for is entitled "Here's Another View: Tobacco May Be Harmless." Dr. Garland frequently broadcast similar views. On July 9, 1964, he told those who came to hear him speak at the Commonwealth Club of San Francisco that his many years of "study" had failed to find any link between smoking and disease. He also declared that "cigarettes in moderation are regarded by many as one of the better tranquilizers." According to Rorvik, both men were publicly accused of accepting $50,000 testimonial fees from the tobacco industry. Dr. Garland, a chain smoker, died of lung cancer. Dr. McDonald died from burns inflicted by a bed fire which was reported to have been caused by his smoking in bed.

Incidents such as those just described are inclined to set one to thinking. I wonder how many people died as a result of the publicity spread widely by these two medical doctors concerning cigarette smoking? I wonder how many more people died because of their interference with the use of Laetrile for therapy or prevention of cancer? They might be able to compete with some of the great killers of history. A rather sorry comparison with what the Hippocratic Oath specifies. Surely these men are not typical examples of what one can expect from medical doctors, yet they were leaders of their profession. Could it be that the overwhelming majority of medical doctors are so busy caring for their patients, frequently saving their lives, that they simply do not have time for engaging in politics? Hence, the predatory types have a golden opportunity to take over control of their hard-working colleagues. And the predatory types are especially likely to recognize a golden opportunity when they see it; hence, they accumulate in the medical profession. Could it be that this is the factor which is generating such great problems in HMOs, which are threatening to take over the practice of medicine, with their officers receiving million dollar salaries? And this is the "business" on which all of us must depend. There is no alternative; all of us must depend on the medical profession to protect us from dying prematurely and in pain.

Most, although not all, of the problems encountered by the Laetrile defenders in their struggles with the cancer establishment have been involved with government agencies or the American Cancer Society; however, I think that there is some justification for illumination of such egregious behavior as that of Drs. Garland and McDonald, for these men were among the leaders of the CMA. When a medical doctor gives advice, most people tend to think that the advice is "right." Otherwise, medical doctors would be unable to give assistance to their patients. At the same time, it is important that there be a general understanding that medical doctors are ordinary mortals; some of them are scoundrels, and some of them are incompetent, as is the case in every profession or group. Thus, it devolves on each individual to do some thinking and not be deluded by the news media, which thrives on scandal and other gruesome affairs. At the time of this writing, the news media have developed the medical profession as a prime target. This is good for the protection of all of us; hence, the great importance of a general understanding that the medical profession, as a whole, is doing the best that it can under difficult circumstances. The news media is a much more liable whipping boy than is the medical profession.

Although I am not ignoring my words in the preceding paragraphs, I am forced to report that there is one organization, which seems to be at least loosely associated with the American Medical Association, which I rate as all bad. I have been unable to discover any redeeming feature in this organization. Because of my lifelong association with the medical profession, which has been cited earlier in this chronicle, and my close involvement with the cancer controversy dating back to 1938, it is not surprising that my attention was attracted to the American Cancer Society (AmCS) long ago. (I will be using an unusual abbreviation for the American Cancer Society throughout this chronicle. I simply cannot bring myself to use the same acronym as that used for more than a hundred years by the American Chemical Society. I have been a member of the ACS for more than sixty years, and so I hope that I can be pardoned for this action.)

Soon after my arrival in California in 1945, I began to hear complaints from various quarters about the tiny fraction of the money collected as a tax-exempt organization that was spent in direct benefit to cancer victims. Without spending much time in searching, I have been able to collect the following data regarding the AmCS budget for the fiscal year ending 8/31/75. Although there have been many changes in the AmCS since 1975, these figures remain of interest as an indication of how their donations are spent; the dollar values are in millions.

Salaries and benefits for 2,900 employees	35.0 [28.7%]
Cancer research	31.2 [26.6%]
Travel; support of publications and 2,850 offices	24.0 [19.7%]
Deposit to the treasury, raising unspent assets to 155 M	21.0 [17.2%]
Direct aid to cancer victims	5.7 [4.7%]

It seems particularly interesting to note that more than 20 percent of donations for this fiscal year were put into savings. The 24 percent of their income, in the middle category, certainly brought in large dividends. I presume that this same category includes money spent in promoting the importance of early detection. However payment for this program is categorized, I object to it strenuously for two reasons: first, it enriches the hospitals and medical doctors, probably billions per year, with money paid by the public in general, either as taxes or insurance premiums. Second, I have good reasons to believe that this money is not just wasted, it is likely to cause more cancer than can ever be cured, alleviated or prevented by early detection. Of course, my first objection is either moot or obsoleted if my second is favorably received and adopted. If I should see this happening, I will know that I am dreaming.

First, I will consider the evidence that early detection does increase the chances of "cure," as defined. I am aware of numerous publications on both sides of this issue; considerable space is devoted to it in the Rorvik letters. Numerous medical doctors and others have testified on both sides of the question; however, it seems to me conspicuous that most of those in favor of seeking early detection stand to be blessed financially by that decision. The AmCS leads the pack, and certainly benefits handsomely. Since there is no obvious way that anyone could benefit personally, it seems that the fact that anyone at all is against searching for early detection suggests that there are some saints among the medical doctors and researchers. This is especially true since anyone publicly advising against the frequent mammary scans is likely to be asked questions—by a medical doctor or hospital personnel—such as "How would you feel if your wife should come down with breast cancer and die from it?" My answer to that question is that I would not be at all convinced that early detection would have done anything other than increase the misery of her last days. In any case, I would want to travel to the great beyond with her. However, most people are likely to fold up like a door hinge before such questioning. Anyone who resists such a question is likely to be classified either as having the courage of his convictions, or else being "a stubborn son-of-a-bitch." I have been publicly classified as the latter but never the former. Perhaps a third category might be suggested. Perhaps some people have more knowledge of the subject than others have.

As has been described in Chapter 7, I had pressing reasons, long before coming to California, to direct a lot of attention toward the causes and cure of cancer, especially the causes—and by association, the detection. Consequently, I paid attention to what I heard and saw, and thought a lot about same. I became impressed that such things as x-ray examinations and yearly physical exams sometimes involved a certain amount of biological insult but, more importantly, tended to make people feel more or less perpetually apprehensive that a carcinoma might be lurking somewhere in their system, waiting to break out and make them die a horrible death. I heard people worrying out loud that maybe that physical exam failed to detect that sneaky tumor, or worse yet, that their next exam would show up a tumor. I was not exempt from such worries. As described in Chapter 1, I was a rather pitiful worry-wart in my childhood, and it was at about the time I entered college that I began to get some control over such nonsense. Nevertheless, such instincts hang on, with me as well as with other successful people. The reason that I refer to successful people is that a person is unlikely to be successful unless he or she worries about his or her future. I will describe an event which illustrates my concern about the successful efforts of the AmCS to keep people perpetually concerned about the possibility of having a cancer lurking within their bodies.

At a time soon after 1950 I was returning from an ACS meeting in the East, and had a change of planes at the old Dallas Airport. As usual, I had a few hours layover before my plane for SFO would arrive, so I began wandering around the airport searching for some way to kill time. Eventually, I came upon this beautiful big spread set up by the AmCS concerning cancer of the esophagus, citing the symptoms and suggesting an immediate visit to "your doctor" in case such symptoms were noticed. I knew that I had been plagued with a sore throat for a couple of days, and I knew that I was hurting in the throat—except when I concentrated on just where I was hurting when I swallowed. But this attractive advertisement was quite seductive—better than anything that was to be accomplished at a later date in Joe Camel ads. I could hardly wait to get to my doctor when I got home, and he told me there was nothing wrong with me except for the sore throat that came along with my cold. But I had an upper GI x-ray anyway. The climax to this story involves two papers which I have seen and filed—but cannot now find; we did not have computers in those days. One was by an oncologist and the other was by a psychologist. Each gave a similar report—differing as might be expected in the different professions. A surprisingly large percentage of their cancer patients were subject to depression. Judging from my own experience and other stories I have heard, this is the worst aspect of the efforts of the AmCS to keep a major segment of the population perpetually worried for fear of cancer. The AmCS hit the jackpot with that program, and it seems to work better all the time—even Medicare says that they will pay for it once a year. I have just read in the San Francisco Chronicle that came today about a surgeon who worked for two years and spent $100,000 of his own money in the campaign that convinced Congress to pass the law which has resulted in issuance of the stamp regarding breast cancer. The AmCS is not really getting its fair share of the billions of dollars involved here.

With the AmCS enlisting the federal government as an ally, opposition seems fruitless, but I will invoke a paper on the subject of early detection of cancer by Hardin Jones, a friend of mine and a professor of medical physics at Berkeley. This paper was published in The Annals of the New York Academy of Sciences during the 1950s. I was well acquainted with Hardin and know that he was an honest man and capable at interpreting epidemiological studies. He also had no ax to grind, except that he was trying to make a useful contribution to knowledge. Ergo, it should not be surprising that I have more confidence in Hardin Jones than in a million items presented by the AmCS. Professor Hardin Jones found that cancer victims who refused any kind of therapy lived longer and experienced a better life than those cancer victims who accepted any kind or combination of orthodox cancer therapy. He made a separate comment about victims of breast cancer, for he found that those victims who refused any kind of treatment lived on average four times longer than those who accepted therapy. I did not learn of this report until after my mother had died of breast cancer. Nobody knows how long she lived with the cancer, but it was more than five years and may have been more than ten years. She was a firm believer in predestination, a doctrine of the Presbyterian Church, and was not about to report her condition, even to her older son who was a medical doctor, until the pain became unbearable. A next-door neighbor who was an RN dressed the lesions for "many years." Whenever I think of the pitiful letters I received from Memur during her last days, where she said that she could not understand why "the Lord is keeping me around for so long," I become even more bitter against agencies of our own federal government, a segment of the medical profession, and the AmCS, all of whom cooperate to kill off about two hundred thousand cancer victims per year.

At this point in my chronicle, after having read or re-read quite a stack of printed sheets, and having not read a somewhat larger stack of printed sheets, I have concluded that such a formidable amount of opinion and analysis has been presented on both sides of the issue that any further addition to this argument by me is unlikely to have a significant effect. There is an abundance of evidence available. There remains only the simple fact that many people are unwilling or unable to base a conclusion on an analysis of the facts, rather than accepting the opinion which is most attractively presented. There is nothing new about this in politics, but now this matter of life and death has become intertwined with politics. In view of this situation, of which I am well aware, I will end the presentation of facts in this chronicle by presenting two items, written by me at different times, which will serve as brief surveys that will bring this report up to the last time of my involvement in the cancer controversy. The first of these items is an article written, by invitation, for publication in The Vortex, which is a publication of the California section of the American Chemical Society. With respect to this article, I must recognize the much appreciated assistance with the writing supplied by Bob Grinstead, who was editor of The Vortex at that time. This article resulted in many letters to the editor, nearly all of them in support of the article. Those opposed came from two individuals, and I was able to give adequate answers to their objections. The object of including this article at this point is, hopefully, to make clear the nature of metabolic therapy and how it works to prevent cancer or to act as an effective therapy against cancer which has already attacked a victim. As I have been reading too much of the lurid language used by the detractors of metabolic therapy, I have come to realize two things. First of all, I believe that those attacking metabolic therapy know exactly what they are doing, and also know a lot about mob psychology and bigotry. On the other hand, much of the audience of these detractors do not know enough about metabolic therapy and the nature of cancer to understand that they are victims of a con game. If this sort of logic is near the facts in the case, I hope that some of the victims of the cancer establishment will read my article, which is reproduced below, and consider the facts in the case.

After the following article, which appeared in the June 1978 issue of *The Vortex*, I will present a letter to the editor by me which gives brief statements referring to events occurring after the publication of the following article.

ASCORBIC ACID, AMYGDALIN AND CARCINOMA
by James Cason

The objective of this report is to present a brief summary of some of the things known about the prevention and therapy of cancer by utilization of proper nutri-

tional factors. This type of cancer therapy is aptly described as metabolic therapy, for reasons which will be developed subsequently; however, the news media usually refer to this approach to cancer therapy as Laetrile therapy, on account of the political attention directed to this component of metabolic therapy. Indeed, the entire subject of cancer therapy has become so entwined with politics and social principles that a sober and thoughtful examination of the facts in the case has become difficult; some of those who have been on the firing line for a few years would say impossible. It is not surprising that emotions would run high regarding the subject that I have the temerity to address, because there is involved lingering death in agony of some 380,000 U.S. citizens per year, as well as the jobs of those who depend on the cancer industry, which involves many billions of dollars per year.

Brief consideration suggests that therapy of cancer is of little importance compared to prevention, except of course in the case of present cancer victims and their families. However, since some 1% of our population is afflicted with cancer at present, this leaves about 99% who are deeply interested in not becoming cancer victims, ie, in prevention. In spite of this truism, we hear much about therapy and little about prevention, except concerning the search for low levels of carcinogens in the environment, which has produced no visible reduction in incidence of carcinoma. I will try to work these two aspects of the cancer problem into a coherent presentation.

In order to understand the principles of metabolic therapy, I have searched in both conventional and unconventional places, and have had the good fortune to become acquainted with two of the MD's who are proponents of this type of therapy. Perhaps a good starting point is to present a few concepts, according to my understanding of them.

The Nature of Cancer and of Orthodox Therapy

The most prominent physical evidence of cancer is the growth of a malignant tumor, but this is merely a symptom of the disease. The cause of the tumor is failure of the immune system to throw out the foreign cells. Treating the tumor is comparable to taking antihistamines for allergy problems. The symptoms may be relieved temporarily, but there is no cure or even alleviation of the disease. Nevertheless, orthodox cancer research and practice has concentrated solely on the tumor. Indeed, the Food and Drug Administration, with support from the National Cancer Institute, Sloan Kettering Institute, and other agencies, has specifically decreed that the only valid cancer therapy is that which causes remission of the tumor—further, this must be demonstrated in test animals before use on humans is allowed. If a specific tumor is destroyed by x-ray or surgery, and another appears later, it is said that the "original" tumor metastasized, ie, spread to a new site. Evaluation of damage to the host animal is subordinated to the effect on the tumor. I am unaware of a statement in the "orthodox" literature that the second tumor grew for the same reason that the first one did. Metastasis is the term always used. There is something wrong with the immune system when a tumor appears, but the orthodox methods of attacking a tumor invariably damage the immune system severely. As a matter of fact, the chemotherapeutic agents are mitotic poisons, and radiation is widely recognized as carcinogenic. Small wonder that the epidemiological studies of the late professor Hardin Jones, first published more than 20 years ago, found that cancer victims who refused therapy lived longer and experienced a better life than those who accepted any kind or combination of orthodox cancer therapy. He found that victims of mammary cancer who refused treatment lived on average four times longer than those who accepted therapy.

Metabolic Therapy

The metabolic therapist declares that treatment should not only specifically avoid anything known to be damaging to the immune system, but should adopt unusual procedures in order to help the animal to build up his immune capability so as to reject the foreign cells. First let us mention use of a nitriloside (a beta-glucoside of an alpha-hydroxy nitrile) whose function is to inhibit or stop tumor growth. That is certainly a good start in helping the immune system in its fight to eliminate enormous numbers of foreign cells. (In case the tumor is physically interfering with normal bodily functions, and is accessible, the metabolic therapist will recommend surgery—minimally as required to eliminate the interference.) Before proceeding to other methods of helping the animal fight back by building up the immune capability, perhaps something should be said about how a nitriloside such as amygdalin (Laetrile, vitamin B17) is believed to function. Amygdalin is a nitriloside commonly used because it is readily available in sufficiently pure condition.

HOW DOES A NITRILOSIDE WORK?

There are some twenty different nitrilosides occurring in at least twelve hundred different plants, many of which are used as food, both historically and at pres-

ent. All those which have been investigated are accompanied in the plant by two enzymes, a beta-glucosidase which rapidly cleaves the beta-glucoside to yield a sugar and the alpha-hydroxy nitrile (in the case of amygdalin this is mandelonitrile), and a lyase which cleaves the alpha-hydroxy nitrile to HCN and the carbonyl compound. When a nitriloside-containing food, such as apricot kernels or bitter almonds, is chewed, this macerates the plant tissue and allows the enzymes to get at the nitroloside, hence the bitter taste due to release of benzaldehyde when apricot kernels are chewed. As soon as the material hits the mammal's stomach (except ruminants), the acid of the stomach inactivates the beta-glucosidase so that the alpha-hydroxy nitrile is released only by acid-catalyzed hydrolysis, slow at 37°C. Thus, ingestion of a nitriloside supplies a low but steady level of HCN in the animal's system. (Parenthetically, HCN has about one twentieth the toxicity of ephinephrine or acetylcholine, which are normal, indispensable regulatory components in animals, including man.) Man and other animals have an enzyme rhodinase, which converts cyanide to thiocyanate, which has useful functions in metabolism (including control of sickle cell anemia crises). It should be noted that development of this enzyme requires a steady supply of cyanide during the evolutionary process, and furthermore suggests that the animal having rhodanase experienced an advantage which helped it to be a surviving species. Nitrilosides are the only food component which supplies the required low level of HCN, and they occur in twelve hundred plants!

There are at least three theories as to how the HCN interferes with tumor growth, but all theories regarding the action of nitrilosides recognize a steady low level supply of HCN as an active agent. The simplest theory postulates that malignant cells do not have rhodanase, hence are poisoned by the cyanide. (Metabolic therapists report that non-malignant tumors are not inhibited by nitrilosides.) Two items bearing on the function of HCN will be mentioned. Some years ago, German investigators found that low levels of cyanide injected into mice inhibited tumor growth. The technique was not pursued because of the difficulty in regulating a steady input of HCN below lethal levels but at tumor-inhibiting levels. The nitriloside does this "automatically." Second item: it has been noted as strange that so few cigarette smokers actually come down with lung cancer, when they are gas chromatographing on the epithelial lining of the lungs (hence concentrating in spots) the most potent known carcinogens. Even cigarette smokers who do come down with carcinoma, generally experience it after a considerable period of time, and many who die of something else have "incipient" tumor for-

*mation in the lungs. Various explanations of this phenomenon have been pro-
posed, but I want to mention that cigarette smoke contains considerable HCN!*

PREVENTION OF CANCER

*If nitrilosides inhibit even massive malignant tumors from growing, then they
must be capable of preventing tumor cells from getting a foothold. There is, indeed
an abundance of epidemiological data in support of this thesis, from all over the
world, but we must be limited here to a few illustrations. Let us start with African
nations where nitriloside-containing foods is a staple of diet among numerous populations. In a 1958 publication famous African physician Albert Schweitzer stated
that for "several decades," his hospital in Lamberene in Gabon did not see a single
case of cancer among the Cassava-eating tribes. In 1971, Oshawa reported that the
natives in the Lamberene area obtain eighty to ninety per cent of their calories from
cassava, with the remainder being green bananas, wild herbs and occasional meat.
Cassava tubers contain about 0.5% of a nitriloside.*

*Next I refer to studies by the Loma Linda Hospital and the USC Medical
School of the incidence of cancer among Seventh Day Adventists in the "carcinogenic" Los Angeles basin, where the Adventists live and work and play amongst
the rest of the people. Except that the rest of the people have more than three times
the incidence of cancer suffered by the Adventists. The religion of the Adventists
forbids killing any animal, so their diet is heavily vegetarian, and that is where the
nitrilosides are. It has been estimated that the average daily consumption of
nitrilosides by the US population is less than 1 mg. per capita, whereas the average consumption among the Adventists is 6-8 mg. At the other end of the scale,
among the Hunzakuts (natives of the Himalayan Kingdom of Hunza), it has been
estimated that the average daily intake of nitrilosides per capita is greater than 100
mg. The Hunzakuts are Moslems, but with a few local twists on the religion, such
as eating apricot kernels; and the priests see to it that the brethren abide by that
part of the faith. Indeed, a young woman is regarded as not properly marriageable
unless she has at least seven apricot trees in her dowry. In a report from The World
Health Organization, after a study of morbidity of the Hunzakuts covering one
hundred years, not a single death from cancer was reported.*

BUILD-UP OF THE ANIMAL'S IMMUNE CAPABILITY

*Immune capability depends on many things, and varies greatly among indi-
viduals; however, it seems generally true that an animal in top physical and men-*

tal condition will have a more potent immune capability. The terms "fighting spirit" and the "will to live" are often heard in the medical profession. This factor is well recognized by the metabolic therapist, who does everything he can to improve the cancer victims physical condition, as well as his state of mind—the will to win the fight and lead a good life free of pain and physical disability. Build-up of the physical condition depends heavily on diet. For example, no animal protein is included in the diet; the necessary amino acids are taken in pills and obtained from plant proteins; also, proteolytic enzymes are included in the diet. The idea is that digestion of proteins requires the most energy of any type of foodstuff, and the cancer victim, being under extreme stress, profits from any relief of burden, particularly on the liver. In general, however, the diet is not unduly restrictive, includes all fresh fruits, vegetables and grains. The most important part of the diet, perhaps, is inclusion of a large amount of vitamins, especially ascorbic acid.

THE ROLE OF ASCORBIC ACID

The idea that vitamin C is intimately involved in the mechanism by which animals fight stress was first promoted by Irwin Stone some forty years ago. Few people paid much attention to Stone's ideas, but some did.

When Linus Pauling began to support Stone's ideas, people began to listen, but when Pauling went so far as to declare that ascorbic acid is beneficial to cancer victims, the Federal Government refused repeatedly to provide financial support—just as they have for everybody else who declines to follow the lines of research decreed in Washington. Pauling is one of a very short list who had the reputation, ambition and determination which makes research possible under those circumstances—hence the inevitable paucity of published research on "unorthodox" (not prescribed in Washington) methods of cancer therapy and prevention. (At least Pauling has not yet been officially accused of being a criminal, which is a better fate than has befallen those who persisted in providing metabolic therapy to those desperate, dying cancer victims who came to them and asked for such therapy.)

There is an accumulation of evidence that ascorbic acid is indeed critical in an animal's capability to fight stress, and it is remarkable that humans, one of a very few species with a genetic deficiency of being unable to synthesize ascorbic acid in the liver, have been able to prosper. Their ability to think and to use tools overcame even the inability to make ascorbic acid. Of course the abundance of ascorbic acid in raw food was no doubt helpful. Among significant items, as regards the role of ascorbic acid in resisting stress is the following: a one hundred fifty pound goat makes about thirteen grams of ascorbic acid daily under ordinary circumstances, but if a goat is put under stress it will produce up to twice that amount. It seems reasonable, then, that ascorbic acid would help man to resist stress—such as generated by virus infections and cancer. It has long been known that under ascorbic acid deficiency, wounds simply do not heal, but heal rapidly under high ascorbic acid intake. In the populations of low or no cancer incidence, it is well documented that they eat considerable nitrilolsides, but I am unaware of any quantitative reports regarding how much vitamin C they eat. It is true, however, that they eat a lot of the stuff. The above-mentioned study of Oshawa of the diet in Gabon referred to green bananas and wild herbs. It is no doubt proper to say that vitamin C may be as important in prevention of cancer as are nitrilosides, or at least that the supporting role of vitamin C in enabling the animal to resist stress is so important that it is integral to the specific attack of HCN on malignant cells. Cameron and Pauling have published data showing that vitamin C alone is certainly helpful to a cancer victim.

ASCORBIC ACID THERAPY OF CANCER

In 1976, Cameron and Pauling published the results of an ongoing investigation of cancer therapy with vitamin C at a hospital in Scotland, where Dr. Cameron is in residence. The investigation applied to eleven hundred cancer victims who had been diagnosed as "terminal." One hundred (matched for sex, age, and type of cancer for comparison with a control group) were given 10 g./day of vitamin C, and the remaining one thousand were the comparison group. The ascorbate-treated patients lived on average about four times longer than the comparison group. At the time of publication in 1976, all the comparison group were dead, while sixteen of the hundred who received ascorbate were alive. One year after this publication, I quote Pauling, "Thirteen of these 'hopeless' patients are still alive, some as long as five years after having been pronounced untreatable, and most of them are in such good apparent health as to suggest that they now have normal life expectancy."

FDA: LAETRILE IS WORTHLESS

The FDA pronouncements on metabolic therapy (always termed Laetrile therapy) are developed along two principal lines:

1. The demonstrated fact that thousands of people with well documented clin-

ical histories which declared them to be terminal cancer victims, are enjoying a good life years later, after going to metabolic therapy, is simply rejected by the FDA as "anecdotal" evidence, therefore of no merit.

2. The FDA has decreed that it is unacceptable to "experiment" with any drug on humans until after efficiency and safety are proved in animal tests. They further declare that animal tests have "repeatedly" failed to demonstrate efficiency of Laetrile against cancer; therefore, use on humans is forbidden by simple decree. Neglecting the considerable expert opinion, including employees of Sloan Kettering Institute, which vigorously disputes the reality of these "failures", I wish to suggest that it is not difficult to report failure in animal tests of this sort if (a) "only " Laetrile is used, with no support of the animal's immune system; (b) the effectiveness of the agent tested is judged solely by whether the tumor goes away (longer life of the animal and lack of metastases not acceptable as positive evidence). After all, this is merely a re-run of the tactics that have failed to accomplish anything at all in alleviation of cancer, after about thirty years and hundreds of billions of dollars.

Last year, Dr. Harold Manners, biologist at Loyola University, reported on several years of experimental work in which not just Laetrile but metabolic therapy was applied to mice. Using pure strain mice from Jackson Laboratories which develop spontaneous tumors, Manners reported a hundred per cent cure. The tumors degenerated and went away. Therapy was begun only on mice where the tumor had reached the "lethal" stage. He invited the FDA or other government scientists to observe and repeat his work. About eight months later, I have not heard any reports that his invitation has been accepted.

Those in my audience who receive no message from this report need not feel lonesome; you are accompanied by virtually all those whose livelihood depends on a flourishing cancer industry. For your benefit, I would like to close this report with a bit of philosophy. If I believe that eating 100 mg. of nitriloside and 2 g. of vitamin C per day will prevent me from becoming a cancer victim, and I live according to my stated convictions, and I am wrong, I suffer no penalty for my poor judgment, because I am doing nothing other than eating food that is commonly regarded as nutritionally beneficial. If one who believes that all this stuff about cancer resulting from nutritional deficiencies is nonsense, lives by his convictions, and he is wrong , that individual stands a very good chance of paying an awesome penalty for his faulty judgment.

(End of article entitled VITAMIN C, LAETRILE AND CANCER)

Before proceeding to the next item which I plan to introduce, I will pose a question related to the last paragraph of the above article: This paragraph presents two options, of which the first appears to me to be a win-win situation, while the second appears to me to be a lose-lose situation. Why would a person who appears to be intelligent and reasonable choose the second option?

After I have entered the next item, I will pose another question. Next, I will consider possible answers to these rather puzzling questions. Here is the March1982 letter which I submitted to The Vortex:

SIR: In view of the considerable publicity which has been generated recently, especially in THE VORTEX, regarding the "official" trial of Laetrile (amygdalin) sponsored by the National Cancer Institute (NCI), with cooperation of the Food and Drug Administration (FDA), I would like to present a few facts in the case. I do not propose to offer opinions, only facts which may be readily verified by anyone wishing to do so.

1. The NCI sponsored clinical trials admitted to the testing program only patients that have been pronounced terminal; that is, the medical profession had declared that there was no hope of saving the lives of these cancer victims. Ergo, the "test" of amygdalin could tell only whether it is better than any combination of orthodox therapies. The test was arranged so that no information concerning the comparative effectiveness of Laetrile and orthodox therapies could result.

2. After only a few months into the test, alleged major scientific conclusions were announced to the news media with no peer review at any time, with no presentation of raw data, and with announcement that a scientific publication would be "several months" away.

3. According to the NCI data, amygdalin injections were made for twenty-one days, at which time 70% of these terminal cancer victims were said to be "stable." The injections were then discontinued, and it was reported that "within one month of beginning Laetrile treatment, 50% of the patients showed evidence of disease progression and 90% showed progression within three months". [Insert to the original letter: Note that no injections were made after 21 days, but the just-cited reports were made after one month and three months. Thus, the "official tests" were made according to a protocol which bears no resemblance to the protocol developed by John Richardson, M.D.]

4. The amygdalin (Laetrile) used for these tests actually could not have contained more than about 15% amygdalin, since its infrared spectrum (supplied by the FDA) showed no detectable absorption at about 4.4 mu, the position of absorption by the nitrile group. Ergo, there is no evidence that the "amygdalin" used for the tests contained any amygdalin. An authentic sample of amygdalin shows absorption at this wavelength, as it must.

I believe that an outline of the sequence of events surrounding the statement in Item 4 is in order. Since this will require the remainder of this letter, I will start a new sequence of items.

A. After the NCI concluded, from observed benefits to a majority of about 15 people with cancer who had received metabolic therapy, that an "official" test was in order, the FDA declined to approve of the test on the grounds that they permitted tests on humans only after benefits to animals had been demonstrated. [Insert to the original letter: As for the allegation that benefit to animals had not been demonstrated, this is purely fictional, as has been demonstrated in different laboratories; cf. my Vortex article.] About a year later, the FDA announced that it would support the NCI tests; no public explanation was provided. They also stated that they would supply the amygdalin (Laetrile) for the tests.

B. At this point Robert Bradford, President of American Biologics, a major supplier of legal amygdalin in the U.S. offered to furnish the amygdalin for the tests at no cost. The FDA declined on the grounds that this would give advertisement to American Biologics.

C. Bradford then requested a sample of the amygdalin to be used, for purposes of examining its purity. FDA refused, so Bradford invoked the Freedom of Information Act. FDA refused, on the grounds that this was not information but material.

D. Bradford then demanded the specifications for the material to be used, under the Freedom of Information Act, so FDA sent technical data, including the infrared spectrum. There was no absorption at about 4.4 mu in this tracing.

E. Bradford demanded that the trials be held up until Laetrile that was Laetrile (amygdalin) could be provided. FDA refused. Bradford threatened to go to court, so FDA persisted in its refusal.

F. In June, 1980, Bradford, Michael Culbert (for the Committee for Freedom of Choice in Cancer Therapy), and Bruce W. Halstead, M.D. (for me personally and my cancer patients) filed suit in U.S. District Court, northern District of California, seeking an injunction to stop the trials until such time as authentic, identifiable amygdalin should be used.

G. On November 5, 1980, the judge entered an order that the case was thrown out of court on the grounds that the plaintiffs "had no standing" to sue an agency of the federal government.

H. So the tests proceeded.

I. On January 5, 1981, plaintiffs in above-cited case appealed to the U.S. Court of Appeals for the ninth Circuit. That case remains pending.

J. Plaintiffs in the above-cited lawsuit have never asked anything except for the federal and state governments to cease blocking privately financed efforts to accumulate information concerning metabolic therapy as provided to those cancer victims who asked for it.

JAMES CASON

Berkeley

A few comments concerning the events just described are in order.

1. All of the people involved with this "test" of the efficacy of amygdalin in cancer therapy were completely ignorant of the chemistry of amygdalin; otherwise, they would have never sent an infrared spectrum to Bradford which showed no absorption at 4.4 mu.

2. The people at the NCI and FDA were so anxious to avoid a test of the efficacy of amygdalin that they resorted to both cheating and lying to avoid such a test.

3. After the test was in progress, the appeals court rejected Bradford's suit on the grounds that it was moot; the trial was already in progress. This certainly has the odor of cooperation of the courts.

4. After these tests were announced, but before they were started, Nobel Laureate Linus Pauling wrote a letter to the NCI, in which he stated that any cancer patient who had received chemotherapy should not be included in the "tests," on the grounds that such a person's immune system had been damaged to an unknown extent. Such a person is obviously not a proper subject for testing the efficacy of anything, including Laetrile. When the raw data was finally published, it was revealed that only patients who had received chemotherapy were accepted for the test.

We are now ready for my second question; my first question was presented after the end of my Vortex article. The second question: During a period of some forty years, there has accumulated an abundance of irrefutable evidence that metabolic therapy has never injured anybody and is more effective than any known type of orthodox therapy. In contrast, all orthodox therapy, except surgery, is known to be carcinogenic, frequently lethal for an otherwise healthy person. By what rational procedure of reasoning can nearly all high officials of state and federal government institutions and of the American Cancer Society continue to fiercely fight against a FAIR TEST of the efficacy of metabolic therapy?

Since an answer to this question is likely to be so closely associated with an answer to my first question, it seems rational to consider the two together. The most obvious and simplistic answer to these questions is to conclude that any people who are demonstratively guilty of lying, cheating, and often-repeated breaking of federal and state laws are such black-hearted criminals that they would not hesitate to kill off some three hundred thousand people per year with cancer in order to protect their respectable positions in society. So far as concerns the AmCS and numerous government officials whose behavior is well known to me, I am inclined to believe that such a simplistic idea might well apply to a majority of the people involved. However, it simply does not make any sense to even consider the possibility that this sort of idea applies to the many millions of dedicated professionals in the area of health care: medical doctors, registered nurses, and all the other professionals involved in the most important industry in our society. And, as I pointed out in an earlier chapter, members of the medical profession clearly rate, in comparison with other professions, as the highest in regard to intelligence and faithful devotion to their profession. The most rational answer to this dilemma that has come to my attention is presented in a commentary by Patricia Griffin, R.N., co-author with John Richardson, M.D., of Laetrile Case Histories. Griffin wrote the introduction to this book. Among the words of wisdom which she presented in this introduction are the following:

"The hardest pill for many professionals to swallow is the thought that they have been wrong and, further, that they and their colleagues have strongly criticized those who have been right. How humiliating! There comes a point, after years of administering drugs for almost every human ailment, and after scoffing at 'those silly food faddists' for preaching nutrition as an alternative, when the professional finds himself backed into a corner. He has put down drugless medicine so hard and so often that his reputation now is at stake, and he has a vested interest in his own error.

"I know because I went through it. It was not easy to accept drugless medicine as a scientifically valid approach to health care. And it especially wasn't easy to let go of all the pet theories about cancer etiology and to view this seemingly complex disease as merely variable manifestations of a single vitamin and enzyme deficiency. But a person can deny reality only so long. My personal experience with patients on Laetrile therapy since 1972 no longer leaves room for skepticism. What I have seen with my own eyes is convincing beyond any doubt. Laetrile is effective in control of human cancer."

I think that there is not much that can be added to Pat Griffin's wise statement. However, perhaps I can amplify it slightly. She states, "But a person can deny reality only so long." That statement applies if the "person" has a strong character and is honest. Otherwise, the "person" will do anything, including kill off droves of people in order to avoid admitting his error. Quite discouraging; but if there is understanding of the problem, there is hope. Sometimes, the "right" person comes on the scene, such as James Madison, who put together our Constitution after spending years of travel studying governments. I have read that Madison's putting together such a document is not as remarkable as his ability to persuade a gang of politicians to adopt it.

Stanislaw Burzynski, M.D.,Ph.D.

I have had no personal contact with Burzynski; however, his history looms as such an important chapter in the history of cancer therapy that I have decided to include a brief report of his activities. It fills the gap between my report on this subject and the time of this writing (1998). Most of the things presently reported by me have been gleaned from the twenty page report which I have received from the Dr. Burzynski Legal Defense Fund. There are many interesting aspects of the Burzynski story which are entirely different from the other things covered in the present chronicle. First, his work deals only with the therapy of cancer, not with its prevention. Second, he worked for years and established a reputation as a research biochemist prior to his involvement with cancer therapy. Most interesting of all, his first contact with the FDA, in 1978, was friendly. They inspected his small manufacturing plant and gave him some constructive criticism. The inspectors were cooperative and gave excellent advice on how to improve his processes. Burzynski later commented, "It was exactly as I thought the government should act in such a situation." After the AmCS put Burzynki's procedure on its "Unproven Methods" list, the behavior of the FDA was very different indeed. And so who is the lead villain in this sordid story?

Stanislaw R. Burzynski was born in 1943 in Poland. His father taught classical Greek and Latin, and attempted to persuade his son to study languages and the violin. However, "Stash," as he was known to his friends, showed great interest in chemistry and won an award for his performance in the chemistry "Olympiads." By the time he reached the medical academy, he had developed a passionate interest in biochemistry. His first published papers on amino acids and peptides appeared while he was still a medical student. He graduated from the Medical Academy in Lublin in 1967, and stood first in his class. He received his Ph.D in biochemistry in the next year. He was one of the youngest people in his country to hold both M.D. and Ph.D. degrees. His dissertation for the Ph.D.degree was concerned with investigation of amino acids and small peptides by use of paper and thin-layer chromatography. Amino acids are the building blocks from which proteins are made. Peptides are small chains of amino acids, whereas proteins are very long chains of amino acids. While still working for his Ph.D., he discussed with his chemistry professor three "lines" on his strips of paper chromatography. He was told that these lines had been observed before but that nobody had investigated them. His continuing investigation of these "lines," many years later, led to his publication of several papers and eventually led to his study of cancer therapy.

When Burzynski graduated from college with his two advanced degrees, he encountered problems characteristic of brilliant, independent-minded people. His status as a "boy wonder" in college inevitably generated jealousy rather than admiration among his associates. (As has been said by some wise man, "A prophet is not without honor, save in his own country".) Exacerbating of this situation, he refused to join the Communist Party. Ergo, he found himself drafted into the Polish army, one of two doctors drafted into the army from the Medical Academy that year. After he suffered through two years of that kind of service, with the help of influential scientists, he was able to secure permission to emigrate.

When Burzynski arrived in the United States in 1970, he initially stayed with an uncle in the Bronx. Since the prophet was now out of his own country, he soon landed a position as a researcher and assistant professor at Baylor College of Medicine. His appointment was in the anesthesiology department, working under Dr. George Ungar. He had an arrangement with Dr. Ungar: he would work half-time on Ungar's projects, and would be free to pursue his own projects. This arrangement proved to be mutually beneficial, and Burzynski was able to move quickly ahead on examining the small peptides which he had encountered in his graduate studies. He continued his work using his own blood, but later switched to urine. Another Pole, S. Bondzynski, had discovered in 1897 that urine also contains peptides, and Burzynski found the composition to be similar to that in blood, only more complex. In Houston, he was able to make rapid progress in his investigations. In 1974, he received an NCI grant, which enabled him to add to the equipment available at Baylor by buying a free-flow electrophoresis machine.

With this excellent equipment at hand, Burzynski was able to make rapid progress to evolving a theory that these small peptides were actually messengers able to give commands to the body such as "stop cancer."

He coined the term "antineoplaston" to describe these peptides. (Neoplasm is a word, based on Greek, which means "new growth," and is commonly used to mean "cancer"; hence, an antineoplaston is a substance which issues commands to stop new growth, such as cancer.) Burzynski's research with antineoplastons was greeted enthusiastically in the scientific community and the press. He presented a paper at the 1976 Anaheim meeting of the Federation of Associations for Experimental Biology (FASEB). The work was done in conjunction with the vice-chairman of the Department of Experimental Therapeutics at M.D. Anderson Tumor Institute. Out of 3,700 papers presented at the meeting, this paper became the lead AP story on the gathering. This event proved to be the beginning of the end of Burzynski's peaceful life with his wife, as he worked as an inconspicuous researcher in Baylor's anesthesiology department. After the AP story appeared, the Baylor Cancer Research Center came to regard Burzynski as an "Important Find," working in their own backyard (the anesthesiology department). He was asked to become a member of the Cancer Research Center, and the University gave him a $30,000 grant to support his research. There was one "condition" attached to the offer to become a member of the Center. He must give up his private medical practice, which had been the principal source of money to support his research. Burzynski declined the offer!

As for the reasons for this action, the writer of this chronicle can understand them. After all, I was well acquainted with John Richardson, whom the FDA killed off. I was well acquainted with such emotions in earlier years, but, fortunately, only a few people were involved. Perhaps Burzynski remembered his earlier encounter with the Polish bureaucracy; perhaps he had not come to America in order to become a cog driving a larger wheel. He has been reported to have said in later years: "Most medical breakthroughs have happened because there was some lack of suppression by the supervisors of people doing some innovative work. Look at insulin, discovered by a graduate student while his supervisor was on vacation in Europe."

In the year before the FASEB event, George Ungar, who was responsible for bringing Burzynski to Baylor, was ousted from the university in a power struggle. He was replaced by a 70-year old anesthesiologist brought out of retirement to become head of the department. He did not like

Burzynski, who was his predecessor's protege. Just before Christmas 1976, Burzynski was informed that his laboratory space would be cut in half. He applied to the NCI for money to save his work. His grant was approved in 1977, but funding was delayed. He knew that he might have to wait as long as four years to get the money, during which time his entire project might well collapse. He realized that he must leave the university—a very difficult decision, for academic life was in his blood, but it had to be made. When he left Baylor he was given a "certificate for meritorious service" by Dr. Michael DeBakey, famous president of Baylor College of Medicine. However, parting words from the chairman of his department were not auspicious: "Just wait, Burzynski, they are going to kick your ass."

On leaving Baylor, Burzynski made the most important decision of his life. He decided to proceed with the testing of antineoplastons on people. As he must have realized, this spelled the end of his peaceful life devoted to research. Apparently he also realized that getting clearance from the FDA would entail such long periods of waiting and cost so much money that it would be unlikely that he would ever get his antineoplastons into use for the benefit of cancer victims. And so he made another fateful decision. He decided that he would go ahead with tests on people, and worry about the FDA when that problem should arise. This writer is well aware of what would have happened if Burzynski had not made the difficult decision to simply detour around the FDA. As will be recounted in Chapter 16, I waited some 15 years for a small drug company to get approval from the FDA for an arthritis therapy which had been proved by tests on me, some friends and some animals to be very effective. The sad ending of that story is recounted in Chapter 16.

After Burzynski left Baylor University, he was able, by diligence and hard work, to gain permission for testing his antineoplastons in two hospitals. His results were very successful, and became publicized in the news. In 1978 he experienced his first visit from the FDA, which was friendly and cooperative, as has been reported earlier in this chapter. Unfortunately, his local colleagues appeared to become jealous of this young upstart who was attracting so much attention. In 1978, the Board of Ethics of the Harris County Medical Society launched an investigation of Burzynski, repeatedly called him in for interviews, and instructed him not to give interviews to the press. He followed this demand for about two years, at which time a New York health crusader named Gary Null published a story in Penthouse magazine entitled "The Suppression of Cancer Cures." Publicity about Burzynski's antineoplastons reached a climax in 1981 when ABC's 20/20 aired "The War on Cancer: Cure, profit or politics?" Following this event, literally hundreds of cancer patients began flocking to Burzynski's Houston clinic. After this publicity, Burzynski heard nothing more from the Harris County Medical Society, but the killer instinct of the AmCS was aroused.

In 1983, the AmCS put Burzynski on it's "Unproven Methods" list. This list is effectively a blacklist of practitioners of whom the AmCS does not approve. It serves as an overt warning to researchers about the kind of research for which the AmCS will provide funding. Shortly after Dr. Burzynski landed on the AmCS blacklist, the previously friendly FDA filed a civil suit in federal court to stop Dr. Burzynski from manufacturing his drugs or treating patients with them . Robert Spiller, the FDA's Associate Chief Council for enforcement, issued a warning to Federal Judge Gabrielle McDonald, as follows: "If this court declines to grant the injunctive relief sought by the government, thus permitting manufacture and distribution of antineoplastons by defendants, the government would then be obliged to pursue other less efficient remedies, such as actions for seizure and condemnation of the drugs or criminal prosecution of individuals." In her decision, Federal Judge McDonald issued an injunction prohibiting Dr. Burzinski from shipping his drugs in interstate commerce; however, she specifically refused to interfere with his treating patients in Texas.

This battle has continued to the present time, with the FDA marshaling more manpower and money, and the Dr. Burdynski Legal Defense Fund raising enough money and enough contributed manpower and womanpower to hang in there and hold them off. In spite of the AmCS's best efforts, Dr. Burdynski is still saving people's lives. A high point, hopefully a turning of the tide, was reached on September 7, 1995, when Joe Barton, Chairman, Committee on Oversight and Investigations, U. S House of Representatives, wrote a letter addressed to the Honorable Janet Reno, Attorney General of The United States. The beginning of this letter follows:

Dear General Reno,

As Chairman of the Subcommittee on Oversight and Investigations, I am requesting a full investigation of very disturbing charges involving employees of the Department of Justice in Washington and the Office of the United States Attorney in Houston, Texas.

The body of the letter was more than a page of single-spaced typing. At this point, the very highly abbreviated story of Stanislaw Burdynski, M.D., Ph.D., which I have introduced as an epilogue to Chapter 15, merges into current times. I have before me a VCR tape bearing the following label:

Congressional Hearings on FDA Abuses of Authority
July 25, 1995 and November 15, 1995
1996 Burzynski Legal Defense Fund

So far as I have heard, in May 1998, The FDA is still trying, but Dr. Burzynski is still healing patients. And AmCS is still collecting money by the bucketful.

CHAPTER 16

ARTHRITIS AND ME

My mother developed arthritis during middle age, and the symptoms became more severe as she grew older. During her last several years, she was able to get around in the house only with the use of a walker. Thus, I was aware that I might expect to encounter problems with arthritis; however, my brother, who was eight years older than me, and my father, who was forty-five when I was born, had no arthritic problems at all. Thus it was not surprising that I had no expectation of such problems until I began to feel such pains myself. As has been reported in Chapters 1 to 3, I led a vigorous life during my youth. This strenuous activity continued during my early years at Berkeley. In 1955, I first noticed some pain on a few occasions while walking the long distances required to move around on the hilly Berkeley campus, but there was nothing chronic or severe. I had no problem at all climbing around the mountains on skis to get to a good viewing position for watching the downhill races at the 1960 Winter Olympics. It was in 1965, at age 53, when I realized that my days of skiing were over. It was on a beautiful day for skiing, when there was about a foot of fresh powder over a hard base—skier's paradise. I was sailing downhill as fast as I could handle it when I caught a tip in the deep powder on a downhill turn and went head over heels down the steep slope. I managed to keep my skis together and parallel so that I stopped the tumbling by digging my skis, which I had gotten crosswise to the slope, into the soft snow to stop my skidding down the slope. I actually did all the right things to stop my tumble, but when my lower ski hit the hard base beneath the powder it stopped me so suddenly that my fanny was jammed down hard against my heels. This was very painful to my right knee, where a lot of cartilage had already been built up. As I was lying in the snow, rubbing my right knee as I straightened it out slowly, a ski patrolman came up and asked if I needed a toboggan to get down to the bottom of the slope. I declined and told him I did not want to end my skiing career on a toboggan. Before I got down to the bottom of the slope, I was sorry that I had declined the offer. I had no instinct to do any more skiing. I have always been a firm believer in the old adage, "Stop while you are ahead." That is why I was able to defeat the Peter Principle.

Rebecca and I started skiing when we were forty years of age, under the encouragement and coaching of Joel Hildebrand, a colleague of mine on the chemistry faculty at Berkeley. Our primary objective was to be able to take our kids skiing, on the grounds that it is a very useful device for generating companionship with the kids and getting them into an activity very useful for growing children. What growing children need most is a strenuous physical activity which is a lot of fun, dangerous but rarely fatal, and generates no problem of conflict with the law. This was a perfect fit with skiing in the days when we were involved with it. This is not the only activity that has changed so much as our society developed over the years that the usefulness of the activity has also completely changed. Everything about skiing has changed, but the most fundamental and damaging change is the incredible increase in its cost. This factor attracts a different kind of people to the slopes—rich people and those who prey on rich people. In the days when we were skiing, if one went into the building usually present near the bottom of the slope to get a cup of coffee or some food, one stuck his skis and poles into the snow and went inside. Only a fool would do that today. This picture tells the story about what is wrong with skiing today, and also makes clear why raising children today is so much more difficult than it was in days of yore. We are grateful that I was not forced out of skiing until our sons were "out of the nest." Our sons continued to enjoy skiing for many years, and were able to handle the disadvantages because of their early introduction to the sport, and their financial capability.

By 1975 my arthritic problems had increased to a point where I began carrying a cane on some occasions. During this period, I learned that aspirin was far better than other analgesics that were for sale over-the-counter. As time went by, I found it necessary to use more aspirin in order to carry on my usual activities, which included such things as felling trees at Camelot, our timber property; driving tractors and other machinery at our almond orchard in Yuba County, and building walls in our steep yard in Berkeley. In the course of these activities, I frequently did heavy lifting, especially when building rock and concrete walls in Berkeley. The muscles I had built up from seven years of gymnastics during prep school and college continued to serve me well. I continued doing this kind of work without intolerable pain by increasing the dosage of aspirin. After about 1970 I began to be troubled by leg pain awakening me several times during the night. I began keeping a record of the amount of aspirin taken and the number of "Ups" I experienced during the night. As long as the number of Ups was between 2 and 5 times during the night, on most occasions I was able to handle this without excessive difficulty by staying abed longer in order to get sufficient sleep. I studied several things: (1) What relation is there between the amount of hard work during a given day and the pain in my legs the next day; (2) what relation is there between the amount of work during the day and the amount of pain and number of UPs during the following night; (3) what relation is there between the amount of pain during the night and the amount of aspirin taken during the day; (4) does the amount of aspirin taken during the night have an effect on the night pain during the same night?

Item 1. The amount of work in a given day had a relatively minor effect on the amount of pain the next day, except when very heavy work was done for an hour or more. Very heavy work refers to such things as driving my 5.5 h.p. chain saw, which has a gear drive and 33-inch bar. On some occasions, as will be described in Chapter 18, I had to cut logs 5 feet in diameter to clear log jams from our creek. In order to cut such a log with my 33-inch bar, it is necessary to cut from both sides. In such a cut, pushing down on the saw as hard as the engine will handle it is hard work, and at least a half hour is required for one cut. Fortunately, we had finished with clearing log jams including that kind of logs by 1973, when my arthritic pain began to get worse.

Item 2. The effect on night pain related to the amount of work during the preceding day was similar to the effect on the next day, only more pronounced. I learned not to overdo the very hard work during the day, because of paying for it during that night.

Item 3. I was unable to establish any relationship between the amount of aspirin taken during the day and the amount of night pain. I spent considerable time on this effect because of the possibility that the night pain might be caused by metabolic products of the aspirin. This is possible because the effect of aspirin as an analgesic could result even if its metabolic products caused night pain. By considering items 1 and 2, one can conclude that the night pains are not due to a causative agent which is derived from the aspirin.

Item 4. It was difficult to get more than a qualitative answer to this question; however, I did learn some other things. The amount of arthritic pain definitely depends, in a non-linear manner, on the extent that the muscles and joints are being worked at the same time. During sleep at night, one is doing very little work, even if quite restless, so the effect of the analgesic is less noticeable. On a very bad night, resulting from too much very hard work during the preceding day, aspirin does exert a very helpful analgesic effect.

As a final commentary, I will note that unless the arthritic pain is rather mild, aspirin is unlikely to completely eliminate the pain, but it certainly has been very helpful to me in rendering arthritic pain tolerable over many years. As is widely observed, an "ordinary" headache may be completely relieved by two or three aspirin tablets. As is also recognized, migraine headaches are in a completely different category. I am fortunate to have not had difficulty with this sort of headache. During the years of my large, chronic consumption of aspirin, I had no "ordinary" headaches, and mild bruises were also no problem. Arthritic pains are also different from other pains, as is clearly indicated by my experiences, as presented above.

In view of my misfortune in having a very large amount of experience with aspirin over many years, perhaps it is in order for me to make some comments about the sorts of truths and untruths that have been spread concerning aspirin, not only in gaudy advertisements making grossly exaggerated claims of every sort, but sometimes from the mouths of medical doctors who ought to do a little more homework concerning many types of new information being made available during the times in which we live. The claims of Bayer aspirin have been going on for decades: it dissolves faster than ordinary aspirin, it has no acetic acid in it to aggravate the stomach; etc. As for the rate of solution of anything while standing in a glass of water, in comparison with its rate of solution while being churned around in the stomach, that is nonsense. The only tablet that can last for a significant time in the strongly acidic stomach is an enteric coated tablet specially designed to survive the stomach and reach the intestine. As for the presence of acetic acid in the aspirin tablet—enough to smell on removing the cap to the bottle—that also is nonsense. Acetic acid, the flavorful constituent of vinegar, is a weak acid, ionized to less than 10 percent. (The strength of an acid depends on the amount of ionization; a strong acid is 100 percent ionized.) Meat cannot be digested by humans unless the required enzyme is activated by acid. That is why the stomach is well supplied with hydrochloric acid, which is a strong acid, completely ionized. A little vinegar in the stomach is harmless except being worthless for promoting digestion of meat. I happen to be somewhat under-supplied with hydrochloric acid in my stomach, so I must be careful about eating too much meat at one sitting. When I burp, it is very uncommon for me to get that acid feel in my throat. I have an acquaintance who must take daily capsules of hydrochloric acid to retain her ability to digest meat.

The most publicity about aspirin in recent years has resulted from the discovery that aspirin interferes with the agglutination of platelets in the blood, and thus interferes with blood clotting. There followed the concept that one should not eat aspirin for a few days before an operation. This was clearly sound advice, but was overdone until it was recognized that aspirin does not cause internal bleeding, but greatly exacerbates the condition if the person already has a condition causing internal bleeding— such as stomach ulcers. Even at the time of this writing, one continues to hear that aspirin causes internal bleeding. I think that it may be worthwhile to report at this point an experience of mine which clearly reveals a great deal about what aspirin can and cannot do.

On December 23, 1986, I developed an incarcerated inguinal hernia which put me in great pain. It also can lead to perforation of the intestine if not attended to promptly. After toughing it out overnight, I telephoned Peter Patch, my longtime family doctor, and gave him my symptoms. He responded: "You have given me a textbook description of an incarcerated inguinal hernia; do not waste time by coming to my office; go directly to

EMERGENCY at Alta Bates hospital and tell them I have sent you. I will come there as soon as I finish the physical exam I am giving and have located a surgeon who will attend you on the day before Christmas." I was very happy to see the surgeon arrive by the time the hospital had finished processing my papers. He began squeezing the painful lump in my abdomen, which greatly increased the pain until it suddenly abated. When he asked, "Do you feel any better?", I responded very enthusiastically in the affirmative. He then said, "Peter's telephone diagnosis was right on the mark; I will arrange for your admission to surgery." When I told him that I had been eating twelve to fifteen tablets of aspirin per day in order to control my arthritic pains, he responded, "That is not good, but we can handle it; you will experience a lot of internal bleeding which will drain down into your leg, but that will not interfere significantly with your healing." I was quite relieved to hear that, and I told him that I usually heal rapidly on account of eating two or three grams of vitamin C per day. When the surgery, under local anesthetic, was completed at about one o'clock, I was held up for about an hour until my "vital signs" had become normal. Rebecca then took me home for some lunch. When the surgeon examined me on the seventh day after the operation, he took out the surgical clips and said, "You have healed remarkably rapidly; you can now do anything that you want to, so long as you do not develop enough strain to cause pain at the incision." When I asked how much pain, he said that I was intelligent enough to know when to back off if pain developed. I was driving a tractor at our almond orchard the next day, and continued to heal rapidly. I felt very grateful to my family doctor, Peter Patch, the surgeon, Walter Rohlfing, and Alta Bates Hospital for treating me so efficiently and effectively on the day before Christmas. I also chalked up another victory in my mind for vitamin C.

Before leaving the subject of aspirin, I should remark about the great publicity that has developed regarding the taking of one tablet of aspirin per day in order to decrease the probability of a heart attack. This certainly sounds reasonable, and is surely a great improvement over feeding victims of a heart attack with carefully controlled amounts of "blood thinning" drugs. These are the same type of chemical compounds that are used in rat poisons such as Warfarin. It seems to me that the use of aspirin is much safer than use of blood thinning drugs, which are well known to be lethal if mishandled. All of which leads me to wonder why I have never heard about a large scale computerized investigation of the frequency of heart attacks among the millions of people who must be out there who have taken large quantities of aspirin for years. There are other reasons that it would be surprising for me to have a heart attack, but we are now reporting on that pestilence known as arthritis.

By 1975, either my arthritis had gotten worse, or aspirin had become less helpful, so I began searching for some more effective remedy or palliative. Charlie Koch, a friend of mine on the faculty in the chemistry department at Berkeley who has been mentioned several times in this chronicle, knew of my search, and so he reported to me a story which he had heard by chance from an acquaintance in Santa Rosa. According to this report, this man in Santa Rosa told Charlie of an acquaintance of his who had been hobbling about with a cane when last seen, several months previously. When encountered recently, the man was walking along the street showing no signs of arthritis. Inquiry concerning this remarkable change brought forth the information that a friend of the man, a veterinarian, had given him a treatment which the vet had been testing for some time as one of those assigned by the FDA to test the efficacy of this material on animals. Further inquiry by my friend Charlie Koch, brought me the information that the material being tested by the vet was being made on an experimental basis by a company named Diagnostic Data, Inc. On consulting our local library, I discovered—to my great joy—that the company was located in Mountain View, California, which is adjacent to Palo Alto and located in what has come to be known as Silicon Valley. Such was the beginning of my acquaintance with the enzyme now known as superoxide dismutase, commonly referred to as SOD.

My first move was to consult my broker and buy stock in this company. As soon as this stock arrived, I wrote a letter addressed to the president of the company, identifying myself as a professor of chemistry at the University of California. I said that I had been plagued for years by arthritis, and was very much interested in the material which they manufactured that was known in the veterinary trade as Palosein. After a short period, I received a telephone call from Wolfgang Huber, the original developer of Palosein and the founder of the company, Diagnostic Data, which had undertaken the development of Palosein. He was director of research for the company. He said that he would like to have me visit the company as his guest and would like to learn what times in the near future would be convenient for me. I gave him a few dates and times, and he said that he would contact me soon to set a definite time for my visit. I was overjoyed to receive a call a few days later giving me a date and time.

When I arrived at the company I was warmly welcomed by Dr. Huber, who proved to have a Ph.D. degree in organic chemistry which was earned by working under a prominent chemist in Germany. He introduced me to Dr. Mark Saifer, who had a Ph.D. degree in medical physics from the University of California. He gave me much information about the history of the company and his development of the substance called Orgotein, which had proved identical with the substance isolated by another investigator, an enzyme called superoxide dismutase. A dismutase is an enzyme which destroys something, so superoxide dismutase destroys superoxide, which is a free radical quite damaging to biological systems. At this time, Orgotein was the generic name for this substance, while Palosein was the trade name of DDI's product, which was used for intramuscular injection into animals. The more highly purified material, for intra-articular injection into joints, was still under development and would be called Ontosein. He told me that Palosein had been approved for use on animals, but that approval for humans had not yet been sought from the FDA. He finally took me, his wife, and Dr. Saifer to lunch at a club in Palo Alto. His wife was Swedish with a Ph.D. degree in a biological science, and was directing the biological testing of their product. He subsequently sent me several reprints of papers that had been published on their research. I returned to Berkeley quite cheered up over the prospect of a product that was expected to be marketed eventually, which would give me relief from arthritis. That was before I learned about the years and the millions of dollars required to get anything approved by the FDA, with a high probability that approval would never occur.

The 1978 annual meeting of DDI stockholders proved very interesting. The President of DDI, who was named Smith, was not an accomplished speaker, so the main part of the meeting, devoted to usual topics of finances, expectations, and current activities, was rather dull. When the period for questions and answers arrived, however, things became very lively. After a few questions about when they expected to submit a proposal to the FDA for the use of Orgotein on humans, a man named Lyle Baker arose from the floor and stated that he would like to make a report to the stockholders. Mr. Smith addressed Baker by his first name and said that his report would be welcome. Baker started by saying that he was a veterinarian in a small city in California's Central Valley, and had been in charge of testing Palosein on large animals in the program which had resulted in FDA approval of Palosein for animals. He then related a few specific instances where the treatment with Palosein resulted in spectacular improvement in dogs, horses, and cattle. Just before sitting down, he stated, approximately, "It also works on humans." When the meeting closed, Lyle Baker was immediately surrounded by stockholders. Since my arthritic legs prevented me from closing in as fast as many others could, I was on the outer fringes of the crowd, but Baker spoke distinctly and loudly so that I could hear his story.

He had been so favorably impressed with the effectiveness of Orgotein on animals that he decided to try it on his mother, who was confined to a wheelchair with one knee swollen to the size of a football from rheumatoid arthritis. He first gave the prescribed sequence of intramuscular injections to himself, and experienced no unfavorable results whatever. Therefore, he treated his mother according to the protocol recommended for horses. A few weeks later she was working half time in his veterinarian hospital for large animals and spending the rest of her time driving around the county delivering hot meals to the poor. At the end of his story, there was a loud expression of joy and much conversation among members of the crowd with each other. I heard one person say that he was going to call his broker at once and buy more stock in the company. In view of the rise in price of the stock for a few days, there were others besides me that had reached that conclusion. I was much more interested in learning whether I could get Palosein for treatment of myself. When the crowd finally thinned out, I asked Baker if it would be possible for me to buy Palosein from him. He responded that if I would give him a telephone call, he would discuss that matter with me. I had already learned from Wolfgang Huber that it was illegal for the company to sell Palosein to anyone other than a registered veterinarian.

When I telephoned Baker, he said that he would be glad to sell Palosein to me, for he would be pleased to be instrumental in allowing other people to be relieved of the kind of misery that was experienced by his mother prior to the Palosein treatment. He also said that he was unaware of any law against his selling Palosein to others as long as he made no claims for it other than that it was Palosein. He also said that he would be liable if anyone should have unfavorable results, such as anaphylactic shock, on injecting the Palosein. He said that he would be willing to take that risk in order to bring the benefits of Palosein to other people; however, he expected to be very careful about whom he sold it to, and said that he had no hesitation about selling it to me. I assured him that I would be no risk at all, even if anaphylactic shock should be encountered. I told him about my years of experience with injecting vaccine for ragweed allergy, following instructions given me by an allergist in Boston. I also told him that I kept epinephrine at hand in case I should make a mistake. He gave me the price of the injection doses, and I ordered enough for two rounds, following the horse protocol.

After I received the Palosein and started injections, both Rebecca and I were doing what is sometimes called "sitting on pins and needles" while waiting for results. Lyle Baker had told me that it was uncommon to start getting results until after the sixth injection. After the seventh injection, I thought that I was better while working in the yard, but I didn't report anything to Rebecca because I was fearful that I was engaging in wishful thinking. By the tenth and last injection, there was no manner of doubt that I was better, and the swelling of my right knee had decreased. For the next several weeks, I continued to improve to the extent of doing some climbing around the mountains at Camelot. I was in a rather euphoric state of mind, although I continued to find it necessary to continue with some aspirin in order to retain the decrease in leg pains. My fingers, which had become rather deformed, seemed to show no decrease in pain or joint swelling. The swelling of my right knee did decrease considerably.

At this encouraging state of affairs, we communicated with two of our friends who were afflicted with arthritis to about the same extent that I was. One of them was my friend, George Jura, professor of physical chemistry in my department, who was two or three years older than me. The other was Muriel Giauque, wife of Nobel Laureate Bill Giauque, who was also a Professor of Chemistry in my department. Muriel had a Ph.D. in physics, but did not work professionally after marrying Bill and starting a family of two sons. Muriel was Rebecca's friend, but I became better acquainted with her than most of the chemistry wives, partly because of her interest in horticulture and also because she was a very witty and interesting person. Muriel was several years older than me. Both of them were very interested in trying Palosein, so I gave them Lyle Baker's telephone number, and suggested that they make sure that Lyle would regard them as reliable people. He shipped them the Palosein without hesitation. Muriel said she did not need any instructions about making the injections. I had George watch me make an injection, and cautioned him about pulling back on the plunger of the syringe in order to make sure that he was not in a blood vessel. Injections were uneventful for both of them, and of course we exchanged numerous telephone calls giving play by play reports. Since we were following the protocol for horses, on one occasion, I asked Muriel how the Old Gray Mare was getting along. On her next call to me, she inquired about the health of the Old Stud Horse. I introduce this bit of levity to indicate that we were in high spirits. On one occasion, Muriel reported that she was able to sleep on her right side for the first time in years. George reported that he was able to play the violin for the first time in ten years. I include these items to make it clear that there was no manner of doubt about the beneficial effect of Palosein on three different individuals with entirely different backgrounds and early childhoods.

There was also an event involving a dog. My younger son and his wife bought a German shepherd dog soon after they were married. Quite a few years later they were divorced, and the wife kept the dog, to which she was quite attached. As often happens to large dogs, in old age his legs began to give out. It became necessary to force the poor dog outdoors to attend to his biological urges, and so Diane was quite distraught. I suggested to her that she should take the dog to a vet and tell him that she wanted him treated with Palosein. Of course I gave her the background for my suggestion. The vet told her that he had never heard of the stuff, and that it was probably another brand of snake oil that was being peddled. She insisted and told him the story I had told her, and so he finally agreed to try the stuff. "After all, its your money." After the eighth injection, when Diane came home from work preparatory to picking up the kids at school, the dog ran to the door and jumped up on her. The vet wanted to know the name of the company which produced the stuff so that he could buy some stock in it.

As I continued Palosein therapy for a couple of years, making injections whenever they seemed to be indicated, my rheumatoid arthritis disappeared. My knees appeared perfectly normal, on visual inspection or examination by an orthopedist. However, my legs began to hurt me more, which was reasonably attributed to osteoarthritis. In 1980 my age was sixty-eight. I visited an orthopedist who was recommended by my family doctor, and he took x-rays of my knees while I was standing upright. He reported that my trouble was indeed osteoarthritis, and explained the x-ray evidence to me. There was no space between the bones at the knee joint, caused by the fact that the cartilage had worn off and left the bones grinding together. The only cure was to replace the joint. I found this outlook quite unattractive, and so I launched an investigation as I continued with Palosein therapy, which was still giving me significant relief, as confirmed by periodic interruption of the injections. After two or three rounds of this, I remained a believer in Palosein, even for osteoarthritis.

The first step in my investigation was to call my prep school roommate, Bill Massie, who had become a prominent orthopedic surgeon, as has been mentioned in earlier chapters of this chronicle. Bill's report on replacement of knee joints was not encouraging. It was about as follows: "Replacement of a hip joint is not difficult; it is a simple ball and socket; I do it frequently. However, replacement of a knee joint is another matter; it is a hinge joint involving two bones. If I should have occasion to get a knee joint replaced, I would have it done by an orthopedic surgeon who was under 45 years of age and did nothing but replace knee joints. In that case, I would judge that I had about two chances in three that it would be satisfactory and would last for ten years or longer." That gave me a permanent chill about replacing knee joints.

Bill also told me that there was a possibility that the recently introduced operation on the knee called arthroscopy might help me, but the small amount of data available on the procedure gave conflicting results. He also said, however, that he had never heard about any damaging results from arthroscopy. I consulted two orthopedists in my area and both of them gave me the same answer I had received from Bill. One of them, after saying that he had never encountered any damage from arthroscopy, added: "That is more than I can say about some other operations I have done." That set in stone my opinion about replacement of knee joints. I had the arthroscopy done, using a spinal block for anesthesia. I felt no pain and enjoyed the conversation of the surgeon with the anesthesiologist as he was peering around inside my knee joint. Rebecca picked me up at the hospital following the operation and brought me home. I forget whether I used crutches for a few days, or relied on my cane, but the knee had completely recovered after a few days. Immediately after the surgeon had finished the operation, he told me: "I think that I did not do you any good." He was right. Also, everybody was right in that the joint showed no evidence of damage.

At about the time that I had arthroscopy on my knee, I received interesting news from Diagnostic Data, Inc., which had now become known as DDI Pharmaceuticals. The news was that DDI had made an agreement with the German company, Grunenthal, for it to market Orgotein in Germany under the trade name Peroxinorm, which would be the purified material suitable for intra-articular injection. I had previously received a letter from my friend Peter Tavs, the Austrian who was a post-doctoral fellow with me in 1959 and 1960, in which he had reported that if I should need a drug made in Germany he could probably get it for me. He had rapidly advanced to a high position with BASF in Germany, and his wife was working in a pharmacy. Naturally enough, I immediately wrote Peter and gave him the information about Peroxinorm. He responded that he could get it, and so we made arrangements about how much I would need to pay him, and how he would ship it in order to make it pass through U.S. customs. The decision about shipping it was that he would address it to Professor Dr. J. Cason, Department of Chemistry, University of California, Berkeley CA 94720, USA. The green tag for customs would read: "Enzyme for experimental use only, no market value in USA." Incidentally, the statement on that green tag was strictly true. At that time, the FDA had not approved shipment of Orgotein into the U.S. After some time, there came the day when I found that package with that address in my mail box. I will never forget that moment; I could hardly believe my eyes. I find it difficult to properly express my emotions, so I will simply say that I was ecstatic.

Until I actually had the Peroxinorm in my refrigerator, I did not dare search for a surgeon who would be my benefactor and make the intra-articular injections. I found a surgeon who had some of the instincts of John Richardson. When I told him that the material which I wanted injected had not been approved by the FDA, he responded, approximately, "I am not afraid of the FDA." After the first injection had been made, the surgeon asked me if I felt any pain or other sensation. When I replied that I felt no difference from before the injection, he responded, "thank God for that." I realized that he was a little on edge, which I was not. The injection into the second knee developed in exactly the same way as the first. When I came into the office for the second round of injections, he immediately asked if I felt any better or worse than before the first injections. I replied that I could report no difference of any kind. This scenario was repeated for the third and fourth injections, but when I arrived for the fifth injection, I told him that my knees seemed to feel better than they had before the start of the injections. When I arrived for the sixth and last injection, I reported that there was no manner of doubt that my knees felt much better. When I left the office after this last injection, I went to the corner of the waiting room where I had been leaving my cane, and found that my cane was not there. I did not want to spoil such a historical event by complaining about somebody stealing my cane, so I left quietly, while radiating great pleasure. I did have a few bad thoughts about the kind of person who would steal a man's cane out of a doctor's office, but when I got home I found that my cane was standing where I always left it. This improvement continued for about two years, and was especially conspicuous by my being awakened much less often at night by aching legs. I also continued to find that aspirin gave some additional improvement. I was able to work for several hours at Camelot without significant increase in leg pain.

During the same year that I was greatly encouraged by getting injections of Peroxinorm, I also gathered information about the cause of osteoarthritis. Remarkably enough, I obtained this information from a front page article in a June issue of The Wall Street Journal. This article, which dealt with the mechanics of animal locomotion, was a report on the work of Dr. C. Richard Taylor, a physiologist who did his research at Harvard's Museum of Comparative Zoology. Early in his investigations, Dr. Taylor discovered that any large animal, including humans, uses less energy to cover a given distance when it runs rather than walks. Naturally enough, this unexpected discovery attracted most of his attention for many years. His findings may be summarized as follows: When a running animal takes a stride, he pushes off of one foot to rise into the air and plunk the other foot down ahead of him. The tendons in the leg act as springs, which are compressed when the animal drops onto the leading foot. As the animal swings forward and pushes from the foot now leading, the spring expands, as a compressed spring always does when the weight is taken off of it. Thus, a part of the energy used to leap into the air is recovered by expansion of the compressed spring and added to the next stride. Dr. Taylor determined the amount of energy expended by measuring oxygen consumption by the animal while walking or running. The hardest part of the work was training the animals to walk and run on a treadmill. Dr. Taylor estimated that a human sprinting at top speed would draw as much as 50 percent of his energy from expansion of the tendons as springs. The kangaroo proved to be the champion at speeding up with little or no increase in energy, partly because the kangaroo is such a clumsy walker. When the treadmill was speeded up with a kangaroo aboard, as his speed increased from 7 miles per hour to 21 m.p.h., his oxygen consumption per minute dropped by 5 to 10 percent.

When I finished reading this article I realized that I could now understand some things which had puzzled me for years. A phenomenon which I sometimes observed at Camelot was especially puzzling to me. A deer weighing about a hundred pounds could charge ahead at top speed, jump off a cliff eight or ten feet high and land running on a solid rock, without missing his stride. How could that animal, with legs near the hoofs not much bigger than my thumb, withstand such a tremendous shock without showing any injury? Thinking about it simply boggled my mind. Now I can understand. The tendons in that deer's legs absorbed the shock by being compressed by the severe thrust of the animal landing, then expanded to give the deer a noticeably long leap. Most phenomena become simple when one understands the causative factors!

With these factors in mind, one can also suggest a reasonable explanation of why the cartilage becomes worn off the bone ends in a joint as the animal ages and loses the elasticity in his tendons. As the tendons progressively lose elasticity, the shock to the joint increases at every step, especially if the step results in the upper bone coming down hard against the cartilage. According to one of the orthopedic surgeons whom I visited, the sensory cells at the nerve endings which send the pain signals to the brain are in this cartilage. The body responds by building up the cartilage which encases the joint to become thicker and wider. This results in several things happening, among them: the joints become enlarged; they may become deformed by the process; the joints may become sensitive to pain, even from a light blow from the side, but especially if the animal comes down on the joint hard because of a fall, or even losing its balance and lurching to avoid a fall. Even getting off balance enough to put unusual pressure on one side of the joint without actually developing the threat of a fall may cause enough pain to encourage the arthritic victim to start carrying a cane. I have just presented a brief description of a part of the pain I have suffered during the past thirty years of struggling with arthritis.

The cause of osteoarthritis is loss of elasticity in the tendons as the animal ages. Before this gets very serious, the buildup of cartilage encasing the joint is likely to cause swelling of the joint as the body seeks to make room for this newly shaped joint, and this may also cause a poor fit of the joint and generate pain. This stage is called rheumatoid arthritis. This stage may disappear when the abnormal situation at the joint reaches the point where the enlargement and deformation of the joint has run its course, but the pain from physically damaging the cartilage remains, and may increase. Naturally enough, the progression of the arthritis from rheumatoid to osteoarthritis is likely to vary greatly from one individual to the next in accordance with the large variation in environment and activity among individuals.

In all my conversations with medical doctors, including at least three orthopedic surgeons, I have never encountered one who had the slightest idea as to the cause of arthritis. Their attention is focused on the symptoms of arthritis, and the only treatment known to the medical profession in general is cutting and sawing out the joint and replacing it with plastic and steel. Since this is likely to destroy the cartilage that had been built up around the joint, and the sensory cells are in the cartilage, this draconian treatment is likely to relieve the pain. Anything short of a perfect performance of this delicate operation may generate pain for other reasons. In any case, it is likely that considerable time may be required in a knee operation before the person can learn to walk in the new configuration. According to a statement I heard from one orthopedic surgeon, the principle reason for people submitting to the operation is inability to tolerate the pain. And, according to my friend Bill Massie, with excellent surgery "the operation may last for ten years or more."

There is a conspicuous similarity between cancer and arthritis as viewed via the tunnel vision of the medical profession. In both cases, there is a sharp focus on the symptoms of the disease rather than the cause of it. There is a conspicuous difference, however, in the results of this perspective of the medical profession. In cancer, the only possible result of orthodox treatment is a shortening of the life span but an increase of pain. In the case of arthritis, the victim has at least two choices: submission to a draconian biological insult in order to relieve the pain; or live in pain and do the best that he can to manage it. I feel fortunate in being free from legal restraints in choosing the latter course of action. However, the combination of legal incompetence and competence of political activity in business and in nations has presented me with a perplexing sequence of events. At times, I have experienced some difficulty in maintaining my cheerfulness and confidence in my capability. And so the time has come to return to said perplexing situations.

As has been reported earlier, the weapon available for controlling the pain in arthritis is use of superoxide dismutase (SOD), so the mechanics of the action of SOD must be considered. As implied by its name, the enzyme superoxide dismutase has the specific action of destroying the free radical superoxide (SO). There are two ways that SO causes damage to an arthritic. One of these is damaging the elasticity of the tendons, which in turn causes a decrease in the ability of the tendons to soften any blow to the joint. This has been previously discussed. A second way in which SO damages an arthritic is by decreasing the viscosity of the sinovial fluid which bathes the bones inside the capsule which encases the joint. In experiments on animals, it has been found that the viscosity of the sinovial fluid is increased after injection of SOD. The less viscous fluid is squeezed out of the junction of the joints when pressure is applied, and the higher the pressure and the less viscous the sinovial fluid is, the more damage to the joints. In the exacerbation of this situation by a decrease in the animal's ability to supply SOD in old age, the sinovial fluid may become so thin that it is comparable to running an automobile engine without oil in the crankcase. This causes a wearing of the cartilage off the bone ends and thus creates the situation which an orthopedic surgeon observes by x-ray of the joints. When the x-ray shows no space between the bone ends, cartilage on the bone ends must be absent. Since continued grinding of bone against bone is occurring, the surgeon declares that this will eventually destroy the bone ends unless the joint is replaced. This diagnosis omits consideration of the fact that an animal builds new cartilage to replace that which is worn away, and further takes the pressure off the bone ends by building new cartilage around the entire joint. Since the sensory cells that send pain signals to the brain are in the cartilage, this process generates pain for the arthritic, even from a light side blow, but especially when the weight of the animal is put on the joint..

In summary, SO gives a one-two punch to the arthritic. Conversely, SOD deflects both punches. In order to understand how to apply SOD therapy effectively, it is necessary to consider the dual effect of SOD against arthritis. One effect which SOD has is directed against the effect of SO in thinning of the sinovial fluid. Since the joint is sealed by an encasement of cartilage, entry into the joint is possible only by way of the blood vessels. It follows that SOD must be applied into the joint by injection through the cartilage encasement. As has been described earlier in this chronicle, this application of SOD is very effective in reducing the pain of walking; however it has no effect on the tendons because of being confined to the joint. Conversely, intramuscular injection of SOD puts it into contact with all the body fluids, including the blood, so attack on SO can occur where it is needed; however, a larger amount of SOD will be required because of the territory that must be covered. The effect of SOD on the arthritic is interference with the attack of SO on the tendons, which reduces the flexibility of the tendons during compression. This reduces the pain that results from the use of "stiff" tendons, and also reduces damage to the knee bones which results from the stiffening of the tendons acting as springs. It follows that the effect on the knee joints is protection from further damage; it does nothing to cure the damage already done in times past. In its effect on the tendons, pain is also reduced by SOD injected intramuscularly. My experience is that the effect on the tendons is modulated by how much the compressibility of the tendons has been affected by the aging process. When I made intramuscular injections at the beginning of my therapy, before any intra-articular injections had been made, the effect of relieving arthritic pain was quite dramatic. As time went on, and my tendons aged, the relief of pain by intramuscular injections decreased markedly, to the point that I was prompted to again seek intra-articular injections.

The effectiveness of SOD therapy depends on the many variables which apply to different animals. There is one characteristic of SOD which is especially important to humans. The specific arrangement of amino acids in SOD is species specific; that is, SOD from humans differs slightly from bovine SOD. Fortunately, this difference is not enough to prevent the effectiveness of the bovine SOD on injection into humans, but it is reasonable to expect that human SOD would be more effective. It is entirely possible to develop a synthesis of human SOD, since the amino acid sequence in both the human and bovine SOD has been worked out.; however, the magnitude of such an investigation is such that it can be done only by expenditure of sums of money likely to be available only by grants from the federal government. Thus far, the FDA has shown no tendency to encourage such grants. Instead it has worked rather effectively to prevent approval of SOD for use in the U.S. This obstruction has also caused—perhaps I should say allowed—competition in industry which has discouraged significant progress in any research on SOD other than its production from cattle. After I finish with the saga of my efforts to obtain SOD for alleviation of my immobility and pain, I will proceed with a report on the remarkable interferences with the success of my struggle to keep my arthritic problems under control while hoping for ultimate relief.

I diverted the chronicle of injections of Peroxinorm after I had received welcome relief from injection of Peroxinorm into my knee joints by an orthopedic surgeon. As a result of the spectacular improvement of my arthritic pains after these 1981 intra-articular injections of Peroxinorm, I decided to learn if I could get additional Peroxinorm from Germany. In view of the frequent surprises which I had encountered during my quest for relief from arthritis, I had become rather apprehensive about the unknown future. Contact with my benefactor in Germany, Peter Tavs, revealed that there was no problem about his securing additional Peroxinorm for me. I ordered and received enough Peroxinorm to serve for two additional rounds of injections. I stored this material in my refrigerator, since it was marked as good until 1988 if kept under refrigeration.

By 1985, the pain in my knees had remained sufficiently under control with aspirin; however, I had developed considerable pain between my ankles and knees along the shins and along the outsides of my legs. I remembered from my prep school days how those running high hurdles complained of "shin splints," pain along the shins. I had also learned from an orthopedic surgeon that tendons run up the outsides of the legs between the ankles and knees. From these considerations, I decided that intramuscular injections might prove helpful, as had been the case years before. When I contacted the veterinarian, Lyle Baker, from whom I had previously obtained Palosein, I was upset to learn that he had been killed in an automobile accident. To make matters worse, his son, who had taken over the veterinary business thought it was "not right" to sell Palosein to people who would use it for self-injection. I was unable to learn anything about his reason for this conclusion, but his instincts were very different from those of his father, who was widely known for his compassion and pleasure in helping other people. However that may be, the son died of cancer a few years later, and I was left without access to Palosein. I asked Mark Saifer, the head of research at DDI Pharmaceuticals, with whom I had become acquainted, if he could help me to "beg, borrow, buy, or steal" Palosein. He declined. And so the gods and fates were ganging up on me again.

I had lost contact with the orthopedic surgeon who had previously made injections of Peroxinorm for me, and so I decided to use the Peroxinorm which I had on hand to inject myself intramuscularly. This was done in May and June of 1986. There was some improvement after a series of ten injections, but less than what had occurred previously. As I was unable to think of anything better to do, I decided to use the rest of my Peroxinorm for intramuscular injections. After these injections in April and May of 1988, I made this entry in my notes: "There was probably improvement, but nothing spectacular." Needless to say, my spirits were not very high, so I set out to learn if I could make arrangements with an orthopedic surgeon to make intra-articular injections for me.

Fortunately, I was able to make arrangements for the intra-articular injections. Furthermore, Peter Tavs was able to get more Peroxinorm for me. Since he was expecting to retire soon from his position with BASF and move back to his native Austria, I ordered and received without mishap enough Peroxinorm for two series of injections. When I reached my contact at DDI in order to find out what the latest protocol was for intraartic-ular injections, I learned that only two-thirds as many injections were being used. This gave me enough Peroxinorm for three series of injections. This proved to be very fortunate.

This series of intraarticular injections was started on February 21,1989, about seven years after the end of the 1981 injections. After the first injec-tion in this series, I experienced such marked improvement that I began to think about the fact that Rebecca had begun to have enough pain in her legs that she had decided not to ride around the almond ranch any more on her three-wheeled bicycle. On inquiry, she said that she would like to try injections into her knees, since we had more material than expected. Injections in her knees were started at the same time as my second injec-tions. These injections in both our knees proceeded uneventfully. After 120 days, the entry in my notes regarding these injections included the follow-ing quotation from Rebecca, "I have no pain at all in my legs or hips on walking." I have never reached that admirable condition, even in my first series of intra-articular injections. From this latest series of injections, I experienced great improvement, although less than after the first intra-articular injections. I continued with aspirin as before.

As time went by, there developed an increasing difference between the reaction of Rebecca and me to the Peroxinorm therapy. She continued with little change after her injections were made, but I began to notice a signif-icant difference in the pain in my legs, especially after working. The most conspicuous increase in pain occurred between the knees and ankles. Since Rebecca continued on an even keel as my tendons began showing signs of increasing stiffness—losing their function as springs—I concluded that there might be some improvement from intramuscular injections, which would give the SOD a chance to destroy the SO that was causing the increased stiffness of my tendons. Ergo, I used the Peroxinorm which I had left over from the last intraarticular injections to make a series of intra-muscular injections. The results were disappointing. There was little improvement.

As time has gone by, I have experimented with the many NSAIDS (non-steroidal anti-inflammatory drugs) on the market and have experi-enced some improvement over aspirin with the use of ibuprofen. No other therapy that I have tried has been useful to me; however, at the time of my writing this chapter, I am experiencing hopeful results from a naturally occurring substance called glucosamine. Since this is a natural product, the FDA cannot interfere with me or the many thousands of others who are using this substance. The FDA launched a determined drive to acquire authority over natural products, but Congress refused to give them such authority. I suspect that the great publicity over Burzynski's antineoplastons (c.f. Chapter 15) was helpful in influencing Congress, but I think that a major factor was the amount of money spent by the drug and vitamin industry in lobbying Congress. Or maybe even an average congressman was bright enough to realize what an expensive fiasco would have resulted if Congress had yielded to the FDA.

The gloomy outlook for my receiving further significant help from the use of SOD was due to a significant extent to the failure of those in charge of DDI Pharmaceuticals to spend the money necessary to secure approval by the FDA for use of the drug in the U.S. Mr. Smith, the president, seemed to be preoccupied with making sure the company was "financially sound." He overdid this commendable principle to the point where more than a million dollars of unused cash became accumulated. That sum of money could have gone a long way towards securing approval of the New Drug Application (NDA). This became increasingly annoying to Mr. Henry Lerman, who was by far the largest stockholder of DDI. His business was operating a family-owned furniture store in New York, and I never did inquire how he had become the largest stockholder in DDI. A good guess would be that he had some personal experience with the fact that Orgotein (SOD) does work as a palliative or short term cure for arthritis. This would explain his becoming the leader of a proxy contest which succeeded in ousting Smith. Lerman became president while Mark Saifer and Wolfgang Huber retained their positions. Huber advised me to vote our stock in favor of Lerman.

As I have previously quoted Robert Burns, "The best laid plans o' mice and men gang aft agley." Or as it might be stated in modern terminology, even the most carefully crafted plans sometimes suddenly go to hell in a handbasket. Lerman did indeed push hard to get approval of Ontosein by the FDA; however, whatever he learned about managing a small family owned business proved to be no match for the ability of the FDA to stall approval of the NDA. The NDA was finally sent to the FDA, which held up further consideration until a laundry list of new investigations were carried out. At some time after this, DDI attracted the attention of a clever and unscrupulous individual named Ray R. Rogers.

Ray Rogers was engaged in setting up small biochemical companies in Oregon, wheeling and dealing to set up additional companies, merging one company into another until he wound up by 1991 as president and chief executive officer of International Bioclinical, Inc (IBC). Soon after this he targeted DDI for takeover. Although Rogers never stated that what he wanted from DDI was the large cash reserve for a company that size, the officers of DDI were well aware of his intentions. The device that Rogers used was called a consent solicitation, and was allowed in a company incorporated in Delaware, as DDI was, unless the articles of incorporation specifically disallowed such a solicitation. As Rogers discovered, DDI did not have such a prohibition in its articles of incorporation. According to the provisions of a consent solicitation, a group of stockholders holding a not very large percentage of the total stock outstanding could call a stockholders' meeting to vote on replacing the present board of directors. The notice of this consent solicitation could be mailed to all stockholders only a few days before the meeting to vote was scheduled. This caught the present officers and major stockholders with their pants down. Although the notices of annual meetings of DDI listed large amounts of stock in the hands of insiders as "beneficial owners," Rogers read the fine print, and learned that Henry Lerman was listed as beneficial owner of 531,252 shares, although he actually owned only 126,252 shares. The remainder were actually warrants to buy at low prices, probably less than $2 per share, since the company had been selling in that range for years. And so the insiders thought they had a way to retain control of the company without spending any money for it. Rogers and associates had the same opportunity. Henry Lerman and associates panicked and did something which indicates that they were handicapped by a weakness of intellect. They filed a complaint in court and mailed a copy of it to all shareholders. This complaint contained numerous false and/or misleading statements, and so it never came to trial. The "Committee" filed a cross complaint in which the false and misleading statements were documented. The judge threw out the DDI complaint. The "Committee" won by default and took over DDI in 1993.

From this point onward any hopes for further development of SOD rapidly deteriorated. The new owners rapidly phased out any significant development of SOD, and pushed development of various biological diagnostic products belonging to IBC. Most of the cash money acquired by the DDI takeover, which was left over after the costs of the "takeover" were paid, was devoted to buying other small companies. In the annual report for the year ending December 31, 1993, a loss of $1,485,000 (0.30/sh) was reported, of which loss $1,531,000 was attributed to the "control contest."

In a memo to shareholders dated April 6, 1995, the opening sentence was: "We officially changed our name from DDI Pharmaceuticals, Inc. to OXIS International, Inc., following a merger with International BioChemical, Inc. and acquisition of a French company, Bioxytech S.A." The last sentence in this paragraph was: "We have raised enough capital and taken the steps required to continue through the first quarter of 1995, but raising the additional capital required to enable OXIS to realize its potential remains our primary focus." In the annual report for 1995, the next to last sentence of the auditors report by Deloitte & Touche LLP, follows; "As discussed in Note 1 to the financial statements, the company has incurred losses in each of the last three years, and at December 31, 1995, the company's current liabilities exceeded its current assets by $1,469,000, raising substantial doubt about its ability to continue as a going concern." Thus, in a little more than two years, Ray Rogers had taken DDI from a company with a large cash reserve to a company with such a large deficit that the auditor cited the possibility of bankruptcy.

The last report that I have received from OXIS was a form 10-K for 1996. They appear to have not issued an annual report since 1995. According to the 10-K, the stock continues to trade on the OTC market at between one and two dollars per share. In the report on Research and Development, the only reference to SOD was the following:

"Bovine superoxide dismutase (bSOD) has been previously studied in numerous clinical trials by OXIS and other companies. OXIS is not currently pursuing an active research program in bSOD but supplies bulk bSOD for human use and sells an injectable dosage form of the drug for veterinary applications under the registered trademark Palosein."

It is a pity that clinical use of superoxide dismutase for help to sufferers from arthritis seems dead, in spite of the established fact that SOD does alleviate the pain for arthritis victims, both osteo- and rheumatoid arthritis. I have lost hope that the outstanding questions that need to be answered will be answered. There are many millions of people worldwide who are living day and night in pain from arthritis. I sometimes remember comments heard at a lunchtime conversation around a table at the University of California Faculty Club. One person commented, "Well, there is one thing about arthritis; seems as if it never actually kills anybody." There was a following comment, "Is that good?" My only remaining hope is that glucosamine will prove as effective as is currently advertised. For me, the jury is still out on that one, as of the date of this writing, which is in the last quarter of nineteen ninety seven.

GLUCOSAMINE

By the end of 1997 I had tested many things that had been presented enthusiastically in the arena of "alternative medical treatments" for arthritis. Most of them were various mixtures of "herbs," and there were few descriptions that were adapted to repetition or assay of the actual contents of the ingredients alleged to be active. Arthritis can vary so much from day to day for reasons that are difficult to pin down, that even an experienced researcher may be challenged frequently as to the meaning of his experimental results. To make matters worse, there is little evidence of any useful research behind the claims made by most of the alternative medicine practitioners. This situation has been vociferously cited by the Food and Drug Administration and others as a powerful argument in favor of giving the FDA authority to control the activities of all types of "alternative medical activities," including vitamins. I was quite happy when Congress refused to give the FDA this authority. If Congress had vested this authority to the FDA, I have no doubt whatever that glucosamine would not have been approved during my lifetime—or ever, if my experience with superoxide dismutase (SOD), as reported earlier in this chapter, is an example.

What this country badly needs is removal of authority from the FDA to test the efficacy of all drugs, and insistence that the FDA do a much more rapid job of testing the safety of drugs. The FDA was initially set up to test the safety of drugs, and they did a good job of it. Later, Senator Estes Kefauver of Tennessee, in an effort to get elected president of the U.S., built up a big campaign against the drug companies selling worthless drugs at a high price. Kefauver did not get elected president, but he did succeed in having the FDA assigned authority over the efficacy of drugs. This led to the development of an ever-expanding system for testing the efficacy of drugs. This testing of efficacy came to depend on statistical analysis using placebos. In several tests using placebos, which I have examined in the Physicians Desk Reference (PDR), there is always a certain percentage—rarely less than 15 percent—of side effects from placebos. A low point among those I have examined involves the arthritis palliative, Naprosyn (now marketed over the counter as Aleve). Among the side effects listed are constipation and diarrhea. When I started taking Aleve according to directions on the bottle, I developed severe diarrhea. I had read the part just cited in the PDR, but assumed I should pay no attention to the reported side effects since millions of people had taken Naprosyn over about thirty years. It seemed reasonable to not be impressed when a small percentage reported diarrhea and another percentage reported constipation. The end of this story is that I persisted in taking Aleve for long enough that considerable Imodium was required to salvage my digestive system.

The objective of the above narrative and critique is to suggest that the marketplace may be as good a test of efficacy as placebo testing and other types of statistical analysis. In my many tests of arthritic "remedies," I have encountered some adverse effects, but none so damaging as occurred when I became seduced into depending on tests by the FDA. When the public is free to hold the manufacturer or purveyor of a drug liable for the performance of the drug, the supplier of the drug is under considerable duress to supply "drugs" that are effective. That particular aspect of the drug business remains competitive if the FDA can be gotten out of it.

All of the preceding narrative has been generated by the fact that I am thankful for the development of glucosamine derivatives (polymers) as an arthritic remedy. My search for information on glucosamine polymers has led to my learning about some other interesting glucosamine polymers. A later section will be devoted to this.

Location of reports on drugs in the "alternative" medical literature is rather tedious and time consuming, and I presume will remain that way until the PDR organization comes out with the promised "PDR for Nonprescription Drugs and Dietary Supplements" and the "PDR Medical Dictionary, First Edition." I presume that there were earlier reports on glucosamine, but my attention was first directed to it at about the time that I finished writing this chronicle—except for the present Epilogue. A rather effervescent description of it was given in one of the articles sent to me by my friend George Gillies, who spends much time in collecting a library of "alternative medical reports." Very useful to have a friend engaged in this sort of thing! By the time that I received the report on glucosamine, I had concluded that I would not experiment with anything for which I could not draw a chemical formula At about the same time that I received the report on glucosamine, I had also received a report on cetyl myristoleate (CM as it was designated), for which I could easily draw a formula. I ordered a supply of each of these two things at about the same time. The supplier of CM promised to ship my order at once, which was done; so I began taking the stuff according to directions. After about two weeks, I had not received the glucosamine preparation, so I telephoned the supplier, and was told that their inventory had been so badly depleted that it would be a while before I received my order. At about this same time, I received a copy of the September 1997 Medical Letter from Chris Jolles, a surgeon located in Salt Lake City. Chris and I had remained in touch with each other since we became friends while he was taking a class I taught at Berkeley. According to Chris, The Medical Letter is a very conservative publication. They had a report on successful tests on glucosamine for relief of arthritis, but stated skepticism that the tests were properly done. A final statement in the brief report was, "Glucosamine may be useful for therapy of osteoarthritis." Consider that this "reluctant" report on glucosamine caused the market for the stuff to be cleaned out. Next, compare this with the failure of human SOD to gain approval by the FDA, even after SOD had been approved for animals after testing prescribed by the FDA. The only people more dangerous than politicians are bureaucrats.

To continue my adventures with glucosamine, after failing to get any of the stuff by mail order after a lapse of time, I decided to call my excellent pharmacist, Wing Gee, and ask what he knew about glucosamine. He replied, "I sell lots of the stuff, but I have some on hand". When I went down to the drugstore, I found that he had two big bottles (180 capsules), and four small bottles (90 capsules). I bought the two big bottles. Within a few weeks, everybody and his brother were selling the stuff—at least two advertisements on TV in my area. It has turned out that only one company sells only to "licensed medical suppliers," and this product has about equal amounts of glucosamine and chondroitin in it, along with a little manganese ascorbate. (ascorbate is vitamin C). Other products contain many different things, including a laundry list of herbs, and many variations in relative quantity of the components.

At the time that I received the information on glucosamine, I had been taking the CMS preparation for about two weeks, without any observable results, either good or bad. Thus, I naturally started taking the glucosamine,chondroitin preparation which my pharmacist was selling. (More about the nature of chondroitin later.) I followed the protocol on the bottle and in the little pamphlet about the preparation, which Wing gave me.

For more than three years before the arrival in my life of the glucosamine,chondroitin preparation (termed G,C for convenience in my records), I had been keeping records of my "adventures" at night, which were directed toward learning which combinations of material would give me the most comfort and sleep. Efforts to quantify this sort of thing proved very difficult indeed. I had developed a card with entries for such things as number of "UPs" between retiring and arising; "B to B", which was the time between getting up and getting back to bed, for such things as visiting the bathroom, adjusting the bed covers, adjusting the room temperature, etc. I arbitrarily defined an UP as getting out of bed for such reasons as just mentioned. Waking up, stretching or exercising legs, then going back to sleep did not qualify. Another arbitrary decision was that I must arise between a time lapse of 7.5 and 8.5 hours after retiring. There were involved so many other variables, such as receiving good, or bad news near bedtime; weather, especially barometric pressure; noises that awaken one; thunder and lightning, etc., ad infinitum, that I spent a lot of time in frustration. I had never been able to develop a protocol for incorporation into my circadian cycle that would allow me to make reliable comparisons. I have included this short description of my efforts in hopes that any readers will realize why it takes forever to get a drug approved by the FDA. This situation will never change unless Congress removes from the FDA authority to approve the efficacy of drugs.

About five weeks after I started a consistently regular use of G,C, I became convinced that my legs were hurting me less on walking. This is a rather fuzzy thing to compare, since there is no zero point for reference, and things being compared are separated in time by weeks. And the same person may react differently to the same pain at different times. In spite of my awareness of such things, I felt that I was experiencing less leg pain. It is reasonable to conclude that the difference was significant. In any case, I was happy about it, even though the difference may have been exaggerated.

A comparison which is probably more reliable is the matter of number of UPs per night as described in an earlier paragraph. Instead of getting up

4 or 5 times per night, sometimes more on a bad night, I was getting up three or four times, rarely more. Thus, I decided to try some experiments with other things which I had held constant in order to give a test of G,C. During this test, I had taken at bedtime the following: 5 mg. of hydrocodone (as Hycodan, the only hydrocodone preparation on the market which is not accompanied by acetaminophene, which gives me severe diarrhea); 4 x 2 tablets per day of Ibuprofen (which I will term IBU), the last two at retiring; 50 mg. of Benadryl (as Genahist, or one of the other generic names for Benadryl, which cost half as much as in a bottle labeled Benadryl)). Benadryl is inclined to cause drowsiness; hence it suffers a handicap as an antihistamine, but is very useful at bedtime—and much safer than hypnotics.

In the first experiment, I deleted the 3x2 tablets of IBU which I had been taking during the daytime. To my surprise, there resulted only a small difference in leg pain during the day. As time went by, I encountered some other surprises. Tests on eliminating the two IBU on retiring, showed that there resulted significantly shorter times for the first two UPs when the IBU was eliminated. Of course this indicates that IBU at bedtime is helping with my sleeping. Furthermore, as time went by, it developed that taking two IBU when I wanted to do things involving exercise of my legs resulted in a very significant decrease in pain for three or four hours. Although these events seem rather mysterious and difficult to explain, I will report that the Physicians Desk Reference (PDR) reports experiments which showed that at some point during increasing the dose of IBU, the side reactions increase at a faster rate than the desired analgesic effect. There occurs at least twice the statement: "always use the minimum dose that gives the desired analgesic effect."

As for the hydrocodone, I began to notice that although my number of UPs at night was decreasing, the difference seemed to result from much longer sleep for the UPs at the end of the night. I had previously noted that the hydrocodone seemed to be helpful in getting to sleep only on certain nights. Thus, I decided to kick the hydrocodone and find out what happened. I began to get to sleep much more reliably, with only Benadryl and IBU included in my bedtime protocol. Narcotics have a variety of actions, most of them undesirable, and my experience indicates that promoting sleep is not one of the effects of hydrocodone, unless the level of pain is high enough that sleep can be promoted by relief of pain by a narcotic.

And so I finally established a highly reproducible protocol, involving no IBU during hours of being awake, except for two IBU tablets before or during unusual activity involving the legs; two IBU tabs and two Benadryl capsules on retiring. On a few occasions, I took two IBU twice during the day, and they seemed to be effective, not detrimental to the usual behavior at night. On a bad night, occasionally encountered for any of various reasons, I also took two IBU after the second UP.

After about a month on this "new protocol," my sleep had definitely improved by a significant factor, and there was nothing on my cards indicating a previous night as good as those being experienced since glucosamine came on the scene.. On one occasion I had 19 nights of three UPs consecutively, before there was a four UP. There were also three isolated nights of two UPs, but I attach little significance to those, for it was an accidental night when everything happened to come together at once. I do, however, attach significance to the fact that the observed improvement had occurred as I was growing older.

As I am gloating over this development, I must also recognize that this improvement is due only to pain associated with joints. This is what glucosamine is touted for—the repair or replacement of the cartilage in joints. There remains the fact that aging tendons lose their elasticity, and this is the fundamental cause of joints losing cartilage on bone ends, and thus causing the symptoms of osteoarthritis. I continue having pain along the tendons between the knees and ankles, especially along the shins. Continuance of application of pressure to the springs (tendons) causes them to ache at night. This appears to be the major cause of my continuing to be awakened at night, and this type of pain has not changed perceptibly since my having established a reproducible night protocol in my circadian cycle. For younger people—kids of only sixty or sixty-five—whose tendons have not lost so much of their elasticity, the relief provided by glucosamine would be expected to be more spectacular.

As has been noted earlier, night pain is helped by use of IBU at night. As of the present writing, I think that the best time to take IBU at night is after the second UP. Also, I have not yet been able to determine what relationship there is between activity of the legs during the day and pain from the tendons at night. There is a relationship, but it would be a mistake to assume that the relationship is linear. In many biological relationships, there is a threshold below which the effect of the irritant is not significant. This is prevalent in allergic reactions.

Another factor of much importance to old people concerns the fact that relief of joint pain does not necessarily engender any improvement in the sense of balance. Thus, a relief of pain may cause an old person to become careless about the way he or she walks, perhaps stop using a cane—which can result in a fall. And a fall can be serious, or even fatal. Two of my friends died as the result of falls.

Before concluding this topic, I should mention that the May-June 1999 issue of Arthritis Today, published by the Arthritis Foundation, has two very interesting articles: one refers to the several ways that arthritis can affect the eyes; the other is a few answers to questions received from readers concerning glucosamine. The latter article reflects the position nearly always adopted by medical doctors. One sentence reads in part: ". . . there is no data to suggest that [either glucosamine or chondroitin] can help rebuild cartilage once it is lost." This is no doubt a true statement, but there is also no proof that these supplements do not help rebuild cartilage. This is why it is so important that Congress should remove from the FDA authority over "efficacy" of drugs. The present situation is similar to what happens if the defendant in a courtroom should be judged guilty unless proven innocent.

Additional Importance of Glucosamine as a Structural Factor

Before leaving the subject of glucosamine, it is probably in order to describe some of the interesting developments which have resulted from my investigation of the chemistry of glucosamine. In spite of the fact that my Ph.D. dissertation was under the direction of the then-editor of The Journal of Biological Chemistry, and my post-doctoral work was under Louis Fieser on carcinogenic compounds, I had no knowledge of the importance of glucosamine as a structural element in the animal organism. The little that I have learned has surprised me considerably more than somewhat.

The carbohydrate polymer which glues together tough protein fibers to form cartilage is chondroitin. The importance of glucosamine is that it is one component of the disaccharide, whose polymerization gives chondroitin. This is the same type of reaction by which proteins are formed by polymerization of structural units called amino acids. Chondroitin is rather unusual in that it is formed by polymerization of a disaccharide, which is a sugar formed by junction of two small sugars. Nearly all of the polysaccharides are formed by polymerization of one small sugar. Starch and cellulose are formed by polymerization of the sugar glucose. The other half of the disaccharide which gives chondroitin on polymerization is glucuronic acid,which is expensive and not as readily available as is glucosamine. This is why glucosamine attracted attention as a precursor of chondroitin. Chondroitin is also readily available and is frequently added to the glucosamine, in ignorance of whether the preformed chondroitin is useful. Chondroitin is so insoluble in water and body fluids that there seems to be considerable doubt that it is likely to be very useful for incorporation directly into cartilage; however, it seems quite improbable that adding chondroitin will do any harm. A case of "when in doubt, use the shotgun approach." In any case, after a couple of months using the G,C complex, with good results, I am now on night number 20 for use of four capsules per day of glucosamine and none of the G,C complex. The G,C complex I have used contains approximately one glucosamine to one chondroitin, and the protocol I have been following specifies three caps per day. Thus far, I cannot detect a significant difference when the chondroitin is omitted and the glucosamine is increased by one third. I will proceed to explain the idea behind using more glucosamine.

There is a carbohydrate polymer whose name is dermatan, which differs from chondroitin in only one respect: Carbon #5 in the glucuronic acid moiety of the disaccharide which is polymerized to give each of the compounds is epimeric in chondroitin and dermatan. This means that the two compounds differ from each other only in the sense that a right hand and a left hand differ from each other. As everybody knows, a glove for a right hand does not fit a left hand. And it is true that nearly all of the essential biological processes involve such compounds, which are known as being asymmetric. Further, it is true that nearly all of the important biological compounds do their thing by fitting together with other asymmetric compounds. For example, the compound adrenaline, which elevates blood pressure, belongs to the left-handed conformation. The compound which is identical except for having the right-handed arrangement, has no effect on the blood pressure.

Since dermatan and chondroitin are epimers, it is entirely possible that they could have rather different functions. This proves to be true. Whereas chondroitin occurs as a binding material in tissue such as cartilage, dermatan occurs in soft tissue, such as arterial walls, heart valves, and skin. Anything with such a pedigree as that should command some respect. I seem to have no problem with my arterial walls and heart valves, but I do have problems with my skin. My doctor tells me that the horny growths that plague me, especially on my face and scalp, are called skin keratoses, and are malfunctions of the skin. I gathered that the cause of their formation is not necessarily understood, but I have the strong impression that mine are sometimes—if not always—caused by my scratching a little place on the skin because it itches. Some of it is done in my sleep. The doctor tells me that I should avoid injuring such places, for if such a place "breaks out" of its location, I will have to see a dermatologist about getting rid of same. I have had particular trouble with two or three places on my nose, where a little bandage is difficult to keep in place. A few months ago, these pesky places began to improve, and shortly thereafter I learned about dermatan. Ergo, I stepped up the amount of glucosamine. I have only one place left, and it is smaller than it was originally.

There is another competitor for consuming glucosamine. Chitin, which is a polymer of a very simple derivative of glucosamine, acetyl glucosamine, is the substance of which fingernails and toenails are made. Chitin is also the substance of which the exoskeletons of many insects and marine animal are made. I seem to have experienced an improvement in my fingernails, which tend to get brittle and split in "old" people, but I have no satisfactory way of knowing if it is real or a product of wishful thinking.

As a parting shot, I will comment that there certainly are several reasons for increasing the supply of glucosamine, and it is reasonable to expect that these several consumers of glucosamine would compete with each other. However, it is also reasonable to assume that during the millions of years of evolution, the animal would have worked out a system of distributing the glucosamine where it is needed. If the need should exceed the capacity of the metabolic system to generate glucosamine, then supplying more glucosamine from outside sources would, hopefully, be distributed according to need. However, as the capacity for generating glucosamine should decrease with age, the capacity for using it might also decrease. Thus, there probably should be some restraint exercised about immoderate increase in eating of glucosamine. Thus far, I have noticed no difference, plus or minus, resulting from elimination of chondroitin and increase of glucosamine by one-third.

CHAPTER 17

A PLACE CALLED CAMELOT

By the latter half of the 1950s, Rebecca and I began to think about buying some rural land. Except for very large purchases, such as our home, we had never bought anything that we could not pay for with cash on the barrelhead, and we had no intention of buying this rural land until we could pay for it. Our older son, Roger, was out of college in 1960, and our younger son, Marsden, was well on his way. We had begun to accumulate some money from my extra stipends from working in the chancellor's office and as acting dean of the College of Chemistry, and we had increased our reserves significantly by conservative investments in the stock market. In those days it was possible to make money in the stock market by doing one's homework and not being greedy. This sort of thing is no longer possible, but we profited from it while it lasted. Thus, we felt that we were in a position to start looking for attractive land that we could afford to buy.

At this time—prior to 1960—we had become significantly involved in skiing, which we had started at age forty under the tutelage of my friend, Joel Hildebrand. Our objective in learning to ski at that age was so that we could take our sons skiing. We had concluded that skiing was the ideal form of recreation for teenage or preteen youths. This conclusion was based on the concept that what growing children need to facilitate proper development is something to do that has the following characteristics: (1) It is strenuous physical activity which requires significant learning in order to be able to fully enjoy the activity. The more proficient one becomes, the more respect he receives from his associates and the more self-confidence he has. (2) The activity should be dangerous; failure may result in injury, sometimes serious injury; however, the likelihood of fatal injury should be very low, although possible. Nothing is as attractive to children of all ages as flirting with danger. (3) There should be a low probability that excessive daring on the part of one person will cause injury to other people. (4) There must be a very low probability that the activity will promote—or even condone—illegal behavior. It should not attract people whose instincts are directed towards causing trouble for others.

In reviewing this list of specifications one might be inclined to say that it is impossible, and this may well be true if one is speaking in terms of perfection. However, considering anything in terms of its relation to perfection is not a good system for evaluating anything, including one's spouse. I spent some time trying to develop a system for providing a healthy climate for the raising of children, and was unable to come up with anything that seemed to be anywhere near to being as hopeful as skiing. In any case, we spent a lot of happy times with our children skiing. Furthermore, our interest in skiing led us to investing in a very small corporation called the Saxon Creek Corp. This company was formed by a group of chemists who worked for Shell Development Corp., located in Emeryville, California, which is a very small city sharing a common boundary with Berkeley. Although this corporation was formed by a group of chemists at Shell, they had friends at Standard Oil of California(now Chevron) and the University of California, so they decided to let us into their closed corporation.

At the time that Rebecca and I joined the corporation, they had completed the purchase of a magnificent tract of land in the high Sierras, about two miles from Lake Tahoe. It was heavily wooded, and the corporation had also bought the timber rights. There was a beautiful small stream flowing through it on its way to emptying into Lake Tahoe. Since we had been assiduously saving our money in anticipation of buying rural land, this was a marvelous opportunity! Without hesitation, we bought an amount of stock which gave us three lots, one for each of our two sons and one for us. I plunged into the affairs of the Saxon Creek Corporation so enthusiastically that I became a member of the board of directors. We picked out our three lots, one with a magnificent big boulder on it. In view of later developments, I should mention that this land was completely surrounded by U.S. Forest Service land. This did not bother us at the time, for we knew that in the case of "landlocked" land, an owner of adjacent land is required by law to give access to the landlocked parcel. The owner of the adjacent land could specify the point of entry, as long as it was practical to use it. We were not concerned about the point of entry since the Forest Service already had a road which ran immediately adjacent to our property.

We had a prominent San Francisco lawyer named Dick Leonard on our board of directors. He was not a member of the corporation, but had agreed to serve as its lawyer because of his interest in the Sierra Nevada mountains. He had a cabin on one of the high altitude lakes in The Sierras which could be reached only by skis in the winter. Of course he charged us for his services, but lawyers were not so astronomically expensive in those days. At the first board meeting I attended, Dick presented the document by which we requested permission for a subdivision in El Dorado County. There were six or eight members on the board, but four of us went to Placerville to attend the meeting at which the board of supervisors considered our petition. We were shocked to hear them turn us down without any discussion of the matter. They were not about to allow a subdivision back in the woods surrounded by Forest Service land, where school buses would have to be sent in the winter. We assured them that this was a vacation subdivision where there would be no residents sending children to school. They said that we had no way of knowing what would happen as the years went by, and besides, they would probably get involved with keeping the roads open in winter so that vacationers would be able to get in and out. We said that we would sign an agreement that keeping the roads open in winter would be paid for by the subdivision. The exchange of opinions continued until the supervisors declared that they had discussed this thing more than enough, and the answer was no subdivision in that place.

When we consulted Dick Leonard about our predicament, he said that he had recently read about a similar case in Colorado where the land owners sued the government for depriving them of the highest and best use of their land. They won the case! Dick recommended that he write the board of supervisors, advise them of the Colorado case, and notify them of our intent to enter a court action against them on the same grounds. This got their attention to the extent that they agreed to meet with us to discuss the matter. Dick recommended that we hire a Placerville lawyer, which we did. After discussions extending over several months, and carried out mostly by Martin Bayer and me, eventually our Placerville lawyer advised us that this board was not going to back down, even if we actually filed a lawsuit. Dick Leonard advised us that the board knew perfectly well that we were unlikely to invest the amount of money necessary to carry a lawsuit which might last for years. He also advised us that the board would be glad to get this thing settled, and that we should discuss the possibility of some kind of compromise with our Placerville lawyer. It turned out that the board and the Forest Service had already discussed the matter, and were just waiting for us to smarten up.

We finally recognized the fact that we were not going to build a subdivision on our property, and that it would be necessary to recover our investment by swapping our property for property that the Forestry Service would put up for exchange. After some exchanges by mail, Martin and I made another trip to Placerville. We had to wait until Martin could get off from work before we started for Placerville, so we arrived after business hours, but the head of the Planning Commission had told us he would be in his office until seven o'clock. We arrived at about six-thirty and went to the Planning Commission office. The head commissioner was still in his office as he had promised. He told us that the Forest Service had a map showing parcels that they would be willing to trade for our property. Martin said that we could not stay overnight, so would it be possible to have the map mailed to us? The commissioner said that it would be much better for us to confer with the head man at the Forest Service, and he sometimes stayed late in his office, so he would give him a phone call to see if he was still there. He was there—at about 7:15 P.M. That was when we realized that there were a lot of things going on that we had not yet heard about. We were acting as pawns while the head honchos were developing a scheme to get that privately owned land out of the midst of Forest Service land. The creepy feeling that we were being manipulated intensified as time went on.

We got the map from the head man at the Forest Service, and received several comments on how to get to each parcel. This meeting was followed by a meeting of all the stockholders of the Saxon Creek Corporation. There were three or four people, mostly on the board of directors, who volunteered to inspect the parcels of property which were being offered. We were among the volunteers, so we took our younger son, Mardy, with us, dropped him off at Fallen Leaf Lake with his fishing gear, and went on to explore the parcels marked on our map. Some of them were accessed by a road which was hard to distinguish from the surrounding terrain. We had no serious objections to only one of the parcels. By this stage in our negotiations, we had given up on getting a parcel on which we would want to build, so we were making our evaluations on the basis of value to a developer who would subdivide it for building small houses on small lots. By the time we had finished our investigation, a summer storm that is typical in the Sierras was developing, one that has a little rain and lots of lightning, and carries a threat of forest fires, Thus, we picked up Mardy and headed for Berkeley.

At the next meeting of the corporation, it turned out, as we had expected, that all of the "inspectors" had reached the same conclusion that Rebecca and I had reached. The people at the meeting also agreed that we would probably have to drive a hard bargain with the Forest Service to get a trade for all of this parcel. This supposition was borne out in spades. Martin Baeyer, the president of the corporation, bore the brunt of it, but several others, including the Casons, helped whenever they could make a useful contribution. Things eventually shook down to where there was a three-way deal. The Forest Service would trade the whole of the desirable parcel to us, and we would accept the trade only if we could close a pending deal whereby the parcel would be traded to a real estate developer by a certain date a few months in advance of the date when the contracts were signed. Martin Baeyer, as well as the other Saxon Creek members who had been involved in the seemingly endless negotiations, felt that this was not likely to happen since negotiations with the Forest Service brass in Washington would be necessary. All of us had confidence in Martin, who had a law degree as well as an engineering degree, but Dick Leonard, who had carried the ball for us in writing the contracts, insisted that we should try it. To put it briefly, we learned a lot about the entwinement of politics with real estate development. At one point, the representative of the real estate developer told Martin: "You ought to quit worrying about this affair; we have had a man in Washington for two months working on this. Please be assured that this deal is going through." He was right.

We were paid over a period of five years, and it was about twice what the corporation had invested in our original property. As one member of our corporation commented, "I am so disappointed over losing my dream of a vacation home on that beautiful property that I cried all the way to the bank with my money." I think that I have heard a similar comment before—and since—but it certainly was appropriate for the Casons in this situation. As that money came in and was added to the investment we had been making for years in anticipation of the day we would buy rural property, we were able to save a substantial sum of money when we bought 160 acres that were destined to become the nucleus for the place called Camelot.

After Rebecca and I had done some exploring in various places, we arrived at a point where we decided to investigate the big timber areas in northwestern California. We took advantage of the Thanksgiving holidays in 1963, and drove up US route 101 to Garberville in a hard rain on Thanksgiving Day. At that time all of route 101 north of Willets was a narrow, winding two-way road, and we left Willets after dark. I thought we would never get there, and we thought of turning back to Willets to remain overnight, but we stuck it out, and got a nice motel room in Garberville. The next day, we found that the only real estate agent in Garberville, named Brisbin, was not in his office, but when we contacted him in his home and told him we were interested in buying an acreage of timber property, he came to his office promptly. The rain had become a drizzle, with occasional harder rain. He first showed us a sixty acre parcel of old growth redwoods, mixed with Douglas Fir, which belonged to an elderly Italian man who needed some money in his old age, but could not bear to log the trees which he had owned since childhood. Thus, he was selling the sixty acre parcel, which was forested except for a small area where his home was located, for fifty thousand dollars. An attached provision was that the trees could not be logged until both he and his wife had died. We had no intention of getting into the logging business, and we had enough money to make the required down payment; however, we were unsure whether it would be interesting to have our vacation home in the dense shade of a redwood forest. That was before we knew that the average rainfall in that area was about 125 inches per year; however, as we were looking around and thinking, Brisbin gave us some information that completely changed our intentions about what we wanted to buy. He told us that the practice in California at that time was to tax standing timber on its estimated market value at the time the timber land was bought. He also told us that the value of the timber in this parcel would likely be set at no less than four times fifty thousand dollars. We immediately asked him how land that had been logged would be taxed, and he said that the tax would be set on the price paid for the land. He answered our next logical question by saying that he had several hundred acres of land along a good creek that would sell for $150 to $200 per acre. We began thinking of hundreds of acres rather than acres.

We went back to Garberville, got some lunch, and went to Brisbin's office. He called Frank McKee, owner of the land which was for sale, and told him that he had customers who wanted to buy logged land. Would he be able to show them the Bridge Creek land? Judging from our end of the conversation, Frank McKee was not very interested in driving about twenty miles in the rain to show that land unless there was a good chance of a sale. At one point, Brisbin said, "I'm sure they are." Finally, McKee agreed to meet us an hour later at a private road which went off of the Shelter Cove road at a point about two hundred yards beyond the steel bridge across the Mattole River. Little did we dream of how familiar that location would become to us.

We arrived at the appointed spot after about forty-five minutes, and McKee arrived soon thereafter. We followed him along an old logging road, which I would not have traversed if there were not a car in front of us that kept moving. After passing along a place where the road had been cut into the steep side of the mountain, with the creek flowing through a gorge far below us, we soon arrived at a place where the valley opened up to a wide place on the side of the creek that we were on. The mountains rose up on all four sides of the valley, which seemed to amount to some fifty acres extending along the creek. Relatively speaking, the land in this area was not very steep. The old logging road on which we had driven extended to the creek and continued on the other side, but there was no bridge. I concluded that the log jam in the creek at that point was what was left of the old log bridge. I asked Frank McKee where the old logging road went on the other side of the creek. He said that it went up along the creek very steeply and cut into the side of the mountain until it began to level off at a point where it was about two hundred feet above the creek, after which it turned downhill and eventually came back to creek level on the other side of the mountain. He said that the part of the road beyond the creek where we were standing could be reached only by removing the log jam, then fording the creek in a 4-wheel drive vehicle during low water in the summer. He also said that he had not been up that road in years, and there might be a couple of places where it was washed out. When I asked him what other entry there was to this valley we were standing in, he said, "None, except by climbing over the mountains on foot." We began to think that this place was rather attractive.

The part of this area where we had entered was wider than the rest of it and had been used as a landing for the logging which had been done in a rather wide area. It was filled with piles of dirt, pieces of tractors, and randomly piled with logs—it had the general appearance of a battle-ground. A little above the old logging road was a house with most of the roof gone and supported on redwood posts based on concrete blocks. Some of the posts were leaning five or ten degrees. I told Frank that I did not like the looks of the house; it was falling down. He said that was no problem: "You wait until it gets wet in the winter, as it is now, and burn it. That is the way we get rid of everything we don't want." I asked him why piles of logs were left near us, and he said that sort of thing is not allowed anymore.

As Rebecca and I were walking around and thinking about whether we should buy the place without further ado, we went around a curve in the road with an embankment on the uphill side and met a big buck who examined us and then went trotting away. I think that was what did it. We decided that we would buy some of the land, but not until we had thought about it for a day while we drove over to the North Fork of the Eel River, looking for rocks for use in our hobby of cutting, grinding and polishing rocks. We told McKee that we would be interested in buying 160 acres of the land which was in four contiguous forty acre parcels, and he gave us a price. When we told him that we wanted to think about it before making a decision while we took a trip over to the North Fork of the Eel tomorrow, he seemed rather perturbed. On telling him we were rock hunting, he assured us that there were lots of nice rocks around here. We told him that we were interested in hard rocks such as quartz and chert, and said we would be ready to talk to Brisbin about the sale after we got back from the North Fork. When we asked him what was a good place to get dinner, he recommended the Shelter Cove Grotto in Redway, so that was the place that we went to eat. It was at the junction of Route 101 and the road we had used to get out to the land we examined. We realized as events unfolded that McKee thought that we were going to look at some more land, and that this rock-hunting story was just a smoke screen.

After we had finished our dinner and were waiting for the waitress to bring us our check, she came in and told us that Mr. McKee had picked up our tab and would be in to talk to us right away. Now we knew why McKee had recommended the Grotto. What he talked about was that since we were buying four forty-acre parcels, he had decided to reduce our price. We told him that was welcome, we talked some about characteristics of the land we were considering buying, and then we went to our motel in Garberville. The next morning, when we came out from the restaurant where we had breakfast, we met Frank McKee walking down the street. He said that he had come down to get a paper. After some chitchat, he said that he had been thinking that if we would pay him cash he would reduce the price by 12 percent, since he would have to pay that to the money grubbers who would buy our note from him. As I was telling him that this pleased us greatly, Rebecca said, "I want to get a paper before we leave; I will be right back." Frank then said, "Take mine; I take it at home anyway." This was the first occasion on which we realized that in those days, a person who drives a Volvo must become accustomed to being recognized wherever he goes. Just as that situation had begun to change in 1982, we shifted to a 4-wheel drive International Scout, a vehicle more adapted to our needs at that time, and more likely to be regarded as indigenous to the area.

When we got back from our trip to the North Fork of the Eel River, we contacted Brisbin and told him to draw up the necessary papers to put our purchase into escrow. This was simplified by the fact that it was a cash deal, and we asked for only two weeks before the close of escrow. That gave us plenty of time to raise the money by selling stock which we had on hand for this purpose. After Brisbin had made out the contract of sale and other necessary papers, we signed everything necessary to put the purchase into escrow, then went back to the Grotto for dinner.

While we were eating, a waitress came in from the back and yelled at a group of men sitting around a table, "Mary just called, and if any of you see Frank tell him that the big deal just went through." We surmised correctly that Mary was Mrs. Frank McKee. When the waitress brought us our bill marked "paid" and told us that Frank would be there soon, Rebecca commented to me, "I should have ordered that big New York steak." Frank soon showed up bearing maps, and told us about the "King Peak National Recreation Area," which was quite close to our property. We explained to him that we would need a few days to sell stock to raise the money, but we would send him a cashier's check by registered mail as soon as we had it in hand. Frank replied, "I will come down to Berkeley to pick it up; I will visit my father, who lives there."

I had no class on Monday, so Rebecca and I decided to stay an extra day in order to go out to Bridge Creek and take another look at our property. We found more log jams in the creek and still more logs that had been left lying around, but we were quite pleased with the remote location surrounded by mountains. We were especially pleased with the spring we found located just opposite the staging area. I estimated that it came out of the ground about a hundred feet above the edge of the creek bank. This would give good water pressure in our house to be built. We were to learn a few years later that Bridge Creek and the springs that feed it were the best water supply in the upper Mattole Valley. We lucked out on that one.

When I got back to the university late Monday afternoon, Bill Dauben told me that the personnel representative from Proctor and Gamble had been interviewing students that day and was sorry to have missed me. When he asked me why I was late getting back after Thanksgiving, I told him, "Well, we saw this mountain that we liked, so we bought it." Bill repeated that comment to several people.

Our purchase of this mountain was not recorded until early January 1964. During that year, my duties at the university made rather large demands on my time, and family affairs added to the load, with the result that we visited our newly acquired property only twice. On one of these visits Roger and his wife Priscilla, along with their two-year old daughter, Kristen, came up and all of us stayed at the Sherwood Forest Motel, which was the nicest motel in Garberville at that time. The back part of the property of this motel was wooded and extended down to the South Fork of the

Eel River, where there were boat docking facilities, so it was often patronized by fishermen. All of this is no more, for the freeway came through right behind the motel buildings. However, during the two years we worked at our property before our house was ready for occupancy, we enjoyed staying at the Sherwood Forest. During one spring that we were staying there, except for about ten hours per day that we were working at our property, a pair of hummingbirds built their nest just outside our window. We saw the whole operation, from building of the nest to the fledging of the young ones. The fledging occurred during the last few days we were there before we were ready to "camp out" in our house. As things worked out, it was just as well that we did not become involved with development of our property during 1964. That was the year of a once-in-a-century flood in northwestern California. Starting in early December, rain began pouring down; each day the rain seemed to be heavier than the preceding day. At the climax reached just before Christmas, according to the reports that we received, water was running knee deep in some of the streets of Garberville. Mile-long stretches of US 101 were wiped off the mountainside, so that its location could no longer be determined. This highway was the only route between the rest of the state and the part of northwestern California around Eureka and north of there, except for the narrow-gauge freight railway, much of whose tracks were along the North Fork of the Eel. This track was in worse shape than US 101. The bridge across the Eel River near its mouth went down in the floodwaters; however, several miles of US 101 north of that bridge was four lane freeway. This strip of freeway was used as a landing strip for the steady stream of big cargo planes bringing in food and other necessities. It was a small scale operation reminiscent of the famous Berlin Airlift.

As is often the case after record-breaking floods, there was hardly any rain for two months after the deluge. This was very helpful for rebuilding US 101. Most of the road construction equipment in California and some from neighboring states was assembled for the job. It is incredible what a CAT the size of a D-9 can do in earth moving. This must have been a little ahead of the time of the paddle wheel scraper, which can move dirt even more efficiently than a big CAT, for we heard nothing about such a device at that time. During the past fifteen or twenty years we have seen many paddle wheel scrapers working on the huge landslides that continue to develop along US 101. In 1996, a mountainside fell on about a mile of four-lane freeway several miles north of Willets. For about a year, the traffic was routed around this place on the "old" 101. This is a real slow-go affair because of the heavy truck traffic, winding road and steep grades. Ever since the "great flood," the state of California has spent very large sums of money on keeping open that lifeline to Eureka.

Near the end of March, 1965, US 101 became open to two-way traffic, with frequent delays. The Highway Department issued stern warnings against pleasure traffic to northwestern California, but we figured that we were certainly going on business in order to find out what had happened to our property. Since the whole area was still occupied by "relief" workers and construction workers, we had to wait a few days before we could get a room at Sherwood Forest. We had a really slow trip up there, of course, with numerous delays for construction work. When we got out to the private road where we turned off to access our property, we found it heavily rutted but dry, since there had been no rain for several weeks. When we arrived at our property line, whose location we knew because of a little wet weather stream which had flowed through a culvert pipe under the road, we found that the culvert had gotten stopped up so that the downpour had flowed over the road; the road had not washed out, but a pile of dirt about five feet high was on our road. We had expected such things, so we had two shovels and a pick with us. After about two hours we had thrown enough dirt below the road so that we could squeeze through with the Volvo. Nice that we had a relatively narrow car; and so we set out to proceed further. After about a quarter mile, where the road was good because of the rock bluff on the uphill side, we came around a bend in the road where I saw nothing ahead of me except space, with a pile of dirt closing off the road about fifty feet away. Rebecca rose up in her seat and exclaimed, "Where's the road?" I pointed down into a hole which was about the size needed to bury a D-8 CAT and said, "My recollection is that it was there." Our only recourse was to back up about three-quarters of a mile to a spot where we could turn around, with much seesawing back and forth, and head back to the Sherwood Forest, where we had stayed overnight. It was apparent that we would have to hire a big CAT to come in and fix that hole in the road, so this project had to be deferred until summer when I would not have pressing duties at the university, and could spend enough time at this timber property to start some extensive activities.

During the summer of 1965 we spent considerable time at our timber property. Naturally enough, we first directed our attention toward getting our road repaired so that we could get into the place, look around, and decide what to do about a house in which to live. The first thing that we learned was that Frank McKee had decided that he was such a poor manager of his business that he had turned over the management of the large amount of property he had inherited to his brother Max, who lived in Willets. After telephoning Max, I drove down to Willets to discuss with him getting our road opened. He had a D-9 CAT working on property on the Mattole River below the steel bridge which was at the confluence of Bridge Creek with the Mattole. On the side of the Mattole where our property is located, the road to Shelter Cove was cut into the mountain and rose steeply to become higher and higher above the Mattole River. This road was the northern boundary of our property. During "the flood," about two hundred yards of our mountain had slid onto the road and carried it toward the river. Repair of this road had received much attention, for other approaches to Shelter Cove are long and tedious. By midsummer, the repair was rather tentative—a Band Aid job—and further work was delayed pending the results of efforts to secure aid from the federal government.

In contrast to the situation on our side of the Mattole, there was a nice wide valley on the other side, with low hills set back from the river. It was among the trees in this valley that we found the CAT which belonged to Max McKee. The CAT skinner was not about to take the CAT off of the job he was working on without hearing directly from Max McKee. Fortunately there was a telephone in the old house on the property of which we had bought a part. We were able to persuade the CAT skinner to call McKee, who gave him the go-ahead to work for us. Since he had to stay off the road with his big CAT, he drove up the Mattole, under the steel bridge, up Bridge Creek to a place where he could get out of the creek, and then to our private road. As soon as we saw him on our road, we went in behind him to the location of the washout. He was looking across the hole to where a landslide had piled dirt about thirty feet high on the road. Apparently the road had stopped the slide from carrying all the way to the creek far below.

The CAT skinner said that there was no problem; he would put the land-slide that was on the road into the hole. I started to ask a silly question about how he planned to get the CAT across the hole in order to move the dirt, but managed to keep my mouth shut. I told him we would go out to the county road and eat the lunch we had with us, then come back in. He told us not to be gone too long. When we got back, he was sitting on the CAT inspecting his job. He said, "Where ya been, I been waiting for ya to inspect the job and let me know if anything else is needed." When I asked how much I owed him, he said that McKee would send me a bill. The bill was for one hour of work. It must have taken him about a half hour to get from the job he was working on to our job and back. When I first looked at that yawning cavity, I had anticipated a big expensive job. It was later that I learned more about what a bulldozer can do, even a small, ancient trac-tor that we later acquired.

Where from Comes the Name Camelot?

We arrived at the name Camelot for our timber property after we had owned it for several years; however, it is appropriate to discuss that mat-ter at this point so that we can refer to the name rather than other longer and less definitive designations. After we had been in residence for about fifteen years, we could look back with pleasure on our accomplishments. Some of the more pleasant recollections "among our souvenirs" are the fol-lowing: Rebuilding an old falling-down house with trees growing up through the floor boards into an attractive residence convenient to live in during both winter and summer. Clearing numerous log jams extending throughout our mile of creek, with the climax being clearing a massive jam at the downstream side of our property, during which we wore out four chains on each of two chain saws, and shed a lot of sweat and a little blood. Keeping deer hunters off our property, as a result of which we accumulat-ed a herd of some fifteen to twenty deer which Rebecca fed from our Scout until the authorities prohibited feeding wild animals, and which we watched with pleasure as their fawns appeared in the spring. Clearing brush, trees, old logs and other debris from a large area around our house, which serves as an attractive and impregnable fire break around our house. Planting hundreds of redwood trees in cleared areas, some of which are now about one hundred feet high. In a separate clearing project, removed hundreds of tan oak trees, which are a fire hazard, with the assistance of our property caretaker, who used them or sold them as firewood; and transplanted or protected small Douglas fir trees already in place, with the result that in these areas we now have valuable timber trees that are sometimes as much as twenty five feet tall, and serve as another effective fire break. Furnishing assistance to the firefighters during the Finley Creek Fire which burned 180 acres of our property, and giving a little assistance at the fireline by climbing up the mountain with a chain saw and felling a grove of tan oak trees touching the lower edge of the fire break.

In view of these activities and others, we felt it would be appropriate to name our timber property Camelot, as described in the song of the same name as "a most equitable place to live." In particular, we were mindful of a comment by King Arthur, addressed to a young knight who had come from afar to help the king in his battle against his bastard son Mordred. This comment, as remembered approximately by me, was, "Let it always be remembered, Thomas, that there was once a place on earth called Camelot, where might was for right." We hope that the Casons' Camelot will last longer than did Camelot in the stage play. We think that it will.

Our Home at Camelot

As has been mentioned earlier in this chapter, I had considered getting rid of the old falling-down house by burning it. As a matter of fact, we had selected a spot where we would build a house on the creek bank where a projecting promontory had the creek on three sides of it. There was a U-bend in the creek with this promontory in it. It was indeed a beautiful sight, except that we discovered during the winter that this place was totally shaded by the mountain across the creek from it during about five months in the winter. The ground remained frozen there for several months during the winter we observed it. This caused us to re-evaluate the old house above the road, and I began to recall my experience when my brother John, Kit Haynes and I built a cabin on the Rocky River in Tennessee. The thing which gave us the biggest problem was setting the rafters on the frame. The frame with the rafters on it was about all this old house had left. There were only two partitions between rooms inside it; there were plenty of places where Dougfir trees were growing up through the floor. About a fourth of the shingles were gone off the outside walls;

the roof had no sheeting on it, just redwood shingles nailed across two planks in each row, with more than half the shingles gone. There was no ceiling below the roof; the wall at one end of what would be the living room was leaning out at an angle of about five degrees; and last but not least, there had been a hole burned about three feet across at a corner of the "living room" at the end opposite the leaning wall, and the sleeper at this hole was badly burned. Except for these things, the house seemed to be in good shape! I began to think about how many years would be required for us to accumulate enough money to pay for having a house built. If I should rehabilitate the old house, with Rebecca's help on numerous things not requiring carpentry or plumbing skills, I could start at once and proceed just as fast as time and availability of funds would allow. After reviewing what would be required to rehabilitate the old house, I decided that I could do it all. The most important thing was putting a concrete foundation under the house, and I had learned a great deal about that sort of thing by watching the workmen put concrete walls beneath the brick walls of the Old Chemistry Building at Berkeley before excavation of a hole for construction of the Low Temperature Laboratory immediately adjacent to the Old Chemistry Building. Ergo, the decision was to rehabilitate. A final advantage to rehabilitating was that we would hope to have a bigger—and probably better—house than anything we could afford to have built. While working hard on our house for years, we kept our spirits up by dreaming of how nice things would be by the time I reached retirement. In our wildest dreams, however, we did not visualize the sort of house in which I am now sitting as I write on my word processor. This house has three bedrooms, one very small with a double decker bunk bed and a soundproof wall between it and our bedroom—in anticipation of grandchildren; a large two-story living room with a Franklin fireplace; a dining room with a table accommodating eight people comfortably, and a bookcase and a four by eight foot corner table at one end, on which my "old" electronic typewriter and my word processor are located; a small kitchen separated partly from the dining room by a dish cabinet with a microwave oven on top of it, and also containing the water heater and gas-fired refrigerator; two bathrooms, one of which we paid a carpenter to build a few years ago—it has a large shower with a corner seat for arthritics. As this chronicle proceeds, we will encounter numerous other things, such as our water system, electrical system, irrigation system for our tree and grass plantings, etc.

A few days after we had made the decision to rehabilitate, we were stopped on our road as we were driving in by an elderly man named Jim Rinard who was living in the old house on the McKee property as a caretaker, to prevent destruction of the old house by hunters and other vandals. Those days antedated the hippies, who were followed by the marijuana growers. Jim Rinard, who was living with an elderly woman whom he described as his wife (she probably was) was typical of a sort of person living on Social Security in the timber country, who often fulfilled useful functions in order to earn enough money to live a little better than they would otherwise—or maybe to buy a little more red wine. We learned at the outset that Rinard was not really typical of such people. When he introduced himself, using excellent English, he said, "Now, I'm no fox," and spelled his last name. He then said that Mister McKee had told him that we were planning to rebuild the old house on our property, and so he thought maybe we would like to hire him to help us. When I asked if he was a carpenter, he said that he was not a carpenter, but had worked for years as a carpenter's assistant and knew a lot about carpentry. When I asked if he could rip off what little was left of the roof and put on new sheeting over the rafters, followed by fire resistant shingles, he replied promptly that he could. All we would need to do would be to furnish the materials. When I asked him how much he would charge us for that job, he said that he had never figured anything like that, but he would think about it and talk to a friend who was a carpenter. Would we stop by his house tomorrow afternoon?

Rebecca and I talked it over and decided that if he asked for less than $1,200, we would hire him. Rebecca had noticed several bird houses on poles around Rinard's house, being used by bluebirds, and so she decided that if he liked birds that much he could not be all bad. "You can't fool a bluebird." When he asked for $900, we accepted promptly. When I asked him if he would like a hundred dollars in advance before he started the work, he brightened up and said that he would get his saw sharpened. We then arranged that if he started to work within a day or two, we would pay him an additional hundred dollars on Friday of the next week, and on each succeeding Friday until $900 dollars was reached. If he finished the job in ten weeks or less, we would pay him an extra hundred dollars. I told him that we were anxious to get that roof on before the rains set in, and said that we would have other jobs for him that could be done after the rains started. We immediately began ordering the material needed for the roof from Southern Humboldt Building Supply, and advised them that we had told Rinard that he could charge to our account any small items needed for the job he was doing. We assumed that Rinard would not be allowed to buy any large items or items that would not be appropriate to the job. This arrangement worked out very satisfactorily.

This proved to be the start of a very helpful relationship with Jim Rinard. After he finished the roof, we started him to work on the shingles on the side walls. Many of the shingles were missing, but fortunately there was an "old timer" in the neighborhood who was still splitting off three-foot shingles. Frank McKee instructed Rinard on how to properly put shingles on a sidewall. We bought sliding aluminum windows for each of the windows in the house, and Rinard knew how to set them in window frames. After Rinard had finished these jobs, he borrowed a "come-along" from somebody, and we worked together to straighten up the leaning wall at one end of the living room. Nailing this wall into position took quite a while, and it was also necessary to build a triangular wall to fit between the top of the end wall and the roof rafters. This space was vacant when we arrived; apparently, it had fallen out when the lower one-story wall slanted out but did not fall. After this wall was in place, I went to work on door frames and doors for front and back doors to the house which were in the living room. We bought beautiful exterior doors from Montgomery Ward at their sales warehouse in Oakland and hauled them to Camelot on top of the Volvo. While I was working on hanging the doors, which took me several days because of my having never hung a door previously, Rinard was working inside on interior walls. The wall between the living room and the bedroom, which later came to be known as "the guest bedroom," consisted only of studs and the plate on top of them. The studs were parallel to each other, but not perpendicular to the floor. Rinard knew how to straighten them up using the come-along, then he nailed diagonal boards between them to make a very sturdy wall. We worked together on building the soundproof wall between the "master" bedroom and the small bedroom, and also built a short wall between the master bedroom and the guest bedroom in order to generate a space for the bathroom. By this time we had the outside of the house closed off, and the inside was finished except for putting wall paneling on some of the inside walls. There was no ceiling at all above any of the rooms; it was open to the roof. There was also no flooring except the rough boards nailed over the sleepers to hold the house together. However, we solved that problem by using large pieces of corrugated cardboard which we got by careful cutting of the boxes in which the windows were shipped. This provided good temporary flooring for two bedrooms and the bathroom. At this point the house was ready for occupancy after essential conveniences had been provided. One set of these conveniences involved the bathroom and kitchen facilities, which I planned to install, except for the septic tank. The other set involved installation of a propane system which would fuel space heaters and the propane fired refrigerator. For this installation, we would depend entirely on Blue Star Gas in Garberville.

While this work on the house was going on, Rebecca and I had been coming up to Camelot as often as I could get away from my obligations at the university. We planted about a hundred redwood seedlings, most of them during hard rain. The soil at this location was very loose, with much sand and pebbles in it. When we dug a hole to plant a tree, working in the rain, the water drained out of the hole into the gravelly soil below, and so we could plant trees in heavy rain, which we did several times. On some occasions Rebecca would be planting trees while I worked in the house. After we got the roof on the house, we had bought what we needed in the way of plumbing supplies, always from Montgomery Ward, which had a central sales warehouse in Oakland. Such things as a wash basin for the bathroom, shower, toilet, and kitchen cabinet sink, we had delivered to the mail order store that Montgomery Ward had in Garberville. We then hauled them to Camelot in the Volvo. In late March or April, we had the septic tank installed. Putting first things first, I installed the toilet, bathroom wash basin, and kitchen sink, then installed the drainage plumbing and connected it to the newly installed septic tank. Bringing water down from the spring up on the mountain was a major job, so we pumped water from the creek for an interim period. We used a small pump, which was supplied with electricity by a portable electric generator. The water was stored in three 50-gallon plastic containers; two for toilet flushing, dish washing, etc., and one for drinking water and other purposes requiring clean water. Each flush required two buckets of water, and the flusher was expected to fill up for the next use.

The last item needed before we could live in the house was installation of a two-hundred-fifty gallon propane tank, installed by Blue Star Gas at a required distance from the house. This tank was connected to two propane fired space heaters and a refrigerator, also fired by gas. A crew from Blue Star Gas attended to all this in two or three days. At one point, when Rebecca, Jim Rinard and I were watching the activity, Rinard commented, "If this old house could talk, it would have a lot to say."

In anticipation of the refrigerator coming into the house, I had nailed long boards between all the slanting posts, with each post having boards in two directions at right angles to each other. I then chose the place where the refrigerator, our heaviest object, would be located and built my first supporting wall in the foundation beneath that spot. At this point I took our little concrete mixer from Berkeley to Camelot, hauling it on a rented trailer with the Volvo. Concrete blocks, rebar, some bags of cement ordered from Southern Humboldt Building Supply, and a load of aggregate ordered from Randall Sand and Gravel put me in business to build the reinforced concrete wall beneath our house. Since there has long been a lot of seismic activity in northwestern California, I was not about to work for a few years on our house only to have an earthquake shake it off its foundations. Subsequent events proved the wisdom of that decision.

I used concrete blocks to build a reinforced concrete wall without the necessity of building forms and handling large amounts of concrete at one time. With one man working intermittently, this procedure was necessary. The supporting redwood posts were at rather variable distances from each other, usually six to eight feet, but this was no handicap to my method of operation (MO). The house had a center row of supporting posts parallel to the long dimension of the house, which was necessary to reduce the length of the sleepers. In this center row, where the refrigerator was located, I dug an eight-inch wide trench in the ground between the two posts, getting as close to the posts as the concrete footing would permit. Pieces of rebar of suitable length were driven into the ground with a spacing of about 32 inches to fit into the central holes in the concrete blocks. I judged this spacing to be close enough because of the light load the wall had to support. A crosspiece of steel was wired to the upright pieces at about four inches from the bottom of the trench. Pouring concrete into the trench to a depth of six inches then resulted in a reinforced concrete base on which to put building blocks to make a wall. The length of the vertical pieces of rebar was such that a concrete block could be placed over the rod and let down onto the concrete base. The wall was then built up in the usual fashion, using concrete as mortar between the blocks. Only the blocks with steel in them were filled with concrete. Next, the wall was built up to where only the space was left which allowed the blocks to be put over the steel. These blocks were added and filled with concrete in places where the steel was located. In those spots where a vertical piece of rebar was located, a second, short piece of rebar was pushed into the wet concrete for about a foot and wired to the vertical piece. This piece of rebar was allowed to extend above the top block in the wall so as to come near to the sill supporting the sleepers. Before the wall was built up too high, spikes were driven into the sills at a point above each piece of vertical rebar. Finally, a piece of rebar was then set across between the sill and the top of the wall, and wired to the spike in the sill and the steel which had been pushed into the wet concrete. The next step occurred after allowing at least a day for the concrete in the blocks to begin setting. For this next step, which I learned from watching workmen shore up the Old Chemistry Building, I mixed a batch of concrete which had more cement and less water in it than normal. This was packed into the space between the top of the concrete blocks and the sill, where rebar was located. It was packed in firmly from each side until water stopped draining away from it. After a period of an hour or more of standing, this material was tested periodically to determine when it did not spring back after being pressed hard with a strong trowel. This gave a solid seal against the sill which had spikes in the wood projecting into the concrete. NO EARTHQUAKE WAS GOING TO SHAKE MY HOUSE OFF ITS FOUNDATIONS. After two big shakes in subsequent years, the preceding statement has held up.

I actually finished the wall just described about a week after the refrigerator was delivered—a characteristic underestimation of the amount of time required to do a job with which I had not had previous experience. I did not feel at all relaxed until that top layer of concrete had hardened, but this time the gods and the fates did not punish me. The next section of wall to be built was at the southwest corner of our house, beneath the "small" bedroom. At the corner the sill was about five feet off the ground. I proceeded with that wall after I had put some very provisional wiring in the house so that we could get some electric lighting from our portable generator. This wiring was really a quick and dirty job, but I put a fuse block between the house and the generator, which was placed about fifty feet from the house because of the noise. Our little generator was rated at 1850 watts, which is enough for several light bulbs, but not enough to run our table-top toaster and more than one light bulb.

After all these advances had been made, we decided that we were ready to camp out in the house rather than commute from the Sherwood Forest Motel in Garberville. Since it was near the end of May, and we had the propane heaters installed and blankets on the bed, we figured that we would be able to keep warm even with no ceiling, no wall paneling on the interior walls, and a rather porous floor. We were wrong. It was not much better than sleeping in a tent, and we were not prepared with sufficient blankets. Fortunately, the weather began to warm up so that we had no further problems with being cold in our rather open house. We were surprised at hearing no animal noises during the night; there was complete silence. This was probably my first experience with that sort of thing since the days when my brother John, Kit Haynes and I were sleeping in our cabin on Rocky River. Since then, I had been an urban animal, and I really enjoyed the silence.

About two weeks after we had begun to camp out in our house, we had a phone call from Rebecca's brother, Ralph, saying that he and his wife, Eileen, would like to pay us a visit to see our new house and forest property. Rebecca told them that we had just begun to camp out in the house, and so they would have to stay at a motel in Garberville if they did not care to brave camping out in our house. Ralph said that they enjoyed camping out, so we arranged to pick them up at the Arcata airport. We drove through some of the redwood parks on our way from Arcata, then into our valley. Since we had done nothing to clean up the part of our valley that was to become the "meadow," the nearby view was not attractive, but Ralph and Eileen were impressed with our location, which was surrounded by mountains. They were a little surprised at how Rebecca had not been exaggerating when she said we were "camping out" in our house.

They were especially impressed with the lack of doors to any room, including the bathroom. We told them that the heavy drape we had hung across the bathroom door was in their honor. Ralph made some wisecracks about the necessity for hauling water in order to flush. I told him that it was just a matter of time until I had cold spring water running into our house from a spring a quarter mile up the mountain. We had a nice visit with them, and went down to the stream in places where we knew that there were no piles of logs. After they stayed overnight, we took them back to the Arcata airport where they took a plane to San Francisco, then changed planes to go back to Los Angeles.

Just before our visit from Ralph and Eileen, I had started construction of the pipeline up to the good spring we had located. This spring flowed a small stream into Bridge Creek all year round, but I went up the steep bank far enough to get a pressure of about 25 pounds psi, which is a good water pressure for house use or irrigation with sprinklers. After some calculations, I decided that a plastic pipe of 1.25 inch-diameter would give us adequate volume. Of course I had no idea at all of putting steel pipe up that mountainside, even if it had not been much more expensive. Putting the pipeline across our meadow-to-be was just a matter of digging a ditch about six inches deep, laying the pipe and covering it up. Crossing the old logging road required a lot of digging in very hard ground and putting it farther below the surface in order to protect it against damage from tractors or heavy trucks that might be using the road. I continued to remind myself that this water line was to bring water to our house, and hence was in a different category from an irrigation line. I could have rented a backhoe to dig the trench across our meadow, but that was such a small part of the job that I also did that "by hand."

The most time-consuming part of the pipeline construction was taking it across the creek. A small chain was used as a suspension support for the pipe. In order to keep the low point in the catenary curve from being any lower than necessary in order to meet the geometric requirements of a catenary, it was necessary to have firm anchors at the ends of the chain. This low point in the catenary must be as high as practical in order to avoid the rapid deposit of sand and dirt at that point, which would eventually plug our water line to the house. Up to a point, this low point in the catenary is raised by tightening the chain, hence the need for firm anchors. On the side of the creek where our house was located, there were trees that could provide the necessary firm anchor. On the other side, it was necessary to run the pipeline along one bank of the small stream from the spring in order to avoid ups and downs which would cause the same problem just described for the pipeline as it crossed the creek. For about fifty feet from Bridge Creek, the bank of the spring stream was so steep that no trees were growing on it. This problem was solved by driving a heavy steel post into the shale rock to serve as an anchor. Lighter steel posts were used to reach a point where the bank was not so steep and trees and brush were able to grow on it. This work had to be done on a ladder. Of course, the chain did not extend beyond the anchor; the pipe was simply laid on top of the posts, which were driven into the bank at an angle. For the part where the chain was suspended, the pipe was supported under the chain with suitable hangers. Several days were required before I reached a place where the bank was not so steep that I could work on the ground. When I reached this point I was elated; however, I was well aware of several hundred feet of dense forest that had to be traversed.

I continued working up the mountain with the pipe until I reached a point about fifty feet below the point where the intake was planned. In this way I continued to have tools available as I went up the mountain, carrying them but once for the entire trip. I also had a clear space behind me in which to travel as I went down and up the mountain once or twice a day. Of course, I always left the tools where I was working. Since this work was very soon after our arrival at Camelot, I had not yet gotten acquainted with a chain saw. Naturally I looked ahead and altered my route slightly in order to miss big trees, but there was a rather complete cover of brush which I had to chop out with an axe. After some days, I reached a point less than a hundred feet below the planned site of the intake, and at this point I could walk up the spring stream with my tools. Thus, I decided to build a little dam to make a small pool for the intake, and run the pipe down from there to meet the pipe that I had brought up the mountain after many days of work. My next move was to go down the mountain over the path I had cleared, which now had the pipe underground beneath it. I brought back up the mountain the fittings necessary for the intake, the tools required for that, and a nice heavy redwood stake to be set at the point where the uphill pipe met and joined the downhill pipe. Of course, I was thinking of the golden spike that was set where the eastbound and westbound tracks of the transcontinental railroad met.

I set that redwood stake at about 7 P.M. on July 4,1966, after working hard since 8 A.M. that morning, except for eating lunch. Rebecca had climbed up the mountain near noon with our lunch: sandwiches, Fritos, a couple of oranges, and a thermos of coffee. We spent about an hour eating our lunch, and exulting over the imminent arrival of water in our house. I lay down on a nice grassy spot and rested while we talked. After I set the stake, I left all my tools where they were, walked and stumbled down the mountain, down to the Bridge Creek level, back up to our "meadow," and into the house to get a shower with nice warm water. We then set out for Berkeley, with Rebecca driving, as she still does on the first stint of our travels back and forth to Camelot. On this occasion we stopped for dinner at Garberville, at the restaurant we had frequented during the days when we lodged at the Sherwood Forest Motel. I did a lot of sleeping as she drove to Willets, the point where we changed drivers. We arrived at 486 Michigan Avenue at about 2 A.M. We were so hyped up by the adrenaline we had been generating in our systems that we did not feel like going to bed at once. As we were unwinding, Rebecca got a bright idea. She would send a straight telegram to be delivered at once to her brother Ralph. The telegram would be: "Celebrated the glorious Fourth by flushing toilet with running water." After she had given this message to the male Western Union operator, she turned to me and said: "He won't send it; he thinks I'm drunk, and he says that he has orders not to send telegrams from drunks in the middle of the night." I got on the phone and explained that this was a family joke, that my wife was not drunk, furthermore had never been drunk, and finally I said, "She doesn't have to be drunk to act that way." After that crack, the operator broke out laughing, and said that he would take a chance on sending the telegram. So much for Ralph's wisecracks about hauling water in a bucket to flush.

After getting running water to the house, I regarded my remaining urgent priority as putting a section of reinforced concrete wall under that southwest corner of the house which was about five feet above solid ground. I did this following the same protocol used for the section of foundation under the refrigerator. This work required some waiting for the concrete to harden. At such intervals, I went to work on building a structure whose dimensions were about six feet by twelve feet, and which would serve as the powerhouse, containing our 6.5 kilowatt electric generator. This electric plant had been ordered from Kohler for us by Blue Star Gas. This generator was wired to feed a standard three-wire system used in houses so that either a 120 volt or 240 volt electric outlet could be used. It was also wired for an automatic start whenever a load of 50 watts or more was put on the line. Whenever all load on the line was turned off, the generator would stop. This feature was convenient for saving the propane which fueled the generator, and became more important as the price of propane increased from twenty-five cents per gallon to $1.10 per gallon. The system carried some disadvantages, however. When Roger and Priscilla stayed in the house with their small children, Kristin and David, in 1967, the kids had lots of fun turning on the lights, especially in the middle of the night.

While I was busy getting the foundations and the framework of the powerhouse set up, Rebecca was nailing wall paneling onto the studs in the house. We were pushing to get the house comfortable for living in when the cold weather arrived. This objective was actually accomplished because I had no duties at the university for that summer. We lived at Camelot for most of the summer. Driving small nails into Dougfir studs which had been seasoned for at least seventy years was not easy. We first tried the classical procedure of soaping the nails, but this was insufficient. We finally learned that it was necessary to drill a small pilot hole before each soaped nail was driven. This slowed things down, but Rebecca soon mastered the art. I had much less trouble putting larger nails into the framing; soaping was sufficient for that.

When I had gotten well along on the powerhouse, enough that I was putting on the roof sometime in September, Rebecca went to Garberville to bring back the door we had bought for the powerhouse from Montgomery Ward. As I was sitting on the roof, nailing on the sheeting, I heard Rebecca come roaring in on our dirt and gravel road at a rate that suggested she thought she was on the checkered flag lap at Indy. When she arrived in front of the powerhouse where I was sitting, she slammed on her brakes, skidded to a stop, throwing up gravel, turned off her engine, jumped out of the car and ran as if a demon was after her. I was not worried, since she seemed in excellent physical condition, but I was curious about such bizarre behavior. In answer to my query, she said, "I had to open the tail-gate of the Volvo because the door was too long to fit inside, and I didn't have the carrier on top, so I just drove out here with the tailgate open. This worked fine and gave me lots of ventilation to keep me cool, until I turned off the county road onto our dusty road. At that point, the wind from over the top of the car swooped back into the car and fed dust to me. I had to go that fast to keep ahead of the dust until I got to the gravel road near our house." Makes sense.

Rebecca started nailing shingles onto the walls of the powerhouse as I was installing two windows and the door, and putting fire resistant shingles on the roof. We took delivery of our electric generator sometime in September, but getting power into the house was held up for a few days until I installed the line to the house. This was put inside an aluminum conduit which was buried about a foot below the ground. Use of the conduit was a precaution against hitting the wires with a pick while doing garden work. We had two reasons for burying the wire: We prized the natural appearance of our house with no wires strung around. We wanted every modern convenience in our house, but saw no reason for wires to be visible. Of greater importance, no doubt, is the protection against having our power cut off in a storm. We had already become aware of how often the P.G. and E. power was lost in a storm, and how long it stayed off on many occasions. The population density in Southwestern Humboldt County is the lowest in the state except for deserts, and the power company gives the fastest restoration of service to the places where the most people are. Our generator failed occasionally, but less often than the power company wires were down, and we have been without power for more than one night only three times up to the time of this writing. During the period we have been at Camelot, we have loaned our portable generator to neighbors on many occasions so that they could keep their refrigerators cold. On the occasion of long power outages, several neighbors passed our small generator from one to another, each one keeping it long enough to cool his refrigerator down. This small generator weighed only about 85 pounds.

With our 6.5 kw generator installed and the underground wire connected to our breaker box in the house, we were in a position to continue with work inside the house during the winter. My first move was to put wiring into our bedroom, the bathroom, the kitchen, and the dining room. Thus, the ceiling lights in all these rooms were on a single circuit. We put the ceiling lights in each of those rooms, with our bedroom first, and the others finished by the time that we were there during Thanksgiving vacation. Because of the heavy rainfall, which averaged about 125 inches per year at that time, we were there on only a few weekends and during Thanksgiving vacation in the months of November through March. During Christmas vacation, we were engaged in family affairs in Berkeley. Actually, during the winter of 1966-67, we were at Camelot more than we have been there in any winter since. On two occasions we had to put up quite a fight to prevent our road from washing out. There was no fun and games during those visits to Camelot.

During that winter we hired a man named Bob McKee to do carpentry work inside our house. Bob was a nephew of Frank McKee, from whom we bought our land, and he was a prominent person in our neighborhood. He had taught school at the local Whitethorn School for several years and was reported to have been the best teacher they had ever had there. During recent years, he had made his living doing carpentry work and sometimes, during the winter, he did carpentry work in the Bay Area in order to keep money coming in. Thus, he was glad to get indoor work from us during the winter, and it was convenient for us because we were not there. The first job he did for us, very important to be done when we were not there, was putting floors in all the house except for the small bedroom which I did the next summer. This included our large living room which had served as a workshop during our house rehabilitation. We wanted this to be a two-story living room extending all the way to the roof of that part of the house. This required work on a scaffold with two men, which went beyond our capabilities or ambitions. Bob and the assistant he hired did a beautiful job for us, with fiberglass insulation in both walls and roof. In the rest of the house, Rebecca had put the fiberglass insulation in the walls and on top of the ceiling in our attic. Except for the floor, which is unimportant for insulation, our entire house was insulated. At our insistence, Bob put knotty pine paneling in the living room, and all the floors were Dougfir. We wanted local lumber in this house. With the redwood shingles on the outside walls, it presented a rather indigenous appearance.

In April 1967, as soon as the heavy rains had let up, we had Bob start on the construction of our garage, which was 20 X 20 feet in size, large enough for a car and a small tractor, with a workbench in front of the tractor. We had left enough space in front of the powerhouse for this garage to fit between the powerhouse and the end of the road to our house. Bob changed my original plans enough to allow the garage to fit against the front of the powerhouse so that the front wall of the powerhouse became part of the back wall of the garage. The ground at this point presented a slope steep enough that excavation to give a level floor to the garage caused the floor of the garage to be about seven feet below the floor of the powerhouse. Bob put stairs on the left side of the garage so that a landing brought the stairs against the back wall of the garage. Three stairs along the front wall of the powerhouse reached the level of the powerhouse, where a landing was built in front of the powerhouse door. At the intermediate landing a door opened to the outside at ground level at that point. I mention these details to indicate the problems which must be surmounted in building on steep slopes. I have mentioned previously that one corner of our house was about five feet above ground level, but I did not mention that the diagonally opposite corner was at ground level. Bob did his usual strong construction of our garage. The entire front wall had to be two doors for entry of vehicles. The only support of the beam across the front above these doors was at the ends and in the middle; otherwise, no entry for vehicles. Bob used a four by eight inch redwood beam to span this twenty foot entry. This beam has attracted the attention of some of our visitors who had never seen that much redwood in one piece of lumber. The doors, which were in two parts mounted on each side and swinging together in the middle, were made of 2 x 4 redwood studs which were nailed together by cross pieces of redwood. Of course, the floor of the garage was concrete. That garage has stood up over the years, during two earthquakes, and shows no signs of getting out of shape.

Our house also has withstood two earthquakes without damage; however, that was after I had put reinforced concrete walls under the entire house, built a screen porch at one end, and a stone and wood patio in front of the front door. These were built after our present reporting.

CHAPTER 18

SAGA OF THE GREAT LOG JAM

When Rebecca and I looked over the property we subsequently bought, we saw quite a pile of logs in the creek at a point directly below our house, which was about a hundred feet above the creek at that point. Frank McKee told us that these logs had resulted from the collapse of a log bridge which was left after the logging in the late forties. He did not mention that the dirty logging, still prevalent in those days, had left logs lying in many places, especially in places where they would end up in the stream. As we began to get near to the end of the immediately urgent things that were obviously needed, we began taking hikes to explore our property. Since the linchpin of our property could well be regarded as the creek, we explored there first. We were rather shocked with what we saw, but not discouraged. After the passage of a couple of years, we realized that there would have applied to us at that time a statement which became publicized during World War II: "Show me a man who does not crumble under these conditions, and I will show you a man who does not understand the gravity of the situation." Or maybe we were so young—only fifty-five years old—that we just didn't think much of anything except what we wanted to accomplish. However that may be, we found the creek strewn with logs of all sizes and conditions of decay. One day during Thanksgiving vacation in 1967, we set out upstream with a shovel, pick, matches and a satchel of paper to start burning logs and smaller pieces of wood. We pried and pulled together as many things as were amenable to such primitive methods. When we reached the edge of our property, we started back downstream setting fire to the piles of debris as we went back towards our house. Later on in the winter, during the few trips we made during that period, we continued with this sort of operation except for a few refinements, such as taking along an eight-foot piece of one inch galvanized pipe to act as a pry bar. On about our third trip, we went downstream to the edge of our property to where a massive log jam rested. We deferred any further action until after we became better equipped for log clearing.

This monstrous log jam was at the very edge of our property, with its lower edge a few feet above the mouth of a nice creek flowing into Bridge Creek from the south. Thus, this side creek was not on our property, although a part of the headwaters may have been on our property. At its face, this log jam stood about twenty-five feet above the creek bed. During the summer the creek below the log jam was a rivulet running from beneath the logs. It was about a hundred yards upstream from the face of the log jam before the rivulet appeared, running over the gravel in the creek bed. After a heavy rain in the winter, a mighty torrent poured over and through the logs in the jam. Apparently this monstrous log jam developed because the creek flowed through a gorge at this point and a large log became lodged crosswise in the narrow stream. This caused other logs and debris to pile up so that the resultant dam caused erosion of the bank on the north side, where there was a significant area of dirt in front of the rock, in contrast to the south side, where there was a rocky bluff at the creek edge. The height of this log jam at its face could be estimated to within a foot or two because there was a log lying on the ground near the face of the jam, atop the rocky bluff which formed the creek bank on the south side. This log extended out from the bank, over the creek for fifteen or twenty feet. On the first occasion when I came walking downstream, watching my step as I climbed over the logs, I bumped my head on this log. Since that log remained after we had cleared the jam, measurement of the distance from the creek bed to that log could be done at any time.

At the point on the north side of the creek where the log jam built up, there was a magnificent Dougfir about five feet in diameter. Presumably the loggers had left this tree because of its inaccessibility. After years of erosion this mighty tree became undermined, fell across the creek, and allowed the buildup of the monstrous log jam which dammed the creek. In retrospect, it seems almost unbelievable that we should have had the determination, perseverance, and/or bloated self-confidence that would have prompted us to attack that log jam. Perhaps it was a little bit of all three, plus the fact that we did not realize the gravity of the situation. All that we could see were the logs protruding from the gravel or on top of those that were protruding. Naturally enough, perhaps, we did not realize that for about a half mile upstream from the face of the jam, logs were buried in the accumulated gravel. An analogy might be drawn: all that we could see was the tip of the iceberg.

However this may be, our love of our land, which had been abused so badly, strengthened our determination to repair the damage to our creek. Prior to our discovery of the log jam we had become acquainted with Wesley Simpson and his wife, from having bought a hundred grape stakes from Wes, to be used to put fences around the tiny redwood trees we had started planting in 1966. This was to protect them from deer. At that time, redwood grape stakes were still widely used in vineyards to support grape trellises. They have since been supplanted by metal stakes. Wes was a real old timer who began felling trees at age sixteen, pulling one end of a cross-cut saw. His stories about proceeding first to the clumsy drag saw and then to the chain saw were rather fascinating. Wes was also the last of the split redwood workers; split stakes are much stronger than sawed stakes. He came to our place to deliver the stakes we had bought, since we did not have a pickup truck. He arrived as I was almost through with building our powerhouse. After he inspected my work, he asked if I was a carpenter. I said that I was not a carpenter, but had worked with my dad who was also not a carpenter by trade but had built several houses. This started a friend-ship which was very helpful to us, as well as quite enjoyable. In spite of our entirely different backgrounds, we seemed to agree on just about any discussion that might arise. Both of us respected people who worked hard and honestly and did a good job.

About a year after we first met the Simpsons I asked Wes if I could hire him to buck a log into several pieces, for it was in a good position to build up yet another log jam. When I asked him how much I owed him, he said, "Nothing; that isn't much to ask of a neighbor." I went on to tell him about our log jam and said that I needed his advice on buying a chain saw. He went down with me to look at the log jam. After one look, he said that this was a very big job, and did I realize how big a job it would be? I said that

I probably did not realize how big a job it would be, but that I wanted to try it, and if it proved to be too much for me, I could always hire somebody to help me. He said he didn't expect me to quit, and that was why he warned me. He told me that I would need a saw with at least a thirty inch bar and a gear drive, and said that I should go down to French's saw shop and tell him he had sent me there. At French's saw shop, I learned for the first time that being a friend of Wes Simpson's generated a lot of respect for me. After I came back with the saw, a Homelite Wiz 55, Wes came over and spent quite a bit of time showing me many things by bucking a log. He then gave me some advice on how to fell trees and buck logs in all sorts of positions. He emphasized certain situations that were very dangerous, where one should do a lot of thinking before starting the saw. He must have been a good teacher, for I spent many hundreds of hours clearing log jams, and later felling trees, and I never had a serious injury. An injury is more likely working with heterogeneously piled logs, but a fatal accident is more likely in felling trees.

In 1968 we decided that with the two sections of concrete foundation at strategic positions under the house and with ceilings and minimum wiring in the bathroom, bedroom, and kitchen-dining room combination, I should start to work on the log jam as a first priority. Rebecca concentrated on planting trees and watering the trees already planted. Watering the plantings using the small generator to pump water from the creek and moving long hoses around was slow and laborious. Although we had heavy rains during the winter, it rarely rained at all during the summer. Early in the summer, I started to work on the Great Log Jam at the point where the small summer stream of Bridge Creek disappeared under the log pile to reappear below the face of the log jam. Since I had never used a chain saw before progress was slow, and slowness was accentuated by the fact that I was very careful indeed. I certainly did not want to spoil everything by having an accident. I was also slowed down by the fact that these logs, which had been washed downstream grinding in the gravel, had much gravel embedded in cracks and beneath the heavy bark of the Dougfir logs. Half a minute grinding against a piece of gravel, and the saw needed sharpening. As I gained experience I learned to spot cracks that might harbor gravel. Also, when Rebecca was not occupied with the irrigation of our new plantings, she came to where I was sawing bearing a big screwdriver and hammer. As she became more expert at locating pieces of bark that needed investigating in search of gravel, my sawing speed leaped ahead in proportion. The thing which made progress possible was that I sawed the logs into pieces about eight feet long, after we had increased our sophistication.

This increase in sophistication involved two factors. We had learned from my coach and benefactor, Wes Simpson, that he was going to sell us a small tractor which he had no further use for, and which had been sitting idle in his back yard for several years. He would put it in good running condition and sell it to us for $900. This machine was manufactured during the 1930s by the Oliver Tractor Co. We began at once to refer to it affectionately as Oliver Twist. I had already done enough log clearing to realize that this machine might make possible our objective of clearing the log jam in one way or another. It was a tracked vehicle which had a loading bucket on it which could also be used for minor bulldozing. It also had a blade which could be used for bulldozing, but I never attached it to the tractor because the bucket was adequate for everything we needed, including putting a chain around the bucket and using it for a lift. As time went by, it developed that we used the tractor as a lift more than for anything else, in spite of the fact that we developed many uses for Oliver Twist that we had not anticipated, such as dragging logs to put in a base for filling a road washout, and dragging brush to a burn pile. We even used its bucket to mix ready-mix concrete, and then carry the concrete to the site of its use. Later on we bought a small winch and attached it to the rear slab of steel which was mounted behind the driver to balance a heavy load in the bucket. Even with this counterbalance, I had to be careful not to try to pick up too heavy a load, such as wet gravel. If I should try to pick up too heavy a load, instead of Oliver's hydraulic system picking up the bucket, the bucket picked up Oliver's rear end. Oliver's first use after Wes delivered it to us was using its bucket with a chain as a lift for moving sawed logs into a pile for later burning. For this operation I drove the tractor and Rebecca set the chain around the log to pick it up with the desired balance. In the parlance of the logging country, where we quickly began to feel very much at home, Rebecca was the "choker setter" and I was the "CAT skinner." In case an eight-foot log was too heavy for Oliver to lift, this was usually resolved by setting the choke near one end and dragging the log to the desired site. In the case of a log three feet in diameter, which Oliver could not lift, it could be rolled to the desired site. If everything else failed, the log could be sawed into two pieces. One way or another, we got the logs into suitable piles for burning.

As for the other reason for not having logs that were too long and heavy, we began to look forward to the possibility of clearing a lesser log jam downstream from our property so that we could send our logs to the sea rather than burn them. The Mattole River is one of a very few streams where a log put into the water near the headwaters will travel to the sea during the high water after a storm. The thing which caused us concern about this was the very old one-way steel bridge across the Mattole River on the Shelter Cove Road. This bridge was supported on two slim concrete piers. Bridge Creek flowed into the Mattole just slightly upstream from the bridge. A log coming down Bridge Creek in high water would be aimed directly at the east pier of the bridge. I did not have any nightmares about a log of ours taking out the Mattole River bridge, but I certainly had no inclination to saw the logs into longer sections in order to save time, money, and labor.

During the academic year 1968-69, I applied for and received a sabbatical leave in residence in order to make the second revision of the laboratory manual which I had written with Rapoport. Rap had become so heavily involved in research that he felt unable to carry his share of the revision, so we arranged for me to receive three-fourths of the royalties on this third edition, with Rap receiving one-fourth. In recognition of my increased participation, Rap would revise only a few chapters where his expertise was required. For a sabbatical leave in residence, I was relieved of teaching except for one course in one semester. Since I could do this writing at Camelot better and faster than I could in Berkeley at the university, we spent a lot of time at Camelot during that year. At that time we did not have a telephone at Camelot, which was a nuisance and not really safe; however, it certainly was an insulation against interruptions.

During the month of December 1968, and the following months of January and February, I spent much of my time working on the book revision, but both of us worked on repairing storm damage and especially, clearing brush, whenever weather permitted. Most of the land around our house, for several hundred feet in each direction, was covered with a thick stand of whitethorn and manzanita. In many places the brush was so thick that a deer could not get through, except for an occasional path which they kept beaten down. Lots of rabbits and pack rats lived happily under the brush. The pack rats built huge nests, sometimes as much as five feet high and ten feet across. These nests were built of branches of brush, leaves, and other debris from the ground. These pack rats were quite a nuisance in several ways, for they would steal tools and other shiny objects and take them to their nests. Occasionally we invited neighbors to view with amazement the size of some objects which the pack rats had moved. Aside from the fact that Rebecca did not enjoy association with these animals, perhaps the greatest objection to them was that their nests would be marvelous fuel for spreading a forest fire. In any case, we cleared brush, including pack rat nests, from areas near our house.

Earlier in 1969 we had concluded that we needed another chain saw smaller than our WIZ 55, not only for sawing the many smaller logs in the log jams and lying around on the ground, but especially for brush clearing. We had rapidly become very sensitive to the danger of a forest fire sweeping over the mountain and roaring through the mass of brush in the wide area surrounding our house. After consulting Wes Simpson, we bought a Homelite EZ saw, with a twenty-three inch bar but light enough for Rebecca to handle. Since we had bought the saw primarily for brush clearing, and most of that would be done by Rebecca, we called this Rebecca's saw. In logging country, it was OK for a woman to handle a rifle, but a chain saw was a no no. Those things are dangerous! Somehow the word circulated around in the Whitethorn area that I had given Rebecca the saw as a Mother's Day present. The obvious conclusion was that the crazy professor up Bridge Creek had flipped his lid. Wes Simpson assured people that I was not crazy, but that my wife was a very unusual woman. Wes was right on both counts. This incident was responsible for our getting acquainted with several people in the Whitethorn Grange. We enjoyed this association, but did not join the Grange because our interests were so different from those of most people in the Grange—but not Wes Simpson, who was an accomplished musician. We became somewhat concerned after a robbery of everything in the house of another "outsider," and we took steps to discourage the idea that we were "rich." On every possible occasion we pointed out that there was nothing in our house worth stealing (which was true), and we never left any firearms, liquor, or chain saws in the house. Liquor we never had in the house, but our guns and chain saws we carried back and fourth to Berkeley for many years—until we had a caretaker for our place.

Returning to the matter of Rebecca's brush clearing. One morning in the fall of 1969, before the heavy rains set in, Rebecca was working in the dense brush below our road, about two hundred feet from the house. I was working in the house, installing the last of our electric wiring, when I heard Rebecca screaming my name. I was very frightened, hoping it was nothing worse than cutting of a tendon or losing a finger. I scrambled down from the attic where I was working and set a record for dashing up the road to where I knew Rebecca was working. I was so relieved that I had to laugh when she said, "Get your saw and get me out of here; I ran out of gas, and I don't want to get any more chummy with these damn pack rats." I didn't ask any questions; I just headed for my saw, which was in the "garage." I knew what had happened. There was no practical way to deal with whitethorn, named because of its abundance of vicious big thorns, except to cut a track into the center of the bush, which was some-times twenty or thirty feet across, then start cutting off limbs from the trunk. There was nothing that could be done with the brush except to throw it behind the sawyer as she moved in toward the trunk. After all the limbs had been cut off, the sawyer would then proceed to cut her way out in the same manner used to come in. But if she ran out of gas, what to do? Yell like hell for Jim!

During this winter of 1968-69, in addition to clearing brush, we worked on the Great Log Jam whenever the rain and high water in the creek would permit it. After the heavy rains had let up in March both of us worked on the log jam, with Rebecca sawing smaller logs whenever she was not needed for digging out gravel. We brought Oliver into the creek by driving down an old logging road. This place was about a quarter mile upstream from the Great Log Jam, and was the only place that Oliver could be put into the creek except for another place about a quarter mile upstream. After a period of sawing logs we would use Oliver to pile them on a gravel bar along the creek beside the log jam. After working at this all summer we had quite a log pile, about twenty-five feet wide at the base, ten feet high at the center (as high as Oliver could reach), and a hundred yards long. This represented quite a tonnage of logs, which could be disposed of only by burning. This part of the creek was in a gorge which made removal of the logs quite laborious, even with a big tractor winching them to the road above; however, this whole consideration was moot, for the gravel in the logs made sawing them in a sawmill impossible. Not only would a big circular saw blade be damaged each time it hit a piece of gravel, but sometimes the blade would be fractured and kill anybody hit by a flying fragment. This matter was well understood by the insane environmentalists, whose favorite tactic for interfering with logging of which they disapproved was driving steel spikes into trees scheduled for logging. These crazy people seemed to feel they had received a message that came down from the mountain which justified any action they might devise against whatever they disapproved of. Never mind little details such as the laws of our land.

The time to burn these logs was early in the winter, before the first high water in the creek would pile them against a small log jam downstream from us on somebody else's property. Furthermore, it was imperative that we get Oliver out of that gorge before the onset of high water. I took Oliver out of the creek by the same route that we had brought it into the creek. As I drove Oliver onto the ground beside the creek, I felt a little black cloud above me vanish. Subconsciously, I had worried about something happening to Oliver which would prevent me from getting it out of the creek before the high water arrived. When we consulted Verne Bonham, who was in charge of the nearby fire station of the California Division of Forestry, he was very helpful to us. This good relationship continued through the years we were clearing our creek of logs. His help even continued to the time of the Finley Creek Fire. There was a problem about burning our log pile, which resulted from a regulation that no burning without a permit was allowed until December 1. The permit had to be signed by the head of the fire station, but we were in Berkeley, unable to leave until after my last class on the Wednesday before Thanksgiving—and a storm was forecast. In view of the magnitude of the problem, Verne stretched the regulations a bit and agreed to put a signed permit in the fire station mailbox if he judged it safe to burn the next day. If there was no permit in the mailbox, we did not have permission to burn. When we got there at about 10 P.M. it was raining, so we were not uncertain about the permit being in the mailbox, which was the case. When the rain was pouring down each time one of us woke up during the night, we became rather alarmed, for fear that our pile of logs would be washed away.

When we got up in the morning the rain had let up and stopped by the time we had finished our breakfast! We took our pile of paper, matches, and two boxes of "fuel boosters" and set out for our road, which was cut into the mountainside above the creek. At this time, the "boosters" were widely used for starting a fire in order to avoid excessive smoke until the fire got to the roaring stage. I think that they were devised for giving a quick start to a backfire during the fighting of a forest fire. In any case, each of our boxes contained twenty-four sausage-shaped plastic packages of a petroleum gel. At about nine o'clock, Rebecca and I, wearing our hip boots and carrying our incendiary materials, climbed down the steep bank and waded across the creek to our monstrous log pile. The water in the swollen creek was lapping at the edge of our pile in some places but was not high enough to threaten washing any logs away. I began firing at the lower end of the long pile and Rebecca started at the upper end. We spaced our boosters according to our judgment in order to consume all of them. This close spacing was used to make sure that the fires we started would take hold in enough spots to get the fire roaring in spite of the wetness of the logs. At each spot we placed a thick pad of newspapers on top of a few pieces of newspapers crumpled to facilitate lighting with a match. As soon as we had split the booster skin, we put a match to the paper. After watching for a few minutes to make sure that the fire was taking off, we went on to the next site for firing. We were concentrating so heavily on our business that when we came together in the afternoon, with only four fuel boosters left, we were surprised to find that it was about four o'clock. We were so tired and wet and hungry as we climbed up the bank that we did not pay much attention to the appearance of what we had wrought, except to note that the fire was burning.

After getting some supper and taking a nap, we drove back after dark to the road above the fire. Before reaching the site above the fire, we realized that the entire gorge was lit up so that we could have read a newspaper standing on the road. The top of the fire was higher than the road on which we were standing. Instinctively, I was a little worried about the size of that fire. When Rebecca said "We have started a forest fire!" I reassured both of us by reminding us that it had been pouring rain all night, and not only that, but Verne thought it was safe. After feasting our eyes on the conflagration for quite a while, we went to our house and got a good night's sleep, the sound sleep of the weary.

The next morning, when we went down to view the scene of the fire, we experienced an even greater euphoria than when we were watching the burn. There was very little left of that monstrous pile of logs; just a few of the largest logs still smoldering were scattered about. Later, we learned from Verne that he had calls from as far away as Garberville, reporting a large fire in the Mattole River Valley. He told the callers to relax, that everything was proceeding according to his permit and was under control.

After the winter storms had let up, we found that so much gravel had been washed out and sent on its way towards the sea as a result of our efforts in clearing our creek that we could no longer get Oliver into the creek. At the place where I had previously taken Oliver into the creek, there was a projection of bedrock which presented a drop of about five feet to what was now the gravel bed of the creek. This was only the beginning of the surprises we experienced as we examined the creek down to the site of our big fire. The few smoldering large logs left after our fire were gone, as was inevitable, since the creek bed was now six or eight feet lower than before our last year's clearing. This revealed a whole new log jam extending upstream to a point above where I had put Oliver into the creek. I had a feeling like I had walked through Alice's looking glass. Going downstream to the face of the log jam, we found that the logs were now piled up to a height of only eight or ten feet. At this point I realized for the first time that the creek was full of gravel and logs upstream to a point where the top of the gravel was at the same level as the top of this log jam at its face. A rather sobering thought. At the time that we decided to tackle the clearing of the log jam, we were able to see only one-fourth or less of the problem! I spent no time speculating as to whether we would have decided to clear our creek if we had known the size of the problem. I also spent no time thinking about whether we would continue, now that we had a better view of the problem. Only a fool or a congenital quitter would stop at this point. So, in 1970, we went to work on phase two of the Great Log Jam, which we tended to call the "second log jam."

Since we were now unable to get Oliver into the creek—and out of it—

we had only one recourse for continuing our salvage of the creek. That was sending the logs to the sea, if that route were open. Wes Simpson told me that if Bridge Creek were clear to the Mattole, the logs from Bridge Creek could go to the sea. A waterfall which was interfering with salmon coming upstream to spawn had been dynamited several years earlier. Exploration downstream in Bridge Creek revealed two problems which I felt able to resolve, although it would require a substantial effort. By this time I was ready for anything that seemed possible, so we went to work downstream in 1970, from early March to mid-September.

Taken in the order in which we encountered them, the first problem was a considerable pileup of logs in a bend about a quarter mile below our property. Apparently accumulation of logs in the bend had resulted in the high waters going around the log pile onto a low bank on the outside of the bend, and thus washing out about a half acre of land to open a passage for the logs subsequently coming down. By the time of our arrival logs had accumulated in this area in the outside of the bend (probably logs released by us upstream) until they were piled higher than those in the original stream bed. My analysis of the situation, based on a little knowledge of rheology, suggested that if we should buck the logs in the original stream bed to our usual eight-foot lengths, with shorter lengths when indicated, with a little bit of luck the outside logs in the bend might generate enough obstruction for the high water to blow the logs in the stream out of the way and send them to the sea, leaving the pile of logs outside the normal stream bed. The "little bit of luck" would involve a favorable ratio of high water coming down in sufficient volume to move the logs already there before additional logs coming from above would generate a sufficient blockade to cause a repetition of the creek flowing outside the bend in the original stream bed, without breaking through the log jam in the original stream bed.

There was a second obstruction downstream from the one just described. This was a very large Dougfir tree which had been undermined by high water and had gone down directly across the creek. It was suspended on each side of the creek at a level where the bottom of the log was about four feet above the creek bed. This was obviously at just the strategic level to guarantee that logs would pile up behind it in high water. It followed that work on any log jam upstream would be futile unless we should decide to settle for getting the logs out of our property and onto somebody else's property. Neither Rebecca nor I had any inclination toward the latter alternative, and so it was a matter of attacking that big log, which measured five to four feet in diameter, proceeding from the end towards the base to the other end.

There was also another sticky little situation with which we had to contend. The creek where these problems were located was not on our property. The property on the left side of the stream, facing downstream, belonged to people with whom we were well acquainted and with whom we had friendly neighborly relations. Both of them expressed strong approval of our clearing their stream. The land on the other side of the stream belonged to a hippie commune which was not of an uncommon makeup. The mother of the man (boy) who was the master of the commune had bought the land and was furnishing him with the money needed to support the operation. There were no buildings, but some tents and lots of "happenings" (LSD sessions), which were often quite noisy. Naturally enough, the people on our side of the creek and right opposite them were very antagonistic toward the hippies. One of them was especially antagonistic and sometimes did things such as fire a rifle into the trees above their heads. Relatively speaking, we were lovely neighbors to the commune, having had some friendly exchanges with the head honcho, Paul Byers. We told them that we regarded them as OK neighbors as long as they did not do hunting or fishing on our property.

When we were ready to start on the downstream work, I decided to start first with the log jam in the bend, to see what would develop with the hippies. It was about eight o'clock in the morning when I started my saw and began bucking a log. I had prepared my pitch, for use if Paul should come down and accost me. Just as I was ready to complete the cut, I heard somebody shouting at me, so I stopped the saw and looked around. Paul was standing on the bank, barefooted, and yelled, "What's going on down here?" (Note the absence of profanity.) After I had apologized for waking him up so early in the morning, I recounted in detail what a mess the creek on our property was in, how hard we were working to correct it, and how we could no longer pile logs for burning because we could not get our little tractor into the creek. I finally stated that we could not get rid of our remaining logs by sending them to the sea in high water for they would get hung up on this log jam, and we would be simply moving logs from our property to his, which I would not do. I ended my long harangue by saying, "It is a dirty shame that this beautiful creek has been messed up in this way, and I am determined to clean it up no matter how long it takes." As soon as I stopped talking, Paul said, "Do you want me to help you?" I was hoping for a favorable response, but was rather overwhelmed by Paul's offer to help. I could not think of much that he could do that would be safe. I told him that there was not much to be done just now except for driving the saw for many hours, and maybe he would carry my heavy saw downstream to the big log across the creek. He said that he would do so as soon as he got some shoes on. He did so, and stayed around for a while watching me buck the big log for the first time. After that he never came down to the creek while I was working there, intermittently for several weeks.

I continued to work on that big log after Paul left, and made two cuts through it on that day. I did not make more than two cuts in a day while working on that log. Such work is strenuous, both physically and emotionally, because of the danger involved. Bucking a log that is suspended at both ends is a difficult and dangerous job, which becomes more difficult with larger logs. At its larger end, towards the base, I was barely able to make the cut all the way through the log by working from both sides with my saw, which had a thirty-three inch bar. A few inches overlap is required. I had sharpened my saw before this undertaking, and also started at the smaller end in order to develop a little expertise before tackling this job. In a log suspended at both ends, the cut must be made in a specific way. Of course, the cut is started at the top since there is no way that enough pressure can be applied to the saw by pushing up. After the cut has been made to about the middle of the log, working as needed on the two sides, two plastic wedges are driven into the cut at the top, properly spaced. As the cut is continued towards the bottom, the wedges are driven in a little harder. The wedges are to keep the bar of the saw from being pinched when the cut goes through at the bottom. After the bar drops down after making the cut, the wedges are held by the two sides of the log pushing against them by the pull of gravity. The next move is to knock the wedges out of the cut with a big hammer after judging where to stand so that the log on one side of the cut or the other does not roll towards one.

For this particular big log, neither side rolled. They dropped straight down and wedged the ends together, closing the small gap where the wedges had been. This left the log in the same position for the next cut, as was the case for the first cut. If one or both sides of the log had rolled, this would have simplified making future cuts. But such was not the case with this particular log. I remembered Wes Simpson warning me to remember that each log was a whole new ball game.

Additional cuts in the log proceeded in essentially the same way as the first cut. This meant that the entire log that I had cut consisted of eight-foot pieces jammed together. Casual inspection would be unlikely to notice that the log had been cut several times. By the time that I had reached the next to last cut, as the log slowly became larger, I decided to put that off until I could get a fresh start on it in the morning. All along, during this work on the big log, I had worked on the log jam upstream whenever I felt I had had enough of the big log for one day. When I went to work on that next to last cut, I was unusually cautious, for I knew that the problem was getting more difficult. When I finally got down to the bottom, ready to cut through, I spent considerable time reviewing my previous examinations. I decided that if the log rolled when I cut through instead of dropping straight down again, it would have to roll upstream. The first eight-foot piece that I had cut had dropped to the stream bank on ground that had about a forty-five degree slope, with the low side upstream. So I took my station on the downstream side of the log and proceeded to cut through. In order to do this, I had to have my bar extending as far as it could reach in order to cover the last sliver that had to be cut. This time the log rolled, but did not fall clear and drop into the creek. With my thirty-three inch bar pushed fully into the log, there was no way that I could withdraw it as the log rolled. When the rolling log, carrying the string of eight-foot cuts with it, pinched the tip of my bar against the part of the log not yet cut, that stopped the roll-and left my saw hanging there above the creek bed.

At this juncture, my first thought was that I did, indeed, get on the correct side of the log for protection against the roll. My next thought was that it would be utter folly to try and cut the bar loose with our EZ saw which had a twenty-three inch bar, and so I would have to seek assistance from Wes Simpson. My pride was resistant to that latter solution unless as a last resort, so I did some more thinking. I thought about the slope at the end of the log chain which had caused me to choose the downstream side of the log to make the final cut. That strategy did cause the log to roll, but the roll was stopped by a very thin piece of steel. Ergo, I cut a suitable piece of a log to act as a fulcrum, and as long a piece of a small log as I could lift, to act as a pry bar. When I got the pry bar in place and pulled down on it, the whole string of logs rolled into the creek, thus releasing my saw. Oh! I forgot to mention that Rebecca was holding up my saw before I pulled the pry bar, so that it did not fall into the creek.

After we had finished sawing the big log by making one more cut, and doing as much sawing as seemed necessary on the logs in the log jam in the bend, we returned to working on the "second" log jam on our property. These were the logs that were uncovered by high water in the creek after we had removed the top layer by the big burn described earlier. Since we were not able to get Oliver into the creek, the logs, sawed into eight-foot lengths, were left lying where they fell. As described earlier in this chapter, we worked for several weeks at clearing the big log and the log jam on the hippies' property in hopes that we would have a little bit of luck and our logs would be carried to the sea during high water. By doing a lot of work this summer, we were able to finish what we felt to be needed on this "second layer" in our Great Log Jam.

Among the things that were revealed by the removal of the top layer by our big burn was the base of a tremendous snag (a dead tree). This tree had been growing on the bank about ten feet above the normal water level in the creek, a location where unusually large trees are frequently found. This tree was about four feet in diameter at waist level. Thus, by the time that the Great Log Jam had reached the level at which we found it, some fifteen feet of the trunk of the tree was buried in gravel. Inevitably, the tree was killed. Since Wes Simpson had told me that felling snags was dangerous business, I decided to get his advice before tackling this big one. When Wes came down to the creek to look at that tree, he immediately said, "Jim, it is too dangerous for you to fell that tree, I will do it for you." My response, "I do not want you to do anything for me that is dangerous; I would never get over it if you were hurt." He immediately responded, in a quiet tone, " It is not dangerous for me to do it." I continued to insist that he not do it. He did not say anything more as we looked over our work on the "second layer" of the log jam.

When he complimented me on being able to get the big log down, I did not tell him about the trouble I had with it.

After this conversation Rebecca and I went back to Berkeley for a few weeks so that I could attend to my duties at the university. When we came back, and went down to the creek to go to work on log clearing, we found that Wes had felled that big tree directly across the creek, the direction in which it had a lean. I have included this short narrative in my chronicle in order to give a clear picture of the man named Wesley Simpson. He died in about 1992, afflicted with Alzheimer's syndrome. This seems like a sad end to such an active and honorable man; however, the fact that he lived long enough to become so afflicted is a testimonial to his skill as a logger. He started at age sixteen, pulling one end of a two-man crosscut saw.

We were not there when the first heavy rains came in the winter, but we had a vivid description of the events from a neighbor living on our side of the creek, below where we had sawed the big log. In this winter, the first heavy rains were very heavy indeed, and lasted overnight and into the next day. Our neighbor had been watching our work in the creek; hence she knew what we were trying to do. Thus, she got on her rain gear at daylight, and went up to the site of the log jam in the bend where we had sawed up the logs and left them where they lay. Her report was the following:

"When I got there, many logs from your work upstream had accumulated so that much water was beginning to flow around the logs which had piled up in the creek, and going around the outside of the bend. I was beginning to think that somebody was going to have one big log pile to burn, as the water level behind the jam kept rising. Suddenly, the dam broke up with an enormous roar, and this mass of logs went roaring downstream. I immediately thought of your worries about the east pier of the steel bridge, so I rushed down the creek bank to where I could see the bridge across the Mattole. It was still there spanning the river!"

A few days after we had gotten the report on the log jam going out, we were able to make a weekend trip to Camelot. Naturally enough, I guess, the first thing we did was climb down the steep bank to the creek, at the point where the Great Log Jam had been located. When we got close enough to the creek to see down to where the water was flowing, we stopped and gazed in astonishment. After a while, I said, "That looks to me like the bedrock in the creek bed beneath that clear water flowing down." After a few moments, while Rebecca moved down closer, she shouted, "It is, that is definitely the bluish green rock that we see in the creek up near our house". There was no doubt about it. That last storm, which was a really big one, had swept the remains of that Great Log Jam on downstream, leaving piles of logs on the gravel bars on each side of the stream where erosion had widened the stream. The swollen stream, reportedly running about ten feet deep as it thundered out of the gorge, left logs in an eddy on each side. Investigation downstream, as we waded along in our hip boots, revealed that the log jam in the bend that we had worked on was also swept clean, but, like our log jam above, had left a pile of logs outside the bend. The stream flow was clear, showing a rock bottom with gravel bars over the rocks in various places in normal fashion. Also, the eight-foot sections of four-foot diameter logs were gone. I have not been down to this place below our property for several years, because of the unfriendliness of the person owning the property recently; however, we did our job of salvaging the creek. As for the piles of logs on each side at the site of our Great Log Jam, we removed those later, and also cleared many logs from many eddies along the mile of our creek. We also cleared a massive log jam in the creek in a forty-acre parcel we bought in 1971. This will be reported soon after we finish the present story.

Now for the end of the story. A man named Mixon, who was a retired Air Force officer, had a house on a small parcel of land on the Mattole River about a quarter mile below the steel bridge where Bridge Creek joined the Mattole. During our short trip to investigate the results of our log clearing, Mixon came to demand an explanation of why we were sending big logs, three or four feet in diameter and twenty or thirty feet long, down the Mattole River. We assured him that these logs could not be ours because we never left any size of log that was more than about eight feet in length. He did considerable muttering about how dangerous that was, how it could have taken out the east pier of the bridge. I stood my ground with the truth; we had not left any logs more than about eight feet in length. After Mixon left, I said to Rebecca, "There must have been one helluva lot of things buried in that gravel that we did not know about; I wonder how many of those steel logging cables got hung up somewhere." We immediately investigated the geometry at the confluence of Bridge Creek and the

Mattole River. It proved to be true that the mouth of Bridge Creek was directed straight towards that east pier. The thing that saved us and the east pier was the fact the Mattole River was running more water than Bridge Creek, because of being a larger stream at that point. Thus, as a log's nose came out of Bridge Creek, it was slammed by the pouring tide coming down the Mattole and steered directly down the Mattole to its rendezvous with the sea.

In 1971, after the Great Log Jam was no more, except for a few details, we began working along the creek clearing numerous piles of logs. The last major effort involved a very large log jam in a forty acre parcel of property which we bought in 1972 from a medical doctor named John Blum, who lived in Berkeley. John Blum was not our family doctor, for our doctor was Peter E. Patch, who had taken care of us since he sewed up Mardy's face. Dr. Blum, however, shared one important characteristic with Peter Patch. He belonged to the "old school," as did my brother, John. He believed that taking care of his patients, according to his Hippocratic Oath, was the most important mission in his life. I think of these people with reverence, for they belonged to an endangered species. Dr. Blum and his wife, Joyce, bought this forty acre parcel, and hauled a house trailer up there to live in while John worked on building a house. He started doing all the work himself. Knowing what part of a house was the most important, he first built a structure measuring about ten feet by twenty five feet to serve as a bathroom and a place to store tools, lumber and other things used to build the house. Just as he got to the point where he was ready to put the roof on the "bathroom," tragedy struck. His wife, Joyce, was diagnosed with lung cancer. She was a chain smoker. John was so distraught that all he could think about was getting rid of that property and everything associated with it. He asked us if we would buy it for what he paid for the land, and agree to his leaving the trailer, the building being constructed, and everything else present on the property. We had previously bought two other parcels of property adjacent to our original purchase, so our finances were rather strained; however, we felt it important to assist John in getting rid of the property. We bought it with a small down payment, and immediately set to work getting a roof on the largest bathroom in Humboldt County.

The log jam on this property was a large one, but very different in composition from the Great Log Jam. This one filled a space in the creek about three times as wide as the gorge where the Great Log Jam was located. Apparently, this log jam was initiated by the collapse of an old log bridge used in a logging operation. The road to this old bridge had resulted in bulldozing a considerable part of the creek bank, so when more logs piled up in the main channel of the creek, the torrents of water coming down after a storm began to wash out this low place, adjacent to the jam in the creek. As near as I could judge the situation, it was similar to the jam in the bend below our property. And for similar reasons, the logs which eventually accumulated were deposited in this widened area, and this prevented a buildup of logs in a vertical direction. The base of this jam was on the original creek bed. There was no chance of our encountering the kind of surprise that we did in working on the Great Log Jam. Since we had cleared the obstructions below this point on our original property, we could leave our eight-foot sections of logs where they fell and depend on subsequent high water to take them to the sea.

We worked all summer and into the fall until the fall session at the university started: sawing logs, prying them from on top of others so that more could be sawed. This work went much faster than that on the Great Log Jam, because these logs had never been buried in gravel. This factor made the work twice as fast, ignoring our additional experience. I sharpened our saws only twice during that period of about six months, with three months during the summer being devoted almost exclusively to this job. I had only one significant delay. I was sawing through a rather large log that was suspended at both ends. I was unaware that the bottom of the log was rotten, so I cut into this area without putting wedges in the top. Ergo, the two sides of the cut fell together and pinched my bar. When that happened, with that big saw going at full speed, there was a very sudden stop to the turning of the sprocket that drives the chain. This broke the sprocket, so I had to make a trip to Milt's Saw Shop in Garberville before I could do any more sawing with that saw. I thought of the caution which I had received from Wes Simpson, "Always remember that every log and every tree is different from every other one."

By the time that the fall session put an end to the work on this log jam, there were so many eight-foot sections of logs and so many long logs that we had not cut that I began to worry about such a mass of logs getting hung up some place downstream. Thus, we decided to have another burn, and came up there with a couple of boxes of fuel boosters during the Christmas holidays. We usually came up to Camelot before Christmas to cut a few small Dougfir trees for our living room and those of friends. We had a break in the weather, and no burning permit was necessary because it was after December 1. Wes Simpson wanted to see how the fuel boosters worked, since he was frequently engaged in brush clearing on his property. The three of us hiked up to the site, carrying our equipment. In our cars, we were able to get no closer than about a quarter mile because the bridge for the logging road had washed out long ago, as had those across Bridge Creek. We started firing at about nine o'clock; with three of us working, we finished before noon.

I still remember Wes, Rebecca and me sitting on the bank about a hundred feet from the fire while eating the lunch that Rebecca had packed for us. Rebecca and I were feeling relaxed and elated over a job well done, and we always enjoyed Wes Simpson's company. Naturally enough, I guess, our conversation soon became focused on the incredible amount of damage that could be done by dirty logging. Wes had always operated as an independent, did his own bulldozing, and always left the forest in better shape than before he arrived. He was painfully aware, however, of the amount of damage that was done, such as what we had encountered on our property. He was very much in favor of the present restrictions on logging. He had found it hard to earn a living while doing a proper job of logging. During the years that we knew him, his logging consisted of salvaging redwood logs from creeks where they had been thrown during logging in days gone by. The owners of the property charged Wes nothing for salvaging the logs, since they were happy to get them out. Since redwood does not rot readily, even when buried in the ground, Wes used his big CAT to haul them out to a place where he could work on them. He then sawed them into appropriate lengths, and split them into posts or grape stakes. Such posts are stronger than sawed ones, but making them is very hard work, swinging a big heavy hammer against a steel wedge. Two of Wes's friends wanted a son to go into the split redwood business, and so they induced Wes to take them on as apprentices. Neither of them lasted for a week. Men like Wes Simpson just don't grow any more. He was the last of the split redwood workers.

Rebecca and I bought the last redwood posts that Wes produced. We made two trips in the largest U-Haul truck available to haul these posts into the Central Valley to our almond orchard north of Sacramento. I helped Wes load the truck. I picked up one end of a post and put it on the truck bed, then picked up the other end and pushed it onto the truck bed. Wes then picked up the post and stacked it in the truck according to regulations about such things. For the stack against the front wall of the truck, he had to carry the post from the rear to the front of the truck. He had to lift them higher as the stack reached the ceiling. Wes obviously had the harder job—I picked up one end at a time. When we finished loading the truck, Wes looked a little tired, but I was exhausted. Near the end, I suggested that we take a little rest so that I could finish. Wes said that he was surprised that I could do it. From the vantage point of this writing, while nursing my arthritic joints, I find it hard to believe that I really did it. Those two trips, about 440 miles round trip, were my only experience driving a big truck. Rebecca was apprehensive at the start of the first trip with a load, but she relaxed a little by the time of the second trip. I was beginning to enjoy it by the start of the second trip, looking down on all those little ants crawling around below me. I also developed a lot of respect for big rig drivers. Most of them are real professionals, with big money depending on their skill.

During 1972, most of our time at Camelot was during the summer, since I was occupied with university duties during the school year. The first thing that we did, which was at spring recess, was visit the "Blum log jam" to see how well the winter high water had carried away the logs. This proved to be quite gratifying. All the eight-foot sections which we had cut were gone, and a significant portion of the long logs was gone. By mid-summer we had finished cutting all the logs we felt needed to be cut. The original channel of the creek was clear to bedrock. Our next move was to go downstream, sawing any logs along the way that we felt should be eliminated. This required only two or three days. Finally, we started to work on the piles of logs on each side of the former location of the Great Log Jam. By the start of school in the fall, we had sawed all the logs needed to have a burn on each side.

During the Thanksgiving holidays, we got a burn permit and fired the piles of logs on each side of the creek. This went off routinely except for one event. The log pile on the side of the creek where our road was located was rather large, and there was an old log lying on the bank just above our fire. It was at a right angle to the creek and extended about one hundred feet up the forested bank. Its end was just even with the place where the bank dropped off rapidly to the creek. After our fire on that side had started roaring and throwing flames to the sky, we saw that the above mentioned log was on fire and burning vigorously. Everything was quite wet; otherwise, we would not have been able to get a burn permit; however, I was somewhat worried because of something I had forgotten. Decaying vegetation which is not exposed to the air gives off methane, which is the principal component of natural gas. When this gas is emitted, of course it is very easily ignited; it can be lit with a match in the rain. As it burns, it ignites the decaying wood in the log, which is also easily combustible. Since I did not want to ruin our good reputation with Verne Bonham, we set to work to eliminate the hazard. The log was already burning about twenty-five feet above its lower end, not flaming much at that distance above the fire, but glowing and progressing. Rebecca went to our car on the road and drove to our house to get our "Indian Fire Fighter" which is not very different from a backpack sprayer used in gardens and lawns except that the nozzle is a hose nozzle which can be adjusted to throw a heavy stream. I immediately went to work, sawing off sections of about four-foot length at the bottom of the log. Each sawed section was then pushed with a shovel down the bank and into the fire. When Rebecca got back, she started putting water on the log at the top of the burn. This slowed the progress of the fire up the log. Of course she had to replenish her water after using five gallons, and this meant a trip to the creek and dragging the five gallon tank of water up to the top of the burning section of log. Slow going, but it retarded the fire so that I soon reached the spot where she was working and sawed off a section of log whose top was not yet burning. This section was rolled down to the fire with the others. There was no danger of these rolling logs starting another fire as they rolled down because wet leaves do not burn at all well, and cannot be lit unless first dried. And so the upper section of that rotting log is still there, or rather what little is left of it. Eventually, such rotting logs blend in with the compost on the ground so that it cannot be located unless by digging and noting the different appearance of the soil.

My experiences during about five years that Rebecca and I spent salvaging Bridge Creek have had a profound influence on my thinking about matters of ecology and conservation. During the period that we worked at this salvation, we wore out four chains on each of our two chain saws, produced many gallons of sweat, and lost a little blood. If the fanatical types who call themselves conservationists during this last fourth of the twentieth century had experienced the things that we have, I think their attitudes and actions would be rather different than they have been. Surely they would not have driven steel spikes into trees being logged, or driven around in cars carrying a bomb. They would know that there are heroes among those in the timber harvesting business. Some of them are CAT skinners, some of them are chain sawyers, and some of them do other things, but nearly all of them belong to a fraternity of dedicated individuals.

As is clearly illustrated in this chronicle called Chapter 18, the damage that can be done in a logging operation is so great that it boggles the mind. It is easy to blame such things on the individuals who did it. Certainly there is enough blame to go around, but that is only a part of the story. The whole story should be considered: the times in which such dirty logging was done, and the lack of knowledge about what could result from the invention of the chain saw. Wes Simpson found that it was difficult to earn a living by doing clean logging, so he began to earn a living by salvaging the mess left by others. Should we condemn the inventors and developers of television for giving us this device that makes it so difficult to raise children to become responsible citizens? Should we condemn the French Revolution as bad because its leaders invented the guillotine to facilitate chopping off the heads of their enemies? Should we condemn Harry Truman for approving the utilization of the atomic bomb, which actually saved the lives of two or three million people? How many people know that Ronald Reagan was personally responsible for making it possible for the conservation movement to prosper in California? Probably the answer to this last question is: very few except for those who have read Ted Simon's book *The River Stops Here*. This list of questions could go on for a long time, for there are so many complicated things involved in anything that happens in the time in history in which we live. It would be helpful if those who are seeking the answers would not be so ferociously criticized by those who seem to think that they have been blessed by heaven with the right answers.

There is another side to this coin. Two people with two of those nasty chain saws and a little tractor have demonstrated that property which has suffered ghastly damage done by dirty loggers can be almost completely rehabilitated. The game warden told us that our creek was the best creek in southwest Humboldt County. I am unaware whether there are any other creeks in southwest Humboldt County which were not subjected to dirty logging.

Chapter 19

FIRE!

On the Saturday afternoon following Labor Day weekend in 1973, I was working on the manuscript for a paper I was to publish. I usually worked in our garden on Sundays, but worked at home on professional activities on Saturdays when something associated with my professional activities was urgent—which was not uncommon. When our older son, Roger, was about nine years old, a visitor asked him if he was going to follow in his father's footsteps and be a chemist when he grew up. Roger answered, "No way, Dad is the only father in our neighborhood who works on Saturday!" On this particular Saturday afternoon, my concentration on writing my manuscript was interrupted by the telephone ringing. This was uncommon on Saturday afternoon. Like other professors who held any type of administrative position at Berkeley during the nineteen sixties and thereafter, I had our phone delisted from the telephone book. Thus, I was slightly annoyed to be interrupted by a call that was probably a social call from one of Rebecca's many friends, while she was working in the yard.

As soon as I heard the message coming in, the adrenaline in my system surged: "I am a telephone operator, and I have a man on the line named Guy Seaton who says that the forest fire in Humboldt County is probably burning through your property. Will you accept his call?" My loud and vociferous response was, "Yes, put him on!" We had heard on the radio that a forest fire had been reported at Finley Creek, but were not alarmed because that location was about twenty-five miles north of us. Guy told us that the fire had started on Friday in grassland, but had swept very rapidly into forested land that was full of brush under the drive of a very strong wind from the north. After this fire had burned overnight, it had reached a point south of Shelter Cove. At that stage the wind shifted to the west and began blowing even harder. Ergo, the fire was now burning toward our Camelot along about a thirty-mile front, driven by a strong west wind. Guy said that he had gotten his information from the staging area for the firefight, which was just across the road from his house. He recommended that we get up there as soon as possible and get our water pumps started because the fire was probably burning on our property. There was so much smoke that the phosphate bombers had given up after missing the fire front six times, so nobody knew just where the fire was located.

Needless to say, we went into action at once preparing to set out for Camelot. I first called my secretary in the graduate division, where I was associate dean, to tell her I would not be able to meet my appointments on Monday and might be away longer, but I was unable to reach her. I next called the secretary in the chemistry department and found her at home. This was my term without teaching in chemistry because of my service in the graduate division; however, I was scheduled to attend a committee meeting on Tuesday. I asked the chemistry secretary to advise that committee on Monday that I could not attend the meeting on Tuesday because of a forest fire burning in my timber property. I also asked her to give my message to Ella Sponseller, my graduate division secretary. This left our only remaining problem the fact that we were in the midst of the gasoline shortage generated by our loving government, and we were uncertain whether we had enough gasoline in the Scout to get us to Camelot. Telephoning revealed that nobody in Berkeley or nearby would sell us any gasoline to meet an emergency, so there was nothing for us to do but set out for Camelot and hope that either we could find gasoline on the route, or that we could make it without more gas. I was driving and Rebecca was looking out for any signs of an open gasoline station. As we were going through Santa Rosa, she said she saw a sign a couple of blocks off the freeway that looked like a filling station. Investigation revealed that it was an open filling station, and he would sell us five gallons of gas—at a high price. I thanked him profusely and paid him twice what he asked. This was not the first time—or the last—that I have been saved in an emergency from interfering government regulations by the ingenuity, goodwill, and foresight of ordinary American citizens. About a mile south of Garberville the freeway rises to the top of a long grade where there is an unobstructed view to the west. The entire horizon was glowing a fiery red! Neither Rebecca nor I said or did anything; I already had the accelerator on the floor because of coming up the grade.

It was about midnight when we arrived at the roadblock opposite the staging area for the firefight. We were stopped by a man in a Division of Forestry uniform, who said that nobody was allowed beyond this point except firefighting personnel. When I explained that we owned property on Bridge Creek where the fire was probably burning, and that we had water pumps which I wanted to get started, he responded by saying that his orders were to let no one pass. At that point, I had a bright idea. I asked him who was in charge of this section of the firefight. He answered, "Verne Bonham." I was hoping for that answer because I knew that Verne was the head of the nearby Division of Forestry fire station. I explained to him that I was well known to Verne, so would he ask him if it was OK for the Casons to go through. Same answer. I then asked him, in a more agitated tone as I gunned my engine a couple of times, would he please ask Verne the question; it could not do any harm. Perhaps he got the message that he was not going to be able to stop me. In any case, he agreed to ask Verne the question. After what seemed to us a long time, as we sat there looking across at our smoke-filled valley, he finally returned. When he was about twenty feet from us, he swung his hand with the thumb pointing forward in the manner used by hitchhikers and yelled, "Go ahead, idiots!" I was at least twenty-five feet away before he got his mouth closed.

When we arrived on our private road at the gorge at the eastern edge of our property, we were relieved to note that the smoke pall in our valley was lying about fifty feet above the ground. At least we would not have to fight smoke as we were setting up the defense of our house. Apparently this phenomenon was caused by the fact that our property was completely surrounded by mountains, with the creek flowing out through a deep, narrow gorge. The winds blow over the mountains, dropping into our valley like an eddy in a stream. When we stopped at the roadblock on our way there was a strong wind blowing, but at our house there was only minor air movement. Of course, the first thing I did was start our electric generator. As I approached the main switch, I said, "Please start, please start!" It not only started within five seconds; it did not miss a beat for the next forty-eight hours. I patted it on its radiator.

Cinders were raining down on our house, some of them glowing. We were not worried about anything that size setting fire to our fire-resistant roof, but we were worried about our walls which were redwood shingles. We set up four rainbirds, one on each side of the house, to throw water against all walls of the house. These rainbirds were fed by water pumped from the creek by pumps driven by electricity supplied by our generator. Water was supplied to three of the rainbirds by our 1.5 horsepower pump, and the fourth was fed by our .5 horsepower pump. We were using these pumps to irrigate several acres where we had planted redwood trees, and we had a main water line to our house. All of the water lines were underground. Our drinking water to the house was from a spring up the mountain, as has been described in Chapter 17. We had hoses deployed around the house, attached to outlets from both the irrigation line and the house spring line. From the start of our development of Camelot we had arranged everything for a defense against fire. This included an irrigated meadow of about two acres of green grass extending to the creek bank. This was an impregnable defense against fire from the direction in which this fire would be coming, and we set it up that way on purpose. When we bought our property in the mid-sixties, the mountainside above our spring had two or three hundred snags (dead trees) on it. Frank McKee told us that a fire had swept over the mountains from the south in the mid-twenties, jumped the creek, and burned on our side. And so we were prepared when this fire developed.

After we had gotten the rainbirds set around our house, we bedded down and managed to get a few hours of sleep before awakening. We were too tired and emotionally exhausted to worry about anything except hitting that bed. When we went outside the next morning we discovered that the smoke pall had lifted enough so that we could see to the tops of the mountains in the direction that the fire was burning. This was the first time that we could tell that the fire had not come into our valley. The hail of cinders also had subsided considerably. We set to work raking leaves back a hundred feet from our house and carrying them away to a distant site. There were very few big trees around our house to give shade at that time, so the leaf cover on the ground was dry. When I went outside to look at the mountains towards the south after we had taken a short after-lunch nap, I was rather shaken to see that the fire was coming over the mountaintops crowning. This was the only time during the whole affair that I felt a little like I was coming unraveled. I turned around and looked in the other direction and told myself that the fire I could see was about a mile away. There was a steep rocky downslope between the fire and the creek, and our green meadow was about a hundred yards wide. So there was no theoretically possible way for the fire to ever get to us unless from burning fragments carried by the wind, and our house with fire-resistant shingles was being watered down with four rainbirds. I then went into the house and gave Rebecca a cheerful report that the fire was coming over the mountain. She took it quite well and decided to go over to the staging area for the firefight and tell them we needed help.

She returned from the staging area to report that the people at the staging area had told her that they were doing everything that could be done to head off the fire but it was a tough one. There were about a hundred CATs and more than a thousand people on the line, but the fire had jumped three firelines and crossed the Shelter Cove road without even hesitating. The brush-covered Queen Peak had essentially exploded as it drove the fire forward about a mile in one lunge. We finished the cleanup around our house, noted that our three hundred gallon propane tank was nearly half full, reminded ourselves of that long downslope on our mountain, and went to bed. Some time after midnight, Rebecca woke me up and said that a pickup truck had come in and driven down towards the small cleared area we called the "turnaround." We got up, got flashlights, and went down towards the turnaround. Before we got halfway there, we met the pickup coming back. The man driving the pickup said that he was the Civil Defense Chief and had been called in to direct the firefight because of the magnitude of the emergency. He told us that one of Sid Greene's CATs was expected to arrive at about ten o'clock this morning (Monday), and that the CATskinner would ask us for directions on how to get up the mountain to put in a fireline across our slope. Rebecca thanked him profusely for coming to our assistance. He replied that he was just doing his job, and that he actually welcomed the chance to get into the field and have the chance to get away from his desk and do things which made it clear to him that he was doing something which was of real benefit in the emergency.

We later heard a story from Wes Simpson about Sid Greene's CATs coming to join the firefight. At the time the fire broke out, Sid's three CATs were about a hundred miles away engaged in a logging operation. Early Sunday afternoon Sid came to Wes Simpson's house, which was directly over the mountain from where the smoke showed the fire to be burning. As they were looking up toward the mountain top, Sid said, "Wes, what do you think?" Wes replied, "If that fire comes over that mountain crowning, they will never stop it before it hits US 101." As Sid turned on his heel and headed for his car, he said "I'm bringing my CATs back here." Of course, these quotations are my recollection of what Wes told me. I introduce this item to illustrate the way in which the logging fraternity pulls together in times of emergency.

On Monday morning, after Rebecca and I had finished our breakfast after sleeping late, we went out to sit on the bank beside our road which came from the county road. A few minutes after ten we heard a heavy truck come in and stop just before coming around a bend up the hill. We were sure it was Sid's CAT on a low-bed carrier, so I suggested to Rebecca that she go down to the creek to show the CATskinner how to get up the mountain while I ran up the road to see why the carrier had stopped. At times like these, nobody wants to discuss whether the suggested plan is the best one; they act. The truck driver and the CATskinner were having a conference about where the driver could turn his truck and trailer around after unloading the CAT. They had stopped next to a place where there was a flat area extending out about thirty feet from the road, with a thick stand of tan oak trees beyond the flat area. When they asked me if there were a place further along on this road where the carrier with trailer could be turned around, I said that the only place I knew of where this could be done without demolishing some trees we had planted was about a half mile further around a bend towards the creek. The driver then asked the CATskinner if he could knock down a row of those tan oak trees so that he could back his trailer in and over the trees that were down and get his tractor in to where he could turn and go out to the county road. The answer of the CATskinner was, "Of course." They unloaded the CAT, and the CATskinner cranked his engine, warmed it up for a few minutes, then put his blade about fifteen feet above the ground and moved in on those trees, whose trunks were twelve to fifteen inches in diameter, and pushed them over without much gunning of his engine. He then backed out of the way, the driver backed into exactly the right spot on the first try, and pushed his trailer over the trees, which proved to be lying on a rather steep slope. The CATskinner then drove through the narrow space between the bank and the engine of the carrier, and stopped a few feet down the road. The driver of the carrier waved as he roared away towards the county road, probably rushing to pick up another D-8.

The top of the track on the D-8 was at about the level of my shoulder, but there were some footholds to facilitate climbing up there where I could talk to the driver by yelling. I pointed to a white, decaying log lying on the ground up the side of the mountain, and told him that log was just above our spring intake, then said that if he could put his firebreak above that we would have water for our house and to hose down any hot spots that might develop. He said that he would do his best to keep above our spring, and not to worry because he would put in a "good firebreak." I then told him to go straight down this road until he saw Rebecca standing beside the road; she would tell him how best to get up the mountain. As he adjusted his smoke mask, gunned his engine, and roared down the road, I had a feeling that the man and the machine were a unit that could stop that fire. I ran down past our house and down the hill to where I could see the CAT already climbing out of the creek and up the bank. He did not follow the old logging road which climbed along the bank and went up slowly. He simply took the most direct route up the steep bank, like a fly on a wall. As he was about halfway up, he began sliding sideways, and I heard somebody yelling, "Don't dump over, don't dump over; you are all we've got between us and that fire." As if in response to the shouting, he braked the uphill track, put all that big diesel had into driving the downhill track, straightened up, and proceeded up the hill. After he disappeared into the smoke, I looked around to see who was doing the yelling. There was nobody there.

After the CAT disappeared into the smoke, we could not see where it was but we could hear that big diesel hitting eight to the bar, so we knew that it was still working for us. By noon, the smoke had cleared enough that we could see that the CAT had gotten south of our spring intake. Later in the afternoon, we became aware that "our" CAT was moving towards the north along the firebreak it had just finished. We were alarmed that something had gone wrong with it, so Rebecca went over to the firefight staging area to find out what had happened. She was told that when our CAT reached the deep valley where the small side stream of our irrigation spring flowed, it was unable to proceed further because of the very steep bluff, sometimes nearly vertical, on the north side of that side valley. We were quite familiar with that valley and should have warned "our" CATskinner about it. We called it Gooseberry Valley, for apparent reasons. We had spent many hours laying a one-inch plastic pipe in that valley, up to the point where we had built a little dam to give us a pool for holding enough water to allow irrigation at a rate as fast as the inflow. Fortunately, our CATskinner was smart enough and cautious enough, even under extreme duress, not to make the mistake of going over that bluff.

The director of the firefight decided to bring in a busload of convicts from the low security "Conservation Camp" a few miles down the Eel River. The inmates of these "Conservation Camps" were chosen from those who were regarded as no danger to nearby citizens and nearly all of them regarded it as a privilege to be transferred to such a place instead of being locked up in a jail. They were often used in fighting forest fires, and we were told that they did a good job, and it was only occasionally that there was an escapee. Those that did choose to escape were usually apprehended in a relatively short time and assigned to a very different kind of prison. By nightfall on this particular occasion, it became apparent that even a ground crew could not handle that steep slope, but they were brought back the next night for an important job.

A few hours after nightfall, when the humidity had increased somewhat, the fire crew set a backfire along the bottom of that steep slope. Except for the places where there was an outcropping of rock, the slope was covered with dense brush. Thus, with the fuel above the line where the firing was done, the backfire was—shall I say, vigorous. The people on the other side of the mountain where Wes Simpson lived were quite alarmed by this lighting up of the sky in fiery red; however, they were soon relaxed by word from the staging area that a backfire had been set.

On this night, Monday, a crew of three Pacific Lumber Co. (PLC) D-8's bivouacked in the clear area of the turnaround. We were told that there

---

were numerous suitable places which acted as home base for a few CATs. The drivers worked ten hour shifts, with one crew going off at 2 A.M. The maintenance crew then came in, worked for four hours servicing the CATs, refueling, and examining the big machines to see if any repairs seemed imminent. The maintenance trucks carried everything necessary for repairing most things likely to wear, short of pulling the head on an engine. At 6 A.M. the day crew took over and worked until 4 P.M. Great effort was expended to ensure that a D-8 did not get stranded up in the woods on a mountain slope with a fire approaching. The CATs were supplied by the lumber companies and the drivers were volunteers, but at extra pay. I received no information as to how much coercion might have been applied, either on the companies by the Division of Forestry, or on the drivers by the companies; however, the esprit de corps which I observed suggested strongly that no coercion was needed. Those CATskinners impressed me as heroes. Their job when fighting a fire was dangerous, and they knew it. As a matter of fact, most of the field jobs associated with lumber production are dangerous. These jobs are held by rugged men, the sort of people who, in many industries, have made the youngest major country in our world the most affluent, the nation to which most of the remainder of the world looks for assistance—and gets it. I make no comment about the hoodlums who fight so hard to interfere with the job the lumber companies do so well. My vocabulary is unequal to doing it justice.

The fire advanced down the steep slope of our mountain relatively slowly on account of being on the lee side of the mountain, and thus sheltered from the strong west wind. However, by mid-morning the fire had progressed far enough that I decided to climb up to the fireline in order to get a closer view of the situation. When I got near the line I realized that the firebreak had been bulldozed through a rather thick stand of tan oaks, a tree which is highly combustible. I called Rebecca on the walkie-talkie I was carrying and asked her to start up the mountain with the EZ saw which I had serviced with fuel and chain oil, and continue until she met me coming down. After we met, I started back up the mountain as she went back down to the green meadow between our house and the creek. The trees that were important to cut were adjacent to the fireline, of course; however, I could not fell them until I felled the trees below. The idea was to get those trees along the firebreak on the ground downhill, sheltered from the fire when the tan oaks above the firebreak burned. I started working across the bottom of the little grove of tan oaks, moving up as I got one row on the ground. As I got near the firebreak, I could see that the ground fire burning brush was near, but there was not yet any crowning of the fire in the tan oaks. After one look across the firebreak, I concentrated on getting the last of the trees down without making any mistakes, and keeping my mind off the possibility that I might run out of fuel just at the last moment. I had no idea how long I had been working.

When the last tree went down, I pitched my chain saw over the pile of fallen trees and followed it down, sliding over the trees. Since I was proceeding from the base of the trunk towards the top of the tree, the branches were all pointing in the direction I wanted to go. I picked up my saw and stumbled down the bed of the little stream from our spring to a little grassy spot beside the stream where the largest of the redwood trees we had planted along the spring stream was growing. I was so tired and so winded that I fell on my stomach on that nice green grass and lay there panting. After a short interval, the tan oaks above the firebreak began exploding like bombs, throwing flames into the sky. Rebecca immediately came on the walkie-talkie, which I had propped up with the antenna upright: "Jim, where are you; where are you!" I sat up and responded that I was on the grass beside that largest redwood tree we had planted. She then demanded that I come down immediately. I told her that I was too beat to come down any further until after a rest. She expressed concern that the fire might jump the firebreak, as it had three other times. I told her that this time the fire was burning down a steep slope, protected from the west wind. Furthermore, even if the fire should jump the break, I could get in that little pool of water in the spring stream which was just below me, and the flames could not possibly get that close to the ground in a spot as low as the stream bed. Both Rebecca and I were very familiar with that particular spot because it was where I had driven the redwood stake at the spot where the descending water line met the ascending water line which provided running water in our house. In any case she was convinced that I was safe, so I lay down and dropped into a deep sleep.

Some time later, Rebecca woke me up with a call on the walkie-talkie: "There are two people here who say that they are psychologists from Civil Defense, and they want to know how we are getting along. I told them that we were getting along fine, but you were resting up on the mountain below the firebreak after felling a bunch of trees. They seem skeptical, so how about you talking to them?" I told them that there was nothing wrong with me that would not be cured by some food and a long rest, so they then asked if it would be OK with us if they sent some of the people who were further down in the valley to talk to us and find out that the fire was not going to get them. Of course we said that would be OK. They were our neighbors; that is, they lived within a mile and a half of us.

When I got down from the mountain, not bearing anything on tablets of stone but carrying my trusty chain saw, I learned some things from Rebecca that had happened during my isolation. She reported that while she was sitting on the creek bank waiting for me, a CAT came up the creek and stopped below her. She knew that there was a narrow gorge upstream with a series of holes in the bedrock, with the stream flowing through between nearly vertical rock walls. Not even a D-9 could get through that place, and the CATs fighting the fire were D-8s. So she slid down the bank and asked if she could help him. He said that he had been told to get up to the fireline at this point. She told him to climb up the bank on the downstream side of the little waterfall on Gooseberry Creek that joined Bridge Creek almost opposite where he had stopped. She also told him that when he got just above the waterfall he could turn into the side creek above the waterfall, and then continue up the creek to where the firebreak came into the creek from the north. Of course she knew that the irrigation pipeline which came down that creek from our little dam up above was no more, but that was a minor detail compared to stopping the fire. We were happy that the Sid Greene CAT had saved our spring intake so that we had water in the house.

Later in the afternoon, when Rebecca was down at the bivouac area, two PLC CATS came up out of the creek. The lead CATskinner waved his arms and shouted: "We came all the way to join up with those coming down from the north. The fireline is holding this time." This was greeted with many cheers because it meant that the fire was "contained." It was all over except for watching for "hot spots" for a day or two. One of these hot spots was directly above our house, and a crew from the Conservation Camp came in to monitor that section of the firebreak. The buses were parked along the road above our meadow, and nobody was allowed to get near the buses. Whenever a snag went down above the firebreak or across the firebreak, the "convicts" jumped on it like a swarm of bees, with much loud shouting—and singing—in Spanish. The majority of this crew appeared to be Mexican.

After dark that night, Tuesday, two CATs came on the road above our meadow and stopped below where the convicts were monitoring the fireline. Since I had gotten some rest after my strenuous activity, I decided to go down to where the CATs were parked and see if I could get any recent news from the fireline. Happily enough, the only recent news was that the firebreak was holding. An occasional hot spot had been quickly extinguished, as when we heard an occasional commotion, with shouting in Spanish, up the mountain above us. Naturally enough everybody was in a relaxed mood, and the CAT skinners were swapping stories about their experiences. One of them told about the enormous boulders he had encountered going along the top of a mountain ridge. He found it necessary to put a detour in the fireline to get by them. Another one gave the following report: "I was coming up Bridge Creek, looking for a way to get up the mountain to the fireline so that I could go south from the point where I was told that the southbound CAT had been stopped by a bluff where they backfired. When I got to the side creek which I figured was my target, I stopped to examine the situation because there was a little waterfall where the side stream came into Bridge Creek. As I was sitting there wondering what to do, this gray-haired woman comes walking around my blade." At this point, another CATskinner broke in with, "Gray-haired woman, what in hell was she doing down there?" The first narrator continued: "She said that she owned this property, that she was very grateful for all that we were doing to stop the fire, and that she wondered if she could give me any assistance in getting up to the fireline. When I told her about my problem with the waterfall, she told me that if I would go up the bank on the left side of that waterfall I would find that I could get into the side stream above the waterfall. I was kind of skeptical about all this, but I obviously had to try what she said. When I got up there, I found that there was just enough room for me to go between the bluff and the waterfall, so I waved to the woman and went on my way up to the fireline. I was the one who met the CATs coming from the south". The second speaker then came in with, "Well, I'll be damned, you ain't kidding us are you?" At that point, I came in with, "He's giving it to you straight; that woman is my wife, and she told me about her contact with 'that nice CATskinner.' " Next comment, "Your wife! I thought you were with the Division of Forestry". Apparently, he was faked out by the "forest green" clothes I always wore while working at Camelot.

When we got up late the next morning, Wednesday, everything was quiet at Cason's Camelot. No CATs, buses, trucks, or pickups charging around our peaceful valley. It seemed so unreal that all of this could have happened since Saturday, when I was jolted by a telephone call from our neighbor and friend, Guy Seaton, who had retired to Humboldt County from his job as head of the welding shop at Bigge Brothers. He was a type we frequently encountered in the area around our Camelot. Wes Simpson and Bob McKee I have already mentioned. I have not had occasion to previously mention Wally West, the man who left his job as an electronics technician at Livermore in order to escape the "rat race." Wally's shop, located on his private road off Shelter Cove road a few miles from Redway, is called "Wally's Westside Repair." He says that his wife suggested the name. We would be unable to operate and keep up our machinery if it were not for Wally. We put in a call to Wally last week to find out why the winch on our little tractor stopped while we were using it to help with tree felling by our caretaker, Richard Donscheski, who retired from his teaching job in a San Diego high school to "escape the rat race." I cite these individuals as representing a different breed from the assorted undesirables in southwest Humboldt County who get all the attention from the news media. There were lots of hippies in days gone by, and the marijuana growers of today, but we have had the privilege of knowing many admirable people such as those cited above.

CHAPTER 20

NEW ZEALAND

During 1975, the year of our fortieth wedding anniversary, Rebecca and I had a lot of discussion about what sort of special thing we should do to commemorate this momentous occasion. Ultimately we decided to take a trip of about one month to New Zealand. Our interest in New Zealand had developed from our friendship with Noel Vietmeyer and his wife. Noel was a native New Zealander who had come to California to do graduate work in chemistry at the University of California. He was doing his Ph.D. thesis work under the direction of Bill Dauben, but his research laboratory was only two rooms away from my office in Latimer Hall. Both Rebecca and I had been interested in horticulture ever since our marriage, and we were well aware of the interesting and unique flora of New Zealand. This led me to strike up an acquaintance with Noel, and this rapidly grew to frequent social meetings between the Casons and the Vietmeyers. The principal topic of conversation at these meetings was New Zealand flora, but we also learned other interesting things about New Zealand. The ultimate outcome was that Rebecca and I reached a firm decision to take a trip to New Zealand.

Although we were quite interested in making the trip to New Zealand without delay, we decided that it would be much better if we waited until I could get a sabbatical leave, which would be in 1977, two years after our fortieth wedding anniversary. By taking a sabbatical leave in residence, which I wanted to do in order to write a textbook for teaching Chemistry 8, I could use a month of this leave for our trip to New Zealand. The requirements for a leave in residence were that I do what I had stated to be the purpose of the leave, and teach one course for one term. This fit perfectly for us to take the New Zealand trip, and for me to do much of the book writing at Camelot, where there would be no interruptions.

Our older son Roger, who had done considerable international air traveling in connection with his accounting profession, advised us that for a non-stop flight as long as the one to New Zealand, we should go first class, even if we had to forego something else. We took his advice, and it was fortunate that we did. We left San Francisco in the afternoon of October 12, 1977, and arrived in New Zealand early the next morning, which was October 14, landing in Auckland in the rain. This was our first experience at crossing the International Date Line. Even during our flight, we began to learn some things about the Kiwi brand of the English language. Several hours into the flight, I asked a stewardess what time it was in New Zealand. She gave me a time which she said was "Oakland" time. After I replied that I wanted to know the New Zealand time, she said that is what I gave you, Oakland time. After a few more exchanges, she realized my problem, and explained how to pronounce the name of the largest city in New Zealand, Auckland. We learned some things on the flight which the rest of the world seemed to know. At our dinner, served on an upper level of the plane, we had the good fortune to share a table with a Pan Am pilot named Grubin and his wife. In conversation with these interesting people, we absorbed a great deal of interesting and useful information about the South Pacific and aviation there. On such a flight bedtime was rather arbitrary, and so we looked around a bit to see how this was handled. Several people were using the same system, so we decided to give it a try. The seats were rather ample, and so we took out the center arm; I sat up in the aisle seat, adjusting the back to my comfort; Rebecca took both pillows to put under her head, which was against the window, and put her legs across on top of my thighs, with the backs of her heels on the arm rest and her toes sticking out into the aisle a few inches. Rebecca was just the right height to fit into this arrangement. It worked fine. Everybody seemed careful not to bump people's feet.

After landing in Auckland and passing into the waiting room, the most conspicuous thing which attracted our attention was a large sign which read, "In many countries, tipping is customary; in New Zealand, tipping is not customary and is not recommended." I turned to Rebecca and said, "I think that I am going to like this country". Everything we saw and did in this remarkable country served to reinforce that first impression. Everything that Noel Vietmeyer had told us proved to be true—in spades. When we passed through the customs inspection, I followed the printed instructions we had received and showed the inspector the plastic bag I had which contained about a pound of apricot kernels. The inspector said that fruits and nuts were not allowed. I explained that I would be very upset if I were deprived of my bag of apricot kernels, for I would worry a great deal for fear of coming down with cancer. He said that he would have to consult his superior and went away with my bag of nuts. In a short time, probably five minutes, he returned, gave me the bag, and said that one bag for the two of us was allowed. On the return trip to our homeland, my treatment coming through customs at Los Angeles was very, very different.

Our next step after clearing customs with our baggage was renting a car from Avis, which proved to be a Ford Escort four-door sedan. Since this vehicle was not marketed in the U.S. at that time, we had never seen one before. Any misgivings we may have had about a completely unknown car were rapidly dissolved. After about seven thousand kilometers, utilizing a total of three different cars, we concluded that it was the best car that we had ever driven. No problem of any kind, and some of the roads our cars were taken over were challenging—such as a hairpin turn on a steep, narrow two-way road with a mirror at the bend of the hairpin so that a driver could see a car coming from the opposite direction. When we turned in the car that we drove on the South Island without a scratch on it, the attendant was astonished.

A very pleasant young lady took us and our baggage to the rented car, and after I was seated in the driver's seat on the right side and Rebecca was on the other side of the front seat, I asked our attendant to explain the controls to me. She zipped along pointing to various things and commenting as she went. Only problem was that I could not understand anything she said. I still remember her last few words, delivered just before she went on her way. The nearest I can describe those words in English was: "Sigh, owl stritefowd." After about two weeks, I was getting sufficiently familiar with the New Zealand brand of spoken English to know that she had said, as translated into English: "See, all straightforward." As a matter of fact, I began to become rather intrigued with understanding the New Zealanders with whom I talked, and sometimes ostentatiously displayed my new knowledge while talking to New Zealanders as Rebecca listened in bewilderment. She did not enjoy learning new things.

After our attendant left us I tried out a few levers, then said to Rebecca, "You drive first." Response, "She was talking to you". JC: "But I couldn't understand one damn word she said." RMC: "Neither could I." End of conversation. I drove around in the parking lot until I could locate the necessary controls as needed. At the Avis desk, we had received a map on which was marked the airport and the route to the DB Mangere Hotel, where we had a reservation. This was one of only two reservations we had made before leaving the U.S. We wanted to be footloose and go wherever we decided we wanted to go. We were warned at the DB Mangere that we should make reservations at least one day ahead, and we did so. It was the off-season for tourists, but native New Zealanders do a lot of touring about the country. Later, we were surprised at the density of traffic, especially on holidays. I drove cautiously to our hotel, with Rebecca watching to warn me of any mistake I might make. I was surprised to find that I had no tendency to drive on the right side of the road because of being surrounded by cars on the left side. There was a problem with remembering which side to expect the traffic from at an intersection; looking up and to my right in order to look at the rear-view mirror but finding only the corner of the roof; reaching for the gearshift lever with my right hand and hitting it against the door; and other details. Somehow or other, we made it to the hotel.

Since we had not eaten since our dinner on the plane, as soon as we got unpacked we went to the dining room for dinner. We had a good dinner, as was usual in New Zealand, but learned a few things about local customs. The most remarkable event involved asking for a glass of water with our meal. After a long absence, the waitress came back and asked if we wanted this water in a cup or a glass. We told her anything would do, but we usually drank our water from a glass. After a much longer wait, she came back with a pitcher of water with orange slices in it, along with two large glasses on a tray. Apparently the kitchen was not equipped to fill our order, so our waitress went to the bar. We had a rather hilarious time at our meal, frequently learning something new. After we finished, we restrained the impulse to tip our waitress, but thanked her for her excellent service in filling our unusual orders. About ten minutes after we got back to our room, there was a knock on the door. It was our waitress, bringing Rebecca's handbag, which she had left at the table. Rebecca was so flabbergasted that she didn't even think of tipping the waitress, but thanked her profusely. There were several hundred dollars worth of travelers checks in Rebecca's bag, but we had not yet gotten any New Zealand money except for about a hundred dollars which we had gotten at the San Francisco airport on the advice of our travel agent.

After we took a nap for an hour or so, I decided to go to a bank in a shopping mall across the street from our hotel and get a few hundred dollars of New Zealand money, using my travelers checks. The exchange rate proved to be about 1:1. When the woman at the window gave me my New Zealand money, she said, with a big smile, "Now you have some Kiwi money." After that I began to refer to the New Zealand brand of the spoken English language as "Kiwiese." We next drove around for a while to practice, then had a light meal and went to our room to plan our next day. We decided to drive up to Whangarei and stay there for two or three days as a base while we investigated that interesting part of the North Island. The Kauri Forest National Park was not too far away. When we called the desk and asked them to reserve us a room at the DB Onerahi Hotel at Whangarei, it was done at once by telex. We had learned that the best hotels were likely to be DB hotels. DB is a beer company; however, they also had a large chain of hotels. Rebecca and I are not beer drinkers, but we certainly enjoyed the DB hotels.

As we drove up to Whangarei the next morning, we noted a rather constant litter of small dead furry animals along the road. When we inquired about this at Whangarei, we were told that this little animal was an opossum which had been introduced from Australia to supply skins for the fur trade. During geological events extending over millions of years, New Zealand became isolated from the rest of the world with unique flora and fauna. There were no ground animals, but a great variety of birds, including large predatory birds. When Europeans first arrived in New Zealand, there were only three land animals present: a rat, a dog and the Maoris (humans) which had come across the open Pacific Ocean in the "great canoes" which brought the Maoris to this Garden of Eden. As to whether the rat and dog were included intentionally or accidentally, that story is found only in the history of long ago. It is reasonable to assume that even though the great canoes were big boats in those days of yore, there would hardly be enough secluded space to allow at least two of each species to escape notice. In any case, Homo sapiens became dominant in this isolated sub-world; and, as usual, made a few mistakes in their interaction with the other animals. The opossums from Australia prospered in this world without natural enemies to such an extent that by the time of our arrival there was a large program in place to control the rate of increase of these little animals. New Zealand has had a program in place for at least one hundred years to improve both flora and fauna for the benefit of their people. In overall consideration, these innovations have been quite successful, especially for flora, because of the remarkably benign climate. I will later report on the interesting introduction of trees and cultivation of native trees, after we have visited the Forest Research Institute at Rotorua.

Whangarei is located on the north shore of a bay, and the tip of the south shore of this bay is named Marsden Point. This Marsden was a distant ancestor of Rebecca's. In view of this personal relationship, we decided to visit Marsden Point by making only a slight detour from our route to Whangarei. This site is unlikely to become a tourist attraction; there is a petroleum refinery there. Nevertheless, we were glad to have visited it so that Rebecca could tell her relatives about it. We arrived at Whangarei well before dark and enjoyed watching a Maori marriage ceremony—the costumes were spectacular. We also had time to read a newspaper, something we had already found to be a must for getting acquainted with this remarkable country and people. We began to learn such things as MP is a member of parliament, but PM is Prime Minister. We learned why there are so many locations along the east shore of the North Island which begin with "whanga". Whanga in Maori means bay in English, and there are lots of whangas along the east shore of the North Island. We also noted that there were several Maoris in Parliament. It was later that we learned a great deal about the cordial relationship between Maoris and "Europeans," which bears no resemblance to such relationships in any other country with which I am familiar. We made our plans for spending two more nights in Whangarei, visiting the Bay of Islands area on the first day and the Kauri Forest on the second day.

A major point of tourist interest at the Bay of Islands is the town of Russell, which is situated on a peninsula which juts out at a strategic place to give a view of the Bay of Islands in three directions. The foot of this peninsula is reached by taking a ferry across Waikare Inlet. We reached the ferry landing just after a boat had left for the terminal on the Russell side of the inlet, so we had time to look around before the ferry came back to our landing. I was a little jumpy about driving onto the ferry boat, since it was only my third day of driving our Escort, so I went down to the shore where the ferry landed. At the point where the ferry docked there was no barrier to prevent a car from driving into the water if no boat was docked there. When I started back to where I had left our car, behind the only other car waiting for the ferry, I found that Rebecca had gotten out of our car and come up to visit with the people in the other car. This was consistent with the policy we had already adopted of getting acquainted with New Zealanders whenever possible. This contact proved to be especially interesting. The man was a neurosurgeon from Auckland whose name was David Robertson. He and his wife had a second home on the shore of the Bay of Islands, a few miles north or east of the peninsula where Russell was located. As I entered the conversation, I expressed surprise that there was no barrier to prevent a car from driving into the bay. He seemed not to understand what I was talking about, so I explained that in my country there would be a strong gate across the space where the boat docked, and a siren would sound if a car got too close to the barrier. After thinking for a moment about my explanation, he responded, "If a person is so drunk or so stupid as to drive into the water, why stop him?" I told him that I thought his system was better than ours.

When Dr. Robertson learned that we were from California, he said that we must drive behind him to his home on the bay, for he was growing a grove of redwood trees on his property and he would like us to see them. I explained that we would like very much to see his grove of redwoods, but that would not be possible because it would make us miss the last ferry. He said that was no problem because we could take a road along the strip of land between Waikare Inlet and the ocean. This road then joined Route 1 just north of Hikurangi, which was not far from Whangarei. By this time it had become apparent that there was no polite way that we could refuse his invitation. Not only that, but we wanted to accept. So we followed the Robertsons at such high speed, and on gravel roads, that I had trouble keeping up. I spun out once, but they waited at the next intersection until I caught up.

Our visit with the Robertsons was very interesting indeed. Of course, our first interest was directed to the redwood trees. This was the first occasion on which we learned that the redwood tree grows at about one-fourth the rate in New Zealand as in California. Later, at the Forestry Research Institute, we learned that a great deal of effort had been directed towards learning what special requirements are necessary for the growth of trees in New Zealand. A particularly interesting thing the Robertsons were doing involved the weka bird. The weka is a large flightless bird which is endemic to New Zealand; i.e., not native to any other place in the world. It was not regarded as endangered, but its numbers were being reduced rapidly by rodents which ate the eggs of the flightless birds. The Robertsons were engaged in a project to build up the numbers of the weka bird. They had a feeder situated about a hundred feet below their house, towards the bay. Dr. Robertson said that the weka was a very curious bird, and if he went out in the yard they would probably investigate to see what he had done. A few minutes after he went out and put some food in the feeder, these large birds began coming out to investigate. We watched from the porch as we enjoyed the tea they served, and engaged in interesting conversation about the different practices in our two countries. As I understood it, in one respect medical practice was the same as in the U.S. at that time, in that each person chose his doctor or doctors; however, there was a large difference in another respect. The New Zealand government paid all of the bills; indeed they would pay all expenses for medical attention that we might need during our visit. I have no idea whether this system has survived to the present time, but if it has I would think that it ought to be investigated. Dr. Robertson said that he had no complaint with the system, and that he enjoyed being free of any worry about finances. In view of the spread which he had on the shore of the Bay of Islands, I certainly did not detect any financial strain.

As sunset approached we reluctantly bid a fond farewell to the Robertsons and thanked them for their splendid hospitality. When we had gotten south of Waikare Inlet as nightfall was approaching, we noted two things which we had neglected: our petrol gage was near zero, and we had not seen a filling station since we had left the Robertsons. As the road turned inland and began to climb over the mountains, our map suggested that we were not going to see a filling station before we got to Route 1. In addition, we had seen very few cars on our route. There was no problem about the hairpin turns, for there were no lights coming toward us except on very rare occasions. We could think of no alternative except to continue and hope that we had a little fuel when our gage showed zero. We made it to Hikurangi, which was six kilometers south of the intersection with Route 1, but before we exhaled with relief, we discovered another problem. After about 6 P.M., everything in New Zealand is closed up and dark. After we had gone a few blocks, we came to an engineering company which had a petrol pump in front of it, but all was dark. There was barely enough light to read the sign on the wall of the building, which read Hikurangi Engineering. Across the street was a little grocery store which seemed to be the first floor of a residence, and there was a light on in the store. The door was open, so I went in and found a man examining the bins of vegetables. I explained our problem to him and asked if there were any way we could get enough petrol to get to Whangarei where we had stayed last night and had our room reserved for tonight. He answered approximately as follows: "I own the engineering company across the street, and I usually am closed by this time, but I will be glad to open up and sell you some petrol as soon as I finish picking out my veggies." I don't remember just what I said, but I certainly expressed my thanks in the strongest terms. After my benefactor had selected his veggies, he called upstairs and said he was ready to check out. He paid his bill, went across the street and turned on a light in the building, then came out to sell us petrol. He said I should come inside to pay him, which I did. When I told him we were going to the Kauri Forest the next day, then south to Hamilton on the day after that, he said that Hamilton, which was in an agricultural region, was not very interesting. I should take the road to the east and visit Mount Maunganui, which was a very interesting drive. He gave me a book of maps and marked our route to Mount Maunganui. When I asked him the price of the book of maps, he said he was giving it to us so that we would enjoy our trip in New Zealand more. When I got to the car, I found that there was a price of $2.00 marked on the book of maps. We decided that it would be a mistake to go back and

offer to pay him. Everybody that we met in New Zealand simply overwhelmed us with their hospitality!

When we set out from Whangarei for the Waipoua Kauri Forest it was
raining lightly, and that continued throughout the day. We later learned
that frequent light rain was common in the North Island, in contrast with
the South Island where torrential rains on the west coast are frequent.
Waipoua is the largest of the kauri forests and is the headquarters of the
government agency which controls all the kauri forests. Government control of the kauri forests is necessary because the kauri wood is probably the
best of all woods for many different purposes, and the growth cycle for
harvest of kauri trees is about 200 years. During the days of sailing vessels,
ships came from over the world to get the trunk of a kauri tree to be used
as a mast (more about the growth habits of this remarkable tree will be
given later). During World War II many kauri trees were logged to meet
the emergency need for wood for construction; however, there has been
very little logging of kauri trees since then. We noted that power poles are
frequently made of small beams of reinforced concrete.

When we arrived at the Waipoua Forest, we found that considerable
road repair and construction was in progress—during the off-season for
tourists. Nevertheless, we persisted. After all, kauri trees were a major reason for our deciding to visit New Zealand. The roads through the kauri
forests were not built for commercial traffic, and both the construction and
rain exacerbated the problem for a driver not accustomed to driving on the
left side of the road. Curves were banked rather steeply to reduce the hazard of skidding on the gravel road. Soon after we got into the mountain-
ous terrain, I noticed that Rebecca was really terrified when we went
around a curve to the left. When I asked what the problem was, she commented: "When we go around those tight turns with me on the inside, and
I look out to the side, I see this gully that is almost straight down. I feel like
one of these motorcycle riders in a carnival where they ride around on a
circular vertical wall." I had not noticed anything because I had good reasons for concentrating on the road, not looking off to the side. On the next
curve to the right, I took a quick glance to my right and found I had to look
down to see anything besides tree tops. What a sensation! That glance
must have lasted for about a millisecond, for I realized how important it
was to keep my mind and eyes on my driving. Apparently the expression

on my face prompted Rebecca to say, "See what I mean?" I restrained myself from saying anything properly illustrative of my reaction; I knew that I could never do it justice, so I just said, "Yes." After some consideration of the fact that we were not going to give up our visit to the kauri forest, we decided that the problem could be solved by Rebecca never looking down, always up, in whatever direction she might be looking. This required much self-discipline, but Rebecca did quite well at it, and soon began to enjoy the interesting things we were encountering. Since I could not take my eyes off the road for even a millisecond, she also advised me of interesting things which I could see after slowing down or parking. Since we were almost alone on this rainy day, there was no problem about parking in the road at a place not too near a curve in either direction. Although the curves attracted much of our attention, actually they were a rather small fraction of the road.

All along our drive we noted the features we had read about in books on the kauri tree. It was quite rare to see what could be called a grove of kauri trees. It was rare to have more than half a dozen of these trees in view at the same time, and some of the larger ones were alone, surrounded by several other varieties which were packed close to the trunk of the kauri tree, which was always bare of branches. As a young kauri tree grows, it sheds its lower branches so that the lower part of the trunk is bare, with no marks to indicate where branches had grown. As the tree grows, the shedding of branches continues above the bare trunk. In very old trees, the trunk becomes a bare log extending upwards to the branches high above.We did not have a chance to really appreciate the form and size of the kauri tree until we arrived at a place where a parking area had been developed at the road. A trail had been cleared for several hundred feet from the parking area to one of the largest of the kauri trees, which was named "Tane Mahuta" (Lord of the Forests). The surrounding forest had been cleared around the massive trunk for a few feet to allow a view of the manner in which the trunk and its buttress had developed. In one direction, at right angles to the trail, a swath about twenty feet wide had been cleared for a distance of about fifty feet from the tree. This was to allow a picture to be taken of at least a part of the tree. Using our wide angle lens, we were able to show where the trunk had limbs growing out from it. Tane Mahuta is estimated to be about 1,200 years old, and its height is 169 feet.

The first limbs occur at 41.5 feet above ground, and its crown spread is 11,600 square feet. Its girth at 15 feet from the ground is 45.17 feet, from which the diameter may be calculated as 14.38 feet. The reason that the girth is measured several feet from the ground is that the base of the tree is a huge buttress extending like a collar about three feet beyond the trunk. As I stood transfixed looking at this phenomenon, I realized that my mind was not really comprehending what I was looking at. If one considers a round tank 14 feet in diameter, such as used for water or oil storage, and then considers that tank extending 40 feet into the air before presenting a crown of limbs for another 130 feet, then one begins to have some inkling of what I was looking at.

When we got back to our Escort, with our heads still spinning from trying to comprehend what we had seen, we met a group of New Zealanders getting out of their car. As usual, we proceeded to get into conversation with them by commenting on what an incredible sight Tane Mahuta was. As soon as one of us opened our mouth a few times, they knew that we were from America. In answer to a query, we said that we were from California, and that really stirred up some conversation. They were quite interested in what they had heard about California redwood trees; that in California redwood trees grew to heights greater than that of the kauri tree, in contrast to the redwoods growing in New Zealand, where the oldest ones were slender trees less than 100 feet in height. I told them that the tallest redwood trees were about 270 feet, but that old growth trees of about 200 feet were not unusual, and that redwoods we had planted in 1947 were 40 or 50 feet in height. Finally, they asked whether we thought the kauri trees or the redwood trees were most impressive and interesting. I replied that this was a question which could not be answered in useful terms. Answering this question would be even harder than deciding whether oranges or apples are the best fruit. Any superlative that might be applied to each of these trees would be likely to fit the other. As the conversation was ending, I told them that we had decided to visit New Zealand in celebration of our fortieth wedding anniversary, and that the Kauri Forest was our most important target. Road construction and rain had not turned us back, and we enjoyed every minute of our day in the Kauri Forest. They replied that they were anxious to visit America, and that California and its redwood forests would be their first target. I told them not to be disappointed if the redwood parks were overrun with people; they should look at the trees and not the people. There were plenty of people to look at in lots of places.

On the day before we left Whangarei, we had the DB Onerahi Hotel call the DB Mt. Maunganui Hotel to make a reservation for us. On each occasion that we had a reservation made for us, the recipient of the call asked how we would pay for our reservation. Our reply was always, "Kiwi money." Before our supply of Kiwi money became low, we would stop at a bank and exchange travelers checks for Kiwi money. We had no inclination to explore the question of who would take traveler's checks, for it rapidly became apparent that use of cash would expedite matters. Otherwise, why would the question always be asked, and our answer accepted immediately? We had provided ourselves with an adequate supply of travelers checks. As a matter of fact, we returned to the U.S. with about half of the traveler's checks with which we started, in spite of the fact that we bought numerous presents for various people as well as ourselves. Noel Vietmeyer had told us that traveling in New Zealand was relatively inexpensive, but we found it even less costly than expected.

Since the drive to Mt. Maunganui was about twice as long as we had previously driven, we got an early start and bought "take aways" for our lunch. Every small or large eating place along the road would have a large sign promoting "take aways." These items were somewhat like what would be bought at McDonalds or Denny's except for the absence of anything that could be regarded as a hamburger. The analog was something called a meat pie, which was kept warm in a customer-accessible oven. We ate our lunch in a beautiful little park stretching along the shore of Hauraki Gulf, above the central section of Auckland. Fortunately, the man who sold us petrol at Hikurangi had given us a map with the route to Mt. Maunganui marked on it. Otherwise, we would not have enjoyed the beautiful drive along the shore above Tauranga Harbour.

Mt. Maunganui is located at the tip of the south peninsula which is one side of the narrow entrance to Tauranga Harbour. Thus, there is water on both sides of this city, and we enjoyed watching the activity of all kinds of small boats in the harbor. The thing which I remember most vividly about Mt. Maunganui is a small area of very green grass on the shore of the ocean. There was a small, low building in the center of this site, with the inside of the building consisting mostly of one room. In the center of this room was a stand with an inscribed stone tablet on it. I failed to write down this inscription; however, it made such a vivid impression on my mind that I recall the gist of it, as follows: "This memorial is dedicated to those who gave their lives that the rest of us may live in peace." As I read this inscription, I realized that it reveals a great deal about the character of so many of the New Zealand people. Many years later, I was able to understand certain behavior of the state of New Zealand which was not admired by many other people with whom I had talked. I refer to their banning from their waters any ship carrying nuclear material.

It is a short trip from Mt. Maunganui to Lake Rotorua, which is at the heart of the thermal region in New Zealand, so we had time to check in at the DB Rotorua Hotel and then proceed with almost a full day of exploring this interesting area. In retrospect, I have concluded that the area around Lake Rotorua is by far the most interesting part of New Zealand. Of course, the thermal activity is the center of attraction and is the only part of this region that most tourists see or remember. However, we found many other things which are almost as unique and far more interesting. We left after two nights there, regretfully, in order to see some of the many interesting things that were on our list. We fully intended to return to New Zealand soon, and find out if it would be possible for foreigners to own land among the beautiful string of lakes east of Lake Rotorua. New Zealanders were well aware that they had developed a land which is the closest thing to the Garden of Eden as there is on this earth; and they were very jealous of it and very wary about an influx of foreigners. When we stayed at the James Cook Hotel in Wellington, after returning from the South Island, we learned about Guy Fawkes and some of the history of the development of modern New Zealand.

Alas, "the best laid plans o' mice and men gang aft agley." We became wrapped up in the almond orchard, which we bought in order to give me "something to do" besides sit on my dead end until I die. Probably a bad choice, but who knows? The orchard certainly gave me something to do, but that comes in the next chapter, which is several thousand miles from this chapter. And so I must shift gears, and start thinking of those golden days of yore.

On our first day at Rotorua, we decided to drive first along the string of lakes which has a paved road, Route 30, running south of them. There are several other lakes southeast of Lake Rotorua, and we visited them later. The three lakes north of Route 30 are, in order from Rotorua, Rotoiti, Rotoehu, and Rotoma. The largest of these three lakes is Rotoiti, so this must be with reference to Rotorua. Obviously, roto means lake in Maori language, and the small list of adjectives in one of our books of maps includes iti, which means small. (Could this be the origin of the English expression, itty bitty?) Rua means hole or cavity, which I presume refers to the steam that pours out of the ground in many places around Rotorua. There must be a big hole down there someplace. These lakes have beautiful blue water in them with green mountains rising around them. Occasionally we saw a sailboat, and automobiles on the road were only slightly more numerous than the sailboats. As we stopped several times in order to drink it all in, we kept thinking, "What a marvelous place to own a piece of mother earth." There was a small motel on high ground above the road which had a place in it which looked like a restaurant. There was a woman there who said that she did not usually have people stopping at this season except for weekends, but she would feed us since we were from America. I have no recollection of what food was served us, but I certainly remember how pleasant it was to be eating as we looked out across Lake Rotoma, and we learned a lot about the country from our "hostess." She was a little upset because she learned, after she had bought this property on which to build the little motel and restaurant, that she did not strike steam when she drilled her well. This meant that she had to spend money for electricity for heating purposes. By the next day we learned much more about the extent to which steam from the ground was used for most heating purposes.

At the DB Rotorua Hotel that night, we learned how a hotel could take advantage of thermal steam for most heating purposes. There was an indoor swimming pool heated by steam to a temperature at which I would not like to take a bath. The entire building seemed to be heated by thermal steam—quite a cheap source of heat. Rebecca went down to the laundry room to wash some of our clothes, but she could not find any facility for drying them. When she inquired of the office if they had drying facilities, a woman came down and pointed to a bank of steam pipes on the wall. When we looked out our window over the city of Rotorua, we got the impression that every building was venting steam into the air.

The next day, we visited some of the places that were arranged for tourists to view the results of the thermal activity. We were quite interested in a stream which was flowing water that was so hot that it smoked. Of course, the stream bed was volcanic rock, but very close to the water on each bank of the stream lush green foliage was growing. Most areas in and near the city showed no sign that thermal activity was affecting the surface flora. We spent some time visiting several interesting sites, such as the Maori village that had been buried under lava in a volcanic eruption during the preceding century. It had been excavated to show the remaining walls and sometimes things such as cooking utensils. We spent much of our time at the Forest Research Institute, where we were treated cordially and supplied with much information about their work.

This institute had been investigating ways of improving the supply of trees suitable for making lumber since the preceding century. Although New Zealand was home of the kauri tree, whose lumber was probably the best in the world, this lumber was of no commercial value because of a harvest cycle of about two hundred years. There had been no reward for their efforts to introduce other trees into the large area of the North Island which appeared to be excellent for growing trees, until it was discovered that the problem resulted from a lack of traces of a certain element in the soil. I cannot find my notes on this subject, but I think that the element was cobalt. After this discovery many trees were introduced from several countries and cultured for a sufficiently long period to determine their worth.

The results of these studies were rather interesting. The redwood tree is still being studied, but there had not yet—as of 1977 when we were there—been discovered any means of encouraging the redwood to grow at a rate anywhere near that experienced in California. The Douglas fir tree (Pseudotsuga taxifolia) gave the strongest and best lumber for construction purposes; however, that tree also grew more slowly than in California. The lumber was used only for special purposes requiring strength. The tree that was the most successful as a lumber tree or for paper pulp was the Monterey pine. This surprised us, since the Monterey pine is a rather small tree in the U.S.. In New Zealand, this tree is planted in dense stands, and as they get to a suitable size they are pruned up very high so that the foliage appears above a bare trunk. I presume that this is done to mitigate the way that a pine tree produces many small limbs and thus many knots in the lumber. There are some eighty different species of pine trees that are endemic to the Northern Hemisphere, but none in the Southern Hemisphere; so this makes the success of the Monterey pine in New Zealand even more interesting. This reminds me of our failure to grow kauri trees from seeds which we obtained from a ranger at the Kauri Forest.

Our next objective after Rotorua was New Plymouth, on the west coast near the base of Mount Egmont, in Egmont National Park, which dominates the skyline in the bulge of land on the west coast near the southern tip of the North Island. On our way to New Plymouth, we stopped by the Glowworm Cave, which is a favorite stop of the tourist buses. This is a remarkable geologic formation, including a rather large stream flowing through one part of the extensive cave chambers. The glowworms are in the roof of this chamber where the stream is located, and they can be observed from a boat on this stream. The people are taken through in a group in the boat. Since we were alone, we had to wait for a group with two vacancies in it. Of course, this is a perennial problem with any tourist trap anywhere, but we left feeling glad that we had been avoiding favorite tourist attractions. Rebecca was feeling rather set upon when we left, and she commented to the attendant at the gate about the "puny redwood tree" near the entrance. The tree was about twenty-five feet tall. The attendant replied with some heat that this was not a puny redwood tree; it was about forty years old. At this point I pulled Rebecca's arm and led the way to our car.

The last part of our drive to New Plymouth was along the road near the coast, with the view ahead dominated by Mount Egmont. We had been told that the top of Egmont was rarely seen on account of being perennially shrouded in clouds. When we were several kilometers from New Plymouth, we noted that the top of Egmont was clear, so we took several pictures. Before we arrived at New Plymouth, Egmont was again shrouded in clouds. It was raining in New Plymouth, and our trip was longer than usual because of our stop at the Glowworm Cave; however, we enjoyed several of the beautiful gardens in that city after we had checked in at the DB Bell Block Hotel, which was on the coast just above the city of New Plymouth. This was our first close view of the ocean on the west shore of New Zealand, and we found the ocean much more violent than on the placid east coast of the northern part of the North Island, with its many bays and harbors. We had not yet been exposed to the violent ocean on the west coast of the South Island.

The drive from New Plymouth to Wellington was longer than we had previously driven in one day, so we did not have time for any side trips; however, we enjoyed the beautiful scenery encountered on this trip. We drove on Route 3 around the eastern base of Mount Egmont, then along the coast of the South Taranaki Bight, past Wanganui and onward until Route 3 joined Route 1 at the Rangitikei River. From there to Wellington was 150 kilometers, most of it close to the ocean. The James Cook Hotel, where we stayed in Wellington, was rather high on the mountain ridge that extends to Cook Strait, which is between the North and South Islands. We had heard so much from friends who had visited Wellington about the strong winds that blow there that we were surprised to find rather mild winds. On our return trip from the South Island, we found out what our friends were talking about.

Since the car rental company did not allow their cars to be taken from the North Island to the South Island, our first move after checking out of our hotel room, was going to the dock where the Avis office was. There was nobody in the office, which was a separate small building, so we were puzzled about how to turn in our car until a man from Australia arrived with the same objective in mind. He stuck his key under the door to the building, and told us that this was routine procedure, so we followed suit. We had already delivered our baggage to the proper place to go to the South Island.

We saw some interesting things while we were waiting for the ferry to depart. We watched in fascination as a man backed his car, with a big trailer on it, at least two hundred yards on a long ramp for loading cars onto the boat. Apparently loading and unloading was done from only one end, and the slow part was done while loading. On reading some literature which we received on board the ship, we learned that loading and unloading all kinds of freight on these large ocean-going ferries was a very elaborate process involving pumping water in and out of tanks to keep the ship on an even keel. After all, these ships were built to operate in Cook Strait, "The Windpipe of the Pacific." On this trip the light winds continued, and the top decks of the ship were filled with people basking in the sun and watching the sea gulls that followed the ship. There was much conversation about what a beautiful day it was.

Another incident which interested us was a minor collision between a bus and a passenger car. The two drivers got out and seemed to be having an amicable conversation while waiting for the arrival of a police officer (it may have been some other official). The official had a short conversation with the drivers while making notes, then everybody went on their way. When we inquired of some people near us about how their system worked, they told us that the government took care of such things. I had heard about the highly "socialized" government of New Zealand, but I did not expect to be so favorably impressed by it. I presume that lawyers are rather scarce in New Zealand. If so, it really is a Garden of Eden.

After the very pleasant "voyage" to Picton, the port where the ferries dock, we rented our car from Avis and loaded our baggage into it. We were anxious to get another Escort since our first one had performed perfectly. We were scheduled for another car of British make, but the attendant did some shifting around which he was not supposed to do—since we were from America—and gave us another Escort. Our accommodation by the people of New Zealand continued!

We decided to stay at Blenheim on our first night in the South Island, principally because it was only 28 kilometers from Picton on Route 1, and was the beginning of Route 63, which we expected to take the next morning. Following our practice in the North Island, we had called ahead for a reservation at the DB Criterion Hotel. The Criterion was an okay hotel but a far cry from the deluxe accommodations to which we had become accustomed in the North Island. Notwithstanding, we had the Criterion call ahead for a reservation for us for the next night at the DB Westport Hotel in Westport. Blenheim is the largest city in what is probably the most intensive agricultural area in the South Island. We were told that its annual rainfall is the lowest for any place in New Zealand, with the exception of a small desert in the North Island. Since there was nothing which attracted our interest around Blenheim, Rebecca and I spent some time planning our trip in the South Island. It was apparent that we would do much more driving between points of interest, partly because of the much greater size of the South Island, and partly because there were so many mountains in the South Island that the population density was very low, except for a narrow coastal zone on the east shore. We decided that our next target would be the Franz Josef Glacier, and that we would reach it by way of Westport, where we would stay overnight.

We got an early start for Westport the next morning, although the distance was only 267 kilometers. From studying the map we realized that about half the distance would be crossing several mountain ranges. For about one third of the distance we drove along the beautiful Wairau River valley; after that, we got into the mountains. In general, we drove along in a deep valley in a direction that was more or less north-south until we came to a place where the road could go over the mountain to the next valley. We then turned west for a relatively short distance of very slow going. Many places on those east-west stretches were much more difficult driving than anything we had seen on the North Island. After three of these cycles, the final east-west stretch slanted off to the southwest and continued until we reached a low area along the coast. At a point 6 kilometers from Westport, Route 6 which we had been following, turned south along the coast, and the road to Westport came in right at the turn in Route 6. Tomorrow we would be continuing on Route 6 all the way to Franz Josef Glacier.

During the final part of our drive it was raining, and we were thankful that we had gotten in just at dark. We were not in a mood for sightseeing. The DB Westport Hotel was a little better than camping out, but we were very cold all night as we listened to the rain pouring down on the metal roof. At the dining room, also under the metal roof, we were asked if we were with the tour bus. With our answer in the negative, we were put at a different table where the food was better. The food was the only thing we enjoyed at Westport; however, stopping there was inevitable, for it was another 293 kilometers to Franz Josef Glacier. There was simply no other road across the mountains north of the glaciers except one from Christchurch, which the maps indicated as even more difficult than Route 6, which we took. It is probably of significance that the route we took was numbered six all the way over the mountain and south to Franz Josef Glacier. There is a fine hotel at the glacier, operated by the Tourist Hotel Corporation of New Zealand. After our experience with two DB hotels in the South Island, we always stopped at the "government tourist" hotels whenever they were available.

During our drive down the coast on Route 6, the rain poured down and the waves pounded against the coast. Since the distance for us to cover to Franz Josef was 293 kilometers, we did very little sightseeing on this trip. We stopped briefly at a place where the pounding waves blew huge waterspouts through blow holes. Another place that we stopped was Hokitika, which was of interest to us since we were rock hounds. Jade is mined near Hokitika, and there was a large display in a shop near the highway. We bought a few items made of jade and also bought a couple of pieces of raw jade to work on in our rock shop. We were surprised at how much they charged us for these items when we went through customs at Los Angeles. Thus, we congratulated ourselves on how little we had paid for them.

When we arrived at the Franz Joseph Hotel about an hour before dark, the rain had stopped for the first time during our trip. There was a flat area of one or two acres around the hotel which was a beautiful garden; however, the entire area was a sea of water, with the paths and road to the parking area standing just above the water. We cautiously drove our car to the dry parking area in front of the hotel, checked into our room, and heard that this appearance of things around the hotel was quite common at any season, but especially during the spring. Since the skies had cleared, except for a few billowy clouds, we figured that these would be ideal conditions for pictures, so we rushed out with our cameras. After we had taken a few pictures, a large husky individual in knee-high boots came sloshing through an area that we assumed to be grass. As soon as this individual spoke, we realized that it was a woman. She told us that she was the gardener at the hotel, and hence very familiar with the area. She suggested that we should not waste our film by taking pictures today because tomorrow would dawn as a beautiful sunny day, with the mountains freshly covered with snow, glistening in bright sunshine. When we expressed some skepticism, she said that there was no doubt about this scene developing; we would find that the large room in the hotel, whose outside wall was all glass, would be full of people before and after breakfast. We learned that this gardener was a European (I forget which country), but spent most of her time in New Zealand.

It turned out, the next morning, that the predictions of the gardener were right on the mark, but the view out that window was even more spectacular than represented. The room was set up with rows of seats arranged as in a theater, with that glass front wall the stage. I have never seen anything on a television screen that could compare with that spectacle. As Rebecca and I were watching this scene while sitting at the end of a row of seats and chatting with each other, a group of four people stopped beside us, and one of them said, "I judge from your speech that you are from America." When we admitted the accuracy of his judgment, there followed a normal sequence: where are you from? California. So are we, where in California? Berkeley. We are from Walnut Creek, just over the hills from you. We have good friends in Berkeley, Charlie and Tess Koch; he is on the faculty in the department of chemistry at the university. This stimulated much conversation, and a get-together arranged by Charlie and Tess after our respective returns to California. Charlie Koch has been mentioned more than once in earlier chapters in this chronicle.

We left the Franz Joseph Hotel rather early in the morning because the distance to Wanaka was 293 kilometers, and the road was described by a tourist from England as the worst road he had ever driven on, even in Yugoslavia. We hoped it was not worse than the Kauri Forest road, which we had driven on in the rain when it was under repair. Fortunately the Haast Pass road proved much less difficult than the road over the mountains to Westport, which we drove in the rain. In any case, we decided that since it was not raining and we had an early start, we would take the short drive to the foot of the glacier in order to examine the moraine in front of the present foot of the glacier. This rubble was left as the glacier receded during the past many decades, and I wanted to see it. I had read about such a moraine in my early studies of geology but had never seen one. Actually, the southern part of the South Island is probably more convenient than any other place in the world for observing Alpine conditions. There are hundreds, perhaps thousands, of square miles of nothing else.

The first part of our drive was on a twisting road along the Tasman Sea. On account of the clear, sunny weather, we were exposed to one magnificent view after the other. At the end of this drive along the coast we came to a one-way bridge across the Haast River, about a quarter of a mile long. We had frequently encountered one-way bridges in New Zealand, even on main roads, but this was the longest such bridge in New Zealand. It was the only one-way bridge we had seen which was so long that there was a short two-way section near the middle where one car going in one direction could wait for an oncoming car coming towards it from the other direction. This system of watching and waiting for a car already on the bridge was used in all the one-way bridges, but the Haast bridge was so long that it was difficult to see whether another car had already started from the other end. On another occasion on the South Island, I arrived at the bridge as another car was already on it coming towards us. While waiting I was looking at the river, whose gravel bars were of white rock, and I did not start across the bridge at once when the oncoming car had passed. Rebecca told me that there was another car on the other side of the river which was waiting there. I was rather puzzled by the situation and sat there trying to decide what to do, when Rebecca said, "Go ahead, he is obviously waiting for you." And so I went ahead. The other driver waved as we went by, and so I waved in return. When we stopped for petrol at the next town, I told my story to the attendant who sold us petrol, and asked him why the man had waited for me. His reply was, "It was your turn, you were there before he was as the other car was crossing the bridge." I responded that I had studied the traffic regulations carefully and had found nothing about that. His response, "We don't make laws about that sort of thing." And so I had learned more about the character of the New Zealand people.

As we proceeded up the Haast River a magnificent panorama of beautiful snow-covered mountain peaks unfolded before us, with no clouds in the sky. Although we were on the outside of the road, i.e., the side of the precipitous drop to the river below, the road was not as bad as the route to Westport. At just about any place our camera was pointed there would be a beautiful scene, so Rebecca, from her position on the left side of the car, took pictures as I drove. When we got to the top of the grade, the road turned sharply to the right and proceeded across the mountain ridges, which were oriented in an east-west direction at this point. After getting over several mountain ridges, we went down into a valley where Lake Wanaka is located. Wanaka, and the Wanaka Tourist Hotel are at a beautiful site at the southern end of this large lake.

We were quite pleased to find such a fine tourist hotel as that at Wanaka, for it is at a strategic location 212 kilometers south of Mt. Cook on a relatively good road. The only other approach to Mt. Cook was by a difficult road from Timaru on the east coast, all the way across the mountains of the South Island. We were told that the expensive road over the Haast

Pass, which we traveled, had been constructed relatively recently in order to develop an alternative to the difficult route from Timaru. In any case, we certainly enjoyed the Wanaka Hotel, which was located in a beautiful setting in the mountains of the South Island.

Although the drive from Wanaka to Mt. Cook was only 212 kilometers, we left Wanaka early and arrived at the Mt. Cook Tourist Hotel in time to check into our room, get a late lunch, and buy a ticket for the bus which drives up over the moraine to the glacial ice. This gave us a good view of the moraine, and the opportunity to get out and walk around on the glacial ice. Our pleasure was diminished somewhat by the fact that nearly all the occupants of the bus besides us were members of a group from a tour bus. As we had encountered in other contacts with a tour bus, this group had a self-appointed master of ceremonies. This individual made running comments rather steadily, and occasionally drew loud guffaws from his group. This is just one of the problems arising when one crosses the path of a tour bus. Frequently we figuratively patted ourselves on the back for having planned our own trip as we went, with avoidance of tourist buses. As mentioned earlier, Mt. Cook was the only advance reservation we made, except for our first night after our arrival in New Zealand. As a matter of fact, our decision to stay an extra day in Rotorua necessitated our changing our reservation at Mt. Cook to one day later. Since we made this change from our hotel in Rotorua, we were able to get a room the next day, but it was on the side of the hotel rather than in the front, facing Mt. Cook. Our luck held out; this change proved to be at least as good as our original location would have been.

After dinner that night, we went out on the lawn area near the hotel wearing the heavy coats (from our days of skiing) that we had been warned to bring; sat on one of the benches which were provided; and literally soaked up the beauty with which we were surrounded. In any direction we looked there was bright moonlight shining on snow-covered mountains. We were the only people enjoying this magnificent scenery, although there were plenty of empty benches around us. At breakfast the next morning, I asked a waitress why nobody was outside last night enjoying the magnificent scenery. Her answer, "After dinner, most everybody is in the bar."

After about an hour on the lawn bench we were beginning to get cold, even with our warm clothes, so we decided to go inside and up to the observation room on the top floor of the hotel, which faced towards Mt. Cook. There were two or three rows of benches there, with the rear ones elevated above the lower ones so that everybody had a view. Again, we were the only ones there. After a short period, a nice looking elderly gentleman with a drink in his hand came in and asked if we would be bothered by his joining us. We assured him that we would be simply delighted to have him join us. He told us that this hotel was built on land owned by his grandfather. After that the conversation got still more interesting. He told us about some of the early history of this area. Near the end of the conversation, he complained about how he could not get a room in the hotel any more without making a reservation a few weeks in advance. The place had been spoiled by tour buses. We expressed enthusiastic agreement with that statement. The last thing he told us before leaving was that we should get up before sunrise the next morning and get in a position, such as in this room, to see Mt. Cook; we would see the sun shining on the east slope of the tip of the mountain for a short period of time. He said that if we did that, and it remained as clear as it was now, we would be two in thousands of visitors to Mt. Cook who had seen it. We assured him that we would be ready with cameras in hand at sunrise, and we thanked him profusely; said that we felt very lucky to have met him.

When we got back to our room, our first act was to call the desk and ask them about the time of sunrise. The woman at the desk said that sunrise here depends on what place you are viewing. When we told her the tip of Mt. Cook, she immediately gave us a time, and so we left a call for forty-five minutes before that. We next examined our little balcony, and were delighted to discover that we could see the tip of Mt. Cook. The next morning we were at our stations, me in the observation room and Rebecca on our balcony. It was clear at sunrise and we got our pictures. I then went back to our room carrying my camera and Rebecca's bag, which was standing right where she had left it the night before. I wonder if there is any place in the world besides New Zealand where this sort of thing could happen. Notwithstanding, we decided that in the future we would store most of our travelers checks in our bag in the car, and I would carry most of the Kiwi money in my billfold.

Our early arising, because of the picture taking, fit in well with our desire to get to Queenstown early enough that we would have time to do some things on the day of our arrival. Queenstown was a little south of Wanaka, and so it was 268 kilometers from the Mt. Cook Hotel. We arrived at about 2:30 P.M., and checked into our room at the Travelodge. We found Queenstown very different from any other place where we stayed in New Zealand. We were told that this was due to the fact that Queenstown was a favorite vacation spot for New Zealand people. We were not interested in such things as powerboat rides on Lake Wakatipu, or riding the cable car lift to the top of the adjacent mountain. We decided that we would enjoy more driving our car along the top of the interesting looking mountains across the lake, which were called the Remarkables. We did not see anything very remarkable about those mountains when viewed from Queenstown, and the same held true after we drove along the top of them. There were some nice views of all of Lake Wakatipu, but we took only a few pictures because the wind was blowing so hard that I was afraid of being blown down and/or blown away.

We did not leave for Te Anau until just before noon because we went to the travel bureau before leaving, in order to make our reservation with Pan American for our return trip to the U.S. In order to get a non-stop flight for the return trip, it was necessary for us to go to Los Angeles. In spite of our late start, we arrived at Te Anau at 3:30 P.M. The distance was only 181 kilometers, and the road was better than those we had traveled recently. During the last part of our trip, after we had turned onto Route 94 and were facing directly towards the west, we became aware of a pronounced haze in the air, and a strong wind blowing from the west. After we had checked in at the Fiordland Motor Lodge, we inquired at the desk of the motor lodge about the haze in the air. We were told that this was smoke which was being blown in from Australia, where they frequently had extensive brush fires at this season of the year. When I expressed amazement that smoke could be blown such a great distance, our informant said that this happens when a strong west wind brings in heavy rain, with snow in the mountains. This reminded me of our drive down the coast from Westport in heavy rain and pounding seas against the shore. When I asked if we should expect heavy rain soon, the answer was, "Before daylight." After the gorgeous weather we had at Mt. Cook, and the clear skies we encountered for our drives on the difficult mountain roads,

I could hardly feel disappointment over the current development. However, I did wonder if the weather would permit us to take our trip on Doubtful Sound, for which we had bought tickets in Queensland when we made our reservation at the Milford Sound Hotel.

The rain started at about midnight. Since our motel room was beneath a metal roof, as is so characteristic of New Zealand buildings, we had no uncertainty that the rain was a downpour. When we asked the waitress who served us our breakfast if the Doubtful Sound trip would be called off, she said that she did not know about that operation, but she had never heard about anything around here being canceled on account of rain. Thus encouraged, we drove the 21 kilometers down to the head of Lake Manapouri where the boats for the Doubtful Sound trip docked. When I went inside the small building at the dock and asked if the Doubtful Sound trip would be operable this day, the woman at the desk showed great surprise that I would ask such a question: "Of course we will operate; we would be out of business if we did not operate in the rain." Following advice we had received, we bought a box lunch at the little restaurant which was in the same building.

The first leg of our trip, to the West Arm of Lake Manapouri, required about an hour in a powerful motor launch. According to my recollection the launch seated about forty people: ten rows of seats with two people on each side of a center aisle in each row. The launch obviously had a very powerful engine, for it traveled at high speed and threw up quite a wave in its backwash. About halfway to our destination at the lower end of Lake Manapouri, the pilot of our boat came on the loudspeaker and said, in a rather worried tone, "The launch which is overtaking us on our right is much faster than we are, and I don't know what is going to happen." What happened was that the faster boat cut in front of us, throwing the massive wave of his backwash against our side—only our pilot turned sharply to his right so that the nose of our boat struck the wave at a sharp angle, and we rode through with only a mighty shake-up. This was repeated at least twice, as all the passengers chattered nervously. I commented to the people in the seat in front of us that if this were in my country, the pilot of the other launch would be among the unemployed before he docked his boat. In view of some other events on this trip, I decided that this event was all fun and games for the entertainment of the customers. Of course, this sort of thing is strictly forbidden in the U.S. In this instance, contrary to some other comparisons I have drawn between these countries, I take a dim view of such practices in New Zealand. I do not see any point in doing things "just for the fun of it" when there is an obvious hazard involved.

When we arrived at the dock at the West Arm of Lake Manapouri, it was still pouring rain, as was the case throughout our trip. There was a short wait before the bus which took us to the head of Doubtful Sound departed. This gave those who had brought lunches, including us, a chance to eat their lunch. The bus trip to Doubtful Sound from the West Arm of Lake Manapouri passed over Wilmot Pass, and was reported to be the most expensive road in New Zealand, costing about five dollars per inch. It was built to bring the enormous electric generators from the head of Doubtful Sound to the hydroelectric generating plant which is located 800 feet below the level of Lake Manapouri. This plant is located in a vaulted room which was blasted out of the solid igneous rock. Thus, the generators were powered by a column of falling water 800 feet high. The bus we rode in to the generator site passed through a tunnel blasted out of the rock. This tunnel was not of small diameter; it was built to permit passage of each of the seven generators which were lined up in the vaulted cavern. One generator was ordinarily not in operation; it was held in reserve, ready to go on line if another generator failed for any reason. I did not ask how often more than one generator was off line. Ordinarily, this would not be serious; it would reduce the amount of electric power available in New Zealand by a small percentage.

As I stood in this tremendous man-made cavern, with the whir of the generators in my ears, I was rather overwhelmed by the magnitude of this Manapouri Project. This sort of thing requires people of great imagination, tremendous self-confidence, and faith that it can be done. According to the report I received, the project was initiated by Australians, but designed and supervised in construction by the Bechtel Corp. of California. The turbines which turned the electric generators came from Scotland, while the generators came from West Germany. It all sounds fictional, but it was not. Those generators have continued over the years to supply a significant part of New Zealand's electric power.

After our side trip to the hydroelectric power station, the bus continued over Wilmot Pass to the head of Doubtful Sound, where we transferred to a boat. Because of the heavy rain, we were rarely out of sight of falling water in the steep beds of the numerous streams. The rain continued as we set out along Doubtful Sound. As we were to learn later, Doubtful Sound is much narrower than Milford Sound, so one is much closer to the waterfalls. The heavy rain produced large amounts of water in the falls. Picture taking became a matter of just how many waterfalls one wants to record in pictures, so we soon settled down to just enjoying the experience without any thought of pictures. For a significant part of the trip I climbed on top of the cabin and sat on the bench under a tarp. I was wearing a trench coat with a slicker, which had developed a rip in it, over the trench coat, and a rain hat which came down over my back. After a few minutes I was soaking wet up to my knees, and rather wet in some other places, but the view of the close-up waterfalls was simply terrific. Apparently, I was generating so much adrenaline that I was only vaguely aware that I was wet until we got to the bus which took us back to the West Arm. There was no one else on the roof when I first climbed up there, but soon thereafter, an elderly gentleman climbed up, sat down beside me, and introduced himself as the former head of the New Zealand Tourism Office. He said that after he retired he decided to visit some of the places he had read a lot about, but had not previously visited. I greatly enjoyed my conversation with this gentleman as we watched the waterfalls.

By the time our bus got back to the dock at the West Arm I knew that I was wet and cold; however, there was one incident that took my mind off of how cold I was. At a a shelter, our bus stopped as an apparition came out of the rain. He had a knee-length coat as his only protection from the rain, and immediately went to the baggage compartment, opened the door, threw his big pack into it, closed the door and got onto the bus. After paying the driver with some bills, he threw his wet coat on a vacant seat, sat down beside a person whom he appeared to know, and said, "My god, I almost missed it." We learned later that the only motor vehicles on this short road had to be shipped in via Doubtful Sound, so they were frequently used by hikers in the area. Hiking under extreme conditions seemed very popular in New Zealand. Even "tracks" such as the Milford Sound Track are downright dangerous in spots.

My remaining recollection of this day concerns how grateful I was for the heaters under the seats in the motor launch that took us back to the dock where our trip originated. Nonetheless both Rebecca and I have agreed, in retrospect, that the Doubtful Sound trip was the high point of our trip to New Zealand. The torrential rain no doubt added a great deal to the trip. It was not only the amount of water pouring down from the nearly vertical walls of the fiord, but the congeniality that develops among people involved with such an event. I particularly remember the gentleman who was retired as head of the Tourism Office. We obviously had something in common or we would not have been the only two people who elected to sit on top of the cabin in the rain.

As we left Te Anau the next morning, on our way to the Milford Sound Hotel, the rain had let up but the weather remained unsettled. We were so pepped up by our glorious day in the rain on Doubtful Sound that we were undaunted by the dark clouds hanging over the mountains. We had no way of knowing that Milford Sound would prove to be the low point in our visit to New Zealand. The drive from Te Anau to the Milford Sound Hotel is only 121 kilometers; however, we were aware of a wait of up to 25 minutes before getting through the one-way Homer Tunnel, which cuts through the top of the mountain. So we left Te Anau sufficiently early to allow enough time to get aboard the cruise ship on Milford Sound. We had bought tickets for this cruise while in Queenstown. Our schedule worked out okay—except that we were unaware that Daylight Time became effective on October 30 that year!

There was nothing to do, of course, except make the best of it. Actually, it was a great day for pictures. The two most famous targets for pictures were Mitre Peak and Bowen Falls. Mitre Peak was covered with snow almost to the water's edge, and Bowen Falls was pouring out a record flow. When we had our film developed after arriving back in Berkeley, one of our slides of Mitre Peak was better than the one we bought from the tourist's store there. When it began to snow again while we were having our dinner, we were not worried until we were reminded that the Homer Tunnel was several hundred meters above sea level. It snowed all night, and there was some snow on the ground around the hotel, which was only a few meters above sea level. Since the snow had stopped falling, and the hotel personnel said that there might not be enough snow on the road to stop us, we decided to check out of our room and try to get up to the Homer Tunnel. Since the other side was downhill, we should have no problem if we could get to the tunnel. It turned out that before we got more than about two kilometers up the grade we began to slide around without making any progress. We had noticed that there was no traffic coming towards us, which convinced us to try and get turned around, then go back to the hotel. We backed up a little to where there was a wide place inside a turn. With Rebecca driving and me pushing, we managed to get turned around, mostly by my pushing sideways. We then changed back to me driving, and managed to get back to the hotel. We passed two cars that had gotten stuck at a lower level than we had been.

The hotel management was not at all amenable to giving us our room back; it had been reserved for months. Of course there were others besides us who were stranded, and so the group of us were able to make progress with convincing the management that there was no place for us to go, so they would have to arrange for us to sleep in the lobby. By the time that they had decided that they would put us in tiny rooms where the employees slept, cancellations began coming in over that one wire that was thrown on top of the bush, with no poles. We finally unloaded our baggage into the same room we had the preceding night. The people in charge of the cruise ships on the sound also made a decision to have a cruise for those who were faked out by Daylight Time, plus any others who were stranded and would like to buy tickets. Thus, the Tourist Hotels Corp. came through quite well under difficult circumstances. We enjoyed the cruise on Milford Sound just as much as if we had not already had the Doubtful Sound cruise. As we had been told while on the Doubtful Sound cruise, Milford Sound was much wider. As a matter of fact, we were told that the Queen Mary cruise ship from England was scheduled to come into Milford Sound a few weeks later.

During this period with people stranded, an epidemic of flu broke out, brought in by people from Australia. At that time I had been taking large quantities of vitamin C each day since the early fifties, as reported in Chapter 14, and I did not come down with the flu. Rebecca had not started taking a couple of grams of vitamin C every day, and she got the flu. She had not begun to feel the full impact of the flu, however, by the next morning, which was November 1. We waited until after lunch before leaving for Invercargill, to allow time for the snow to melt. Buses had begun to come in from the east. We had no difficulty getting up to the Homer

Tunnel, and after that we had no problems. We were familiar with almost half of the route to Invercargill because it was the same road that we had traveled on our way to Te Anau.

The distance to Invercargill from Milford Sound is about 280 kilometers, but the road was good, and we arrived there at about 5:30 P.M. Since the single wire, lying on top of the bush, to the Milford Sound Hotel was overloaded with communications because of the storm, we were unable to make advance reservations at Invercargill. When we arrived we found that the city was overrun with people because of the occurrence of an important series of horse races—sulky racing, not with riders on the horses. We went to a hotel in search of lodging and food, but encountered, "booked solid." Someone in the hotel told us that a place called the Candlelight Restaurant was not well known to tourists and might be able to accommodate us for dinner. The restaurant was a small place on the top floor of a building, approached by a long narrow stairway, with a small sign beside the door which gave the name of the restaurant and nothing more. We had lucked out again, partly, perhaps, because of the instincts of New Zealanders to help Americans. The restaurant was a rather small room in the shape of a T, and seemed to be run by a middle-aged couple and their daughter. As soon as we opened our mouths, as usual, they knew we were from America, and so all three, as well as a couple of patrons, gathered around us to ask questions about America and answer our questions about New Zealand. For example, we learned that no one would think of putting a thoroughbred racehorse out in the fields without a blanket fitted over it, because of the cold nights and cold rains. We had been noticing these horses wearing blankets as we were driving down the road that day. We also learned some more useful things, such as a new motel that had just opened about two miles out of town, and was not fully ready for the races. Maybe they would have a room for us. To cap all this, Rebecca got the best medium rare sirloin steak she had eaten in New Zealand. In fact, she had given up on beef and shifted to lamb. I ate venison most of the time, which I really liked when prepared the way that New Zealanders prepared it. They cooked thick pieces slowly with a gravy that was not thick or greasy, and it was very tender. They sometimes hunt the red deer that were introduced from Australia many years ago, but these same deer were sometimes grown on ranches, like cattle.

This pleasant experience at dinner helped to raise Rebecca's morale, which was most welcome, for the Australian flu was really hitting her by this time. We did find a room at the Ascot Motel, named in honor of the races, I presume. Rebecca was so tired from the long day on the road that she got some good sleep in spite of the flu.

The next day we drove to Dunedin, which had been described as "more Scottish than Scotland." I presumed this to be a slight exaggeration; however, we did see the school children walking around in short plaid skirts for the girls and pants above the knees for boys, always in uniform. It was cold there, and the knees of the kids were really red. Again we came in without reservations, and the motels were mostly out on a peninsula which was on the far side of the harbor. We finally found a place run by an elderly couple with four or five units.. There was no heat in the place except heaters embedded in the floor, with no controls accessible by us; not so good for a person with the flu. I finally hit on the idea of turning on the hot shower in the bathroom with the door open, and this was a big help. During the night we were saved by a heater under the bottom sheet of the bed, for we had control over this. Rebecca was better by the next day, saved by the "electric sheet."

Dunedin had no particular attraction for us, and we left early the next morning and arrived at Christchurch at about 2:45 P.M. This city had been described as "more British than Britain." We have never been to Britain, but Christchurch was very different than any place we visited in New Zealand. At no other place have I ever seen a banker sitting at his desk in the bank with coat and tie and knee length pants on. We had made reservations at Christchurch, but were never able to find the place—very strange. We finally found a very nice place near the gardens we wanted to see, called the Commodore Motor Inn. It was not very British, in that the rooms were nicely heated.

Rebecca's flu had improved sufficiently for her to enjoy the plethora of parks in Christchurch. Hagley Park in the center of the city is a very large park containing playing fields as well as many types of ornamental shrubs. We were particularly interested in the Botanical Gardens, which contained everything from succulents and bulbs to cherry trees and huge rhododendrons. Christchurch is a lovely place, entirely different from the remainder of the South Island, where magnificent spectacles attract tourists.

We left Christchurch early the next morning so that we would have time to cover the 350 kilometers to Picton by late afternoon. This road was Route 1, which was good all the way. In addition, I had driven several thousand kilometers in New Zealand by this time, so that everything was coming naturally to me. This made the driving more pleasant, as well as more safe, without such total concentration. After we had checked in to our motel, we asked a clerk in a store about a good place to get dinner. She directed us to what sounded like "Whilersin." When Rebecca said that she did not understand, the woman made motions with her hands which were supposed to indicate a fish swimming. My Kiwiese had gotten to be pretty fair by that time, so I cut in and thanked her for the information and asked her where the restaurant was located. She pointed down the street, so we left going in that direction. As soon as we got out of earshot, Rebecca said, "Did you know what she was saying?" I replied, "If we come to The Whalers Inn after two or three blocks, the answer is yes." We had a nice dinner there.

The next morning we checked out of our motel and took our Escort, to which we had become quite attached, to the Avis office and turned it in. This "voyage" on the ferry was quite different from our trip coming down to the South Island. We had been warned about the weather, so Rebecca was fortified with motion sickness pills. There was so much of interest on this trip that Rebecca got so absorbed that she handled the rough seas without a flicker. When we got out of the inlet, at the end of which Picton was located, we learned why Cook Strait had been dubbed "the Windpipe of the Pacific." This ocean-going ship was pitching and rolling and burrowing into the waves. As we were nearing the entrance to Wellington's harbor, we began to see fishing boats making a run for it. At times one of them would disappear entirely as a wave rolled over it, but it would come out right side up and holding to its course. I decided that the hardy souls in these boats either had nerves of steel, or lots of faith in God. Or maybe they were the same type that loves to hike the Milford Track.

At the Wellington dock we checked out our third Escort and then returned to the James Cook Hotel for our second stay there. What a difference from our first time! As the bellhop and I were unloading our bags we had to hang onto them, without a moment of lax vigilance; otherwise, our bags would have been blown to God knows where. As I was helping the bellhop wrestle with our bags, Rebecca was checking us in at the desk, according to our usual practice. When she came up to our room, on the top floor, she reported that a dinner with my favorite venison and her lamb was $16.30 for the two of us, with an additional charge of $5.50 for room service. I did not ask her any silly questions about whether she had ordered room service. After about thirty minutes our dinner arrived, borne by two young men. There was a large glass-top table in front of an even larger plate glass window looking out across Wellington Harbor. Our servants set out our dinner with us seated side by side, facing out the window. They advised us to call the office when we were ready for our dessert, and departed without any indication whatever that they might get a tip. Rebecca looked at me, then looked out the window, and said, "Nobody will ever believe it." When I checked out the next morning, the total bill was $52.80, from one of the finest hotels in New Zealand, located a few blocks up the hill from the Parliament Building. Small wonder that we returned from New Zealand with about half of our travelers checks not cashed. While writing this chapter, I have been wondering how much this situation has changed. This would be especially interesting since the U.S. dollar is now worth a lot more Kiwi dollars than was the case when we were in New Zealand.

To add to our pleasure, there was entertainment outside our window, down in the harbor. This just happened to be Guy Fawkes day, one of the biggest holidays in New Zealand. We heard some folklore about the origin of Guy Fawkes day; however, we learned of its true origin from our friend Noel Vietmeyer. It was an importation from England, where Guy Fawkes was executed for leading a group that plotted to blow up the Parliament building. Just at dark, fireworks started all over the harbor—all over that large harbor! It seemed as if new fireworks began pouring up from another boat at frequent intervals. We told the young woman who brought our desserts that we certainly enjoyed the show put on for us while we were eating such a fine dinner. We have already mentioned that "our best day" in New Zealand was the wet day in Doubtful Sound. Our most enjoyable evening in New Zealand was that night in front of the big window on the top floor of the James Cook Hotel. No doubt about it.

During the fireworks we hardly noticed the howling wind around our hotel. Even at our elevation, there was continual booming. I assumed that there was no concern about fires being set by the fireworks during such a strong wind, for all of the fireworks were over water. After bedtime we had a little trouble getting accustomed to the howling wind, but it then became a part of the environment—like sleeping on the airplane when we flew to New Zealand. The next morning we discovered a large bank of louvers across the side of the hall on that side of the building. I knew that they were installed to prevent the strong wind from reducing the pressure outside the building enough to cause the windows to pop out. This happened to a building in Boston several years ago.

The distance from Wellington to Taupo was 378 kilometers, our longest drive in a single day during our stay in New Zealand; however, it was certainly not our most difficult. The roads on Route 1, which we followed all the way to Taupo, were very good. Our trip to Taupo was uneventful, although we did run through a rather violent thunderstorm as we were driving through the only desert in New Zealand, east of the mountains in the Tongariro National Park. This was quite interesting to us since we had been unaware that such a thing as a desert could exist in New Zealand. This was especially surprising to us since we were just returning from the overabundance of snow and water in the South Island. Since we arrived late in the afternoon, we located a motel before eating our dinner. We stayed at the Oasis, which advertised itself as a "beach resort motel." We were not interested in swimming or sun bathing, but the view across Lake Taupo was quite interesting. Since our older son, Roger, had become quite involved with sailboats at that time, we were especially interested in the variety of sailboats on the lake.

When we made our plans that night, we decided to stay a second night at Taupo since we had a little time available. When we left on the morning of November 8, we paid our bill for two nights lodging and one dinner for the two of us: $65.30.

We visited several interesting places within driving distance of Taupo, but the one thing which stands out in our memory was the Wapahihi Botanic Society in Taupo. This was a small-scale organization which had been formed years ago by a group of local people for the purpose of developing and beautifying a hillside. Our impression was that the original purpose was to provide a place where the members could work on it essentially as if it were the garden of each of them. One day each week was designated as Members Work Day. All the members who were so inclined gathered for a day of garden work and the accompanying socializing. This seemed to provide most of the labor for the development of the property. By the time of our arrival, it had functioned so well that they had numerous members from various locations in New Zealand, as well as a few international members. After our return home, we applied for and received an international membership. We later supported a special development of new facilities by buying a "Membership in Perpetuity," which seems to differ from a life membership by lasting after death.

On our last night in Taupo, we decided to try and find a better restaurant than the one at The Oasis. There were numerous restaurants all around the lake. We decided to try the restaurant at the Tui Oaks Motor Inn, which proved to be a good choice. Their venison seemed unusually good. Our bill for two venison dinners with added salads, at 0.95 and 0.80 for each , and two coffees (the tag says "black water") at 0.80 for the two, amounted to $13.55. OK, so I would not believe it either, if I were not looking at the tag from the restaurant as I write.

Our drive to Auckland the next morning was only 279 kilometers; part of the road was a motorway, and I felt rather relaxed on my last drive in New Zealand, except in the city of Auckland. I found driving in Auckland interesting, but not relaxing, even after four weeks of driving in New Zealand. Since the DB Mangere Hotel was near Route 1, on which we were driving, we naturally had made reservations for our room there. Its proximity to the airport also made it convenient for turning in our third Escort just shortly before boarding our plane to Los Angeles.

We had allowed ourselves one day in Auckland in case of an unexpected delay in getting back there. We had no unexpected delays, so we had a chance to see and do a few things in Auckland, as had not been the case on our first stay there. We decided that our first activity would be buying some New Zealand stamps as a gift for our friends Mary Dee and Ted Vermeulen. The traffic jam, noise and confusion at the location of the Central Post Office was a surprise to us, but once we got involved, we decided to persist in our mission. I let Rebecca off as close as I could get to the post office building, then set out to drive around a few blocks and then return to pick her up. Fortunately, we had designated a specific spot where she would stand and wait for me to pick her up. It turned out that driving around a few blocks was handicapped by one-way streets, "no right turns," various irregular shaped blocks, and a few other things. It was something like a half hour before I got back to the appointed place, so I expected Rebecca to have worried that I was hopelessly lost—which happened more than once. Instead, there was no Rebecca at the appointed spot. I pulled into a place marked "No parking," where I could see this spot. I figured that if I should be accosted by a traffic policeman, I would plead ignorance on account of being an American, and hope to be treated as well as I had been treated so many times during our New Zealand adventures. Actually I was not accosted, and Rebecca showed up in about five minutes and apologized profusely for being so slow. And she got the stamps she wanted. Our New Zealand luck seemed to be holding out to the very end. I began to think that maybe there is something about New Zealand that promotes good luck.

There are numerous parks, gardens, museums, and scenic reserves in Auckland. We decided that the things of most interest to us were located in what is known as the Auckland Domain. This is a large expanse in the central part of Auckland which includes a park, sports fields, museums, and a large botanical garden featuring a variety of tropical and sub-tropical plants. Although we had visited many beautiful gardens in several places during our trip to New Zealand, we decided to visit the garden concentrating on tropical plants, with which we were not familiar. We enjoyed seeing many of the plants we had read about. We also enjoyed the variety of New Zealand people who were visiting this garden. There were many Maori children there, with the girls wearing colorful clothes. Many of the children were playing games, always in a well-behaved manner, even when the playing was rather boisterous.

The last site that we visited was the Auckland War Memorial Museum, specifically, the floor devoted to one of the finest collections in the world of Maori relics and carvings. There was a reconstruction of one of the "Great Canoes" which brought the original Maori people across the open ocean from Polynesia. I was quite intrigued by the construction of this oceangoing canoe. It was situated in the museum in front of a typical Maori temple. While we were there a group of children from one of the schools came to visit the temple. Although the group was rather evenly mixed with Maori and "European" children, several Maori songs were sung. We also saw carvings and paintings of Maori history, which were especially interesting to me because of my long standing interest in history.

As all things must, our cherished trip to New Zealand finally ended. Since we were now veterans, there was no hitch to delivering our baggage to be loaded on the plane, turning in our third Escort, and finally boarding the plane for Los Angeles. As we took off it was raining, just as it was when we first landed at Auckland—and just as it usually is, according to all reports. We enjoyed the light rains we encountered in the North Island much more than the downpours characteristic of the South Island. Our best day in New Zealand was in heavy rain on Doubtful Sound; however, this was an anomaly, resulting from the convergence of several coincidences.

Our flight to Los Angeles was uneventful. Much of it was in daylight, in contrast to our trip to New Zealand, but this was a trivial difference, since the view from forty thousand feet is rather uninteresting. We found the customs agents at Los Angeles to be very nasty. The inspector said that there was a ban on bringing furs into the US, so I could not bring in the opossum fur slippers we had bought as presents. I told him that the opossum in New Zealand is a serious pest which is being systematically killed off by a government agency; in the northern part of the North Island, we found the roads to be littered with road kill of these pests. He was unimpressed, but finally agreed to consult his superior—while the people in line waited. He finally returned and begrudgingly allowed us to take the fur slippers with us. In the general confusion which was occurring throughout the customs area, Rebecca and I got separated from each other, but somehow or other finally got together in time to board the plane where our baggage had already been loaded. We could not help but contrast our experience with that at Auckland, where our bag of apricot kernels caused only a minor, friendly delay. But "All's well that ends well" (with apologies to Shakespeare).

Our flight to SFO was entirely uneventful, and seemed to us like taking a street car to the other side of town. Mary Dee met us at the airport, waited for us to collect our baggage, and took us to 486 Michigan Avenue. After a light lunch we slept the sleep of the weary, with some interruptions by dreams of Maoris; glaciers; beautiful lakes and streams;

delightful people called New Zealanders; steam pouring out of a thousand chimneys in Rotorua; and, most vividly, the roaring waterfalls lined up one after the other on the nearly vertical banks on each side of Doubtful Sound. How unfortunate that the turn of events has prevented us from seeing such things again—except in our dreams.

Chapter 21

THE ALMOND ORCHARD

During my first twenty years at Berkeley, a time when I was very busy, I gave exactly zero attention to the retirement system in effect at the University of California; however, several older professors, including Professor Axel Olson in the chemistry department, were directing a great deal of attention to the UC retirement system. It was especially inadequate in years of great inflation. Working through the Academic Senate, this group of professors succeeded in convincing the Regents to introduce significant improvements in our retirement system. By the middle of the1970s, when mandatory retirement loomed close enough to me that I could see it through the haze, I realized what benefactors Axel Olson and his group had been for all of us. According to the improved system which was in effect at that time, mandatory retirement for academic personnel was set to occur at the end of the academic year in which the sixty-seventh birthday occurred. My natal date was in August 1912; therefore, my retirement date was July 1, 1980. If my natal date had been sixty days earlier, my retirement date would have been one year earlier.

As early as 1975 I began to direct significant attention to the question of what I would do after being forced to retire. From observing the behavior of numerous people as they approached retirement, and after retirement, I realized that I would need something to do after retirement that required my attention on a regular basis. I was accustomed to working in positions where failure to do my job and do it well would cause trouble for other people, sometimes many other people. How could I be satisfied with traveling around the world, with no particular objective other than traveling around the world? I knew that I would need something to do which would go to hell in a handbasket if I failed to pay attention to my duties. Some kind of business suggested itself, of course. I knew that I would not thrive in a retail sales business, such as running a rock shop, because of my having no appetite for bickering with people about such things as price. Rebecca and I eventually settled down to the idea of engaging in some kind of agricultural operation, since both of us had great interest in horticulture. Next we decided that something which continued from year to year, such as trees or vines, would be our choice. Neither of us had interest in growing row crops where there is no continuity from year to year except for the land on which the crops had been grown. Rebecca had grown up on an orange orchard, and stated unequivocally that she did not want anything to do with one. Among other comments: "There may be worse problems in other kinds of agriculture than in orange growing, but I know what the problems in orange growing are, and I do not want to contend with them any more." Sounded logical. We finally decided on an almond orchard for several reasons which appeared to be well based. The most convincing factor that influenced us was the fact that the operation of an almond orchard can be made nearly 100 percent mechanized.

After looking at several other orchards that were for sale, we bought an orchard of about 75 acres, of which about 60 acres were planted with almond trees. By an ironical twist of fate this purchase occurred at about the time that the federal government finally got around to legislating against discrimination against older people, the last large group of people to be given relief. California passed laws to essentially duplicate the federal legislation. Prior to that time, discrimination against older people was not only rampant, but generally regarded as quite acceptable. This turn of events had no effect on my pleasure, and that of Rebecca, in having bought the almond orchard; however, it did affect our activities during the next few years because my retirement was delayed for three years. For one thing, this gave me time to apply for and get a sabbatical leave in residence, which gave me the opportunity to write a textbook and also spend a glorious month in New Zealand, as recounted in the preceding chapter. It also caused a delay of two years before we devoted significant attention to the almond orchard, on account of having spent much time working out the details of my retirement, which I will be discussing next.

As might be expected, this legislation was controversial, and was debated for a long time before its actual passage. As a result of the debate certain exceptions were included in the final form of the legislation. One of the exceptions deferred for three years elimination of discrimination against College Professors.

At first consideration, this sounds like an example of the old adage: "If you want to discriminate against some group of people, pick a group that is too small to successfully defend itself." Actually, this was not the case— at least not the most important thing involved. During the debate about this legislation, college administrators descended on legislators with an argument that was so powerful that the three-year hiatus for college professors was included in the law. The argument in favor of a hiatus for college professors may be briefly summarized as follows: "Our college faculties are being increasingly populated with old professors who are the despair of the students, the administrators, and the rest of the professors. They should have retired years before, but we cannot dismiss them for they have tenure; and the concept of tenure among college professors has been inscribed on tablets of stone." If I had been an administrator at the time, I would have vigorously supported the idea of giving the colleges a few years to get adjusted to this "new deal." During my many years as a professor, and mercifully few years as an administrator, I became familiar with many of these unfortunate situations. As a brief illustration of this sort of situation, I will recount a conversation I had years ago with Joel Hildebrand concerning the dismissal of a tenured chemistry professor during the time that Joel was dean of the College of Chemistry. He told me that since he came to Berkeley in 1914, he was aware of only two instances in which a professor with tenure rank at the University of California had been dismissed. I will avoid naming the individual involved, but will give an approximate quotation with which Joel ended the conversation: ". . . and I was the one who was stuck with the job of dismissing this man." If I should give a many-page account—which I will not—of the alternating hilarity and despair generated by "this man," it would make clear the magnitude of the problem generated in colleges by the concept of tenure.

However may be the justification of the hiatus of three years before the relief of college professors from discrimination, the fact remains that this was the law. And it is also true that the colleges devoted a great deal of time to deciding what should be done about the professors who would be forced to retire during the hiatus. I was one of the "Berkeley Seven" involved with this predicament who did not want to retire at the specified date, according to present regulations. Thus, I attended many meetings on the subject. Finally, the university developed a plan for the "Berkeley Seven" who refused to go away. (Incidentally, there was only one other professor at all the other campuses who adopted the position of the Berkeley Seven. This resulted from the fact that Berkeley was the only campus old enough to have many professors of the age that caused them to be included in the hiatus.) The plan for us was called "phased retirement," and all of us welcomed the opportunity provided. Each person who elected to participate in the phased retirement plan would be allowed to continue in phased retirement for three years beyond his previously normal retirement date. The statewide regulation seemed to be rather vague as to details of "The Plan," but the basic plan was clearly set up to discourage participation. As noted above, the last word in the previous sentence actually should be read "participation by the Berkeley campus." According to the plan, each department on each campus would set the ground rules for participation in phased retirement, and there would be no increase in the campus budget to pay the cost of phased retirement. I asked for teaching two-thirds of my normal load, but with the department paying only one half of my normal salary. The other half would be paid by the UC Retirement System. The dean of the College of Chemistry told me that they would try to scrape up the money for one-half of my salary, but they could not promise anything until the time and the budget arrived each year. Fortunately my mind was relieved of this uncertainty before the time arrived. The chancellor at Berkeley during this period was Michael Heyman, who had been recruited from our Law School where he had been a professor for a long time. For many years he has been director of the Smithsonian Institution. As soon as he got the word that the Berkeley campus would have to pay for the phased retirement of the Berkeley Seven, he announced, approximately, "I guarantee that the phased retirement of the seven professors on this campus will be funded, whatever else must be sacrificed." From this point, as far as concerns the Berkeley Seven, Mike

Heyman could do no wrong. Indeed, this was only one of the many things that Mike did which endeared him to nearly all the Berkeley faculty—especially those who had been aboard for many years. They knew that an important part of the duties of the Berkeley Chancellor was to defend us against the pressure applied to the statewide administration by all the other campuses. The other campuses were anxious to derive benefits from what Bob Sproul had done in previous years in building up the University of California as an internationally famous institution.

In spite of the introduction of federal laws regarding discrimination against old people, and the adoption of a plan for phased retirement by the University of California, Rebecca and I had already bought the almond orchard. As a matter of fact, we remained very interested in operating and improving the orchard we had bought. We bought the orchard from two people, Ernest Rubke and Frassie Speckert, who were not married but lived together on a parcel of a few acres immediately adjacent to the orchard. They retained this parcel with the house on it when they sold the orchard. This unusual arrangement had originated because of the fact that Ernest Rubke and Otto Speckert had worked as partners in farming for many years and had lived together. When Otto married Frassie, Ernest continued to live with them and work with Otto as before. When Otto died, that left Ernest and Frassie as co-owners of the orchard and the house thereon.

Since Ernest was more than eighty years old at the time that Otto died, he and Frassie decided to sell the orchard. A part of the sale agreement for us to buy the orchard was that Ernest would manage the orchard for the year following the sale, including harvesting the 1977 crop for us. Our buying of the orchard included our progressing to the ownership of the membership of the orchard in the California Almond Growers Exchange, known widely as Blue Diamond. Blue Diamond is a large agricultural cooperative which handles about one half of all the almonds grown in California. Since California markets about three-fourths of all the almonds marketed in the world, this makes Blue Diamond the largest factor in the world almond market. Our sale agreement also specified that Ernest would handle all the expenses, including providing us with necessary data for the federal income tax. In turn, we would reimburse him for all expenses, and would instruct Blue Diamond to pay him a specified percentage of the gross income from the 1977 crop. We would receive the remainder of the 1977 income. This made it possible for us to take our New Zealand trip described in the preceding chapter, but provided us with hardly any contact with the 1977 harvest. I did have brief instruction in use of the tree shaker, the nut sweep and the pickup machine. The crop of nuts that year was rather good, about 60,000 lbs.; however, we had nothing to compare it with, except that Ernest Rubke told us that it was the best crop he had ever harvested from this orchard. So we were quite pleased with the outcome of our first year of owning the orchard. In retrospect, it is clear that we were very fortunate indeed to have had so many good experiences during our first years of operation of this orchard.

During our second summer of owning the orchard, we hired a man named Ray Brusasco to manage our orchard, and Frassie allowed him to stay in her house until Labor Day when they came back from Montana, where they owned agricultural property. Ray lived in Gridley which was only about twenty miles from our orchard, and he commuted from Gridley on his motorcycle after Ernest and Frassie came back. Our contact with Ray was one of numerous fortunate circumstances which allowed us to solve the many problems encountered when we, as really green tyros, set out to learn how to operate a thing as complicated as an almond orchard. Ray entered the University of California at Berkeley in 1976, one of the years in which I had volunteered to be the "mentor" of a Cluster Group, a very worthwhile system which the campus had developed to help students who were unaffiliated with any organization to get acquainted with other students early in their freshman year. The group of which I was mentor was composed of students who thought they would be interested in becoming chemists. There was no stated or implied commitment for the student to continue in the field of the Cluster Group; its function was purely social, and the concept worked very well. In my Cluster Group, which met weekly for lunch, which they brought, except for beverages supplied by me, the students became well acquainted with the mentor as well as with each other. It followed that I became the adviser of the students in my Cluster Group, on any and all kinds of subjects, social, academic, and personal. Ray Brusasco was uncertain whether he wanted to be a chemist, so I told him that I was interested in his report because I had no intention of becoming a chemist when I entered college. I told him some personal history which is included in early chapters of the present chronicle. We became so friendly that he saw me often in the years following his year in my Cluster Group. I learned that he lived in Gridley with his parents and had worked for several summers in almond orchards. To get to the bottom line, when 1978 arrived, I offered him a job for the summer managing the culture of the orchard, and working on harvesting the crop when that began in August. He accepted with pleasure, and so that was another problem solved for us.

In 1978 we learned how bad a crop year could be. The problem was not Ray's management but the weather. As we would learn as the years went by, the principal problem in growing almond trees is the weather, a thing over which mortal man has no control. In this year there was much rain during the blooming season, which starts in February for almonds, earlier than for other tree crops. Before harvest time it was apparent that the crop would be poor. The poor crop was exacerbated by a rain during the harvest season. This is much less important than the weather during bloom, but when the crop is already poor, rain during harvest makes it worse. We harvested only about 14,000 lbs. of nuts.

Before reporting on the 1979 crop, which proved to be the best we would ever have, I will outline the procedure for harvesting almonds by the modern methods which have been developed in California, the only state that produces significant amounts of almonds. The completely mechanized harvesting of almonds requires more than a hundred thousand dollars worth of equipment, for which reason small growers frequently hire a harvesting company to do their harvesting. This is very expensive, and is a handicap to small growers. Other small growers buy second-hand equipment, frequently at auction sales where a business is closing down or a large grower is replacing old equipment. In our case, when we bought the orchard we acquired the equipment necessary to do the harvest. Thus, we did our own harvesting; however, we had a lot of repairs done on our equipment; and after a few years, we began to replace the old equipment as it became obsolete or too expensive to repair.

Although small growers of almonds are subject to handicaps in relation to large growers, this is no different from the situation of small operators in other industries, especially other branches of the food industry. In spite of the handicap under which the small almond grower operates, there are probably more people operating small almond orchards than is the case in growing other kinds of food. There may be a good reason for this. An almond orchard is probably the nicest and most enjoyable of any other type of food production. There is no stench (perfume and beauty in the blooming season instead), less noise than from a busy highway, and dust only for a short interval during harvest. A well-kept almond orchard is more attractive than most city parks. And finally, as a contribution to the economy of our country, California is able to export almonds to Europe and market them at a price lower than that at which Spain, with the cheapest labor in Europe, can market them. Spain is the only other significant producer of almonds except California. When Spain joined the European Common Market, they persuaded the EC to put a tariff on almonds. That tariff persists until today, but political maneuvering led by Blue Diamond has succeeded in getting the tariff applied only after a certain number of tons of almonds have been marketed in the EC. And so let us return to a description of this remarkable feat which American Ingenuity has brought about, even in such a prosaic industry as growing almond trees. Not all the modern American miracles are in the spotless production facilities in Silicon Valley. Some of them are in greasy machine shops where such inventions as tree shakers have been developed.

The first stage in almond harvesting is preparing the ground for picking up the nuts after they have been shaken from the trees with a tree shaker. Preparing the ground obviously takes a varying amount of time, depending on how much grass and weeds are present and how much manpower is applied. This requires an estimate on when the earliest maturing trees are ready to be shaken. Since almonds require cross pollination there must be at least two varieties in every orchard, and it is common to find three varieties. Our orchard had six varieties planted in it when we bought it. The variety which is ready to harvest first is called Non Pareil, and it is the variety which, traditionally, has been planted in the largest numbers, for it gives the best yield. New varieties have been introduced in recent years, and some of them are being planted in new orchards.

The next stage after the ground is prepared is shaking the trees at the time it is judged that the nuts are dry enough to be shaken from the trees. Tree shaking is the part of harvest that requires the most skill. The tree shaker must shake off most of the nuts without tearing the bark off the tree trunk or limb where the clamp to the tree is applied. After we had developed our technique, we settled down to having the shaking done by me and our ranch hand, Pedro Tagle, whom Ernest had hired and who was destined to be with us for the duration of our operation of the orchard. The division of the shaking between Pedro and me was variable, depending on what other tasks required our attention; however, Pedro usually did more than half the shaking. He was faster than me and was able to carry on longer, especially if the temperature in the orchard was hitting a hundred or higher. The only time I did as much or more shaking than Pedro was when he was still preparing the ground in part of the orchard while I started shaking in another part. This sometimes happened when a sudden hot spell made our prediction of the time of shaking later than it proved to be.

After the shaking of the trees, the nuts must be left on the ground until they are dry enough to be hulled, which is determined by frequent inspection and judging when that time has arrived. This is the time when rain generates a lot of extra work and possible loss of product. When dry, the nuts are swept into windrows using a nut sweeper designed to leave the nuts in windrows. At first we hand-raked the nuts from the ends of the rows to get the ends of the windrows into a position where the pickup could get them. This was hard work requiring no skill, and we frequently hired temporary laborers before Pedro learned how to do this job with the sweeper. This occurred when we bought a new sweeper, and the salesman showed us how to do it with the new equipment. Pedro did all the sweeping because of the skill required. We bought a dust helmet for him to protect his nose, mouth, and eyes from the dust that is unavoidable during the sweeping operation. A little fan operated by a battery blows air through a filter and out around the face.

The last stage in the harvest operation is driving the pickup machine, which is pulled by the big tractor. It takes the nuts from the windrows and sends them up a conveyer belt that feeds into bins, whose dimensions are about four feet on each edge. When the bin is full it must be exchanged for an empty bin. This is done by the fork lift driver, who first parks an empty bin beside the pickup which has stopped for this operation. He first lifts the full bin off the cart and sets it on the ground. He then sets an empty bin on the cart which carries the bins in position to receive the effluent from the conveyer belt. The pickup driver has gotten off her tractor in order to clamp the empty bin firmly in position as the fork lift driver holds it in place. The fork lift driver then retracts his forks from the empty bin on the pickup, puts them under the full bin, which weighs about a thousand pounds, and takes it to the staging area. Soon after the forklift is on its way, the pickup driver has started to fill the empty bin. When a suitable number of bins has been accumulated, a hauler who has been contracted to do the job is called and told to take the bins to the huller. At this point our job is done. After the huller has cleaned and hulled our nuts he sends them to Blue Diamond, which processes them and markets them.

These latter operations require considerable skill. After some experimenting and practicing and conferring, we settled down to Rebecca being the pickup driver and me being the fork lift driver. I was the only one who drove the forklift, although Pedro could do it rather slowly. After Rebecca tried driving the forklift she announced that she did not want anything more to do with that machine. Both Pedro and I could drive the pickup but did so only in unusual circumstances, for Rebecca was much better at it. The pickup driver has many things to watch all the time, and experience is a great teacher. A small mistake can consume quite a bit of time; this is important if rain clouds are gathering and Pedro is getting tarps ready to put over the bins the moment they are delivered to the staging area by the fork lift driver. On a few occasions we had rather exciting times, but always came through with dry nuts.

As has been indicated before, the first time that Rebecca and I and Pedro did the harvest was in 1979, when we had the very heavy crop. Knowing that the stakes were high we approached the task with some qualms, but never a doubt that we could do it. By that time in our lives, we had weathered enough storms that we had developed a slogan: "We have done it before, and we can do it again." We knew from having inspected the orchard during the summer that there were many weeds and grasses throughout the orchard, on account of very little having been done since the preceding harvest. This fit in very well with our decision to take grandchildren Kristen and David with us to work for us during the harvest, since they had already obtained their work permits from school. David was under sixteen, and so he was allowed to work only twenty hours per week. Also, we had obtained agreement from Frassie Speckert for the four of us to stay in their house during the time they were in Montana supervising the harvest of their cherry crop.

We were not able to get into the Speckert house until about the first of August, because that was the time that Frassie and Ernest went to Montana. As soon as we were installed in the house we assembled proper hand tools, such as weed cutters and rakes. Pedro was already mowing weeds, pulling a flail mower with the tractor, but there was a great deal of additional hand work necessary. In about two-thirds of our orchard, the trees are only eighteen feet apart in the tree rows, so a sprinkler midway between two trees leaves no room for the tractor to get through between the riser to the sprinkler and the tree. Thus, at each sprinkler location, weeding in the tree row had to be done by hand, so the four Casons and a woman we hired went to work weeding.

As we approached the end of this long job of weeding, I began to spend some time shaking limbs to learn if the nuts would fall off, then putting those that fell off in the sun for a few days to find out if they would dry out rapidly. I was working under the handicap of conventional wisdom, which held that an early harvest was important to keep down damage to the nuts from the navel orange worm (NOW). Long before we became involved in almond growing, the navel orange worm had found a happy home in the large acreages of almonds. It was by far the worst pest for almonds at the time of our entry into the business. After a few years of experience I learned that the concept of the early harvest is not necessarily correct. At the least it should be considered in connection with other factors, such as the number of nuts left on the trees after shaking. However, at this first harvest I had no alternative except to act without reservations on the basis of conventional wisdom. Ergo, we left a lot of nuts on the trees, probably not more than 10 percent. As to whether this sort of thing is better to happen in a good crop year or a bad one, such considerations are a waste of time. We were very happy with the very large crop we harvested in our year of being tyros. Having no powers of prophecy, we had no way of knowing that this would be by far the best yield that we would ever have. In spite of several handicaps with which we had to contend during this first year, we had a yield of about 103,000 lbs. of nuts delivered to Blue Diamond. In order to properly recognize such an auspicious start, we had a "gleaning party," to which a few friends were invited. We had Pedro shake a few trees for them which had an obviously large number of nuts left on them. One of those attending the party commented, "If this is gleaning, I can hardly imagine what the trees looked like before your original shaking." After several years of experience in operation of the orchard, I began to have a similar feeling.

As already implied, our first harvest was not without difficulties. Our largest problem resulted from the fact that we did not have a fork lift. Ernest was a big strong guy, and he felt no need for a fork lift to handle those bins weighing half a ton. He did have a system that worked, but only David and Pedro in our crew could handle it. Arthritis was beginning to give me too much trouble to allow me to handle that sort of thing. What we began to term the "Ernest System" involved having two carts for holding the bins as they were drawn behind the pickup rig to receive the nuts from the conveyor belt. When a bin was full, the pin holding the cart to the tractor was withdrawn and the cart pulled by hand to one side. On the other side would be a cart carrying an empty bin, which had been hauled to the site by a small tractor. This cart, with the empty bin thereon, was then attached to the pickup rig, taking the place of the cart with the full bin which had been detached. As the pickup rig proceeded picking up nuts, the small tractor was used to haul the full bin to the staging area; the clamp holding the bin to the cart was opened and the tractor hauling the cart was driven suddenly forward to drag the cart from underneath the full bin. The tractor driver then dragged an empty bin, which weighed about 175 lbs., onto the cart, remembered to close the clamp holding it on the cart, then drove back to the place where the pickup rig was working; then did it all over again. Sound complicated and laborious? It is!

The situation was made somewhat easier by the fact that Ernest had bought for us a small, old tractor which was large enough to haul a full bin. There was also a third cart on hand. Thus, when the rate of pickup was very heavy, as was the case in a part of our orchard, Pedro could drive one tractor and David the smaller tractor. Even with this laborious system of changing bins, it was possible to keep the pickup moving without any waiting for a bin change. Also, Pedro would always be assigned the task of changing bins on places where there was a hill. A hill caused a very great increase in the difficulty of changing bins. David became quite attached to the small tractor, and always regarded it as his during the years he assisted us at harvest time. It was an International Harvester Farmall tractor, made in days of yore for use on small agricultural operations.

Our system of operation under normal conditions was for Pedro and I to share the shaking of the trees. There was always a push for keeping the shaker going as long as possible. With big operators, it was common to keep this most expensive machine going around the clock. With us, we did the best that we could without paying Pedro time and a half for overtime work, which was after ten hours per day. Pedro started shaking soon after daylight and shook until noon. I ate an early lunch and shook for an hour while Pedro took his lunch break. I then came on again when Pedro's ten hours were up and shook until it was too dark to see well enough for setting the clamp. In years where Pedro was finishing the flail mowing to prepare the ground, as I started the shaking, I shook for about eight hours in one day.

For the remainder of the harvest there was not such a rush as in the case of shaking, for one part of the orchard could be worked for one operation while another part was worked for a different operation. As mentioned previously, Pedro did all the sweeping while Rebecca did the pickup driving, with me filling in on long days. As soon as the pickup started, Kristen had the job of marking the bins as they came in to the staging area. This included the following: Rubke Cason Ranch; variety of almonds in the bin; date of the bin pickup; and number of the bin for the particular variety involved. This numbering continued sequentially throughout the pickup of one variety, even if the pickup was intermittent over several days. This notation was necessary for us to know whether any of our nuts failed to get all the way to Blue Diamond. Kristen was advised of the importance of her getting all the notations correct.

This description of the harvesting process applies in the same way to each variety; however, all varieties besides the Non Pareil are in much smaller amounts. The Non Pareil amounted to more than one half of the trees in our orchard, so we felt that the big push was done as soon as the NP had been harvested. Things were also facilitated by the fact that different varieties mature at different times, and this makes it easier to arrange to keep the machinery busy all the time.

In subsequent years, following the record harvest in the third year, our general procedure for the harvest remained about the same; however, the specific details varied considerably because of several factors, including improvement of our machinery by purchasing additional machinery to replace the old machinery which came with the orchard. Also, fighting pests was not as simple as in 1979 when the crop was so large. We were assisted by David for two more years after 1979, but Kristen became involved with other things during the summers.

In 1980, we had a fairly good crop of nuts, about the same as in 1977, and our harvest was greatly facilitated by the fact that we bought a new sweep, and learned how to use the sweep to eliminate the hand raking of the row ends. We also had David's assistance and therefore got along well with changing bins without a fork lift. We had a lot of trouble with crows eating a part of our crop. We had three "crow guns," which automatically fired a mixture of propane and air at a set interval to give a loud boom. The crows had already gotten educated about crow guns, however, and ignored them as soon as they got hungry. Our next move was to provide Pedro with a shotgun. After he killed a few, they found that the loud bang was sometimes accompanied by a man with a shotgun. This made it difficult to get near enough to kill more crows, but it also made them flee when anyone came around in a tractor or motor cart—until they learned that the person was not dangerous unless accompanied by a gun. And so the struggle went on.

In 1981 we had another fairly good crop, which would have been better if Ernest, who was still doing some managing for us in the spring and early summer, had not gotten the big idea of pulling a cultivator through the orchard to dig up the surface. He then had Pedro pull the land plane over that to give a smooth surface for the harvest. Sounds all right if one ignores the fact that the ground must be allowed to dry out before harvest. Otherwise, the heavy machinery will tear up the ground so that there is no longer the smooth surface from which the nuts can be swept into windrows. When that powdered surface dried out after the last irrigation it became dust, and so we were sweeping our nuts from a layer of dust about four inches thick. This was known to us as the "dust year," and our losses were enormous, so we had no measure of what our crop actually was.

Stimulated by my anticipation of a poor harvest in this dust year, I took a further step against the crows and bought three electronic scarecrows. These devices were powered by a storage battery and emitted an intermittent noise which was supposed to imitate birds in distress. These devices proved disappointing. They seemed to hold off the crows for a little while, but after they got hungry it was back to the shotgun and crow guns. This was also the first year that we began to have big trouble with ground squirrels. I bought a second shotgun, and between Pedro and I we kept the squirrels down, but we also encountered the same situation that developed with the crows. Before a man came within range to use his gun, the squirrels would have ducked into their holes. However, driving around in a motor cart or tractor without a gun worked better than it did for the crows, for a squirrel underground could not tell whether the vibrations were associated with a gun. No doubt for similar reasons, the squirrels rarely came out again in less than an hour. During actual harvest in a given area, there was never any evidence of squirrels.

The year 1982 stands out as the worst of all the years that we operated the almond orchard. Early in that year, during the blooming season, problems began with persistent heavy rains. By the end of March it was clear that we would have an insignificant crop; however, we were not discouraged because of the good years before 1981. During this dismal year we did several things designed to improve our future operation of the ranch. Major improvements were stimulated—indeed, required by the problem we had with staying in the Speckert house during much of the blooming season. We began to have problems with Frassie's obnoxious sister, Bertie, who insisted on staying in the house during the time we had been staying there in previous years. This led to our having to discontinue having David help us with the harvest because of the expense and great inconvenience of all of us staying in a motel several miles away. In order to accommodate to this development we had to do two things before harvest set in: buy a fork lift, and arrange for lodging and feeding for Rebecca and me.

We were able to attend to the first item by having Ernest search for a secondhand fork lift in the Marysville area while I searched the Bay Area. Surprisingly enough, I was the first to find a suitable fork lift and arrange for the seller to deliver it to our orchard near Marysville. As we expected, this really revolutionized the harvest of our almonds, and our ag mechanic, Don Perkins, was able to attend to the repairs that fork lifts seem to need frequently. At a later date, David commented, with a knowing smile, that his job with us was the victim of mechanization. Actually, this was only partly true, for David became interested in more important things in future years.

The second matter, arranging for board and lodging for Rebecca and me, was not as readily solved; however, at the last minute, Bertie decided that she had harassed us enough and moved out of the Speckert house. This fit in with the fact that we had been so slow about making up our minds to solve our problem by buying a mobile home that we were unable to get it installed until after the harvest was completed. In order to bring the mobile home to our chosen site at the north edge of our orchard without taking out several more almond trees, it was necessary to bring it across about a quarter mile of vacant land adjacent to us. This was accomplished exactly one day before heavy rains set in and continued through the winter. The mobile home was a very good single wide one, with two bedrooms and two adjacent baths at opposite ends, and a nice living room and food room in the middle. One door opened into the living room, and the other opened into a short hall giving access to the bedroom, the bathroom, and a utility room where we put a clothes washer and dryer. This door opened from the back side of the house into the orchard. When we came in from working in the orchard hot and dirty, we took off our clothes and put them into the washer, then proceeded to the shower. The other bedroom with adjacent bathroom, where we slept, was at the other end of the house. We bought the house with ducts for an evaporative cooler already installed, and we had a carpenter install two large air conditioners in the wall of the living room and our bedroom. Thus, we were able to handle even the hot weather in the valley. We had a large front porch and a small back porch added after the house was installed. The entire layout, including septic tank; telephone and power brought in; and connecting the plumbing to the pressure system which also supplied water to the ranch hand's mobile home, added up to an expense of $27,000 dollars, which was reported as a capital improvement for our orchard. For the federal income tax, the amortization period was ten years. We found living in our mobile home so comfortable and pleasant that cleaning out and selling it was the most heart-breaking part of closing down and liquidating our orchard.

After 1981, as far as production of almonds was concerned, things turned down and stayed down for a decade in our orchard. This rather sudden turn for the worse affected the almond industry as a whole; however, the impact on us was worse than average. There were several factors that affected us; however, the greatest problem for us was the age of our orchard, which was planted in 1964 to 1969. Thus, our trees were nearing twenty years old during the mid-1980s. By that date it had become clear that after twenty years of age an almond orchard starts going downhill, and things get worse with time after that. This situation was exacerbated for us by the fact that our trees had been planted too low in the ground, and we began to lose trees from root fungus. Furthermore, when our trees were young, they had been pruned with the limbs coming out of the trunk too near the ground. This interferes with the shaking of the trees. Finally, in 1985, by which time the trees had become much larger than they were when we bought the orchard, we finally decided that something had to be done to stop our loss of the nuts that we could not shake off the trees. We bought, second hand, a new shaker which was more powerful and also capable of limb shaking. This improved our situation; however, we continued to have trouble in getting all the nuts off of the trees, especially the largest trees.

The problems cited above resulted in our having a worse crop than average for the state, especially in a bad year when the take by ground squirrels and crows becomes a larger percentage of the nuts. In good years, we would not be so far below average, but the price would be down in response to the abundant supply of almonds. A general problem in the farming industry is that the better the crop, the worse the price. This factor would have been worse if it had not been for the stabilizing influence of Blue Diamond, and the amount of cold storage available. Almonds keep indefinitely in cold storage, and Blue Diamond was able to influence the industry to withhold nuts from the market in years of overabundance, to be sold in poor years. Even so, our price from Blue Diamond was below one dollar per pound through most of the 1980s.

Even with all our difficulties, as far as making money was concerned, we still enjoyed operating our beautiful orchard, and striving to do the best that we could under the circumstances with which we were confronted. The Old Professor, after a lifetime of research, still enjoyed solving problems, and we sometimes got a lift by being able to solve a problem.

One problem that we did solve was the control of ground squirrels, and that problem remained solved until we closed down the orchard after the tornado of 1995. We solved this problem by killing the squirrels in a relatively humane way. Probably more important, our system was rather inexpensive and completely harmless to the ecology. Even with such serious pests as crows, I always held off killing them until it became absolutely necessary, with no alternative except closing down the orchard. It was rather shocking to discover that a hundred or so crows can clean all the nuts off a hundred trees in a day or less, even in a good crop year. In one poor year, in which we had some other difficulties which kept us away from attacking crows for two or three weeks, our crop was wiped out. We did not even harvest three varieties of nuts.

With the ground squirrels, things were different. We drowned them. I bought a small water pump which was operated from a twelve volt storage battery, and also bought two "deep cycle" twelve volt batteries. This made it possible to operate the pump for many hours in a day, and charge the batteries overnight. We had lots of five gallon cans on hand, in which we had bought various kinds of oil and grease for the various machines which we operated. We loaded seven or eight of these cans full of water into the bed of our motor cart, then pumped water into a squirrel hole until the water backed up to the surface. Either nothing happened, or else a half-drowned squirrel staggered out of a nearby hole. This squirrel was not in a condition to quickly run away and was easily disposed of with a shovel. We soon concluded that there was a network of interconnected burrows underground. So we began to plug all but one hole in an area, and put water in that hole until the hole filled up to ground level. No squirrels were able to come out the hole where the water was applied, so we assumed that this particular den had been eliminated. Subsequent observation showed that this assumption was justified.

The next chapter in this description of our attack on the squirrels relates to our change of the battleground to an area where the ground for several hundred square feet was riddled with squirrel holes. As expected, this area could not be handled in a practical manner with cartloads of thirty-five or forty gallons of water. Fortunately, we had a 500 gallon water tank mounted on wheels that we could haul around with a tractor after filling it with water. We picked the hole at the lowest elevation to apply the water. We learned how we could have lost so many nuts to ground squirrels when we pumped 250 gallons of water into one hole before the water rose to ground level at that hole, and wet squirrels had run out of holes at higher elevations. This event is particularly impressive if one remembers that ground squirrels were not eating most of the nuts they gathered; they were storing them for the winter. With our deep cycle batteries and our 500 gallon water tank,we could handle even this, although it did take some time. We eliminated the ground squirrels. The next year the squirrels began moving back on us from adjacent properties; however, the problem was much more simple when we did not have to contend with large, well established colonies.

Prior to 1981, we had employed a spray program in our orchard, following what was regarded as a minimal program: dormant spray and fungicide applied at the pink stage of blossom. I was rather uneasy about this "minimal" program because Pedro had told me about finding dead birds in the orchard. Since both Rebecca and I have long been bird lovers, and since this fungicide spray was in the spring when there was much bird activity—pecking around eating insects of all kinds—I took a particularly dim view of the fungicide spray. For this reason, we discontinued the fungicide spray and used only the dormant spray during the period 1982 to 1984.

As a result of two papers I read during the period just mentioned— one in Science magazine and the other a report to a national meeting of the American Chemical Society—I decided, starting in 1985, to discontinue all spraying of the trees. The only spraying we did in 1985 was herbicide spraying on the ground. Even that proved to be a mistake. The herbicide that we used damaged our trees badly and our crop was so poor that we could not use the data from that year in order to conclude anything about the utility of dormant spraying of the trees. After that, we used only Roundup herbicide for ground spraying. Roundup enters green plants through the leaves, but kills plants by affecting the roots. Thus, ground spraying of Roundup when there is no wind affects only the weeds and grasses on the ground and cannot affect the trees, whose lowest leaves are several feet above the ground.

We did no spraying of the trees during the period 1986 to 1988, in order to make a comparison with the years 1983 and 1984 concerning the rejects reported by Blue Diamond for the nuts we delivered to them. The object of spraying is to reduce worm damage to the nuts, which causes them to be rejected as having no commercial value. The results of this comparison were so interesting that we published a paper reporting our results in Almond Facts, a magazine published by Blue Diamond for the benefit of its members, but which is also distributed to a few thousand almond handlers and other people interested in the almond industry. The title of this paper is: "Grower has good results with no-spray program." The results of this investigation are summarized, in part, in the following table:

Rejects of Almonds by Variety

Crop year:	1983 dormant spray only	1984 dormant spray only	1986 no sprays	1987 no sprays	1988* no sprays
Non Pareil	6.65%	1.95%	5.9%	0.5%	1.1%
Ne Plus	7.6	2.3	No harv.	0.4	2.8 (100%)
Norman	6.8	6.5	3.7	3.5	5.3 (86.7%)
Thompson	4.2	2.7	15.5	0.6	4.5(83.4%)
Price	6.4	1.4	No harv.	0.5	1.2
Total Wt. of our crop (lbs.)	12,715	91,417	8,098	82,846	48,742

* The numbers in parentheses are the percentages of the rejects for the respective varieties which were caused by gum, as reported to us by Blue Diamond. Gum is caused by difficulties during development of the nuts, such as extremely hot weather, and is not caused by NOW, thus is not related to the spray program. The percentages reported in this table which are not in parentheses are total rejects for all reasons.

In most years, nearly all rejects are caused by worm damage, and the naval orange worm (NOW) is the prime offender. The peach twig borer (PTB) is less damaging and not as difficult to control. The very hot weather in 1988—a long string of days with the thermometer above 100°, some of them above 105°—obscures the normal distribution of damage in the rejects. Thus, the most informative data is that in the two good years of 1984 and 1987. It seems clear that spraying causes more rejects! How could that be? Actually, the answer to that question is quite clear and straightforward. The spray chemicals being used were doing a better job of killing off the pest predators than killing the pest for which they were targeted.

For those skeptics who question the validity of the preceding statement, there is interesting evidence in support of that statement developed by Rebecca, who spent much time in studying the pests in our orchard and the literature concerning them. Beginning in 1985, Rebecca found that our orchard had been heavily invaded by tiny black beetles with a few spots of color on them. Sometimes there would be a dozen or more of these tiny beetles on one nut, between the hull and the shell, but there was never any evidence of damage to the nut! An analysis at the state laboratory identified the beetles as Hyperaspis lateralis, a type of ladybird beetle which was cultured as a beneficial predator in the years before the introduction of chemical sprays. Yet, the field man for the chemical distributor from whom we bought our agricultural chemicals, said that he had never seen the beetle before. I asked him if he had ever inspected an orchard before which had not been sprayed with chemicals designed to kill pests. His answer: "Of course not."

As an additional report on this subject, I will note .that it has been years since we have had mite trouble in our orchard. In one year when we had a few trees which were losing their leaves, I asked Errol Storm from the Yuba County Agriculture Commissioner's Office to inspect our orchard and advise us if there was mite trouble. After a careful inspection with a magnifying glass, Errol reported, "It can't be mites because I can find only an occasional dead mite. You must have a mite predator in your orchard."

Since this clear evidence against use of chemical sprays was made available to several thousand people in much more detailed form in our published paper, would it be reasonable to expect a rush to stop using chemical sprays in almond culture? Of course not! When an "expert" on ag chemicals (who earns a living by selling them) tells an almond grower that he is likely to lose half of his crop if he does not spray, most growers will continue spraying. However, since my getting out of touch with almond growing, I understand that several moderately large operators are doing experiments on gradually reducing spraying and observing the results. This is not the right way to do it, but it may eventually produce results—which will be a boon to everybody except chemical manufacturers.

For the benefit of those who might reach the logical conclusion that I am one of those who is trying to interfere with the progress of science by dinging the chemical industry, I would like to remind such people that I spent my professional life as a professor of chemistry. I will always do what I have always done—search for the facts in the case, and disseminate any knowledge that I may be fortunate enough to acquire. The chemical industry has brought simply enormous benefits to civilization, and in the U.S., has taken great pains not to damage the ecology in so doing. I am in a good position to know that the chemical industry has taken a bum rap from the news media and wild-eyed conservation types. Furthermore, I am in close contact with the lumber industry, as has been indicated in pre-vious chapters. I am inclined to become rather intemperate discussing the attack of the wild "conservationists" on that important industry. Ergo, I have nothing to say about that situation.

In consideration of the age of our orchard, the yield of 82,846 lbs in 1987 was very good indeed; however the price of about 75 cents per pound was so low that we had no profit. The 1988 crop of 48,742 lbs. was better than any other year of orchard operation after that. About the only thing that could be said about those years was that the orchard provided us with a "tax shelter"; however, I would prefer a tax shelter that did not involve so much hard work in the hot sun.

In 1994, the last year before "the tornado," our crop of 37,323 lbs. was the best yield since 1988, and the harvest at the end of that year stands out in my memory as one of the most pleasant ones during our tenure in the orchard. We had defeated the ground squirrels; we held off the crows bet-ter than in recent years; and most of all, we had a very pleasant and capa-ble man named Ralph Woodmansee to haul our nuts to our huller. In recent years we had been having a lot of trouble finding people to haul our nuts. As harvest approached in 1988 we had no one lined up, and so we asked our huller if he could help us. A few days later I had a phone call from a man whose last name was difficult for me to understand, but I could understand that our huller had told him that we were looking for a nut hauler. I confirmed our need, and he visited us on the same day at our mobile home on the orchard. It turned out that he had grown up in Chico, the earliest center of almond growing in California, and had recently returned to Marysville by buying a trucking company there. He outlined the system he would use in hauling our nuts, which I recognized at once as quite superior to all others we had tried. He had the equipment to do the job right. I would call him when we had nuts ready for him to haul, and he would bring his semi-trailer to our staging area and leave it there, after he disconnected his tractor and went on to do other business with it. The semi held sixteen bins in two rows of eight, so that I could load it from each side. When we had that many bins ready to go, I would phone him and he would come to get the loaded semi within twenty-four hours. He always arrived in less than the specified time, took our bins to the huller and returned to leave the empty semi for me to load with our next sixteen bins.

During the time of harvesting we became quite friendly with Ralph Woodmansee. He was fascinated with these two octogenarians doing all the labor on the orchard except for their one ranch hand. He told his mother that we were assisted by a young fellow who did a lot of the really heavy work. He told her that this man was only sixty-eight years old. This was true; Pedro worked until he was seventy years old and we had to close the ranch down because of the tornado. I had explained to Pedro several years earlier that if he worked beyond age sixty five it would greatly increase his benefits when he did retire. Since this was the last year of our operation of the orchard except in a liquidation mode, it is rather nice that Rebeca and I have pleasant memories of it.

It was early in the morning of March 11, 1995, that Rebecca and I received a call in Berkeley from Pedro, reporting that they had a terrible storm during the night which roared so loudly and shook his mobile home so badly that he and his children were "scared to death." He had not been out yet, because of the continuing heavy rain, but he could see from his house that many trees were down. None had hit his house.

By that time in our life, Rebecca and I had discontinued driving an automobile at night or in heavy rain. Nevertheless, we decided that we should get to the orchard at once, since there was no indication that the rain was letting up. I had not driven in such heavy rain since I drove down the west coast of the South Island of New Zealand. I concentrated very heavily on my driving, most of which was on freeways, and we made it without incident. In spite of the downpour which we encountered during our drive from Berkeley to the orchard, the rain let up significantly just before we arrived. As we drove in the gate, the visibility was good for about a hundred yards. What we saw were piles of trees scattered about at random where neat rows of trees had been. Neither of us said anything as we drove to our house which was about a quarter mile from the gate. At our house, we spoke out loud to congratulate ourselves on the fact that it was intact. A large tree about ten feet from the house went down along a line that was parallel to the long dimension of the house. Our electric power was okay, but our telephone was out, not due to any problem on our property, for our line was underground as soon as it came down from a pole at the edge of our property. Lack of a phone was a nuisance during the two or three days before Pacific Bell found where the break in their line was located; however, our good neighbor, Berry Woods, kindly provided us with access to their phone.

As soon as Rebecca and I had a long talk with each other in the process of getting our wits assembled, we went to work salvaging what was left of our orchard. We soon found that the view we had on entering the orchard was the worst area for storm damage, and this lifted our spirits considerably. It turned out that the tornado had come in from the west, and our entrance to the orchard was on the west side. After about three hundred yards from our west boundary, damage dropped off rapidly. After examining the situation, we decided to harvest any remaining nuts left on the trees, in spite of the few nuts that were left. We knew that we would have to clean up the mess, whether or not we harvested, because of demands by the fire department.

Our first move was contacting a wood cutter which we had used before, and arranging to sell him the trees for four dollars per tree. His contract was to fell any windthrown trees not already on the ground; cut what he wanted for his sale of firewood, and leave the brush. We started Pedro on moving the brush as soon as the ground dried sufficiently to allow taking the old tractor which had a brush buck on it, into the orchard without tearing up the ground. From the time of the tornado to the time when weed control had to be initiated, Pedro moved brush during all days that the ground was dry enough for that work. Storms on March 22 and 27, which added approximately another hundred windthrown trees to Pedro's herculean task, was discouraging, but Pedro kept on working hard and managed to clear the land by harvest time.

I also finished my task of rearranging the irrigation system to throw water from the sprinklers as much as possible where trees were left, and as little as possible where only weeds would be irrigated. This involved using several kinds of sprinklers, including more than a hundred hose nozzles which could be adjusted to irrigate a single tree. This task also was finished barely in time for the fall harvest. Naturally enough, Pedro and I and Rebecca were all disappointed that our harvest for 1995 yielded only 753 lbs. of nuts, which is approximately none.

There is an ancient expression, probably written by a poet: "Hope springs eternal in the human breast." Whatever the origin of that expression, it seems to apply to me—at least on some occasions. Incredible as it seems in retrospect, I was able to convince myself that we should have one more harvest from our crippled orchard. My reasoning was as follows: Even though we had only about half of our trees left, we had our modified irrigation system in place to irrigate them, and the price next year should be high because of the trivial carryover from this disastrous year. If we had anything like a good blooming season, we should make money. Each year that we had had a high yield of nuts followed a poor year. This sequence was first observed in 1979.

However good, bad or hopeful my reasoning might be evaluated, it contained a fatal flaw. There was an if in the reasoning, which depended on things over which I had no control. Although we had a beautiful bloom, the best in years, there was persistent rain. The bees got out some, but they could not scatter the damp pollen over the orchard. Contrary to classical wisdom, bees do not accomplish pollination by carrying the pollen from one tree to an adjacent tree of a different variety. Pollination is effected by the pollen falling off the legs and wings of the bees as they fly back to their hives. Anyone who spends some time observing bees during a blooming season will note that they flit from one bloom to a nearby bloom to another adjacent bloom, and so forth until the bee being watched suddenly zips off towards his hive.

Ergo, our yield in 1996 was only slightly more than in 1995. To make matters worse, the yield over the state was moderately good, and so the price was not bad. Of course, the price had only a minor effect on us, for we had such a tiny crop.

We were forced to liquidate the orchard. We were assisted in this most unattractive job by Bob Hoving, from whom we had rented bees for many years. Bob put us in contact with an excellent auctioneer named Dennis B. West. His company was named D. B. West Auctioneers, and his slogan was "Best in the West." He auctioned all our machinery, along with assorted boxes of tools, plumbing fittings, etc., on December 12, 1996. Bob Hoving proved to be a good ag mechanic, and was of great value in getting our machinery ready for the auction. He also sold our remaining trees to a woodcutter for more than one-third what the auction of our machinery brought in. Almond wood is probably the best of all firewood in terms of maximum calories output and minimum ash production. Bob also located a chipping company which had enormous machinery for chipping brush, large limbs, and even stumps. The chips were sold as fuel to such a business as a generator of electricity using "unconventional" fuel. This disposal of our brush was at no cost to us.

In follow-up operations subsequent to the orchard closedown, Bob and his wife Bobby loaded on one of their trucks and carried to Camelot for us: two slightly used beds with mattresses and springs and accessories from our "second bedroom" in the mobile home; several wall hangings and small items from the mobile home; and last but not least, the motor cart with dump bed, Comet clutch drive, and 16 h.p. Briggs and Stratton two cylinder engine, which had been so useful in the orchard. It has proved to be even more useful at Camelot. It has a bench seat which will carry Rebecca and me together, along with a load of a few hundred pounds of firewood, or brush, or tools, or anything else with which we may be working. Unless there is a heavy load in the bed, it will also accommodate a third person on the seat if that person does not have too broad a spread.

As a final hurrah, Bob and Bobby cleaned out and cleaned up and repaired our mobile home and sold it by advertising. All of these proceedings were quite traumatic for us, but Bob and Bobby made it possible with no undue strain. We had nobody available to blow taps on a bugle, but it would have been appropriate. We were left with only the cleared land and the old mobile home which our ranch hand had occupied. We would have sold the old mobile home, which Bob and his son put into tip-top condition, if Yuba County had not passed an ordnance that a mobile home manufactured before 1976 could not be moved onto any private property. Never mind that we had equipped this particular mobile home with a full-house air conditioner, and it provided better quarters than occupied by about a third of the people living in Yuba County. So we started renting it in December, 1996, for $300 per month. By the present time (September 1998), we have collected more rent money than the amount for which we had planned to sell it. Strange things happen when politicians are in charge of things. Please pardon the understatement, when interpreted in terms of 1998.

I will close this chapter on a cheerful note: our adventures with the Internal Revenue Service while reporting our disaster loss resulting from the March 1995 storms. Let me say at the outset that I have been making out my own income tax returns (Form 1040) since 1940, and all my relations with the IRS have been pleasant, including a few years when I was investing in limited partnerships. Furthermore, I was never stymied so that I could not get straightened out by phoning IRS offices. I suspect that a part of my success was due to good advice given me by older son, Roger, who was a CPA at a public accounting firm at the time; however, I also did my homework. But Form 1045, Application for Tentative Refund, was different. This is the form used to report a disaster loss and apply for a refund, if any, due on taxes paid in earlier years, going back first to the third year preceding.

The 1045 which I first submitted did not even get off the ground. I had reported the disaster loss on Schedule A, as I had done years before when a forest fire burned through about 170 acres of our Camelot property. Since our present loss was a business loss, not a personal loss, it must be reported on page 1 of 1040. Thus, I did not even get to 1045 on this first try. My second try came back with the red ink used to make it out correctly as far as an early step. The third try was similar, except that the red ink went to the next step that was wrong. The first and third of these returns were signed by Examiner M. Alex, while the third was signed by Examiner L.

Sant. I really worked hard and carefully on this fourth submission, and on the bottom of the form to accompany my return, I wrote the following note:

Dear M. Alex,

Enclosed is what I hope is my final submission of form 1045. I want to state that I greatly appreciate the patience of you and Examiner L. Sant in correcting the errors which I persisted in making. I have been making out my own income tax forms since 1940—the year before that fateful date of 12-7-41. And I have never been stymied before. It may be that form 1045 is a tough one, but I think that I am getting too old for this sort of thing. Now that our almond orchard has been wiped out and closed down, we are hoping for smooth sailing.

Sincerely, James Cason

I received my refund in the mail on the third day after I mailed this form.

Don't try to tell me that the IRS is not cooperative and helpful. On three previous occasions, I have had pleasant and helpful exchanges with the IRS after they questioned my return. On two other occasions, they simply paid me a refund, along with a form explaining that I had made an error. I am suspicious that those who complain so loudly about the vicious tactics of the IRS are mad as hell because they were caught cheating. I say more power to the IRS, so that I will not have to pay taxes that ought to be paid by the cheaters.

And so I close this chapter on what is hopefully a pleasant note.

CHAPTER 22

OLD AGE IS HELL

A title such as this, which expresses an opinion, is likely to stir up opposition from those who disagree before they read further in order to find out what the author has to say on the subject. For this reason, such titles have been eschewed in the first twenty one chapters of this chronicle. However, I believe that this specific title is different. The word "hell" has been used so widely and so indiscriminately by so many people that it really has no meaning unless, perhaps, from the context in which it is used. In Chapter 2 there are quoted a few satirical lines from a poem entitled "Hell", which decries the widespread use of the word in order to avoid thinking of appropriate words. Nevertheless, I believe there is a pervasive idea that "hell" usually connotes some degree of badness. Thus, my title to Chapter 22 states that there is some degree of badness about old age, and goes no further. The reader must read further in order to learn whether he disagrees with me. I am well aware that one frequently hears about the "Golden Years," and Robert Browning went so far as to write. "Grow old along with me, the best is yet to be, the last of life for which the first was made." I am inclined to disregard such statements as these on the grounds that they indicate a lack of contact with reality, or else are made with the intent of promoting something to the advantage of the promoter. The term, "Golden Years," is a favorite of those selling something, whether an insurance policy, real estate, or various kinds of presents. I have made the following statement in the presence of groups of old people, or even to groups of people containing some youngsters no older than sixty: "There is absolutely nothing about old age that is good, except that it is better than the only alternative—up to a point." I do not remember having heard any outspoken disagreement with that statement; however, I have heard a lot of discussion about that "point." Indeed, that "point" is a major factor in making old age hell.

I believe that most of the problems involved with making old age hell can be categorized under three headings: (1)deterioration of the mental processes; (2) poor health, with its various ramifications; and (3) very little that is attractive to which one can look forward.

Deterioration of the Mental Processes

Since the first of these categories inevitably affects all people as they age, varying only with time of onset and rate of progression, perhaps this is properly discussed first. This condition, when it has not progressed to the advanced stage which is characterized as Alzheimer's Syndrome, is frequently referred to as "absentmindedness," which is a misnomer. Obviously the mind is not absent. It is unable to handle several cyberspace channels simultaneously, whether output or input, without one or more channels hogging so much attention that, for all practical purposes, the remaining channels are "absent" from the brain at that particular moment. The brain is still there, and normally is working perfectly otherwise. As a matter of fact certain notoriously capable scientists, while still far from "old," have been able to successfully concentrate on certain channels, completely ignoring everything else so that they can accomplish almost unbelievable mental achievements. Many of these people have received a lot of public attention for their "absentmindedness." One of these whom I never had the good fortune to meet was Johnny von Neumann, a member of the Institute for Advanced Studies at Princeton, New Jersey. He lived a moderate distance from the Institute. According to the stories, which I heard repeated more than once, there was an intersection on his route from home to office where he had had so many minor automobile accidents that it became know as "von Neumann's Corner." One person said that there was a sign at this corner giving it the above-cited name, but I have never been there and have no idea whether this part of the story is correct.

I could consume many pages reporting the humorous anecdotes that have circulated regarding the absentmindedness of prominent and capable scientists; however, I have no intention of doing so. I am not trying to record any history; I am trying to illustrate a very important point. As people age, they begin to make mistakes, such as knocking over a glass of water or wine at the dinner table. The person who does this is certain to feel very bad about it, and he (please understand he or she) needs support, not criticism or advice. He is already feeling a sense of despair, since he has nothing to look forward to except this sort of thing getting worse until he dies. If a person becomes repeatedly bruised by criticism in such a situation, he may become the victim of Alzheimer's Syndrome. Or before it gets that bad, he may wisely decide to cash in his chips while he is still ahead in the game.

Rebecca and I have developed a system of looking for humor in such things, rather than thinking about the misery. We got started on this track after reading a humorous story that appeared in some publication—perhaps an AARP Bulletin. According to our best recollection, this story applied to an aging woman whose minister called on her, and suggested, among other things, that she should begin thinking about the Hereafter. She replied, "Oh, I think a great deal about the Hereafter, many times each day. No matter whether I go into the kitchen or the bedroom, or some other room, I find myself standing in the middle of the floor, thinking, 'Now what am I in here after?'" This sort of thing is subject to a lot of variation, and never seems to get old with us—a typical family joke. We have agreed that there is one room where we never stand on the floor thinking, "What am I in here after?" That is the bathroom. A twist on this occurred years ago when I was serving on a university committee. We were meeting to generate a report on a rather important matter, but we were having a problem on reaching a meeting of the minds. Finally, the chairman said, "I hereby officially adjourn this meeting to the men's room; at least all of us know what we come into that room to do." Somehow this broke the ice, and we reached a conclusion after reassembling. This digression has a meaning: it is especially important for old people to understand the virtues of humor—and it is free.

Another consequence of the aging of the brain is deterioration of the sense of balance. An old person who may have been an amateur gymnast in his youth, as I was, may discover, at age such as the biblical three score and ten, that he no longer feels comfortable about carrying a chain saw as he walks across the creek on a log suspended far above the water. At some later date, he may find that walking along on rough ground requires some attention in order to avoid falling down. If distracted by trying to discover the identity of a bird that happens to fly by, he may fall on his face. After that, things get worse rather than better. In retrospect, I think that I was saved from having serious accidents because my arthritic legs began to hurt me enough to drive me to getting a cane. In walking, one is always balancing on one foot while moving the other one forward. Small wonder that a second contact point with the surface is a very big help. And there is no reason to think that arthritic pain while walking will develop at just the right time to cause a person to start using a cane in order to compensate for deterioration of the sense of balance. It is almost enough to make a person conclude that arthritis is not all bad. In any case, it is a helpful thought at times when it seems that the gods and the fates are zeroing in on one.

It is very important indeed that every person who has aged sufficiently that his sense of balance is deteriorating must understand the significance of recognizing this development when it occurs. There are several natural instincts which tend to deceive a person into acting too little or too late. It is quite a blow to one's morale to recognize that he is deteriorating from age. And when he does face up to it, he tends to think that he is going to have to do something about it eventually. The hospitals and nursing homes are well populated by people who have had a fall. And the funeral parlors enjoy a significant amount of business from the same type of people. It is also important for each aging person to recognize that debilitation with age occurs to all of us, the intelligent and the less intelligent. As a matter of fact, when a successful person is accustomed to being right most of the time, he is especially prone to thinking that he is not susceptible to the same considerations that most people are. He is dead sure that he will know just when the time has come for him to get that cane, or stop driving at night, or stop rushing around doing things in a hurry. This latter point deserves special attention.

When an older person must use several of his mental channels to carry out such a simple process as walking, or even standing still without falling down, it is apparent that doing anything in a hurry is likely to result in accidents. Another factor involved with walking, or doing other things involving movement of joints, is the slowing of differential movement of the bones because of poor lubrication of the moving surfaces. This poor lubrication results from a thinning of the sinovial fluid, the lubricant in the joints, by an action of the superoxide radical. As has been described in Chapter 16, thinning of the sinovial fluid is a major factor causing pain in the knees while walking. It also causes the joints to move more slowly, as happens in any poorly lubricated joint. I learned years ago that walking more rapidly causes more pain because the joint may be not quite set in a new position before weight is put on it. On some occasions when I have been walking at my normal slow pace, I have been distracted by some event, such as a blaring automobile horn, with the result that I make a step without proper attention to what I am doing, and there results a sharp pain. This pain persists if I continue to step on that leg, presumably because the joint was forced into a wrong position. If I sit down, flex the knee a few times and rub it where it hurts, this usually gets my leg back to normal. If there is no place to sit down, I can support myself on the other leg and my cane, then flex the knee until it does not give unusual pain while being stepped on. Tactics of this sort and use of the analgesic which I have finally found to be the best for me have kept me walking around about twenty years after I was first told by an orthopedic surgeon that I had no reasonable expectation of continuing to be mobile without a knee joint replacement. Another surgeon told me that the principal motivation for a joint replacement operation is hope for relief from pain. I believe that this surgeon was right; this belief is supported by other experiences with him.

Avoidance of rushing is especially important in some activities, such as driving an automobile. It is apparent that it is important for everybody to avoid rushing while driving an automobile; however, this precept is ignored so persistently that it becomes important for an older person to understand that this is one activity where this difference between him and the rest of the people can become a matter of life and death. There are other activities that are more subtle and more likely to be ignored by old people, but where rushing can also result in serious, or even fatal injury. One of these situations which is likely to occur frequently among older people is getting up from a sound sleep at night with an urge to relieve oneself. This is an ideal combination of events likely to lead to an accident: urgency and half asleep. Many falls are reported among older people in this situation, and it can be fatal. An accident of this sort happened to a friend of mine who was about seventy-five years old. As he rushed to the bathroom at night, he fell and landed with his chest on top of a pointed newel post at one corner of the bed. The pointed tip of the post passed between two ribs and pierced his heart. He died instantly. I suppose that a critic of this story might wonder how many people are likely to die in such an improbable accident. True enough; however, I hope it illustrates the point that an older person should get in the habit of attempting to quell the urge to rush to the bathroom at night. My friend is just as dead as if he had had some commonplace accident.

Poor health, with its various ramifications

Older people may die of any disease, of course; however, the incidence of infectious diseases is less among old people, for those who were susceptible are likely to have died at an earlier age. On the other hand, older people are more likely to be afflicted with degenerative diseases than are the rest of the population. In contrast with a machine made of steel, a biological machine has the remarkable ability to repair itself; however, the biological organism does age, and so becomes more susceptible to diseases which result from wear and tear of the organism. The three diseases which plague old people the most seem to be arthritis, atherosclerosis—usually stroke or heart attack—and cancer. Of these, arthritis certainly kills the least people, even indirectly. Arthritic victims usually live for a long time in constant pain. Although arthritis has been discussed at length in Chapter 16, I will add a few comments which are appropriate in this chapter.

The medical profession has made great strides during the past century in comparison with related professions such as chiropractic and osteopathy. Indeed, the success of the medical profession has been so overwhelming that it has gained monopolistic control over health care in the U.S., presumably over most of the world. The reason for this spectacular success is that medical science was based on the principle that diseases are infections caused by micro-organisms, as set forth in the latter part of the nineteenth century by Koch and Pasteur. The success of that principle in curing or ameliorating the diseases that plague humans and animals alike is now history. The success of the medical profession in controlling infections has also made possible the spectacular accomplishments of surgery. I have good reasons to be acutely aware of the impact on surgery of the increasing discovery of drugs for controlling infections. In 1930 I slipped on takeoff for a pole vault and landed on my outstretched hands in the sawdust pit. Somehow, because of the twisting way I landed, one bone in my right forearm snapped. Because of the heavy musculature in my forearm, due to years of gymnastics, the surgeon was unable to properly set the bone. There was only about a fifty percent overlap between the two pieces. The only cure for this would be an open operation which would expose the bone to air, hence to an airborne infection. Naturally enough, I and my parents consulted my brother, John, who was in medical school at the time. John reported that the odds of getting such an infection were moderately high, and if such occurred, there was no cure which would save the patient's life except amputation of the limb. Needless to say, the set of the arm was not tampered with, and so to this day I have no rotation in my right forearm. A bit of a nuisance, but I have had no real difficulty in adapting. I learned to continue my gymnastics with no big difference. Occasionally there is a situation which is more amusing than troublesome. When I am receiving change after a store purchase, the cashier will invariably present the change to my right side. I cannot hold a fork or spoon properly in my right hand and put food in my mouth, so that is avoided by using my left hand for my spoon and fork, with the knife in my right hand. This has proven to be a better system, apparently a custom that is widespread in continental Europe.

The remarkable accomplishments of the medical profession have contributed a great deal to the progress of civilization, and have traditionally been much appreciated, frequently viewed with awe and admiration. However, this same progress in civilization to which the medical profession has contributed so much has had a great impact on that same profession. As more and more people survive the infectious diseases and grow "old," the degenerative diseases become more important. Since new doctors are trained by old doctors, adaptation of the medical profession to recognition of the causes of degenerative diseases and treatment of such diseases has, inevitably, been painfully slow. This situation has been discussed in some detail in Chapter 15, Cancer, and Chapter 16, Arthritis. The problems resulting from this situation have been more traumatic in the case of cancer, and more highly publicized. However, the problems with arthritis have been much longer lasting in most instances, and the medical profession can offer no assistance unless for replacement of joints, which is a rather draconian procedure and does not cure the problem; it is just a palliative. I have never talked to a medical doctor who understands the cause of arthritis, or who is willing to accept the facts when presented. Refer to Chapter 16.

Atherosclerosis causes more deaths than cancer; however, it receives little attention in the news media. This can be rationalized in several ways. One is that a heart attack rarely involves pain for a long duration. I dare say that many people have thought, after reading of the death of a friend by a heart attack, "What a nice way to go. I hope that I am so fortunate." Another probable reason for so little public attention to atherosclerotic diseases is that this type of disease generates a trivial amount of income to hospitals, medical doctors, and other health providers. Since this type of disease is responsible for so many deaths, it seems a pity that there has developed hardly any attention to information which has been published in reputable journals, and clearly indicates simple non-medical procedures which reduce liability to death from heart attacks by a large factor, probably tenfold.

I first heard about the involvement of Vitamin B6 with heart attacks in the early 1950s. An old friend of mine, Karl Folkers, who was head of Pioneering Research at Merck and Co. at that time, visited Berkeley, during most years, on a recruiting trip for chemists graduating with a Ph.D. degree. Karl usually invited Rebecca and me to have dinner with him while he was at Berkeley. On an occasion in the early fifties, Karl was quite excited about a research paper that had been published by two professors at the UC medical school in San Francisco. One of these professors was named Greenberg, and I think that the other was named Rheinhard. These investigators had kept apes (it could have been monkeys) on a diet completely free of vitamin B6 for a long period. After several months, the animals had developed plaques in their arteries which appeared identical to the cholesterol-containing plaques in the arteries of humans which cause the snagging of blood clots that eventually cause arterial occlusion, and thus a heart attack. Karl was so excited about this work because he had been director of the group at Merck which had earlier developed the commercial synthesis of vitamin B6. He could hardly wait to get back to Rahway and persuade Merck to immediately start a check on this research in order to confirm the results.

I heard no more about this affair until Karl visited Berkeley about a year later. Merck had refused to fund the research on the grounds that it would cost more than Merck could ever profit from selling more vitamin B6. This attitude was entirely different than was the case at Merck prior to the recent arrival of a new president. Karl asked me if I knew of any academic positions that he might be interested in investigating. Not long after this event, Karl became president of what was then known as Stanford Research Institute. He was there for several years, but eventually departed because of a disagreement with the trustees of the institute. It seemed that a majority of the trustees did not approve of Karl spending a lot of time in the laboratory directing the research of a group under his direction, rather than sitting in the president's office. After a period of time, Karl became director of an institute at the University of Texas. We kept in touch with him for many years, and he later advised us to step up our daily input of Vitamin B6 from 25 mg. to 50 mg. Starting at some time after 1960, there was further investigation of the relation of Vitamin B6 to heart attacks, and the mechanism of its action was established. I have not been able to find my reference to this work.

Another important line of defense against heart attacks involves ingestion of lecithin. Lecithin is a type of fat which occurs widely in nature, but differs from other fats in that one part of the molecule has phosphorus included in its structure. This gives lecithin a variety of uses because of its ability to form complexes with numerous compounds. It tends to form emulsions which are difficult to break, and for this reason is widely used in food, especially foods containing chocolate. Most people have found that putting chocolate in the refrigerator, which breaks the emulsion by cooling with formation of crystals, ruins the flavor of the chocolate. The ability of lecithin to form molecular complexes is the property that is of use as a defense against heart attacks.

There have been several papers on this subject, but the first one that came to my attention was by a man named Jacobus Rinse and was published in the April 1978 issue of the scientific magazine called American Laboratory. This work was predicated on an experimental fact that has been known for years. In the laboratory—termed in vitro—lecithin forms a molecular complex with cholesterol which is somewhat water soluble. The reasoning was that since cholesterol is a major component of the plaques in the arteries which lead to heart attacks and other atherosclerotic diseases, perhaps lecithin, in vivo, would tie up cholesterol as a water soluble complex and thus greatly reduce, or even eliminate the liability for a heart attack. Tons of printer's ink and other resources have been expended in discussing the relationship of cholesterol to heart attacks, and I will later direct some attention to this controversial affair. However, our present attention is directed toward a different and specific effect of lecithin on atherosclerotic diseases. This effect is reduction of the incidence of heart attacks by ingestion of lecithin.

The involvement of lecithin as a protective agent against heart attacks cannot be studied by use of the widely touted statistical methods called epidemiology. In my opinion, this is just as well. Epidemiological studies are subject to so much difficulty in identifying the factors involved that the interpretation is likely to become highly controversial. This results in a situation that is not too different from what is involved in a judicial court. The winner of the controversy is the most eloquent or the best supported financially, or both, and is not necessarily the one who is right. This is why the war on cancer has failed so miserably; and is also the reason why billions of dollars have been wasted on a wrong theory of the causes of the pestilence known as AIDS.

I became interested in the involvement of lecithin with atherosclerotic diseases because a large segment of my research was being directed toward fats, frequently termed lipids by chemists. As a matter of fact, the title of my Ph.D. thesis at Yale was "The Lipids of the Bovine Strain of Tubercle Bacillus." Since I was quite convinced of the importance of lecithin and vitamin B6 in defense against cancer, I supplied information on the subject to friends who had experienced a heart attack.

One friend to whom I supplied information was Bill Stanley, who did his thesis work for a Ph.D. degree under my direction. Bill suffered a heart attack at about age sixty. There seems to be a general consensus that the younger a person is when suffering his first heart attack, the more likely he is to die of a heart attack later. Bill continued to work at the Western Regional Research Laboratory until he retired, and enjoyed very good health. After retirement, he served on an advisory board concerning citrus culture, and spent a considerable period of time advising about citrus culture in Crete and also in Israel. Recently, he and his wife have been living in Monterey during the winter and during the summer, in a house they have in the Sierras. In his 1997 Christmas card, he reported that they were considering disposing of the mountain place, since they were getting a little too old for traveling back and forth. I have heard no reports from Bill regarding the performance of his heart, so I presume that it is still doing its job in a normal fashion.

Another old friend to whom I provided information about heart attacks was Tom Weaver, my gymnastics partner at Vanderbilt University. Tom was in Vanderbilt Medical School during the same four years that I was an undergraduate at Vanderbilt University, which was on the same campus as the medical school. After Tom graduated from Vanderbilt Medical School and did his internship elsewhere, he returned to Nashville to practice medicine as a pediatrician. Later, he cared for the children of my two nieces who were living in Nashville; a natural development since my older brother, John, also a graduate of Vanderbilt, was practicing medicine in nearby Murfreesboro. The last time I saw Tom was when he attended my brother's funeral in Murfreesboro.

A few years ago I received word from one my nieces in Nashville that Dr. Weaver had experienced a heart attack. (I have reported on my close association with Tom Weaver in Chapter 3.) Ergo, I immediately sent Tom all the information I had on lecithin and vitamin B6, along with an accompanying letter reporting some of the reasons for my sending him this material. After a few days, I received a letter from Tom in which he thanked me for my interest in his welfare, but said that the medical profession took a rather dim view of this sort of thing. I had realized long ago what enormous pressure the members of the medical profession are under to ignore the existence of "alternative medical procedures"; however, I was quite saddened by this letter. I was much more upset, a few months later, when I received a clipping from a Nashville newspaper which was Dr. Thomas Weaver's obituary. At my age, I have received many such disappointments, but this one hit me harder than any other—even Bill Massie's death. I develop a feeling of helplessness, combined with rage against the social and political forces that have created such disastrous situations. How can the most civilized country that the world has ever seen continue to be plagued and crippled by such things? So far, I can see very little light at the end of the tunnel; however, I have noted one hopeful sign. Alta Bates

Hospital in Berkeley has recently been advertising the development of a new program in "Alternative Medical Procedures." They are advertising for donations from the public to help finance the program, and I hope that they get a response from the millions of people who are suffering from the lack of medical attention to degenerative diseases.

About a decade after World War II, Jack Gofman, professor of medical physics at Berkeley, published a series of very interesting papers on the relationship of lipids (fats) to atherosclerotic diseases, with most of the emphasis focused on heart attacks, as usual. I and one of my graduate students, George Gillies, were co-authors on one of the papers published by Gofman's laboratory. So many investigations were rapidly focused on Gofman's work that the original proposal, which identified lipids as the villains in causing heart attacks, was modified in two respects, more or less concurrently. The idea that fats were the villain had to give way before the criticism that Italians, who are prone to become overweight by middle age because of the quantity of olive oil that they eat, had a low incidence of heart attacks. Further investigation, especially by Gofman's laboratory, was able to develop general agreement that the villain was saturated fat. Certain components of unsaturated fat proved to be actually beneficial. This concept has withstood the test of time, and seems to be generally accepted at the time of this writing.

During the period that "fat" was being replaced on the no-no list by "saturated fat," there was developed the concept that the greatest villain of all is cholesterol. This was initially proposed because cholesterol is a component of the tough plaques in the arteries which snag clots and cause an occlusion. Although there had accumulated very good evidence that vitamin B6 and lecithin have a great effect in reducing heart attacks, there remained numerous investigators who insisted on pursuing the idea that elimination of cholesterol was very important because it definitely is a major component of the plaques. Never mind the fact that cholesterol does form a water-soluble complex with lecithin, and the well-established effect of vitamin B6 on plaque formation. Furthermore, investigation of the relationship between cholesterol in the diet and heart attacks is a simply marvelous opportunity to expend large sums of money on massive epidemiological investigations. To add to the attractiveness of such investigations, no scientific expertise is required either on the part of those setting up the experiment or on the part of those hired to man the computers. All that is required is statisticians eager for yet another place to apply their specialty.

One of the earliest investigations of this concept involved the search for drugs that lower the level of cholesterol in the blood. This investigation hardly got off the ground because of the damage inflicted on people who ingested the cholesterol-lowering drugs. According to my recollection, a few people were actually killed. One might think that these results would alert people to the fact that cholesterol has some important function in controlling metabolic processes. However, this did not occur, in spite of the fact that it had been well known for many years that one important bodily function, control of blood pressure, is monitored by two chemical compounds whose structures are well known. Epinephrine (adrenaline) is the compound in the body which raises blood pressure. There are other compounds belonging to the class of pressor amines which raise blood pressure, but I believe that none of them are naturally occurring in humans. Lowering blood pressure is monitored by a compound called acetylcholine. This compound knocks down blood pressure so drastically and with such tiny amounts that the body has developed an enzyme, choline esterase, which destroys acetylcholine and prevents more of its formation when sufficient has been made to meet the situation occurring in an animal at any given time. Ergo, any substance which destroys choline esterase or interferes with its normal function is a deadly poison. A tiny bit of enzyme causes a chemical reaction to occur over and over ad infinitum, without the enzyme being used up. The class of compounds known as nerve gases, discovered during World War II, destroy the enzyme choline esterase. One tiny drop of the deadliest of these compounds, placed on the back of the hand, will cause the death of a one-hundred-fifty pound animal in twenty minutes or less. The facts just cited may not be widely known, but they certainly are well known. In spite of this situation, and in spite of the fact that, so far as I have been able to discover, nothing is known about the obviously important function of cholesterol in human metabolism, nevertheless, large sums of money continue to be spent in epidemiological investigations of the role of cholesterol levels in the diet as a cause of heart attacks. It would seem wiser to channel the money into investigations of the actual role of cholesterol in human metabolism. Unfortunately there has continued the expenditure of money on epidemiological investigations of the effect of cholesterol levels in the diet on the frequency of heart attacks.

One investigation compared a large group of people on a low cholesterol diet with a similarly chosen group on a "normal" diet. After the computerized statistical analysis had been completed, the conclusion was that the group on the low cholesterol diet had a slightly higher rate of heart attacks than those on the normal diet; however, the difference was so small as to be insignificant. The rest of the epidemiological investigators were not about to take this quietly. It was declared that the investigation was flawed. The subjects of the investigation had been picked at random from the population at large. Another large investigation should be carried out on subjects who were "at risk"; that is, had high cholesterol levels in the blood. The results of this investigation were reported as showing that the subjects on the low cholesterol diet had a slightly lower rate of heart attacks; however, this difference was declared to be significant. I know nothing about statistical analysis, but an acquaintance of mine who is known to be a skeptical sort once declared: "There are three classes of liars, which can be ranked in order of the least proficient first and the most proficient last. These classes are plain ordinary liars, damn liars, and statisticians." In view of my ignorance about statistics, I am more inclined to make a rather plebeian statement; "Anyone who believes that those multi-million dollar investigations are significant probably also believes in the tooth fairy." In view of the millions of dollars that are being spent in guiding people about cholesterol in their diets, it seems probable that my statement is wrong, and the statement concerning the ranking of liars is correct.

As a final shot which should have shot down the whole cholesterol investigation before it was airborne, I will refer to the research of Professor I. Chaikof, which was carried out in Berkeley during the 1950s. In the late 1940s, Chaikof approached me on the idea of synthesizing a natural fat, except that it would contain an atom of carbon-14, which is radioactive carbon. He proposed to feed such a fat to animals, then determine whether carbon-14 appears in the cholesterol in the fat depot of the animal. It had been determined at that time that cholesterol is synthesized in the body from acetate which the animal produces as a part of the process of digesting fat. Therefore, if carbon-14 appears in the cholesterol in the fat depot of the animal after it has been fed the synthetic fat containing an atom of carbon-14, it follows, beyond any possible doubt, that the animal synthesized at least a part of its cholesterol from the food it was fed. I declined to undertake the job of synthesizing the fat containing carbon-14 on the grounds that I was not equipped to handle radioactive compounds in my laboratories. I suggested that he consult my friend and colleague, Bill Dauben, who was working with carbon-14. He did so; Bill did the synthesis; and Chaikof did the animal experiments. The carbon-14 showed up in the cholesterol in the fat depot of the animals in a rather short time. This is very clear and definitive evidence that animals are able to synthesize cholesterol from common components of food. A lot of work by several people for a few years, but the answer is clear. I would like to depart from rigid scientific expressions in order to make a flourish taken from Sullivan of Gilbert and Sullivan, approximately as follows, from memory: "On this there is no manner of doubt; no possible, probable shadow of doubt; no possible doubt whatever."

As a matter of fact, Chaikof decided to undertake his experiment as soon as the disastrous results of lowering the cholesterol level were published. If cholesterol is necessary for some bodily function, it would be quite remarkable if the body was unable to synthesize it. Thus, it may be truthfully stated that when one eats eggs, he saves his liver from the work of synthesizing cholesterol. Come what may, that statement is true.

Humans are unable to synthesize vitamin C, but they do not die if deprived of it; they are handicapped. Humans were able to become the dominant species on earth in spite of this handicap. They were powered by the ability to think—to eventually reach the conclusion that they should eat enough vitamin C to overcome their handicap.

Very little that is attractive to which one can look forward

As a person grows older, he tends to think less and less about what he is going to do tomorrow and more about what he is going to do in the future. In retrospection I realize that, while in college, most of my attention was directed towards such things as getting in a tennis game during the lunch hour; when I was going to study for tomorrow's classes; getting a new ribbon for my typewriter, etc. On certain occasions I would get together with my brother John, or my friend Kit Haynes, or others to make plans for the summer, or for some other occasion in the near future. Only in my senior year in college did I begin to make serious plans for what I would do after graduation. Since the glamorous air force in the U.S. army, at that time, refused to accept anybody who wore glasses, I went to graduate school at Berkeley. After going to Berkeley, I soon began to focus my short-range plans on that sun-kissed blonde, but after a few months we began to plan our futures to marriage and beyond. And so it went, on down the years. Even after I had been in Berkeley for ten or fifteen years, my thoughts did not reach as far as retirement. At some time after age sixty I could not escape noticing that nobody was interested in my ideas about the future, and so I began adjusting to the fact that I was going to be completely out of the picture in the near future—declared obsolete. Initially I reacted by devoting more time to the teaching of the organic chemistry course for non-chemistry majors. As related in Chapter 12, I even went so far as to write a textbook for the exclusive use of teaching this course. I enjoyed teaching this course more than courses designed for chemistry majors which I had previously taught. The premedical students are usually the best students in any university, and they seemed much more interested in the course than were the students in the course for chemistry majors. The premeds frequently asked questions during office hours which did not directly involve anything in the course, but things they thought I might know something about. This encouraged me to sometimes look up answers to their questions, and on a few occasions I discussed appropriate things in class. Of course, all this helped me to keep that inevitable date of retirement out of mind.

As the retirement date approached, I devoted considerable time to deciding what would be my best activity. As discussed in the preceding chapter, the almond orchard was my choice. This demanded so much of my time that it was helpful in getting me through the years after retirement. It was about ten years after retirement that I really recovered. By the time the tornado hit our orchard, I was in good shape to handle the situation. I began to plan things for the future, just as I did when I was sixty-five; things like writing a book.

During the period which seems to be commonly regarded as old age, perhaps starting at the time that Medicare takes over much of one's medical expenses, both Rebecca and I have been either fortunate or smart or some combination of both. Or maybe we have good genes. After studying several generations of young people as they passed by me in my capacity as a teacher in three different universities of three different sizes, I have reached some conclusions about the importance of genes in shaping one's lifestyle. The "right" genes do not guarantee that a person will lead a happy and useful life; they act as a prerequisite. The situation is similar to setting algebra as a prerequisite to calculus. If a person has the "right" genes, that is no guarantee that he will lead a happy and successful life, but he has the opportunity to lead such a life. (Please understand that I use he for lack of a satisfactory pronoun which refers to either sex and does not lead to verbose and/or clumsy diction.) At some time, perhaps starting at the subteen level, the ball is in each individual's court. It is his responsibility to make the shots which will win the game. It is my impression, in observing literally thousands of young people go by, that for about ten people that have the "right stuff," one delivers the goods. Environment and something frequently called "character" are what counts when the chips are down. Maybe "character" is a combination of several genes, and this makes it harder for everything to click.

Whatever may be the arcane reasons that cause some individuals to be happier than others, make greater contributions to society, make those who meet them happier rather than more unhappy, see a doctor less often, live longer, and so forth for a long list of important characteristics, the fact is apparent that these differences are the very basis of the success of our society. I firmly believe that it is also true that each individual can improve on the character determined by the genes which he received by chance. Paderewski was born with the "right" genes, but he also worked long and hard in order to become one of the world's greatest pianists, while he also became a statesman. Mark McGwire was born with the "right" genes, but he also worked long and hard to hit seventy home runs in one baseball season. The right genes are necessary, but they only present an opportunity.

This discussion of factors involved in a person's success is probably in order in this concluding chapter of my chronicle. The older a person becomes, the more necessary it is for him or her to make many changes in his or her lifestyle. Some of these changes to which one must adapt are directly and obviously the result of changes in a person as he grows older. To pick an extreme case, the attack of arthritis on me began to exert a serious interference with my lifestyle at about age sixty-five. From that point onward, the interference of the arthritis increased intermittently, because of my persistent efforts to counteract the changes, but inexorably. Ergo, I had to steadily change my lifestyle in very fundamental ways. And this sort of necessity attacks one when the normal instincts of old age exert a powerful pressure to not change habits which have served one so well for so long. There is an ancient expression which states that you can't teach an old dog new tricks; however, it becomes very important for an old person to fight to learn new tricks. This can be very frustrating and painful, and is one of the reasons that old age is hell. I know! I have been involved in that fight for about twenty-five years. And as time goes by, one can hardly expect things to get any better before they get worse. As the end point, which is death, gets closer, it becomes all the more important for a person to try and develop things to which he enjoys looking forward. Since no one in the real world actually has any powers of prophecy, a person only knows that this end point gets closer as each day goes by. Thus, an old person lives with a steadily increasing realization and apprehension about dying.

Apprehension about dying derives largely from social customs in our society, and resultant legal regulations. Any logical consideration of the phenomenon known as dying indicates clearly that the only reason for apprehension about dying is the fear that the process will be painful and long-lasting. Indeed, just about everybody has read about, heard about, or been closely associated with an individual who has endured a simply ghastly amount of despair and pain before finally being released by death. I still have difficulty in not weeping whenever I think about a letter which I received from my very religious mother a short time before her death. It contained the sentence: "I simply cannot understand why the Good Lord is keeping me in this world for so long." The early chapters in this chronicle include a description of a tiny fragment of the good deeds that my mother performed throughout the years of her long life. She was anxious to escape torture in this world so that she would receive her reward in Heaven for working hard her entire life to help other people. Surely she deserved something better than suffering years of torture before being allowed, due to interference by humans, to reap her richly deserved reward. Surely any court which was able to judge on the basis of what is right and what is wrong, rather than on the basis of a complicated, arbitrary set of rules, would judge those responsible for her suffering as guilty of a heinous crime. Moreover, such a court would judge this crime as more reprehensible than the average murder. Murderers usually send their victims into the hereafter by means which are quick and with short duration of pain. Even O. J. Simpson, who murdered his ex-wife by chopping her up with a butcher knife, was decent enough to cut her jugular vein.

I have found it difficult to identify those faceless people who are responsible for spending enough money and putting out enough labor to be successful in persuading a large number of people who vote to keep our society imprisoned by laws which require continuing torture for indeterminate periods before death is allowed to free the victims. However, if one judges by what can be learned from the news media, the Catholic Church is certainly one of the ring leaders in the organized effort to accomplish two things: (1) prevent any and all women from using their own judgment about whether to have an abortion; (2) force those who want to die to live until nature takes its course, however long and painful and expensive such a course may become.

The most frustrating part of such things is that those who fight mercilessly to force these things on the rest of us actually never give any reason for their determination which bears scrutiny in the real world. The only reference is to things originating in somebody's mind, sometimes in centuries long past. I am reminded of the dictionary definition of religion: "A set of beliefs concerning the cause, nature, and purpose of the universe, especially when considered as the creation of a superhuman agency or agencies, usually involving devotional and ritual observances and often having a moral code for the conduct of human affairs."

As set forth in early chapters of this chronicle, I became a research chemist by instinct and by my own choice. I was trained to search for the true facts in nature, and to administer them for the good of society. I have lived according to that concept to the best of my ability. Ergo, it makes me especially nervous and apprehensive to realize, at age eighty-six, that I am bound and fenced in by such concepts as are criticized in the preceding paragraphs.